Research Methods in Public Administration and Nonprofit Management

Research Methods in Public Administration and Nonprofit Management

Quantitative and Qualitative Approaches

Second Edition

David E. McNabb

M.E.Sharpe
Armonk, New York
London, England

Library of Congress Cataloging-in-Publication Data

McNabb, David E.
Research methods in public administration and nonprofit management: quantitative and qualitative approaches /
by David E. McNabb.—2nd ed.
    p. cm.
Includes bibliographical references and index.
ISBN 978-0-7656-1767-5 (cloth : alk. paper)
1. Public administration—Research—Methodology. 2. Nonprofit organizations—Management. I. Title.

JF1338.A2M38 2008
658.0072--dc22   2007022267

Printed in the United States of America

The paper used in this publication meets the minimum requirements of
American National Standard for Information Sciences
Permanence of Paper for Printed Library Materials,
ANSI Z 39.48-1984.

BM (c)   10   9   8   7   6   5   4   3   2   1

Once again, dedicated to Janet, Meghan, Michael, and Sara—none more appreciated, none more deserving, none more loved.

BRIEF TABLE OF CONTENTS

DETAILED TABLE OF CONTENTS

LIST OF TABLES, FIGURES, AND BOXES

TABLES

FIGURES

BOXES

PREFACE TO THE SECOND EDITION

Although it follows a similar emphasis and structure, this second edition features a number of improvements over the first. These changes include a number of recommendations made by students in Master's degree programs, professors who have used the book in their classes, and the well-appreciated suggestions of anonymous reviewers. The underlying objective of the book remains the same—helping students and public and nonprofit organization administrators recognize that the research process can be both easy to understand and rewarding at the same time.

This book is primarily intended for students in a graduate-level research methods course. Graduate students researching and writing a thesis or dissertation in public administration, public and nonprofit organization management, or related social science academic programs will find the book a useful, easy-to-read guide to the research process. The book is also appropriate for upper-division social science research courses. It is also intended as a research guide for consultants, practitioners, and those who contract for and supervise research projects in the public and nonprofit sectors.

CHANGES TO THE SECOND EDITION

In addition to changes that reflect the rising importance of qualitative research methods, the changes in this edition also reflect the growing availability of statistical software and personal computers. I have made a judicious effort to remove the unnecessary repetition found in some sections of the first edition.

Some of the material included in the first chapter of the first edition has been moved to a new Introduction. Chapter 1 is now a strengthened treatment of the fundamental principles and philosophy of research, research methods, and strategies. A chapter on how to prepare a research proposal has been added, immediately preceding the chapters on quantitative and qualitative research methods. The research proposal chapter was requested by a number of professors who require preparation of a comprehensive research proposal as an early step in students' thesis or dissertation research.

Illustrative of the importance I place on the subject, the chapter on ethical research practices has been moved forward to become the second chapter in the text. Chapter 3, "The Building Blocks of Research," is also a new chapter. It includes a discussion of the debate over which ontological foundations and epistemological positions are most appropriate for public administration and nonprofit management research.

A significant improvement in this new edition is the expanded discussion on research in non-profit organizations (NPOs) in chapter 5. This additional material adds to, but does not supplant, the earlier stress on research in public administration. There are also more examples of research in nonprofit organizations in the chapters on specific research methods, and a discussion of some of the issues found in current research in nonprofit organizations.

Part 2 of the book has been expanded from three to four chapters with the addition of a new chapter on the steps and components necessary to produce a solid research proposal. Part 3, which covers quantitative research methods, has been revised and improved. Part 4, with its nine chapters on quantitative research designs and methods, has also been brought up to date with additional information on multivariate and nonparametric statistics. The last chapter in this section explains how to use the popular statistical software, Statistical Package for the Social Sciences (SPSS). Instructions on how to use Microsoft Excel to organize, tabulate, and analyze quantitative research data are included within the several chapters.

The chapter on qualitative research strategies in Part 5 has been extensively revised and another new chapter added. Chapter 26, the revised chapter, focuses on three models of action research. Chapter 27, which is also concerned with critical research, discusses empowerment research and the feminist research model in greater depth than in the first edition. The last two chapters in Part 7 of the first edition have been combined into a single chapter on organizing, structuring, and writing a final report of the research findings. The chapter includes a modernized and expanded emphasis on APA style.

ACKNOWLEDGMENTS

Many people—students, faculty, and administrators—helped with the second edition of this text. Among the greatest contributors to this project are my colleagues at the schools where I have been privileged to spend the years since the appearance of the first edition: Pacific Lutheran University, The Evergreen State College, the Stockholm School of Economics at Riga, Latvia, and the University of Maryland–University College; I owe you all a debt of gratitude that I can never fully repay.

I wish again to extend my appreciation to the many members of the excellent staff at the book's publisher, M.E. Sharpe, Inc.; thanks are particularly due to Angela Piliouras, managing editor, and Jerry Altobelli, copyeditor. Throughout the writing and editing processes, these talented people have provided knowledgeable, insightful criticism and assistance that only improved the final product. I again wish to particularly thank executive editor Harry Briggs for his continued support and encouragement.

Finally, I wish thank the students and professors for their great feedback and the many contributions they have provided for this new edition. Their assistance is, as always, greatly appreciated; the book could not have been written without their help. As always, I thank my family for their continued support.

David E. McNabb, Ph.D.
Hartstene Island, Washington

INTRODUCTION

This book is about some of the many different forms and directions that research in the public and nonprofit sectors can take. Its chief objectives are first to explain the fundamental principles that underlie the activity of research, and second to instruct students and practitioners of government and nonprofit organizations in the ways to conduct research activities. Throughout, the discussion follows an applied rather than a theoretical emphasis. This is exemplified in the definition of research upon which the focus hangs: *Research* is the process of systematically acquiring data to answer a question, solve a problem or problems, or guide an action.

The collected knowledge about research and research methods continues to grow rapidly. Of particular importance to researchers today is the increasing acceptance of qualitative research methods. Little more than a decade ago, many thought that following behavioral research principles was the only truly scientific way to conduct research, with analysis focusing primarily on measurements and statistical analysis. This is no longer the case; today, qualitative methods have become part of the mainstream in political science and public administration; they stand on an equal footing with quantitative methods. The fall 2004 newsletter of the American Political Science Association's section on qualitative methods included a note that illustrates this growing acceptance. Section President Andrew Bennett of Georgetown University reported that section membership was then "well over 700," with attendance at the annual *Institute on Qualitative Methods* in 2004 nearly double that of 2002.

Equally vital qualitative research sections also exist in the Academy of Management (AOM), and the American Society for Public Administration Association (APSA). These and similar organizations publish newsletters and journals on qualitative research methods. However, before proceeding with the instructional elements of the text, it is important that to establish working definitions of both public administration and nonprofit management.

PUBLIC ADMINISTRATION IN SOCIETY

Understanding the evolution of public administration in society may help explain why so much of the research in the public sector is practical. Public administration in the first decade of the twenty-first century includes the study of local, state, and national governance, policy-making, and political activity; interorganizational operations; human and stakeholder relations; organizational theory; communications; human behavior; and the historical and legal foundations of governing. Thus, public administration from the point of view of research can be described as a diverse and constantly changing field of inquiry into the behavior of individuals and groups involved in the administrative and managerial activities and processes. Researchers study people involved in analyzing, planning, organizing, implementing, and controlling the programs and activities of government agencies, units, and systems for the purpose of meeting the needs of society.

The research conducted in this discipline addresses the many organizational and management questions that arise from this wide-ranging field. As the discipline continues to grow in scale and scope, some researchers have argued that the *positivist* approach, with its emphasis on quantitative methods, is still the only valid way to conduct research in this field. However, a growing body of researchers has come to believe that the positivist approach alone is no longer able to answer many of the problems facing public administrators. As a result, they have adopted qualitative research methods to find answers to these problems. Richardson and Fowers described these evolving attitudes that call for a shift in methodological emphasis in the following terms:

> [I]n spite of tremendous effort, enormous methodological sophistication, and many decades of efforts, mainstream social science [including public administration] has failed to achieve anything even resembling the kind of explanatory theory that counts and as truth and is needed for precise prediction and instrumental control. Just describing interesting patterns of variables—which always have many exceptions—does not yield the sort of technical control over events we associate with modern physics, biology, or engineering. (Richardson and Fowers 1998, 471)

Public administration researchers have looked at a wide variety of topics while maintaining a largely practical focus using a wide variety of research approaches, methods, and tools (Garson and Overman 1983; Stivers 2000; Lan and Anders 2000). The focus is still on *applied* or *empirical research* for the resolution of practical problems faced by public and nonprofit organization administrators and managers. Although very little pure or theoretical research is published in public administration professional journals, interest in theoretical research is on the increase. In recent decades, a small but growing number of researchers have directed their attention toward establishing or building on a *theory* of public administration—that is, finding the "truth" of public administration. This research has not proved to be particularly rewarding, however, as Stivers has noted:

> In my view, the field of public administration has been marked since the early twentieth century by a largely fruitless search for scientific truth. I say "fruitless" because the attempts to identify generalizations about administrative practice that hold across all or even most situations inevitably runs up against what seems to me to be an undeniable aspect of our subject matter—that is, any particular situation is simultaneously similar to and different from any other situation. (Stivers 2000, 134)

The bulk of public and nonprofit research is applied research. However, over the past several decades, a growing body of research on public administration theory has emerged. Today, a loosely organized group of academics and practitioners are joined in an effort to advance theoretical knowledge. The Public Administration Theory Network (www.PAT-Net.org) allows interested persons to share their ideas on political and social theory, philosophy and ethics, theory of institutions and organizations, and other related concepts, problems, and issues. The group publishes a quarterly journal, *Administrative Theory & Praxis* (ATP).

RESEARCH IN THE NONPROFIT SECTOR

It is difficult to generalize about nonprofit organizations, and equally difficult to come up with a definition that applies equally across their wide-ranging scope of activities (Hall 2005). To differentiate them from business and government, nonprofits may also be referred to as the third, the independent, the voluntary, the philanthropic, the social, the tax-exempt, or the charitable sector (Luckert 2005). Fundamentally, any organization formed to serve a social need or for the benefit of its members, and which does not include making a profit among its objectives, can be considered a nonprofit organization. These organizations are not legally restricted from making a profit; clearly they must earn more than they spend. However, any excess income over expenses must be retained for use by the organization; if any part of the net earnings of the organization is distributed among the organization's owners, members, shareholders, or private individuals, the organization stands to lose its tax-exempt status. Nonprofits are defined by the Nonprofit Resource Center (NRC) as:

> In a nutshell, a nonprofit corporation is an organization formed for the purpose of serving a purpose of public or mutual benefit other than the pursuit or accumulation of profits. A Nonprofit is not a way for ordinary businesses—or people—to shield assets or avoid paying income tax. It is not an alternative business form for any regular type of business. (NRC 2006, 1)

The Internal Revenue Service (IRS) separates the more than 1.2 million U.S. nonprofit organizations into two broad classes, both of which are exempt from paying federal income tax: charitable [(501(c)] organizations and civic or noncharitable [501(d)] organizations. The IRS considers donations made to charitable organizations to be tax deductible. Although civic organizations have tax-exempt status, donations made to them are not deductible.

Beyond this simple dichotomy, nonprofits are further categorized as (1) charities, (2) foundations, (3) public welfare or advocacy organizations, (4) professional and/or trade organizations, and (5) religious organizations. Charities include such organizations as the United Way and the Red Cross; foundations include such organizations and the Bill and Melinda Gates Foundation and the Ford Foundation; public welfare organizations include such groups as the American Civil Liberties Union and colleges and universities; advocacy groups include such groups as the National Rifle Association and Nature Conservancy; professional and trade organizations include local chambers of commerce and the American Dental Association; religious organizations include church denominations (Luckert 2005).

There are twenty-two classes of organizations included in the IRS 501(c) classification. However, according to the Nonprofit Resource Center, people are most familiar with religious organizations and what the Center calls "public benefit corporations." These are organizations that exist for scientific, artistic, literary, education, or charitable purposes. The IRS groups these organizations together in its 501(c)(3) category.

Nonprofits can be local, regional, national, or international. Those that operate globally—the nongovernment organizations, or NGOs—have acquired great importance in the world's economy. They have filled in for individual nations or existing international government bodies (such as the United Nations) during international disaster and famine, when health relief agencies provide their services regardless of ethnic, political, or cultural boundaries.

GETTING STARTED IN RESEARCH

When beginning researchers embark on what too often seems to be an extremely daunting and thoroughly confusing research task, they find themselves faced with finding answers to such questions as:

- What is the purpose for doing this research?
- What is a research problem?
- Who has the needed information?
- What is the best way to ask questions?
- Which research design should be followed in this situation?
- How should the data be gathered?
- How should data be processed?
- What does all this processed data mean?
- What is the best way to communicate these findings?

It is equally important that researchers know what questions *not* to ask, what questions cannot be readily answered, and how much research can be conducted in the time allotted and with the people and money available.

PURPOSES OF RESEARCH

Research is conducted for many different purposes. At its most fundamental level, the purpose of research may be either *basic* or *applied.* Basic research, which is also called *pure* or *theoretical* research, is conducted to increase the general storehouse of knowledge. Basic research is concerned with coming up with theories about what things are and why events happen the way they do. An example of basic research is the study of the fossils of life forms that existed on earth millions of years ago. This is the science of paleontology, and is characterized by an emphasis on *theory building* rather on the application of solutions to real-life problems. A typical theory in paleontology may be concerned with why the dinosaurs disappeared. The findings of paleontologists are interesting indeed, but to many people they have little immediate, practical value.

On the other hand, applied research is conducted to solve practical problems or to help researchers understand past behavior in order to predict future behavior. Applied researchers are concerned with developing theories why something happened; they look for *causal* relationships. They conduct research in order to describe in detail what happened or to plan programs that will cause events to happen. In this way, they hope to be able to predict future events or consequences.

Categorizing the Purposes of Research

There are many ways to characterize purposes for a research study. Neuman (2000) has suggested that all social science research is conducted for any one or more of four different purposes: to answer some practical question; to gather information that will enable them to make better decisions; to add to the body of knowledge about a topic or field; and to change society in some way.

A number of authors have tried to develop a set of purposes that are specific to the topics and questions found in public administration. Babbie (2001), for example, identified three purposes for research in the social sciences, including political science and public administration: (1) the *exploration* of a topic; (2) the *description* of a topic, situation, or event; or (3) to *explain* some phenomenon. In their discussion of the comparative method in political science research, Pennings, Keman, and Kleinnijenhuis (1999) identified three purposes for research: (1) regularities regarding the relationship between societal and political actors, (2) the processes of institutionalization of political life, and (3) the changes in society that emerge from the first two forces.

Stallings and Ferris (1988) identified three categories of research: *conceptual, relationship,* and *evaluative.* The purpose of a conceptual study is to establish the fundamental concepts that underlie a problem. Conceptual studies are designed to identify critical variables for further research or to frame a problem for which another study can be developed. The purpose of a relationship study is to describe relationships between variables or investigate the potential for causation resulting from a relationship. Finally, evaluative studies are designed to explain or evaluate an event, a program, a policy, or some other phenomenon.

A different approach was taken by Lathrop (1969), who described four purposes in research methods: (1) theory testing, (2) extending the range of applicability of existing research, (3) resolving conflicting research findings, and (4) replicating previous studies.

Identifying Research Objectives

Another way to categorize purposes for research is to view them as *research objectives.* In science, research objectives and research purposes are nearly interchangeable terms. For example, three common objectives for research are: (1) to *explore* a topic for the purpose of gaining insights and ideas, (2) to *describe* a topic, which typically has the purpose of counting the occurrence of one or more phenomena, or (3) to establish and/or measure *causation* to determine the power of one or more independent variables to influence change in a dependent variable. These three purposes could just as easily been termed "objectives."

PURPOSE OF THE BOOK

The purpose of this book is to provide in one location information about how to design, conduct, interpret, and report on research projects. It should serve as a tool for reading and writing on any administrative or social science discipline or topic. Its emphasis, however, is on research methods for students of public administration and those already embarked on their careers. It can also aid students who have little or no experience in writing a scholarly paper or article for publication in a professional journal.

This book is organized around a discussion of the two major research strategies: quantitative and qualitative research. The text defines and explains some of the major variations and processes employed in these strategies, focusing on the different research methods used today in public administration and nonprofit organization research. A few studies combine elements of both approaches; these are mentioned throughout the work.

Graduate students will find the book useful for designing and completing assignments in a research methods course, and for the research phase of their degree thesis or dissertation. Managers in administrative and managerial positions may use the book as a step-by-step guide for designing and conducting a research project with their staff. In addition to a review of the basic features of researching and reporting, a number of discipline-specific requirements and examples are provided.

SCOPE OF THE BOOK

This book has been written to help students and administrators in public administration and nonprofit organizations successfully complete both simple and complex research projects. It covers such important topics as research design, specifying research problems, designing questionnaires and writing questions, designing and carrying out qualitative research approaches, and analyzing both quantitative and qualitative research data. Also covered is the evolution of the research philosophy from the positivist approach to postpositivist theory and critical research.

The book was developed to fill a need for a text on research methods that incorporates the latest thinking in public administration and nonprofit organization management. It includes discussions and examples of research topics and research methods found in the current professional literature. It incorporates the latest developments in social science research, management and organizations research, and research in the social and administrative sciences, and also provides specific instructions in the use of available statistical software programs like Excel and SPSS.

STRUCTURE OF THE BOOK

The book is organized into seven major sections, each with one or more chapters. The first section, "Research Fundamentals," contains five chapters. Chapter 1, "Introduction to Research Methods," includes working definitions of research and the scientific method, as well as a rationale for students to develop the skills to conduct research projects and interpret and report their findings. The chapter also introduces the chief philosophical approaches to research and science: the *quantitative* and the *qualitative* approaches (the *positivist* and *postpositivist* epistemological approaches).

Chapter 2, "Research Ethics: Doing the Right Thing," begins with an overview of the fundamental moral principles upon which ethical decisions are founded and concludes with a discussion of the key moral concerns and ethical dilemmas encountered by researchers. Special emphasis is placed on research with human subjects. Chapter 3, "The Building Blocks of Research," is a discussion of the fundamental issues currently influencing the form and content of public administration and nonprofit organization research.

Chapter 4, "Public Administration Research: Theory and Practice," provides an overview of the art and science of research in public administration. The chapter discusses positivist and postpositivist research models. It includes a discussion of the purpose and rational of social science research in general, and in the public sector specifically. The chapter also includes a discussion on the use of research for theory building, and on research in its practical, applied approach. Chapter 5, "Research in Nonprofit Organizations," follows the lead of Chapter 4 by providing an introduction to the scale and scope of ways research can improve management decision making in this important economic sector. Research in this sector typically addresses normative issues. This chapter describes the processes and issues driving research in nonprofit organization management.

Part 2, "Understanding the Research Process," provides a basic understanding of the necessary steps that must be taken when conducting a research project. Chapter 6, "The Eight Steps of the Research Process," explains the steps researchers follow when designing and conducting research. If followed closely, these steps, have the power to improve the outcomes of research—regardless of the type of research problem or issues they study. Chapter 7, "Selecting a Research Topic," explains what is necessary to define a research problem. It also provides suggestions on how and where to begin the literature search. Literature searches involve detailed examination of textbooks, journals, electronically stored and retrieved articles, and other materials in sources inside and outside of the researchers' organization. Most researchers' early research proposals tend to be far too broad for the resources at hand (particularly time and money). Therefore, a discussion on the importance of a *research focus* is included in this chapter.

Chapter 8, "Choosing a Research Design," discusses the three chief ways to design and conduct research projects: *quantitative, qualitative,* and *combination* strategies. Combined designs include parts of both quantitative and qualitative strategies and methods. Chapter 9, "Putting Together a Research Proposal," includes instruction on how to develop a *research proposal*—a critical early step in a research project. The chapter includes several different organizational structures for proposals.

Part 3, "Quantitative Research Strategies," consists of three chapters that introduce readers to key elements of quantitative research designs: statistical analysis, sampling, and survey instruments. Chapter 10, "Fundamentals of Quantitative Research," begins with a discussion of the characteristics of measurements and includes an explanation of the categories of statistics used in the public and nonprofit sectors. Chapter 11, "Introduction to Sampling," discusses the sampling process, explaining how and why researchers use simple random samples (SRS). The chapter also introduces readers to the concept of measurement distributions. Chapter 12, "Writing Questions and Developing Questionnaires," is a practical guide to writing the kinds of questions and developing the survey instruments that have the best promise of returning the needed data.

Part 4, "Quantitative Research Methods," is one of the largest sections in the text. Chapter 13, "Summarizing Data with Descriptive Statistics," is a practical guide to producing the several categories of statistics that form the foundation of quantitative research. Chapter 14, "Using Tables, Charts, and Graphs," describes how graphic tools can improve the readability of research reports. It describes specific software steps needed to produce tables, charts, figures, and graphs. Chapter 15, "Research Hypotheses," discusses the various types of hypotheses used in by researchers. Hypotheses establish the basis or benchmark upon which the design of all data collection and statistical analysis should be based.

In Chapter 16, "Testing Hypotheses About Two or More Groups," readers are introduced to some of the more commonly used approaches to testing hypotheses about differences. This chapter focuses on *inferential statistics*—that is, the statistics pertaining to samples, in which probabilities play an important role. It reviews the *t*-test and analysis of variance approaches for measuring statistically significant differences between two or more groups or subgroups.

Chapter 17, "Testing Relationships with Correlation and Regression," also deals with hypothesis testing. It discusses two important statistical methods used in association analysis: correlation and regression analysis. Chapter 18, "Experiments and Experimental Design," focuses on the tasks and analysis concepts associated with designing and conducting experiments; it also introduces the statistical tests used in experimental or cause-and-effect research designs. Included are single-factor, multiple factor, and regression analysis methods.

The next two chapters are new to this edition. Chapter 19, "Nonparametric Statistics," examines nonparametric analogs of popular statistics used in studies involving samples and populations. The chapter explains how to use statistical software to calculate many nonparametric statistics. Chapter 20, "Exploring Multivariate Statistics," introduces three popular families of multivariate statistical designs: multiple regression analysis, factor and cluster analysis, and multiple discriminant analysis.

Chapter 21, "Conducting Statistical Tests with SPSS," describes how to use the powerful statistical software package the Statistical Package for the Social Sciences (SPSS) to process most if not all of the statistical tests used in public administration and nonprofit organization management research.

In Part 5, "Qualitative Research Strategies and Methods," readers are introduced to ways to plan and implement the major types of qualitative research designs. Chapter 22, "Introduction to Qualitative Research," describes the purpose and scope of some of the more common qualitative research strategies. It also discusses how qualitative designs can contribute to understanding public and nonprofit organizational culture and its impact upon employees and the public. Chapter 23, "Research Using the Case Study Approach," describes both the single- and multicase approaches to research. The case method is considered by many to be one of the most productive qualitative designs in public administration and nonprofit organization research.

Chapter 24, "Research Using the Grounded Theory Approach," looks at a strategy that is becoming increasingly popular among researchers in education, sociology, and social psychology as well as public administration and nonprofit organization management. In these studies, researchers approach a situation, event, or relationship with little or no preconceived theoretical bias. The researcher seeks to construct a theory only after the in-depth analysis of the study data.

Chapter 25, "Research Using the Ethnographic Approach," is a discussion of some ways that this culture-based strategy is used in public administration. Ethnography was originally developed to describe and explain phenomena in distant and what were considered to be "primitive" societies. It has also been successfully adapted to research on modern cultures and subcultures. Chapter 26, "Critical Research: Action Research Approaches," is the first of two chapters on critical research designs. This revised and expanded chapter examines three models of action research. Chapter 27, "Critical Research: Empowerment and Feminist Models," is the second chapter on critical research. This new chapter is designed to help readers understand how empowerment research and feminist research strategies have expanded the horizons of public administration and nonprofit organization research.

Part 6, "Analysis and Interpretation of Qualitative Data," includes two chapters on methods used for analyzing qualitative data. The first, chapter 28, "Analyzing Qualitative Data," introduces the fundamentals of qualitative data analysis. It includes a brief introduction to several software programs that have been developed to analyze large amounts of qualitative data. Chapter 29, "Analyzing Texts, Documents, and Artifacts," introduces readers to a number of research approaches to qualitative data analysis of the symbolic meanings of texts, documents, concepts, ideas, and things. Typically, researchers using these tools are interested in determining how events are interpreted and written about in narrative or graphic form. Narrative and discourse analysis are becoming increasingly important in social and administrative science research. The content analysis method of researching published documents, internal memos, and similar secondary sources is also discussed.

Part 7, "Preparing the Research Report," consists of a final chapter that provides instruction on how to organize, structure, and write a final research report. Chapter 30, "Writing the Research Report," provides instruction on how to organize and structure the report and takes a brief look at the various styles, rules, and requirements researchers must deal with when writing a research report.

SUMMARY

Research has many definitions. The definition that serves as the backbone upon which hangs the subsequent meat and sinew found in this text is: *Research is the process of systematically acquiring data to answer a question, solve a problem or problems, or guide an action.* This means that research is always a purposeful activity of management. To achieve the goals for which it will be intended, research must be systematically planned and carried out.

PART 1

RESEARCH FUNDAMENTALS

1

INTRODUCTION TO RESEARCH METHODS

Knowing how to conduct research is an important skill needed by all administrators and managers in public and nonprofit organizations. *Research* involves collecting, processing, analyzing, and interpreting data, then intelligently and cogently communicating the results of the analysis in a report that describes what was discovered from the research. Knowing how to interpret and evaluate research that has been conducted by academics, administrators, or contract research organizations is equally important. To learn the skills needed to conduct and evaluate research, students of public administration participate in one or more courses in *research methodology*. Designing and conducting a research project is usually a requirement in those courses. This book has been written to help students and practicing public and nonprofit organization managers successfully complete research projects. It is organized around a discussion of both quantitative and qualitative research strategies, as well as some studies that combine elements of both approaches. There is no magic to the activity of research; at its most fundamental, all it takes is the ability to ask questions and record and interpret answers.

FIVE REASONS TO DEVELOP RESEARCH SKILLS

There are at least five very good reasons for developing or expanding the skills needed to use research methods and prepare written research reports. The first reason is that it will help develop and hone critical analysis and communication skills. Government and nonprofit organization employers have long identified these skills as the most important characteristics of successful leaders and managers. Employees who are able to gather relevant information, analyze and interpret data, and communicate their findings effectively to others are valuable assets in all organizations.

A second reason is that by engaging in the research process, the public administrator can become aware of what others in the career field are doing and saying about what may be common problems. Nearly every issue of relevant periodical literature contains one or more reports about research on topical issues and concerns in public and nonprofit organization administration. Reviewing this research literature—an important early step in all research projects—can help administrators and managers save time, money, and other resources when addressing similar problems.

A third reason for learning how to do research has to do with *credibility*. Credibility is closely associated with the concepts of *replicability*, and *reliability*—both ideas that are fundamental to the scientific method. To be considered credible, a theory that is developed according to the scientific method must be testable; that is, the research behind the theory must be able to be replicated by

Box 1.1
What Happens When Research Findings Cannot Be Replicated?

Alzheimer's disease is considered to be a result of degeneration of the neurological system. Testing of an experimental Alzheimer's vaccine was halted in 2002 when researchers discovered that some patients experienced brain inflammation in reaction to the vaccine. The patients' autoimmune system reacted with an attack.

However, other researchers working on neurological studies with laboratory mice reported achieving positive results—in ways not anticipated. Results of their early lab experiments showed promise for repairing nerve degeneration, which is also associated with such conditions as glaucoma and spinal injury.

On the basis of these findings, the researchers concluded that a mild autoimmune reaction might actually benefit the body. The medical community's reactions to the results remained mixed, however, as other researchers have not been able to replicate their laboratory mice findings. As of 2006, the once-promising research results remained little more than an interesting theory.

Source: Minkel 2006.

others. Only through replication of results can the theory become credible. Furthermore, conclusions that are derived from such theories must be developed following methods that are repeatable, predictable, and supportable. Thus, for research to be considered "scientific" anyone reading a report of the research must be able to achieve the same or similar results by following the same research design. If not, the findings may simply not be believed.

A fourth reason is the way new information is passed on to future generations. The findings of research studies are often published in scientific and professional journals. Research findings are also disseminated in papers presented at professional conferences and scholarly or professional meetings. Scientists and others with an interest in a field of inquiry often consider the research unreliable or unfounded unless the findings are published—typically in peer-reviewed journals (Gubanich 1991). Following well-established guidelines for conducting research and writing research reports makes verification through publishing more likely to take place.

Since professional journals usually present the most current information available, editors try to publish information on the "cutting edge" of their discipline or profession. In this way, journals provide the new information needed for success in a career field, and researchers come to know which publications in their field are the best resources for this information.

A fifth reason is that in this era of rapid change and uncertainty, public and nonprofit agency administrators must have the ability to make quick, intelligent decisions. The best decisions are almost always made after all the available information pertaining to the outcomes of the decisions is gathered, read, and weighed. This usually involves some research activity, whether it is formal or informal.

Research and writing are important skills required of all public administrators. Researching means gathering, processing, and interpreting data of some kind. Research results must be communicated in intelligent and well-written reports. Public administrators also must interpret and evaluate research reports that have been produced by academics, administrators, or contract-research organizations. Producing clear, cogent reports is an important ingredient in producing effective research.

Box 1.2
What to Do When Research Findings Generate Skepticism

Scientific research generates knowledge that is founded upon observation, study, and experimentation. This knowledge, in turn, generates testable theories. For a theory to become an accepted explanation of a phenomenon—that is, to become a *law*—other researchers must have access to the study's findings and methods. Skepticism is a natural artifact, and dictates that other researchers are able to replicate the findings. Pseudo- or non-scientific research, on the other hand, does not welcome debate or criticism. Pseudoscientific research produces findings that cannot be reproduced and are based upon the researchers' faith or hopes alone. Examples of nonscientific theories include intelligent design (scientific creationism), crop circles as messages to or from alien beings, and "free" energy from cold fusion.

Public and nonprofit sector administrators and managers must arm themselves against purveyors of pseudoscientific research findings. The following four principles are good points to remember when reviewing all research findings:

1. *Extraordinary claims demand extraordinary evidence.* The more counterintuitive a claim or the more it contradicts existing evidence, the greater the need to provide proof that it is not the result of error or even fraud on the part of the researcher.
2. *Proof for extraordinary claims is the responsibility of the researcher.* It is not the task of the administrator or recipient of the findings to prove the researcher right or wrong, but rather to point out questionable or problematic contentions and wait for the proof to be provided.
3. *To be taken seriously, findings must be testable.* Claims must be verifiable, clear, and presented logically. This means that other researchers must be able to achieve similar results employing replicated methods. The researcher must state what is used as evidence for a claim, as well as what constitutes an acceptable amount of evidence.
4. *The evidence must be accessible to all critics.* Researchers who are unwilling to share their methods, data, and findings with other researchers lose any claim to believability.

Source: Beyerstein 1995.

RESEARCH—THE SCIENTIFIC WAY

Conducting "good" research—that is, doing research the *scientific way*—means following a fundamental set of rules and approaches to problem solving that have shaped most of the advances in science, learning, and technology. That set of rules is what we call the *scientific method*. The scientific method includes a set of procedures and a philosophy or mind-set that shape the way people approach a research activity (Achinstein 1970). Rosenthal and Rosnow (1991) emphasized this concept of mind-set in their definitions of research and the scientific method. They considered the scientific method to be a distinct way of approaching problem resolution that can be used regardless of the problem addressed or approaches and methods employed.

Following the scientific method means approaching a research problem without any preconceived answers; it requires avoiding any hint of subjective bias. This does not mean leaping into a research problem blind. It means developing ideas about what might be happening—coming up with a *hypothesis,* and in some types of qualitative research, *testing a theory.*

Research the scientific way can be applied to many different problems or questions. However, the goals of most scientific research typically fall into these categories: (1) research to *describe* some event, thing, or phenomenon, or the procedures by which events and their relationships are defined, classified, catalogued or categorized; (2) research to *predict* future behavior or events based on observed changes in existing conditions; or (3) research to provide greater *understanding* of phenomena, how variables are related, or of the underlying causes of the occurrence of a phenomenon (Shaughnessy and Zechmeister 1994). Key elements of research conducted for all these purposes include: defining issues, terms, and concepts, forming hypotheses and/or theories, and applying an appropriate quantitative or qualitative research method and data analysis technique. These will all be discussed in greater detail in the chapters that follow.

Activities in Scientific Research

Typically, the triggering activity in researching the scientific way is the *recognition of a problem.* For example, an administrator or manager is assigned the task of developing a plan to reorganize an agency. The administrator recognizes that many facts about the reorganization problem are not known or understood. For example, how might the reorganization affect the agency's ability to carry out its mission? How might the reorganization affect staff morale? What other outcomes will impact which agency stakeholders? The administrator needs information to devise the research plan. He or she believes that the unknown information is important enough that an effort should be taken to collect and interpret its meaning. Thus is born a research project.

To begin the research, the administrator must collect data. One way to do this is to make observations and/or measurements of the "things" (variables) associated with the problem. To know what questions to ask in order to collect the right data, the administrator will have to have some ideas about what might happen during and after agency reorganization. These ideas are called *hypotheses.* A hypothesis is simply a statement of what the researcher thinks might or might not happen, or might cause something else to happen.

The administrator may then test the hypothesis or hypotheses in a number of different ways. In quantitative designs, *objective* statistical tests are used for this purpose. In qualitative designs, the researcher makes a *subjective* determination of the validity of the hypothesis. If the administrator determines the hypothesis is valid, he or she may then look to the literature for other applications to which the hypothesis can be applied, thus reinforcing belief in the conclusions.

Collecting Data

The process of gathering or accumulating data might include asking clients or staff to complete a survey questionnaire. Or it may involve interviewing those who will be affected by the reorganization; observing or reading about events, or examining case studies of similar agency reorganizations.

However gathered and arranged, these data must be coded, tabulated, analyzed, and interpreted. First, the collected data must be organized into some meaningful order, often according to their similarities or dissimilarities. The collected and organized data is then subjected to analysis and interpretation by the administrator. Through this process the data becomes the information the administrator needs for answers to questions. These answers then make it possible for the administrator to make the best possible decisions and plans.

If the reorganization plan assignment was for hypothetical purposes rather than for actual implementation, the administrator might formulate a *theory* about the potential impact of a reorganization of the agency. Theories are statements about hypothetical future events. For example, the administrator might propose a theory that states that, assuming the existence of similar variables and/or relationships, similar cause-and-effect results may be expected to occur with a similar reorganization plan.

To arrive at a theory, the administrator may employ two different types of reasoning. If *inductive reasoning* is used, a conclusion is reached by moving from the *specific to the general*. The inductive reasoning process involves the act of making an *inference*; that is, applying data from a single case or small sample to a larger population or future results. Or the administrator might use *deductive reasoning*. In deductive reasoning, the researcher concludes that the facts of the case speak for themselves; they constitute a theory. Following the deductive reasoning process means moving from the *general to the specific*. The conclusion reached from analysis and interpretation of the collected data is assumed to explain what took place in earlier situations as well the case at hand; the resulting *theory* that explains what will happen in reorganizations.

The final activity in this scientific approach to research is the verification of conclusions derived from the research. This may entail replication of the design with a different sample. For example, the researcher asks, "If X occurred once, will it occur in similar circumstances?" If it does, then the researcher may propose a *theory*. If others accept the theory, the researcher may attempt to have it accepted as a *law*.

THE SCIENTIFIC METHOD

While there are other ways to go about conducting research, the scientific approach underlies them all. This approach emerged during the Enlightenment, the explosion in scientific investigation and artistic creativity that began in Europe in the seventeenth century. Early scientific investigators proposed the scientific approach to research as a way of maintaining rigor in scientific investigation. The method, simply put, meant not coming to a conclusion on a basis of preformed beliefs alone, but instead on only what can be observed or tested by the senses. Authority, custom, or tradition—the stuff of metaphysics—should not be the source of knowledge and understanding. Instead, these should come from the reality of objects themselves (Richardson and Fowers 1998).

Bernard Phillips (1976) described how knowledge and understanding are achieved in the following terms:

> [The scientific method is] an effort to achieve increasing understanding of phenomena by (1) defining problems so as to build on available knowledge, (2) obtaining information essential for dealing with these problems, (3) analyzing and interpreting these data in accordance with clearly defined rules, and (4) communicating the results of these efforts to others. (p. 4)

Out of the scientific outlook described by Phillips emerged the idea that the world and everything in it was a giant collection of objects that could be mapped and understood by empirical observation. From this belief, natural scientists developed a faith in a formal and objective method of observing the world and its parts. Richardson and Fowers (1998) have described that faith as being "an almost boundless confidence" in the ability of science to explain the world. This belief came to be known as *positivism* or the *positivist* approach to science. The positivists saw this "faith in method" as the only path to true knowledge. That faith was eventually adopted by the social sciences that evolved in the nineteenth and twentieth centuries as well. Those early social scientists insisted using the same correlational and experimental methods used in the natural sciences, regardless of the subject matter being investigated.

LOGIC AND REASONING IN RESEARCH

Logic is the subfield of philosophy that relates to how people make judgments. The word evolved from the Greek *logos,* which in its translation to English is generally used to refer to the activity of *reasoning.* Reasoning refers to how people come to various conclusions. In the fourth century BC, Aristotle concluded that humans employ two types or methods of reasoning: deductive and inductive. Deductive reasoning means arriving at a conclusion on the basis of something that you know, or that you assume to be true—a general law. Deductive reasoning is usually demonstrated with a *syllogism.* A syllogism has three parts: a major premise, a minor premise, and a conclusion. In deductive reasoning, the conclusion *must* be true if the premises are true. A syllogism is often used to illustrate this concept. A syllogism is an argument that includes two premises (assumptions or definitions) and a conclusion. For example: (1) Socrates is a man; (2) all men are mortal; therefore, (3) Socrates is mortal (conclusion).

Deductive reasoning requires only that the premises be accepted as true in their own terms—that is, as they are defined by the researcher or assumed to be so. Truth, then, is what the researcher decides it is, or what it has always been; it is based on a *faith* that does not have to be empirically tested or proven. Deductive reasoning is the paradigm that underlies qualitative research.

For example, a cultural anthropologist might gather information about the mating habits of young islanders in a primitive society by observing their actions over time. The researcher may then conclude that these are the mating habits of all young people in that society. This may or may not be true for all subjects. Rather, it may be true only for the subjects observed by the researcher—or may even be what the subjects want the observer to believe is true. Thus, it can only be seen as a conclusion (or faith) of the researcher. It is not *Truth.*

Inductive reasoning, on the other hand, is the paradigm of *positivism.* This is the approach normally followed in research in the natural sciences and is typically *quantitative* in application. Positivism is the belief that knowledge can only be gained through direct observation and experimentation, not through metaphysics or theology. When following this approach, researchers identify a problem, gather data from observation or through an experiment, measure their results, and then draw an inductive conclusion from (and only from) the data. In this model, a conclusion is never considered to be final; it is always open to further question (verifiability). In inductive reasoning, the researcher uses a set of established facts (research data) to draw a general conclusion, but that conclusion remains open to revision if new facts are discovered.

The positivist approach emerged in the early twentieth century in Vienna, Austria, where a group of philosophers—the Vienna Circle—were concerned with what they saw as a rash of theoretical speculation in the new sciences that were appearing (Dusche 1994). These speculative concepts included evolution, natural selection, thermodynamics, and molecular theory. The Vienna Circle philosophers were worried that science was returning to its early metaphysical foundations. Their reaction was to propose a philosophy of science—positivism—that stressed the need for the researcher to follow a process that moves from observable evidence to accurate predictions. The positivist tradition remained the dominant research method in the natural and social sciences until the late 1970s. This approach follows the scientific method approach, and typically involves the following steps:

- Selection of a hypothesis
- Observation
- Data collection
- Hypothesis testing
- Acceptance or rejection of the hypothesis.

Competing Paradigms

A philosophical split exists between those who hold that the positivist approach is the only valid, truly scientific approach to follow in research and those who Phillips (1976) described as rejecting mathematics in favor of a *qualitative* or *empathic* research approach. The empathic approach supports arriving at scientific conclusions through application of thought rather than interpretation of observed phenomena. It is called qualitative to contrast it with the quantitative approach, which refers to measurements.

Positivist researchers argue strongly for the use of the positivist approach for public administration (Houston and Delevan 1990). They hold that a quantitative or measurement strategy is the best approach to use when studying problems in the public and nonprofit sectors. Early positivists believed that public administration could only be understood (and public policy be framed) through the study of human behavior known as *behavioralism*. Today, most public and nonprofit administration researchers agree that both the qualitative and quantitative models have a place in research. Moreover, both deductive and inductive reasoning can make valid contributions to research in the social and administrative sciences (White 1986, 1999).

Until very recently, inductive and deductive reasoning were considered to be two completely separate and competing paradigms: the positivist approach (discussed above) associated with inductive reasoning and quantitative research approaches; and the *postpositivist approach*, associated with deductive reasoning and qualitative research methods and emphasizing understanding as well as description or measuring of phenomena.

It is important to note that today most public and nonprofit administration researchers agree that no single method is the only appropriate way to conduct all research. Rather, there is a place and a purpose for all approaches and methods. There is a growing awareness of the need to use research to better *understand* as well as to describe human events and phenomena. Description has been the traditional domain of quantitative methods, whereas understanding involves the researcher in qualitative methods as well.

Periodically, conflict arises between these two philosophical camps, expressed in attempts to influence the direction of research in public administration and nonprofit organization management. However, much of the research carried out today involves elements of both approaches. Therefore, they are treated as equally as possible in this text.

THE QUANTITATIVE APPROACH TO RESEARCH

Quantitative research involves the use of *numbers* to describe things. It involves the statistical analysis of collected data. Statistical analysis can be as simple as counts and measures of central tendency (averages) or as complex as multivariate analysis of data and their relationships. Statistical tests are used to establish whether the differences in the way groups respond to a stimulus are "real" (that is, statistically significant), or whether they reflect a naturally occurring variation. Interpretations of statistical tests are usually based upon principles of *probability;* that is, we can never believe in the answer to a statistical test with 100 percent confidence. However, with some lesser degree of probability, such as 95 or 99 percent, researchers can be reasonably certain about the accuracy of their results.

The quantitative approach to research owes its growth in popularity during the 1920s and 1930s to the reemergence of *logical positivism* as a requisite principle of scientific inquiry (Phillips 1987). As previously stated, the positivist approach holds that a thing, idea, or concept is meaningful only if it can be seen or measured. As stated by Kaplan and Norton (1996, 21): "Measurement matters; if you can't measure it, you can't manage it." The qualitative argument, on the other hand, can be summarized in the obverse: "If you can count it, that ain't it" (Holsti 1969, 11).

The positivist approach was initially an attack on reasoning that was considered to be meta-physical—that is, based on faith alone—rather than scientific, which could be measured or seen. Positivists based their argument on what they saw as the inability of metaphysical phenomena to be verified.

During the first half of the twentieth century, this argument was extended beyond faith-based knowledge to bring all qualitative research methods into question. Recently, however, the argument against qualitative approaches has lost much of its acerbity, though it does flare up from time to time. Such statements as: "In all fields there is a growing tension between the so-called 'qualitative' and 'quantitative' paradigms," indicate that the debate between the two views is not entirely resolved (Phillips 1987, 27).

THE QUALITATIVE APPROACH TO RESEARCH

Qualitative strategies fall into one or more of three types of study techniques. These are *explanatory, interpretive,* and *critical* (White 1999). These approaches or research designs can be applied to many different study methods, including ethnography (the study of social groups); kinetics (the study of movement); atmospherics (the study of influences on the physical environment of places); phenomenology (the study of things and events as people perceive them); and proxemics (the study of special relationships in social settings).

Data gathering in qualitative studies can occur through many different means. Chief among these methods are focus-group interviews, individual and group interviews, and the use of un-obtrusive measures such as simple observation and analysis of documents and/or artifacts. Two qualitative research approaches that are often used in the administrative sciences are ethnography and the case study approach. Data gathering in ethnography usually takes place during observation or researcher participation in group activities. Researchers studying native cultures developed ethnographic methods, which were then picked up and expanded upon by sociologists and public administration researchers. The method has a long history of use in studies of group behavior in business and government. Case studies in which data were gathered during ethnographic studies are used extensively in public administration, nonprofit and business management research.

Ethnography allows researchers to gather information while acting as participants in a group situation, thereby identifying *patterns* in human activity. According to Gill and Johnson (1991), ethnography focuses on the way that people interact and cooperate. Ethnographic research is often considered to be *unobtrusive* because subjects' behavior is observed but not intentionally manipulated.

Another qualitative research method is the case study. Two types of case studies are used in the administrative sciences—the single case approach, and one that uses a limited number of closely related cases. For both approaches, Van Evera (1997) identified five main uses for case studies in political science and public administration: (1) to create theories, (2) to test previously established theories, (3) for identifying preceding or contributing conditions, (4) for testing the importance of these antecedent conditions, and (5) for explaining cases of fundamental or intrinsic importance.

A Combined Approach

Combined studies employ both qualitative and quantitative methods. Several broad classes of studies are considered to be combined approaches, including document analysis, the study of archival data, media studies, and artifact interpretation. In these approaches, data collection and analysis are interconnected. Techniques used in these types of studies include *hermeneutics, content analysis,* and *in-situ analysis.*

Hermeneutics

The analysis of documents and texts is possibly the most commonly encountered combined approach. The qualitative technique often used in such research is called *hermeneutic analysis* or simply *hermeneutics.* Hermeneutics is the science of subjective interpretation of the content in printed texts and documents. It was originally an approach to the study of biblical texts, but has been expanded greatly in scope and is now a fundamental method underlying all learning. Accordingly,

> Hermeneutics has come forward as that comprehensive standpoint from which to view all the projects of human learning. For those of us who have been puzzled by the new intellectual dominance of hermeneutics, the key is that the term no longer refers to the interpretation of texts only but encompasses all the ways in which subjects and objects are involved in human communication. From "theories of everything" in natural science, to the textualizing of every act of communication, hermeneutics has become an essential reflection upon knowledge claims and a recategorization of the act of making knowledge claims. Under this conceptuality, hermeneutics or interpretation has come to be regarded as shorthand for all the practices of human learning. (Richardson 1995, 8)

This definition of hermeneutics includes an underlying philosophy of science and a particular way of analyzing textual material (Myers 1997). In its philosophical role, hermeneutics provides the foundations for the concept of *interpretivism.* As a method of analysis, its focus is on answering the question: What is the meaning of this text (or language)? In what is called "a hermeneutic circle," it involves first developing an understanding of the text as a whole and then moves to an interpretation of its parts, in themselves and as they relate to the whole. It also involves understanding the context in which the text or artifact was first created.

As a caveat, it is important to mention that by itself, the hermeneutic approach to document analysis does not result in the establishment of any fundamental "truth." Rather, it is truth as the research believes truth to be—and as the original author of the text intended it to be. As Maas (1999) has noted:

> Though the influence of hermeneutics is far-reaching, its efficiency must not be overstated. Hermeneutics does not . . . rectify false philosophical principles or perverse passions . . . of itself, hermeneutics does not investigate the objective truth of a writer's meaning . . . it does not inquire what is true or false, but only what the writer intended to say. Hence, a hermeneutic truth may be an objective falsehood. (p. 2)

Content Analysis

Content analysis is the quantitative component of document analysis. It is used to describe attributes contained in documents and other forms of messages, but is not intended to determine the intentions of the sender. The process involves breaking the written material down into researcher-selected categories or units. The researcher then prepares an "item dictionary" in order to clearly define identified constructs. Measurements of the occurrence of these items in the text make statistical analysis of the data possible.

Holsti (1969, 14) defined the content analysis process as "any technique for making inferences by objectively and systematically identifying specified characteristics of messages." The point he was making is that content analysis does not illuminate "truth." It can only measure *usage*.

Holsti did not limit analysis of data gathered by the process only to quantitative analysis, stating that he believed that a "rigid qualitative-quantitative distinction seems unwarranted." He concluded that researchers using content analysis should use both qualitative and quantitative methods to supplement each other. In this way, Holsti can be said to have combined aspects of hermeneutics with the traditional quantitative interpretation of content analysis.

Bernard (1994, 339) defined content analysis as a "catch-all term" used to describe a variety of techniques for making inferences from textual material: "The idea [of content analysis techniques] is to reduce the information in a text to a series of variables that can then be examined for correlations." He noted that the major difficulty with the process is the subjectivity inherent in identifying the original codes and categories that are to be counted. It is nearly impossible to avoid interjecting some researcher bias into this step of the analysis.

In Situ Analysis

In situ analysis is very similar to content analysis in that it involves both interpretive and quantitative analyses. The researcher must go beyond simply counting phenomena, for this only provides a partial picture of the concept under study. For full understanding, the researcher must also determine the meaning underlying the event or behavior under study.

This process examines the artifacts and inventions of human and organizational cultures in the environment in which they exist. The growing discipline of urban archeology incorporates these techniques. Examples of in situ studies include examining refuse sites to determine such things as product usage, waste generation, and consumption rates. The technique has great potential for public administration research, but has not yet been widely adopted.

THE FUTURE OF RESEARCH

What is the importance of this "competing paradigm" to today's students of public administration and nonprofit organization management? A number of implications can be drawn from these differences of opinion. First, the emphasis on research topics that address practical, organizational administrative issues over theory building is still very much alive, as a glance through the top journals in public administration and nonprofit organization management will attest. Second, despite this remaining emphasis, there seem to be few if any restrictions on the nature of the study problems addressed in public and nonprofit organization research. Third, public and nonprofit sector researchers use qualitative and quantitative research methods in generally equal proportions. Academic researchers still favor adopting quantitative research, although a growing number of researchers appear to favor qualitative approaches.

SUMMARY

Research in the public and nonprofit sectors is conducted by students, academicians, people working in public agencies, and by consultants. Most of this research is concerned with problem-solving issues as they occur at all levels of government and nonprofit organization management.

Three types of research strategies are used in public sector research: qualitative, quantitative, and combined. Qualitative research strategies are marginally preferred over quantitative strategies. Qualitative strategies involve such mainstream social science research methods as ethnography, phenomenology, case studies, and the like. They may be explanatory, interpretive, or critical designs.

Quantitative strategies are statistical designs. They may be exploratory, descriptive, or causal, or they may involve all three approaches in a more comprehensive, large sample design. Most quantitative studies did not go much beyond the use of simple descriptive statistics.

Combined strategies employ components of both qualitative and quantitative methods. Hermeneutics is emerging as a major direction in the philosophy of science and is, hence, influencing the manner in which qualitative research in public and nonprofit organization administration is conducted.

Content analysis is the process of breaking written material down into researcher-selected categories or units for statistical analysis. In situ analysis is similar to content analysis in that it involves both interpretive and quantitative analyses. Simply counting phenomena provides only a partial picture of the concept under study; for full understanding, the researcher must also determine the meaning that underlies the event.

ADDITIONAL READING

Beyerstein, Barry L. 1995. *Distinguishing Science from Pseudoscience.* Monograph prepared for The Center for Curriculum and Professional Development. Victoria, BC: Simon Fraser University.

Collins, Harry, and Trevor Pinch. 1993. *The Golem: What Everyone Should Know about Science.* Cambridge, UK: Cambridge University Press.

Couvalis, George. 1997. *The Philosophy of Science: Science and Objectivity.* London: Sage.

Holsti, Ole R. 1969. *Content Analysis for the Social Sciences and Humanities.* Menlo Park, CA: Addison-Wesley.

Hughes, John, and Wes Sharrock. 1997. *The Philosophy of Social Research.* 3rd ed. London: Addison Wesley Longman.

Schwab, Donald P. 1999. *Research Methods for Organizational Studies.* Mahwah, NJ: Lawrence Erlbaum Associates.

2

RESEARCH ETHICS: DOING THE RIGHT THING

Why do some people select careers in public administration over work in the private sector? Why do others elect to devote their working life to helping others by laboring in nonprofit agencies and organizations—what are sometimes collectively referred to as *nongovernment organizations* (NGOs)? Pay in government and NGO service is often much less than in industry; the hours are often longer; the personal rewards, such as expense accounts, company cars, and attractive retirement programs are often fewer and of less monetary value.

There are many answers to these questions, of course. Some people choose careers in government or nonprofit organizations because they believe it is the best place to exercise their particular skills. The military, public safety, wastewater management, and child welfare are just a few of many examples that come to mind. Others do so by accident; they might have begun as an intern during college and stayed on after graduation. Still others do it because of a sincere desire to serve. Their own quality of life is enhanced because they know that every day they are doing something to make life better or easier for people less fortunate than themselves. Finally, some do it specifically to lie, cheat, and steal.

No matter how honorable, how thoroughly upstanding and professional we would like to think our public servants are, the truth is that some public administrators are no more immune to unethical pressures than are other professionals. Bad choices can be made by anyone—and often are. This is not to make an excuse for unethical behavior in the public sector. Rather, recognizing the *universality* of the potential for unethical behavior is the necessary first step in ensuring a climate of ethical operations in government and NGO bodies.

Academics, administrators, and the popular press are alike in their increasingly strident calls for moral reform, passage of ethics laws and codes, and greater education and training in ethical behavior for public employees.

Calls for ethics reform have been directed at every level of government, from the Office of the President of the United States to the smallest local special service district. Ethical problems in government run the gamut from sexual harassment to embezzlement of millions of dollars. When they occur, they are loudly proclaimed by the press as examples of the poor quality of public servants in general. For example, in one week, newspapers contained stories of the alleged sale of presidential pardons and diplomatic passports (*New York Times,* June 17, 2001, A1+), charges that the town president (i.e., mayor) and nine others stole $10 million in taxpayer money in Cicero, Illinois, and the conviction of a former mayor of Camden, New Jersey, on charges of laundering drug money and accepting bribes from racketeers (*San Francisco Chronicle,* June 16, 2001, A2 and A5, respectively). Citing a recent Gallup poll, *USA Today* reporter Karen Peterson (2001) wrote that, for only the second time in half a century, ethics and morality are near the top of a list of the major problems that people believe are facing the nation. Gallup reported that 78 percent of the public feels that the nation's moral values are weak and getting weaker.

Those were not isolated, seldom seen instances. There has long been both an ethical and a political aspect to public administration. It has been, in fact, one of the major reasons for developing a *profession* of public administration and separating administration from politics (Rohr 1998, 4). It is becoming increasingly important today.

According to one widely cited author on the topic, Terry Cooper (1998), interest in administrative ethics appears to have mushroomed. This has resulted in a growing demand for in-service training, publication of many ethics articles, and professional conferences devoted solely to ethics problems in government. In addition, more and more public administration graduate education programs are requiring or offering courses in ethical behavior.

This heightened interest in public administration ethics has also included the practice of research. For example, J. Mitchell described the growing interest in ethics in public administration research as follows:

> Public administration research and analysis involves ethics. This is evidenced by newspaper headlines questioning the veracity of government reports and by legislative hearings on research misconduct in public agencies. (1998, 305)

Mitchell included most types of research in his analysis, including "pure" social science, as well as more "applied" studies such as policy analyses, and program evaluations. He considered ethics to be an issue in research whether it is conducted to describe problems, predict outcomes, evaluate solutions, or measure agency performance.

THE MEANING OF ETHICS

Ethics, a branch of philosophy, is the study of the *moral* behavior of humans in society. It has also been defined as the set of principles that govern the conduct of an individual or a group of persons, and briefly as the study of morality or moral behavior (Velasquez 1998). *Morality* refers to the standards that people have about what is right, what is wrong, what is good, or what is evil; these standards are the behavior norms of a society. *Moral behavior* is acting in ways that follow the moral standards that exist in society. *Moral standards* are the rules by which a society functions. Examples of moral standards include the moral commandments: *Do not kill; do not steal; do not lie,* and so on. They tell us what behavior is acceptable, what is "right" and what is "good" in society, and their opposites. While moral standards differ from time to time, they remain relatively constant for at least a generation or more. When they do change, they tend to do so very slowly.

Moral standards vary from society to society; there are few absolutes in ethics. However, the fundamental standards of behavior tend to be quite similar throughout the industrialized nations of the world. This is so because, if standards were wildly different, nations would have a difficult time cooperating in such value-laden areas as international relations, commerce, and other global activities. Countries having difficulty in achieving most favored nation (MNF) status—valued in international trade because it provides lower tariffs—is a case in point. Some say that a key barrier has been the government's behavior on certain human rights issues, a moral standard that is considered unacceptable in the West.

What distinguishes moral standards from standards that are not moral? Velasquez (1998) has identified five characteristics of moral behavior that make this distinction. First, moral standards are concerned with matters that people think can seriously injure or benefit human beings. Second, people absorb their moral standards as children and revise them as they mature. Therefore, moral standards are neither established nor changed by the decisions of authoritative bodies; ethics cannot be legislated.

Third, by their very nature as fundamental norms of behavior in a society, moral standards are preferred over other values, including self-interest. Fourth, moral standards are based on impartial considerations; they apply equally to all persons in society. Finally, moral standards evoke special emotions, including guilt and shame, and are associated with a special vocabulary; words such as "good," "bad," "honesty," "justice," and "injustice" are examples.

SOURCES OF OUR MORAL STANDARDS

Moral standards have evolved from a number of different philosophical traditions, some of which are as old as recorded time. Similar codes of behavior evolved some 5,000 years ago in both Egypt and Babylonia (present-day Iraq), for example. A key concept in those early codes was the idea of *justice*. It continues to underlie moral standards in many modern societies. In the United States and Europe, codes of ethics have roots in the Judeo-Christian tradition. In the Middle East, behavioral standards are founded on writings in the Koran. In parts of Asia, moral standards spring from either Confucius or Buddha. In the last half of the twentieth century, a renewed interest in the *rights* of human beings emerged as an integral part of modern ethical standards—it has been expanded to include the rights of animals as well, a point with great implication for medical researchers.

At least five different ways to approach an ethical situation have evolved from those earliest guidelines for moral behavior. These include: *utilitarian, rights, justice, caring,* and *virtue ethics* (Velasquez 1998).

Utilitarian Ethics

Utilitarian ethics is based on the view that the "right" action or policy is the one that will result in the greatest benefit (or the lowest costs) to society. Thus, decisions on actions and polices must be evaluated according to their net benefits and costs. Utilitarianism is concerned with the consequences of an action, not the means to achieve the results. Modern cost-benefit analysis is based on this principle. Because it supports the value of efficiency, utilitarianism is often used in the resolution of public administration dilemmas.

A key characteristic of utilitarianism is that the benefits need not be equally distributed; some people may not benefit at all, and some may be negatively impacted. What counts is the greatest good for all concerned—but the moral dilemma is determining who is to decide what is good (Malhotra 1999).

Rights Ethics

Rights ethics are another approach often seen in public administration. A *right* is often defined as a person's entitlement to something. Because of this focus on the individual, rights ethics differs from the utilitarian approach, where the focus is on the greater good of a society. Two types of rights are included in ethics: legal rights and human rights. Legal rights are based upon laws; consumer protection and contract rights are examples. Human rights, on the other hand, are culturally based; they provide people with a way of justifying their actions; they are also associated with *duties.*

Today's basis for rights ethics comes from the writings of philosopher Immanuel Kant (1724–1804). Kant believed that all human beings possess some rights and duties, and that these exist regardless of any utilitarian benefit they might have for or against others in a society.

To make this point, Kant proposed moral principles he called *categorical imperatives*. Kant's first categorical imperative states that an action is morally right if—and only if—the reason for doing it is one that the person would be willing for everyone to act upon in a similar situation. There are two parts to this concept: (1) *universality* (it applies to everyone), and (2) *reversibility* (a person would be willing to have others use the concept in the way they treat him or her). Kant's second imperative holds that an action is morally right if—and again, only if—a person performing the action does not use others as a means for improving his or her own interests. When making the decision, administrators must respect the right of others to choose freely for themselves.

Several key concepts in public administration are founded upon Kantian rights theories, including the idea that all people have positive rights to work, clothing, housing, and medical care; that everyone has a negative right to freedom from injury or fraud; and that humans have the right to enter into contracts.

Justice Ethics

Moral standards based on the idea of justice include the concept of fairness. Together, these ideas contribute to three fundamental bases for moral behavior: *distributive justice, retributive justice,* and *compensatory justice.* Distributive justice is concerned with the "fair" distribution of society's benefits and burdens. A just distribution based on a person's contribution to society is the value behind the capitalist system, whereas distributive justice based on needs and abilities underlies socialism, and justice, defined as the freedom to do as a person chooses, is the idea behind libertarianism.

Retributive justice is concerned with the providing of punishments and penalties that are just. Thus, a person should not be considered to be morally responsible under conditions of ignorance or inability. This principle is the idea behind the standard of enlightened consent for participation in research studies. Compensatory justice supports the idea of compensating people for what they lose when they are wronged by other individuals or by society (including government itself).

Caring Ethics

The ethics of caring means making a decision in the face of an ethical dilemma based upon a genuine caring for the best interests of another individual. Key virtues of the caring administrator include friendship, kindness, concern, and love for fellow human beings. As might be expected, these ethical standards are often employed in describing decisions made in social welfare agencies and NGO activities.

The care ethic emphasizes two moral demands (Velasquez 1998). First, because people live in their own web of relationships, they should preserve and nurture the valuable relationships they have with others. Second, they must care for those with whom they are related by attending to their particular needs, values, desires, and well-being. This also means responding to the needs, values, desires, and well-being of those who are vulnerable and dependent on their care.

Three different types of care ethics come into play in social situations: caring *about* something, caring *after* someone, and caring *for* someone. In public and nonprofit organization administration, the applicable ethic is caring for someone. It focuses on people and their well-being, not on things.

Virtue Ethics

Based upon the writings of Aristotle and others, virtue ethics refers to the idea of using society's virtues as the basis for making ethical decisions. Aristotle identified four "pivotal" virtues: courage, temperance, justice, and prudence. St. Thomas Aquinas added three additional virtues: faith, hope, and charity. In today's society, the virtues considered most important include honesty, courage, temperance, integrity, compassion, and self-control—terms often used to describe the "ideal" public servant. Vices are the opposite of virtues; they include such examples of "bad" behavior as dishonesty, ruthlessness, greed, lack of integrity, and cowardice. These are considered to be undesirable because of the way they can destroy human relationships.

Velasquez (1998) described the thinking that shapes decision making in virtue theory in the following way:

> An action is morally right if in carrying out the action the agent exercises, exhibits, or develops a morally virtuous character, and is morally wrong to the extent that by carrying out the action the agent exercise, exhibits, or develops a morally vicious character. (p. 137)

Which Approach Should You Follow?

Which, if any, of these ethical principles should guide the researcher when preparing, conducting, and reporting the results of research studies? Some of the underlying principles have resulted in the passage of laws that define specifically what a researcher can and cannot do. However, it is not enough to simply do what is legal; researchers have a moral responsibility that goes far beyond adhering to the letter of the law. Because there is no one comprehensive moral theory that is capable of stating exactly when a utilitarian consideration should take precedent over a right, a standard of justice, or the need for caring, the public administration researcher is forced to follow his or her conscience when faced with an ethical dilemma.

Ethical dilemmas that cause the most difficulty for public administrators and researchers in public and nonprofit administration are not those associated which what Orlans (1967) described as outright "knavery—lying, bad faith, conscious misrepresentation to get money, or the deliberate breach of the terms on which it was obtained (i.e., research grants)." These are practical problems of a legal nature rather than problems of ethics. Although he attributed the problems specifically to funded or sponsored researcher, Orlans' (1967) description is applicable to all research:

> The persistent ethical dilemmas in . . . research are those in which the right course of action is *not* clear, in which honorable (researchers) may differ and no consistent rule obtains. They involve issues in what is reasonable to one (person) is ignoble to another; in which honesty must be reconciled with tact and effectiveness; in which the disinterested pursuit of innocent truth can abet the interested selection of useful knowledge; in which the judgment of the pragmatic (person) of affairs confronts that of the academic moralist. (p. 4)

Reynolds (1979, 43) identified five problem areas where research dilemmas occur most often:

1. *Research program effects:* the positive and negative effects of an overall research program
2. *Research project effects:* the positive and negative effects that result from a specific research project

3. *Participation effects:* the effects of participation in the research on each participant
4. *Overall distribution effects:* the even distribution of the key positive and negative effects of research
5. *Consideration of participants' rights and welfare:* the features of the research program and project that ensure that the rights and welfare of participants are, or will be, respected

Physicist Richard Feynman has been given credit for providing the following final guiding principle for all researchers:

> The key to science (research) is a kind of scientific integrity, a principle of scientific thought that corresponds to a kind of utter honesty—a kind of leaning over backwards. For example, if you're doing an experiment, you should report everything that you think might make it invalid—not only what you think is right about it.

WHAT ARE PUBLIC ADMINISTRATION ETHICS?

Is there a distinct ethics for public administration? Most professionals like to think that their profession is in some way unique, that it has an ethics or a morality of its own, and that their ethics take precedence over the ethics of ordinary people (Goss 1996). Of course, public and nonprofit administrators feel the same about their professions.

What Do Administrators Think Is Important?

How do public administrators perceive the ethical climate of their profession? Goss (1996) compared the attitudes of 378 public administrators with 100 elected state officials and a random sample of 250 voting citizens. Attitudes were measured across twelve dimensions arranged in two scales of six items each. One set of items covered the professional (bureaucratic) ethos; the second set of six items covered the service or democratic ethos. Public administrators valued *professional competence* above the other eleven value characteristics, and rated *being an advocate of the public interest* as the least important characteristic. Clearly, practicing administrators were more concerned with their professional skills than they were in serving the public.

Both the state legislator and general public samples rated *trustworthiness* as the most important behavioral characteristic for public servants. If Goss's one-state case study is valid—if his results can be considered to be representative of administrators everywhere—it appears that administrators are out of touch with the publics they serve. They apply their skills to the job at hand in ways that are different than the public and their elected legislators would have them do; they are less sensitive to the public interest and individual rights than the public, directly or through their elected representatives, would prefer them to be.

This difference in moral focus has important implications for public administration and nonprofit researchers. Administrators value competence, including knowledge, experience, and skill, above all other things. They believe that it is most important to conduct or purchase research that is competently conducted, informative, and skillfully presented. These are skills that can be readily learned. What is not so easily learned is the ability to do research that is compassionate, caring, thoughtful, and, above all, ethical. However, caring, compassionate research may not be funded, and if it is, it may not reach its intended audience. It is critical, therefore, for researchers to strike a balance between the two points of view—but erring always on the side of ethics over expediency.

The Two Ethos of Public Administration

Ethics in public administration functions on two dominant levels or *ethos* (Garofalo and Geuras 1999; Woller and Patterson 1997; Goss 1996; Denhardt 1988). The term ethos refers to the characteristics that distinguish a particular person or group. First, public administrators are faced with a professional or bureaucratic ethos. This has to do with the way people perform their jobs. According to Garofalo and Geuras (1999, 48), it is based "on hierarchical control and obedience to political superiors." In some ways, the ethics of public administration are not much different than the ethics of any profession; the major distinguishing characteristic is the lack of a profit factor that motivates behavior in the private sector.

The second defining moral standard of public and NGO administrators is the underlying belief and commitment to public service. This is the *democratic ethos*—possibly an unfortunate selection of names since it can exist in nondemocratic societies as well; a better choice might have been a *service ethos*. The democratic ethos deals with such values as liberty, justice, human rights, and equality (Garofalo and Geuras 1999).

Managers in public and nonprofit organizations face ethical questions in both of these areas of morality. For example, while maintaining a sense of fiscal responsibility and professional competence across the principle areas of administrative activity, administrators are also expected to live up to several distinctive values of the service ethos in order to retain the public's trust. These include: (1) avoiding conflicts of interest, (2) maintaining impartiality toward the public and stakeholders with conflicting interests, (3) avoiding any appearance of impropriety, and (4) regularly submitting to public disclosure in most every detail of their existence (Petrick and Quinn 1997).

Because research projects are carried out for all levels and functions of public administration, the ethical conduct of research is extremely important. There are dual responsibilities involved. First, research projects must be done ethically by the researcher, who must treat respondents fairly. In addition, the sponsoring agency has a moral obligation to be honest, to do research that is complete, and to support ethical methodological choices. Morality, public administration functions, and research ethics are closely interconnected. This is illustrated in Figure 2.1.

How people behave in their roles as public administrators depends in large part upon the core beliefs and values that they bring to their position. Some of these are moral in nature; they reflect the administrator's sense of moral duty. Ethics may not be able to be taught, but it is clearly apparent that people can be made aware of the ethical principles that underlie their organizations. Administrators must also be informed of the potential consequences of unethical behavior.

Establishing and maintaining a climate of ethical behavior in an organization begins with an overtly communicated commitment by the chief executive. Workers take their behavior cues from their leaders.

WHAT ARE RESEARCH ETHICS?

Research ethics refers to the application of moral standards to decisions made in planning, conducting, and reporting the results of research studies. The fundamental moral standards involved are those that focus on what is right and what is wrong. Beyond this, however, J. Mitchell (1998) has identified the following four practical ethical principles that shape morality in public administration research: *truthfulness, thoroughness, objectivity,* and *relevance.*

The *truthfulness principle* means that it is unethical for researchers to purposefully lie, deceive, or in any way employ fraud. Deliberately misrepresenting the purpose for a study, not informing subjects of the dangers of participation, hiding the identity of the sponsor of the study, or inflat-

Figure 2.1 **A Hierarchy of Public Administration Research Ethics**

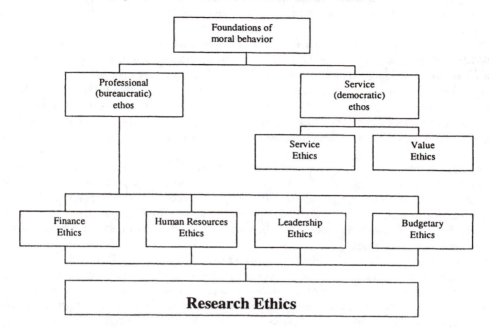

ing or understating the findings of a research project are all examples of research that fails the truthfulness principle.

Despite the belief that truthfulness is a fundamental standard for all human endeavors, it sometimes gives way to expediency in some research applications. When it does, a rationale for not telling the truth is usually provided. For example, some researchers believe that certain research could not be conducted without deception of some sort or that disclosing the true sponsor of a study will unnecessarily bias the findings. Researchers who use deception use two arguments to justify their actions: (1) they assume that participants will not suffer any physical or mental harm as a result of the deception, and (2) they take on the responsibility of informing the participants about the deception after the research study is completed (Zikmund 1994).

The *thoroughness principle* demands that researchers not "cut corners" in their designs. It means being "methodologically thorough" (Mitchell 1998, 312). It means "doing good science" by following all steps in a study. Researchers are morally obligated to include the following in the study reports:

- Definitions for all key concepts used in the study
- Selection of appropriate samples or group participants, including full descriptions
- Identification of all limitations of the research design
- A description of the analysis design

Furthermore, remaining methodologically thorough means that all results and findings must be reported—both good news and bad. It means guaranteeing that participants will not be physically harmed or emotionally distressed. Thoroughness is not a simple concept, however, and can cause a great deal of difficulty for a researcher. Mitchell (1998, 313) summarized this difficulty in the following way: "In short, thoroughness is evidently at the core of methodology; the ethical problem is defining exactly what thoroughness means in the actual conduct of research."

The *objectivity principle* refers to the need for the researcher to remain objective and impartial throughout all aspects of the study. Objectivity is one of the cornerstones of the positivist scientific tradition. "Doing good science" means that the researcher does not bias the study in any way. The researcher should never interject personal feelings or biases into the design of a study, selection of participants, writing and/or asking questions, or interpreting results. This means using probability methods to select a sample, wording questions is such away as to avoid any hint of leading the subject to give a desired answer, and not allowing the researcher's own values to color the results.

Not all researchers believe that remaining neutral is the proper role for a researcher to take in conducting research for public and NGO organizations. Some say that it is impossible to do so. These researchers object to the positivist philosophy of science and instead purposefully place themselves as one with the study participants. These researchers follow a postpositivist approach and employ such qualitative methods as ethnography, case analysis, grounded theory, and action or participatory research methods.

The final ethical research principle discussed by Mitchell is *relevance*. Research should never be frivolous or done because the researcher wants to punish the persons or groups involved in the subject organization. According to Mitchell, research in a democracy has a moral responsibility to be understandable to people and useful. Research that fails this test can be open to ridicule and worse. From 1975 to 1988, former Wisconsin senator William Proxmire often used the press to disclose what he deemed to be wasteful, irrelevant, and often childish government-funded research projects. He awarded the sponsoring government agencies his Golden Fleece Award. An example was a $27,000 study to determine why some inmates want to escape from prison (TFCS 2001).

Senator Proxmire's public ridicule of federally funded research that he called a "wasteful, ridiculous or ironic use of the taxpayers' money" should serve as a warning signal to all researchers in public and NGO organizations. The phrase, "it if sounds ridiculous, people will think it is" applies to all research. Kumar (1996, 192) has summarized the need for relevance in the following way: "If you cannot justify the relevance of the research you are conducting, you are wasting your respondents' time, which is unethical."

RESEARCH WITH HUMAN SUBJECTS

The modern acceptance of ethical standards as a guiding principle for all research with human subjects is based upon decisions made during the Nuremberg Military Tribunal on Nazi war crimes held after the end of World War II. The standards that emerged from those trials resulted in adoption of what is known as the Nuremberg Code (Neuman 2000; Neef, Iwata, and Page 1986). Although originally applied to medical experiments only, the principles in the Code are today used in all research that involves human subjects, including the social and administrative research employed in public administration. Included in the code are the following principles:

- Subject participation must be completely voluntary
- Participants must not undergo unnecessary physical or mental suffering
- The experiment must not take place if death or disability is likely to result
- The experiment must end if continuation will cause injury or death

- Experiments should be conducted only by highly qualified researchers
- Results should be for the good of society and unattainable by any other method

A sample of a human subjects research application for use at Evergreen State College in Olympia, Washington, is displayed in Figures 2.2 through 2.4. Figure 2.2 describes the college policy and its history; Figure 2.3 is the form required for all research involving human subjects; and Figure 2.4 (p. 25) is a sample human subjects review committee application form.

The following instructions are included with consent forms distributed with each human subjects research application:

- Prepare an abstract of your research project by summarizing the nature and purpose of your research.
- List the procedures to which humans will be subjected, such as questionnaires, interviews, audio or video recordings, etc.
- Explain when, where, and how these procedures will be carried out. In the case of questionnaires or interviews, please attach a copy of the questions you will be asking.
- Explain how subjects will be recruited for the proposed work, including your recruitment criteria and procedures.
- List the possible risks to the human subjects. Outline precautions that will be taken to minimize these risks, including methods to ensure confidentiality or obtaining a release to use attribute material. *Note:* The concept of risk goes beyond obvious physical risk. It could include risk

Figure 2.2 **Background and Requirements for Human Subjects Review Form**

The Evergreen State College
USE OF HUMAN SUBJECTS

Background. The Human Subjects Review policy at Evergreen took effect in January 1979 to protect the rights of humans who are participants in research activities. If you are conducting a study using information from people or if you are recording them is some way for that study, you must complete this application with the collaboration of your faculty sponsor.

General Principles. All students, staff, and faculty conducting research at the college which involves the participation of humans as subjects of research must ensure that participation is *voluntary,* that *risks are minimal,* and that the *distribution of your study is limited.* All potential physical, psychological, emotional, and social risks should be considered, and explained to the participants in the study. This explanation must be clear, in letter form, and accompanied by a written consent form, which the participants sign. Similarly, the researcher must explain the benefits to the participant, the course of study, and intellectual inquiry. Participants must not be asked to expose themselves to risk unless the benefits to the participants or society are commensurate.

Please note that in most cases, keeping the participants' names confidential significantly minimizes risk.

Source: Forms and instructions are used with permission from the Evergreen State College.

Figure 2.3   **Sample Informed Consent Form**

The Evergreen State College
Sample Informed Consent Affidavit

I, _____, hereby agree to serve as a subject in the research project entitled
_____ . It has been explained to me that the purpose of
this study is _____and that the
proposed use for the research obtained, now and in the future, is _____ .
I   understand   that   the   possible   risks   to   me   associated   with   this   study   are:
_____

Medical treatment and/or compensation is _____ / is not _____ available for projects presenting
physical risks; if available, treatment or compensation consists of _____.
I may not receive any direct benefit from participation in this study, but my participation may help
_____ .
_____ has offered to answer any questions I may have about the study
and provide me with access to the final report or presentation.

I understand that the person to contact in the event I experience problems as a result of my
participation is _____ at _____.

I hereby agree to participate as a subject in the above-described research project. I
understand that my participation in the project is voluntary, that I am free to withdraw from
participation at any time, and that my choice of whether or not to participate in this project
will not jeopardize my relationship with the Evergreen State College. I have read,
understood, and agree to the foregoing.

Participant's Signature: _____ Date: _____

Parents' Signature (required if subject is a minor): _____

to the subject's dignity and self-respect, as well as emotional, psychological, and behavioral risk. Risk could also include a potential for jeopardizing one's employment or standing in an academic program.

- List specific benefits to be gained by completing the project, which may be at an individual, institutional, or societal level.
- Describe how the information gained from this study is to be used, to whom the information is to be distributed, and how the promise of confidentiality, if made, will be carried out in the final project.
- Prepare an Informed Consent Affidavit and a cover letter.

Receiving Permission to Interview Subjects

Every participant included in a survey has the right to refuse to participate and to know what the study is about, who is sponsoring the study, and for what purpose the results will be used.

The sample consent form included in Figure 2.5 (p. 26) was patterned after a similar form used in a World Health Organization study on women's health and domestic violence against women (Ellsberg and Heise 2005). It is recommended that researchers make their own modifications to suit the needs of their study and sample. The point is to make sure that every research subject knows that they are being asked to participate in a research study and that their replies will be kept confidential.

Figure 2.4   Sample Application for Human Subjects Review Board Approval

---

Human Subjects Review Application
Please return this application to:

The Evergreen State College, Olympia WA 98505

The Evergreen State College (Revised Application 1/12/00)

Research project title: _____

Name of project director(s): _____

Mailing address or mailstop: _____

Phone number: _____

Proposed project dates: _____

Date application submitted: _____

Immediate supervisor, faculty sponsor, or dean: _____

Funding agency/research sponsor (if applicable): _____

INDICATE IF THE PROJECT INVOLVES ANY OF THE FOLLOWING:

___ Minors   ___ Pregnant women   ___ Developmentally disabled
___ Prisoners   ___ Abortuses   ___ Random sample
___ New drugs   ___ Fetuses   ___ A cooperating institution

Certification: We understand that the policies and procedures of the Evergreen State College apply to all research activities involving human subjects which are being performed by persons associated with the college and, therefore, that these activities cannot be initiated without prior review and approval by the appropriate academic dean and, as required, by the Human Subjects Review Board.

X _____
   Signature of the project director   *Date*

X _____
   Signature of the supervisor or project coordinator   *Date*

ETHICS IN THE RESEARCH PROCESS

Public administration and NGO researchers are most concerned with ethics at four times in the research process: (1) when they are planning to gather data, (2) while they are gathering data, (3) when they are processing and interpreting data, and (4) when they are disseminating the results of their research. The interrelated nature of these four situations is displayed in Figure 2.6 (p. 27).

Figure 2.5 **Sample Participant Consent Form**

Hello. My name is _____. [Show credentials or name tag]

I am helping in a study being conducted by [university or nonprofit organization] to learn more about _____. You have been selected by chance to be a participant in this study. May I ask you a few questions?

No one will ask you for your name or address, and all your answers will be kept completely secret. You can stop your participation anytime you wish and can skip any question you don't want to answer. Also, every answer you do give is a "right" answer; there are no "wrong" answers. At the end of the interview, and if you agree, I will ask you a few simple questions that are only used for classification purposes.

Some of the questions might be hard to answer. However, we have found that sometimes people benefit from sharing their thoughts or beliefs about such things. Anything you can contribute will be very helpful, I promise you. Your participation is completely voluntary.

The survey will take around _____ minutes to complete.

Do you have any questions before we begin?

For the Interviewer:

I certify that I have read this consent form to the participant in its entirety and have received permission to complete the survey.

Signed: _____

Date: _____

Source: Original from WHO 2005; included in Ellsberg and Heise 2005, 37.

Ethics When Planning Research

A key activity in planning a research project is deciding who will be the participants in the study. In a positivist design—what most people call a quantitative study design—this typically entails the use of *sampling*. Use of the proper sampling design is a critical decision factor in these designs. If the study is an interpretive design, participants may be as few as one person in a case study, or in

Figure 2.6   **A Model Illustrating When Ethics Are Particularly Important in Research**

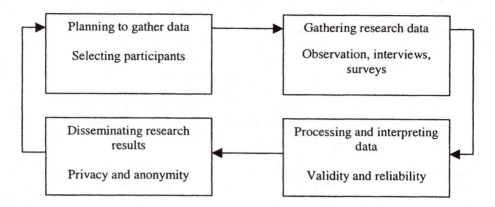

an action research study, everyone in a group, organization, or a community. The most commonly used probability sampling design is what is called a simple random sample (SRS). In an SRS, every subject in the population has an equal chance of being selected for the sample.

In all designs, special care must be taken to ensure that participants voluntarily agree to participate, that their privacy is protected, and that they are not physically or mentally harmed in any way. Six questions must be answered before involving a subject in the study (Neef, Iwata, and Page 1986):

1. Has the participant given his or her *informed consent* to be included in the study?
2. Has the subject *voluntarily agreed* to participate, or has some form of coercion been used to force the subject's participation?
3. Has the subject been *fully informed* of their right not to participate and of any risks and/or benefits that might accrue from the study?
4. Will the subject be *harmed, either physically or mentally,* in any way as a result of participation in the study?
5. Is it necessary to use *deception* to disguise the research, or use covert research methods in order to collect the data?
6. Will a jury of external professional peers *validate* the study?

Informed consent. The idea of informed consent is based upon Western society's ideas of individual freedom and self-determination, as spelled out in the body of common law (Neef, Iwata, and Page 1986). A person's right to be free from intrusion by others is supported by a number of court decisions, including the 1973 *Roe v. Wade* decision. From this and other court actions, the following components of the informed consent are of particular interest:

- The capacity of the person to consent to participation
- The free and voluntary giving of consent
- Consent that is informed and knowledgeable

Courts have held that the capacity to consent requires that the person giving consent knowingly and rationally understands the nature of the experiment or study, any associated risk, and other relevant information. At the same time, researchers are not permitted to decide whether the subject is competent enough to make the decision; all people retain the right to manage their own affairs.

In research involving children, parents have traditionally been allowed to give consent on their behalf, but Neef, Iwata, and Page (1986) noted that the courts have not always accepted that as a right. Therefore, researchers are advised to acquire the consent of parents and the child, as well as that of relevant organizations (such as schools).

Voluntary consent. There are two aspects to the concept of voluntary consent. First, the agreement must be entirely free of any coercion. Second, the subject must understand that the consent can be withdrawn at any time without any harmful consequence (Neef, Iwata, and Page 1986). Often, academic researchers use the students in their classes as participants in research studies. Students are not required to participate, and must know that their performance in the class will not suffer as a result of their not participating.

Knowledgeable consent. All potential research participants must be made aware of all aspects of the study. This means that they must be told (1) that they have the right not to participate, (2) that they can withdraw at any time, (3) what risks might be involved, and (4) the potential benefits of the study, if any. If the study is an experiment, they must also know the risks and benefits of any alternative treatments.

Freedom from harm. A fundamental ethical principal that must be followed in all research studies is that no harm shall fall on the participants as a result of their participation in the research (Neuman 2000; Oppenheim 1992). *Harm* is broadly defined; for example, it can mean physical, cultural, social, or psychological distress as well as physical pain.

Ethics When Gathering Data

Kumar has identified five key points in the research when an ethical concern for respondents is particularly important: (1) when seeking consent from the subject, (2) when providing incentives to participate, if any, (3) when seeking sensitive information or information that might embarrass or otherwise cause discomfort to the subject, (4) when there is a possibility of causing harm, and (5) while maintaining confidentiality for the respondent.

Data-gathering methods used most often in public administration and NGO research include observation, interviewing, and survey questionnaires. Deciding which subjects to include in a research study and which to exclude is also affected by which of these methods is chosen. For example, personal interviews may take as long as two or more hours to complete. As a result, sample sizes may be quite small; researchers must be very selective in their choice of participants. However, if the design calls for use of a self-administered questionnaire, it is often relatively easy to add more subjects to the mailing list.

A number of ethical issues come into play when conducting interviews or writing questionnaires. The ethics of data gathering in all forms continue to raise controversial questions among researchers (Oppenheim 1992). The two problems that cause the most difficulty are the potential for *bias* on the part of the interviewer or in the wording of the question, and the *response distortion* that such biases can cause. Most researchers concede that it is impossible to eliminate all interviewer bias; conscientious training of interviewers is the only way to reduce it.

Ethics in Processing and Interpreting Data

Researchers are sometimes asked to design and conduct a research study and analyze the collected data in order to provide "scientific credence" for preestablished conclusions. Other researchers have been asked to compromise their ethical standards as a condition for receiving a contract to conduct research. Both of these situations present ethical dilemmas. The researcher has three options in these situations (Neuman 2000): (1) The researcher may feel that loyalty to an employer or group overrides any ethical considerations and quietly go along with the request; (2) he or she may overtly oppose the request, making the opposition a part of the public record. This places the researcher in the role of a *whistle-blower* and may cause loss of credibility in the agency, elimination of future research opportunities, or even loss of a job; (3) he or she can simply refuse to make compromises and walk away from the request, aware that another researcher may be found to do the work.

Making the right moral decision in such situations is not an easy choice. Opting for the first path may not only cause the researcher undue personal stress, but may also open the door to criminal prosecution. On the other hand, refusing to go along with the request exposes the researcher to accusations of disloyalty to the organization and disregard for the well-being of fellow workers.

Ethicists often encourage selecting the path of becoming a whistle-blower; it is clearly the most "moral" of the three options. However, whistle-blowers are seldom rewarded for their willingness to publicize unethical activity. They must be in a position to prove their allegations in a court of law, where deliberations may take years to complete. In the intervening time, they are often ostracized by fellow workers, removed from any meaningful work in the organization, eliminated from potential promotion, and ultimately forced to suffer loss of a job. The popular press has aired many reports of whistle-blowers who have not only lost their job, but their home and other possessions as well. It takes a brave person to adopt this role; fortunately, many still do.

Refusing to do the study may be the easiest way out of the dilemma. If morality can exist on a continuum, this path is less immoral than going along with the request and less moral than publicly disclosing the request. This does not mean to imply that it is an easy solution. Choosing to not do the research may mean loss of income or professional standing. On the other hand, complying with the request because someone else will do it anyway is never an acceptable justification. Neuman (2000, 103), discussing the conflict that often appears in such situations, concluded, "Whatever the situation, unethical behavior is never justified by the argument that 'If I didn't do it, someone else would have.'"

Ethics in Disseminating Research Results

Researchers are faced with two broad classes of ethical considerations when disseminating their findings. First, ethical considerations come into play with the distribution and/or publication of the findings. Second, researchers have the moral obligation to protect the privacy of the participants in the research.

Researchers must consider several factors when communicating the results of their research. These include (1) telling the entire story rather than just a few significant portions; (2) presenting insignificant, adverse, or negative findings; and (3) contributing to the general storehouse of disciplinary knowledge. Telling the entire story relates to the idea of methodological completeness discussed earlier. The obligation to include findings that reflect negatively on the sponsoring agency, the research method, or the researchers themselves is based on the ethical standard of honesty. Telling only part of the truth is little different from not telling the truth at all. Contributing to knowledge in the field refers to the researchers' obligation to the ethos of the profession, both as administrators and as researchers.

In addition to the ethical obligation to be truthful when preparing the research report, the researcher must also protect the rights of participants. Three issues are of particular importance when disseminating the results of a research study: (1) protecting the privacy of participants, (2) ensuring the anonymity of participants, and (3) respecting the confidentiality of individuals involved in the study. Protecting participants' privacy is a fundamental moral standard as well as a legal requirement affecting all researchers. While this is primarily a concern during the sample selection and data-gathering steps, the researcher must take great care to ensure that the identity of participants cannot be deciphered from the findings. Participants must know that their privacy will not be invaded as a result of dissemination of the findings.

Ensuring the anonymity of participants is closely related to the privacy standard, except that it is primarily a concern during the preparation of the findings stage. An integral part of every study is, or should be, a description of the sample participants. This description should always be done in the aggregate, focusing on characteristics of the group, such as measures of central tendency, variation, and the like. The results of any single participant should never be made known, except in interpretive studies, which can focus on a single case. The confidentiality standard means that no one other than the primary researcher should know the sample members' names and addresses. A single list must be kept by the researcher.

Researchers also have a moral obligation to avoid reporting incomplete research results or issuing misleading or biased reports (Malhotra 1999). Incomplete reports are more likely to be disseminated when the researcher uncovers adverse or negative information. Misleading results are released to intentionally mislead an audience, even if it is not an actual lie. For example, say that more than 90 percent of the citizens of a community prefer that a ten-acre parcel at the edge of town be left undeveloped, 5 percent want a new shopping center on the site, 3 percent want an industrial park on the site, and 2 percent want a park with softball and soccer fields. It is unethical for the city planning commission to announce that more citizens prefer a shopping center to any other development scheme for the parcel without also saying that 90 percent want no development at the site. It is misleading not because it is false but because it does not give all the facts.

Biased research is often conducted to provide justification for a preconceived result or solution. It also occurs when researchers do not follow the required steps in a research process, when the problem is incorrectly defined, the questionnaire is not pretested, questions are written to almost force respondents to answer in a particular way, or respondents are asked questions that they are unable to answer.

Finally, ethical decisions during dissemination of research findings arise regarding disclosure of the limitations of the study. The sponsoring agency, respondents, and the recipients of the research report are justified in their right to know how much credence they can give to the findings.

Detecting and Preventing Research Misconduct

Grant-awarding institutions are becoming more concerned about research misconduct and are taking steps to prevent researchers from performing unethical activities. For example, in accordance with federal policy on research misconduct, the U.S. National Endowment for the Humanities (NEH) has published a comprehensive set of guidelines for dealing with allegations of research misconduct. Portions of those guidelines are included here to remind researchers that all funded research is subject to a severe examination to ensure that ethical procedures are followed. The NEH guidelines apply to all basic, applied, and demonstration research (NEH 2001).

Section I: Definition of Research Misconduct

- Research misconduct includes all fabrication, falsification, or plagiarism occurring in proposing, performing, or reviewing research or presenting research results. Research misconduct does not include honest error or differences of opinion.
- Plagiarism refers to using other researchers' ideas, processes, results, or words without giving (citing) appropriate credit.

Section II: Findings of Research Misconduct

- To be found as misconduct, there must be a "significant departure" from the accepted practices of the research community; that is, the social and administrative sciences, humanities, management, and other applicable fields.
- The accused must commit the misconduct intentionally, knowingly, or recklessly, and the allegation must be proven by a preponderance of evidence.

Section III: Responsibilities

- Grant-receiving organizations, the NEH, and researchers are equal partners in sharing responsibility for any misconduct.
- While the NEH has final oversight authority for NEH–funded research, grant-receiving organizations have primary responsibility for prevention and detection of research misconduct and for inquiries, investigations, and adjudication of alleged misconduct.
- If, after an investigation, the NEH Inspector General believes that criminal or civil fraud violations have occurred, the case will be submitted to the Department of Justice for action.

SUMMARY

The potential for unethical behavior is a universal problem; it affects administrators at all levels of government, nonprofit and nongovernment organizations (NGOs). Academics, administrators, and the popular press have called for moral reform, passage of ethics laws and codes, and greater education and training in ethical behavior for public employees. These calls for reform have been directed at every level of government, from the Office of the President of the United States to the smallest local special service district.

Ethics, a branch of philosophy, is the study of the *moral* behavior of humans in society. *Morality* refers to the standards that people have about what is right, what is wrong, what is good, or what is evil. *Moral behavior* is acting in ways that follow the moral standards that exist in society. *Moral standards* are the rules by which a society functions.

Moral standards have evolved from a number of different philosophical traditions. Today, at least five different ways to approach an ethical situation have evolved from these earliest guidelines for moral behavior. These include *utilitarian, rights, justice, caring,* and *virtue ethics.* Researchers draw upon these traditions when faced with ethical dilemmas.

No one approach is more correct than any other. For example, because no one comprehensive moral theory is capable of stating exactly when a utilitarian consideration should take precedent over a right, a standard of justice, or the need for caring, the public administration researcher is forced to follow his or her conscience.

Ethics in public administration functions on two dominant levels, or *ethos.* First, public administrators are faced with a professional or *bureaucratic* ethos. The second defining moral standard of public and NGO administrators is the underlying belief and commitment to public service. This is the *democratic ethos*—possibly an unfortunate selection of names since it can exist in nondemocratic societies as well; a better choice might have been a *service ethos*. These ideas deal with such values as liberty, justice, human rights, and equality.

Research ethics refers to the application of moral standards to decisions made in planning, conducting, and reporting the results of research studies. The fundamental moral standards involved are those that focus on what is right and what is wrong. Four additional, practical ethical principles that shape morality in public administration research are *truthfulness, thoroughness, objectivity,* and *relevance.*

Although originally applied to medical experiments only, the principles spelled out in the Nuremberg Code are today used in all research that involves human subjects, including the social and administrative research employed in public administration. The key clauses of the Code ensure that participants have the right to not participate, that they are informed of all risks, and that they will not be intentionally physically or mentally harmed.

Public administration and NGO researchers are most concerned with ethics at four times in the research process: (1) when they are planning to gather data, (2) while they are gathering data, (3) when they are processing and interpreting data, and (4) when they are disseminating the results of their research.

ADDITIONAL READING

Elliott, Deni, and Judy E. Stern, eds. 1997. *Research Ethics.* Hanover, NH: University Press of New England.

3

THE BUILDING BLOCKS OF RESEARCH

Many new scientific disciplines were born during the last half of the nineteenth century when the study of human sciences was separated from that of the natural sciences. Among the first of the "new" human or "social" sciences to emerge were anthropology, economics, psychology, and sociology. Combinations and derivatives of these, such as cultural and physical anthropology and social psychology, soon followed. Similar transformations occurred in communications, industrial psychology, organizational behavior, and the administrative and management science disciplines. As these disciplines grew in influence, specific research methods were developed. Some of those methods employed measurements and quantitative analysis of numerical data, while others involved a variety of qualitative approaches to data analysis.

Public administration was one of the new disciplines, having evolved out of antecedents in political science and sociology. It was recognized as a legitimate field of study in the late 1880s, but the first university education program in public administration was not established until 1926. It remains, however, the least understood aspects of government (Smith and Licari 2006). From its beginnings, there has been a continuing debate on what should be the nature of questions studied in public administration: Should it be considered a social science, along with sociology and psychology? Or, should it be considered an administrative science akin to professional education, such as business administration? The debate is important because it influences the scope and direction of research in the field (Coleman, Brewer, and Brudney 1999).

The issues shaping the approaches and methods used in public administration and nonprofit organization research are directly related to the argument over the nature of all science and research. For example, researchers asked, what is the most appropriate methodology for research, quantitative or qualitative methods? Early researchers argued that the positivist approach, with its emphasis on quantitative methods, was the only valid way to conduct research. However, a number of dissenters argued that the positivist approach would not be able to answer many of the human problems facing public administrators. Those dissenters concluded that a more interpretive approach was needed. That interpretive approach is what is now referred to as postpositivism and involves the use of a variety of qualitative research methods. Richardson and Fowers (1998, 471) described the emerging attitudes calling for a shift in methodological emphasis this way:

> [I]n spite of tremendous effort, enormous methodological sophistication, and many decades of efforts, (mainstream social science, including public administration) has failed to achieve anything even resembling the kind of explanatory theory that counts as truth and is needed

for precise prediction and instrumental control. Just describing interesting patterns of variables—which always have many exceptions—does not yield the sort of technical control over events we associate with modern physics, biology, or engineering.

THE BUILDING BLOCKS OF RESEARCH

Research involves collecting relevant data that can be analyzed and digested for the purpose of adding usable knowledge. Research is not a casual, off-the-cuff activity. Rather, it is built upon a solid foundation of philosophy, practical experience, cultural characteristics, and social institutions and traditions. The activity of research involves an interrelated progression of theoretical positions and processes that make up the six fundamental building blocks of research activity. At every level of the process, researchers are faced with deciding from among a wide variety of options. Moreover, researchers often disagree about which option is best in any given research situation. When this disagreement surfaces, the alternatives become issues.

The six key building blocks of research range from the greatest to the least levels of abstraction. The ontological or theoretical foundations that individual researchers bring to the activity are at the most abstract level. These are followed by the epistemological positions that shape the types and forms of questions addressed in research projects. These two basic conditions establish the framework upon which research projects are planned and implemented. Once a framework has been established, the researcher must decide which specific research strategy to follow and determine which approach or approaches will be employed to collect data. The final activity in this process is selection of the methods that will be used for analyzing and interpreting the collected data. The elements in this integrated framework are displayed in Figure 3.1 and discussed in greater detail in the following pages.

ONTOLOGICAL FOUNDATIONS

Researchers study the issues that they think should be examined and design research activities the way that they believe will produce the greatest amount of needed information. Whether they are aware of it or not, researchers in all disciplines are guided in the way they design and conduct their studies by the underlying philosophical positions they bring to the research activity (Marsh, Stoker, and Furlong 2002). The foundations for these positions are embedded in *ontology* and *epistemology*, which are philosophy constructs concerned with the way scientists and researchers develop knowledge.

Ontology deals with *what* people can learn; it asks what is "out there" that can be known. Ontology has to do with questions about the nature of the world humans can experience. The ontological position of each individual researcher is a product of the researcher's own experience and culture; different experiences lead each person to be concerned with different research questions, or approach similar questions from different points of view. This represents the *theory* that each researcher brings to the research process (Denzin and Lincoln 1998). The ontological questions in public administration typically deal with what it is about institutions, political behaviors, or other administrative or political phenomena that can and should be studied and known.

EPISTEMOLOGICAL POSITIONS

Epistemology is concerned with questions about the *way* that people learn. It is expressed in the methods humans use to gain knowledge. Epistemology is also concerned with the *validity* of knowl-

Figure 3.1 **The Building Blocks of Research**

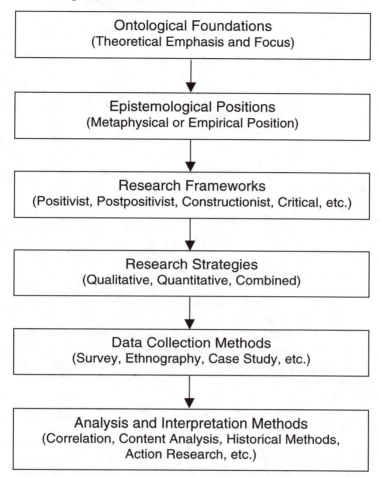

edge; how humans can know anything and be certain what they know is "true" (Plotkin 1994).

Researchers approach the act of research from two separate-but-related epistemological positions: a metaphysical or theoretical position or an empirical or observational position. In practice, these two positions are not diametrically opposed. Rather, they should be seen as opposing positions on an epistemological continuum (Figure 3.2). On the left side of the continuum are the purely theoretical concepts that are not based on observation but instead on belief or faith. At the other extreme are empirical statements formed from scientific observation or measurement (Alexander 1985).

These two major methodological positions—theoretical and empirical—that guide political science researchers reflect the epistemological positions of the researcher. The positivist falls closer to the empirical pole of the epistemological continuum, with the postpositivist closer to metaphysical position. The positivist approach is commonly associated with *quantitative* research strategies, whereas the postpositivist approach—also referred to as realist, interpretist, hermeneutic, or narrative research—is typically associated with qualitative strategies.

Figure 3.2   **The Scientific Continuum and Its Components**

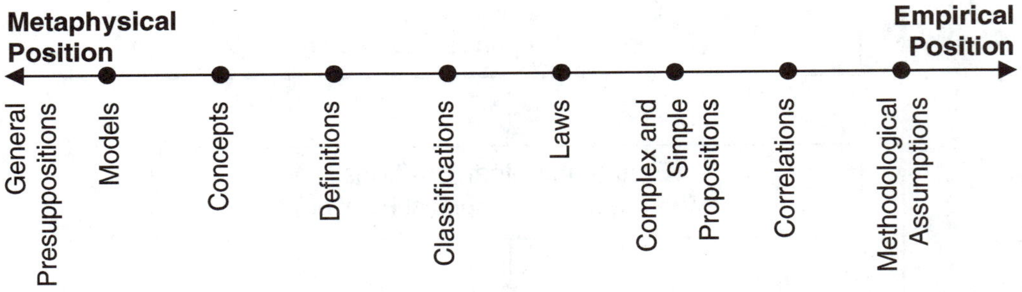

Source: Alexander 1985.

The important thing to remember about this continuum is that research strategies or designs seldom, if ever, exist exclusively at either of the poles. Nearly all research elements exist at more than one place on the continuum and typically include aspects of both positions. This characteristic of research is clearly stated in the following observation:

> Science can be viewed as an intellectual process that occurs with the context of two distinct environments, the empirical observational world and the non-empirical metaphysical one. Although scientific statements may be oriented more toward one of these environments than the other, they can never be determined exclusively by either alone. The differences between what are perceived as sharply contrasting kinds of scientific arguments should be understood rather as representing different positions on the same epistemological continuum. (Alexander 1985, 2)

RESEARCH FRAMEWORKS

A number of different theoretical models guide the approaches that researchers take in research in any subject (Gubba and Lincoln 1998; Heron 1996). The four models used in public administration and nonprofit organization research are the *positivist, postpositivist, constructionist/interpretive,* and *critical theory* models. Other approaches also exist, such as the emancipatory models (for example, the Marxist and the feminist models) and the poststructural model. However, the positivist and postpositivist models are usually treated as the chief methodological approaches that political scientists follow to gain knowledge about the world (Denzin and Lincoln 1998; Marsh, Stoker and Furlong 2002; Oakley 2000). The questions studied and the research methods researchers employ are framed by these theoretical positions (Figure 3.3).

For the past several decades, the epistemological argument between positivist and postpositivist approaches has been a major reoccurring issue in social science research (Oakley 2000, 26–27). This debate is often couched in arguments about whether quantitative or qualitative research methods are the most appropriate means for collecting data and producing information. Although some still argue that only one or the other approach is the true way to conduct research, most social science researchers no longer consider the question one worth arguing about. Because scientific research does not follow one position exclusively, it makes little sense for researchers to adopt and defend either position as the sole approved approach to research. The positivist and postpositivist

Figure 3.3   **Basic Theoretical Frameworks for Research**

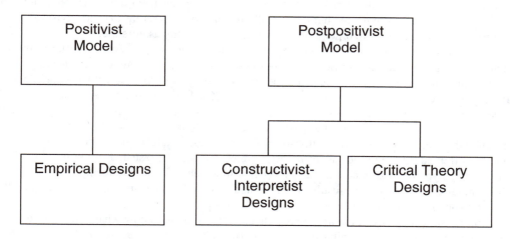

epistemologies—and, therefore, both quantitative and qualitative methods—should be accepted as valid in public and nonprofit administration research. The researcher's choice should be based on the objectives for the research, not because of an irrational bias.

Early Positivist Rationale

The positivist approach to scientific inquiry emerged as a reaction to the metaphysically based philosophy of science that existed until the Age of Enlightenment, which lasted from roughly 1600 to 1800 (Bryant 1985). Before 1600, knowledge developed under ecclesiastical (church) sponsorship was believed to be attributable to supernatural or deific (God-like) forces (Trochim 2002). That early research was based on a belief that God created the world in its entirety; research could describe that world as it was, but the underlying processes could not be known. Thus, all knowledge about the world involved reasoning that was speculative at best, producing conclusions that were not based upon true understanding or confirmed by observation.

The new awareness and thirst for knowledge that characterized the Enlightenment made it possible for a new approach to scientific learning to emerge with the Industrial Revolution. The theocratic foundation for knowledge gave way to what became known as positivism—a "philosophical doctrine that only experience can inform us about reality. Reality . . . can be perceived by our senses and represented by thoughts and language" (Stahl 2003, 2879).

During the 1800s, the positivist view of the world came to have a tremendous influence—first on the natural sciences, then on philosophy, and eventually on the social sciences. It came to full flowering in the writings of the Vienna Circle, a group of philosophers and social scientists working in Vienna, Austria, during the 1920s. In 1929, the Circle issued a pamphlet that stated their belief that all scientists' conceptions of the world are based upon two characteristics:

> *First* it is *empiricist and positivist:* there is knowledge only from experience, which rests on what is immediately given. This sets the limits for the content of legitimate science. *Second,* the scientific world-conception is marked by the application of a certain method, namely *logical analysis* (Bryant 1985, 111; Bryant's emphasis)

Early positivists argued that the only experience can be measured and that meaningful knowledge comes from the senses. All other knowledge is speculation at best. Postpositivists contend that reality can only be approximated but never really understood. Therefore, postpositivists employ multiple research methods in order to learn as much about reality as possible.

The positivists' reaction to science based on metaphysics was *empiricism.* Empiricism means that knowledge does not just exist; it must be *sensed* to be real. Faith alone—a "knowing" that something is true because you believe it to be so—was deemed an insufficient basis for explaining a phenomenon or as a foundation for knowledge. The idea that *phenomena that cannot be measured should not be studied* was a logical extension of this reaction to metaphysics. These early positivists also believed that the goal of all sciences—natural and social—is to describe everything that can be experienced. Positivists proposed cause-and-effect theories about phenomena, and then framed those theories as *hypotheses,* which can then be tested. The preferred method of testing a hypothesis is to conduct an *experiment* in which variables are manipulated—that is, their values changed—and the results observed and recorded. This pattern of inquiry eventually became known as the *scientific method.*

Empiricism is the way of learning things that says we can only know what our senses tell us. However, another way of learning is through a process of *mental reflection.* E. Terrence Jones (1971) called this approach "rationalism." To make the jump to a rational way of learning, researchers have increasingly been forced to adopt qualitative approaches for conducting their research. Pennock (1966) believed that the aim of positivists—and particularly the behavioralists—was "to apply the scientific method vigorously and rigorously to every nook and cranny" of social science. It was his contention that the rationalist goals of the postpositivists emphasize *ideas* more than researcher-formed constructs that must be observed and measured. In a critical paper on the position, Pennock (1966, 46) explained:

> Empirical scientists have often made a fetish of measuring. Worse still, they have confused efforts to avoid bias caused by unconscious or uncritical values with the avoidance of all evaluation. They too have developed a crude positivism that most philosophers, if they ever held it, have long since abandoned.

Dependence upon Logical Reasoning

The scientific method employed in empirical research relies on *logical reasoning* rather than speculative reasoning. This approach emphasizes experience (observation) and a commitment to measurement. While it was originally developed as a way of researching in the natural sciences, by the end of the nineteenth century the scientific method—hypotheses, experimentation, observation, and quantification—was also being applied in the social sciences; it is the model of scientific inquiry that positivist researchers still follow today. Public administration researchers who follow the positivist tradition tend to study the operational aspects of government, including the institutions and organizations of government and the stakeholder groups that try to influence the decisions of governments (Stocker and Marsh 2002). Marsh and Furlong (2002, 22–23) have identified four key concepts that characterize the positivist approach to research:

- The world exists independently of our knowledge about it; the world is real, not something socially created.
- Natural science and social science—including public administration—are both similar in outlook and require the same methods, including forming hypotheses that can be tested by direct observation.

- A key objective of research in public administration is to identify causal relationships between social, political, and administrative phenomena.
- The proper goal of public administration research is to focus on the empirical—"what is" questions—with "what should be" questions delegated to the province of religion and philosophy (metaphysics).

Another fundamental tenet of positivism is that science must be objective; it must be *value free*. Scientific knowledge must be based upon what is observed, not on the opinion or beliefs of the researcher. Positivist researchers emphasize "precise quantitative data" that is gathered and analyzed using experiments, surveys, and statistics; they employ "rigorous, exact measures by carefully analyzing numbers from the measures" (Neuman 2000, 66). Neuman summarized this concept in the following way:

> Positivism sees social science as an organized method for combining deductive logic with precise empirical observations of individual behavior in order to discover and confirm a set of probabilistic causal laws that can be used to predict general patterns of human activity.

The Postpositivist Reaction

Not every researcher accepts the emphasis on positivist methodology and quantitative research methods; they would replace the traditional positivist position with one that permits an interpretive approach. Their charge is that public administration researchers still place too great an emphasis upon empirical or applied research. As a result, researchers are making few if any contributions to advancing the state of knowledge in their fields. Moisés Naím, editor-in-chief of *Foreign Policy* magazine, compared what he called "the extraordinary progress in the revolution in technologies, biology and electronics, computer processing, and even astronomy" with what he identified as the dearth of comparable results in the social sciences, particularly in economics and political science [including public administration] (Naím 2002, 38–39).

Richardson and Fowers (1998, 471) echoed the critical view of social science research with the statement that, "in spite of tremendous effort, enormous methodological sophistication, and many decades of efforts," social science has not achieved anything close to the type of "explanatory theory that counts as truth and is needed for precise prediction and instrumental control. Just describing interesting patterns of variables—which always have many exceptions—does not yield the sort of technical control over events we associate with modern physics, biology, or engineering."

Referring to the positivist mind-set of some researchers as "a silent civic disease," Boyte (2000, 49) offered the following example of their criticism:

> Our implicit theories of knowledge assume the specific understanding of scientific inquiry that derives from positivism, for a time the dominant philosophy of science. This model deligitimates "ordinary knowledge" and depreciates the capacities, talents, and interests of the nonexpert and the amateur. It is antagonistic to common sense, folk traditions, and craft and practical knowledge mediated through everyday life experience. Of course, "common sense" is not always right, nor "science" always wrong. I argue only that many different kinds of valuable knowledge support public life and that conventional academic approaches slight the nonexpert.

As previously stated, the theory of empiricism holds that humans can only know what their senses tell them (Jones 1971). Adoption of the postpositivist approach was a "radical shift" away from objective, value-free, universal knowledge that characterized the rationalist, positivist, and behavioralist approach to research (Locher and Prügl 2001). Hempel (1966, 15), an early critic of the positivist focus, identified what he saw as a problem in research: "There is wide agreement today among philosophers of science that scientific hypotheses and theories are not derived from observed facts, but invented to account for them."

Written before what has become a nearly general acceptance of the validity of qualitative research, a 1993 study by Bartels and Brady (1993, 121) examining more than 2,000 articles in six important journals and several different collections of papers revealed that quantitative methods dominated public and nonprofit research. One striking conclusion from the Bartels and Brady discussion is that as late as 1990s, a matching qualitative research methodology category was not considered important enough to be included in the research papers they examined.

Also studying the quantitative/qualitative research argument, Lan and Anders (2000) reviewed 634 research papers published over a three-year period in eight public administration and political science journals. They found that most published research was empirical, dealing with specific managerial issues in federal, state, or local government, with the emphasis on state and local levels. A smaller number of studies dealt with public sector issues in general, while only a small portion addressed international issues. The primary emphasis of the examined research was on government in general or issues that concern the executive branches at all levels.

No Single Method is Best

Today, most political science researchers agree that no single method is the only appropriate way to conduct research. The appropriate choice from among the growing variety of research traditions in political science must be "contingent upon time and place and a given set of socio-political circumstances" (Dryzek 1986, 315). Researchers are more likely than not to agree with the following conclusions: "there is no one method of acquiring knowledge" (Stoker and Marsh 2002, 15), and "[T]here now exist not only multiple approaches to empirical research, but also multiple agendas for the discipline as a whole" (Farr, Dryzek, and Leonard 1995, 2). Denscombe (2002) feels there is a growing tendency to combine the use of different methods and different research strategies within the same studies. Researchers in the twenty-first century are able to eclectically select one or the other model, drawing on the models' individual strengths and compensating for their weaknesses.

Constructionist, Interpretive, and Critical Designs

Since the early 1970s, qualitative research has evolved into more than the predominant positivist way of approaching scientific inquiry in public administration. The research methods that fall under these broad models are more likely to use qualitative than quantitative designs. In addition to the traditional *explanatory* approach taken by the early postpositivists, additional strategy approaches receiving growing support in research today are the *constructionist, interpretive,* and *critical* approaches (Neuman 2000; White 1994). In the constructionist and interpretive approaches, researchers follow an inductive approach rather than the deductive approach followed in positivist research. Researchers begin with a set of assumptions and a theory or theories about a research question or phenomenon. They then build understanding of the phenomenon by observations, refining the theory as they add additional observations.

The Constructionist Model

The constructionist (or social constructionist) approach to research refers to the idea that what we see and experience is determined or defined in accordance with society and culture; meaning is "constructed" out of a subjective interpretation of phenomena. Thus, meaning (or "truth") is a reflection of what Potter (1996, 2) described as a process by which people's experiences, abilities, common sense, and knowledge are both forged in, and reproduce throughout, their societies and/or communities. According to Stahl (2003), constructionism is the idea that reality is what society says it is; it comes into being only as product of the interaction of people in society. Reality must be "constructed by the observers" (Stahl 2003, 2879). As a result, knowledge about the world is only possible because humans create the world in the act of perceiving it; meaning is constructed in communication, discourse, and share narratives.

Wright (2004, 11) applied a constructionist approach to analysis of a private sector firm's planning process when, citing A.L. Cunliffe's 2003 paper in the journal *Human Relations,* he described the intellectual processes by which constructionist research occurs thus (his emphasis):

> Social constructionists argue that we construct and make sense of social realities in various forms of discourse: conversation, writing, and reading. Radically reflective researchers recognize their own place in this process, suggesting we *construct intersubjectively* the very *objective realities* we think we are studying: we are inventors not representers of realities. . . . Constructionist research explores how meaning is created between research participants.

The constructionist model is not without serious flaws. If truth can only exist as a result of a consensus reached through social interaction, then truth can only be the result of the individuals that form the group consensus. With different groups there is a different consensus—and different truth. Thus, constructionism does not allow for any absolute truths; therefore, constructionism cannot claim to be a true theory or even a theory that can be verified. Finally, there can be no basis upon which to decide whether a given construction is good or viable (Stahl 2003).

The Interpretive Model

Interpretive research has been defined as "the systematic analysis of socially meaningful action through the direct detailed observation of people in natural settings and interpretations of how people create and maintain their social worlds" (Neuman 2000, 71). In practice, the interpretive research method is not used to test researcher-determined hypotheses using previously defined dependent and independent variables. Rather, the aim of interpretive methods is "to produce an understanding of social context of the phenomenon and the process whereby the phenomenon influences and is influenced by the social context" (Rowlands 2005, 82).

Dirkx and Barnes (2004, 1), concluding that virtually all types of inquiry and research are designed for interpreting some phenomenon of interest, explain the process:

> We seek to explain, understand, or some way make sense of an aspect of [the] world that has, in one way or another, become problematic. Our motivations for engaging in this process of interpretation vary widely, and the process itself is shaped by a host of presuppositions and assumptions that we bring to the inquiry, including our worldviews, paradigms, perspectives, theories, and beliefs.

The underlying theoretical rationale for interpretive research is the belief that knowledge is acquired by social interactions that take place through language, group consciousness, and shared meanings (Klein and Myers 1999). An example of this is the diffusion of cultural norms from generation to generation. Interpretive research also recognizes that meaning (knowledge) is a reflection of the relationship between the researcher and what is being studied, as well as the situational factors that exist at the time (Rowlands 2005).

As with the constructionist model, the interpretive approach to research is burdened with problems. Rowlands (2005) identified two of these problems. First, unlike research in the positivist model, researchers using interpretive methods do not have a generally accepted model for communicating the findings of their research. Second, few common rules exist to guide researchers through the inductive reasoning process that characterizes interpretive research. The lack of commonalities in these two key steps is not surprising, considering the wide variety of interpretive research data-gathering methods, such as single and multiple case studies, action research, grounded theory, ethnography, participant observation, and others (Banister 2005; Rowlands 2005).

The Critical Model

The critical approach to research is sometimes referred to as *emancipative* or *empowering* research. The key objective of this approach is to help research participants identify and understand the causes of their circumstances, and then to empower them to bring about the change that they feel is required. The approach is "a critical process of inquiry that goes beyond surface illusions to uncover the real structures in the material world in order to help people change conditions and build a better world for themselves" (Neuman 2000, 76). Feminist and Marxist political science research approaches are considered to be "emancipatory" models.

For several reasons, the critical approach is more likely to be found guiding research in social work and other social disciplines than in public administration research. Box and King (2000) discussed reasons behind this conclusion:

> Critical theory has only a small audience in public administration today, in part because public administration is an applied professional field, and in part because critical theory offers broad narratives about oppression within capitalist society and the need for emancipation of whole classes of people, allowing them to realize full human potential. Such an all-inclusive theoretical system makes it difficulty to accept and use critical theory in a time of competing views on research and politics, skepticism about grand narratives such as elite domination or class consciousness, and the triumph of Western liberal-capitalist economic and political systems. (p. 758)

SELECTING A RESEARCH STRATEGY

Once the ontological and epistemological positions are established and a research framework has been determined, the researcher must decide which strategy to follow in order to meet the objectives specified for the proposed research project. The two chief strategies are referred to as *quantitative research* and *qualitative research,* with a combined approach also possible. The chief activity in positivist research is quantitative and involves counting. The tools used in quantitative research are carried out to provide measurements, including demographics, lifestyles, attitudes, and opinions.

Traditionally, public administration research has involved the use of positivist research traditions with an emphasis on quantitative methodology. In fact, a majority of social science research still seems to follow a positivist-quantitative design (Boyte 2000). Researchers who use quantitative designs are encouraged to remain detached from their subjects and to remain "value free" in their approach to the data collection and analysis research processes. Quantitative studies are conducted to produce predictive theories that are based on experimentation and emphasize mathematical and statistical methods in their analysis. Smith et al. (1976) described this quantitative tradition in the preface of their text on research methods:

> [Research] has changed substantially in the last thirty years. Many textbooks and most professional journals cannot be understood fully without some minimal acquaintance with the philosophy of science or social science and a wide range of empirical and statistical methods including computer science, various forms of statistical analysis, content analysis, survey research, and many others. (p. xi)

DATA COLLECTION, ANALYSIS, AND INTERPRETATION METHODS

Quantitative data are gathered by surveys, experiments, case-control studies, statistical records, structured observations, content analysis, and other quantitative techniques. Postpositivist designs tend to favor qualitative research strategies. The chief activities in postpositivist research are theory building and understanding. Qualitative designs include case studies, ethnographic observation, grounded theory, historical and legal studies, action research, and similar strategies. Quantitative data collection methods include interviewing, observing, story recording, and analysis of texts and physical artifacts.

Qualitative or interpretive political scientists often employ the tools of anthropological research, participant observation, and field research. The major research activity followed in all postpositivist/interpretive research approaches is observation, either as a participant in a group under study or as a silent, often hidden, observer. Specific data-gathering techniques employed include participant observation, in-depth interviewing, action research case studies, life-history methods, and focus groups (Oakley 2002, 27). Typical analysis approaches are content analysis and heuristic evaluation of texts and materials. Later chapters of this book cover typical analysis approaches.

Analysis and Interpretation Methods

Along with methodology, the analysis and interpretation of research findings is the focus of the remaining sections of the text. Here, however, it is worth stating again that the choice of strategy, method, analysis, and interpretation processes should be a reflection, not of researcher preference, but of the research question and objectives.

SUMMARY

There has been a continuing debate from its beginnings on the nature of public administration: Should it be considered a social science, along with sociology and psychology? Or should it be considered an administrative science akin to business administration and law? The debate is important because it influences the scope and direction of research in the field.

A persistent problem with the debate over approaches and methods used in public administration research sprang from disagreement over the fundamental nature of the discipline. As interest in public administration and nonprofit organization management grew in scope and acceptance during the 1900s, researchers argued that the positivist approach, with its emphasis on quantitative methods, should be the only valid way to conduct research. However, others questioned whether positivism was able to answer many of the human problems facing public administrators. As a result, they turned to postpositivist research models.

Research is about collecting data that can be analyzed and digested for information for the purpose of adding to usable knowledge. Research should be built upon a solid foundation of philosophy, practical experience, cultural characteristics, and social institutions and traditions. The activity of research involves an interrelated progression of theoretical positions and processes.

The six key building blocks of research range from the greatest to the least level of abstraction. The ontological or theoretical foundations individual researchers bring to the activity are at the most abstract level. This is followed by the epistemological position that shapes the type and form of questions addressed in a research project. These two conditions establish the framework upon which the project is planned and implemented. Once a framework has been established, the researcher is able to decide which specific research strategy will be followed. The researcher must then determine which approach or approaches will be employed to collect data. The final activity in this process is selection of the methods that will be used for analyzing and interpreting the collected data.

The positivist and postpositivist models shape the design of research. The positivist model is often described as an objective approach, with an emphasis on measurement. The postpositivist model involves subjective interpretation; three manifestations of the positivist model are the constructionist, interpretive, and critical theory models.

ADDITIONAL READING

Popper, Karl. 1959. *The Logic of Discovery.* London: Heinemann.
Woolgar, Steve. 1988. *Science—the Very Idea.* London: Tavistock Institute.

4

PUBLIC ADMINISTRATION RESEARCH: THEORY AND PRACTICE

Researchers take many different approaches to the study of administrative, managerial, economic, behavioral, and political questions that are addressed in public administration and nonprofit organizations. This chapter will serve as a conceptual overview of research in the public sector. The chapter begins with an overview of three research designs for each of the two chief epistemological positions and then looks at some of the topic areas addressed in public administration research.

As discussed in the preceding chapter, the two major epistemological positions in research are the positivist and postpositivist. Each of these supports a variety of research designs. Researchers are in general agreement that different research methods and research topics are both valid and appropriate. Researchers are likely to agree with the following conclusions: "there is no one method of acquiring knowledge" (Stoker and Marsh 2002, 15), and, "[T]here now exist not only multiple approaches to empirical research, but also multiple agendas for the discipline as a whole" (Farr, Dryzek, and Leonard 1995, 2). Denscombe (2002) believes that there is a growing tendency to combine different methods and research strategies in the same study. This chapter will look at three popular positivist designs in public administration before examining four common postpositivist designs.

POSITIVIST RESEARCH MODELS

Principal positivist approaches used in public and nonprofit sector research include *institutional analysis*, *behavioralism*, and *rational choice theory*. A slightly disproportionate emphasis is given to the discussion on behavioralism because it is still the epistemological position of preference for many researchers and academicians.

Institutionalism

For most of its history as a social science discipline, public administration was considered to be a subfield of political science; it remains so in many academic programs. For more than one hundred years, the dominant methodological focus in political science—and, therefore, public administration—was *institutionalism*. This positivist institutional focus remained the direction of choice until the 1950s, when it was replaced by a *behavioralist* approach.

The focus of institutionalist research was not the *organizations* that make up the political world, but rather such concepts as the formal and informal rules, political standards, norms, and guides for accepted political behavior. The term "political" does not refer exclusively to party politics but to the broader view of governance in general. Political phenomena are, after all, social phenomena. Therefore, the rules that enable society to function are also necessary for government to function. *How* governments work—not how they *should* work—were the questions that institutionalists sought to answer. One of the earliest examples of an institutional study is Woodrow Wilson's 1885 investigation of the American Congress. That study (*Congressional Government*) sought to explain the way Congress actually worked instead of the way the Constitution says it should work (Shepsle 1995).

During the institutionalism era, most public administration research dealt with identifying and understanding the rules and conventions that made it possible for state and local government to serve the needs of citizens. The research topics were often concerned with describing—often by the comparative method—such formal institutions as constitutions, legal systems, and government structures and their changes over time. During this period, public administration research topics were typically concerned with resolving administrative problems encountered in institutional operations.

Nineteenth-century American students of government were particularly interested in the concept of the state. Discussing the government meant discussing the rules, conventions, traditions, and cultural influences that enabled the collaboration and cooperation necessary for it to function. According to Shepsle (1995, 277), "Government for the most part was conceptualized as the institutional manifestation of the state, and the agenda so set . . . carried on into the early decades of the twentieth century." Good administration was equated with efficiency and effectiveness, and the research of the time focused on improving all aspects of agency operations. Political science—the parent discipline—retained its focus on *government*, whereas the new public administration discipline focused on the practice of *governing*.

The influence of the institutionalists began to wane as the twentieth century reached its halfway point. Arguments against the institutionalist approach centered on several points; one of these criticisms was that the focus of research on the formal institutions of government was too narrow to answer many of the larger issues of the discipline. Increasingly, institutionalists were studying the formal rules and organizations rather than informal solutions, and spending more of their time attempting to define what it is that constitutes "good government" rather than looking for the causes of good and bad political and administrative behavior. The behavioralist approach was adopted largely because its focus was on individual behavior rather than organizational behavior, which was far more difficult to pin down.

Today, institutionalism is enjoying a renewed popularity among students of government, although in a format dramatically different from the institutionalism of the past. Today, it no longer focuses only on explaining political organizations by comparison. Instead, new institutionalists are interested in the ways that power is gained, held, and exercised in various circumstances and how political and citizen groups share and disseminate their values. There is also a renewed focus on the broader issues of organizational design, as seen in the President's Management Agenda of George W. Bush.

According to Lowndes (2002, 91), new institutionalists are now concerned not only with how political institutions affect individuals, but also with the interaction between institutions and individuals. Lowndes identified six changes helping to make the institutional approach more palatable. She was clear to point out that the changes are occurring on a sliding scale—they should be considered to be points on continuum. The points of change in focus for the new institutionalism in government and administration research are from:

- An old focus on organizations toward a new focus on rules
- A concentration on formal concepts to informal definitions of institutions
- A view of political institutions as static to a dynamic view
- Submerged (or ignored) values to seeing values as critical to understanding institutional relationships
- A holistic view of institutions to a focus on their individual parts and components
- Institutions as independent entities to seeing them as embedded in societies and specific contexts

Behavioralism

Beginning in the middle to late 1950s, some researchers began looking for ways to improve society by enhancing political institutions, increasing public participation, and otherwise addressing governmental and politically based social problems. The institutional focus was unable to meet the needs of the new researchers, who felt that the purely descriptive approach of institutional methods was not able to successfully address the important issues of the discipline. A new science of analysis was needed; they found that new approach in the rigorous application of scientific principles that was being followed in other behavioral sciences.

This new way of studying government phenomena was, in the words of Shepsle (1995, 279), "Tremendously important . . . because it emphasized, in its many variations, precise observation, counting and measuring where possible, the clear statement of hypotheses, and unambiguous standards for accepting or rejecting them." Furthermore, the new direction called for a "radical shift" away from the rambling narratives that characterized much of the institutional research of the period. To study administrative behavior and apply the same scientific rigor to their studies, some academic researchers turned to the behavioralist approach as expressed in works of experimental psychologists such as John B. Watson and B.F. Skinner. According to Gunnell (1983, 15), the objectives of behavioral research were reached by "the formulation of systematic concepts and hypotheses; the development of explanatory generalizations that would raise inquiry beyond mere factual empiricisms; interdisciplinary borrowing; empirical methods of research; (and) direct observation."

Behavioralism was introduced as a social science research approach in the 1920s. By the 1940s, the concept was deeply entrenched in the minds of academic researchers in political, public administration, and other social science departments. Social scientists began to move their data-gathering activities out of the laboratory or classroom and into the real world, which made it even easier to apply behavioralist research principles to public administration research. For example, experimental social scientist William S. Verplanck (2002, 4), describing the lessons he learned while conducting research at the Naval Medical Research Lab during World War II, stated, "If you're really going to learn about behavior, unless you settle for a kind of myopia, you have to do research in the 'real' world, that is, the world in which we all live every day, and not solely in the restrictive environment of a laboratory. Neither what is theoretically best nor is what works best in the lab necessarily the best elsewhere." By the 1950s, behavioralism had become an accepted way of conducting social science research, and by the 1960s, the primary focus of public administration and political science had shifted from the study of political institutions to the study of the behavior of people in the real world.

The following eight assumptions and objectives are characteristics of behavioralist concepts and methods in political science research that differentiate the approach from the traditional institutionalist approach (Easton 1962, 7–8; Somit and Tanenhaus 1967, 177–179):

1. *Regularities:* These are discoverable commonalities in political behavior. They are expressed as generalizations or theories. Political science is capable of prediction and should avoid the purely descriptive studies that characterized most institutionalist research.
2. *Verification:* The validity of generalizations must be testable and tied to relevant political behavior. Political science researchers should focus on observable phenomena—what individuals do and say. This data can then be studied together as "political aggregates." Institutional behavior is the behavior of individuals.
3. *Techniques:* The means for collecting and interpreting data about the generalizations and behavior must exist; they must be examined using rigorous means for observing, recording, measuring, and analyzing behavior. Research must be theory oriented and theory driven.
4. *Quantification:* Precise measurement requires quantification and application of mathematical (statistical) analysis. Data must be quantified to make the discovery of precise relationships and regularities possible.
5. *Values:* Ethical evaluations are not empirical explanations, and they require different methods of evaluation and interpretation. Extreme care must be taken not to mistake one for the other. The "truth" of values such as democracy, equality, and freedom cannot be proven scientifically and therefore should not be a part of political science research.
6. *Systemization:* Research should be systematic. Theory and research are closely associated parts of the orderly development of knowledge. Research untutored by theory may prove trivial and theory unsupported by data, futile.
7. *Pure Science:* Political science research should focus on *pure* research. Pure research advances our knowledge of the political world. Behavioralists contend that applied research is an "unproductive diversion of energy, resources, and attention."
8. *Integration:* Political science research must not ignore the other social science disciplines; only by integrating all knowledge about human behavior will political science be brought back to its earlier high status and return to being considered as one of the social sciences.

Sanders (2002) summarized the position of behavioralism at the start of the twenty-first century by pointing out that, for behavioralists and postbehavioralists alike, the main objective of social scientific research is to *explain the behavior of individuals and aggregates of individuals.* The underlying research question that these studies pose is: Why do individuals, institutional actors, government agencies, and nation states behave the way they do? Referring to the central position that theory plays in the approach, Sanders (2002) added:

> Embedded in the behavioralist notion of explanation is the idea of causality. Although behavioralists are aware that causality may be as much a reflection of the way we think about the world as it is of "reality," they nonetheless insist that, unless a theory makes some sort of causal statement, it cannot be deemed to explain anything. (p. 63)

Rational Choice Theory

Rational choice theory (RCT) is a way of explaining human behavior which states that people and organizations make decisions for the purpose of providing themselves the greatest possible benefits. In economics—where most of the principles of the theory were developed—this is referred to as the process of maximizing utility. Social scientists began to employ RCT during the 1960s and 1970s, partly in reaction to the behavioralist contention that human behavior is not a matter of personal choice but is instead shaped by psychological and social accidents to which humans are exposed—often against their will. The essential focus of RCT research is the analysis of the ways that groups of individuals respond to challenges in government agencies, political institutions, public policy, and related phenomena.

In its most popular form, RCT is closer to the institutionalist position than it is to behavioralism. Shepsle (1995) described how rational choice theory differs from behavioralism in this way:

> In place of responsive, passive, sociological man, the rational choice paradigm substitutes a purpose, proactive agent, a maximizer of privately held values. A rational agent is one who comes to a social situation with preferences over possible social states, beliefs about the world around oneself, and a capability of employing these data intelligently. Agent behavior takes the form of choices based on either intelligent calculation or internalized rules that reflect optimal adaptation to experience. (p. 280)

A key concept in RCT is that all human behavior occurs for a purpose. Given a set of options and information about the costs and benefits of their choices, people will act in the way that provides them the greatest payoffs—they make a *rational* decision. Thus, all behavior is centered on the self. People play games in order to win. Another key concept in RCT is that all the players know—and generally adhere to—the rules of the game. "Rules" in this sense are similar to the standards and norms that are a focus in the institutionalist approach to research.

Rational choice researchers use methods such as game theory and other mathematical models from economics. They apply logic to sets of assumptions about human behavior in an attempt to develop basic laws and make predictions. According to Binmore, Kirman, and Tani (1993), game theorists have "absurdly broad" objectives for this approach to research: to develop a theory of conflict and cooperation that is universally applicable and which covers the same topics now addressed by other social sciences. Game theory is used in public administration to predict future behavior and events, to explain phenomena, to investigate problems, to describe events, and for prescriptional purposes.

POSTPOSITIVIST RESEARCH MODELS

The many postpositivist research approaches now finding their way into use in public administration have been grouped together under the label of *interpretive theory* (Bevir and Rhodes 2002). Interpretive approaches to research involve the use of *subjective narrative*. Narrative methods are believed to produce knowledge that is different from knowledge gained by traditional (positivist) science (Wapner 2002).

Interpretive research brings the researcher into the research process instead of the detached, impartial, value-free investigator positivist tradition. Interpretive public administration seeks to uncover the *sense* of an action, practice, or idea. It does this by first discovering the intentions, desires, conceptual schemes, and experiences of the humans involved in the research, then attempting what has been called, "seeing how they fit into a whole structure which defines the nature and purpose of human life" (Fay 1975, 79).

According to Denscombe (2002, 18), some writers use the term *constructionism* to categorize the same approaches that fall under the interpretist label. Constructionism means that the researchers do not agree with the idea that the world of reality is "out there," waiting only to be discovered. Rather, they believe that humans construct all social phenomena and that no single construction is better than any other. Denscombe found that most of the different approaches falling under this label share a number of common points. First, all reality is subjective; it is constructed and interpreted by people. Second, humans react to the knowledge that they are being studied. When people become aware of this fact their behavior changes in a subtle but real manner. Hence, the researcher can never know the "true" behavior of a group. Third, it simply is not possible to gain objective knowledge about social phenomena. Despite all their efforts, researchers cannot be objective. Fourth, there is little or no prospect of producing grand theories explaining the social world. All reality is subjective, created by individuals, and subject to change.

Interpretive/constructionist research includes the *feminist, Marxist,* and *anti-foundationalist* (or *postmodern*) designs. These studies are often small-sample investigations, typically analyzing just one or a few cases. Although quantitative analyses are not rejected outright, researchers working in this tradition place greater emphasis upon qualitative methods. An integrative characteristic of each of these approaches is their emphasis on *narrative.*

A Second Classification Scheme

Using a somewhat different approach, Robson (2002) summarized the many different types of nonpositivist research into three broad strands. The first two, the *postpositivist* and the *constructivist* approaches, represent an evolutionary drift away from earlier quantitative and qualitative traditions; the third emphasis is known by many names, including *interpretive research, critical research,* and *emancipatory research.*

The postpositivist approach, although often leading criticisms directed at positivism, has not disregarded all aspects of positivist thinking. For example, a basic tenet of positivism is objectivity. While postpositivists generally accept this principle, they break with positivism in their willingness to admit that the theories, hypotheses, knowledge, and values of the researcher can influence what is observed. Positivists contend that one reality exists and the role of the researcher is to discover what that is, while postpositivists contend that reality can never be precisely known because of the intervention of the researcher's prior experiences and knowledge limitations.

Constructivist researchers do not accept the idea of a single objective reality. Rather, they consider that reality is socially constructed. It is established by the researcher and is a reflection of that context. In constructivist research, the research participants help the researchers to establish the reality. Hence, participant observation is one of the research methods often used by constructivists.

Emancipatory research, the third qualitative research theme noted by Robson, includes a number of different approaches. The three most common emancipatory approaches are *feminist research, Marxist research,* and *action research,* all of which share similar concerns and the following four principal characteristics:

- They focus on studies of the lives and experiences of groups that have traditionally been marginalized by society, such as women, minorities, and persons with disabilities.
- Their research focuses on analyses of how and why such groups are subjected to inequities and imbalanced power relationships.
- They examine how results of social inquiry into the inequities can be linked to political and social action and empowerment.
- They all use an emancipatory theory to develop their research approaches.

Feminist Research

The feminist approach to research and to science in general is based on the value-free fact that women see things differently than men. Moreover, education research has shown that the genders have different ways of learning and different ways of describing meaning. Thus, how females and males view research phenomena often differs in many meaningful ways.

For centuries, males have dominated the academic, administrative, and managerial career fields; most research in these areas was designed and conducted by males for male readers. Hence, the extensive and important role of females in society was often ignored or, at best, glossed over. However, many believed that the centuries that females were forced to accept a lesser status in the academic and political spheres demanded that a new, more equal approach to science be implemented. This resulted in establishment of the feminist-oriented approach to research in public administration, nonprofit operations, and political science. The feminist research model—which today is used by researchers of both genders—was seen as the methodological emphasis that would aid in this critical emancipatory effort.

Researchers who employ the feminist approach contend that gender-based political theory and political writing have long been both overtly and covertly gender biased. Thus, many feminist researchers saw traditional positivist research as possessing a gender bias that was misleading at best, and potentially insulting and derogatory at its worst.

When feminist researchers in public administration and political science examine such political phenomena as international relations and politics, state formation, war and peace, revolutions, international political economies, and global governance, they now discuss the role of gender in these events. Thus, gender is finally considered to be a relevant factor in all international politics, public administration, and other writing on governance phenomena (Locher and Prügl 2001).

The Marxist Approach

Classical Marxism may have been the first critical approach to social science research. It was based on the idea that conflict between the haves and have-nots, workers versus owners, the worker class versus the capitalist ruling class, are at the root of all political behavior. Therefore, Marxist research focused on ways to highlight disparities and identify the economic structures that form and restrict development of society, and on studies in egalitarian and emancipatory principles (Marsh 2002).

Four main principles are associated with classical Marxism: *economism, determinism, materialism,* and *structuralism.* Economism refers to the concept that economic forces determine social conditions. The determinism principle is the idea that capitalist production methods determined a person's role in life; humans were not free to choose their lot. Materialism refers to the materialism of the ruling class, the owners and operators of factories and the ruling classes they supported. Finally, structuralism refers to Marx's contention that economic and political structures established the actions of human beings. However, modern Marxism is radically different from the classical version. According to Marsh (2002):

> [W]hile modern Marxism is characterized by diversity, most of it rejects economism; rejects determinacy, emphasizing contingency; rejects materialism, acknowledging an independent role for ideas; rejects structuralism, accepting a key role for agents; no longer privileges class, acknowledging the crucial role of other causes of structured inequality; and, to an extent, privileges politics. (p. 161)

Marsh concedes that Marxism's influence on political and administrative research is in general decline. This decline may be attributed to several factors: the collapse of the Soviet block of nations, the renewed strength of conservative ideologies, and recent changes in capitalism, including widespread ownership, global economic development, and entrepreneurial activity. Despite its decline, Marsh believes Marxism still has much to offer. Foremost is its potential contribution to the critical analysis of existing social and political institutions; societies still contain inequalities and exploitation still dominates many Third World economic systems.

Because of its concern with righting social wrongs, the Marxist model is more likely to be found in research conducted by public administration researchers with strong backgrounds in sociology; they often are referred to as *political sociologists* rather than public administrators. Robson describes this emancipatory model as remaining closer to earlier qualitative traditions established in anthropology, psychology, and sociology.

Marxist research in Western social sciences emerged during the 1950s. Social scientists writing after World War II broke with traditional Marxian sociology that was characterized by "Marx's iron law of history, irrevocable evil of capitalism, and the proletariat as the privileged subject and anticipated agent of social transformation" (Kincheloe and McLaren 1984). Instead, they came to believe that the transformation of the social sciences taking place at that time could eventually lead to a more egalitarian and democratic social order, that men and women could determine their own existence, and that the emerging emancipatory form of social research would free research from the stigma associated with Soviet expansionism and the Cold War.

Kincheloe and McLaren (1984, 139–49) defined a Marxist researcher as a *criticalist* or theorist who:

- Tries to use his or her work as social or cultural criticism
- Accepts the basis assumption that power relations shape all thought; these relations are socially and historically established
- Believes that ideological thought shapes all facts

In addition, these researchers also believe that:

- The relationships between an idea and an object and between an identifier and what is identified are not stable or fixed; rather, social patterns in capitalist production and consumption always shape those relationships
- Language is the key to the formulation of conscious and unconscious awareness
- Some groups in a society are privileged over others and, while the reasons why may vary, oppression in society is reinforced when the nonprivileged accept their status as natural, necessary, or inevitable
- Oppression has many shapes; focusing on only one, such as class oppression versus racism, often misses the interconnections among them
- Established research practices generally (although usually unwittingly) reproduce the systems of class, race, and gender oppression

Except for stories about "dalliances and misdeeds," most people have less interest in politics than previous generations (Agger and Luke 2002, 160). As a result, much of the public sector research that might have focused on emancipatory issues is no longer in vogue. Other than feminist research, emancipatory research is seldom found in U.S. public sector graduate studies. Students are not taught the reasons for or how to conduct Marxian research models, nor is it generally known that Karl Marx, with Max Weber and certain members of the Frankfurt School, was one of the founders of sociology, particularly political sociology (Crotty 1998).

Despite these problems, there remains a large role open for anyone wanting to follow a Marxist research approach to empower the disenfranchised and marginalized of society. Agger and Luke (2002, 168–169) agree that modern Marxists:

> ... recognize the crisis tendencies of capitalism, without offering any hard-and-fast guarantees about the imminence of socialism and communism. This is because revolutionary change requires people actively to work for it, using their consciousness, ingenuity, strategy in order to throw over the old order. This capability of active decision-making and change is what philosophers call *agency,* suggesting a human being who is self-creative and proactive and not simply determined by impinging social forces. . . . Marxism is not deterministic. People are free to change their history, effecting social change made possible by a combination of free will or agency and propitious social and economic circumstances for revolutionary intervention. . . . The main variable for Marx, in determining the susceptibility of social circumstances to revolutionary transformation is ideology, or the degree of false consciousness. Ideology is produced by the political state, as well as by culture and religion. Ideologies are systematically interrelated belief systems that close the door of radical social change just as they open the door of personal salvation and self-betterment within the framework of the status quo.

Crotty (1998, 113) described Marxist research as a contrast between research that seeks to describe and understand, and research that challenges the status quo. It contrasts with research that sees a social situation in terms of interactions between social actors because it sees the situation as conflict and oppression of one or more groups. Instead of research that accepts things as they are, it is research that seeks to use the power of ideas to bring about change.

One of the key characteristics of Marxist research is that it continues to ask questions about current ideology while at the same time calling for action to redress perceived social injustice. Marxist researchers challenge traditional social structures and plan and participate in social action. Underlying this approach is what has been described as an "abiding concern with issues of power and oppression." Thus, these researchers focus on power relationships within society in order to expose inequities and injustice (Crotty 1998; Ray 1993; Habermas 1979).

Finally, critical research such as Marxist research is never really finished; rather, it is an ongoing, cyclical process of reflection and action. While the underlying goals of a just society and freedom and equity for everyone may seem utopian, critical researchers believe that they can accomplish change that leads to these goals.

Postmodern Approaches

Among the postpositivist research approaches that have gained some acceptance since they appeared in the last decades of the twentieth century are the *postmodern* or *anti-foundationalist* positions. These approaches to research have their roots in the *critical theory* found in art, music, and literature of the 1960s. Several key principles of postmodernism are that no single fundamental truth exists; there is no one certain way to gain knowledge; and no rules exist to guarantee the rationality of science.

According to Oakley (2002), postmodernism emerged from the extensive cultural changes in Western societies since the end of World War II, such as the emergence of a global economy, the weakening of radical politics and collapse of the Soviet Union, a lost faith in the power of rationality to bring about freedom, the rapid and pervasive spread of technology, and the spread of popular culture. Postmodernist critics hold that, since social science is part of the modernist condition, evolving changes in the philosophical foundations of public administration research make it necessary to adopt a postmodernist approach to research in these disciplines.

The postmodern approach has been adopted by a variety of researchers and philosophers who, according to Dwight Allman (1995, 69), "dispute the viability of modern civilization." For them, this means that the positivist approach of searching for an all-encompassing "true" picture of a social event is a waste of time. Each event must be described individually, taking into consideration the intentions of the actors, the experience of the investigator, and the external circumstances at the time of the event.

To determine the meaning of a phenomenon, the postmodernist believes that the time, situation, and intent of the social actor must be considered in addition to the event or behavior itself. Furthermore, there is no one best way to investigate, describe, or define a social event or social behavior. Therefore, one of the researcher's most important tasks is to interpret the phenomenon itself before it can be researched. The researcher must first frame the act within a larger context that includes the objectives of the social actors and the specific circumstances existing at the time of the action (Fay 1975).

The postmodern researcher cannot simply progress from a known and accepted foundation of basic assumptions. To the postmodernist, the meanings of the concepts we usually take for granted, such as democracy, the "sovereignty of nature," honesty, and ethical behavior do not really exist; they are, instead, human *constructs,* products of the human intellect. As such, the interpretations placed on these constructs are only one of many possible meanings. For example, Wapner adopted a postmodern approach in his discussion of the apparent lack of an international consensus in the importance of degradation of the environment and how that lack of consensus limits public environmental policy. Thus, there is no *better* or *best* view of nature. Nature is what society makes of it, and people in different cultures and circumstances have different points of view about nature that are equally legitimate. Wapner (2002) concluded that:

> Postmodern critics have shown . . . that "nature" is not simply a given, physical object but a social construction—an entity that assumes meaning within various cultural contexts and is fundamentally unknowable outside of human categories of understanding. This criticism raises significant challenges for global environmental politicians. (p. 167)

RESEARCH IN PUBLIC ADMINISTRATION

Regardless of the theoretical approach taken in research in the public sector, the questions most likely to be addressed are those with practical application for administrators in public organizations. Examples of the practical side of this research can be found in such journals as *Public Performance and Management Review* (PPMR) and *Public Administration Review* (PAR).

Researchers have developed an interest in both practical and theoretical aspects of research in public administration and nonprofit organization management. However, the research emphasis in both of fields has long been on the practical side (Rutgers 1997). Such research has primarily been concerned with resolving issues and problems in skills and decision-making that characterize the business of running an administrative organization. Thus, this research has focused on ways to improve the *practice* of public and governmental administration, particularly in urban and local government agencies (Garson and Overman 1983). This also means that research in both the practical (or empirical) and theoretical focus are grist for the research mill; in the words of

Alexander (his emphasis): *"All scientific development is a two-tiered process, propelled as much by theoretical as by empirical arguments"* (1985, 30).

While maintaining this largely practical focus, public administration researchers have looked at a wide variety of topics (Garson and Overman 1983; Stivers 2000; Lan and Anders 2000), and a wide variety of research methods have been used. Research in public administration has involved most if not all of the methods developed by the natural, social, human, and administrative sciences. The focus has not changed, however; it is still *applied research* for the resolution of practical problems faced by public and nonprofit organization administrators.

Although very little "pure" or theoretical research is published in public administration professional journals, interest in theoretical research is increasing. In recent decades, a growing number of researchers have directed their attention toward research aimed at establishing or building on a *theory* of public administration. This research has not proved to be particularly enlightening, however, as Stivers (2000) noted:

> In my view, the field of public administration has been marked since the early twentieth century by a largely fruitless search for scientific truth. I say "fruitless" because the attempts to identify generalizations about administrative practice that hold across all or even most situations inevitably runs up against what seems to me to be an undeniable aspect of our subject matter—that is, any particular situation is simultaneously similar to and different from any other situation. (p. 134)

Criticisms of Public Administration Research

A number of studies on the scope and focus of public administrative research have criticized published public sector research. Perry and Kraemer (1986) found that public administration research has been deficient in three important methodological areas. First, little theory testing is performed. Second, the research lacks cumulativeness—little attention is given to earlier studies and little effort is given to build upon that earlier work. And third, the published research has seldom been funded by outside sources.

Some observers believe that much if not most of the research conducted in public administration has been of low quality (McCurdy and Cleary 1984; Perry and Karemer 1986; Stallings and Ferris 1988; Houston and Delevan 1990; Cleary 1992; Cozzetto 1994; Brewer et al. 1999; Lan and Anders 2000). Brewer and colleagues (1999) put it this way:

> Over the past fifteen years, scholars have sought to address the quantity and quality of research in the field of public administration by examining dissertations written by public administration students and articles published in public administration and related journals. The results have been most discouraging. (p. 374)

RESEARCH TOPICS AND THEMES

What sorts of topics and themes do public administration students, practitioners, consultants, and academics research? Public administration research can be grouped into just two broad categories: *generic* research and *mission-specific* research. Generic research is conducted in order to advance knowledge or understanding of management processes and is likely to have wide applicability. Mission-specific research, on the other hand, focuses on a specific purpose, program, agency, or policy and is likely to have only limited applicability to the field.

Table 4.1

Topics in Early Published Public Administration Research

- Policy output
- Adaptation to scarcity
- Local attitudes and leader opinion
- Licensure effectiveness
- Policy outcomes
- Organizational costs
- Attitudes, beliefs, and values
- Cash-management strategy
- Tax limitations
- Research validity and reliability

- Staff-planning methods
- Productivity measures
- Effects of federal aid
- Public participation
- Cooperative management styles
- Job managing effectiveness
- Staff burnout
- Program effectiveness
- Risk-management practice
- Affirmative-action effectiveness

Source: Adapted from Garson and Overman 1983.

Garson and Overman (1983) established a list of topics (Table 4.1) from their examination of sources published during the 1970s. Those topics mostly dealt with management and administrative concerns and covered all organizational functions. The focus of the approach has been almost entirely on how these problems affect local and state government administration.

Houston and Delevan (1990) examined a sample of 123 papers published in six different public administration journals between 1984 and 1989. Most were written primarily to develop conceptual themes for further research. Most of the remaining (28 percent) were categorized as empirical efforts to examine relationships between variables. A very small number were reports of public policy evaluations.

Houston and Delevan concluded that descriptive statistics (frequency distributions, measures of central tendency, and variability) are the most commonly used statistical techniques in reported public administration research. These statistical methods served three main functions in the sixty-one papers Houston and Delevan coded as "relationship studies"—*description, inference, and control.* Nearly 69 percent of the papers used statistical hypothesis testing, suggesting that inferential statistical methods are widely understood and applied. Table 4.2 contains a breakdown of the statistical techniques found in the quantitative methods papers.

Richard Box (1992) examined 230 articles published in *Public Administration Review* (PAR) over the five-year period from 1985 to 1989. The majority (67 percent) of the papers published in PAR dealt with issues pertaining to the practice of public administration. The remainder were almost equally divided between public administration theory and assorted specific issues, such as the research task itself. Eight papers dealt with politics and/or administration; four papers each were concerned with the public/private dichotomy, and four dealt with reorganization issues. Motivation, regulation, and conflict resolution were the subjects of three papers each. Eleven papers were about public administration theory in general; six each were on either public administration research or theory in the public/private issue. Another five were on the politics/administration issue, and two dealt with bureaucracy. According to Box, none of the articles contained complex or sophisticated statistical techniques.

The new editors of PAR published an editorial in the January/February 2006 issue that clearly stated the journal's editorial policy and gave four reasons why PAR is still vital (Stillman and Raadschelders 2006, 1–3):

1. First and foremost, for advancing generalists administrative expertise. The new editors agree to attempt to integrate theory with practice.

Table 4.2

Statistical Techniques in a Sample of Published Articles (n = 61)

Statistic(s)	Frequency
Univariate	37
Bivariate correlation	20
Multiple regression	25
Cross-tabulations	22
Factor analysis	5
Chi square	4
ANOVA	3
Path analysis	3
Bivariate regression	1
MANOVA	1
Nonlinear regression	1
Other	3

Source: Adapted from Houston and Delevan 1990, 678.

2. Second, for building a share sense of professional identity. From its first issue, PAR has been an important way for academics and practicing administrators to share their interests.

3. Third, for fostering ethical responsibility. Applying administrative activity to public issues requires a special sense of social responsibility among administrators and academics.

4. "Fourth, for ensuring balanced representation. PAR must include a balance of research in all areas of public administration and related disciplines, with coverage of a wide variety of issues and concerns.

As a further indication of PAR's responsibility to the profession, the editors stated their commitment to include "state-of-the-art administrative research" on such topic areas as motivation, budgeting and forecasting, and implementation theory.

Major Topics in Recent Published PA Research

A comprehensive analysis by Lan and Anders (2000) reviewed 634 research papers published in eight academic and professional journals over a three-year period (1993–95). They found that most published public administration research dealt with managerial issues relating to federal, state, or local government, with the emphasis on state and local levels. A lesser number dealt with public sector issues in general, while only a small portion addressed international issues. The primary emphasis of the research they examined was on government in general or issues that concern the executive branch (at all levels). The topics were almost all focused on solving managerial or administrative problems.

Lan and Anders also found that researchers in their sample studied a wide variety of administration and function topics within this applied framework. Most focused on such organizational management issues as personnel management and human resources planning, political/legal institutions and processes, finance and budgeting, administration theory, policy design and analyses, social and economic issues, and research methodology. Less than 2 percent addressed ethics issues.

Research Methods

No single research method has overwhelmingly dominated the articles investigated by any of the authors who surveyed published public administration literature, including doctoral dissertations. At best, a small majority of these studies favored a *qualitative* approach. Quantitative approaches were followed in a little less than 41 percent of the papers; qualitative approaches were followed in 59 percent.

Of the quantitative papers, 15.4 percent used simple descriptive statistics and/or simple correlation analysis. Another 15 percent applied some intermediate statistics, which included hypothesis testing and some inferential statistics. More advanced statistical tests, including regression analysis, time series, and more sophisticated inferential statistics added another 13 percent.

Lan and Anders concluded that nearly all the qualitative methods used in social science research were represented in the sample of articles they investigated. The case study was the preferred qualitative research method (it was not clear if these were single case or multiple case studies). A small number used ethnography methods. The remaining third were grouped into the "others" category, which included literature reviews, reports of interviews, and other qualitative approaches. Slightly more than 44 percent used existing literature (other than government statistical reports) as the basis of their analysis; 27 percent used self-collected data; and almost 21 percent used data from government publications.

SUMMARY

Modern public sector researchers approach their studies from several different traditional philosophical foundations. The two major traditions are *positivism* and *postpositivism*. Each of these philosophical foundations has its own preferred body of designs and methods. For example, positivist researchers emphasize quantitative data that is gathered and analyzed using experiments, surveys, and statistics. Postpositivism includes several different narrative-based approaches, including explanatory, critical, feminist, and postmodern research. While in decline, some experts feel that Marxist research could also be useful to investigate commonly held assumptions and address social injustice.

The social and behavioral sciences include public administration, political science, sociology, psychology, economics, economics, and cultural anthropology. The topics and methodologies of public administration research are rooted in several different methodological traditions and framed within different conceptual elements that are also found in the other social science disciplines. In studying a government agency, one researcher may use a variable-based approach, with heavy emphasis on quantification and statistical analysis. This is in keeping with the positivist research tradition. A second researcher may follow a comparative case study approach, in which the most common themes are derived from an interpretation of a body of narrative.

Despite the continuing discussion over methodology issues, research into issues, controversies, and questions in public administration is alive and well—and probably better off for its differences of opinion and focus. Obviously, the research on public administration, governmental institutions, and the behavior of citizen clients and service providers is not yet complete. The good news is that there are many different topics to examine and many ways to go about conducting research studies that contribute to the body of knowledge in this important field of inquiry.

ADDITIONAL READING

Chalmers, A. 1985. *What Is This Thing Called Science?* Milton Keynes: Open University Press.
March, J., and J. Olsen. 1989. *Rediscovering Institutions.* New York: Free Press.
Peters, G. 1999. *Institutional Theory in Political Science: The "New Institutionalism."* London: Pinter.

5

RESEARCH IN NONPROFIT ORGANIZATIONS

Although charitable activity may be as old as civilization, nonprofit and charitable organizations have occupied their positions of importance they now hold for only a little more than fifty years. The nonprofit, or *third sector* as it is often called, appeared as a full-blown, complementary sector to business and government only after the end of World War II (Hall 2005). Certainly nonprofits existed in relatively large numbers before then—in 1940, there were approximately 12,500 charitable and 60,000 noncharitable nonprofit organizations in the United States, as well as nearly 180,000 religious congregations. By 2004, the total number of nonprofit organizations had grown to more than 600,000 charitable organizations, 400,000 congregations, and another 600,000 noncharitable nonprofits. More than 90 percent of these nonprofit organizations came into existence after 1950.

The nonprofit sector is big by any measurement. For example, the Federal Reserve Bank of St. Louis estimates that American individuals and organizations donated a record $248.5 billion in 2004 (Hernández-Murillo and Roisman 2005). Of that amount, foundations donated $33.6 billion, corporate giving added another $3.6 billion, and community organizations added another $3.2 billion. Individual donations made up most of the remaining total of more than $198 billion (CRC 2006). In 2003, U.S. individuals, estates, foundations, and corporations gave $240.7 billion, an increase of 2.8 percent over the $234 billion donated in 2002 (AAFRC 2004).

These statistics are included here to reinforce the idea that great research opportunities exist in this sector. The leaders of these nonprofits must make decisions in all the management disciplines, including accounting and budgeting, finance, human resources, marketing, and planning and operations—and must do so in an environment of uncertainty exacerbated by their dependence upon voluntary contributions of time, participation, and money.

Although different in scope and focus, in many ways researchers investigating issues in nonprofit organizations do so with the same objectives and scope as researchers in public administration. Most research conducted in and for nonprofit organizations is empirical; it is typically concerned with normative issues—that is, it is research that looks for better ways for the organization to operate. Thus, the published literature on nonprofit organizations is filled with reports of studies on fund-raising; identifying potential donors; recruiting, training, and supervising of volunteers; and similar normative issues. However, there is also a small but growing body of research pertaining to theory development in the area of volunteerism and citizen participation in planning and program operations.

Typical research topics in nonprofit organization are case studies dealing with organizational

Table 5.1

Examples of Research Topics in NVSQ

	Research Area	Example Article Title	Author(s)	Issue/Pages
1.	Organization and leadership	"A Study of Organizational Effectiveness for National Olympic Sporting Organizations."	David Shilsbury and Kathleen A. Moore	2006 35(1): 5–38
2.	Philanthropy	"Do Public Subsidies Leverage Private Philanthropy for the Arts? Empirical Evidence on Symphony Orchestras."	Arthur C. Brooks	1999 28(1): 32–45
3.	Volunteerism	"Men's and Women's Volunteering: Gender Differences in the Effects of Employment and Family Characteristics."	Hiromi Taniguchi	2006 35(1): 83–101
4.	Public Policy	"The Strategic Choices of Child Advocacy Groups."	William T. Gormley Jr. and Helen Cymrot	2006 35(1): 102–38
5.	Civil Society	"Comparing Faith-Based and Secular Community Service Corporations in Pittsburgh and Allegheny County, Pennsylvania."	Kevin Kearns, Chisung Park and Linda Yankoski	2005 34(2): 206–31

and volunteer needs analyses, situation analysis, and strategies for attaining objectives, operating programs, and managing people and processes. The goal of this chapter is to bring to light some examples of research taking place in and for nonprofit organizations, so researchers may see for themselves how various methods are applied in this sector as well as in the government sector.

ISSUES IN NONPROFIT ORGANIZATION RESEARCH

As expected, much of the research carried out in this field focuses on the key issues of interest to the managers and administrators of nonprofit organization. For example, most of the research reported in the nonprofit sector journal *Nonprofit and Voluntary Sector Quarterly* (NVSQ) is directed at topics in these five areas: (1) organization and leadership, (2) philanthropy, (3) volunteerism, (4) public policy, and (5) civil society in general. Examples of the types of nonprofit sector research projects published in recent issues of NVSQ are displayed in Table 5.1.

RESEARCH IN ORGANIZATIONAL LEADERSHIP

Nonprofit organizations have long benefited from research findings on many of the same organizational management issues addressed in the private and government sectors. For example, a small sample of the titles of typical research studies in recent management literature of nonprofit organizations include: *Strategic Planning for Public and Nonprofit Organizations* (Bryson 2004), *The Jossey-Bass Handbook of Nonprofit Leadership & Management* (Herman 2005), *Making Nonprofits Work* (Light 2000), *High Performance Nonprofit Organizations* (Letts, Ryan, and Grossman 1999), and *Third Sector Management* (Werther and Berman 2001). The *Jossey-Bass Handbook,* for example, includes sections on context and institutions, leadership issues, operations management, managing financial resources, and managing people.

Research in Nonprofit Organization Issues

With more than 1.5 million nonprofit organizations in existence in the United States in 2006, it is impossible to determine what organizational topics are of most interest to managers or researchers. Typical of the research conducted on nonprofit organizational issues are a study in the March issue and two in the June 2006 issue of *Nonprofit and Voluntary Quarterly Sector Quarterly:* "Communalities and Distinctions in the Measurement of Organizational Performance and Effectiveness" by Baruch and Ramalho appeared in the March issue. "The Larger They Get: The Changing Size Distribution of Private Human Service Organizations" by Tucker and Sommefeld; and "Worker Motivations, Job Satisfaction, and Loyalty in Public and Nonprofit Social Services" by Borzaga and Tortia appeared in the June issue.

The papers included a comparative analysis of the way researchers measure and report organizational effectiveness and organizational performance outcomes; a report on how the rapid growth in the number and size of private human services organizations is likely to cause a decline in the numbers of small, independent human services organizations; and a report on how workers in nonprofit and public organizations determine which factors influence loyalty and satisfaction.

Academic institutions have a rich tradition of research on nonprofit organizations. For example, such diverse universities as Harvard, Seton Hall, the University of San Francisco, and Case Western Reserve in Cleveland run just a few of the many university-sponsored programs that focus on research in the nonprofit sector. The program at Case University's Mandel Center is typical. The Center publishes the *Nonprofit Management and Leadership* journal, and lists the following as some of the issue areas for their research efforts (CASE 2006):

- The history and status of nonprofit organizations
- Law of nonprofit and charitable organizations
- Ethics in nonprofit organizations
- Various elements of organization management
- Program evaluation and performance measurement
- Strategic alliances involving nonprofit organizations
- Leadership in nonprofit organizations
- Nonprofit organization human resource management
- Accounting and financial issues
- Foundation operations and other related topics

The University of San Francisco's Institute for Nonprofit Organization Management is another example of an academic center of research on nonprofit organizations. The USF Institute researches and publishes regular reports on the state of the nonprofit sector and philanthropy in California. The Institute describes its mission as working to improve the management and leadership of nonprofits through application of the following programs (USF 2006): (1) Carrying out and publishing research for use by nonprofit managers, leaders, policy-makers and the academic community; (2) supporting and improving management development through professional education in nonprofit management; and (3) planning, programming, and holding relevant events and meetings of professional nonprofit organization managers, academic leaders and researchers, and other individuals for developing strategies designed to strengthen nonprofits and develop philanthropy.

Other academic research centers can be found at the University of Maryland, Grand Valley State University, and Indiana University, to name only a few. Additionally, a number of associations sponsor or conduct research on nonprofits (Harrison 2006). A partial list includes:

- Association for Healthcare Philanthropy
- Association for Research on Nonprofit Organizations and Voluntary Action (ARNOVA)
- Association of Small Foundations
- The Council of Michigan Foundations
- The Council on Foundations
- The Foundation Center
- The Independent Sector
- National Center for Charitable Statistics
- National Center for Family Philanthropy
- New Tithing Group
- Philanthropy Roundtable

A Crisis in Leadership?

In the December 9, 2004, issue of the *Chronicle of Philanthropy,* contributing writer Pablo Eisenberg charged that U.S. nonprofit foundations and organizations were suffering from what he termed "a critical lack of leadership." Eisenberg based his conclusion on the following points (2004a, 44):

- The extraordinary growth of new, one-issue organizations has stifled creative leadership and resulted in narrow agendas.
- Loss of government funding and greater competition for private resources that has made it necessary for organization executives to spend a disproportionate amount of time on fund-raising.
- A shift from the sector's historical social focus to one of "corporatization," with growing commercialism; this has resulted in lapses in ethics and favored "managers, not leaders; entrepreneurs and deal makers, not visionary designers of new programs; and egoists, not institution builders."
- Emergence of "celebrityhood" that has seen nonprofits rush to sign up celebrities ("nationally known hotshots") as managers in the mistaken belief that such high-profile public personalities will be successful in running the organization; this has resulted in a loss of teamwork, which is an essential ingredient in all nonprofit organizations.
- The high cost of a university education, which has led graduates away from careers in the nonprofit sector.
- Lack of advocacy and the unwillingness of participants in federal volunteer programs, such as the Peace Corps and AmeriCorps, to move into leadership positions in voluntary organizations.

Eisenberg did not just cite problems in nonprofit leadership—he also proposed a number of actions designed to alleviate the problems. These remedial steps included (1) subsidizing nonprofit sector entry-level jobs for young people; (2) strengthening leadership training in academic centers on nonprofit management and public policy; (3) increasing campus involvement in community problem-solving and citizen participation; (4) renewed emphasis on civic education and requiring more courses in civics, history, and citizenship; and (5) encouraging nonprofit organizations to focus on the leadership problem. Ideally, researchers would study and compare each of these potential solutions, thus developing a database that could help future managers when faced with similar management questions.

RESEARCH IN PHILANTHROPY

When it comes to philanthropy, most people respond generously to calls for contributions of money, time, and voluntary labor. Americans donated nearly $250 *billion* to charities in 2004 (Hernández-Murillo and Roisman 2005). Americans are not alone in their willingness to share their time and money with others less fortunate. This fact has been made abundantly clear in reactions of people around the globe to three recent catastrophic events. The first was the September 11, 2001, terrorist attacks on the World Trade Center, the Pentagon, and the aborted attempt to crash an aircraft into the White House. The second major event was the 2004 tsunami in which an estimated 180,000 lives were lost in India, Indonesia, Sri Lanka, and Thailand. The third event, in 2005, was the damage from Hurricane Katrina in New Orleans and the nearby Gulf Coast. After all of these events, outpourings of donations and voluntary action came from countries around the world.

As part of a larger study dealing with the terrorist attacks, an Indiana University Center on Philanthropy (IUCOP) survey found that Americans were very generous in their contributions related to the September 11, 2001 disasters; nearly 75 percent of the sample said they performed some type of charitable activity related to the event—donating money, food, clothing, blood, or volunteering their time (IUCOP 2002).

Managers of nonprofit organizations are encouraged by the willingness of people and corporations to contribute their time, possessions, and cash to charitable causes. However, they worry that such contributive largess might dry up their own sources of funds and voluntary participation. For this reason alone, research into philanthropy and how it can be sustained even in the face of unexpected shocks is becoming increasingly important.

In addition to "feast or famine" issues, managers of nonprofit organizations often find themselves faced with making decisions in the face of what are often conflicting research results. Indiana University economics professor Mark Wilhelm addressed this issue in a comparative study of six different research studies—each with widely different estimates of the percentages of households that donate to charity and the amounts they gave (Wilhelm 2002). The percentage of households that contribute was found to be 68.5 percent in one study and 89.9 percent in another. Four possible factors contributing to the disparities include: (1) results are adversely affected by missing data; (2) respondent recall differs based on the type of cue system employed; (3) interviewers with skill in ferreting out other financial data came up with lager amounts of giving; and (4) disproportionate amounts given by upper-end respondents may have skewed the results—points that researchers should be aware of.

RESEARCH IN VOLUNTARISM

Voluntarism, or volunteering, is the lifeblood of most nonprofit organizations. The term *volunteer* refers to people of all ages who perform any type or amount of unpaid activity for a nonbusiness organization; *organization* refers to associations, societies, or groups of people who share a common interest. People give their time, labor, and money, without which the nonprofit sector could not function. The federal government groups these organizations into eight major categories, including but not limited to civic and political, education and youth, environment or animal, hospital or other health, public safety, religious, social or community service, and sport, hobby, or the arts. A ninth catchall category is also used (BLS 2005).

Nonprofit organizations of all types are interested in knowing why people do or do not volunteer, who volunteers, when and where they volunteer, how to stimulate voluntary activity, and everything else that might increase the level and quality of volunteering and participation in civic associations and organizations. Therefore, they regularly commission, fund, or conduct research projects to increase the knowledge base about this topic.

Volunteering in the United States

Research opportunities in the nonprofit sector are illustrated by questions such as, who volunteers in America? Every year, the U.S. Department of Labor's Bureau of Labor Statistics (BLS) provides quantitative answers this question by surveying a sample of more than 60,000 citizens across the country. From September 2002 to September 2005, the BLS reported that approximately 65.4 million people—28.8 percent of the total U.S. population—volunteered in some way at least once. About one in every three women and one in four men did some volunteer work during the twelve-month period. In all age groups, more women than men were likely to volunteer (Table 5.2) (BLS 2005).

Nearly 70 percent of U.S. volunteers limited their activity to working with just one organization. Religious organizations and faith-based groups enrolled more volunteers than any other type of organization, with almost 35 percent of the total. Older volunteers were most likely to work with faith-based groups than any other type of organization.

Fund-raising was listed as the most commonly reported activity (29.7 percent of all volunteers) in the survey of voluntary participation in the United States. Other activities included collecting, preparing, distributing, or serving food, general labor, supplying transportation, and tutoring or teaching. Among the reasons given for not volunteering were: lack of time, 45.6 percent; health or medical problems, 15.2 percent; and family or childcare problems, 9.3 percent.

Voluntary Activity in Canada

Similar studies are conducted in Canada. Canadian citizens also participate regularly in charitable giving, volunteering, and participation in charitable organizations and actions. In Canada, almost four out of five people donate to charitable or nonprofit organizations or causes; as in the United States, the largest proportion of these donations was funneled through religious organizations (McKeown et al. 2004).The Canadian government, in cooperation with various nonprofit organizations, regularly surveys voluntary activity in an effort to track the state of giving and volunteering in Canada. Beginning in 1997, the Public Health Agency of Canada (PHAC), along with other government and nongovernment voluntary organizations, sponsored a National Survey of Giving, Volunteering, and Participating (NSGVP)—the *Voluntary Sector Initiative* (VSI)—with a plan to conduct the survey every three years. This survey has been described as "the most comprehensive assessment of giving, volunteering and participating ever undertaken in Canada and, perhaps, in the world" (Hall, McKeown, and Roberts 2001).

The NSGVP survey series asks questions about how Canadians give money and other resources to individuals and to charitable and nonprofit organizations; how they volunteer time; and how they participate in organizations. Highlights of the 2004 survey include (Hall et al. 2006):

- The nonprofit and voluntary sector in Canada accounts for 6.8 percent of GDP; when the value of volunteer work is included, this increases to 8.5 percent of GDP.

Table 5.2

Volunteers by Sex and Age Characteristics

Characteristic	September 2002 Number (000s)	Percentage of Population	September 2005 Number (000s)	Percentage of Population
Sex				
Total, both sexes	59,783	27.4	65,357	28.8
Men	24,706	23.6	27,370	25.0
Women	35,076	31.0	37,987	32.4
Age				
Total, 16 and older	59,783	27.4	65,357	28.8
16–24 years	7,742	21.9	8,995	24.4
25–34 years	9,674	24.8	9,881	25.3
35–44 years	14,971	34.1	14,809	34.5
45–54 years	12,477	31.3	13,826	32.7
55–64 years	7,331	27.5	9,173	30.2
65 years and older	7,687	22.7	8,712	24.8

Source: Bureau of Labor Statistics 2005.

- Nonprofit and voluntary organizations employ 12 percent of Canada's workers, and 13 percent of its nonagricultural employment.
- Service activities dominate nonprofit and voluntary activity in Canada; about 74 percent of workers in this sector work in the delivery of services, including education, health, and housing. This compares to 64 percent in the rest of the world.
- Canadian nonprofit and voluntary organizations receive more funds from the government than similar agencies elsewhere in the world (probably due to funding of hospitals, universities, and colleges).
- Philanthropy accounts for 9 percent of all income for nonprofits. When volunteer work is included, this represents 20 percent of the total income. It is the main source of revenue for environmental agencies and the second largest for foundations and culture, recreation, and social services groups. However, it is less than the 28 percent of the total income average for all developed nations.

RESEARCH IN NONPROFITS AND PUBLIC POLICY

In the United States, the first decade of the new century has seen a growing reliance upon cooperative arrangements between public agencies and for-profit and nonprofit organizations to solve local social problems. This growth in the number and variety of partnerships is due to purposeful changes in public policy.

One example of these policy shifts at the highest level of the federal government is the *faith-based initiative* recommendation in the 2002 President's Management Agenda. This policy is designed to make it easier for faith-based organizations and government agencies to collaborate in finding solutions to social problems (OMB 2002). Although such partnerships became possible with passage of 1996 federal welfare reform law, which made it possible for faith-based community organizations serving a community to apply for direct or indirect federal support for such service, progress had been spotty at best.

The faith-based initiative has three main goals (OMB 2002): (1) to identify and eventually eliminate federal barriers to funding and cooperating with effective faith-based and community service programs through legislative, regulatory, and program reform; (2) to stimulate greater private contributions to nonprofit, faith-based community service programs and community groups by increasing tax deductions and other incentives; and (3) to pioneer a new model of cooperative federal and state government and nonprofit organizations that collaborate with faith-based and other community groups in programs such as after-school and literacy services, help for the children of prisoners, and support for other children in need.

By 2001, the 1996 law had not been well or fully implemented; no faith-based organization from any state had become a service provider supported with federal funds. However, newly elected President George W. Bush made the concept a centerpiece of his plan to transform the way government functions. A faith-based initiative was included in the Management Agenda introduced in 2002. President Bush signed two executive orders: one created the White House Office of Faith-Based and Community Initiative; the second set up parallel offices at five federal departments—Health and Human Services, Justice, Housing and Urban Development, Labor, and Education.

The White House Office is charged with promoting a federal policy of cooperation, respect, and collaboration with religious and grassroots organizations. Full implementation of this charge may be the first time the federal government has made it a matter of open policy to fund groups with religious affiliations, thus making it one of the most promising public policy developments affecting nonprofit organizations since the Great Depression of the 1930s. It is also an issue area that cries out for much new research if it is to grow and prosper as foreseen.

Additional Collaborative Programs

This trend toward great collaboration in policy making on nonprofit issues is occurring at the congressional level as well. In early 2005, the U.S. Senate Finance Committee's investigation of abuses of the laws affecting charities and foundations resulted in what one observer termed a "historically unprecedented example of participatory policy . . . [by making] extraordinary efforts to get the views of nonprofit leaders and experts" (Goldman 2005, 39). The Senate committee asked more than one hundred executives of nonprofit organizations to work together in drafting suggestions for the committee. One of the suggestions was for elimination of barriers that make it difficult, if not impossible, for nonprofit groups to work closely with government and businesses in serving society.

Public and nonprofit sector collaborations are typically formed to accomplish (1) what a government agency cannot as effectively and efficiently do alone, (2) what a government agency group might have difficulty in accomplishing on its own, or (3) to provide improved or enhanced services to a segment of the public (Becker and Patterson 2005).

These partnerships are formed for varied purposes, many of which fall into five general categories: (1) health and human services; (2) public land conservancy management; (3) neighborhood and regional redevelopment and economic growth; (4) planning, construction, and management of infrastructure; and (5) recreation and cultural programs. As the number of partnerships continues to grow, so does the number and scope of the research activities that deal with related issues.

RESEARCH IN CIVIL SOCIETY

Civil society refers to the collection of civic and social groups and organizations outside of formal government; they include service organizations, booster groups, volunteer agencies, and other similar groups. Collectively, they are also called the "third sector," with government and business being the other two.

A 2000 Institute of Development Studies (IDS) and Ford Foundation study reported on the state of civil society in twenty-two different nations across Africa, Asia, Latin America, Eastern Europe, the Middle East, and the United States. The study discussed the state of civil society in each country, the local government's attitudes and reactions toward civil organizations, and potential interactions between civil society and the state (IDS 2000). Professor Yu Keping was one of the researchers. He looked at the connections between political institutions and a newly emerging civil society in modern China.

Keping identified four key distinguishing features of civil society organizations that have relevance in all societies. First, they are unofficial. That is, although they may carry out services for a government, they are separate civil organizations. Second, they are nonprofit. While some may charge a fee for some portion of their services, earning a profit is not their primary objective. Rather, they exist to provide a service to society or one or more stakeholder groups. Third, they are independent of government. Although some may receive some financial support from government in the form of grants or payments for services they provide, their management, organizational leadership, and funding are expected to remain independent of government and politics. Finally, they are almost always voluntary; members are not forced to join, serve, or contribute (Keping 2000).

Categories of Civil Society Organizations

There is wide variety in the numbers and types of projects that researchers might address in the civil society category. Prior to a 1999–2000 restructuring, a North American coding system for nonprofit organizations identified 645 separate categories of organizations for which the Internal Revenue Service could grant tax-exempt status. Even after the reorganization, the system still categorizes nonprofits into approximately 400 groups—all of which are fertile soil for research (NCCS 2006).

Redesignated after 2000 as the *National Taxonomy of Exempt Entities—Core Codes* (NTEE-CC), the classification scheme divided North American civil society into twenty-six major groups organized under ten broad categories. The ten categories and the coding-system groups for each are identified in Table 5.3. In addition to the ten categories and twenty-six major groups, nonprofit types are further broken down into additional codes. For example, the largest category in the classification scheme is Group V—Human Services—with eight major subgroups coded from I through P (Table 5.4). The largest of these subgroups is the Human Services P category.

There are forty-four subgroups under the Human Services P group. They range from such diverse operations as fund-raising and fund distribution (P12), to neighborhood centers (P28), family counseling (P46), group homes (P73), and homeless centers (P85). Information about these and other classifications can be found at the NCCS website: http://ncss2.urban/org/ntee-cc/index.htm.

SUMMARY

There are conflicting opinions about the future of the nonprofit sector in society. In just a little more than fifty years, nonprofit organizations have become fully engrained into global society; as a group, they make up what is now recognized as the Third Sector, and are well on the way to becoming equal partners with the private (business) and public (government) sectors as essential elements of an economy. No one doubts that nonprofits are here to stay; they fill too many needs of society to disappear. As governments find themselves forced to retreat from direct involvement in the arts, rapidly growing needs for health care, shelter, food, and basic education and training, nonprofit organizations have stepped forward to fill the void left from reductions in government funding.

Table 5.3

The NTEE-CC Classification System

Code	Category	Major Groups
I.	Arts, Culture, and Humanities	A
II.	Education	B
III.	Environment and Animals	C, D
IV.	Health	E, F, G, H
V.	Human Services	I, J, K, L, M, N, O, P
VI.	International, Foreign Affairs	Q
VII.	Public, Societal Benefit	R, S, T, U, V, W
VIII.	Religion Related	X
IX.	Mutual/Membership Benefit	Y
X.	Unknown, Unclassified	Z

Source: Bureau of Labor Statistics 2005.

Table 5.4

Major Groups in the Human Services Classification

Group	Group Services	Number of Subcategories
I	Crime and Legal Related Services	25
J	Employment	15
K	Food, Agriculture, and Nutrition	19
L	Housing and Shelter	19
M	Public Safety, Disaster Preparedness and Relief	14
N	Recreation and Sports	30
O	Youth Development	24
P	Human Services	44

Source: Bureau of Labor Statistics 2005.

Because they fill such a vital and growing need, we may be entering upon a "Golden Age of Nonprofits" (Werther and Berman 2001, 215). Corporate, foundation, and personal philanthropy has never been greater in the United States. On the other hand, some observers believe that citizens' confidence in charities has declined as a consequence of published lapses in the integrity, transparency, and commitment to serving the public interest among some nonprofit organizations (Eisenberg 2004b). Accusations that some agencies lobby for preferential treatment are also a part of the criticisms facing the nonprofit sector.

Research on areas of concern to nonprofit managers includes ways to improve their operations, become more efficient at raising funds, recruiting and using voluntary workers, and other normative issues. Little research focuses on theory building, but is not completely absent. This chapter has followed the practice of the Association for Research on Nonprofit Organizations and Voluntary Action (ARNOVA) by grouping nonprofit research topics into five broad classes: organization and leadership, philanthropy, volunteerism, public policy, and civil society.

ADDITIONAL READING

Hogan, Cecilia, and David Lamb. 2004. *Prospect Research.* Boston: Jones and Bartlett.

PART 2

UNDERSTANDING THE RESEARCH PROCESS

6

THE EIGHT STEPS OF THE RESEARCH PROCESS

All research activity takes place in a sequence of steps. First, someone is faced with a problem, conflict, event, or situation that requires a decision (a *study problem*). That person or someone else is instructed to design a method of collecting data that will help achieve a solution to the problem (planning a *research strategy*). Information is then collected (a data-gathering activity). Once the data are collected, they must be processed, analyzed, and interpreted to find their meaning. Finally, all the pieces are put together in a report that helps bring about resolution of the problem. *How* these steps are put together is called the *research process.*

There is no limit to the number of possible choices of study questions, research strategies, data collection methods, data processing and evaluation approaches, and interpretations of results. It is possible to put these together in many different combinations, no one of which is inherently better or more correct than another. Today, these combinations are all seen as valid research strategies. The validity of their selection and application is based on the nature of the study question, the objectives for the study, and the researcher's level of skill and comfort with the research method.

The same can be said for the sequence of steps that researchers follow in conducting their research activities. The eight-step research process presented in Figure 6.1 has been tested and refined over decades of scientific investigation. It is a product of years of teaching and conducting research activities, tempered by a review of many different types of research guidebooks and can be used to guide research activities in all the social, administrative, and natural sciences.

IDENTIFY THE RESEARCH PROBLEM

Research in public administration, nonprofit management, and related disciplines may be either theoretical or applied. The first step in a theoretical study is to select a topic that is of interest to the researcher and has the promise of contributing in some meaningful way toward the continual development and evolution of public administration theory. However, for studies with a more applied orientation, researchers usually begin a study only after they have identified a problem or situation for which more information is needed.

Whether the goal is to develop theory or solve an organizational problem, knowing what to investigate is the critical first step in public administration and nonprofit management research; it is when the research *identifies the research problem clearly and succinctly.* This is the most

71

Figure 6.1   **The Eight Steps of the Research Process**

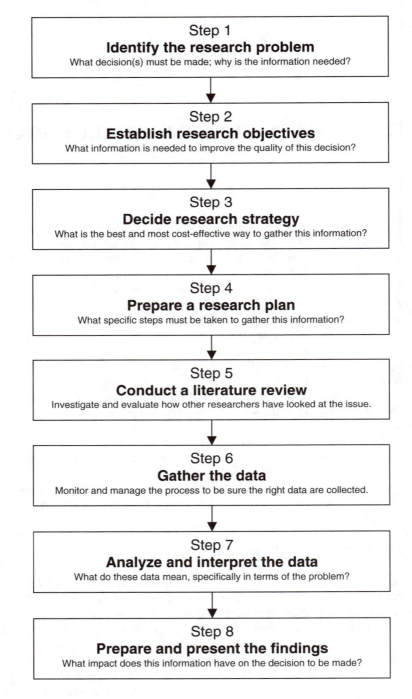

important step in the process—it may also be the most difficult step to accomplish (McMillan and Schumacher 1997). If this first step is not done correctly, the remaining activities will be a waste of the researcher's time and labor. Data will have been gathered, but the relevance of that data will be questionable.

The label *research problem* often confuses students and administrators; it implies a situation or condition needing discussion and resolution. Instead, sometimes the term describes the purpose that underlies a proposal to collect or develop information. In the social sciences, it is often replaced with the phrase *defining the study question.* It is sometimes referred to it as a process of *establishing a rationale for the study,* and has been called the *research topic,* the *research situation,* the *information need,* and other things. They all mean the same: establishing what it is you want to know, and why.

If the research is going to be an academic or scholarly project, there are a few tips that will make the research process easier to manage. First, be sure to pick a topic that interests you. Second, be sure that the topic is not so large that there is no way for you to get a handle on it in the time allotted. On the other hand, make sure that the topic is not so narrow that you will not be able to find enough information to complete the study. One way to resolve this problem is to begin with a large topic, then narrow it to a subtopic of that main topic. If these subtopics are still too large, you can select even more specific parts to focus on. Keep doing this until you have a relevant topic on which to focus.

To help guide you in the study design and data collection phases of the research process, it is a good idea to state your research question or study topic in the form of a question. For example, consider the question: "What effect does the home production of methamphetamine in Thurston County have on the health of children less than twelve years of age living in the same residence?" Not only does this question inform the researcher what data to look for, it also specifies the study area limits and identifies research subjects. The key is to include the main concepts or keywords in the question (Olin and Uris Libraries 2006).

ESTABLISH RESEARCH OBJECTIVES

Step two in the research process is to make clear what each step of the research is to accomplish. This means writing clear, attainable, and time-framed objectives for the study and each person involved. Clearly, this step depends upon the first step—identifying the research problem. Both the first and second steps address the reasons for doing the research. However, at this stage in the process the objectives may still be tentative; a final set of objectives may not emerge until after a review of the literature pertaining to the study question has been completed.

While the research problem is a statement of the reason for doing the research, the research objectives are statements of what you want the research to accomplish. Say, for example, that you manage a statewide program to improve high school students' awareness of the prevention of sexually transmitted diseases. A study question might be to determine the best way to accomplish this task. Specific research objectives might be to determine the students' current level of awareness of the diseases, their causes, spread, and methods of prevention.

A second objective might be to determine where the students receive their information about sexually transmitted diseases. Another might be to identify their preferred medium of communication and its ability to effectively convey persuasive messages. The researcher may also want to know who makes up the population at greatest risk. There are usually no simple answers to study questions and objectives; instead, each involves many subcomponents and antecedent factors.

DECIDE ON A RESEARCH STRATEGY

Step three of the research process is deciding on the research strategy that provides the most cost-effective way of gathering the needed information, and the strategy that produces the best possible answer for the research question. The three broad classes of research strategies are qualitative, quantitative, and combined. Each of these strategies provides the researcher with a variety of data-gathering methods and data processing and analysis techniques. The researcher's selection must be based on the first two steps in the research process.

PREPARE A RESEARCH PLAN

The researcher must prepare a plan for the research activity. This means identifying in advance the research subjects or sample, the methods planned for gathering and processing data, and a timeline for completing the project. Thus, designing an effective research plan requires decisions on (1) data sources, (2) the research approaches, (3) the data-gathering instruments, (4) a sampling plan, (5) and methods of contacting study subjects. Each of these steps will be discussed in detail in subsequent chapters.

CONDUCT A LITERATURE REVIEW

An important part of any research project is an activity called a *literature review.* This is an analysis of prior research on the topic at hand. It typically involves reading and analyzing published material in books, professional and academic journals, government documents, and other sources.

The focus of a literature review should always be on the key ideas that may function as leads for further investigation. Previous investigators may have already stated and tested hypotheses about your topic. The task of the literature review is to gather these previously published ideas, evaluate their usefulness as they relate specifically to your research, and determine whether they suggest new ways of looking at the problem that you might have missed (Selltiz, Wrightman, and Cook 1976).

GATHER THE DATA

Step six, an action step, involves gathering the data needed for meeting the study objectives and answering the study question. Depending on which research strategy is selected, data may be gathered by: (1) participating in a social situation and recording the findings, (2) passively observing subjects, (3) interviewing subjects one at a time or in groups, (4) preparing a questionnaire to survey a sample, (5) recording discussions of panelists in a focus group session, (6) recording the self-administered responses of a panel of subjects, or (7) reviewing documents, artifacts, or other information sources. The researcher may gather primary data, secondary data, or both. These data can come from internal sources, external sources, or both. A classification of data sources is displayed in Table 6.1.

Primary data are original data that the researcher gathers from original sources. Examples of primary data include responses to a questionnaire, an interview, agency performance data, or some other type of measurement. Secondary data are data that have been collected by someone else or for another purpose. Examples of secondary data include government statistical reports, articles in professional journals, and city or agency records. Neither data type is inherently better than the other, although care must always be taken in the interpretation of secondary data to ensure that it meets the specific research objectives.

Table 6.1

A Classification of Data Sources

I. Qualitative Data Sources
   A. Existing documents
      1. Books, periodicals, published reports, domestic and foreign
      2. Local, state, and federal government documents
      3. Trade and professional association reports
      4. College and university documents
      5. Minutes of meetings
      6. Commercial databases
      7. Other
   B. Primary sources
      1. Interviews
      2. Life histories
      3. Case analyses
   C. Internal sources
      1. E-mail
      2. Memorandums
      3. Reports and other documents
II. Quantitative Data Sources
   A. Surveys (in-person, mail, telephone, interactive)
      1. Questionnaires
      2. Attitude and lifestyle surveys, psychographics
   B. Experiments and field studies
      1. Laboratory experiments
      2. Field experiments
      3. Observation studies
      4. Interviews
      5. Videotaping and audio recordings
   C. Internal sources
      1. Company or organizational annual reports
      2. Company or organizational invoices and/or accounts payable records
      3. Production and services records
      4. Human resources records

ANALYZE AND INTERPRET THE DATA

Step seven is the payoff step; it is also the activity that may be the most difficult for beginning researchers to master. Once the data are in hand, the researcher must establish some order in the data and determine its meaning and/or implications. This interpretation must be carried out so that the findings can be related to the original study question and research objectives. Figure 6.2 illustrates how the data-information-knowledge cycle functions to provide administrators research results that help in decision making.

Researchers are often faced with the task of finding meaning in a large mass of data. First, they will want to know what is "typical" in the sample. This means getting some idea of the central tendency of the responses. In everyday language, they want to know what the averages are and how to describe a typical sample subject.

Second, they want to know how widely individuals in the sample vary in their responses. In a community economic development study, for example, the director might want to know whether local citizens have similar or widely diverse attitudes about proposed development of a ten-acre parcel on the city limits.

Figure 6.2   **How Data, Information, and Knowledge Move through the Knowledge Cycle**

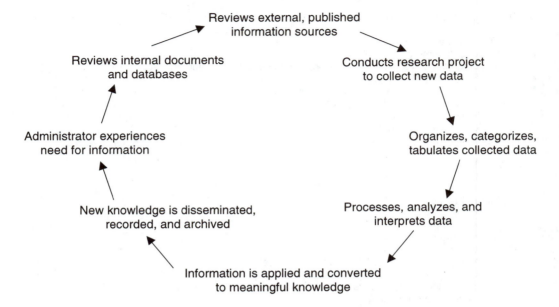

Third, researchers want to see how subjects are distributed across the study variables. For example, is the number of people who prefer a new park for the ten-acre site the same or greater as the number who prefer a new shopping center or single-family housing on the site? A good way to display this type of information is to use charts or graphs showing the frequency of responses.

Fourth, the analyst will want to show how the different variables relate to one another. It may be important to know, for example, that the preferences for different types of uses for the parcel seem related to certain characteristics of the population, such as age, gender, occupation, or annual income. Finally, the researcher will want to describe any differences among the two or more groups or objects. It might be important to know, for example, whether females in the sample respond differently about their preferences for the site than do males in the sample. This type of understanding is important because much public administration research focuses on comparisons of groups of citizens (Selltiz, Wrightman, and Cook 1976).

Tabulating Responses

The first step in data analysis is to tabulate the responses to all items in the study. In a quantitative study, this could mean counting all the answers to each question or schedule item. These counts of responses are referred to as *frequency distributions;* they are easily produced with statistical software processes that count responses and prepare summary data for the researcher.

Frequency distributions and summaries prepared for one variable at a time produce *univariate statistics.* Counts of how many subjects answered "yes" to a question and how many answered "no" and the distribution of males and females in a sample are both examples of univariate frequencies. Univariate statistics include measures of central tendency, variation, and location.

Once univariate statistical tabulations are completed, the researcher then begins *bivariate* tabulations. In this process, responses to one variable are tabulated with a second variable. The

Table 6.2

A Crosstabulation of Bivariate Data

	Gender	
Response	Males	Females
Yes	47	81
No	76	53

information is usually presented in a table (called *crosstabulations* or *crosstabs* for short). For example, responses to a yes-no question are displayed broken down for males and females in this crosstabulation table (Table 6.2).

In addition to simple counts of responses, crosstabulations can also display some summary information for each of the responses. The individual boxes with counts displayed are called *cells; rows* always run across the page; and *columns* always run down the page. Summary statistics included the percentage of the total represented by the number of responses in each cell, the cell's percentage of the row total, and the cell's percentage of the column. Row, column, and total percentage values are provided along the sides of the crosstabulation table. Finally, a wide variety of statistical tests for nominal, ordinal, and interval/rations data can also be produced with crosstabulation software.

Qualitative Responses

For a qualitative study, the researcher often begins the analysis by reviewing the data to establish a structural skeleton that will provide for meaningful interpretation and discussion. For qualitative research, the typical data analysis has been the *narrative text* (Miles and Huberman 1984). This is often a comprehensive rewrite of the researcher's field notes, with the researcher's verbal interpretation and conclusions from the data. There are few agreed-upon styles and formats for the broad scope of qualitative analysis methods. Selection is left up to the researcher. Accordingly to Miles and Huberman (1984, 79):

> Valid analysis requires, and is driven by, displays (i.e., narrative text and graphic presentations of qualitative research findings) that are as simultaneous as possible, are focused, and are as systematically arranged as the questions at hand demand. While such displays may sometimes be overloading, they will never be monotonous. Most important, the chances of drawing and verifying valid conclusions are very much greater. . . . The qualitative analyst has to handcraft all such data displays . . . each analyst has to invent his or her own.

PREPARE AND PRESENT RESEARCH FINDINGS

In the eighth and final step, the researcher prepares a written report and presents the findings. Although it is the final step in the process, it is second in importance only to clearly defining and focusing on a research problem/study question. An outline for the research report follows the same outline developed during the planning process. Some portions of the report, such as a description of the research problem, delineation of research objectives, the review of the literature, and the rationale for selecting the strategy employed, may have already been written as the researcher completed the earlier steps in the process.

Although there are many different ways to gather data and to communicate the research find-ings, research reports tend to follow one of a few different organizational forms. The results are often passed on to a supervisor, a fellow employee, or members of a funding organization or, if possible, even published in a brochure, report, or professional journal., following a standard format makes it easier for readers of the research report.

"Doing good research" means more than using good scientific methods to select the sample, gather data, and tabulate the results. It also means interpreting what the data mean in terms of the study objectives and writing research reports that clearly and effectively communicate the findings of the research effort. Using an appropriate s*tyle* is critical in all research writing. Style refers to the words, syntax, and punctuation that are used or not used. It includes the way these components are placed into sentences and paragraphs. It involves the structure and organization of the report, and whether it conforms to the traditions of the discipline. It also refers to the way that the author's sources are cited, identified, and credited. It is important to remember that there is no one best style. One or more may be more appropriate for a given discipline, but often that fact seems arbitrary. The best style to use in all research reports and organizational papers is writing that is *clear, concise,* and *readable.*

The processes necessary for producing a research report for the social and administrative sci-ences are similar to those that are used for research in chemistry, physics, biology, or any other natural science. Slightly different research, analysis, interpretation, and presentation processes are involved, however.

Following an accepted style enhances the readability of the research report, regardless of its discipline. Administrators and managers are typically pressed for time. If a paper is written in a familiar format (style), it will be easier to read—and take less of the reader's time. This often results in greater acceptance of the research findings—an extremely important point for research that comes up with negative findings. This benefit alone should be a desired outcome.

One problem making professional writing difficult for researchers and students is the *lack of conformity* in formats required by different disciplines and their journals. The format demanded by the editors of a journal sponsored by the Academy of Management, for example, will probably result in rejection of the paper by the editors of *Public Administration Review.* Researchers must determine which style is required in their field, and which styles are unacceptable. The only thing consistent about writing styles may be inconsistency!

SUMMARY

The research process can be defined as *the process of systematically acquiring data to answer a question or solve a problem.* Research is done to help managers, administrators, and academics achieve a better understanding of how the world works. Research *methodology* refers to the approach researchers take as they examine their study questions or problems. It includes a philosophical mind-set that researchers bring to the research activity as well as a set of procedures. This mind-set is what we now call *the scientific method.*

Humans employ two types or methods of coming to conclusions about things: deductive reasoning and inductive reasoning. Deductive reasoning means arriving at a conclusion on the basis of something that you know, or that you assume to be true—a general principle or *law.* Inductive reasoning, on the other hand, is the logic model or paradigm normally followed in scientific research.

The research process involves eight steps, beginning with establishing what and why the research is necessary and ending with a comprehensive report of the findings that emerge from the research process. These steps are (1) identify the research problem, (2) establish research objectives, (3) decide on a research strategy, (4) prepare a research plan, (5) conduct a literature review, (6) gather the data, (7) analyze and interpret the data, and (8) prepare and present the findings.

ADDITIONAL READING

Johnson, Janet B., Richard A. Joslyn, and H.T. Reynolds. 2001. *Political Science Research Methods.* Washington, DC: CQ Press.
Martin, Maner. 2001. *The Research Process.* 2nd ed. New York: McGraw-Hill.
Morton, Rebecca B. 2001. *Methods and Models.* Cambridge, UK: Cambridge University Press.

7

SELECTING A RESEARCH TOPIC

Beginning researchers often find themselves at the start of the research process struggling for answers to such questions as: What shall I research? How shall I begin? Once I've gathered my data, how can I make any sense of it? How will I know what my findings really mean? For some, simply choosing a subject to research and write about can be the most difficult part of the entire project. These questions and others will be addressed in this chapter.

The research conducted in public and nonprofit organizations is done to provide information needed to make better administrative and managerial decisions. For example, an administrator of a program to provide financial assistance education to welfare recipients might find that the number of applicants for aid has declined precipitously in the last quarter. She would need to conduct research to find out the cause of the decline.

Another administrator might need to determine the most cost-effective way to communicate information about sexually transmitted diseases to teens and subteens. A third administrator might need to determine whether the morale, attitudes, and beliefs of the agency's personnel are affecting job satisfaction and performance. These are all examples of research projects conducted by employees for the organizations in which they were employed. These were real problems that needed resolution. But how does a student determine what topic to research?

Research topics can come from questions discovered in texts, in the professional literature, from classroom discussions, from hobbies and other outside interests, and, of course, from the life experience of the researcher. An example is the study of a hearing-impaired graduate student who learned that Native American children are more likely to have hearing problems than are children of other ethnic groups with similar socioeconomic characteristics. Determining why this is so and what can be done to alleviate the problem became the student's graduate-program research project.

This is what Sylvan Barnet said about choosing a topic: "No subject is undesirable," and "No subject is too trivial for study" (1993, 177–178). Barnet might have added: *No subject is inherently uninteresting.* It is the way subjects are researched and reported that makes them desirable or undesirable, interesting or uninteresting. Here are a few guidelines to think about when choosing a research project topic:

- Research and write about something that interests you
- Be sure enough material about the topic is available to do a good job
- Make sure that the topic is not so big it is overwhelming

- Be sure the topic fits your abilities and understanding
- Make sure you take good notes once you start reading about the topic
- Ask your reference librarian for guidance on your research topic
- Get assistance from your instructor
- Focus, focus, and focus!

SELECTING A PROBLEM TO STUDY

A key requirement for all research is the clear, concise, and thorough definition of the problem for which the research will be carried out. This doesn't mean answers are known before the questions are asked. Rather, it means that the researcher has a specific goal in mind for the research before getting started. Having said this, it must also be said that it is hardly ever an easy process. Here are some examples:

Administrators are experiencing a decline in enrollments in programs designed to help welfare recipients gain the skills necessary for successful full-time enrollment. A recent state law mandates that all able-bodied recipients of public assistance receive aid for a maximum of five years. At the end of that period, they must be removed from the program, regardless of their employment or dependent status. The administrators of the program do not know the reason for the decline in the skill-development program, although they have some assumptions. Nor do they know what should be done to reverse the trend. Considering that people's lives are involved, making the wrong decision may be extremely costly.

Another example is the difficulty faced by administrators of substance-abuse programs and law-enforcement agencies as they seek to halt growth in the use of controlled substances. Despite billions of dollars spent on public education and abatement programs, drug use continues to be a major problem across the nation. Demand for treatment facilities far outstrips the availability of tested, effective programs. Federal and state legislators, program administrators, and local law-enforcement agencies are all looking for the most effective way to apply their limited resources to deal with the problem. Each agency involved has a different mission, different information needs, and different objectives. Coming up with a clear definition of the research problem is a difficult task for every agency involved, but going through the process of defining the task helps researchers deal with this challenge.

TASKS IN PROBLEM DEFINITION

The process displayed in Figure 7.1 has been designed to help administrators identify and define research problems.

Relate the Problem to the Program Mission and Objectives

The first step in the problem definition process is determining whether the proposed research project will produce information that is commensurate with the purpose, goals, and objectives of the organization, program, or agency. The research project must be worth the effort, time, and money it will consume. The researcher and administrator requesting the research must be absolutely sure of the relevance of the project.

An organizational problem can usually be translated into many different types of study problems. Many of these may be intuitively interesting, but beyond the scope of the agency or ability of the administrator to change or influence. This does not mean that administrators should not

Figure 7.1 **Tasks in the Problem Definition Process**

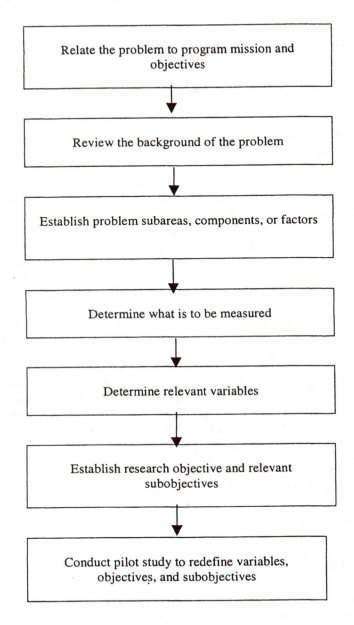

"stretch" to increase or improve their level of awareness of their agency, its client population, and the problems associated with both. It only means that they should first do what can be done. Answers to such questions as these must be found before proceeding with the program:

- What is it specifically that we do?
- Whom do we serve, and why?
- What information do we need to improve the way we function?
- Does what I want to know fit these functions, programs, or operations?
- Do we need this information for personal reasons or is it needed for our operations?
- Is this something I really need to know, or is it something I think I would like to know?
- Has someone else already researched this question, or am I just repeating something that has already been done?
- Could these resources be put to better use elsewhere?

Answers to such questions can often be found by conducting a thorough review of the background and published literature on the topic. Another way is to conduct a series of interviews with several key informants; these are people who have a greater than average familiarity with the problem and its associated antecedents or consequences.

Review the Background of the Problem

There are two aspects to a problem's background. The first is the nature of the problem within the organization; this is called the *internal background.* This is the total body of knowledge on the topic that exists within the organization or its larger administrative body. It may exist as published reports, operations records, or as accounting data; it may reside in the memories of other participants in the organization, or it may be in the historical archives of the organization. It is usually easier to access than external literature. It should always be the first place a researcher looks when conducting organizational research.

The second part is the body of work that already exists on the problem, its causes and cures, its extent and impact, and the way that other researchers have approached the issue. This is the *external background.* External information exists in the body of literature on the topic; accessing this earlier work is referred to as a *review of the literature.* It includes all the published and unpublished-but-available material on the question.

What happens when the researcher is unable to pinpoint a specific research problem before turning to the literature? Not surprisingly, this is often the case when students begin their research projects. The answer to the question is for the budding researcher to use the literature review to achieve a greater focus for the research.

It is a good idea to begin with an idea about some aspect of the general topic that seems particularly interesting—for example, something from the student's life experience or the experiences of friends or family members. It could be an article in a newspaper or a story on a television news or opinion program. It could be something seen in a textbook or an issue discussed in a classroom. It could be a topic as broad as taxation, unemployment, the impact of technology on family life, workplace diversity, gender issues, disproportionate distribution of resources, or environmental degradation—all it takes is an interest in a topic.

The first step in the literature review is to examine a relevant index of articles or a library catalog. The researcher should then scan these journal articles or books to see what parts of the broad topic are of most interest. It will not take long to go from just having a tentative interest in an unfocused topic to becoming focused on an interesting problem that can be researched. Searching the literature to break the larger problem down into subproblems can facilitate the remaining steps in the research process.

Establish Problem Subareas, Components, and Factors

Once the researcher has settled on a problem or circumstance that requires more information, the next step is to break that broad problem into as many parts or subproblems as are feasible. Say, for example, the research problem decided upon is: "How can the level of service provided to outpatient disabled veterans be improved without raising hospital operating costs?" Here is a partial list of relevant subproblems of this question:

- The type of organization (e.g., hospital, outpatient clinic, field provider, etc.)
- Type of service that patients require
- Staffing levels
- Queuing system in effect or not
- Location of facility (urban, suburban, rural)
- Prescreening system
- Attitudes of provider staff
- Attitudes of service users
- Expectations of service users
- Operating and other costs

Normally, not all of the possible subareas can or should be included in the research study. Instead, they are prioritized, and only the most important are included. Limiting the final choice of factors to be included in the study are (1) what the researcher can do in the time allowed, and (2) what will give the greatest payback for the time and labor resources expended.

Determining What Is to Be Measured

Once the researcher has identified the problem to study, the next step is to determine which relevant components should be measured. For example, when studying a problem pertaining to school dropouts, should the researcher collect data on local economic conditions, neighborhoods, schools, ethnic groups, families, peer groups, students who drop out, students who do not drop out, students below a certain age, or students above that age? Each option will provide very different information.

In another example, say that the research problem is gender abuse. Should the researcher gather data on men, women, children, family dyads, parents, or some other combination of subjects? If the research topic deals with problems faced by persons with hearing disabilities, should the researcher study society in general, employers, service providers, persons with hearing disabilities, or persons without hearing disabilities?

Related to this question is one of *accessibility*. If the element or subject to be measured is a person, that subject must have the needed information, be willing to share the information with the researcher, speak the researcher's language, and be able to put into words why they behaved in a certain way. The same problems exist for all possible measurement elements.

Determine Relevant Variables

Researchers investigate and test *variables*. A variable is anything that changes in value or varies in some way. Thus, variables are phenomena that can be "measured" in some way. Said another way, variables are study questions that have been rephrased into testable statements.

For example, the high school dropout phenomenon is a *study question,* whereas the annual rate of dropouts is a *variable* that can be measured. Another variable is the gender of the dropout; others are the dropout's age, ethnic group, the level of education of the dropout's parents, the location of the dropout's residence, and many more.

Another variable relating to this issue could be the dropout's attitudes or opinions about education in general. Other variables could be teacher effectiveness, the dropout's need to work in order to help support a family, or any similar measurement. A listing of some of the types of variables researchers use is displayed in Figure 7.2.

There are several ways to classify variables. One way is to divide variables into two categories based on the type of numerical measurements they provide. These are *categorical* and *continuous* variables. Categorical variables identify a limited number of possible categories. Gender is an example, with just two categories possible: female or male.

Continuous variables, on the other hand, can have an unlimited number of values. Values for continuous variables can be measured on a continuous scale (such as weights or height in inches). They are not restricted to specific, discrete categories or values, as are categorical variables. Attitude scales that provide continuous data are used often in public administration research. Researchers are concerned with mean (average) scores on a scale, not the response category (score) of any single subject.

A second way of looking at variables is whether they are *dependent* or *independent.* This dichotomy is important in causal research designs. Dependent variables are variables that are influenced in some way by another variable or variables. Independent variables are the variables that act upon the dependent variables. For example, the dependent variable *voting behavior* can be influenced by many different factors, such as the type of political contest involved or the income, education, occupation, or age of the voters and nonvoters.

Establish Research Hypotheses

The *hypothesis* is the fundamental building block of all scientific research. It defines the research topic and the researcher's ideas about it. Hypotheses can be defined in many different ways. One way is to look at the hypothesis as the researcher's ideas about a relationship between two phenomena (variables). Shaughnessy and Zechmeister (1994) defined hypotheses as nothing more than a "tentative explanation for something." Hypotheses are tentative answers to the "How?" and "Why?" questions about the research problem. No research should be started before one or more testable hypotheses have been written.

Types of Hypotheses

There are two types of hypotheses: *causal* or *noncausal.* With causal hypotheses, the researcher proposes that *event or activity A causes C to happen.* An example is: "Poverty *causes* juvenile crime." In this sense, the hypothesis is that poverty is the reason for the occurrence of the phenomenon called "juvenile crime."

In a noncausal hypothesis, the researcher surmises that *A and B are associated with C.* In this example, A and B can be said to be *correlated* (associated). However, in the absence of any further proof, it is not possible to say that either A or B "causes" C (Van Evera 1997). An example of this type of hypothesis might be: "High rates of high school dropouts and high rates of teenage pregnancies are associated with poverty." This hypothesis does not say that dropping out of high school causes increases in the rate of pregnancies among teenage females. The high school dropout phenomenon, teen pregnancies, and poverty are related, but neither "causes" the other.

Figure 7.2 **A Classification of Types of Variables**

Variable:

A characteristic, quantity, or anything of interest that can have different values. Examples include saving account amounts, stock prices, package designs, weight, monthly sales, gender, and salaries. The values of variables may be said to be either *continuous* or *categorical.*

Independent variable:

A variable that functions as the causal element in a hypothesis. A change in the value of an independent variable is said to "cause" a positive or negative change in a dependent variable. An example is the independent variable "poverty" in the hypothesis "Poverty causes crime."

Dependent variable:

The second part of a causal hypothesis, a change in the value of a dependent variable is hypothesized to have been "caused" by a change in the level of the independent variable. In the hypothesis "Poverty causes crime," the level of crime is the dependent variable.

Intervening variable:

Sometimes referred to as a *control variable,* an intervening variable lies between an independent and a dependent variable. A change in the intervening variable must be "caused" by the independent variable; this change then "causes" the change in the dependent variable. For example, in the hypothesis "Workplace stress causes physical illness, which causes absenteeism," physical illness is the intervening variable.

Conditional variable:

This variable establishes the antecedent conditions necessary for change in the dependent variable. The values of a conditional variable influence the level of impact that the independent and intervening variables have on a dependent variable. In the example "Poverty causes substance abuse, causing HIV-positive rates to increase wherever needle-exchange programs are proscribed," the existence of needle exchange programs is the conditional variable.

Study variable:

A variable whose cause or effect status the researcher is trying to discover through research. The study variable can be an independent variable, a dependent variable, an intervening variable, or a conditional variable.

Continuous variable:

Quantities that can take any value within a range of measurements, such as weight or percentage of increase in the price of a stock, are said to be continuous.

Categorical variable:

Categorical variables (sometimes called *discrete* variables) have values that can vary only in specific steps or categories.

Hypotheses must be written so no questions can be raised about the concepts that underlie them. This requires preparing clear and concise *definitions* for all variables, constructs, and concepts and spelling out all assumptions relating to the study. Hypotheses must always be written in ways that allow for their scientific testing. Such metaphysical concepts as beliefs or faith should never be used as the basis for a hypothesis because they cannot be empirically tested.

Establish Research Objective and Subobjectives

Research objectives are statements of what the researcher wants to accomplish by completing the research activity. They are related directly to the study question. For example, the director of a program designed to help single parents receiving public assistance make the move to full-time employment might be concerned that the program participation rate is declining while the numbers of parents receiving assistance is not declining. Why enrollment is declining is a key study question. Identifying ways to reverse the decline might serve as the program director's main research objective. Subobjectives might include the following:

- Identify characteristics of clients who participate in the program
- Determine reasons why they elected to participate
- Identify characteristics of clients who do not participate in the program
- Determine reasons why they elected to not participate
- Identify barriers to participation
- Identify what incentives might entice more qualified people to participate
- Determine what successes other programs have had and whether they may be transplanted to the local program

Pretest to Redefine Variables, Objectives, and Subobjectives

Pilot testing the study instrument or discussion guide is a critical step in the research process. No matter how close they might be to a problem, program, or issue under study, researchers are very different from their research subjects. They do not look at variables in the same way. The working definitions of variables and issues are also different. Without a thorough pretest of the data-gathering scheme, the probability of encountering a study error is significantly greater than it would be with a pretest.

An example of the value of a pretest occurred when the author designed a questionnaire to gather information about the declining number of commercial fishermen. In exploratory discussions with key informants, the question "In what area of the industry do you work?" was used to differentiate fishermen from fish processors, suppliers, bankers, and others. The open-ended question was included in the draft instrument. Most respondents assumed the question to imply a geographic location; their answers were "Alaska," "Washington," "Oregon Coast," and so on. The question was changed to a checklist of possible occupational areas before the survey was administered to the full sample. Without the pretest, this question would have provided neither the researcher nor the client the information desired.

SELECTING A RESEARCH FOCUS

The second problem researchers often face is this: *What part of this problem should I study,* and *what parts should I ignore?* This is a question of *focus.* Making a few relatively easy decisions early on about the focus of the study will make it easier to gather the data, interpret what is in the data, and then organize ideas into a meaningful research report later.

One way to address the issue of *research focus* is for the researcher to establish the *point of view* proposed for the topic and the research project. Making this determination early in the study establishes the method of gathering the required information. Narrowing the study's focus also makes it easier to organize the final report. *Organizing* the report means deciding what goes first in the paper, what goes second, and so on.

Once the researcher has decided on a topic, there are many options on how to approach the study of the topic. According to Seech (1993), research studies and their reports can follow one of five different approaches:

- Thesis or "position" studies
- Compare-and-contrast studies
- Analysis studies
- Summary studies
- Basic research studies

A *thesis* or *position* study is one in which the researcher begins by stating a position, either his or her own or some other person's or group's. This is then followed by arguments for or against the point of view. Various types of evidence are presented to support one viewpoint and/or refute the others. Political candidates regularly issue position papers in which they spell out their support or lack of support for such things as tax increases, school budgets, and welfare expenditures. The evidence presented in such papers is usually the product of a research project. For example, it can be acquired by using qualitative research methods to gather anecdotes, testimonials, or analogies, or by using quantitative research methods involving statistical analysis.

Compare-and-contrast studies are used to compare two or more ideas, methods, proposals, or positions. First, each approach is defined and discussed. Research is usually necessary to fully develop each position. This is followed by a section in which key points or themes are pointed out. This is then followed by a more detailed discussion of the differences. The researcher then selects one argument and uses supporting evidence to explain to readers why that argument is best. Again, research is used to come up with the evidence.

Analysis studies are closely related to generic research reports and often follow a similar structure. These studies require the researcher to carry out an in-depth analysis of an *idea*. Examples include such public administration issues as privatizing services, adopting user fees for services, and spending limitations. The researcher's opinions are typically included in analysis reports.

The investigator reviews and summarizes existing literature on a topic, then writes an analytical conclusion in which he or she interprets the information for the reading audience. For example, a researcher might be assigned to research and write a report about how passage of a people's initiative putting a cap on state automobile excise taxes affects the state highway department's plan to reinforce bridges to comply with federal earthquake damage requirements. The researcher will first go to the published literature to review trends and developments on all the topics. This could be followed by a series of interviews with department and budget administrators to establish their opinions about such things as delaying work on some bridges, finding cheaper ways to do the required work, or identifying other revenue sources.

Summary studies are detailed summaries of a topic or issue. They are much like an expanded version of the *review of the literature* section of other types of studies. These summary studies include a brief introduction defining and describing the topic, then move immediately into a conclusion of what other researchers or practitioners have said about the topic. Unlike analysis studies, summary reports often do not require the author to subjectively interpret the previous research, but only to summarize what others have reported.

Seech's last style or approach to research studies is the *basic research study*. The form followed in research studies is rooted in the earliest traditions of scientific research. The scientific method approach to research evolved out of this tradition. Because of this, social science and administrative research usually follows a structure similar to research for such disciplines as chemistry or biology.

When conducting a basic research study, the researcher designs and conducts a data-gathering project. To do this, the researcher may elect to follow a qualitative or a quantitative approach. In either approach, the data is *primary data* or *secondary data*. Collecting primary data means the researcher gathers "new" information. This might mean conducting a survey with a questionnaire, carrying out a series of personal interviews, employing content analysis to published documents, or conducting an experiment. Afterward, the gathered primary data are processed (often with computers) and interpreted. Then the researcher can draw relevant conclusions and make recommendations

Research to collect *secondary data* means getting most of the information from already published sources. These data can be found in libraries, on the Internet, or in internal publications, among other sources. Because this material has already been published, the researcher must use extreme care to report all the sources of material used in the report. The report must not be just a repeat of what others have written. Rather, the research report must include the researcher's *interpretation* of what others have written. In his book on writing about art, Barnet (1993, 176) said this about using secondary data in research reports:

> A research report is not merely an elaborately footnoted presentation of what a dozen scholars have already said about a topic; it is a thoughtful evaluation of the available evidence, and so it is, finally, an expression of what the author thinks the evidence adds up to.

FINDING INFORMATION ABOUT A TOPIC

Writing a research report means that the researcher must first do research. There is no way to get out of it. There are a number of different ways to go about this task. The researcher can work in a library, examining written, recorded, or filmed sources. Or the researcher can sit in front of a computer screen and do the research electronically. The researcher can interview subjects at work, at play, shopping, or anywhere it is possible to gain access to them. The researcher can sit with a telephone in a central location and ask respondents questions from a survey questionnaire. Or the researcher can design and conduct either a laboratory or field experiment, or both.

Assuming that the topic has been narrowed down to something that sounds interesting, the researcher gathers preliminary information about a topic or topics by conducting a comprehensive review of the published literature on the topic and its various subtopics. There are three ways to locate this literature:

1. Dive straight into the library stacks and begin the search by pulling out books, periodicals, reference materials, or government documents and other reference works that just might seem interesting.
2. Examine computerized, online library catalog lists. These list most library material, including books, journals, videos, and CD-ROMs, filing items by subject, author, or title.

(Although highly unlikely, some or all of this information might still be stored in card catalog form. If so, the concepts and methods to follow are the same as if the data were available online.)

3. Refer to a commercial database; almost all will be found online. For example, ABI/IN-FORM, the business periodical CD-ROM database, is available via the Internet, allowing access to information from any networked computer.

Traditional Library Research

Researchers call all previously published information *secondary literature*—regardless of the form in which it is recorded. It is called "secondary" because it is information that has been gathered by someone else. Published government statistics on aging, for example, are secondary data. Accounting information in an agency's annual report is secondary data. A report on regional economic conditions published by the federal government or by a local bank is secondary data. Tables, charts, and graphs from textbooks or city, county, and federal government documents or international organizations such as the United Nations are secondary sources. All information contained in previously published reports, magazines, and journals are secondary data.

It is the nature of academic research to find that, usually, more than one person is or has been interested in the same topic. Like fashions, researchers often follow fads. This means that there will often be many possible sources of information about the chosen topic. Sometimes this means more sources than the researcher can deal with. Therefore, one of the researcher's first tasks will be to narrow the topic down to a manageable scope. For example, for an eight-page report on economics, a researcher cannot cope with 200 sources. Instead, examining something like eight to a dozen at most is manageable. In summary, researchers are encouraged to start their research with a narrowed or focused topic—and begin with a plan (Lester and Lester 1992).

Begin with a Research Plan

Efficient library research always begins with a plan. This means starting with a general topic, then focusing on relevant parts of that topic. The researcher must decide on what keywords to begin with. Say that a student has been given a general assignment to research and write something about how computers have impacted ethical standards and practices in business. The student might start the search in the library catalog (cards or electronic) or in a special index of articles in a discipline looking up a general subject, such as business ethics. These indexes (or indices) are available either in CD-ROM or online databases.

Despite the phenomenal increase in the availability of information from electronic sources, libraries are still filled with books; they add hundreds if not thousands of new books to their collections each year. In addition, they still subscribe to many printed periodicals and other resource materials. Accessing much—but not all—of the information in the library has been made easier and faster through the use of computers and online databases.

It is important to remember that searching a large database might return hundreds or even thousands of titles on a topic. The researcher should narrow the search down by using *qualifiers*. These limit the search to only topics that match the focus of the study. For example, a researcher could narrow down a broad topic like *ethics* to something like *ethics in government,* or *ethics and computers*. The topic can be focused even more this way: *government ethics and computers in Michigan*. Restricting the search to a specific year could make it even narrower.

Most library research begins with periodical literature. Periodicals are scholarly journals, magazines, or newspapers that are published *periodically* (daily, weekly, monthly, quarterly, etc.). Journals contain articles and research reports on relatively narrow topics, written by people who work in or know a lot about a particular career field. They are an excellent source of background information of most topics.

Once the researcher has found an interesting article listing and its abstract (if available), the full article can usually be accessed from the library stacks, microfilm, through interlibrary loan, or using the full-text provisions of many databases. Whatever else is done, it is always good to start the research with a visit with a reference librarian

Research Using Electronic Sources

Electronic sources of information for research studies are often erroneously grouped under the single label "the Internet." The Internet is just one of a wide variety of electronic sources. Other important electronic sources include online databases, CD-ROM databases, local area networks, and library networks. The Internet is a vast international network of computer networks. Hardware ranges in size from individual desktop computers to supercomputers used for complex scientific modeling. All kinds of information have been made available through the connecting of this huge network of computers; not all of it is true, and not all of it is acceptable for research.

Anyone, including private citizens, universities, research laboratories, companies, and government agencies, can place information on the Internet, change it at any time, or take it off. The information stored on those computers is accessed through the *World Wide Web* (WWW, or simply the Web). It is this complete accessibility that creates potential problems for users of the Internet.

The Modern Language Association's committee on new technologies for research had this to say about problems with Internet sources:

> We want researchers to look at more than the Web, for the sake of historical concerns. Many important things aren't on the Web. Also, researchers must learn how to cite Web sites. And we have to learn how to read Web sites critically. . . . How do you know if what you're reading is fact? What are the credentials of the person who posed the information? The very quality that makes the Internet an attractively egalitarian tool—anybody can say anything and send it anywhere—makes it problematic for researchers. (Keller 1998, C2)

Search Tools

Researchers use two tools to search for information on the Web. The first is what is known as an *Internet directory.* These directories index information from many different sources; it is then stored in various databases. There are many different such collections of information; each deals with some particular aspect of research information. For example, one database indexes only economics literature; another index lists articles and papers from 375 life-science journals. An online news and current affairs database is also available for topical information about anything in the news.

The second way to search for information on the Web is using a *search engine.* Search engines make it possible to search the Web for information on any subject, such as companies, products, agencies, and organizations, by using keywords. Search engines such as Google are particularly effective for searching obscure topics because they search multiple sources at the same time, retrieving as many documents as possible with one search. A reference librarian can direct the researcher to these tools.

Online Databases

Today, most literature search information is available via online databases. Until recently, most of these were available only as CD-ROM databases. Now, online citation services provide the same services formerly available only on CDs. CD-ROMs are still used for encyclopedias and special-interest compilations of sight and sound.

A number of different databases may be found in each of several different categories of information. For example, the business and economics areas are served by at least ten different databases; sixteen online databases are available in the natural and health sciences disciplines; and eight or more databases index articles and other information in the news and current events collection.

The following databases contain citations and full-text listings of scholarly and popular articles on public administration, economics, and nonprofit organization administration (Note: Not all libraries subscribe to every possible system).

- *EconLit:* This is the key database for economics information; it also includes reports on public administration and public policy issues.
- *ABI/INFORM Global:* A database covering U.S. and international professional publications, academic journals, and trade magazines.
- *Business & Industry:* This database indexes leading trade magazines, newsletters, the general business press, and international business newspapers.
- *Organizations, Agencies, and Publications Directory:* This is a global directory of new and established organizations, agencies, and publications.
- *EBSCOhost (Academic Search Full Text Elite):* A comprehensive index to more than 3,100 scholarly (academic) journals and general periodicals in all subject areas.

SUMMARY

Information about a research topic can come from already-published sources—what is called *secondary data*—or it can be gathered directly from the first or primary source by the researcher or research team in what is called *primary data*. Most research involves a combination of these approaches. The researcher first identifies a study topic, looks to the published literature to gain more information or additional insights into the problem or issue, and then gathers primary data as needed.

The use of an eight-step process can aid the researcher in defining the research problem. The steps discussed in this chapter are: (1) relate the problem to the program mission and objectives; (2) review the background of the problem, usually by conducting a literature review; (3) break down the problem into its subareas, components, or factors; (4) determine what is to be measured; (5) determine relevant variables; (6) establish testable research hypotheses; (7) establish research objectives and subobjectives; (8) conduct a pilot study to check on the validity of the variables, measurements, and hypotheses. The pilot study is also used to redefine any or all variables and hypotheses, if necessary, and to determine whether the objectives and subobjectives can be achieved.

Once the literature review is completed, the researcher decides on which factors or components of the study question require more information. Then, the researcher either delves deeper into the published literature or designs a research project for acquiring the needed additional information.

ADDITIONAL READING

Anastas, Jeane W., and Marian L. MacDonald. 1994. *Research Design for Social Work and the Human Services.* New York: Lexington Books.
Wildavsky, Aaron. 1993. *Craftways: On the Organization of Scholarly Work.* 2nd ed. New Brunswick, NJ: Transaction.

8

CHOOSING A RESEARCH DESIGN

Researchers in the social and administrative sciences are no longer required to follow a single design for their investigations. Instead, many different research approaches are acceptable. To help clarify this great variety of options in research designs, they can be grouped into just three broad categories: *qualitative, quantitative,* and *combined* designs. Each design supports a variety of methods for gathering data, and each allows the researcher a variety of analysis and interpretation approaches. A key task of the director of the research project is selecting the appropriate strategy for the research problem and study objectives. This selection task is what is known as the process of developing a *research design.*

An important thing to remember about research design selection is that the researcher is never locked into using any one "best" design. There are many acceptable ways to conduct research; the only selection criterion that makes sense is that the method chosen must provide the best possible conclusions. Phillips (1976, 5) described the research process plan as a *Magna Carta* for the researcher; he added:

> [The researcher] is not chained to a set of techniques simply because they have worked adequately in the past, nor must [he or she] defer to the supposedly superior methodological knowledge of other investigators because of their research reputation. It is not necessary for [researchers] to continually look back over [their] shoulder, wondering if others would consider [the] procedure to be "correct" or incorrect. . . . What counts is not what others think of those procedures but how well they work.

The key to good research results is "doing good science." This simply means selecting a research design that best meets the objectives for the study. As Eisner (1997, 261) has noted, researchers are no longer required to slavishly adhere to one or more method, approach, or design:

> Increasingly, researchers are recognizing that scientific inquiry is a species of *research.* Research is not merely a species of social science. Virtually any careful, reflective, systematic study of phenomena undertaken to advance human understanding can count as a form of research. It all depends on how that work is pursued.

Researchers spend considerable time and effort into the design selection process. As always, the nature of the problem to be researched and the data acquired will establish the researcher's options.

Figure 8.1   **Research Methodologies, Approaches, Designs, and Methods**

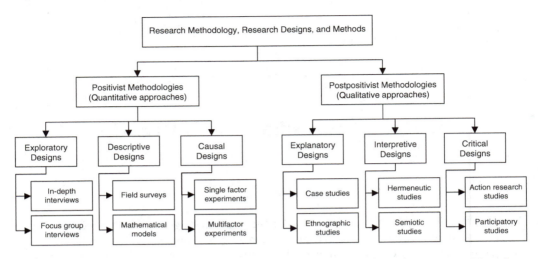

For now, all that is necessary is for researchers to understand what their options are. Therefore, the following pages are devoted to an introductory discussion of the three basic forms of research design: quantitative, qualitative, and combined. The relationship of these three strategies, together with some of the approaches used in each design, is displayed in Figure 8.1.

QUANTITATIVE RESEARCH DESIGNS

Quantitative research designs are employed in a sequence of steps (see Figure 8.2). Until recently, many research traditionalists maintained the opinion that quantitative research methods used in most physical or natural sciences research were the only appropriate approach to follow with any scientific research problem. Among these traditionalists, the watchword for "good science" is measurement: "If it can't be measured, it can't be studied." While this may no longer be the dominant opinion in research, quantitative studies still by far outnumber other approaches. A glance at any social or administrative science professional journal will usually support this contention.

Questions and Statistical Tests

In deciding what strategy to follow in a quantitative design, public administration researchers usually seek answers to these six basic questions (Miller 1991):

1. What characteristics of the people in my sample (such as demographic differences) distinguish them from other groups or subgroups of people who I might have included in my study?
2. Are there any differences in the subgroups contained in this sample that might influence the way the questions are answered or opinions that are offered?
3. Are there any statistically significant differences in the answers of any groups or subgroups in this sample, or did they all answer the questions in roughly the same way?
4. What confidence can I have that any differences that I do find did not occur by chance?
5. Is there any association between any two or more variables in my study? Is it relevant? Is it significant?

Figure 8.2   **Quantitative Strategies in the Research Process**

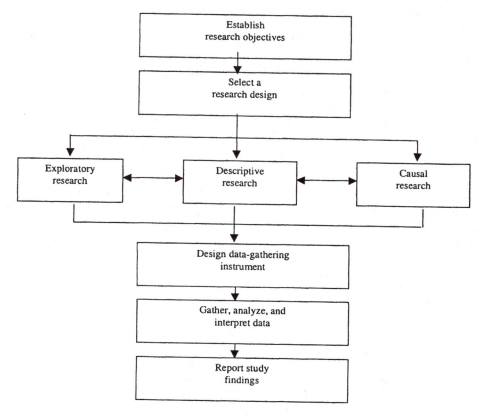

6. If there is any relationship between two or more variables, is it possible to measure how strong it is and whether it is a positive or negative relationship?

The statistical tests typically used in quantitative public administration research to answer questions such as these include, but are not limited to, the following:

- Measures of central tendency, variability, and/or dispersion
- Graphic methods, such as tables, charts and graphs
- Hypothesis tests
- Association (correlation) tests
- Regression analysis
- A few tools for specific purposes, such as time-series and quality tests

THREE TYPES OF QUANTITATIVE DESIGNS

Depending on their research objectives, researchers select from three types of quantitative research designs: exploratory, descriptive, or causal. In each of these approaches, one or more of a variety of statistical tools are used to test ideas or concepts and to communicate research findings. They may begin with a small-sample, exploratory study designed to provide the information needed for developing a questionnaire (also called a survey instrument or simply an instrument) for carrying out a large-sample, descriptive study.

The exploratory study may be used to identify the key dependent and independent variables that will be tested in an experiment (a *causal design*). However, the researcher may elect to use all three approaches, beginning with an exploratory study for insights and ideas, then going to a descriptive study to define the salient variables, and concluding with a causal study to test them for cause-and-effect relationships.

For more complex studies, a host of powerful multivariate statistical tools have been developed to aid the researcher. Some of these will be discussed in later chapters.

Exploratory Designs

Exploratory studies are small-sample designs used primarily for gaining insights and ideas about research problems and the variables and issues associated with those problems. These types of studies are sometimes referred to as "pilot studies." Exploratory studies are often employed as the first step in a multipart research project. Because of their limited scope, however, they seldom stand alone. Exploratory studies help the researcher gain greater understanding of the problem for which more information is needed. They also help the researcher identify variables that may be only tangentially or only marginally related, and thus should not be included in a more extensive research effort.

Data gathering in exploratory research may involve quantitative or qualitative strategies, or a combination of both. The data may come from either primary or secondary sources; that is, it may be gathered directly by the researcher, or it may be data gathered by someone else for a different purpose. Both data types have similar validity in exploratory research.

Exploratory research designs often involve conducting personal interviews with knowledgeable individuals from within and/or outside of the organization. These individuals are called "key informants," and the process is known as *key informant interviews*. These subjects are selected because they are likely to be better informed about the study problem and the issues associated with that problem. For example, the author was part of a team engaged to design and conduct an extensive community needs analysis for a regional general hospital. The team's first step in the study was to conduct a series of in-depth interviews with key local employers, community leaders, hospital administrators, and senior medical staff. These data were then developed into a comprehensive needs-analysis questionnaire administered throughout a three-community region.

The hospital administrative staff also used the findings of the exploratory study in its presentation to the hospital district board of directors. The report provided evidence that a larger, in-depth survey was needed to complete the district's ten-year development plan.

Focus-group interview sessions with groups of six to ten representative subjects are another common exploratory research strategy. A major benefit of group interviews is the potential interaction among participants. This interaction is impossible to achieve in one-on-one interviews. Focus groups are also more efficient than a series of individual in-depth interviews. A major disadvantage of focus groups is the fear of public embarrassment, which sometimes makes it difficult, if not impossible, to bring up sensitive issues.

A third approach used in exploratory research studies is to survey a small random sample drawn from the same population of interest—what is called a "pilot survey." A commonly used purpose of a pilot study is for pretesting a draft of a survey questionnaire. Results of the exploratory study are used only to test the validity and reliability of the study design and the instrument questions.

Problem words, phrases, and entire questions may be edited, deleted, or replaced. Results of such pilot studies should never be included with the findings of the final study.

Another purpose of exploratory research studies is to provide the researcher with greater insight into the study problem and ideas about the variables that should be included in a larger or more comprehensive study to follow. In addition, the findings of an exploratory study can often be used to train data gatherers and help the researcher design and test a data-processing plan. Equally important, the findings of an exploratory study can often provide guidance to the researcher in rephrasing the study question. They can also require the imposition of totally new variables into the study.

Descriptive Designs

Descriptive research designs are used to develop a snapshot of a particular phenomenon of interest. Descriptive studies typically involve large samples. They provide a description of an event or define a set of attitudes, opinions, or behaviors that are observed or measured at a given time and environment. The focus of descriptive research is on the careful mapping out of a circumstance, situation, or set of events to describe what is happening or what has happened (Rosenthal and Rosnow 1991).

Descriptive studies may be either *cross-sectional* or *longitudinal*. The snapshot study is called a cross-sectional design. It is a one-shot assessment of a sample of respondents. Time is an important consideration because the "picture of the sample" usually varies—sometimes substantially—if the research is repeated at a later date or conducted with another sample taken from the same population. Descriptive research that is repeated with the same sample over two or more time intervals is known as *longitudinal research*. Studies using panels of participants are longitudinal studies. The purpose of a longitudinal study is to identify and measure *change* in subjects' responses.

Researchers use two related but different types of descriptive research approaches: *field studies* and *field surveys*. Field studies tend to go into greater depth on a smaller number of issues or items. They may use face-to-face or telephone interviewing techniques for data gathering. The survey instruments often include "branching questions," which require a different set of questions for subjects who respond differently at a given place or "branch" in the instrument. They may also involve one or more open-ended questions. Such questions require far more effort for coding and tabulating than is needed for the fixed response items found in field survey studies.

Field surveys are the most commonly encountered approach in the administrative, social, and human sciences; they make up more than 80 percent of all quantitative research. Surveys are popular because they are relatively easy to design and administer. The wide availability of powerful desktop computers and statistical software today has made them much easier to tabulate and interpret.

Both field studies and field surveys produce data that are used as numeric *descriptions*. These descriptions may be of a *sample* of subjects or from an entire *population*. Many different types of variables can be used, including but not limited to demographic characteristics, attitudes, opinions, intentions, characteristics of organizations, groups, families, and subgroups. In essence, almost anything that can be measured can be a descriptive variable.

Causal Designs

Causal research studies are often the last step in a three-part approach to research into a problem in the administrative and social sciences. They require designing and conducting *experiments*. In experiments, researchers must control for confounding or intervening variables while testing hypotheses about differences and/or relationships. Because they are usually difficult to arrange with human subjects, experiments tend to be used far more often in laboratory or classroom conditions than in practical or applied public administration research.

Causal studies may be either *relational* or *experimental*. The purpose of relational studies is to identify how one or more variables are related to one another. They are sometimes called *correlation* studies. The purpose of an experimental causal study is to identify the cause or causes of *change* in a variable or event—that is, determining "what leads to what" (Rosenthal and Rosnow 1991).

Designing an experiment is the key activity in a causal research project. Experiments involve subjecting two or more samples or subsamples to different treatments. Researchers may manipulate one, two, or more independent variables in the same treatment experiment. Treatments can be any relevant characteristic or phenomena. Examples include:

- Different teaching methods (lecture vs. experiential)
- Testing the effect of a new drug vs. a placebo
- Tests of the impact of two different levels of expenditures on a social program
- Different communications media

Researchers must be careful in the design of experiments and interpretation of the findings so that potential intervening or confounding variables do not muddy the results of the study. The set of experiments conducted at the Western Electric manufacturing facility in Hawthorne, New Jersey, is a classic example of the need for careful attention to experimental design.

A random sample of assembly workers was selected, moved to a special location, and subjected to variations in working conditions, including varying the speed of the production line, different levels of lighting, and varying rest periods. Researchers measured workers' performance under normal conditions (the *pretest*), changed a working condition characteristic (a *variable*), then measured performance again (the *posttest*). To their surprise, production increased with negative environment changes just as it did with positive changes. The design did not consider the effect on workers of being singled out for attention. This unplanned change is what is known as an *intervening* or *confounding* variable.

Experiments can involve manipulating (making changes to) a single independent variable or two or more variables. The changes are referred to as *different treatments*. For example, a park administrator might want to know whether increasing the fee for campsite use will reduce or increase the need for maintenance personal at the campground. Two or three similar sites with comparable usage levels could be randomly selected, with different fees charged in each test site (the "treatment" is the different fees). The administrator might use damage to campsites over the test period as a measurement of the need for more or fewer maintenance personnel. At the end of a designated test period, results at the three sites would be compared.

Manipulating two or more variables is also possible. For example, agricultural researchers often vary amounts of both fertilizer and irrigation, measuring the effects of different combinations on crop production. In a three-factor experiment, the researcher might also include different types of soil conditions (such as clay, sandy loam, etc.) as another of the test variables.

QUALITATIVE RESEARCH DESIGNS

Qualitative research is not based on a single, unified theoretical concept, nor does it follow a single methodological approach. Rather, a variety of theoretical approaches and methods are involved

Figure 8.3 **Qualitative Strategies in the Research Process**

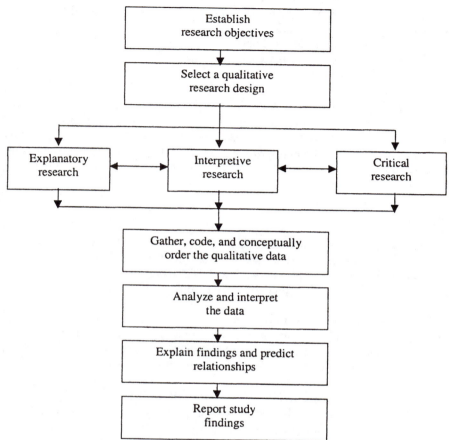

(Flick 1999a). All of these approaches and methods have one common underlying objective: understanding of the event, circumstance, or phenomenon under study. Thus, description is less important than the researcher's interpretation of the event, circumstance, or phenomenon. To achieve qualitative study objectives, researchers analyze the interaction of people with problems or issues. These interactions are studied in their context and then subjectively explained by the researcher.

Figure 8.3 illustrates the interconnected nature of the qualitative process. In all three approaches, several different techniques may be employed for gathering data, including *observation, participation, interviewing,* and *document analysis.* In each, data are coded, placed in some intelligent order, interpreted, and used for explaining and/or predicting future interrelationships in similar circumstances.

Flick (1999a) has identified the following features of qualitative research that help to differentiate these methods from positivist quantitative approaches:

- Diverse theories underlying the approach
- Diverse perspectives of the participants
- Reflexivity of the researcher and the research (i.e., responses to each other)
- Variety of approaches and methods
- Reconstructing cases as a starting point
- Construction of reality as a basis for the research
- Use of text as empirical data

Broadly speaking, qualitative strategies fall into three categories of study techniques. These are *explanatory, interpretive,* and *critical* designs (White 1999). These approaches can be applied to many different study approaches, including ethnography, kinetics (the study of movement), atmospherics, phenomenology, and proxemics (the study of space in social settings). Additional examples include such data-gathering methods as focus groups, elite-group interviewing, and the use of unobtrusive measures.

Explanatory Research

Explanatory research is the approach taken in most mainstream qualitative research. Its goal is to go beyond the traditional descriptive designs of the positivist approach to provide meaning as well as description. The purpose of explanatory research is also broader than descriptive research; it is conducted to *build theories* and *predict events.* According to White (1999, 44):

> Explanatory research strives to build theories that explain and predict natural and social events. Theory building requires the development of a collection of related and testable law-like statements that express causal relationships among relevant variables. The ultimate goal of explanatory research is the control of natural and social events.

Typical objectives for explanatory research include explaining why some phenomenon occurred, interpreting a cause-and-effect relationship between two or more variables, and explaining differences in two or more groups' responses. The design is similar to the traditional positivist approach, and some numerical description and simple statistical analysis may be involved.

Interpretive Research

Interpretive research is characterized by a strong sense of connection between the researcher and the subjects who are a part of an interpretive study. The goal of interpretive research is to build understanding between the participants and the researcher. Therefore, interpretive research often focuses on standards, norms, rules, and values held in common, and how these all influence human interactions (White 1999).

The primary objective of interpretive research is to establish the meaning of a circumstance, event, or social situation. It goes beyond simple description or explanation in aiming to enhance people's understanding of the symbols, artifacts, beliefs, meanings, feelings, or attitudes of the people in the study situation (White 1999).

Interpretive research has much in common with the study of phenomenology in philosophy and the phenomenological approach to sociological research. Public administration theorist Camilla Stivers (2000, 132) has provided this view of interpretive research:

To me, interpretation entails sense-making: taking a more or less inchoate bundle of events and processes—what might be thought of as a situation or group of situations—and putting a frame around them based on more or less conscious assumptions about what is likely to be important, significant or meaningful.

Interpretive research also plays an important role in the third approach, critical research, and provides the common understanding that is necessary for successful attitude change. In this way, the interpretation of ideas that are associated with Freudian psychoanalysis has become an integral part of critical research.

Critical Research

Critical research is the least-used approach in qualitative research in general and public administration in particular. While it has potential for application in public administration, the subjective nature of critical analysis makes it difficult for students to adopt and use in meaningful ways. According to White (1999, 57):

Criticism is the most radical of the three modes of [qualitative] research because it calls into question our most basic assumptions and asks us to evaluate them as a basis for action. Critical research does not always satisfy the critic, nor does it always change beliefs and values, but it has the potential to do so.

Critical research in public administration has been adopted mostly from sociology research methodology. It also has roots in the criticisms of social structures and the capitalist economic system that emerged in reaction to the excesses of the Industrial Revolution. It reached its highest influence in the studies of society's acceptance of tyrannical governments and the public's reactions to propaganda. This research was greatly influenced by the social scientists that fled Nazi-dominated Europe in the 1930s and later helped form the New School for Social Research in New York City.

The purpose of the critical research tradition that emerged from those early foundations was to help citizens overcome the constraints that an oppressive government placed on their freedom and development. As White (1999) noted, critical research assumes that people can misunderstand themselves and their situations. It also assumes that they can be confused about what is in their own interests.

The overriding objective of critical research is to change people's beliefs and actions in ways that the investigator believes will better satisfy their needs and wants. The criticism points out inconsistencies between what is true and false and what is good and bad. It aims to bring people to actions that are commensurate with accepted truth and goodness. According to White (1999), the "truth" of critical research is only realized when people (through a process of self-reflection) finally take action to change their situation.

Gathering Qualitative Data

Three of the most popular methods for gathering qualitative data in public administration and nonprofit organization research are *observation, participation,* and *interviewing.* A fourth method, *document analysis,* is also used, but less often than the first three approaches. However, a variation of document analysis—*hermeneutics*—is rapidly becoming one of the more popular approaches in qualitative research.

Observation

Observation research studies are the least intrusive of all research methods. In this approach, the researcher simply watches and records the social behavior of subjects. This method came into wide acceptance with the growth of *cultural anthropology* for the study of the behavior, beliefs, and customs of primitive cultures. It is still the predominant data-gathering method in anthropological ethnographic studies and is also common in sociological field studies.

With data gathered by observation, researchers must interpret what they see in the light only of the conditions that exist in the culture at the time the group is observed. The interpretation should not be made in terms of the researcher's own experiences within the context of modern culture. Despite this possible limitation, the method is gaining increasing acceptance in the study of organizations in both the private and public sectors (Gummesson 1991). For example, today public administration researchers are using the method to come to a better understanding of the role that organizational culture plays in program effectiveness.

One of the key advantages of observation is that it has a very low impact on the social setting because the researcher only watches and records events in the study group or setting, remaining uninvolved in the group's activities or actions. The researcher's goal is to produce an unbiased record of the events and behaviors. Extensive field notes must be maintained throughout the observation period. This means including what has been described as the "systematic noting and recording of events, behaviors, and artifacts (objects) in the social setting chosen for the study" (Marshall and Rossman, 1999, 107). Subsequent analysis of these descriptive records often occurs as an integral part of the data-gathering process (Miles and Huberman 1984).

Participation

Participation research studies are more intrusive than observation approaches. The researchers' involvement in the culture, subculture, clan, group, or organization under study cannot help but have some influence on the study target. Participation requires that the researcher become wholly immersed in the activities and environment of the study group, thereby experiencing and sensing the same reality as members of the study group.

The researcher's goal in a participation study is to understand what the individuals in the group see, feel, and hear. While acting as a participant, the researcher prepares field notes that include a description of the group members' experiences, reactions, and feelings (Marshall and Rossman 1999). For greater understanding, the researcher often describes or compares his or her experiences in the analysis.

Interviewing

Interviewing is the third method of gathering primary data used by researchers pursuing qualitative research strategies. Interviewing research is the most intrusive of all qualitative research approaches.

Face-to-face or voice-to-voice (i.e., telephone) interviews may be *structured* or *unstructured*. Structured interviews follow a planned discussion guide in which answers are sought for specific questions. Unstructured interviews are more like conversations between friends. Respondents are left free to bring up whatever topic they wish. The researcher may then probe for more detailed information, but is careful to avoid leading questions or communicating any value judgments. The researcher may, however, ask questions when the responses are terse or the respondent is unable to express needed information.

Face-to-face interviews typically take two or more hours to complete. The interviewer must be sure the respondent does not ramble excessively or use the interview to continually vent frustrations or anger (some such information is valuable, of course, but continual repetitions waste time and other resources).

COMBINED RESEARCH DESIGNS

Combined designs entail using both qualitative and quantitative methods. The three broad classes of combined studies are archival, media, and artifact studies. Techniques used in these types of studies include content analysis, document analysis, and in situ analysis (also known as within-site analysis). Several types of multivariate statistical tools are also used in these designs, including canonical correlation and cluster and factor analysis. These statistical tools all require some subjective (qualitative) interpretation of the data.

Flick (1999a, 634) is one of many who now report that good research often requires the use of a combination of quantitative and qualitative approaches:

> It is well known that the juxtaposition "qualitative—quantitative" has sometimes led to not very fruitful controversies and is sometimes used as a schematic demarcation. But the combination of approaches is often truthful as well.

Archival, Media, and Artifact Studies

Archival studies involve the study of historical records and documents in order to establish an understanding of the circumstances that characterized an event or period. Researchers review the published and unpublished records of an organization, a community, or a culture. McNabb (1968) used this design for a study in mass communications history and persuasive communication. The design required analysis of historical documents dealing with the battle for public acceptance by private power firms and public utilities from 1909 to 1939. Documents included pamphlets, press releases, annual reports, and newspaper articles published during the period.

Media analysis is a similar process, although in media analyses the items studied tend to be current rather than historical. Like archival studies, media analysis often employs *content analysis,* which is a way of organizing content into desired categories and weighing the results. In another example, the author once designed and led a study that involved comparative analysis of London's eight daily newspapers for editorial-content emphasis on the then-controversial plan of Britain's joining the European Union.

In a media analysis study, McNabb (1991) surveyed 200 years of publications in the newspaper section of the British Library. These included actual and microfilm copies of seventeenth- and eighteenth-century newspapers and other periodicals. The research resulted in a published report on the first one hundred years of the publication of one of Great Britain's first daily newspapers and consumer magazines as part of a larger description of the history of government regulation and support of the modern consumer society.

Artifact studies (also called *object studies*) owe their emergence to the transposition of archeological methods to the study of modern societies and cultures. An example of a modern use of the method is the investigation and cataloging of items discarded in modern landfills. Researchers use this method to gain a greater understanding of the culture and values of groups.

SUMMARY

This chapter has discussed the various different types of research designs used by researchers in the social, administrative, and natural sciences.

Quantitative research strategies are employed in a sequence of steps. They usually begin with a small-sample, exploratory study to provide information for developing a questionnaire (also called a *survey instrument* or simply an *instrument*). The questionnaire will then be used in a large-sample, descriptive study. The exploratory study may be used to identify the key dependent and independent variables to be tested in an experiment (a *causal design*). Or, the researcher may elect to use all three approaches, gaining insights into the problem with an exploratory study, following with a descriptive study to define the salient variables, and concluding with a causal design to test for cause-and-effect relationships.

Broadly speaking, qualitative strategies fall into three categories of study techniques. These are *explanatory, interpretive,* and *critical.* These approaches can be applied to many different study approaches, including ethnography, kinetics, atmospherics, phenomenology, and proxemics.

The three methods used most often for gathering qualitative data in public administration research are unobtrusive observation, participant observation, and personal interviewing. A fourth method, document analysis, is used less often.

Some of the methods that combine parts of both quantitative and qualitative approaches include archival studies, media analysis, and artifact studies. Content analysis is the quantitative method used in these studies, and hermeneutics is the predominant qualitative method.

ADDITIONAL READING

Miller, Gerald J., and Marcia L. Whicker, eds. 1999. *Handbook of Research Methods in Public Administration.* New York: Marcel Dekker.
Schwab, Donald P. 1999. *Research Methods for Organizational Studies.* Mahwah, NJ: Lawrence Erlbaum Associates.

9

PUTTING TOGETHER A RESEARCH PROPOSAL

A comprehensive research proposal should be the mandatory first step in all research projects. The proposal is a description of what, why, and how you plan to carry out a research project. It serves as a guide that keeps the researcher focused on the tasks that need to be done. It also provides the research sponsor with a rationale for investing in the effort. Preparing a good research proposal in advance makes writing the final report much easier. However a proposal does more than just make conducting research easier, as the following statement from Locke, Spirduso, and Silverman (1999, 3) attests:

> A proposal sets forth both the exact nature of the matter to be investigated and a detailed account of the methods to be employed. In addition, the proposal usually contains material supporting the importance of the topic selected and the appropriateness of the research methods to be employed.

Although the proposal is a critical component of the total research process, it has too often treated as something that everyone intuitively knows how to write. However, nothing could be further from the truth. Poorly written proposals are one of the major causes of failure to receive committee approval of a graduate thesis or dissertation topic or, more importantly, failure to receive funding for a proposed study (Wasby 2001).

After reviewing a number of research proposals at the National Science Foundation (NSF), Wasby concluded that many graduate students were receiving little or no instruction in the skills needed to produce effective research proposals. Although many of the proposals contained exciting research ideas, they were often poorly written or incompletely presented. Wasby concluded that the good ideas that did exist were often "embedded in horrendously constructed proposals" (Wasby 2001, 309). In many proposals, a clear statement of the research problem and a well-executed literature review would be followed by a thin or nonexistent description of the research design. Or, there would not be a transition statement between the literature review and the statistics to be used. Hypotheses, where present, were often not developed from the discussed literature—or for that matter, from any literature.

Wasby considered graduate school curricula responsible for the many poor research proposals. In his view, graduate work in the social sciences—including political science, public administration, and social services—has not always provided students with enough experience in proposal writing. What instruction students had received in their research methods courses was too often inadequate or even inappropriate for the proposed task. For example, Wasby (2001, 309) found that:

Table 9.1

Common Mistakes in Proposal Writing

1. Failure to provide the background necessary to frame the research question
2. Failure to delimit the boundary conditions for your research (proposing to do too much)
3. Failure to cite landmark research on the topic
4. Failure to accurately present the contributions made by earlier researchers
5. Failure to stay focused on the research question
6. Failure to develop a coherent and persuasive argument for the research
7. Too much detail on minor issues; not enough on major issues
8. Rambling—going on and on without a clear direction
9. Missing too many citations and having incorrect references
10. Proposal is too long or too short
11. Failure to follow APA style
12. Sloppy writing
13. Claiming the study is significant without demonstrating it
14. Claiming prior research was poor or inadequate without providing support
15. Stating the need for the research without substantiating your claims

A related aspect of inadequate training is that our methods training seldom focuses on particular methods. For example, elite interviewing and content analysis, and when to use them, are critical components of a well-rounded methods curriculum. That curriculum, however, instead becomes additional training in statistics, with the course in "Methods" becoming "Statistics II or Statistics III," with little if any attention to problem specification or research design. . . . This deficiency helps to explain why proposals often move, without a transition of linkage, from literature review to discussion of the statistical method of choice.

Although they are equally important components of a single systematic activity, the research proposal and the research project are often erroneously treated as entirely separate activities. Instructions on how to prepare a research proposal are likely to be found in the appendix of a textbook—or excluded entirely. In these unfortunate circumstances, beginning researchers trying to prepare a research proposal often do not know how to go about completing the assignment. If they do, their proposals are often incomplete or do not adequately guide the researchers toward completion of the research project. This can doom the project even before it starts, while a well-written proposal properly shows the potential of both the research and the researcher (Wong 2002).

Wasby identified a number of mistakes commonly found in qualitative proposals (Table 9.1). The mistakes range from failure to provide sufficient background information to a misdirected emphasis on small, unimportant information that only blurs what issue is under study.

COMPONENTS OF A RESEARCH PROPOSAL

A chief purpose of the research proposal is to convince the administrator, manager, organization, professor, or committee that the proposed project is worthwhile. It is also shows the people involved that you have the ability and knowledge to design a work plan and the competence to complete the work outlined in the proposal. For this to happen, the proposal must contain enough information about the research process for the approving body to evaluate your proposed study.

There are many different opinions as to what should be included in a good research proposal. As Locke, Spirduso, and Silverman (1999, 7, emphasis theirs) noted, "Whatever the particular situation confronting the writer, it is vital to remember that *no universally applicable and correct format exists for the research proposal.*" Because of this, there are many possible outlines and guides to follow, some of which are displayed in Table 9.2. Elements in the far-left column have been synthesized from McMillan and Schumacher (1997); the far-right column has a simplified version of Salkind's list of elements (2002). The remaining columns are summaries from a wide variety of sources, with terms changed to reflect common concepts.

Common components of these guides include (1) an executive summary or abstract; (2) an introduction, which includes a statement of statement of objectives, key definitions and assumptions, a statement of the problem, and a rationale for doing the research; (3) a review of the relevant literature; (4) a description of the research methods to be followed that includes a plan for data analysis and limitations; and (5) appendices which may include a time line, a budget, and copies of proposed research instruments, discussion guides and results of pilot studies, if any.

Abstract or Executive Summary

Although quite different in form, both the abstract and executive summaries are designed to be brief summaries of the full proposal. Both are written in such a way that the reader will get a moderately complete overview of what the proposal is about. Abstracts range from a low of about 100 words to a high of 300 words; preferably they are closer to 200 words. Some abstracts have exceeded 500 words, but when this happens, they lose their intended purpose as a *brief* summary. An executive summary, which may be written as either a narrative or in bulleted or numbered form, should not exceed one full page. Both the abstract and executive summary should outline the proposed research project and present a brief statement of the research objectives and the methods proposed for accomplishing them.

The Introduction

Introductions are where the author sets the scene for the material that will follow in the body of the paper. Introductions typically explain the *"who, what, where,* and *why"* of the study. In addition to a rationale or justification for doing the research, the introduction should also include a description of the researcher's credentials and prior involvement with the study topic; these help make it clear that the researcher is qualified to conduct the study

If the proposal is to be submitted to a funding organization, the introduction is also where the author can "sell" the value of the proposed project. Thus it must be written in such a way that readers come to believe in the project and your ability to accomplish it as described. The proposal should show that the research will be a good the investment of time and money.

A good introduction can play an important role in helping the researcher establish a clear focus for the study. By including clear statements of the concepts to be examined in the research, the hypotheses to be tested, or the possible theory that may emerge from the analysis, the researcher is far less likely to become sidetracked during the rest of the proposal and the research study itself.

A good introduction may include most or all of the following elements:

1. A statement of the research problem
2. A rationale for the proposed study that clearly indicates why it is worth doing
3. A brief description of the major issues and problems to be addressed by the research
4. If a quantitative study, a statement of the hypotheses; if a qualitative study, a statement of theory, if any

Table 9.2

Some Alternative Formats for the Research Proposal

Sample Format 1	Sample Format 2	Sample Format 3	Sample Format 4
Cover/Title	Cover/Title	Cover/Title	Cover/Title
Table of Contents	Table of Contents	Table of Contents	Table of Contents
Executive Summary	Executive Summary	Executive Summary	Executive Summary
or Abstract	or Abstract	or Abstract	or Abstract
Introduction	Objectives	Background	Literature Review
• Problem statement	Activities	Literature Review	Objectives
• Literature review	Methodology	Scope of the Study	Research Plan
• Research questions	Personnel Involved	Methodology	Methodology
and/or hypotheses	Facilities Needed	Work Schedule	Work Schedule
• Significance of	Other Information	Equipment	Budget
proposed study	Budget	Estimated Costs	References
Design and	Appendices	References	
Methodology	References		
• Subjects			
• Instrumentation			
• Procedures			
• Data analysis			
• Presentation			
• Limitations			
References			
Appendices			

5. Limitations expected and definitions of key concepts
6. A review of the literature on the topic, although this is more often a separate section of the proposal.

Statement of the Problem

The statement of the research problem is the chief component of this section. In most academic research, the problem is derived from the literature; that is, researchers determine what to study from what past researchers have studied or proposed. Beginning academic researchers are advised to follow this same path: study the journals of a discipline, pick a recognized investigator or investigators, and then focus on research that closes identified gaps in the published research. However, in fields of inquiry such as public administration or nonprofit organization management, research tends to be more *applied* than theoretical. Thus, research problems often emerge from problems encountered in the day-to-day operations of existing organizations, or they arise with proposed modifications to existing organizational processes.

In either case, the problem(s) to be investigated should be framed in the theoretical concepts of the discipline. For example, say that the issue has to do with a healthcare administration problem. To address this issue effectively the researcher(s) should have grounding in health care administration. Some of this grounding comes from practical experience in the field. In this way, the research is able to locate the problem within the current thinking found in the literature.

Researchers should keep the following cautionary points in mind as they approach this critical component of the proposal (Paxton and Cox 2000):

Sample Format 5	Sample Format 6	Sample Format 7
Cover/Title	Cover/Title	Cover/Title
Table of Contents	Table of Contents	Table of Contents
Executive Summary or Abstract	Executive Summary or Abstract	Executive Summary or Abstract
Introduction	Introduction	Introduction
Literature Survey	Research Problem	• Problem statement
Problem Statement	Statement of Need	• Rationale
Conceptual Framework	Major Issues and Subproblems	• Objective(s)
Specific Objectives	Key Independent and Dependent Variables	• Hypotheses
Hypotheses (if any)	Hypotheses or Theory	• Problem summary
Methodology	Delimitations	Literature Review
Bibliography	Definitions	• Current status of the topic
	Literature Review	• Relationships between literature and problem
	Methods and Design	Method
	Discussion	• Participants
	Bibliography	• Research design
		• Definitions
		• Reliability/validity
		• Pilot study results
		• Data analysis plan
		Implications and Limitations
		Appendices (instrument, human subjects approval, permission forms, time line, budget)

- Be sure to take enough time to explore the current research in the field. This has two payoffs: it can help you avoid choosing a topic that has already been thoroughly investigated, and it can help you narrow your study to something that can be covered effectively in the allotted time frame.
- Do not try to be "different" in your choice of topic and/or your methodology just to be different; instead, choose a research problem that can *make* a difference.
- Do not choose a topic that is too complicated or too trivial. Attempting to study a highly complex problem is one of the main reasons why many graduate students fail to finish their academic programs.
- Avoid choosing a research problem that you are not truly interested in. Do not take the easy way out.

Review of the Literature

A "literature review" is the researcher's detailed summary and interpretation of the published articles, books, and related materials that pertain to the issues that frame the research problem. A thorough analysis and interpretation of the published literature tells the researcher what has or has not been studied about the issues and the methods used to study them, thereby providing a way to plan and conduct the proposed research. Demonstrating a direct link to previous research in your proposal is always a good idea. A literature review serves a number of additional functions (Wong 2002):

1. Demonstrates knowledge of the problem and its larger theoretical foundation.
2. Demonstrates ability to critically evaluate relevant literature.

3. Shows knowledge of the issues surrounding the research problem.
4. Indicates ability to integrate and synthesize information.
5. Provides new insights and new models for the framework of research.
6. Helps avoid "reinventing the wheel."
7. Gives credit to those who have previously studied the problem.
8. Helps convince reader that research will make a significant contribution to the problem area and discipline.

There is no one best way to organize the literature review. However you choose to structure the narrative of your analysis, remember to follow a logical path of presentation. You must make it easy for the reader to follow—group related topics together and separated by subheads. Remember to synthesize and integrate your findings during the section and summarize the issues and your conclusions at the end.

Study Objectives

The introduction should have a definitive statement of the objectives for the study. Study objectives usually begin with a statement of the problem, a discussion of the need for the project and the questions that the study is designed to answer, and the activities that will take place. The objective (or goal) is a statement of what you expect to determine from the findings. For example, in a research project to determine why a selected minority group exhibits disproportionately low citizen participation in municipal planning sessions, a study objective might be to identify what causal factors influence the group's involvement. The rationale for the researcher is to design activities and programs designed to elicit greater group participation.

Research Design and Methodology

The research design and methods section describes the design or procedures you plan to follow in conducting the research. Methods might be surveys, interviews, library research, lab work, fieldwork, analysis of historical documents, analysis of physical artifacts, and many others. The underlying purpose of the methods section is to inform others how you plan to approach your research project. It must carry enough information to convince the reader that your methodology is sound and appropriate. This section will vary with the type of study proposed. Some elements are more important for a quantitative study than they are for a qualitative project. For example, research in the sciences most often follows a quantitative design. Therefore, the proposal requires a detailed description of the proposed experiments, laboratory work, research subjects, data collection methods, and similar details. Such studies also require identification of the population from which the sample or samples will be drawn, including sample size, sample elements, and related sample data.

Although most social science research is also quantitative, an increasing number of studies follow a qualitative approach. These proposals also require a description of the sources and types of data to be collected, strategies and processes for data collection, and the techniques, if any, proposed for analysis of the collected data. Data collection tools, interview discussion guides, and other related information must also be described.

References and/or Bibliography

The research proposal must include detailed bibliographic data for every source addressed in preparing for and writing the proposal. In addition, the bibliography may also include a list of all the resources the researcher plans to investigate during the subsequent research. Sources are grouped according to whether they are primary or secondary and in what form they exist. Primary sources are those with first-hand data, such as interviews. Secondary sources are those with data collected originally by others, such as journals and databases.

Public administration and nonprofit organization management disciplines tend to follow the *American Psychology Association* (APA) style more often than not, although it is a good plan to check with the sponsors of your research to determine which style they prefer. Some publishers prefer to follow an exact or modified version of *The Chicago Manual of Style*. Other commonly encountered styles include *A Uniform System of Citation* published by Harvard University (a similar volume is published by Columbia University) and *Modern Language Association* style.

DIFFERENCES IN QUANTITATIVE AND QUALITATIVE PROPOSALS

A finished research proposal should be a document that clearly communicates what the research intends to accomplish. Exactly what elements should go into the proposal may vary somewhat depending upon the type of study envisioned. At the most fundamental level, there are small but very real differences in the way that quantitative and qualitative research proposals are structured. Quantitative studies follow a deductive approach, whereas qualitative studies tend to be more open ended, suggesting a final design that is inductive—evolving from the research itself. Table 9.3 has Kelly, Bennett, and Moore's (2002) list of differences between qualitative and quantitative proposals. However, some commonalities do exist. Both proposal types have a statement of the problem, a literature review, a rationale for the study, a design statement or methodology description, and a bibliography.

Preparing a Quantitative Research Proposal

The design and methods section of a quantitative proposal generally includes a description of the subjects, instruments, and procedures for collecting the data, data analysis, and possible design limitations. Quantitative studies may be exploratory, descriptive, or causal. Exploratory projects are usually small-sample studies designed to produce insights and ideas for further research. Descriptive studies provide a descriptive snapshot of a sample at a particular time. Causal projects involve experimentation and are designed to measure relationships between independent and dependent variables.

The data analysis section identifies the statistical techniques to be used in data analysis. In this section, some proposal recommendations explain how the data are to be presented. Statistical tests should be identified for each research question and/or hypothesis, often with a rationale for selecting the test(s). Limitations of the design that should be noted include the scope of the study (research projects typically address one small part of a larger issue or problem), the overall design, and/or the methodology.

Preparing a Qualitative Research Proposal

Unlike proposals for quantitative research projects, qualitative research proposals are necessarily more tentative and open ended. They often must allow for a design and hypotheses that emerge from the research activity. The actual detail to be included in a qualitative study often depends on the amount of preliminary work the researcher performs prior to preparing the proposal.

Some of the points that might be included in the introduction section of a qualitative proposal include site selection; identification of the case or cases to be studies; locating archival collections such as historical, political, or legal documents; and the role of the researcher, including the degree of intrusion (participant-observer) into the group to be studied.

Table 9.3

Differences in Preferences in Quantitative and Qualitative Research Proposals

	Quantitative Preferences	Qualitative Preferences
1.	Precise hypotheses and definitions stated at the outset	Hypotheses and definitions that emerge as the study develops
2.	Data reduced to numerical scores	Data as narrative descriptions
3.	Focus on assessing and improving reliability of scores obtained from instruments	Reliability of inferences is often assumed to be adequate
4.	Assessment of validity with reliance on statistical indices	Validity assessed through cross-checking sources of information (triangulation)
5.	Random selection of samples	Recruitment of expert informants for sample
6.	Precise description of procedures	Narrative/literary description of processes
7.	Statistical control of extraneous variables	Logical analysis in controlling or accounting for extraneous variables
8.	Specific design control for procedural bias (procedural and measurement integrity checks)	Reliance on researcher to deal with procedural bias (integrity checks are still critical)
9.	Statistical summary of results	Narrative summary of results
10.	Breaking down of complex phenomena into specific parts for analysis	Holistic description of complex phenomena
11.	Willingness to manipulate aspects, situations, or conditions in studying complex phenomena	Unwillingness to tamper with naturally occurring phenomena

Source: Kelly, Bennett, and Moore 2002.

The proposal must also identify the data collection methods proposed, with recognition that these might change under exigencies of the collection event. The limitations of the design note the difficulties the researcher can identify in advance, the scope of the study, and methodological, time, and site limitations.

SUMMARY

Research proposals are the critical first step in all research activities. Too often, however, they are not given the attention they need to be successful. Research proposals are often rejected because the research problem is too trivial or broad to be meaningful. Another cause of rejection is the researcher's failure to clearly and cogently describe the methodology to be followed.

Proposals serve several different purposes. First, they show that the researcher is competent enough to carry out the project, that the research is important and should be done, and that the research is connected to prior research in the field. Research proposals should state the problem, convey the importance of the study, give a review of the relevant literature, and state the research questions and hypotheses. Quantitative proposals usually identify the population, sample selection, subjects, instruments, data-gathering and analysis procedures, and references. Qualitative proposals are more tentative, with the design often emerging from the research activity. However, they should also state the selection of the case or cases and how and why they were selected.

ADDITIONAL READING

Elise K. Parsigian.1996. *Proposal Savvy.* Thousand Oaks, CA: Sage.

PART 3

QUANTITATIVE RESEARCH STRATEGIES

10

FUNDAMENTALS OF QUANTITATIVE RESEARCH

A key objective of most public administration and nonprofit organization research is to provide the information needed to improve the quality of decisions made by managers and administrators. Among their many tasks and responsibilities, administrators must establish organizational and resource priorities, identify alternative courses of action, set and manage budgets, and hire, motivate, and, when necessary, fire employees. Administrators receive, interpret, and share instructions, develop and write plans with objectives and strategies, monitor staff performance, and inform higher-level managers about their progress in achieving objectives. Higher-level managers are often called upon to communicate the progress of the organization to internal and external stakeholders, including voters, legislators and other elected and appointed officials, financial analysts, and the general public.

In each of their many tasks, administrators must make decisions. They compare two or more alternatives, weigh the costs and benefits of each, and then select and implement the better alternative. Administrators often conduct research to improve the quality of their decisions. In the past, most of that research followed a *quantitative* paradigm, and much of it still does.

To make effective managerial decisions, administrators must know how to use quantitative research methods and how to interpret quantitative data. The proper use of numbers can make communicating easier, faster, and often more effective than the use of words alone.

In research, these numerical data are called *statistics*. Statistics and statistical methods cannot be applied, however, until the fundamental nature of measurement is understood. Beginning with a discussion of the four types of measurements, the next several chapters are an introduction to some of the most commonly used quantitative research designs. The emphasis is on how to use and interpret statistical methods, rather than on the theoretical side of statistical analysis.

FUNDAMENTALS OF MEASUREMENT

The key to ensuring that everyone who reads a research report can make sense of the findings is the consistent use of the measurement type appropriate for the task at hand. The terms *measurement type* and *data type* are often used interchangeably to refer to the numbers produced by measurements, the variables to which the measurements refer, and to their relevant classes, levels, or values. Researchers use numbers for things that can be counted; they use words to describe things that can't be counted. When different values are assigned to categories of a variable, different but specific meanings are established.

Researchers use four different types of measurement data: (1) nominal, (2) ordinal, (3) interval, and (4) ratio. Statisticians have produced different statistical tests in order to analyze each data type. In differentiating between the scales or types, each must meet one or more rules. The term *scales* refers to measuring tools such as questions in questionnaires and other devices to record measurements. The higher or more powerful scales require more rules that must be applied to each type of measurement.

Nominal Data

Nominal data, which are the least powerful, must pass just one test: *Different numbers must mean different things.* For example, a 1 might be assigned to the female gender and a 2 to the male gender. For a specific categorizing question in a survey, a value of 1 can never mean anything other than female; the same is true for the value 2 for male. Thus, a nominal scale is simply a set of numbers used to name or classify different things. With these scales, the differences in categories to which a number may be assigned represent *qualitative* differences; this means they are numbers subjectively assigned to one category in a class.

With nominal-level data, numbers or labels are used only to differentiate between things. The numbers or labels serve no other purpose or function and supply no additional information. Furthermore, once a number has been assigned to a given category, all other items with the same characteristics must receive the same number or label. Just one variable is singled out, such as gender, and that attribute and only that attribute dictates further classification. Typical examples of nominal or categorical scales include the following:

1. The values of 1 and 2 arbitrarily assigned to the categories of registered and non-registered voters, respectively.
2. The values 0 and 1 assigned to groups of users versus non-users of a service, such as remedial instruction.
3. Numbers used to denote different types of occupations, political party membership, and class in college (freshman, sophomore, etc.), or which newspapers or magazines read.

To repeat, for nominal data there is only one rule: different numbers mean different things.

Ordinal Data

An ordinal scale supplies more information than a nominal scale, so more than one rule applies. The data must first pass the nominal scale rule—different numbers mean different things—but now must also pass a second test. The second rule is that the *things being measured can be ranked or ordered along some dimension.* With ordinal data (often simply referred to as *ranked* data), the differences between measures are *quantitative* rather than just qualitative.

When things are ranked or ordered, they are arranged in some logical sequence. They may have *more* or *less* of a particular characteristic than other items in the set. The limitation with ordinal data is that the numbers never state precisely how much more or less difference exists in the scores of the two groups. These numbers only communicate "more or less," not *how much* more or less.

A typical use for ordinal scales is to measure people's preferences or rankings for services or things. Much of the data collected by public administrators is based upon ordinal scales. Examples include political opinion questionnaires and ranking citizens' preferences.

Interval Data

The third type of measurement data is *equidistant interval*—more commonly referred to simply as *interval*. To qualify as an interval scale, a measurement must now pass three tests. First, the different numbers must mean different things. Second, the things measured can be ranked or ordered on some appropriate dimension. Third—the most important rule—is that *the differences between adjacent levels on the scale are* (or are assumed to be) *equal.*

With interval data, in addition to determining that one scale item is greater than, less than, or equal to another, it now becomes possible to determine exactly *how much* one item differs from another. The differences between levels on the scale can be any size and can include numbers that are positive, negative, or both. Also, the zero point on the scale can be set anywhere on the scale that the researcher wants it to be. The key requirement is that a single-unit change *always* measures the same amount of change in whatever is being measured. However, the unit gradations within the scale may be as broad or as fine as need be. For example, on a five-point scale, the distance between 3 and 4 or between 4 and 5 might be measured in tenths, in hundreds, thousands, or even finer, but they must apply to every part of the scale equally. Thus, one might see mean (average) measurements of 3.3, 3.33, or 3.333, depending on the accuracy desired. The distance between 3 and 4, or 1 and 2, never changes, however. Only the fineness of the measurement may be changed.

Measuring temperature using the Fahrenheit scale is a good example of interval scale data. Fahrenheit scales have a zero point, but it is no more important that any other number on the scale. Others examples are grade point averages, dimensions, and IQ scores. Attitude scales using different levels of agreement are assumed to provide interval-level data. This makes attitude scales a highly desired measurement tool for all social and administrative science researchers.

Interval scales provide more information than either nominal or ordinal scales because of their equal distance between measurement points. There are, however, still limitations to the information provided by interval data. For example, because the zero point is set arbitrarily, it is not possible to say that one measure is exactly twice as great or small as another. We cannot say that 100 degrees Fahrenheit is exactly twice as warm as 50 degrees, or that 35 degrees is half as warm as 70 degrees. We must turn to the fourth level, *ratio scales,* to make such qualifying statements.

When a Nominal Scale Is Really an Ordinal Scale

Some researchers feel it is wrong to assume measurements acquired from attitude scales to be interval-level data and believe that they are really ordinal. This criticism is often put forward as a law: *Do not make interval-level conclusions on ordinal-level data.* Despite this criticism, much published social and administrative science research continues to report statistical processing of attitude scales and their interpretations using statistical tests that assume the data are interval rather than ordinal data.

Ratio Data

As with the other three scales or data types, lower-level rules also apply to ratio scales. Different numbers still mean different things; the data can still be ranked or ordered on some dimension; and the intervals between adjacent points are considered to be of equal value. The ratio-required fourth rule is that *the measurement scale has an absolute or fixed zero point*—even if it is not used in the specific range of items being measured. Examples of ratio scales are time, distance, mass, and various combinations of these; units sold; number of purchasers; and temperature according to the Celsius scale. In applications of statistics in public administration research, the distinction between interval and ratio is of little practical value. The same statistical tests can be used for either data type; they are also interpreted in the same manner. As a result, statistical software packages like the Statistical Package for the Social Sciences (SPSS) have combined the two into a single category called scale data, which includes the same statistical tests for both interval and ratio data.

Nominal and ordinal data have their own statistical tests; they are considered to provide "nonparametric" data. This means that they do not depend upon the normal distribution of the characteristics of a population, such as the mean. They are said to be "distribution free."

It is inappropriate to use lower-level statistical tests on data from higher-level scales of measurement. However, higher-level tests may be used on lower-level data, although there is seldom any reason to. Using higher-level tests on lower-level data will always provide less information than could be gained using a more appropriate-level test. It is much easier to play by the rules.

STATISTICS TERMS AND CONCEPTS

The term *statistics* is used in a number of different ways. It is used to mean the numerical data in a report. Examples include the number of clients served each day, week, or month; hours worked and employees' earnings; costs per unit; turnover rates; performance ratios; age and gender of citizens in the community; and many, many more. The term *statistics* is also used to define the many mathematical techniques and procedures used for collecting, describing, analyzing, and interpreting data. Statistical processes can include simple counts of events or the determination of the central values of a group of counts, conducting hypothesis tests, and determining relationships between two variables.

As in every discipline or management function, a variety of concepts and terms not part of our common language experience are to be found in the study of statistics. Here are definitions for some of these concepts:

- *Descriptive statistics:* Measurements or numbers used to summarize or describe data sets.
- *Inferential statistics:* Statistical techniques used to make estimates or inferences about the characteristics of interest for a population using the data from a sample data set.
- *Sample:* A portion of a population. The sample is chosen as representative of the entire population.
- *Population:* The set of all elements for which measurements are possible. A population can consist of products, workers, customers, firms, prices, or other items about which the decision maker or manager is interested. Another word used to identify a population is a *universe*.
- *Statistic:* A number used as a summary measure for a sample. For example, "The mean age for the 20 students in the sample is 20.3 years."
- *Parameter:* A numerical value used as a summary measure for a population or universe. For example, in the statement "The mean age for all entering college or university freshmen is 19.1 years"; the age of all entering freshmen is a *parameter.*
- *Variable:* A characteristic or quantity that can have different values. Examples include savings account amounts, stock prices, package designs, weight, monthly sales, gender, and salaries. The values of variables may be said to be either *continuous* or *discrete*.
- *Continuous Variables:* Quantities that are measured, such as weight or percentage of increase in the price of a stock, are said to be continuous. Values for these variables can be measured on a continuous scale, such as weights, and are not restricted to specific, discrete categories or values.

- *Discrete variables:* Variables with values that can vary only in specific steps or categories (they are sometimes called *categorical*). Assuming that we assign in advance the value of 1 for female and 2 for male, the variable *gender* is an example of a discrete variable.
- *Univariate statistics:* Statistics describing a single variable. They include such measures as the valid number of responses (frequencies); the mean, median, and mode; and standard deviation.
- *Bivariate statistics:* Measurements with which two variables are described or compared at the same time. A crosstabulation table is an example of bivariate statistics in use. Counts, percentages, correlations, difference tests, and many other statistical tests can be carried out with bivariate statistics.
- *Multivariate statistics:* Statistics, such as *multiple regression analysis,* used when more than one independent variable influences one dependent variable. For example, sales of a product are probably influenced by aesthetics, price, availability (distribution), and advertising.

Some Categories of Statistics

Statistics can be categorized in several different ways. One way is according to how they are applied. Statistics can be used to describe something or to infer similar measurements in another, larger group. The first of these applications is called *descriptive statistics;* the second application is called *inferential statistics. Descriptive statistics* are used to numerically describe events, concepts, people, work, or many other things.

Another use of descriptive statistics is for *summarizing* a set of data. A *data set* is simply a collection of a distinct set of measurements. A data set can be as large as the combined total of all measurements of all U.S. residents taken every ten years for the Census of Population, or as small as a dozen or so test scores from a midterm examination.

Inferential statistics describe a class of statistics that are used for one or more of the following three purposes:

1. To make generalizations about a larger group—called a *population*—from which the sample was taken
2. To make estimates or draw conclusions about the characteristics of a population, or
3. To make predictions about some future event or state of affairs

Note that these three uses employ measurements of a smaller group (a *sample*) for making *inferences* about a larger group (a *population*). This is why they are known as "inferential" statistics. The term *sample* is used to mean some portion of a population. Samples are usually chosen to be representative of some larger population. A *population,* on the other hand, is the set of all elements for which measurements are possible. A population can consist of products, workers, customers, firms, prices, or anything else about which the decision maker is interested. A survey of every unit in a population is called a *census.* Individually, each person, item, or thing in the sample, population, or universe is called a *population unit.*

Another label sometimes used to identify a population is a *universe.* The labels *population* and *universe* are often used interchangeably to mean a complete set or group of people, items, or events from which a sample is or can be drawn.

IS IT A PARAMETER OR A STATISTIC?

Another way that statisticians categorize measurement data is based on whether they apply to a sample or to its parent population. Differences in these applications result in two types of statistics: *parametric* statistics and *nonparametric* statistics.

A *parameter* is a numerical value used as a summary measure for a population or a universe. For example, consider the statement, "The mean age for all entering college or university freshmen in California is 18.8 years." Because 18.8 years is the average of *all* entering freshmen—the population—it is a parameter.

A *statistic,* on the other hand, is a number used as a summary measure for a sample. For example, consider the statement, "The mean age for a sample of thirty Benson College freshmen is 18.3 years." The mean for this sample is a statistic. In this case, the mean for the sample is larger than it was for the population of all college and university freshmen in the country, and statistical techniques have been developed to determine whether the two mean values are *statistically different.*

Parametric Statistics

Parametric statistics require that measurements come from a population (rather than a sample) in which the distribution of variances is normal. This doesn't mean that all the measurements are the same. Rather, it means that the differences vary in what we call a "normal" way. Take the measurements of the incomes of a randomly drawn sample of a thousand households as an example. If each of measurements were plotted, it would be expected that the distribution of incomes for members of the sample would come close to the same distribution that occurred in the population—and this distribution would be expected to be "normal."

Plotting this distribution would result in a typical bell-shaped curve. There would be a few values at either end of the curve but the bulk would fall around the middle value—near what would be the mean for the sample. When discussing measures of central tendency, it would be appropriate to refer to the average or *mean* income of the group with this measurement. Inferential statistical tests could be used as well.

Nonparametric Statistics

Nonparametric statistical procedures must be used when working with nominal- and ordinal-level data. No assumptions can be made about the distribution of these measurements, nor can any assumptions be made about the larger population. Rather, with nonparametric statistics, the distribution must be assumed *not* to be normal.

Testing a sample of new parts coming off a manufacturing line can be used as an example. The parts are examined to see if they work or don't work—often called a "pass or fail" test. Only one of two possible outcomes can occur. There is no way to establish if the distribution of "passes" and "fails" is normal or not. A mean or average score is no longer possible; instead, the researcher can only say something like "three out of one hundred failed," or that "ninety-seven out of one hundred passed." Both the "three" and the "ninety-seven" are nonparametric statistics.

With this nonparametric example, the means must be replaced by the mode. The *mode* is the value that comes up most often. Here, the mode is ninety-seven. It is meaningless to talk about a "mean" score on a two- or three-category item. Rather, the category appearing most often, the "mode," is the relevant information.

STATISTICS AND COMMUNICATION

One of the great advantages of using numbers instead of words to describe something is that it often makes it easier for both the sender and receiver to agree on what is being said. For example, one person might be described as being six feet tall and a second person as being five feet, nine inches tall. Clearly when both people are standing on the same level surface, one is taller than the other. But how great is the difference? It is hard to tell by just looking at the two people. By measuring the differences in height, it becomes possible to know for sure.

Because numbers were used instead of just saying "one is taller," it is now possible to know that one person is precisely three inches taller than the other person. Furthermore, in the English language, the word "three" and the symbol "3" refer to the same amount. Three inches or three bananas are the same number as 3 oranges.

The same communication concept is true for fractions and percentages. Most people will comprehend the idea behind the phrase "one third" and will know that 33.3 percent is very nearly the same thing as one third. One third of a gallon is the same *share* of the whole as is one third of a liter or one third of a pound, even though the absolute quantities are different. One third of anything is always one third of whatever is the unit of measurement. Numbers make it possible to communicate these ideas.

The same goes for other percentages. One hundred percent of anything can only mean all of it, a totality. One hundred and ten percent, on the other hand, is all of something plus ten percent more. Every time you use it or say it, it is the same. That's the beauty of using statistics when communicating—little or nothing is lost in translation. Because things can be measured, they can be described.

Communicating with Statistics

The term *descriptive statistics* refers to the set of measurements (numbers) that are used to summarize a set of larger numbers, and that *have the same meaning for everyone.* Here is an example of how an administrator might use descriptive statistics:

A public assistance program manager might be interested in knowing the size (amount) of clients' allotments. In today's age of desktop computers, it would be a relatively simple task for the manager to call up a list of all client monthly totals, when the last payment occurred, and a host of other information about each client. However, the volume of data that such requests can quickly provide could soon become overwhelming. By themselves, the numbers for any individual would most likely provide little information about the total. What the manager could use instead is a simple set of numbers that *summarized* specific features of all clients' accounts—in a word, a *summary* of the data set using descriptive statistics.

A major use of statistics is to make *inferences.* Researchers assume or infer that measurements of some characteristics of a smaller group (the sample) are held in common by some larger group (the population). One example of inferential statistics is in the periodic testing of small portions of a production run (a sample or samples) to *estimate* the failure or error rate of the entire day's production (a population).

Another example of how inferential statistics are used is the now-famous experience of administrators who determined statistically that taking one aspirin a day may greatly decrease the likelihood of having a heart attack. In the aspirin experiment, some 10,000 medical doctors were recruited to participate in a ten-year experiment. Half were to take one aspirin a day; the other half, an inert placebo (colored chalk). Participants were assigned to their group randomly so that no one knew to which group he or she belonged. After just a few years, the incidence of heart attacks among the aspirin takers was found to be so much lower than the placebo group that the experiment was called to a halt and the results announced. Taking one aspirin a day was deemed to be highly likely to reduce one's chance of (that is, lower the probability of) having a heart attack. Thus, the assumption (or inference) was made that the results (measurements) of the sample applied to the overall population as well.

STATISTICS IN ACTION

Statistics is the collective term to describe numbers used to indicate the measurements of something. The measurements of a particular sample are typically drawn from a larger body called a *population* or *universe.* As we have seen, only the numerical values that apply to the sample are known as "statistics," whereas the values of the population are known as "parameters." In learning about applying statistics to public administration situations, this difference is seldom a problem because managers rarely deal with entire populations.

In statistics, the term *measurement* refers to numbers read from a *scale* or other measuring device, such as a ruler or gauge, or a multi-point answer to a question. With such measurement or recording devices, the numbers are arranged according to some meaningful *set* or *range of values* that has been determined to be appropriate by the person or persons reading the scale. Examples of scales include inches and feet, a set of millimeters and centimeters, foot-pounds of pressure, engine horsepower, computer chip memory capacity, miles per hour, and many others.

Public administration has followed the lead of the social sciences and expanded the concept of a scale to include such phenomena as responses to questions on a consumer attitude or lifestyle questionnaire. Scales have also been established to measure levels or increments of awareness, agreement, desirability, rank order, preference, and many other similar concepts. In all applications, numbers have also been assigned to various "things" such as events, objects, characteristics, responses, and qualities.

Most managers in public and nonprofit organizations have a use for statistics. Some examples of statistics used by public and nonprofit organization managers and administrators are displayed in Box 10.1.

DESCRIPTIVE AND INFERENTIAL STATISTICS

Administrators use both descriptive and inferential statistics. Descriptive statistics are used to describe things numerically. For example, the average age of the workers in a government office is a descriptive statistic. On the other hand, say that a sample of 100 workers is randomly selected and asked to rate their agency's overall effectiveness on a five-point scale; the mean rating score for the sample is 3.8. This average is then used as the mean score for the entire staff of the agency. Sample statistics are inferred to be the population statistics.

Numerical information for both descriptive and inferential statistics may be presented in tables or charts, or as graphical illustrations. Some of the more commonly encountered uses of descriptive and inferential statistical tests are discussed in the following sections.

Descriptive Statistics

The four basic types of descriptive statistics used most commonly by administrators and managers are (Lang and Heiss 1990):

1. *Measures of central tendency.* These include the mean, the mode, and the median values of a data set.
2. *Measures of variability in the data set.* The three variability measures are the standard deviation (SD), the range, and the interquartile range.

Box 10.1
Uses for Statistics

Program Management and Administration

New program planning, acquisition, and distribution administrators use statistical analyses of environmental trends, as well as detailed cost accounting, budgeting, inventory control, and similar systems—all of which are measurements.

Planning and Forecasting

Managers of public health and welfare agencies are regularly required to forecast community needs for their services; managers must determine service-provider staff requirements; client trends and demographics for planning and budget preparations are established with statistical studies.

Decision Making

Decision making includes a broad variety of studies, demand tests, and concept evaluations that involve collection, evaluation, and interpretation about consumer preferences, habits, lifestyles, demographic trends, and the like.

Process Controls

Statistical record keeping and analysis aids quality control managers in maintaining standards and efficient production schedules. Medical administrators and hospital staffs maintain statistical records to monitor patients' reactions to pharmaceutical products.

Human Resources

Today more than ever, human resource managers use statistics to track and predict workplace diversity trends, staff turnover, absenteeism, appraisals, etc. Many more such business applications require statistical record keeping, analysis, and interpretation.

3. *Measures of relative position in the set.* Included are percentiles and standard scores. The most commonly used standardized score is the z score.
4. *Measures of correlation between two or more variables.* Correlation tests are used to show how strongly and in what direction two variables are related, if at all.

A wide variety of statistical tools have been developed for use in these four applications. Naturally, not all of these are relevant to the majority of decisions that managers or administrators face. The tests included have been selected for their extensive use in organization and organizational management literature, their relative ease of application and clear interpretation characteristics, and their availability in most general statistical software packages.

Inferential Statistics

The basic types of inferential statistics (i.e., procedures) used in public administration research are:

1. The *t*-test for significant differences between means of dependent (uncorrelated) groups.
2. The *t*-test for significant differences between the means of paired or correlated groups.
3. Simple correlation and regression analysis for measuring the strength and the direction of relationships between variables.
4. Analysis of variance (ANOVA) tests for differences on one variable for two or more groups.
5. Analysis of variance (ANOVA) tests for differences on two or more variables between two or more groups, and for any *interaction* that might result from the two variables.
6. Analysis of covariance, as used in pretest and posttest experimental applications.

In addition to these easy-to-apply-and-interpret statistical tests, other commonly encountered statistical applications include: (1) the use of probability in decision making; (2) concepts and applications of sampling; (3) prediction and forecasting tools; and (4) statistical applications for managing quality.

Statistics by Computer

Managers of public and nonprofit organizations use statistical tools to help them carry out the decision-making and communication tasks of their position. However, it is no longer necessary for anyone to memorize confusing statistical formulas or to work complex statistical calculations by hand. Most administrators have access to a personal computer. While powerful statistical software has been available almost from the desktop computer's introduction, much of the early statistical software was limited in scope because of hardware restrictions that resulted in slow processing speed. Another limitation was that statistical processing of large data sets required far more memory than was available on early desktop computers.

The majority of modern desktop and laptop computers are powerful enough for managers to analyze large data sets and to conduct sophisticated statistical tests on that data. Throughout the remainder of this book, a variety of statistical software for desktop computers will be referenced, including Microsoft Excel and the Statistical Package for the Social Sciences (SPSS).

SUMMARY

Administrators use words and statistics to communicate with their staffs, supervisors, and with people and groups outside of the organization. Statistics, presented either in tables, graphs, or other illustrations, help to ensure mutual understanding of the data at hand. Statistics are used for two main purposes: (1) as *descriptive statistics,* they are used to summarize a larger set of numbers, called a data set; (2) as *inferential statistics,* the measurements of a smaller group—a *sample*—are used for making assumptions about a larger group—the *population* or *universe* of interest.

The numerical values in statistics are typically measurements taken with some type of scale or measuring device. These scales provide different levels of information, based upon the type of data they are intended to acquire. The four types or levels of data (the terms apply to the data-gathering scales as well) from the lowest in power to the highest are nominal, ordinal, interval, and ratio. Each data type has a body of statistical tests that are appropriate for that level; lower-level tests should not be used on higher-level data.

When the term *statistics* is used, it can mean one or more specific measures or values describing some thing, a sample of some type. The word can also be used to refer to a body of mathematical tools and techniques invented for analyzing and giving meaning to sets of numbers. This latter use of the word is called *statistical analysis*.

Statistics may be *parametric* or *nonparametric*. Parametric statistics require that certain assumptions be made of the host population, such as a normal distribution. With nonparametric statistics, no such assumptions need be made.

ADDITIONAL READING

Einspruch, Eric. 1998. *An Introductory Guide to SPSS for Windows*. Thousand Oaks, CA: Sage.
Green, Samuel B., Neil J. Salkind, and Theresa M. Akey. 2000. *Using SPSS*. Upper Saddle River, NJ: Prentice Hall.
Phillips, John L. 1996. *How to Think About Statistics*. 5th ed. New York: Freeman.

11

INTRODUCTION TO SAMPLING

Research projects are often designed to measure some aspect of very large groups of subjects. Whenever large-group research is required, techniques are available that make it far more economical and nearly as accurate to select a smaller, representative subgroup instead of everyone. The full group is called a *population;* the representative subgroup is called a *sample;* the process of selecting the subgroup is called s*ampling.*

Researchers draw samples from populations, measure the relevant elements or characteristics of that sample, and infer that the sample measurements also apply to the population. Sample measurements are called *statistics;* population measurements are called *parameters.* Researchers acquire sample statistics to estimate a larger population's unknown *parameters.* The process is known as *inference,* and the statistical tests that are used for this purpose are called *inferential statistics.* When inferring that sample results apply to the entire sample as well, researchers can never do so with complete certainty. Rather, they do so with some degree of confidence or probability that is less than 100 percent.

This section begins with a discussion of some fundamental concepts in sampling. This is followed by a comparative description of several different types of samples, the meaning of bias and error in sampling, sample distributions, and concepts of sample size. It concludes with a review of several statistical procedures relating to sampling.

WHEN INFORMATION IS UNAVAILABLE

If all possible information needed to solve an administrative problem could be collected, there would be no need to sample. Decision makers seldom have this luxury. They are typically limited in time and money. Therefore, they use samples and make decisions based on probabilities (Fitz-Gibbon and Morris 1987).

For example, the author once conducted a series of focus groups in ten different cities across the United States. The objective of the study was to determine which features of running shoes male and female recreational runners preferred. Obviously, the study could not require that all runners in the United States or even in a single town be interviewed. Instead, a series of samples of approximately 100 runners were interviewed in each of the ten cities. Opinions were nearly—but not entirely—unanimous across all samples. The results provided a consensus that reduced the potential loss that would have resulted from including less desirable features in new shoe models.

It must also be noted that sometimes it is, indeed, possible and desirable to take a census. The term *census* means that every element in the group or population of interest is measured. Surveys of workers in an organization or small group are frequently conducted as a census.

For example, a caseworker in a public agency working with high school dropouts in an administrative center was able to identify a floating homeless population of teenagers that ranged in size from 35 to nearly 100. The caseworker was charged with coming up with ways to effectively communicate safe sex information to at-risk youth. The objective for her study was to determine how the homeless youth acquired and shared information about health and safety programs. Because of the small size of the population, the researcher concluded that she needed to reach everyone in the subject group.

REASONS FOR SAMPLING

The main reasons why samples are used in place of a census of a population involve considerations of cost, time, accuracy, and the destructive nature of the measurement process. Cost and time are closely related. In planning a statistical study budget, the researcher must address these key concerns:

- How accurate must the final results be in order to make the type of decision required in the particular business situation?
- What is the cost to the organization if the wrong decision is made?
- How much more information must be added to reach the desired level of accuracy?
- What kinds of data are needed? How much does it cost to acquire them?
- Can we afford the extra cost to collect the data?

Sampling Precision

Administrators, managers, and researchers often use measurements of the characteristics of a sample for forecasting similar characteristics about larger samples or populations. In a sense, they use the sample data to *predict* how a population will act or react under the same conditions in some future situation or event. However, researchers can control few if any of the intervening variables that might affect that future event; they are asked to "measure the unknowable." The idea of *sampling precision* refers to how confident the researcher is that sample measurements can be used to make inferences.

The idea of *sampling* is rooted in the fundamental concepts of *probability*. Confidence is typically stated in terms of probability; that is, as a 0.10, 0.05, or a 0.01 level of confidence. These are typically stated as a "point one 0," a "point 0 five," or a "point 0 one" level of confidence. In the language of probability, a value of 1.0 indicates 100 percent confidence in a statistical result; 0.10 indicates that the researcher is 90 percent sure about the results; 0.05 means 95 percent sure; and 0.01 means the research is 99 percent sure.

Predictably, a high degree of precision is often difficult—if not impossible—to attain without greatly increasing the size of a sample. This is not the problem that it might seem to be, however. In most research in the social and administrative sciences, it is seldom necessary to achieve very high degrees of precision or reliability. Instead, decision makers can most often deal very well with information that is only *relative*. Often what is more important is tracking trends (Nye 1997).

The cost of acquiring additional information in order to improve the precision of a measurement is often prohibitive. Precision—and, hence, reliability—increase at a much slower rate than sample size does. Reliability grows at the rate of the square root of the increase in sample size. Thus, to double reliability requires making the sample four times as large.

Using very large samples can have other drawbacks as well. One is the *destructive nature* of the survey process. Simply by being asked questions, subjects begin to think about them. This can result in changes in their attitudes. Exposure to a survey questionnaire may help the subject to verbalize deep-seated attitudes that had lain dormant, but were brought to the fore during the study.

SAMPLING METHODS

There are a number of techniques that researchers can use to achieve greater reliability of a sample study with minimum additional cost. Among the most important of these is the type of *sampling method* employed. Sampling method refers to the way the sample units are selected from a parent population. When deciding which combination of sampling characteristics to use, researchers must make decisions in five basic areas. These, when combined, allow for thirty-two different possible choice combinations. The five basic concerns are:

- Probability or nonprobability sample
- Single unit or cluster of units
- Unstratified or stratified sample
- Equal unit probability or unequal probability
- Single stage or multistage sampling

Probability or Nonprobability Sample?

A *probability* sample is one in which the sample units (people, parts, groups, homes, cities, tribes, companies, etc.) are selected at random and all have an equal chance at being selected. Examples include simple random samples (SRS) and systematic samples. A *nonprobability* sample is one in which chance selection techniques are not used. Examples include *convenience samples* (selected at the convenience of the researcher) and *quota samples,* where only subjects with specific characteristics are added until some predetermined mix is achieved.

A third example of a nonprobability sample often used in practical public administration research is the *judgment sample.* This entails substituting experience or the judgment of an administrator or researcher for a more scientific approach at randomization. It often means deliberately picking a sample that is nonrepresentative of a population.

The choice between a probability and a nonprobability sample is often based on the cost-versus-value principle. The researcher will pick the method that provides the greatest margin of value over cost. A worthwhile rule of thumb to follow in sample selection is that, the more diversified the population, the greater the need to guarantee representativeness by following a probability sampling method.

Single Unit or Cluster Sampling?

A *sampling unit* is the basic element of the population being sampled. When choosing whether to use single unit or cluster sampling methods, the deciding factor is the nature of the sampling unit. In single unit sampling, each sampling unit is selected independently. In cluster sampling, the units are selected as groups. If sampling units are households, single unit sampling requires that all households in the population of interest be selected without reference to any other characteristic. A cluster sample might change the sampling unit to the random selection of city blocks, with some or all households on each selected block then surveyed. Cluster sampling usually costs less per sampling unit than single unit sampling does. As a rule of thumb, whenever a study involves a low tolerance for error with a high expected cost of errors, and a highly heterogeneous population, single unit sampling is favored over cluster sampling.

Stratified or Unstratified Sampling?

A third consideration is the *stratified* or *unstratified* sample question. A sample *stratum* is a portion of a population that has one or more characteristics of interest to the analyst. Examples include political party membership, income level, age, and many others. The final sample is selected so that it reflects the same percentages of the characteristic that are found in the larger population. A stratified sample may help to ensure representativeness, and thus reduce potential for sampling error. Finally, to obtain the same level of sampling error, a smaller sample size is needed with a stratified sample than would be needed if a nonstratified sample were used.

Equal Unit or Unequal Unit?

The question of *equal unit* or *unequal unit* probability sampling (that is, a greater or lesser likelihood of a sampling element's being included) is closely associated with strata in the population. The final sample drawn will include a disproportionately larger (or smaller) percentage of the characteristic of interest.

For example, a furniture retailer conducting a survey of local furniture buying patterns will probably include fewer persons older than 50 years of age in the sample because this group spends a disproportionately small amount on furniture items. At the same time, the retailer's sample will more than likely be heavily weighted in favor of the 24- to 34-year-old and 35- to 44-year-old demographic groups because they spend disproportionately more on furniture than other age groups.

Single Stage or Multistage Sampling?

The final consideration has to do with *single* or *multistage sampling.* The number of stages included in a sampling process is usually dictated by the nature of the population and the sample frame (source of units). For example, sampling fund-raising letters in a printing process is typically a single-stage process; items are randomly selected from the production process (Figure 11.1).

In a comprehensive survey of consumer attitudes across a large area, a multistage process will often be used. Multistage sampling is the method of choice for needs analysis studies when sampling large populations and with population elements disbursed over a wide area. This type of multistage sampling would involve the following three-stage process.

1. The first stage is random selection of census tracts in the various socioeconomic sections of the region.
2. This is followed by the random selection of residential blocks in the selected census tracts.
3. The third stage is the random selection of individual households in each selected block.

Figure 11.1   **Three Stages in a Multistage Sampling Process**

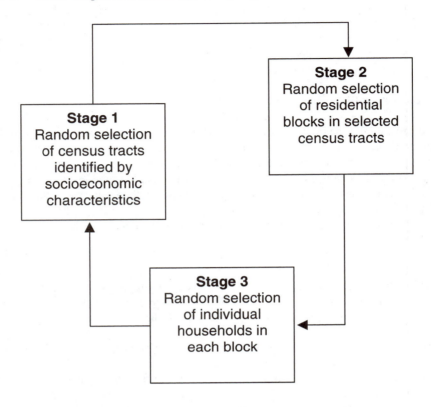

SAMPLE BIAS AND SAMPLING ERROR

The ultimate objective of all sampling is to select a set of elements from a population in such a way that the measurements of that set of elements accurately reflect the same measurements of the population from which they were selected. A number of potential pitfalls exist to make achieving this objective difficult. Among these are bias and several different types of potential error. These are characterized as *sampling error* and *nonsampling error.* Several types of nonsampling error can occur, including sampling frame error, nonresponse error, and data error.

Sample Bias

Bias in sampling refers to the sampling process itself; it is sometimes referred to *systematic bias.* Bias can be intentional or unintentional. Intentional bias is used when a researcher has a particular point to prove and uses statistics to support the preestablished conclusion. For example, an agriculture decision maker might intentionally select a better piece of ground to show more dramatic yield improvements from a new plant seed.

Unintentional bias can occur as a result of a researcher's best efforts to include relevant elements in the final sample. For example, in decision making to determine whether voters might approve a special bond issue for library construction, the researcher might telephone only registered voters.

This results in a *double* bias. First, it includes only people with telephones, and second, it ignores the library users who have not voted in the past, but would in order to improve the library system. The best way to avoid or reduce any and all bias is to maintain random selection procedures.

Sampling Error

Sampling error occurs when a sample with characteristics that do not reflect the population is studied. It is almost impossible to specify a sample that exactly matches the parameters of a given population. The results of a second sample will not exactly match the first. Taking more samples will not increase the likelihood of a perfect match.

Two "laws of numbers" affect sampling error. First, the *law of large numbers* suggests that increasing sample size will reduce the size of the sampling error encountered. However, the *law of diminishing returns* also applies to this error reduction method. Recall that to reduce error by half requires making the sample four times as large. Using a statistically efficient sampling plan is clearly the best way to control sampling error.

DEALING WITH NONSAMPLING ERROR

Nonsampling error can result from many different sources. Several of these sources include problems with the *sampling frame,* with subjects' *nonresponse,* and errors in the *data* itself. Errors that occur randomly generally have little impact upon research findings. However, systematic error can have severe impact upon a study. As a result, researchers devote considerable time and effort to controlling nonsampling error. The greatest source of nonsampling error is when members of the sample fail to respond. The best way to control for nonresponse is to increase the size of the sample—a costly fix, at best.

Sampling Frame Error

The sampling frame is the source from which the sample is drawn (such as a list or a telephone directory). If the study is a test of components provided by an outside supplier, the sampling frame is the collected total of all parts provided by the supplier. If the sample is to be drawn from customers who enter a particular facility, the sample frame consists of the actual premises; the population in this example is all persons who enter the facility during the survey period.

For example, a sociologist conducted a study of the attitudes and concerns about terrorism among a group of regional airline passengers. The sampling frame for the study consisted of the list of passengers with reservations to fly on a specific route on a specific day. Individual passengers were randomly selected from those waiting in the boarding lounge before boarding their aircraft.

The key to reducing *sampling frame error* is to start with as complete a sampling frame as possible. If the sampling frame is a list of clients, it should be up-to-date and include everyone. If the sample frame is all the products produced by a given machine, it should include all products produced during all shifts, under the control of all supervisors, over the entire time period in question.

A way to adjust for potential sample frame error has been developed by researchers who gather data by telephone. Increasingly, private telephone numbers are not included in printed telephone directories. To deal with this problem, the survey operators modified their telephone book sample frames to include unknown, nonlisted numbers. In a process that is called *plus-one dialing,* they do this by adding one number to the numbers taken at random from the directory.

Box 11.1
Some Ways to Reduce Data Error

- Ensure that survey instruments (questionnaires) are well prepared, simple to read, and easy to understand.
- Avoid any internal bias (such as the use of leading or value-laden words).
- Properly select and train interviewers to control data-gathering bias or error.
- Use sound editing, coding, and tabulating procedures to reduce the possibility of data-processing error.

Nonresponse Error

Nonresponse error is another problem encountered in survey decision making. When only small proportions of subjects respond, there is a strong probability that the results are not characteristic of the population. This type of error may be reduced through the use of incentives for completing and returning the survey instrument, and through follow-up telephoning, although there is no guarantee error reduction will occur.

Data Error

Finally, *data error* can occur because of distortions in the data collected or from mistakes in data coding, analysis, or interpretation of statistical analysis. Several different ways to reduce data error in research projects are displayed in Box 11.1.

SAMPLING DISTRIBUTIONS

When researchers talk about *sampling distributions,* they are referring to the way a statistic would be distributed if computed for a series of samples taken from the same population. This concept has several uses. First, it provides the researcher a quick estimate of the validity of the results of the study. Second, it enables the researcher to estimate the values of some variable in a population of interest. Third, it produces a value that is associated with determining sample size.

Sampling distributions represent a fundamental concept in statistics (Zikmund 1994). It is sometimes a difficult concept to grasp, however. This is because it refers to a *hypothetical* distribution of something that will never take place: randomly selecting a very large number of samples (such as 50,000 or more) from a specified population, computing a mean for every sample, and then examining the distribution of those means. The mean of all the means is called the *expected value* of that statistic, and the standard deviation of the sampling distribution is the *standard error of the mean.*

When researchers draw two or more random samples of subjects or items from a given population, the statistics computed for each sample will almost always vary. Such variation is natural and expected. Drawing samples from the same population will produce summary measures that are also different from the first sample or samples drawn. Drawing more and more samples will also produce varying measurements. From this point on, assume that the statistic is the mean value on any relevant question, characteristic, or scale item.

If the mean score for each of the group of samples were displayed as a frequency distribution, the individual sample measurements will be distributed in such a way that they would present a picture of a normal, symmetrical distribution. Most of the values would cluster around the center of the range, with smaller and smaller amounts drifting off toward the edges. This pictorial representation of the frequency distribution would be a traditional *bell-shaped curve.* A key requirement of many statistical tests is that the data be normally distributed.

The Sampling Error of the Mean

It is important to remember that the standard error of the mean is only an estimated standard deviation of a hypothetical series of samples. Still, it does provide an indication of how close the sample mean probably is to the mean of the population. It is an estimate of the sampling variability in the sample mean.

For example, in a study of public agency organizational climate, scale items consisted of such statements about the organization as "Red tape is kept to a minimum in this organization." The mean score on this seven-point agreement scale was 3.50; the standard deviation for the sample was 1.512. A standard error of .535 indicated that the sample mean was within a little more than half a point of what could be expected as the mean for the population from which the sample was drawn.

Central Limit Theorem

A rule of statistics called the *central limit theorem* states that as the number of samples drawn from a population gets larger the distribution of the sample statistic will take on a normal distribution. The number of samples necessary for this to occur is about thirty. What is a "normal" distribution? This term describes a frequency distribution that follows a bell-shaped, symmetrical shape. The two sides of the curve are the same, with the *mean* and *median* both falling at the peak of the curve. Distributions that are not symmetrical are said to be *skewed.* Skewed distributions that have fewer values at the high end (right side) of a distribution are said to be *positively skewed,* or *skewed to the right.* When the values taper off toward the left side of the distribution, it is said to be *negatively skewed,* or skewed to the left. Distributions can also have more than one peak (in what is called a *bipolar* distribution).

The central limit theorem applies for all sample statistics, but is usually applied to the value of the mean. The *sampling distribution of the mean* (sometimes referred to as the sampling distribution of the *average*) is nothing more than a distribution of the means of each of the samples that could be drawn from a population. The phrase "could be" is used instead of "is" because this is a theoretical concept; decision makers typically deal with just one sample. The problem at hand is how to know that the distribution of that sample statistic accurately reflects the same measurement that might be found in a census of the population.

No single sample is likely to produce measurements that exactly mirror the population's measurement. In addition, the measurements of another sample taken from the same population will produce values that are different from every other possible sample. The same is true for the third, fourth, fifth and more samples. Researchers are concerned that the measurements of the sample fall within an accepted range of possible values.

SUMMARY

Sampling in public administration research is used because it is more efficient than studying a full population. Sampling can lower the cost and improve the efficiency of measurement activities. Studying a sample rather than an entire population saves time and money. It is also thought to be less destructive of underlying attitudes (the process of measuring may influence future measurements).

The five fundamental considerations of the sampling process result in many different possible combinations in sample design. Sample design is based on these choices: (1) probability or non-probability, (2) single unit or unit clusters, (3) stratified or unstratified, (4) equal unit probability or weighted probability, and (5) single stage or multistage sampling.

Decision makers must take care to avoid introducing bias and sampling or nonsampling error into the sample design and selection process.

Sampling distributions—the way each individual measurement clusters around some statistic—tend to reflect distinct patterns, with most following what is referred to as the *normal distribution*. In a normal distribution, the bulk of the measurements cluster around the mean value, with a few trailing off above and below the mean. When plotted, they appear in the shape of the familiar bell-shaped curve. Most inferential statistics require that the data be from a normal distribution.

According to the *central limit theorem,* as the size of the sample increases, the distribution of the sample measurements tends to take on the shape of normal distribution, whereas small-sample studies may result in data that are not reflective of the parameters of the larger population.

ADDITIONAL READING

Eddington, Eugene, 1987. *Randomization Tests.* New York: Marcel Decker.

Johnson, Janet B., Richard A. Joslyn, and H.T. Reynolds. 2001. *Political Science Research Methods.* Washington, DC: CQ Press.

Schwab, Donal P. 1999. *Research Methods for Organizational Studies.* Mahwah, NJ: Lawrence Erlbaum.

12

WRITING QUESTIONS AND DEVELOPING QUESTIONNAIRES

Researchers use several different approaches when gathering primary data in quantitative research studies; they may collect data by observing subjects and counting their overt acts of behavior, or they may ask people to respond to fixed or open-ended questions. Questionnaires—also called *instruments*—are the most popular way to gather primary data. It has been estimated that questionnaires are used in 85 percent or more of all quantitative research projects. They are particularly appropriate when the research problem calls for a *descriptive* design.

Regardless of what method is used to gather quantitative data, the researcher must first prepare or acquire either a list of topics to cover or questions to ask. The observation method uses what is known as a *schedule*, which is nothing more than a list of items, events, characteristics, or behaviors that the observer wants to be sure are counted. A questionnaire is a specific set of closed or open-ended questions that respondents must answer. This chapter will discuss the process of questionnaire preparation, including the nature, limitations, and wide variety of ways to write survey questions. Observation methods will be discussed in some detail in the qualitative methods section.

Questionnaires can be used to gather information about large numbers of respondents (populations) and from small groups (samples). Most of the time, public administration research is conducted with *samples*. The sample method used most often is the *probability* or random sample. Samples that are representative of the population are surveyed; the researcher then makes inferences about the population from the sample data. Within some known margin of error, the sample *statistics* are assumed to be a reflection of the population's *parameters*. Careful planning and construction of the questionnaire is, therefore, a critical step in research.

ADVANTAGES OF USING QUESTIONNAIRES

Questionnaires have many advantages. The greatest of these is the considerable *flexibility* of the questionnaire. Questionnaires can be custom designed to meet the objectives of almost any type of research project. Researchers may also purchase the rights to employ many different types of prepared questionnaires. These are instruments that have been developed by other researchers and thoroughly tested with a variety of different samples. They have been applied enough times to warrant strong belief in their ability to effectively measure some phenomenon. These prepared questionnaires are called *standardized instruments* and may be ordered from a wide variety of test catalogs. Reference librarians can direct the researcher to many different lists of these standardized instruments.

Despite the ease of using prepared instruments, most researchers develop their own questionnaires. Questionnaires can be designed to gather information from a wide variety of respondents, in many different situations, and for many different purposes. Questionnaires can be short or long, simple or complex, straightforward or branched. They can be rigidly structured or a loosely organized list of topics to discuss. They can be administered face to face, over the telephone, by mail, and over computer networks. With fixed answer forms, respondents' answers are easy to code and tabulate. This can reduce turnaround time and lower project costs.

Questionnaires can be designed to determine what people know, what they think, or how they act or plan to act. They can measure subjects' factual knowledge about a thing or an idea, or they can be used to measure people's opinions, attitudes, or motives for behaving in certain ways. They can be used to measure the frequency of past behaviors or to predict future actions. When subjects are children, people who are unable to read, or people from different cultures, it is possible to substitute pictures or symbols for words as alternate responses.

Because of the flexibility of the questionnaire, there are very few absolute rules to follow in developing the instrument. However, constructing an effective questionnaire does demand a high degree of skill. Questions must be arranged in a logical order; they must be worded in such a way that their meaning is clear to people of all backgrounds, ages, and educational levels. Particular care must be taken when asking questions of a potentially controversial or personal nature so as not to embarrass or offend respondents. Folz (1996, 79–80) has summarized the concerns associated with questionnaire construction this way:

> Know what you want to ask and why you want to ask it; compose clear, unambiguous questions; keep the survey (questionnaire) as brief as possible; and have a plan for analyzing the result before the instrument is administered.

QUESTIONNAIRE CONSTRUCTION PROCEDURE

When preparing a questionnaire, the researcher must follow a systematic procedure in order to make sure that it fulfills three broad objectives (Malhotra 1999). The questionnaire must: (1) successfully gather information that answers each study question, (2) motivate respondents to answer all questions to the best of their ability, and (3) keep all potential error to a minimum.

The seven-step procedure shown in Figure 12.1 has been designed to help in the preparation of effective questionnaires and questions. Because questionnaire construction is as much an art as it is a science, the list should be considered as a guide, rather than a checklist of steps that must be followed in the order presented.

Determine What Information Is Needed

Before any questions are written, the researcher must be absolutely certain that the objectives for the research are clearly spelled out. It is never enough for a researcher to just think that he or she has an idea of what it would be nice to know. Rather, only questions that contribute to the overall research objective should be asked. This begins with an understanding of the scope of the proposed research: Is the research being done to solve a particular problem in a public administration or nonprofit organization, or is it "pure" research designed to identify or test some theory? This is the dichotomy between applied and theoretical research that appears periodically in the literature on public administration research.

Figure 12.1   **The Questionnaire Construction Procedure**

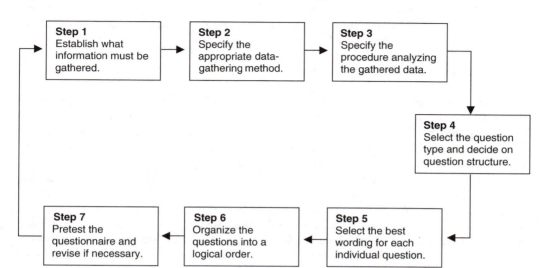

Specify Data-Gathering Method

The three primary ways to collect data with questionnaires are: (1) in-person or *face-to-face* interviews, (2) telephone interviews (also called *voice-to-voice* interviews), and (3) mailed survey instruments that are *self-administered.* In what is the latest method of data collection, data may also be gathered over computer networks. Self-administered questionnaires may be mailed to respondents, handed out in public locations such as shopping malls, or dropped off at homes or offices. Each of these approaches has its own advantages and disadvantages.

Face-to-Face Interviews

The primary advantage of conducting in-person interviews is that they usually make it possible to gather large amounts of information in a relatively short period of time. Also, people who might not otherwise participate in the survey can often be encouraged to do so by a persuasive interviewer or researcher. Another advantage of the personal administration approach is that the data gatherer can often help respondents who might not understand a word or a question. In-person administration is particularly helpful when branching questions are used in the questionnaire. This involves asking people questions based on their response to one or more screening questions. Based on their responses, people are instructed to move to a different section or set of questions.

Although in-person data-collecting methods have many advantages, they also have four major disadvantages:

- They take longer to administer than other methods.
- They tend to be the most costly method of collecting survey data.
- The changing demographic makeup of the country means that fewer adults of working age will be at home during the day.
- Interviewers are subjected to potential personal harm when interviewing takes places in an unsafe location.

One way that researchers get around these problems is by conducting interviews in public places, such as shopping malls or recreational facilities. While this tends to eliminate poor and older citizens from the sample, it does allow a large number of completed questionnaires to be gathered in a very short time.

Telephone Interviews

The major advantages of telephone surveys are (1) the relative speed with which the data can be gathered, (2) their lower cost, and (3) the opportunity for the researcher to ask questions that might not be answered in a face-to-face situation. To reach people at home, most telephone interviews are conducted on weekday evenings or on Saturdays. This allows public administration researchers to use public agency or office telephones after the working day, further cutting the costs of data gathering. Most telephone interviews are conducted from a central location, thus further reducing researcher travel time and its related cost.

The major disadvantages of telephone interviewing are (1) the inability to make eye contact with respondents, (2) not knowing if people with the desired demographic profiles are answering the questions, (3) the limited length of time respondents are willing to give to the interviews, (4) respondents being leery of providing personal information to strangers over the telephone. Respondents may assume that the caller is a telemarketer rather than someone who is conducting legitimate research, or fear that the caller has sinister motives. Finally, no one is as yet aware of the effect the wide use of cellular and car telephones have on response rates for telephone interviewing. Researchers do know that it is becoming increasingly difficult to acquire the desired number of completed instruments in the time allowed for data gathering.

Mailed Questionnaires

Mailing questionnaires is often the least expensive of all data-gathering processes. On the other hand, this method often results in the lowest return rates of all data-gathering methods. Return rates are referred to as response rates when applied to face-to-face and voice-to-voice interviewing. They refer to the number of completed questionnaires received by the researcher. It is important to plan for return rates when planning the sample size. For example, it is not uncommon to achieve return rates of 10 percent or less in a mailed questionnaire, although the typical rate is closer to 25 to 40 percent. This means that for a sample of one hundred, the researcher may have to mail out from 400 to 1,000 survey instruments.

Determine Analysis Procedure

The way that the researcher writes individual questions and develops a questionnaire will directly influence the way that the gathered data will be coded, tabulated, analyzed, and interpreted. Today, computers using readily available, easy-to-use statistical software tabulate almost all survey results. For this reason, most questionnaires are precoded (classification numbers appear beside each question and possible response), making data entry simple and less prone to error. The increasing use of machine-readable answer forms further improves the data entry process.

Coding the answers to open-ended questions can also be done almost entirely in advance. Using responses to a subsample of around twenty instruments from the total number of completed questionnaires typically establishes the most common answers. Major categories can be formed from these response categories and then translated into numerical form for statistical analysis.

Table 12.1

A Classification of Question Types by Content

Cognitive Awareness Stage	Type of Question	Information Acquired
Cognitive stage	Factual Knowledge	The facts about people or things What people know about things
Affective stage	Opinion Attitude Motive	What people say about things What people believe about things Why people act the way they do
Action stage	Behavior	How people act, what they do; how they will react to certain stimuli

Source: Folz 1996.

Select Question Type and Structure

There are many different ways to classify the data produced by different question types. The most common way is by the type of measurements they produce. The four measurement types are *nominal, ordinal, interval,* or *ratio.* Another way data are classified is by the character of the measurement values; that is, the values are *discrete* (as in "yes" or "no" answers) or they are *continuous* (such as incomes, weights, and attitude scale data). A third classification system is based on the form the responses can take; that is, whether the answers are *open-ended* or *close-ended.* A fourth way to classify data and question types is based on the *objective* of the generated response; that is, on the cognitive level of the information produced. Folz (1996) has identified these six broad categories of objective-based questions: *factual, opinion, attitude, motive, knowledge,* and *action* or *behavior* questions. Each question type delivers a different type of information and must be worded in such a way that this objective is achieved.

Table 12.1 displays the question types alongside respondents' level of cognitive activity addressed by each type. These three stages are (1) the *cognitive* (knowledge) stage, (2) the *affective* (attitudinal) stage, and (3) the *action* (or behavioral) stage. Examples of the information each type of question produces is also shown.

Select the Best Wording for Each Question

Very great differences in responses can occur with small variations in the wording of a question. As a result, extreme care must be taken in developing questions. The key things to look for when writing questions are *clarity, brevity, simplicity, precision, bias,* and *appropriateness.*

Clarity

Questions must be worded so that everyone completing the questionnaire understands what is being asked. Each question should address a single topic. Trying to include too much in a question often results in what is called a *double-barreled* question—a question that combines two or more questions into one. They are not only confusing to the respondent, but also to the researcher, who cannot be sure what part of the question generated the response.

Brevity

Questions should always be as short and to the point as possible. Somewhat longer questions can be included with in-person interviews and mail surveys, but shorter questions—less than twenty words—should be used in telephone interviews (Folz 1996). Also, be sure that the questionnaire itself is not too long. A rule of thumb to follow is that interviews should not take longer than an hour or so to complete. Phone surveys should be kept to less than twenty minutes. Mailed, self-administered instruments should be kept to four standard pages or less.

Simplicity

Never ask questions that are complex or difficult to answer. Make sure the question is one that subjects can answer knowledgeably. Use short words and simple sentences. This is not to say that respondents should be given the idea that they are being looked down upon. Rather, focus on words that are in common, everyday use.

Precision

The wording of every question must be as precise as possible (focus, focus, focus!). Never use ambiguous words in the body of the question. Examples of words with ambiguous meanings are "sometimes," "possibly," and "maybe." Also, always make sure that each question asks just one thing.

Freedom from Bias

Avoid asking questions that arouse strong emotions, generate resistance, or result in a refusal to answer. If you must ask these questions, place them at or near the end of the questionnaire, so that they do not result in only partially completed instruments. Such questions will often cause respondents to simply stop answering all questions, resulting in an incomplete instrument.

Do not ask leading questions that direct or influence the response toward one point of view. These, too, will often cause subjects to not respond to the survey.

Large numbers of refusals to answer can greatly influence the results of a survey by introducing what is known as *nonresponse error* or *bias*. Often subjects who do not complete the questionnaire would respond far differently than those who do respond. Thus, not including their responses may color the study results in ways not expected.

Appropriateness

As has been said, be sure that each question is one that needs to be asked. Avoid fishing expeditions where you are trying to produce something interesting that could lead to further research at a later date. Each and every question must relate to the study objectives. Keep in mind that many persons have very strong opinions about what should and shouldn't be asked. Federal privacy laws also confound this issue. This is particularly true with classification or demographic questions. Gender, marital status, ethnicity, income, and the like are potential stumbling blocks in any questionnaire. It is important to remember to only ask such questions if they are critical to the study. It they are not absolutely needed, they are inappropriate and should be left out of the questionnaire.

Figure 12.2   **The Funnel Approach to Questionnaire Structure**

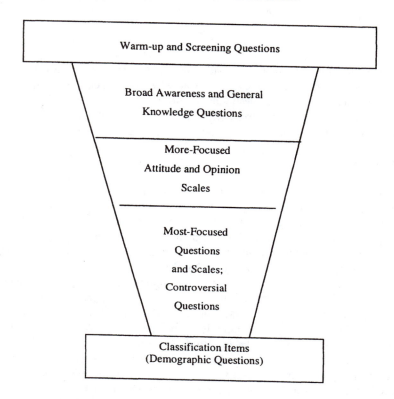

Organize Questions into a Logical Order

The sequence of items in a questionnaire can also unintentionally influence or bias answers to questions that occur later in the instrument (an item is just another word for a question). Therefore, the researcher needs to carefully organize the questionnaire in such a way that subjects are encouraged to follow through with answers to all questions.

Questions are usually arranged in an order that begins with the broad and easy-to-answer questions placed before the more focused, in-depth questions. The latter often require a significant effort on the part of the subject to answer. If the task is too difficult, respondents will often skip the question (Oskamp 1977).

Every questionnaire is composed of five distinct parts: (1) the title and identification of the survey's sponsors, (2) instructions to respondents, (3) warm-up questions, (4) the body of the survey, and (5) classification questions (see Figure 12.2).

Title, Purpose, and Sponsor Identification

Questionnaires should have a title; they should indicate the purpose of the survey, including how the information will be used. The public likes to know who is sponsoring the survey and to know that individual anonymity is guaranteed. These items should all be included at the top of the first page of the questionnaire, although in mail surveys it is also acceptable to include some of this information in a cover letter attached to the questionnaire.

Instructions

Instructions are particularly important for self-administered questionnaires. They should be clear and easy to follow. Care must be taken to clearly spell out what is expected of the respondent. It is also a good idea to introduce early in the questionnaire information about potential points of confusion that might appear later, such as who is expected to answer sections of questions after a screening or branching point. These instructions should be repeated right before the branching occurs.

Warm-up Questions

These are simple, easy-to-answer questions that subjects can answer quickly and with a minimum of effort. They are often dichotomous or, at most, simple multiple-choice questions. These are usually questions designed to discern factual or knowledge information; they seldom dive right into gathering attitudinal data. Items in this section of the questionnaire are often *screening* questions—that is, questions to determine whether the respondent qualifies as a primary target subject. Examples of screening questions are shown in Box 12.1.

The objective of this section is to ease respondents into the questionnaire and to bring them to a level of comfort with the questions and the question-answering process. Therefore, questions that are potentially contentious, controversial, or personal in nature should never be included early in the instrument. The best place for potentially controversial questions is right after the body of the questionnaire and just before the classification questions.

In the past, some researchers have tried to use warm-up questions that have no connection whatsoever to the study, but were asked only in an attempt to capture subjects' interest in the survey process. There have not been any convincing reports in the literature on the effectiveness of this ploy, however. Because of the already-existing difficulty of gaining subjects' willingness to participate in yet another survey, it is probably a good idea not to waste a question this way. Researchers are encouraged to stick to the point and focus all their attention on gaining meaningful data.

Body of the Questionnaire

This is where the most important questions should be placed. Again, the easiest of these questions should appear before the more difficult or complex questions. The questions should be placed in a logical order that does not require the respondent to leap from one idea to another. When changes in direction are necessary, a line or two of additional instructions or words calling the shift to the respondent's attention should be considered.

The first third of this section is sometimes used as a transition section between the introduction and ultimate core section of the questionnaire. Researchers use this section of the questionnaire to ask questions to determine subjects' awareness of the survey issue. Other questions can serve to test their knowledge of component factors, indicators, and possible causal factors. These are usually broad questions that help build an overall view of the study for the researcher.

In the second third of the instrument, researchers often employ more focused attitude, opinion, or other types of scales—*if* scales are included in the design. Because they often require the subject to *think* about the question before answering, this is often where nonresponse error creeps into the survey. Another type of question that is sometimes included in either the second or last third of the

---

Box 12.1
Examples of Screening Questions

1. Do you consider yourself to be a Democrat or a Republican voter?
    Democrat   ☐
    Republican   ☐

2. Do you drive your personal car to work more than three times a week?
    Yes   ☐
    No   ☐

3. Do you own a horse?
    Yes   ☐
    No   ☐

---

body of the instrument is for gathering what is called *lifestyle* information. These data are often grouped together into a category of information called *psychographics*. Lifestyle information is used to develop a more in-depth profile of the respondents, adding *attitude, opinion, value,* and *activity* information to the traditional demographic profile.

The final third of the body of the questionnaire is where the most focused questions should be placed, as should all potentially controversial or personally embarrassing questions. The reason for this placement is that while subjects might skip a threatening question because it appears near the end of the questionnaire, they will have already provided answers for the bulk of the instrument. Questionnaires that are mostly completed are almost as valuable as those that are answered completely.

Classification Items

Classification items are questions that enable the researcher to describe the sample in some detail and to compare the responses of one or more subgroups of subjects with responses of other subgroups. Classification information is sometimes referred to as demographic data because it usually consists of demographic statistics about the subjects themselves.

These data are, indeed, important to the research results, but not as critical as the information contained in the body of the questionnaire. This is because researchers are seldom interested in any one subject's responses, but instead want to know the mean (average) scores for the entire group. Thus, missing a little classification data does not render the instrument completely useless.

Pretest and Revise the Questionnaire

Every questionnaire should be pretested on a group of subjects that as closely as possible reflect the same characteristics as the study sample. This is the critical debugging phase of questionnaire construction. No matter how many times the researcher or members of the research team go over the instrument, some problems are almost sure to surface. Typographical errors and misspellings are the least of these potential problems.

People in a career path will often share a particular sense of meanings for words and phrases that are not likely to be shared by everyone else. Thus, subjects who share the experience and characteristics of the study sample, not the research team, must look at question wording. The best way to do this is to administer the questionnaire to a random sample of subjects from the population of interest. The results from questionnaire pretests should not be included with the findings of the final study sample.

WRITING QUESTIONS

Responses to questions produce what are called *raw data*. Only when coded, tabulated, and interpreted does raw data become information. The way in which questions are worded and structured influences the way responses will be coded, tabulated, and interpreted. Questions may be written in many different ways; they may include a limited set of responses from which the respondent must choose (closed-ended), or they may allow respondents to provide answers freely and in their own words (open-ended).

Most survey questions used in descriptive research designs are closed-ended. These questions force respondents to choose from only those alternatives provided by the researcher. While this results in survey instruments that tend to be more objective than open-ended questions, it can also work as a disadvantage. Closed-end questions force subjects into using the same ideas, terms, and alternatives that the researcher uses—thus following the potential bias of the researcher (Oskamp 1977). Open-ended questions are far more difficult to code and tabulate than are closed-ended questions. Therefore, open-ended questions are used most often in a small sample, exploratory research design, or as a component in an otherwise completely qualitative design.

Open-Ended Questions

Open-ended questions can be divided into two broad types: *completely unstructured response* and *projective techniques*. Unstructured response questions are entirely the subject's own responses to a question. The researcher provides no clues or direction for the response, although subsequent questions may probe for more information. The subject may answer the question in any way desired, with a short or a long answer, and with or without qualifying statements. Projective techniques also allow subjects to respond to some stimuli in their own words. The stimulus can be words, pictures, or symbols. The questions are structured in such a way that the respondent unconsciously *projects* hidden feelings or attitudes into the response. It is believed that in this way projective questions can produce answers that might not otherwise surface.

Five different types of projective techniques are used in social and administrative science research. These are: (1) association, (2) construction, (3) completion, (4) ordering, and (5) expressive techniques.

1. *Association Techniques.* With association techniques, subjects are asked to react to a particular stimulus, such as a word, an inkblot, or other symbol, with the first thoughts or ideas that come to mind. The technique is believed to be a good way to discern the underlying values that certain words or symbols convey.

2. *Construction Techniques.* With construction techniques, subjects are asked to create a story, either about themselves or others, or to draw a self-portrait. The idea is that even though subjects are not told that the story is about them, their underlying values and attitudes will be reflected in the general sense of the story.

3. *Completion Techniques.* These techniques require the subject to finish an already started stimulus, such as a sentence or a picture. In the sentence completion version, subjects

are asked to finish the sentence with any statement that they wish. The rationale for this approach is that the subjects' responses will not emerge from a vacuum; rather, the words chosen for the sentence completion will reflect the subjects' subconscious attitudes.

In the picture version of this process, the subjects view a photograph or a drawing of two characters. One of the characters is portrayed making a statement. Subjects are asked to put themselves in the other character's shoes and respond in the way that the second character would. Again, the belief is that without consciously doing so, the subject will interject his or her own feelings or opinions into the created response.

4. *Ordering Techniques.* Also called classifying or choice techniques, these require the subject to arrange a group of stimuli into some order or to choose one or more items from a group of items. The item(s) selected are supposed to be most representative of the idea or thought involved. This method can also measure what is known as *salience,* which is another way of indicating the importance that a respondent places on each of the items.

5. *Expressive Techniques.* In these techniques, subjects are asked to creatively express themselves in some way, such as by drawing a picture or cartoon or by finger painting. The method is often used in conjunction with the construction technique. The two are considered to reinforce each other. The picture will reveal an underlying attitude, with the subject's description of the events or components of the picture often indicating salience.

It is important to recognize that projective techniques require skilled and empathetic interpretation that goes far beyond the abilities of most students of public administration. On the other hand, in the hands of a trained professional, they can and do provide valuable information that might not otherwise surface in a traditional, scale-driven attitudinal research study.

Closed-End Questions

Closed-end questions can be organized into two broad classes: *structured answer* and *scales.* There are two types of structured answer questions: dichotomous and multichotomous (multiple choice). Structured answer questions are used for the warm-up, introductory, and classification portions of the questionnaire, while scales are more commonly found in the body of the instrument.

Structured Answer Questions

Structured answer questions are the easiest type to write and easiest for respondents to answer. There are two types of structured answer questions: *dichotomous* and *multichotomous.* For both types, the data provided is *discrete* (also known as *categorical data*).

Dichotomous questions require respondents to select from just two alternative answers. Examples include gender (female/male), behavior (do/do not), intentions (will/will not), status (employed/unemployed), and any number of such two-alternative answer forms. Multichotomous, or multiple-choice, questions allow for more than two possible answers. Figure 12.3 shows examples of dichotomous and multichotomous questions that were taken from a public safety agency survey of organizational climate and culture.

Figure 12.3 **Examples of Dichotomous and Multichotomous Questions**

63.	Where do you work most of the time?	Field [2]	Jail [1]			
64.	Your gender:	Male [2]	Female [1]			
65.	Years with the department:	1-5 [5]	6-10 [4]	11-15 [3]	16-20 [2]	20+ [1]

66.	Highest level of education you have attained:	Graduate work or degree [6]	4-year college degree [5]	2-year college degree [4]	Some college [3]	High school graduate [2]	Not a HS graduate [1]

67.	Do you have supervisory responsibility?	Yes [2]	No [1]

Source: McNabb, Sepic, and Barnowe 1999.

DEVELOPING AND USING SCALES

The types of scales that are used most often in public administration research are: attitude scales, importance scales, rating scales, and readiness-to-act scales. Attitude scales are used most often in public administration and nonprofit organization research. An attitude has been defined as a *relatively enduring, learned disposition that provides motivation to respond in a consistent way toward a given attitude object* (Oskamp 1977). Public administrators are interested in people's attitudes for any number of reasons:

- Voters' attitudes toward candidates and issues directly influence the outcome of elections.
- Citizens' attitudes influence the formation and adoption of public policies.
- People's attitudes influence their behavior and the consistency of that behavior.
- Attitudes determine group support for issues and programs.

Many different types of scales have been developed for measuring attitudes. The attitude scale methods that are used most often are (1) Thurstone scales, (2) Likert scales, (3) semantic differential rating scales, and (4) a related semantic differential approach, the Stapel scale.

Thurstone Scales

The Thurstone scale is as much a method as it is a scale. More formally known as "Thurstone's Method of Equal-Appearing Intervals," it was developed in the late 1920s as a way of measuring the precise amount of difference between one subject's attitudes and another subject's.

With the Thurstone process, the researcher collects one hundred or more opinion statements about a subject. These should be positive, negative, and neutral. The next step is to have a large number of "informed judges" rate the degree to which each statement is favorable or unfavorable. Judges then sort the statements into eleven equally spaced categories based on this favorable/unfavorable continuum. When judges disagree widely about a statement, it is discarded.

The remaining statements are then assigned scale values based on the median favorable value assigned by the panel of judges. The statements with highest panel agreement are then included in a final attitude scale that is administered to the sample of interest. While Thurston's method does a good job of scale development, the fact that it is so time-consuming and tedious is the reason it is seldom used outside of the laboratory or classroom.

Likert Scales

By far the most favored attitude-measuring tool in use today is the Likert scale, which was developed by Rensis Likert in the early 1930s. Likert scales do not require a panel of judges to rate the scale items. The researcher prepares a pool of items—each item is an individual statement—that express an opinion about a subject or one of its contributing aspects. While the resulting data are most appropriately considered to be *ordinal-level data,* some researchers treat them as *interval-level* and process Likert data with interval-scale statistics. O'Sullivan and Rassel (1995, 274) summarized the argument this way:

> The level of measurement of a Likert-type index is ordinal. The items do not really measure the quantity of a characteristic, but we can use the items to rank the cases. However, by adding together the numbers assigned to the response categories for each item, we are treating the measurement as if it were interval. This practice allows us to use more statistical techniques for analysis. Many analysts feel that treating Likert-type scales as if they were interval measures provides more advantages than disadvantages.

The objective of the Likert scale is to measure the extent of subjects' agreement with each item. The extent is measured on a five-point scale: *Strongly Agree, Agree, Undecided, Disagree,* and *Strongly Disagree.* The items are assigned values running from 1 through 5, respectively. Depending on how the statements are worded (positively or negatively, approving or disapproving), the researcher can use low mean scores to equate with either positive or negative attitudes, while using high mean scores to reflect the opposite attitude.

Researchers are typically not concerned with subjects' responses to any one item on the scale. Rather, an attitude score is established by summing all ratings of items in that scale. Reverse scoring must be used when items are stated in positive and negative terms are used together in the same Likert scale. An example of a six-item Likert-type scale designed to measure subjects' attitudes or opinions about one aspect of an organization's climate are displayed in Figure 12.4. Responses are coded in reverse order for the first two questions in that scale. Because low scores are assigned to negative attitudes, agreeing with the statement in question 18 is coded with low values. Question 19 is assumed to register a positive attitude toward the company. Positive attitudes are assigned with high values. Hence, agreeing with the statement is coded with high values.

Individual attitude statements to be used as statements or items in the Likert scale are often generated by an exploratory study that uses a series of in-depth interviews with key informants in the organization or sample.

Semantic Differential and Stapel Scales

Two additional scales are often used to measure attitudes and opinions. These are the *semantic differential* and its close relative, the *Stapel scale.* Semantic differential scales are pairs of oppos-

Figure 12.4   Likert-Type Statements to Measure Attitudes Toward Risk in an Organization

	Very Definitely Describes ⇓						Does Not Describe ⇓
18. The philosophy of our management is that in the long run we get ahead fastest by playing it slow, safe, and sure.	[$_1$]	[$_2$]	[$_3$]	[$_4$]	[$_5$]	[$_6$]	[$_7$]
19. You get rewarded for taking risks in this organization.	[$_7$]	[$_6$]	[$_5$]	[$_4$]	[$_3$]	[$_2$]	[$_1$]
20. Decision making in this organization is too cautious for maximum effectiveness.	[$_1$]	[$_2$]	[$_3$]	[$_4$]	[$_5$]	[$_6$]	[$_7$]
21. You won't get ahead in this organization unless you stick your neck out and take a chance now and then.	[$_7$]	[$_6$]	[$_5$]	[$_4$]	[$_3$]	[$_2$]	[$_1$]
22. We do things by the book around here; taking risks is strongly discouraged.	[$_1$]	[$_2$]	[$_3$]	[$_4$]	[$_5$]	[$_6$]	[$_7$]
23. We have to take some pretty big risks occasionally to make sure the organization meets its objectives.	[$_7$]	[$_6$]	[$_5$]	[$_4$]	[$_3$]	[$_2$]	[$_1$]

Low values = negative attitudes; high values = positive attitudes. Positive statements are reverse scored.

Source: McNabb, Sepic, and Barnowe 1999.

ing adjectives, with spaces between each for subjects to mark their opinion. A seven-point scale typically separates the adjectives. Subjects are asked to make a personal judgment about a characteristic or a complete concept. For example, the adjective pairs can be used to help researchers build a picture of how subjects rate the service they receive at a particular agency. They could also pertain to the agency as a whole.

For example, subjects could be asked to rate the overall effectiveness of a proposed public service announcement for an AIDS prevention campaign. Subjects are asked to read the brochure and then rate it on a five-point scale, checking the boxes that most closely match their perceptions of the document. Figure 12.5 shows the paired adjectives.

The Stapel scale is almost identical to the semantic differential scale except that only *one* of the polar adjectives is used instead of both; they are *unipolar* rather than *bipolar.* In practice, many researchers consider the points on both the semantic differential and Stapel scales to be equidistant, thus providing interval-level data. However, because the assigned differences are arbitrarily assigned, other researchers feel that the scales only provide ordinal data. This conflicting interpretation has resulted in a reduction in the use of the scales in social and administrative science research.

Other types of scales include *ordinal* (ranked) *importance scales, comparative and noncomparative rating scales,* and *ratio scales.* Figure 12.6 (see page 150) displays example questions to illustrate these several types of scales.

Figure 12.5 **An Example of an Unbalanced Semantic Differential Scale**

Clear	[ ]	[ ]	[ ]	[ ]	[ ]	Confusing
Simple	[ ]	[ ]	[ ]	[ ]	[ ]	Difficult
Quick	[ ]	[ ]	[ ]	[ ]	[ ]	Slow
Complete	[ ]	[ ]	[ ]	[ ]	[ ]	Incomplete
Realistic	[ ]	[ ]	[ ]	[ ]	[ ]	Phony
Valuable	[ ]	[ ]	[ ]	[ ]	[ ]	Worthless

SUMMARY

Researchers use two different approaches when gathering primary data in quantitative research studies; they may collect data by *observing* and counting overt acts of behavior, or they may use a *questionnaire* to generate responses to specific questions.

Questionnaires are the most popular way to gather primary data. They are particularly appropriate when the research problem calls for a *descriptive* design. Questionnaires have many advantages. The greatest of these is their *flexibility*. Questionnaires can be custom designed to meet the objectives of almost any type of research project.

Seven steps are followed in questionnaire construction: (1) establish what information is needed, (2) specify the data-gathering method, (3) specify procedures for analyzing the data, (4) select question type and structure, (5) select the best wording for each question, (6) organize the question in a logical order, and (7) pretest and revise the questionnaire, if necessary.

Open-ended questions can be divided into two broad types: *completely unstructured response* and *projective techniques.* Unstructured response questions are entirely the subject's own responses to a question. Projective techniques allow subjects to respond to some stimuli in their words. The stimulus can be words, pictures, or symbols. The questions are structured in such a way that the respondent unconsciously *projects* hidden feelings or attitudes into the response. Five different types of projective techniques are used in public administration research: association, construction, completion, ordering, and expressive techniques.

There are two types of closed-end questions: *structured answer* (dichotomous and multiple choice) and *scales.* Structured answer questions are used for warm-up, introductory, and classification portions of the questionnaire; scales are usually found in the body of the questionnaire. The types of scales used most often in public administration research are attitude scales, importance scales, rating scales, and readiness-to-act scales.

Many different types of scales have been developed for measuring attitudes. The attitude scale methods that are use most often today are Thurstone scales, Likert scales, semantic differential rating scales, and their related approach, the Stapel scale.

ADDITIONAL READING

Alreck, Pamela L., and Robert B. Settle. 1995. *The Survey Research Handbook.* 2nd ed. Boston: Irwin McGraw-Hill.
DeVellin, Robert F. 1991. *Scale Development: Theory and Applications.* Newbury Park: Sage.

Figure 12.6   **Examples of Importance and Rating Scales**

I. Ordinal Importance Scales

1. Please rank each of the following public transportation methods in terms of how important it is to reducing traffic congestion in this region. (Use 1 for most important, 2 for next in importance, etc. Do not give any two items the same value.)

_____ Freeway buses
_____ Light-rail system
_____ Vehicle ferryboats
_____ Passenger-only ferryboats
_____ Heavy rail commuter trains
_____ Commuter pool vans

2. In your opinion, would you say that patient waiting time at the veteran's hospital you normally visit is:

_____ Shorter than most
_____ About the same as most
_____ Longer than most
_____ The longest I have ever encountered

II. Comparative Rating Scale (single attribute)

1. Compared with Microsoft® Excel™, how do you rate SPSS® in ease of use? (Check the appropriate bin)

| Much
Easier | | | | About
the Same | | | | Much
Harder |

|___|___|___|___|___|___|___|___|___|
 1   2   3   4   5   6   7   8   9

III. Noncomparative Rating Scale

1. How would you rate this brochure on its ability to inform you of the disadvantages of using tobacco products? (Circle the appropriate number)

Very   About   Very
Good   Average   Poor

  1   2   3   4   5   6   7   8   9

PART 4

QUANTITATIVE RESEARCH METHODS

13

SUMMARIZING DATA WITH DESCRIPTIVE STATISTICS

Two types of statistics are used in quantitative research: *descriptive* statistics and *inferential* statistics. Some descriptive statistics are found in almost every type of research report. Descriptive statistics are used for two major purposes. First, they are used to *summarize* a data set. Second, they are used to *numerically describe* sample units, phenomena, and other variables of interest. Inferential statistics, on the other hand, are used to make assumptions or inferences about populations from the measurements taken of sample units drawn from the population. This chapter focuses on the four major descriptive statistics used in social and administrative science research and includes an introduction to the idea of data distributions.

CONVERTING RAW DATA TO STATISTICS

Neither researchers nor administrators have much use for unprocessed, unorganized collections of raw numbers. Considered in bulk, unprocessed data are, at best, coarse measurements. The data must be brought into some sort of order before their meaning can be found. This occurs in the series of six phases as shown in Figure 13.1. In the first phase, the researcher decides upon an appropriate measurement program. This entails preparing items and questions that produce the most powerful data possible, commensurate with the objectives of the study. In the second phase, the data are gathered using questionnaires or schedules in personal interviews, by telephone, or by mailed surveys. After the data are gathered, the third phase of computer coding and tabulating (counting) all responses occurs. This key organization and structuring phase is followed by the first of two important statistical procedures: the fourth phase is the production of frequency counts and percentage distributions of all responses; the fifth phase is calculation of the desired types of summary statistics needed to describe the subjects and their responses. In the sixth and final phase, the researcher prepares a written report interpreting statistical information produced by whatever statistical software is used.

SUMMARY STATISTICS

Researchers use four different types of descriptive statistics to convey summary information (Lang and Heiss 1990):

Figure 13.1   **A Model of the Phases of Descriptive Statistics Data Processing**

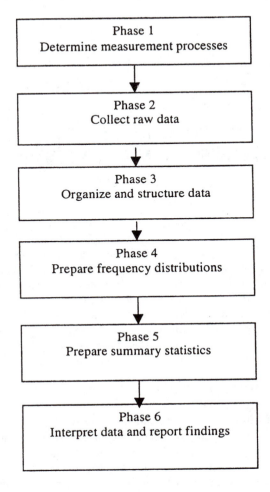

- Measures of central tendency
- Measures of variability
- Measures of relative position
- Measures of correlation

These four types of measures make it possible to reduce a large data set down to a few meaningful numbers that everyone can understand. These numbers can then provide essential information about the internal structure of the raw data.

An example of how the first three of these summary measurements can be used in public and nonprofit organization applications is in the records of the performance characteristics of a sandbag-filling machine used by a state roadway maintenance crew. The quality-assurance processes employed by the department include measuring the performance of the filling equipment by the periodic weighing of samples of filled bags. Since it is unlikely that the weights of filled sandbags are always exactly identical, performance will typically fall within some *range* of values. Wet sand might partially clog the filling equipment one day, with dry sand flowing smoothly the next day. Spillage might occur; an operator might miss an equipment breakdown; or any other random factor may have an effect on the process.

The production manager will want to know the average weight of filled bags and whether the range of bag weights falls within what roadway engineers have established as the acceptable upper and lower weight limits. The manager might also want to know what value appears most often and how widely the filled sandbags vary within the range.

MEASURES OF CENTRAL TENDENCY

The main purpose for measurements of central tendency is to identify the value in the data set that is most typical of the full set. This "typical" value may then be used as a summary value. Several different numbers can be used for this purpose. The easiest way to quickly summarize a set of measurements is to identify the most typical value in the set (sometimes called the "most representative score"). Four types of measurements used to communicate central tendency:

- The arithmetic mean
- The median
- The mode
- The geometric mean

Calculating the Mean

The term *central tendency* refers to a point in a data set that corresponds to a typical, representative, or central value. The measurement used most often for this is the *arithmetic mean*. Means are only valid for use with data that are ratio or equidistant interval (i.e., quantitative). Attitude scales used by decision makers are a typical example of an application where a mean (or "average") score for the total sample conveys far more information than the response of any one subject in the sample. A mean score of 1.2 on a 5-point scale item, with low scores equating with negative attitudes and high scores with positive attitudes, clearly suggests an interpretation for the attitude held by members of this sample.

The Arithmetic Mean

Sometimes referred to as the "average of all scores," the arithmetic mean is the number arrived at by adding up all the values of a variable and then dividing by the number of items or cases in the set. It is used when the distribution of scores is fairly symmetrical about the center value. When plotted, a symmetrical distribution may produce the typical bell-shaped curve.

Mean scores or values are generally not valid for use with categorical (i.e., nominal and ordinal) measurements, although most public administration researchers have accepted use of the mean with certain ordinal data. Say, for example, that a state natural resources agency conducts a series of meetings with outdoor sportsmen to establish preferences for a proposed salmon protection program. Citizens are asked to rank five different programs in their order of preference. The agency wants to know which of the programs has the best chance of being accepted across the state. Normally, a "mean rank" value would not be an appropriate statistic for these categorical

---

Box 13.1
Key Statistical Notations and Their Meanings

N = the total number of cases in a population
n = the total number of cases in a sample
μ = the mean of a population (pronounced "mew")
$\overline{X}$ = the mean for a sample (pronounced "X-bar")

---

data. However, establishing mean ranks is a requirement for certain nonparametric statistical tests. Thus, mean rank values are encountered on some statistical program printouts and are reported by some researchers. It is more scientifically accurate, however, to use the mode rather than a mean in such cases.

In an example with nominal data, subjects are asked to indicate their occupation from a list of eight or nine categories. The number of responses for each category is informative; the modal category is the one that was checked most often. Determining the "mean" occupational category is nonsense.

Frequencies and means are of interest for both populations and samples. Their computation is similar, but separate notation or symbols differentiate them. Box 13.1 lists differences in notation for these key concepts.

The Median

The *median* is the halfway point in a set of numbers. Half of the values are above the median value; half fall below that point. The median should be used when the scores are not symmetrical, such as when they are closely grouped but with a few very high or very low scores. These very high values might have a disproportionate influence on the arithmetic mean.

The median is appropriate for all data types, but is particularly useful with ranking (ordinal) data, or when the data set contains *outliers*—extreme values that could disproportionately influence the mean. Because the median deals with structure or order in the data set, it can be used with ordinal and interval/ratio data, but it is meaningless with nominal (categorical) data.

For a small-sample example of how the median is computed, assume that during the first half-hour of a fund-raising event, a public broadcast radio station received donations in the following amounts: $25, $18, $20, $22, and $100. The mean donation value is the total amount divided by the number of donations, or $185 divided by 5 ($185/5), or $37. It should be obvious that a mean of $37 is misleading, because the $100 donation (an *outlier*) unduly influences the result. A more meaningful measure of location in this case would be the median, which is $22. This is arrived at by rearranging the data in ascending order ($18, $20, $22, $25, and $100), followed by selecting the value that falls in the center. Two donations fall below $22, and two fall above $22. For larger data sets, the median can be computed by subtracting 1 from the total number of cases and then dividing by 2. The formula for computing the median is:

$$\text{Median} = (n-1)/2$$

The Mode

The *mode* is the value that appears most often in a data set. It is the value with the greatest frequency of occurrence. The mode can be used for a quick estimate of the typical or representative score.

The mode is the only measurement that makes sense when dealing with nominal-level variables. It is defined as the value that appears most often in a collection of all counts for a variable. Modes are particularly important when processing scale data; for example, data produced with five- or seven-point Likert scales.

For example, a focus-group study was conducted with university seniors. Subjects were asked which presidential candidate they preferred. Individual candidates were assigned identifying code numbers ranging from 1 to 4. The final tally of subjects' preferences was: 3, 2, 1, 1, 3, 4, 2, 3, 1, 2, 1, 1, 1. The category value "1" appears most often in the data set: six times. This gives the decision maker the maximum amount of information. Since the numbers represent specific persons and are not quantitative, both the mean and the median clearly are inappropriate measures of location in this example.

Public facilities managers and designers are often interested in the modal distribution. They look at distribution of public-area usage in order to provide appropriate space for heavy- and light-use activities in building designs.

The Geometric Mean

The *geometric mean* is the cube root of the product of all items in the data set. It is particularly appropriate when computing an average of changes in percentages. Not all statistics texts include a discussion of the geometric mean—in fact, few social and administrative science statistics texts today do so. This is a mistake. It has many uses in statistical research applications. There are many instances where a geometric mean is far more appropriate than an arithmetic mean.

An appropriate use of the geometric mean is when a program manager wants to know the average change in operating costs from a series of percentage changes. Say, for example, that an administrator has gathered the following figures for a four-year period and wants to know the overall average percentage change (Table 13.1). The arithmetic mean for the 2002–2005 period is 7 percent ($12 + 7 + 2/3 = 21/3 = 7$). Computing the geometric mean, however, arrives at a more appropriate measure. This mean is computed by multiplying each percentage change in sequence; note that each change is the new change plus the base 100 percent (which is the previous value), then determining the root for the cases included (in this case, the cube root):

$$G = \sqrt[3]{(X_1 \times X_2 \times X_3 \times \ldots \times X_n)}$$
$$G = \sqrt[3]{(112 \times 107 \times 102)}$$
$$G = \sqrt[3]{1,234,352}$$
$$G = 6.92\%$$

Table 13.1

Costs in the Portland District, 2002–2005 (in thousands)

	Year			
	2002	2003	2004	2005
Gross ($)	4,000	4,800	4,940	4,890
Change (%)	—	12	7	2

Calculating the Geographic Mean with Excel

Computing the geometric mean is a quick and simple process with Microsoft Excel. The data are arranged in a column array; the GEOMEAN option is then selected from the Function Wizard. Box 13.2 lists the steps to follow.

Because all computations are conducted using the Wizard, the process is easy to complete and provides a geometric mean to four decimal points. The Excel worksheet will look like the material in Table 13.2. As the table reveals, the geometric mean produces a more accurate average rate of cost increase over the period of 6.92 percent, not the 7 percent of the arithmetic mean.

MEASURES OF VARIABILITY

Measurements of variability (sometimes referred to as measures of dispersion) tell the researcher how the individual measurements vary within the set. These statistics include the *range,* the *variance,* and the *standard deviation* of a set of measurements. Percentiles and quartiles are measures

---

Box 13.2

Microsoft Excel Process for Computing the Geometric Mean

- Insert all labels and values into a new worksheet. Cell A1 contains the label for column 1, "Variable."
- In cells B1 through E1, insert the years 1993 through 1996. Type the label "Gmean" in cell F1.
- Insert the labels and data. Percentage changes must be written as hundreds (e.g., a 7 percent increase must be inserted as "107.")
- In cell F4, insert an equals sign (=).
- Select the Function Wizard (*fx*). Scroll down to GEOMEAN. "=GEOMEAN" will appear in the worksheet formula bar for that cell.
- Hit Enter to begin the calculation.
- The value for the geometric mean will appear in cell F4, alongside the last inserted percentage change value.

Table 13.2

Excel Worksheet Setup for the Geometric Mean

			Year		
Variable	2002	2003	2004	2005	Gmean
Costs	$4,000	$4,800	$4,940	$4,890	
% Change		112	107	102	106.9221

106.9221 = 6.92%

of relative position and variation in a range. The last topic to be examined in this chapter, correlation, explores the relationships or associations between two or more variables.

Once the administrative decision maker has determined which measure of location is appropriate, the next concern is to determine how the *distribution* of numbers in the data varies around the central value. The questions to answer here are: *How and to what extent are the scores or values different from one another? How can this variability be summarized?* The three most common ways to express variability are the *range,* the *variance,* and the *standard deviation;* these all provide information about the distribution of responses within the range.

The Range

The *range* is the easiest statistic to compute. It is determined by subtracting the lowest value from the highest value in a distribution. It can be misleading, however, and is not used very often by itself. Alone, the range does not take into consideration the actual variation of scores within a distribution; it is, therefore, only a crude approximation of variability. For example, consider the following two sets of data:

<blockquote>
Data Set A: 65, 80, 81, 82, 83, 84, 98
Data Set B: 65, 69, 74, 78, 87, 89, 98
</blockquote>

Both sets have the same range: 98–65 = 33. However, a closer look at the two sets reveals that Set B clearly has more internal variability than Set A. In Set A, five of the seven values are in the low 80s, whereas in Set B, the values are spread across the entire range.

Also limiting the usefulness of the range is the fact that it uses only two values in the set of measurements: the highest and lowest values. As a result, *percentiles* (also called *fractiles*) are often used with the range to give more meaning to this measurement. Percentiles are values below which some proportion of the total scores or observations fall. The most commonly used percentiles divide the data into *quartiles.* These divide the data into roughly 25-percent segments. A quarter of the values fall below the first (or 25 percent) quartile; half are below the second (or 50 percent) quartile; and, three-fourths are below the third quartile. The second quartile value is the same value as the median.

The Variance

The *variance* is an index of how scores or values in a data set vary from their mean or average value. Because it is only an index of variation, interpreting the variance is more art than science. Statistically, the variance is defined as the average of the squared deviation of all values in the range, divided by the number of cases in the data set minus 1. The size of the value is used for subjective interpretation; larger variance values indicate the data are more spread out, whereas smaller variances mean the values are more concentrated around the mean.

Many comprehensive statistics texts distinguish between the variance of a set of scores for a sample and the variance of a set of values for a population. The formulas for computing each are slightly different: for a population, the divisor is *N,* or the total number of subjects in the population. For a sample, the divisor is n−1, or the total number of subjects in the sample minus one. Similar differences occur with the standard deviation of populations and samples. Because researchers and administrators most often deal with samples rather than total populations, the variance for a sample is the statistic used most of the time.

The Standard Deviation

Because the variance is only an index or rough indicator of variation and, thus, somewhat abstract, it is far more common to find variability stated in terms of the *standard deviation* rather than as the variance. The standard deviation is nothing more than the square root of the variance. Rather than a squared value, which suggests or implies variation, the standard deviation is a more exact measurement, stated in exactly the same units as the original data. Because the standard deviation focuses on variation from the true mean, it is probably the most reliable of all the measures of variability and is the one used most often.

As with the variance, standard deviations for samples and for populations vary slightly in their computation formulas. The divisor for the standard deviation of a population is the total number of cases (N); for a sample, it is n−1.

Excel Instructions

Excel's procedures for obtaining both the variance and the standard deviation for samples and populations are included under the STATISTICS function on the main toolbar. The subcommand for the variance of a sample is VAR; for the variance of a population, it is VARP. To obtain the standard deviation for a sample, the function command is STDEV; for the standard deviation of a population, the command is STDEVP.

MEASURES OF RELATIVE POSITION

Measures of *relative position* are used to compare one score against any other score in the data set. Two types of measures can be used for this: *percentiles* and *standard scores.*

Percentiles

Percentiles are points or values used to indicate the percentage of subjects or measurements with scores below that point. Percentiles are very common in education statistics. Every secondary school student's scores on the SATs include an indication of how that set of scores compares with all other students' scores for that test set. Similar applications exist for the Law School Aptitude Test (LSAT), General Management Aptitude Test (GMAT), and the Graduate Record Examination (GRE).

Say, for example, a graduate school applicant scores 580 on the GMAT. This might be reported as falling in the 85th percentile (P_{85}) of all scores for persons taking the test at that time. This means that 85 percent of all applicants had lower scores than the applicant's 580. If the applicant had scored 450, this might have fallen in the 65th percentile (P_{65}), and so on. The 50th percentile (P_{50}) is always the median value for the set of scores.

One important application of quartiles used in organizational research is the *interquartile range.* This includes all values above the first quartile and below the third quartile, which is the same as the range for the central 50 percent of all cases.

Excel Example

Microsoft Excel includes procedures for obtaining any-level percentiles as well as standard quartiles. These functions are incorporated into the STATISTICS toolbox of the Function Wizard (*fx*).

When the Function Wizard is selected, two lists appear in the window. The left-hand list shows categories of functions, one of which is STATISTICS. Within the STATISTICS master-category function are a variety of specific functions. These appear in the right-hand window. Scroll bars must be used to display all the choices available.

The commands for Excel's percentile function are slightly different from most applications. In Excel, a single-digit value between 0 and 1 must be entered. For example, to arrive at the 90th percentile value, the user must enter 9. In most other applications, the values to be entered are a number between 0 and 99.

With the Excel Quartile function, the user may set the QUART value from 0 to 4. Setting it to 1, 2, or 3 will return the corresponding quartile values. Setting it to 0 or 4 will return either the minimum or maximum values in the data set range. Excel uses the median value for the second quartile.

Standard Scores

Standard scores are the original raw scores of the data set that have been statistically transformed in order to establish a common measurement basis for the scores of more than one test. They are often used to compare one score against another.

The standard-score transformation used most often is the *Z-score*. Z-scores are raw scores that have been converted into standard deviation units. The Z-score indicates how many standard deviation units any one score is from the mean score for the total group.

Z-scores also make it possible to compare a single subject's scores on two different scales. For example, the SAT includes a section that tests communication skills and a section that tests mathematics skills. The mean score for each of these components serves as the common reference point for the test population; standard deviations are the common unit used to measure variability in the dataset. Using Z-scores to interpret individual scores gives us a clear picture of how individual results compare with the groups' total scores.

Excel Example

Standardized scores (Z-values) are easy and quick to compute with Microsoft Excel. All that is required is to highlight the data set and then select the STANDARDIZE optional command from the Function Wizard. Steps in the Excel process are listed in Box 13.3. In this example, data from the sandbag-filling process discussed earlier are displayed in Table 13.3. The results of an Excel standardization of the measurements from Table 13.3 are displayed in Table 13.4.

MEASURES OF CORRELATION

Measures of *correlation* are used to indicate the relationships or associations between two or more variables or subjects. Measures of correlation are commonly included in social and administrative science research reports along with other descriptive statistics.

Data are grouped into two categories, depending upon the type of measurements they represent—*discrete* or *continuous*. Nominal and ordinal data are categorical, and, therefore, represent *discrete numbers*. Interval and ratio data can vary within a set of ranges; they are considered to be *continuous*. Except for interval and ratio data, different correlation measures must be used with different data types, as indicated in Table 13.5 (see page 163).

It is important to remember that correlation should be considered as a summary measurement.

Box 13.3

Empirical Rules That Apply to Normal Distributions

1. Approximately 68 percent of all the items will be within one standard deviation of the mean.
2. Approximately 95 percent of the items will be within two standard deviations of the mean.
3. Most items will be within three standard deviations of the mean.

Table 13.3

Weights of Sample Sandbags, A.M. Shift

| Hour | Sandbag weights (in pounds and tenths) | | | | | |
	Sample 1	Sample 2	Sample 3	Sample 4	Sample 5	Sample 6
1	18.4	17.9	18.6	19.0	17.8	18.7
2	18.2	18.0	18.5	19.1	17.4	19.0
3	18.0	18.1	18.4	19.2	16.9	18.8
4	17.9	18.2	18.6	19.1	17.6	18.5

Table 13.4

Standardized Values for Weights of Sandbag Samples, A.M. Shift

Sample	Raw Score	Sample Mean	Sample SD	Z–score (standardized)
1	18.4	18.125	0.22174	1.24022
1	18.2	18.125	0.22174	0.33824
1	18.0	18.125	0.22174	−0.56373
1	17.9	18.125	0.22174	−1.01472
2	17.9	18.050	0.12910	−1.16190
2	18.0	18.050	0.12910	−0.38730
2	18.1	18.050	0.12910	0.38730
2	18.2	18.050	0.12910	1.16190
3	18.6	18.525	0.09570	0.78370
3	18.5	18.525	0.09570	−0.26123
3	18.4	18.525	0.09570	−1.30617
3	18.6	18.525	0.09570	0.78370
4	19.0	19.100	0.08160	−1.22549
4	19.1	19.100	0.08160	0.00000
4	19.2	19.100	0.08160	1.22549
4	19.1	19.100	0.08160	0.00000
5	17.8	17.425	0.38620	0.97100
5	17.4	17.425	0.38620	−0.06473
5	16.9	17.425	0.38620	−1.35940
5	17.6	17.425	0.38620	0.45313
6	18.7	18.750	0.20820	−0.24015
6	19.0	18.750	0.20820	1.20077
6	18.8	18.750	0.20820	0.24015
6	18.5	18.750	0.20820	−1.20077

Table 13.5

Data Types and Their Appropriate Correlation Statistics

Data type	Measurement statistic
Nominal	Chi-square (χ^2)
Ordinal	Spearman's rho
Interval	Pearson's r (r or r^2)
Ratio	Pearson's r (r or r^2)

Values ranging from 0.0 to 1.0 (±) should be considered as indicators of a relationship between the two variables, not as an indication of causality. In this way, they provide the researcher with suggestions for further research involving experiments and causal designs.

UNDERSTANDING DISTRIBUTIONS

It is important at this point for researchers to have some idea about the role of distributions. A *distribution* is a representation of the way that all the measurements for a single variable would look if each were to be entered onto a plot with an *x*- and *y*-axis. Two commonly encountered distributions are *normal* and *asymmetrical* or nonnormal.

Understanding the information contained in a given set of scores or values requires looking at the ways frequency distributions of scores can be distributed around their mean value. We are most familiar with what are called normal distributions. Normal distributions result in the typical bell-shaped curves that enclose a group of individual scores or measurements. Students' test scores often follow this type of distribution. Normal distributions tend to be symmetric, with the mean and median falling near one another at the middle or high point on the curve. The modal value is often close to this point as well.

Most distributions encountered in public administration and social science research tend to be normal. That is, the bulk of the responses or scores cluster around the mean, with the rest trailing off toward both ends. When the distribution of scores does not cluster around the mean, the distribution cannot be described as normal. The information about normal distributions in Box 13.3 has been found to be true so often that it is now accepted as a "rule."

In normal distributions, one standard deviation value above the mean will include close to 34 percent of all the cases in the data set. Similarly, one standard deviation below the mean will include another 34 percent of the sample, for a total of 68 percent falling within a range of plus or minus one standard deviation. Another 27 percent of the cases will be included if one more standard deviation above and below the mean is included. Thus, together some 95 percent of all cases will fall within two standard deviations above or below the mean. Finally, when three standard deviations are included, 99.7 percent of all cases will be included under the curve (this makes the normal distribution *six standard deviations wide*).

Asymmetrical or Nonnormal Distributions

As might be expected, not all distributions are normal. Nonnormal distributions are known as *skewed* or *asymmetrical* distributions, and somewhat different distribution rules prevail. Some have a majority of the values gathered at either the low or the high end of the scale. Other distributions have the great majority gathered at the center; whereas others may bunch up in two or more points or modes. The terms used to describe these nonnormal distributions are *positively skewed, negatively skewed,* and *bimodal distributions.*

Positively skewed distributions have their peak nearer the *left-hand* end of the graph, with the line stretched out toward the lower right-hand corner. Negatively skewed distributions have greater concentrations at the *right-hand* side, with the left line stretched toward the lower left-hand corner. Bimodal distributions have two concentrations of scores, and have curves resembling a two-humped camel's back. Multimodal distributions have three or more concentrations or peaks.

Calculating Descriptive Statistics with Excel

The Microsoft Excel Data Analysis package contained in the Tools subprogram will produce a complete set of summary statistics with very little effort (Box 13.4). Table 13.3 displays the results from the sandbag packaging process example introduced earlier. The descriptive statistics for the total sample are displayed in Table 13.6. To produce complete descriptive statistics for each hourly sample of six packages, click on the box that indicates that the data are arranged in row (each row is a sample of six packages). Table 13.7 displays the complete descriptive results for each of the four samples.

Box 13.4

Procedure for Producing Descriptive Statistics with Excel

1. Arrange the data in a spreadsheet data array.
2. Highlight the data only (do not highlight the row or column labels).
3. Select the Tools option, followed by the Data Analysis option.
4. In the Data Analysis option, select Descriptive Statistics.

Table 13.6

Descriptive Statistics, Total Sample, Produced by Microsoft Excel

Statistic	Value
Mean	18.32917
Standard error	0.118945
Median	18.4
Mode	18.4
Standard deviation	0.582707
Sample variance	0.339547
Kurtosis	0.061706
Skewness	−0.50748
Range	2.3
Minimum	16.9
Maximum	19.2
Sum	439.9
Count	24
Confidence Level (95.0%)	0.246055

Table 13.7

Descriptive Statistics, Individual Samples, Produced by Microsoft Excel

	Hour 1 Sample	Hour 2 Sample	Hour 3 Sample	Hour 4 Sample
Mean	18.4	18.36667	18.23333	18.31667
Standard error	0.191485	0.261619	0.323179	0.2182
Median	18.5	18.35	18.25	18.35
Mode				
Standard deviation	0.469042	0.640833	0.791623	0.534478
Sample variance	0.22	0.410667	0.626667	0.285667
Kurtosis	−1.45702	−0.67794	1.130976	−0.43236
Skewness	−0.26166	−0.34933	−0.78347	0.132737
Range	1.2	1.7	2.3	1.5
Minimum	17.8	17.4	16.9	17.6
Maximum	19	19.1	19.2	19.1
Sum	110.4	110.2	109.4	109.9
Count	6	6	6	6
Confidence Level (95.0%)	0.492228	0.672512	0.830756	0.560899

SUMMARY

Descriptive statistics are used to summarize data and describe samples. Four categories of descriptive information can be used for these purposes: measures of central tendency, measures of variability, measures of relative position, and measures of correlation. All of these statistics can be quickly calculated with Microsoft Excel.

Four measures of central tendency can be used in descriptive statistics. They include the arithmetic mean (also called the average), the median, the mode, and the geometric mean. Three measures of variability are the range, the variance, and the standard deviation.

Two measures of relative position—percentiles and standard scores—make it possible to compare one score against any other in the data set. The most commonly used standard score is the Z-statistic, which states variation in values of standard deviations from the mean. For most data sets, almost all scores fall within plus or minus (±) three standard deviations of the group mean.

Measures of correlation are used to numerically identify the level of relationships between variables. Care must be taken to avoid unsubstantiated cause-and-effect relationships from correlation values.

When plotted, a distribution of individual scores on a variable can take several different shapes. Distributions that take on the shape of a bell are considered to be "normal" distributions. This is an important fact since a required assumption of many statistical tests is that the data approximate a normal distribution. Most distributions will approximate a normal distribution, although some distributions will be positively or negatively skewed; while others will be bi- or multimodal distributions.

ADDITIONAL READING

Brightman, Harvey J. 1999. *Data Analysis in Plain English, with Microsoft Excel.* Pacific Grove, CA: Duxbury Press.

Phillips, John L. 1996. *How to Think About Statistics.* 5th ed. New York: Freeman.

14

USING TABLES, CHARTS, AND GRAPHS

A principal objective of statistics is to communicate information contained in a data set. When first collected, data usually have little or no meaning for the researcher or decision maker. This "raw data" must be put into some kind of order or structure and then grouped together into sets that have logic and meaning. Numbers do not speak for themselves; they acquire meaning only when they are organized in terms of some mutually understood framework (Wasson 1965).

The nature of the data influences the way they are presented. For example, summary data are often presented in the form of a table or a graphic presentation of some kind. There are a number of different ways to present graphic data, including *scatter plots, histograms, bar charts, pie charts,* and *relative frequency polygons*. These graphic representations of data are able to communicate summary statistics, frequency distributions, relative frequencies, and percentage distributions with greater impact than is possible with simple tables.

Graphic displays and other illustrations make reports more readable and more effective in meeting their communications objectives. In the process, they serve two important purposes: First, they make it easier for the researcher to capture the meaning of the data and to more clearly apply the data to the decisions or actions that are going to be made based on the results of the study. Second, they make it easier for the readers to see how the analyst arrived at the conclusions and interpretations presented in the decision-making report.

This chapter describes how researchers structure and display raw data. It describes how graphic representations can be used to display the meaning of a study and improve the quality of their research reports. The chapter begins with a section on how to make sense of ungrouped or raw data and then discusses how to create and use tables, charts, and graphs.

MAKING SENSE OUT OF UNGROUPED OR "RAW" DATA

A collection of raw data by itself typically contains very little information; analyzing and applying order to the data set are required before research results make sense. Tables, charts, and graphs are used for this purpose.

The researcher can construct a *frequency distribution table,* a *stem-and-leaf diagram,* or a *histogram* to give meaning to raw data. Nearly all statistical-analysis reports include frequency distribution tables and/or histograms; stem-and-leaf diagrams are used far less often. Still, stem-and-leaf diagrams often can be more informative than simple frequency tables because none of the underlying data are lost in the analysis; all values are displayed. Histograms present summary data, but they do not display individual values for a class in the way that stem-and-leaf diagrams do.

The first step to take in preparing any graphic tool is to organize and enter the responses for each of the cases into a computer database. There are several different ways to do this, but today data are usually entered into a simple *spreadsheet data file.* In all spreadsheets, each variable is entered as a separate column, with "cases" entered in rows running across the page.

PRESENTING DATA IN TABLES

The first step in the analysis and interpretation of statistical data in a table is to select a set of classes or categories among which the responses will be distributed. Each category must be assigned its own specific code value. For example, the question, "What is your gender?" has two categories of responses, male or female. For computer processing of the data, a numerical value is assigned to each of these categories. "Female" may be assigned the value of 1 and "male" may be assigned the value 2.

In quantitative studies, the selection of categories and assigning of a value for each usually occurs in the questionnaire-preparation phase of the study. In qualitative studies, categories are selected after the data are gathered in a process known as *content analysis.* Closed-end questions use established categories; the researcher subjectively selects categories for open-ended questions after the data are collected.

Once categories and their individual values are established, the data can then be tabulated, with results presented in a table. Tables are sets of numbers and their identifying labels that the researcher has organized in some logical way. These are called *frequency distribution tables,* or simply *frequencies.* Frequency distribution tables are the most commonly used method of bringing order to raw data. When data are arranged in tables, it is easier for anyone reading the report to spot trends, relationships, and differences in the data. Usually, however, the researcher will want more information than just the counts in a frequency distribution table. As a result, tables often also include the *percentage* of the total each class represents. Percentages are easily understood and typically convey more meaning than simple frequencies.

The following issues or concerns should be addressed when arranging data in a table:

1. What is the total number of classes or categories to include?
2. What are the upper and lower limits of each category?
3. What title, captions, headings, and legends should be included?
4. What additional explanatory numbers should be included (such as the relative percentage each number of occurrences represents, the percentage of each class when there is missing data, etc.)?

Establishing Categories or Classes

The total number of categories or classifications that cover all possibilities is called a *category set.* The number of classes or categories in the set depends on the purpose of the researcher. Simple decisions require less precision in the measurement than do more critical decisions. For example, decisions that involve spending large sums of public money, or that have the potential for loss of life if the wrong decision is made, will require far greater precision than decisions that deal with routine activities.

The number of categories or classes selected for tables is influenced by the nature of the data. For example, dichotomous data (male–female, yes–no, pass–fail, etc.) requires two and only two classes. With multichotomous data, more classes must be selected (*multichotomous* means more

Table 14.1

Daily Permit Application Totals for Quarter 1

Week	Monday	Tuesday	Wednesday	Thursday	Friday	Saturday
1	110	83	95	112	110	72
2	99	121	115	105	112	59
3	120	80	92	103	111	61
4	121	95	87	125	103	63
5	73	113	78	92	93	64
6	91	83	122	107	93	71
7	107	130	85	111	112	56
8	99	69	74	104	106	57
9	123	105	111	101	117	66
10	85	105	109	88	109	55
11	108	99	117	106	109	61
12	102	75	74	128	116	54
13	64	124	91	118	85	63

than two categories). Scales may require three, four, five, seven, nine, or even more classes of responses. There are no hard and fast rules for the numbers of classes to use in a scale. Despite the assumed "scientific" nature of statistics, researchers disagree on the maximum number of classes to include in a table; recommendations vary from five to fifteen or more.

Very large numbers of choices may create difficulties for respondents and for readers of the research report. When people are presented with numbers of classes beyond eight or so, some confusion or loss of continuity can occur. Because a key purpose for presenting data in tables in the first place is to communicate meaningful patterns in the data, it is best to keep the number of categories to a number that makes the most sense to the people reading the tables. This usually means using the *fewest* categories or classes possible. A good rule of thumb to follow is not to have more than ten categories in a table—and fewer if possible.

Establishing Class or Category Widths for Tables

Table 14.1 displays partially grouped (raw) data that records the number of building permit applications processed by a county building department, Monday through Saturday, over a 13-week period. The data are shown organized into rows and columns. Each column is a different day's total (these values are known as the frequency of responses). Rows (across the page) are the numbers assigned to a sample. Sample units consist of all permits processed during the given week.

The width or inclusiveness of each class is influenced by the nature of the data, the frequencies of occurrence, and the guidelines for the maximum number of classes to include. The range is determined by subtracting the lowest value from the highest value. A formula to help establish class width follows:

$$\text{Class width} = \frac{\text{Range of the data}}{\text{Preferred number of categories}}$$

Scanning through the data in Table 14.1, it is apparent that the highest number of permits processed (130) occurred on Tuesday of Week 7. The lowest number (54) occurred on Saturday of Week 12. Therefore, the range is 130 minus 54, or 76.

Table 14.2

Class Widths and Range of Values for 10-, 12-, and 15-Wide Categories

Number of classes	10-wide classes range of values	12-wide classes range of values	15-wide classes range of values
1	50–59	48–59	45–59
2	60–69	60–71	60–74
3	70–79	72–83	75–89
4	80–89	84–95	90–104
5	90–99	96–107	105–119
6	100–109	118–129	120–134
7	110–119	130–141	
8	120–129		
9	130–139		
10			

Suppose the researcher wants to present the data after it is grouped into six classes. To establish class widths, first substitute the range values in the formula to come up with a class width as follows:

$$W = \frac{76}{6} = 12.66$$

A class width of 12.66 is, at best, difficult to work with. However, since the data seems to lend itself to groupings of ten, the researcher could use a class width of 10 rather than the cumbersome 12.66. Or, if this resulted in too many classes, a width of 15 could be tried. Table 14.2 displays class ranges for 10-, 12- and 15-wide classes for the data in Table 14.1.

Ten-wide ranges for each class should be 50–59, 60–69, and so on up to 130–139, rather than 50–60, 60–70, and so on up to 130–140. Nine classes would be needed to include all the data. Class ranges for 12-wide categories might begin with 48–59 and end with 130–141; seven classes would be needed for the data.

With 15-wide classes, the lowest category range could be 45–59, with 120–134 the highest category; only six classes would be required. The important thing to remember is that all the classes must be the same size (equal in width), and that all measures can fall into one and only one class.

Additional guidelines for presenting data in tables begin with numbering each table and including a caption. Most often, it is easier to read the table when the data are arranged downward, as opposed to having it spread across a page. Columns and rows must be identified, with qualifiers placed under the table in the form of footnotes. The caption and figure number of a table is always printed above the table; captions for graphs, charts, and other illustrations are presented below the figure.

Univariate and Multivariate Tables

Tables can be used for presenting any type of data and may be univariate, bivariate, or multivariate. Table 14.3 is a *univariate* table and displays counts of a single variable (gender only); Table 14.4 is *multivariate* (gender, height, and weight) table. Multivariate tables are an excellent way to display comparative information.

Table 14.3

Sample Univariate Table

	Number	Percent
Males	456	78.9
Females	122	21.1
Totals	578	100.0

Table 14.4

Sample Multivariate Table

Gender	*n*	Mean height (inches)	Mean weight (pounds)
Females	18	66.6	139
Males	12	71.3	177

Table 14.5

Weekly Exercise Rates, Total Sample (Frequency)

Weekly hours of exercise	Frequency	Relative frequency	Cumulative percent
3 hours or less	5	.156	15.6
4 to 6 hours	7	.219	37.5
7 to 9 hours	10	.312	68.7
10 to 12 hours	8	.250	93.7
13 hours or more	2	.063	100.0
Totals	32	1.00	

Frequency Distribution Tables

A type of table often used in research reports is the frequency distribution table. Frequency distribution tables present the frequencies or counts of the occurrence of each value (class or category) of a variable. According to Mattson (1986), the idea of a frequency distribution table is straightforward; instead of reporting every measurement or response separately, the individual measurements are first grouped into classes. Then, the number of measurements or responses in each class is reported. The totals for each class are called the *frequency of responses* for that class.

Frequency tables also display the *relative frequency* for each class. Relative frequency is the *proportion* of the total each group or value represents. Knowing the relative frequency of responses can be important for comparing the distribution of responses or measurements. It is conveniently communicated as a percentage. Table 14.5 is an example of a simple frequency distribution table showing responses to a multichotomous scale of exercise participation.

Rules when Preparing Frequency Distribution Tables

There are a few rules to follow when preparing frequency distribution tables. First, the table must be *internally consistent*. That is, groups or classes must be equal in size—except when dealing

Table 14.6

Weekly Exercise Rates, Total Sample (Count)

Weekly hours of exercise	Count	Percent	Valid percent	Cumulative percent
3 hours or less	5	14.3	15.6	15.6
4 to 6 hours	7	20.0	21.9	37.5
7 to 9 hours	10	28.6	31.2	68.7
10 to 12 hours	8	22.8	25.0	93.7
13 hours or more	2	5.7	6.3	100.0
Missing	3	8.6	—	—
Totals	35	100.0	100.0	

with outliers. Outliers are either excessively high or low counts that fall outside of the assumed normal distribution. Researchers should be careful not to lose all information about the case that tossing out an outlier would entail. If the outlier is abnormally high it should be grouped with the highest class; if it is abnormally low it should be grouped with the lowest class. An example for Table 14.5 is if one member of the employer-sponsored fitness program exercised more than three hours a day, six or seven days a week. This would require a "21 hours or more" class in the table. However, the gap between thirteen and twenty-one hours creates the need for two *blank* classes. Including the outlier in the highest "normal" class eliminates the need for blank classes and reduces the outlier's influence on the group average.

Second, frequency distribution tables should include the *relative frequency* and often, but not always, the *cumulative frequency*. Relative frequency is the proportion of the total that each class represents. It can be stated as a decimal or as a percentage. In decimal form the total must always equal 1; in percentages, the total must equal 100 percent. In Table 14.5, the relative frequency of the lowest category is .156, or 15.6 percent.

The last column in Table 14.6 displays the cumulative relative frequency. This represents the sum of a class and all preceding classes. For example, the cumulative relative frequency for the second level, four to six hours, is its value (21.9 percent), plus the value of the 3-hours-or-less class (15.6 percent), for a total of 37.5 percent

Finally, some statistical software packages include provisions for computing relative frequencies when the data contains missing values. A missing value occurs, for example, when a subject refuses to answer a particular question on a survey. When this occurs, the relative frequency distribution column will include the proportion of the total represented by the missing values. A separate column labeled *Valid Percent* will appear in the table alongside the relative frequency column.

BUILDING A STEM-AND-LEAF DIAGRAM

In this example, the supervisor of a state work-training program for at-risk parents is responsible for recording the number of contact hours agency counselors spend meeting with their assigned program participants. In the past, it was determined that a minimum of eighteen contact hours per week was the most time a counselor could devote to personal contact and still keep up with the requirements of the job. Any less time seemed to result in suboptimal progress for participants; more than eighteen hours did not materially improve program performance.

It would not be cost effective to measure the counseling provided to every single participant in the statewide program. Instead, the supervisor could accomplish the task by randomly selecting

Table 14.7

Spreadsheet Display of Total Counseling Contact Hours

Week	Counselor 1	Counselor 2	Counselor 3	Counselor 4
1	18.4	18.2	18.0	17.9
2	19.9	18.0	18.1	18.2
3	18.6	18.5	18.4	18.6
4	19.0	19.1	19.2	19.1
5	17.8	17.4	16.9	17.6
6	18.7	19.0	18.8	18.5

and recording the results of several samples drawn at different times and different offices. Each week for six weeks, the records of six counselors were randomly selected and the time spent in contact with program participants recorded, thus providing a total of twenty-four measurements. The researcher chose to use a stem-and-leaf diagram to summarize the data.

To construct the stem-and-leaf diagram, the data must first be entered into a spreadsheet. A Microsoft Excel Data File can be used for this purpose (Table 14.7). In the spreadsheet, the first column contains the week the measurements were recorded. The next four columns contain the hours each counselor spent counseling program participants. Individual week records are displayed in rows.

Normally, the researcher would be most concerned with the average weight of the six records in each weekly sample (the mean hours for each sample), but for the stem-and-leaf diagram, the important information is the weekly hours of each counselor. The stem-and-leaf diagram displays *variability* in the sample and is a good way to pictorially display the shape of the total distribution of hours. The stem-and-leaf displays at one glance all of the measurements for each major value; the "major values" in this example are the hours. These full numbers become the "stem" of the diagram: 16, 17, 18, and 19. The leaves are the partial-hour measurements (numbers after the decimal point). Examples include: .0, .1, .2, and so on up to 9.

Excel Example

Excel does not include a special function or wizard for creating stem-and-leaf diagrams. However, it is possible to come up with a satisfactory diagram with several simple intermediate steps:

Steps in Preparing a Stem-and-Leaf Diagram Using Excel:

Step 1.   Copy the Table 14.7 data as a spreadsheet data array with the data as a single column (as in Table 14.8, left column).

Step 2.   Copy these data into an adjacent column.

Step 3.   Convert to descending or ascending order (Table 14.8, right column).

Step 4.   Form a stem-and-leaf diagram from the ordered data (Figure 14.1).

The first step is to copy the counselor hours from Table 14.7 onto a new Excel worksheet; this is shown in Table 14.8. The first column should contain the raw data for all the samples collectively. All the data should be entered in a single column. The second step is to copy these data into an adjacent column. The third step is to use the Sort Wizard to sort the copied data into ascending or descending order. For this example, the data were sorted into ascending order (from the lowest value to highest).

Table 14.8

Rank Ordered Contacts per Hour Records

Raw data	Ascending order
18.4	16.9
18.2	17.4
18.0	17.6
17.9	17.8
19.9	17.9
18.0	18.0
18.1	18.0
18.2	18.1
18.6	18.2
18.5	18.2
18.4	18.4
18.6	18.4
19.0	18.5
19.1	18.5
19.2	18.6
19.1	18.6
17.8	18.7
17.4	18.8
16.9	19.0
17.6	19.0
18.7	19.1
19.0	19.1
18.8	19.2
18.5	19.9

Figure 14.1   **Stem-and-Leaf Diagram of Counseling Hours**

15. 0
16. 9
17. 4, 6, 8, 9
18. 0, 0, 1, 2, 2, 4, 4, 5, 5, 6, 6, 7, 8
19. 0, 0, 1, 1, 2, 9
20. 0

Then, to form the stem-and-leaf diagram, enter each stem value into an empty cell, beginning with the lowest value and ending with the highest. Enter the tenths values for each stem value alongside the appropriate stem point. The final stem-and-leaf diagram should look like the example displayed in Figure 14.1.

COMMUNICATING WITH CHARTS AND GRAPHS

Many research reports contain descriptive statistical data that are presented in graphs or charts. Descriptive statistics in particular are often presented in some sort of graphic form, such as bar charts, histograms, or pie charts. The type of chart or graph selected often depends upon the preference of the researcher or administrator presenting the information and the nature of the data. With today's increasingly powerful spreadsheet and statistical software programs, together with color printers, these pictorial or graphic tools are easy and quick to produce. Among the more commonly used types of charts are *bar charts* and *histograms*.

Bar Charts

Bar charts show how many measurements or observations fall into each class or category of each variable. Printers may use asterisks or shading to represent the extent of the relative frequencies. It is important to remember that the bars are not accurate measures; they are *symbolic* only. The bars in any one chart may not appear exactly to scale, but they do give a clear *visual impression* of the variation among the values in the class. Excel produces bar charts in two different procedures. The first requires two distinct steps: (1) establishing categories and (2) selecting from several different chart forms.

The first step in this procedure is for the researcher to decide how to group the responses into distinct classes. Excel labels these classes as "bins" and allows the researcher to create bins of any size. As an alternative, the researcher can let the program divide the data into categories it feels are appropriate, but those categories may not be relevant in the data analysis.

An example of a bar chart produced with Microsoft Excel is displayed in Figure 14.2. The table and chart use the building permit data displayed in Table 14.1 near the beginning of this chapter. In this example, five measurements ranging from zero to sixty are included in the first class; fourteen items with scores from sixty-one to seventy-five are included in the second class, and so on. The bin data are summarized in Table 14.9.

Histograms

Another way to graphically display a frequency distribution is with a *histogram*. A histogram has a visual appearance much like a bar chart, except that in histograms the bars are usually displayed horizontally, while the bars of a bar chart are displayed vertically.

When it is possible to use either a bar chart or a histogram, bar charts should be used when displaying *discrete* data—that is, data in distinct categories such as gender or occupation. Histograms can be used to display both discrete and continuous data. Examples of continuous data include incomes, height, weight, and other similar measures. As with frequency distribution tables, continuous data categories or classes used in histograms must exhibit internal consistency: all classes must be of the same width.

Excel's TOOLS/DATA ANALYSIS/HISTOGRAM Wizard was used to construct the bin width for the frequency table displayed in Table 14.9 and the bar chart in Figure 14.2. Recall that earlier a set of classes was computed and resulted in a value of 12.666, which is a cumbersome span. Bin widths of ten or fifteen measurements can be used with similar results. The histogram in Figure 14.2 was calculated using a bin width of fifteen permit applications. Different bin (or class) widths would have resulted in different bar charts. Remember: There is no rule specifying the number of classes or bins that should be used in either tables or charts. Rather, a rule of thumb is to keep the number of classes around six to eight and never to exceed ten if at all possible.

Figure 14.2   **Bar Chart of Permit Application Data**

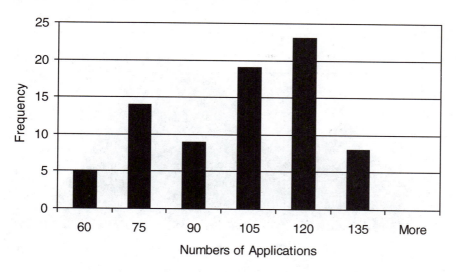

Table 14.9

15-Wide Classes (Bins) of Permits Issued and Frequencies for Each Bin

Bin	Frequency
60	5
75	14
90	9
105	19
120	23
135	8
More	0

Graphs

Graphs are another way to present a visual summary of data. The types seen most often in research report applications are line graphs, frequency polygons, and pie graphs (also known as pie charts).

Line Graphs

Line graphs are used to show how values of a variable change over time. The time periods are always shown on the horizontal axis, while the vertical axis displays the values of the variables being examined. When plotting continuous data, the points at each time period represent the middle level of the class. Simple line graphs are used to display *trend lines* of single variables. Compound line charts displaying the component values of a larger sum are often used to visually display comparisons over time. Figure 14.3 is an example of a line graph produced with Microsoft Excel's *Chart Wizard*.

Figure 14.3 **Line Chart of First Quarter Daily Permit Application Totals**

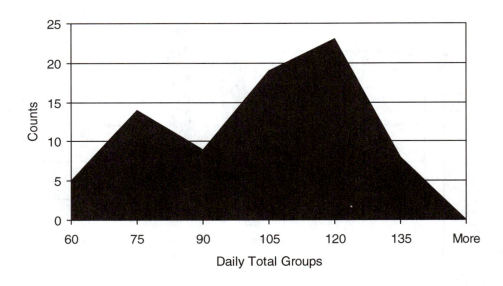

Frequency Polygons

Frequency polygons display data in much the same way as histograms; they show the total occurrences for each value of a variable. In appearance, however, they appear almost identical to line graphs. For many years, when statistical computations were done by hand or, at best, with a hand calculator, frequency polygons were the method most often-used to graphically display frequency distributions because they are extremely easy to construct. However, today they are not used nearly as often as bar charts and histograms.

With all frequency polygons, two axes are needed. The vertical y-axis represents the frequencies; the horizontal x-axis displays the measurement or class values. With grouped data (such as age categories of ten years each), the midpoint of the interval is used. When plotting specific data such as individual scores, the actual score value is used. Lines connect all total frequency values. The lines of a polygon are often extended to one value above and one below the observed data so as to "close off" the polygon instead of leaving it hanging in midair.

Frequency polygons can also be used to plot and compare two or more sets of scores or values that are based on separate scales. In this case, use the relative frequency distribution in place of actual frequency distributions.

Pie Charts

Pie charts (also called pie graphs) are another popular way to graphically display data. In pie charts, the data are presented as portions of a 360-degree circular "pie." Each portion of the pie represents roughly the same portion of the total that each group or category of the variable represents. In the example shown in Figure 14.4 is a pie chart produced from the data presented in Table 14.10. The categories are portions of the United States. The pie chart in Figure 14.4 was produced with Excel's *Chart Wizard*.

Table 14.10

Contribution by Region

Region	Percent
Pacific Northwest	11
Mountain States	12
Southwest	15
Central	27
New England	13
Southeast	14
Total	100

Figure 14.4   **Pie Chart of Contribution by Region**

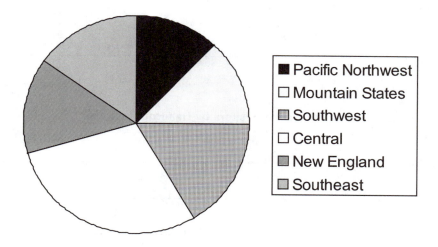

Scatter Plots

Scatter plots are another way to visually present data. Scatter plots are used to display a series of points of two or more variables that are related in some way. When all measures are plotted, a visual picture of the relationship between variables can be seen. Scatter plots are visually similar to line charts, except that no lines connect the various points on the scatter plot. Figure 14.5 is a scatter plot of the data presented in Table 14.11; it was produced with the Excel Chart Wizard.

When all measures are plotted, a visual picture of the relationship between variables can often be seen. In Figure 14.5, the time period variable is plotted on the horizontal axis. This time variable has eighteen classes or categories. Each is one half-hour period during the day. Data for the variable "Number of Visitors" are plotted on the vertical axis. When scatter plots are used to display dependent-independent variables, the horizontal axis should always be the independent variable.

Table 14.11

Number of Museum Visitors by Half-Hour Periods

Period	Time	Visitors
1	9:00–9:29	15
2	9:30–9:59	25
3	10:00–10:29	34
4	10:30–10:59	50
5	11:00–11:29	65
6	11:30–11:59	90
7	12:00–12:29	115
8	12:30–12:59	247
9	1:00–1:29	312
10	1:30–1:59	304
11	2:00–2:29	400
12	2:30–2:59	450
13	3:00–3:29	362
14	3:30–3:59	247
15	4:00–4:29	210
16	4:30–4:59	145
17	5:00–5:29	97
18	5:30–5:59	32

Figure 14.5 **Scatter Plot of Museum Visitors by Half-Hour Intervals**

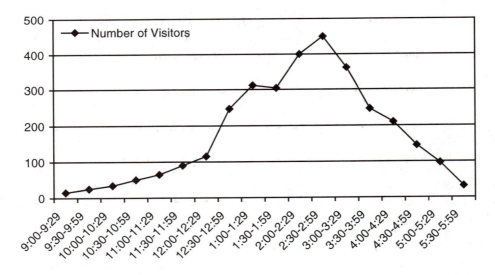

Half-Hour Periods: 9:00 A.M. to 6:00 P.M.

Table 14.12

Differences Between Friendly and Unfriendly Graphics

Friendly Graphics	Unfriendly Graphics
All words in the graphic are spelled out; use of elaborate or cute coding is avoided.	The researcher's abbreviations are used, forcing the reader to refer to the text to find their meaning.
Type runs from left to right, similar to the way normally text is written.	Words are typed vertically, particularly on the vertical (Y) axis, or words run in more than one direction.
Small messages in the graphic help explain the meaning of the data.	No explanations are included in the graphic, forcing readers to refer back to the text.
Complicated, busy shadings and cross-hatching or colors are not used. Instead, labels are placed on the art itself; no legend is required.	Hard-to-discern color or textures force the reader to go back to the text to understand the graphic.
The graphic draws readers' attention by inspiring curiosity and interest.	The graphic is messy and hard to figure out; it is filled with unnecessary "chart junk."
Colors, if used, are picked in consideration of the 5 to 10 percent of readers who are color-blind.	The artwork is insensitive to color-blind viewers. Red and green are used for contrasts.
The typeface is clear—not flashy or cute.	The type is overbearing, taking readers' attention away from the message in the graphic. Examples of typefaces to avoid include Fritz Quadrata, BANKGOTHIC MD, and Compacta BT.
All capitals are not used; the type is upper- and lowercase, and a typeface with serifs (such as Times New Roman) is used whenever possible.	The type is all capitals and/or a sans serif typeface is used. Examples of sans serif typefaces to avoid are ARIAL or MICROSOFT SANS SERIF.

FINAL REMINDERS ABOUT GRAPHICS

Although now mostly forgotten, for many years Princeton professor of public affairs Edward R. Tufte was America's recognized expert on graphic display of quantitative data. Anyone planning to use creative graphic displays in their research reports would be well advised to examine his work before beginning. As a reminder, Table 14.12 offers a comparison of what Tufte described as "friendly" and "unfriendly" graphics.

SUMMARY

Before administrators can use research data, it must be ordered and classified into a structure that has meaning and is relevant to the decision problem. Often, the first step in making sense of raw data is the preparation of univariate, bivariate, or multivariate tables. These present the data in summary form. Stem-and-leaf diagrams are also used for this purpose.

Graphic displays of data are used to make it easier to communicate meaning to readers. Bar charts, histograms, line and area charts, scatter plots, and pie charts are used to graphically display the structure found in data sets.

Statistical software programs like Microsoft Excel and SPSS can make preparing tables, charts, and graphs a simple and quick process. Both of these software programs require that the data be entered in a spreadsheet format.

ADDITIONAL READING

Brightman, Harvey J. 1999. *Data Analysis in Plain English, with Microsoft Excel.* Pacific Grove, CA: Duxbury Press.

Green, Samuel B., Neil J. Salkind, and Theresa M. Akey. 2000. *Using SPSS.* Upper Saddle River, NJ: Prentice Hall.

Moore, David S. 1979. *Statistics: Concepts and Controversies.* San Francisco: W. H. Freeman and Co.

Neufeld, John L. 1997. *Learning Business Statistics with Microsoft Excel.* Upper Saddle River, NJ: Prentice Hall.

15

RESEARCH HYPOTHESES

Risk and uncertainty are present in public and nonprofit organizations; administrators and managers are hardly ever able to predict with absolute certainty the outcome of a decision. One important reason for this is that the predicted outcomes will occur in the future. No one can predict the future; however, an attempt to do so must be made. Experienced administrators can make fairly accurate predictions about outcomes. When decision makers do predict future outcomes, they use probabilities as indicators of their confidence in the likelihood of the outcome.

Because it is usually impossible to test or measure entire populations, researchers use sample statistics to then make inferences about population parameters. This chapter examines the way probabilities and sample statistics are used to form and test hypotheses.

A systematic series of steps must be followed in the application of all statistical analyses. First, someone must establish a purpose or goal for the research. Second, data relating to the issue or question must be gathered. Third, one or more statistical tests are carried out. Finally, the person directing the activity must decide whether the gathered and analyzed data satisfactorily meets the need spelled out in the purpose.

As this abbreviated procedure suggests, before any data are gathered, processed, or interpreted someone must establish a foundation for the activity. In statistics, this foundation is called a *hypothesis* (the plural form of hypothesis is *hypotheses,* spelled with an "e" in the last syllable instead of an "i"). A hypothesis is a *statement that explains or suggests a conclusion about some phenomena.* All subsequent statistical testing follows from this foundation.

In organizations, all data is, or should be, gathered for a purpose. This purpose is established by clearly defining the organization's problem or situation for which more information is needed. Once the purpose is established, the researcher can then decide on a design or method of data collection. Following a design means establishing and following a plan for collecting, analyzing, interpreting, and reporting the findings of the study. As we saw earlier, there are three broad classes of research designs: exploratory, descriptive, and causal. The same steps must be followed regardless of the design selected. These steps are:

1. Define the organization's problem or decision to be made.
2. Form hypotheses about the problem or decision.
3. Select a research design.
4. Select the appropriate statistical test or tests.
5. Select a sample.

6. Collect the data.
7. Analyze and interpret the data.
8. Report the findings or make the decision.

Defining the organization's problem is the first step in the process. This chapter is about the second step in this process: how decision makers write hypotheses about problems, decisions, or situations in their organizations and then statistically test those hypotheses. Hypothesis tests can be made about single samples or two or more samples. Because hypothesis testing is founded in probability theory, most decisions about hypotheses are made on the basis of some level of probability; this is called the *p-value approach* to hypothesis testing. Therefore, this chapter includes a brief introduction to the rationale behind probability-base (*p*-value) decisions about hypotheses.

TYPES OF HYPOTHESES

Management decisions based on inferential statistics are made on the basis of what is *probably* true, not on what is or what will actually be true. Therefore, probabilities are the basis of all statistical inference. Usually decision makers do not have perfect information before them when they are required to make a decision. To gain information and reduce uncertainty, administrators usually use the results of sample studies as approximations of what is actually true for a population.

One of the greatest limitations of sample studies is that a study based on another sample taken from the same population might produce entirely different results. One way to lower the risk of this happening is to increase the size of the sample. Larger samples lower the influence of extreme values—what we earlier identified as *outliers*—in a data set. But collecting data costs money and takes time, both of which are limited resources in organizations. Therefore, decision makers develop formal hypotheses about the problem or situation before actually seeking data. Hypotheses tell them what to look for and what to test.

There are many definitions of hypotheses, but most boil down to the fact that hypotheses are simply statements *or predictions* by someone that explain or suggest some conclusion, event, or thing. Hypotheses are only suggestions or beliefs about something; they are not "true" statements. The manager's degree of faith in the truth of the statement is called the level of *confidence;* confidence levels are typically stated as *probabilities.*

Hypotheses can be written to address *relationships* between variables or as *differences* between values. They can be stated as facts or as distributions. Traditionally, they are written as negative statements. Examples include "There is no association between the age of a machine and its production-error rate"; "There is no difference in a sample of runners' preferences for running shoe brands"; and "There is no disproportionate distribution in the frequencies of responses among different age groups to political party preference."

In formal terms, decision makers deal with three main types of hypotheses: predictive, comparative, and association. Predictive hypotheses are typically predictions about the future value of a measurement. Examples include predictions about client use of medical services over the next several quarters, predictions about the movements of labor costs, and the government's predictions of annual growth in the deficit, in productivity, or in unemployment.

Comparative hypotheses make comparisons among groups of people, companies, countries, products, and the like. These comparisons are often used in hypotheses about differences between scores of one group compared with another. Examples include differences in mean pedagogy preference scores between two samples of school administrators, and rainfall rate differences encountered after a change in environmental conditions.

Association hypotheses deal with the levels of relationship or association between two or more variables. Examples include measuring whether new advertising, a change in price, or facilities modification influences usage levels of state parks or whether temperature variations during the summer season influence failure rates in park trail systems.

THE NULL HYPOTHESIS

As noted earlier, hypotheses are statements about events or things that decision makers or analysts believe are true. Statistical tests are carried out to verify the statement. In practice, hypotheses are employed in pairs. The first hypothesis is typically stated in negative terms: something is *not* true; variables are *not* related; mean scores of groups are *not* different. This is called the *null hypothesis;* it is represented by the symbol H_O. Null hypotheses are always stated as a status quo situation or as if there are no statistically significant differences in the values.

Paired with the null hypothesis is an *alternate hypothesis;* it is represented by the symbol H_A. The alternate hypothesis is the obverse of the null hypothesis and stated in terms exactly opposite from the null hypothesis. Hypothesis tests are used to test for differences between statistic and parameter values that are known or unknown (inferred).

The null hypothesis is what is being "tested" in a statistical test. Researchers gather data to support the alternate hypothesis and to decide against the null hypothesis (or the reverse). Say, for example, descriptive statistics establish the mean value of a sample; the researcher may then conduct a one-sample hypothesis test to establish whether this statistic is "different" from the mean of the larger population. If it falls within an acceptable range of values, the researcher can state that the statistic is not different; the results of the sample can be inferred to be what would occur in the population.

When a statistical test of the null hypothesis fails to support the belief statement, decision makers say that the null hypothesis must be rejected (or "not accepted"). Saying that there is no difference in the way the groups responded to the question is only a *belief* statement and cannot be considered a fact. Rather, the researcher can only state that the null hypothesis of no statistically significant difference must be rejected. For example, say a statistical test is carried out for differences between two groups' mean scores on an attitude scale. The null hypothesis is that there is no statistically significant difference between the two means. The alternate hypothesis is that the two mean scores are not the same. If the difference is great enough and the probability that the difference did not occur by chance is lower than a preset confidence level, the null hypothesis is rejected and the alternate hypothesis retained (or accepted).

Hypotheses can be stated as recognizing no difference or change ($H_O = H_A$); change in one direction (less than or greater than) only ($H_O < H_A$, or $H_O > H_A$); or change in any direction ($H_O \neq H_A$). A one-direction change (either greater or less) is called a *one-tailed test.* When the test involves difference in any direction, it is called a *two-tailed test.* Statistical programs such as SPSS for Windows often print out test statistics for both one- and two-tailed tests for the same data. The *t*-test in Excel also computes a value for a one-tailed test, a two-tailed test, or both.

MAKING INFERENCES ABOUT POPULATIONS

Decision makers almost always use sample statistics as the basis for making inferences about populations. These inferences can be based on confidence levels or confidence intervals established by the manager or from the results of statistical tests. The latter method is referred to as *significance tests.* For most organization statistics, confidence levels are predetermined at one of three standard points: the 99 percent, 95 percent, or 90 percent confidence interval, which is another way of saying the .01, .05, or .10 level of confidence.

Confidence intervals are based on the proportion of sample means that can be expected to fall within a specified range of the estimated population mean. For samples with a normal distribution, 95 percent of all sample means can be expected to fall within ±1.96 standard errors from the population mean, whereas 5 percent will fall outside of these limits (Poister 1978). This is the same thing as the .05 level of confidence.

Confidence limits can be established in two different ways. One possible way is when statisticians use either the Z or t-distribution to establish the probability of a mean falling within a specified number of standard errors of the population mean. Confidence levels are then stated in terms of values for Z or t. A second way is when the probability levels computed with tests carried out with most statistical software packages are used for hypothesis acceptance or rejection decisions.

By itself, the significance level of a sample statistic gives the manager very little information. It tells nothing about the size or magnitude of the relationship or difference between the variables. Therefore, it should be used only as an indicator and not as a final test. Rejecting the null hypothesis on the basis of the significance value suggests that a relationship or a difference exists, but nothing more. Information regarding the strength and/or direction of the connection is of more importance.

Errors of Analysis

Regardless of which confidence level is selected or computed, several errors of analysis may confound the results of a study (Mattson 1986). There are two types of such errors associated with hypothesis tests: *Type I* and *Type II* errors (Figure 15.1).

Type I errors occur when a null hypothesis that is actually true is rejected. This is also called *falsely rejecting the null hypothesis.* Type I errors are related to the confidence level adopted for a decision. Thus, with a confidence level of .10, we can falsely reject the null hypothesis 10 percent of the time. Lowering the confidence level to .05 means we can expect to be wrong only 5 percent of the time. As can be seen, tightening confidence levels lowers the likelihood of Type I errors occurring.

As noted earlier, rejecting a null hypothesis does not mean that something is definitely "true." Rather, it means we reject this hypothesis and accept the alternate hypothesis. Type II errors occur when we do *not* reject the null hypothesis when it is, in fact, false. Type II errors occur less often than Type I errors; procedures for computing their possible occurrence are usually found in comprehensive mathematical statistics texts. In general, decision makers can reduce the likelihood of Type II errors occurring by increasing the size of the sample.

HYPOTHESIS TESTING IN ACTION

Hypothesis tests have been developed for use with one sample and with two or more samples. This chapter will address one-sample hypothesis tests; the next chapter will look at comparisons of the means of two or more samples. Hypothesis tests can also be carried out on categorical (nominal) and ordered (ordinal) data; those tests will be discussed in a later chapter on nonparametric statistics. Hypothesis tests can be carried out in situations involving a single mean, for differences between two independent means, for differences between dependent or paired means, in situations involving single proportion, and for differences between proportions.

Figure 15.1   **Type I and Type II Errors in Hypothesis Testing**

	Reject the null	*Accept (retain) the null*
Null is false	Correct decision	Type II error
Null is true	Type I error	Correct decision

ONE-SAMPLE TESTS

One-sample hypothesis tests are used to determine whether a sample statistic, usually the mean, falls within a set of upper and lower critical values. One-sample tests are also used with proportions and to establish the distribution of the statistic. These tests are important because two key assumptions in most interval and ratio data hypothesis tests are (1) randomness, and (2) a normal distribution. Tests for two or more samples are discussed in the next chapter.

The hypotheses formed and statistical tests employed will naturally depend upon specific decision circumstances facing the manager, the data-collection process to be followed, whether the variance is known, and whether the test is one-tailed or two-tailed.

The decision to accept or reject a null hypothesis is based upon an acceptance value that is called a *confidence level*. The required degree of confidence the manager must have in the decision to be made will dictate the level of confidence to be used. Confidence levels are probabilities that the results of the test could not have occurred by chance. For example, a confidence level of .05 means that the mean values of the sample will fall within the same range as the population parameter 95 out of 100 times. In this way, significance tests are decision tools for all inferential statistics.

With normal distributions, roughly half of the possible values of the sample statistic could fall above the mean and half below. Values falling out of this range are those that would call for rejection of the null hypothesis. The entire set of possible values within this range is called the *confidence interval*. The confidence interval is the range of values within which we expect the "true" value of the population (mean) parameter to fall—with some researcher-selected level of probability. The values delineating the confidence range are known as the *upper* and *lower confidence limits;* together they form the bounds of the confidence interval. That is, with a 95 percent confidence value (and a normal distribution), we expect that only 2.5 percent of the values to be above the statistic value and 2.5 percent below.

Testing Hypotheses with Excel

Inferential statistics involves using measurements of a sample to draw conclusions about the characteristics of a population. We can never know with complete certainty that the statistics of the sample match the population parameters. We do know that drawing other random samples will most likely produce similar but different values for their statistics. The decision maker wants to know with what degree of probability the sample statistic (such as the mean, mode, or median) will fall within an acceptable range of possible values. This acceptable range is called the confidence interval. If all possible samples of the same size were taken, what percentage of them would include

Table 15.1

Sandbag Weights (in pounds) for Shift 1

Hour	1	2	3	4	5	Mean	SD
1	17.36	18.61	18.17	17.37	17.39	17.7800	0.5783
2	17.45	18.62	18.39	17.19	19.03	18.1360	0.7848
3	17.66	17.38	18.31	17.90	19.19	18.0880	0.7042
4	18.18	17.88	17.90	18.09	18.61	18.1320	0.2958
5	18.33	19.10	17.75	18.18	18.53	18.3780	0.4950
6	18.54	18.77	17.28	18.31	18.88	18.3560	0.6403
7	18.66	18.90	19.15	19.54	19.89	19.2280	0.4929
8	19.90	18.11	18.01	18.00	17.99	18.4020	0.8388
				40-observation totals		18.3125	0.6941
			40-observation confidence interval				0.2151

the population parameter somewhere within the interval of their statistic values? Since the actual parameter value is seldom known, an estimate must be made. Microsoft Excel's CONFIDENCE function can quickly establish an estimate for the range of values above and below the hypothesized population mean. Three values are needed to complete the CONFIDENCE test:

1. *Alpha* (the manager-determined significance level to be used to compute the confidence level; a number greater than 0 and less than 1).
2. The standard deviation of the population (since this is seldom known, the SD for the sample is substituted).
3. *N* (the total of sample items involved).

The sandbag production line data in Table 15.1 can be used for an example with the CONFIDENCE test in the Microsoft Excel Function Wizard. The test determines the range of the confidence level for the mean of the population. Say that a machine fills sandbags by weight rather than volume. Some variation is expected to naturally occur within a range of weights. Each bag is labeled as weighing a total of 18 pounds. Every hour in each eight-hour shift, a sample of five bags is randomly selected and weighed. Table 15.1 displays the test results for a single shift.

The selected significance value, standard deviation, and number of cases in the sample must be inserted for the Excel CONFIDENCE function to produce a value that is exactly one-half of the confidence interval. The sample mean of 18.3125 pounds, standard deviation of 0.6941, and sample size of 40 produce a confidence value of .2151. Thus, any mean falling within the range of 0.2151 over and –0.2151 below eighteen pounds (18.2151 and 17.7849) results in a rejection of the null hypothesis and acceptance of the alternative hypothesis: The sample mean does fall within the normal range of the population mean. The decision maker may assume the filling process is in specifications. When a sample mean falls outside this range, a discrepancy is in effect, and an adjustment to the process is necessary.

A significance value of .05 is established at the decision value or cutoff point for accepting the null hypothesis. The mean for this sample of forty observations is 18.31 pounds; the standard deviation is 0.6941 pounds. The production manager believes that the variances for the entire shift's production are the same as those of the samples. A null hypothesis that might be tested is: *There is no statistically significant difference in the mean weights of all samples.*

The means for hours 1 through 4 all fall within the acceptable confidence interval, so change to the process is unnecessary; the null hypothesis is retained. However, the means for hours 5 through 8 all fall outside of the upper limit of 18.2151 pounds (no test statistic falls below the lower limit of 17.7849 pounds). Therefore, the null hypothesis is rejected for the samples for hours 5 through 8. Clearly, an adjustment to the filling equipment is required.

TESTS FOR A NORMAL DISTRIBUTION

A key condition of many statistical tests is the requirement that the samples be drawn from a population with a normal distribution and normal variance. It is common for this to be stated as a hypothesis. Therefore, one of the first tests on a sample data set is often a test for normality—that is, a test to see if the population parameter has a normal distribution. This test should only be done with a probability sample; that is, one in which the cases for the sample have been randomly selected. Thus, decision makers are often required to compute the area under a normal curve and/or to establish probabilities associated with the normal distribution.

Microsoft Excel's statistical analysis capabilities accessed with the *Function Wizard* (f_x) include five functions that pertain to normal distributions. The first of these is the STANDARDIZE function, which computes standardized Z-values for given raw scores. The second function related to the normal distribution is the NORMSDIST function. This function computes the area under the curve (probability) that is less than a given Z-value. The third function, NORMSINV, computes a Z-value that corresponds to a given total area under the normal curve. This function is the opposite of the NORMSDIST function. The fourth Excel normal distribution function, NORMDIST, computes the area (probability) that is less than a given measurement value (X), such as a sample-bag weight in the example from an earlier chapter. The last function in this family of tools is the NORMINV function. This function—the converse of the NORMDIST function—computes the measurement value (X) that corresponds to a given area under the normal curve.

In addition to these five specific normal distribution-related tests, Excel also includes the capability to conduct one-tailed and two-tailed, one-sample *t*-tests; a two-tailed (only) Z-test; and a confidence interval test. These will be discussed in later chapters.

SUMMARY

Before any data are gathered, processed, or interpreted, someone must establish a foundation for the research activity. In statistics, this foundation is called a *hypothesis* (the plural form of hypothesis is *hypotheses*). All subsequent statistical analysis follows from this foundation. A hypothesis is a statement that explains or suggests a conclusion about some phenomena.

Public administration decision makers write hypotheses about problems, decisions, or situations in their organizations and how they then can test those hypotheses statistically. Hypothesis tests are made about one-sample characteristics, as well as about two or more samples.

Hypotheses can be written to address *relationships* between variables or as *differences* between values. They can be stated as facts or as distributions. Traditionally, they are written as negative statements.

In formal terms, decision makers deal with three main types of hypotheses: (1) predictive hypotheses, (2) comparative hypotheses, and (3) association hypotheses. Predictive hypotheses are typically predictions about the future value of a measurement. Comparative hypotheses make comparisons between groups of people, companies, characteristics, responses, services, products, and scores of one group compared with another. These are often used in hypotheses about differences between scores of two groups. Association hypotheses are used to test the levels of relationship or association between two or more variables.

ADDITIONAL READING

Brightman, Harvey J. 1999. *Data Analysis in Plain English with Microsoft Excel.* Pacific Grove, CA: Duxbury Press.

Levine, David M., Mark L. Berenson, and David Stephan. 1997. *Statistics for Managers Using Microsoft Excel.* Upper Saddle River, NJ: Prentice Hall.

Salkind, Neil J. 2006. *Statistics for People Who (Think They) Hate Statistics.* Thousand Oaks, CA: Sage.

16

TESTING HYPOTHESES ABOUT
TWO OR MORE GROUPS

The underlying concepts of one-sample hypothesis testing discussed in the preceding chapter also apply to a body of statistical techniques designed to test hypotheses about two or more samples. These tools permit managers to test whether the different values found in two or more samples are statistically significant or whether they could have occurred by chance. Another way to look at a hypothesis test is to consider it a significance test, the results of which help managers evaluate certain characteristics in measurements. *Differences* are one class of characteristics; *relationships* are another.

As we saw in the last chapter, the null hypothesis is what is tested in statistics. Null hypotheses are always stated in terms of either the status quo or as no difference. This chapter will examine a number of the statistical tools used to test for significant differences between parametric statistics for two or more groups or subgroups. The next chapter will look at hypotheses about relationships.

Statistics for specific measurements vary from sample to sample. Measurements taken after a modification to a process or a change in working conditions will be different from the measurements taken before the change (such a change is sometimes called a "treatment"). Researchers need to know if the differences measured in such measurements are "real" or if they are simply chance-related variations that are seen every time a new measurement is made and that would fall within the normal distribution range of a statistic. They are looking for differences that are *statistically significant*. A difference that is statistically significant is one with a high probability that it did not occur through chance alone. It is important to remember that the analyst will never know if the differences are, indeed, "real." Rather, within a predetermined acceptable *level of confidence,* such as 90, 95, or 99 percent, the procedure entails rejecting or accepting a hypothesis or hypotheses about a difference.

Collectively, these tests are often referred to as "difference tests," although some texts treat them all as "significance tests." A variety of statistical techniques are used to test for differences with all types of data or levels of measurement. Researchers will most likely find themselves using the tests for comparing differences in means. However, the choice of a particular statistical test for differences between measures depends upon the nature of the measurements themselves. For example, a statistic based on nominal data, as in a categorical measurement of two groups, should *not* be tested with the same scale used for continuous variables.

Researchers are interested in significance tests and tests for differences in a wide variety of situations. One of the more basic uses is to determine whether the values of a randomly selected sample statistic are distributed in the same way they are in a population—the test of *normality* discussed in the previous chapter. A similar application is available for testing the distribution of responses for a categorical variable. Called a *goodness-of-fit test,* this looks at the data to determine whether the distribution of response frequencies is disproportionate; that is, whether the frequency distribution is the same as would be expected with a normal distribution. Difference tests also weigh disparities between two or more groups in their rankings or ratings of a set of items, which result in ordinal- and interval-level data, respectively. Probably the most commonly encountered difference tests, the small-sample *t*-test and large-sample F-test, test for differences between the scores of two or more groups. These two tests should only be used with interval or ratio data.

STATISTICAL SIGNIFICANCE

Hypothesis tests are sometimes called *differences tests* or *significance tests. Statistical significance* is the term used to describe the point or value beyond which researchers accept or reject a null hypothesis. Decisions are usually made based on preselected levels of confidence, typically .01, .05, or .10.

In the past, the critical values of a statistic had to be read from a table of values found at the end of most statistics texts. These were then compared with a value that was found by following steps in a formula for calculating the statistical test. Today, the value at which the decision can to be made appears as a *probability* value in the results of inferential statistical tests. This is called the *p-value approach.*

Remember that just because the result of a statistical test is *statistically significant,* it does not automatically mean that it is socially, culturally, administratively, or even logically significant (Poister 1978). A result can be statistically significant and totally irrelevant or trivial at the same time. On the other hand, a small difference can have great practical significance. It is up to the researcher to make these determinations.

INTERPRETING RESULTS WITH *P*-VALUES

Most public administration and social science researchers make hypothesis acceptance decisions at the .05 level of confidence. However, the nature of the study and required level of confidence in the results often require that a level of .10 or .01 be employed. In statistical notation, the low-ercase Greek letter *alpha* (α) is used to represent the confidence value. When analysts use the .05 level of confidence, they are saying they are 95 percent sure about a hypothesis decision. This 95 percent, which is known as the *confidence coefficient,* is the probability that a null hypothesis is retained when it should be retained.

It is important that significance levels are not confused with "importance." The two concepts are not related in any way. Importance refers to the weight or value the decision maker places on the information from a statistical study. Statistical significance is the product of a selected confidence level. Confidence levels are closely related to confidence intervals, discussed in the previous chapter. Before widespread acceptance of the *p*-value approach to hypothesis testing, managers were required to compute acceptance and rejection levels and to look up decision values in tables. Today, most statistical packages, such as SPSS and Excel, compute critical *p*-values along with *t*-test, *z*-test and F-test values. The decision whether to retain or reject the null hypothesis can now be made by comparing the computed *p*-value with the confidence level or *alpha.* The notation for the .05 level of confidence is written as $\alpha = .05$. *P*-values of the same or greater value than the selected alpha result in retaining (or accepting) the null hypothesis; *p*-values less than the significance value require that the null hypothesis be rejected and the alternative hypothesis be accepted.

GOODNESS-OF-FIT TESTS

The term *goodness-of-fit* refers to an evaluation of the frequency distribution of values for any type of measurement. This test compares the actual frequency results against a hypothetical distribution, referred to as an "expected" distribution, assuming a normal distribution. The most commonly used statistical test for goodness-of-fit tests is the chi-square (X^2) statistic, which is one of a series of nonparametric tests. Nonparametric statistics are considered to be "distribution free." While most nonparametric tests were developed for nominal- and ordinal-level data, the X^2 goodness-of-fit test can be used with nominal and ratio data as well, although other, more powerful tests provide more information.

Goodness-of-fit tests are just one of the uses for the chi-square statistic. Among other applications, it can be used as a test of independence between variables, as a test for normality (normal distribution), or as a one-sample relationship test. As a goodness of fit test, it compares two sets of data. One set is the actual collected data (called the *observed data*); the second is a hypothetical data set (called the *expected data*). The hypothetical data represent what the data would be if the null hypothesis of no difference were really true. They also show that there is no relationship between the variables. For a goodness-of-fit test, the null hypothesis might be the distribution of responses found in the collected data is not different from the expected distribution. If the collected data differs significantly from the expected distribution, the null hypothesis must be rejected.

Statistical software packages calculate a chi-square and a *p*-value. Large chi-square values usually suggest that the null hypothesis must be retained. Small chi-square values usually mean the null hypothesis must be rejected. A computed *p*-value is used to make the final decision. *P*-values of less than the selected significance value call for rejecting the null hypothesis. Finally, when carrying out a goodness-of-fit test, it is important that there be at least five responses in each category or cell; if not, the results of the test are considered to be *spurious*—that is, more likely to have occurred by chance and, therefore, not reliable.

TWO-GROUP HYPOTHESIS TESTS

An extensive body of statistical tools has been developed for testing hypotheses about statistics for two or more groups (Figure 16.1). Various tests exist for use with *parametric* and *nonparametric* statistics. Parametric statistical tests can only be used with data at the equidistant interval or ratio level. When the data are ordinal (ranked data) or nominal (categorical), a body of tests known as *nonparametric* statistics must be used. In addition, parametric statistics require that the data be from random samples and have a normal distribution.

When these assumptions cannot be met, nonparametric tests must be used in place of parametric tests. Some parametric tests require that the samples be independent from one another, while other tests have been developed for use with dependent or paired samples. Separate-but-related statistical tests have been developed to meet either independence requirement.

Tests for differences in the mean values of two or more samples can be used for both interval and ratio data. Whether the samples are independent (as most are) or are dependent (or paired), some minor differences will be found in the computational formulas—and associated computer statistics package selection—for several of the tests, although their interpretation is identical.

Two of the statistical tests often used when comparing the mean values for independent samples are the *Student's t-test* for independent samples and the one-way, two-way, and *n*-way *analysis of variance* (F-ratio) tests (ANOVA). When the researcher has any doubt about the independence of

Figure 16.1   **A Schematic Display of Two-Sample Differences Tests**

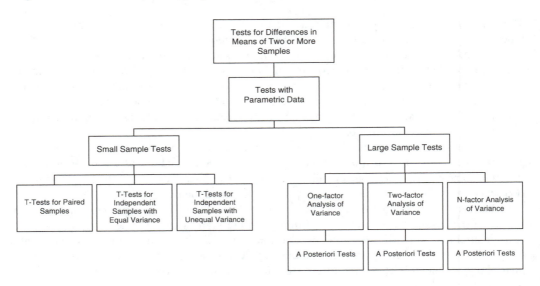

the samples, testing a null hypothesis for dependence with the *Levene test for independence* can be done before selecting either of the difference tests.

Once the decision maker is assured that the samples are independent, he or she must then decide whether the *t*-test or analysis of variance F-test is appropriate. The *t*-test has more limitations than the F-test, but is well suited for comparisons between the means of two, and only two, relatively small samples (typically around thirty cases) when each sample has the same number of observations or cases.

Testing for Differences with the *t*-Test

The *t*-test is used to compare the means of no more than two groups with approximately equal variances—for example, the test scores of two groups of employment applicants. Scores from a group of trainees gathered prior to a training program might be compared with scores for the same group after completion of the training. The *t*-test might also be used to compare different sample means in service delivery situations, such as filling boxes or bottles. Many similar uses are possible. Minimum required assumptions for using the *t*-test are listed in Box 16.1.

Only two sets of means can be compared at any one time using the *t*-test. The DATA ANALYSIS tool in Microsoft Excel contains three different types of t-tests. The *t*-tests in Excel are to be used only when the manager has all the individual measurements available. ANOVA, which compares variances between samples, also requires that the raw data be available. When this is not the case and the researcher has only the mean scores at hand, it is possible to make a similar comparison using just summary data and the Excel mathematical formula capability.

As in one-sample hypothesis testing, the first step must be to prepare the null and alternate hypotheses. It is possible to perform both a one-tailed test and a two-tailed test with the pooled variance *t*-test in Excel. A typical two-tailed test hypothesis pair in a test for a statistically significance difference in population means, would be:

Box 16.1

Minimum Requirements for Applying a *t*-Test

1. The measurements are of at least interval-level data.
2. The samples are randomly selected.
3. The scores are randomly distributed.

$$H_O: \quad \mu_1 = \mu_2$$
$$H_A: \quad \mu_1 \neq \mu_2$$

If a one-tailed test is desired, either a greater or lesser hypothesis pair must be written as follows:

$\mu_1 > \mu_2$	$\mu_1 < \mu_2$
$H_O: \mu_1 \geq \mu_2$	$H_O: \mu_1 \leq \mu_2$
$H_A: \mu_1 < \mu_2$	$H_A: \mu_1 > \mu_2$

The difference between *one-tailed* and *two-tailed* tests is that in one-tailed tests the researcher specifies the direction of the difference: it is either greater or lesser. The probabilities calculated with the *t*-test on a one-tailed test are half of the probabilities for a two-tailed test. It should be noted that selecting either the one- or two-tailed test should not be done arbitrarily. If the manager has no specific reason to expect a difference in one direction, it follows that no prediction can be made in advance. The manager is obligated to use the two-tailed test.

Two factors influence the choice of approach. The first is the nature of the two samples for which measurements are available: *Are they paired or independent?* This question must be answered before selecting one of the several different *t*-test computational methods. The second key characteristic of the data is what is known as *degrees of freedom*. Degrees of freedom refer to the limits to which a set of measurements may vary. The concept is rooted in physics, where an object that can move on a flat plane is said to have *two degrees of freedom*. If it can move in only a straight line, it has just one degree of freedom. In statistics, this idea is used to mean the *number of independent comparisons that can be taken between sets of data*. For example, with two observations, analysis is limited to just one independent comparison. Two "observations" means two independent measurements, such as would be taken from a sample of just two individuals. If there are three observations, then two independent comparisons are possible, and so on. In statistical notation, this is written as "$n - 1$" degrees of freedom (the *n* refers to the total number of observations).

Degrees of freedom are computed differently depending upon whether the data is collected from the same individuals, as in a pretest and a posttest situation, or from different sets of individuals (two independent samples). Data collected from the same individuals at different times are called *correlated data*. Data collected from separate samples are called *uncorrelated data*.

To determine the degrees of freedom for *correlated* data, 1 is subtracted from the total number of cases. To compute the degrees of freedom for *uncorrelated* data, 1 is subtracted from each sample. In statistical notations, this is shown as $df = n_1 + n_2 - 2$. The various *t*-tests contained in Excel include these different values in their computations; all the manager needs to do is to select the correct option.

Table 16.1

Subject Scores Before and After Computer-Assisted Training

Pretest scores (variable 1)	Posttest scores (variable 2)
20.7	19.3
21.7	23.9
17.2	19.9
18.0	24.0
15.1	17.7
21.1	21.5
24.5	25.9
17.8	19.1
23.6	24.0
19.0	19.5

Excel's DATA ANALYSIS function includes a test for paired samples and two tests for independent samples. The two independent sample tests vary in that one assumes the samples were taken from populations with equal variance, while the second test assumes two populations in which the variance is unequal. In practice, this means the manager should select the equal variance option when comparing the means of two samples, both of which were randomly selected from the same larger population. The unequal variance option is to be used when the populations are different. An example would be comparing the means of samples taken from two separate production lines or processing machines.

All two-sample *t*-tests compare sample (or group) means by computing a Student's t-value and comparing the significance of whatever difference is found between the means. Considered to be only slightly less "robust" than the F-test statistic used in analysis of variance procedures, the *t*-test can be used to test the means for either different (independent) samples or paired samples. "Different samples" refers most often to different groups within a larger sample.

For example, the attitudes of nonsupervisory personnel might be compared with the attitudes of management; the responses of females in a sample might be compared with those of males. Paired sample testing refers to testing for differences between two separate variables. Examples include comparing the mean scores on a pretest given before a training activity (variable 1) with the mean of a second test given after the training session (variable 2). Table 16.1 displays data from a paired-sample, pre-and posttest example.

COMPARING GROUPS WITH ANOVA

Analysis of variance (ANOVA) is a powerful tool for comparing the differences in means between any number of groups and for doing so at more than one level. With ANOVA, it is possible to test the role of each of several variables independently and then to determine whether two or more variables *interact* to influence the differences between groups' scores.

A classical example often cited is testing the influence of farm plot location (or any other variable, such as amount of water applied) and the amount of fertilizer on crop yields. Each variable can be tested by itself. Then the two are tested for interactive influence on the yield result. Analysis of variance is also regularly used in social research studies to compare mean attitude scores of potential client groups.

In all applications, analysis of variance uses an F-statistic (actually, a ratio) in a comparison of the variances of mean scores. The test compares the variance of the mean to the overall variance found in the sample. Decisions about the null hypothesis are based on these comparisons.

To make its comparisons, analysis of variance compares the means of two samples or two groups within a sample. Furthermore, analysis of variance results include summary statistics for each sample or group, an F-ratio and a probability value. This makes interpretation simple: The means are "statistically different" if the p-value is less than the analyst-selected confidence level. Interpretation is not as easy when more than two groups or levels are compared. Another way to interpret the test is to refer to the "critical F" value produced along with the F statistic and p-value (in the past, analysts had to look this value up in a table of t-values). The critical F-value is compared with the computed F-statistic (called the *F-ratio*); if the computed F is smaller than the critical value, the null hypothesis is rejected.

The p-value of the F-ratio will indicate whether the null hypothesis is to be rejected, but it will not indicate where the differences lie. Another test, called an *a posteriori* test or a *post hoc* test, is required. When one of these is selected, statistically significant differences will be indicated. Those differences that are statistically "the same" will be so marked. None of these "after the fact" tests are available in Excel, but they are available in more powerful statistical packages such as SPSS.

THREE VERSIONS OF ANOVA

Managers have three different versions of analysis of variance: a one-way version, a two-way version, and an "*n*-way" version.

One-Way Analysis of Variance

One-way analysis of variance is the basic procedure; it is used when two or more groups' means are compared across a single factor. For example, a children's services agency administrator might want to know if teenage and preteen students from high-income families respond differently to a film on underage use of alcoholic beverages than do students from low-income families. The response variable must be at least interval level; the grouping variable can be any level data. In this case, it might be family income. The single factor score might be a measurement of students' scores on a recall test given after viewing the film.

One-way ANOVA compares the mean scores on a scale variable across two or more categories of a single categorical variable. The group of cases or subjects that make up each category are referred to as *subsamples* or *subgroups,* and the categorical variable itself is called a *grouping variable.* Grouping variables are often demographic characteristics, such as gender, marital status, ethnic group, education level, or occupation.

Three different ways of estimating variance are possible: (1) a total estimate of the variance of all cases, (2) a between-group estimate based on the variation of the subgroups' means around a "grand mean," which is nothing more than a mean of the means, and (3) a within-group estimate that is based on the variation of subgroup cases around their subgroup mean. ANOVA divides the between-group variance by the within-group variance to come up with a value that is called the F-ratio, or F-statistic. The total group variance is not used in ANOVA.

When using one-way ANOVA to compare group means, the null hypothesis should be that the means of the subgroups are the same (or equal). Another way to state the null hypothesis is that there is no statistically significant difference in the means of the two (or more) groups.

Degrees of Freedom

The number of degrees of freedom affects estimates of population variance in ANOVA tests. A different F-distribution has been calculated for nearly every combination of degrees of freedom; these values are included in the appendices of almost all statistics textbooks. Until the advent of powerful desktop computers, researchers were forced to manually calculate the three different variances and an F-ratio. This F-ratio was then compared with the appropriate statistic in the F-tables. Tabular F-values were available for both the .05 and .10 levels of confidence. Null hypothesis decisions were based on these comparisons. Today, however, most statistical packages calculate an F-ratio and a significance value for each set of variables. Therefore, it is no longer necessary to determine the number of degrees of freedom. Since they are identified for the researcher, it is still traditional to include the number of degrees of freedom in the ANOVA analysis results.

Remember, if the significance value is less than .05 (the traditional decision point), the subgroups' means are statistically different.

Interpreting One-Way ANOVA

Researchers should include the value of the F-statistic (F-ratio), the degrees of freedom involved in the test, and the associated probability or significance (sig.) value. The following example represents the method used for testing differences in the mean scores of two groups.

A new manager was hired to improve morale at a government agency. The previous manager had alienated volunteers and staff; employee morale had declined dramatically, product quality and customer service were ranked as very poor by the agency's clients, and volunteer retention was becoming a major problem. The manager wanted to determine if both staff workers and volunteers perceived the company climate in the same way. A seven-point composite organizational climate scale was administered to a random selection of twenty workers and fifteen volunteers. Individual scores on the scale are shown in Table 16.2.

The manager's null hypothesis was: "There is no difference in the way staff employees and volunteers rate the organization's climate." To test this hypothesis, a one-way analysis of variance procedure was used. The results of that procedure are presented in Figure 16.2.

To interpret these results, refer to the p-value of 0.000004, which was printed along with the F-ratio of 28.02889. The large F-value alone would suggest that the difference in the two groups' means is statistically significant. This assumption is strongly supported by the very small p-value. In this case, the researcher rejects the null hypothesis.

Table 16.2

Organizational Climate Scales Scores, Staff and Volunteers

			Scores					
		Staff				Volunteers		
3.0	5.0	3.0	4.0	5.0	2.0	2.0	3.0	4.0
5.0	6.0	5.0	5.0	3.0	4.0	3.0	4.0	2.0
3.0	3.0	4.0	6.0	3.0	4.0	2.0	2.0	1.0
7.0	4.0	5.0	6.0	2.0	1.0	1.0	3.0	2.0
3.0	5.0	6.0	4.0	5.0	3.0	2.0	3.0	1.0

Figure 16.2 Results of an Excel Single-Factor ANOVA Test

Anova: Single Factor

SUMMARY

Groups	Count	Sum	Average	Variance
Staff	25	110	4.4	1.666667
Management	20	49	2.45	1.102632

ANOVA

Source of Variation	SS	df	MS	F	P-value	F crit
Between Groups	42.25	1	42.25	29.80722	0.0000	4.067047
Within Groups	60.95	43	1.417442			
Total	103.2	44				

Two-Way ANOVA

Two-way analysis of variance designs are the simplest example of a class of statistical tests developed for what are called factorial experiments or *factorial designs*. In all such cases, the goal of two-way ANOVA is to test the means of two or more groups on two variables or factors at the same time. In addition, the procedure tests the *interaction effect*—whether two or more of the variables working together my have had an impact on the differences.

Here is an example of a two-factor analysis of variance procedure: The administrator of a municipal water department has been authorized to begin an advertising campaign to encourage conservation. The administrator wants to establish which is the best day to advertise in the local paper and in which section of the paper the ad should appear. Thus, the two factors are *day* and *position*. Four days of the week are tested: Wednesday, Thursday, Friday, and Saturday. Three locations are tested: general news (the first two sections of the paper), the sports section, and the family section, which includes the entertainment pages. Readership will be measured by the results of a telephone survey of the paper's subscribers, in which respondents are asked whether they saw the ad. Table 16.3 displays the totals for the two factors. Figure 16.3 displays the results of an Excel two-factor analysis of variance procedure.

The two factors being tested are *position* and *day* of the week. Three levels of the *position* variable are included in order to match the four *days* of the levels. Four measurements are made in each sample unit, making it necessary to record forty-eight total observations. Analysis of variance will compare the means of the four levels of each of the three positions for the four days in each position.

This analysis of variance procedure will compute an F-table with *p*-values and critical F-values for each of the three positions, the four day variables (labeled as "columns" in the ANOVA summary table), and a measurement of the effect of any interaction between *position* and *day*.

There are three results to interpret in the ANOVA results produced in this Excel application of the test. The first null hypothesis was that there is no difference in the *position* factor. These are the groups in the table; each includes four iterations of the response results. The second null hypothesis is that there is no difference in the days of the week on which the advertisement is placed.

Table 16.3

Daily Responses by Position and Day of Week

Position in Paper	Day of the Week			
	Wednesday	Thursday	Friday	Saturday
1	933	979	1,240	1,610
1	1,004	1,112	1,299	1,020
1	933	1,003	1,353	1,003
1	979	980	1,222	1,900
2	1,217	1,172	1,175	1,945
2	1,171	1,034	1,371	1,837
2	1,178	1,011	1,421	1,958
2	1,230	1,021	1,314	1,851
3	1,021	1,871	1,889	1,835
3	1,015	1,735	1,948	1,631
3	1,041	1,642	1,872	1,500
3	995	1,675	1,919	1,720

Figure 16.3   **Two-Factor ANOVA Results with Interaction**

Anova: Two-Factor with Replication

SUMMARY	WEDNESDAY	THURSDAY	FRIDAY	SATURDAY	Total
GENERAL NEWS (1)					
Count	4	4	4	4	16
Sum	3849	4074	5114	5533	18570
Average	962.25	1018.5	1278.5	1383.25	1160.625
Variance	1244.916667	4008.333333	3548.333333	198328.9167	74228.38333
SPORTS (2)					
Count	4	4	4	4	16
Sum	4796	4238	5281	7591	21906
Average	1199	1059.5	1320.25	1897.75	1369.125
Variance	836.6666667	5713.666667	11287.58333	3912.916667	112788.3833
FAMILY (3)					
Count	4	4	4	4	16
Sum	4072	6923	7628	6686	25309
Average	1018	1730.75	1907	1671.5	1581.8125
Variance	358.6666667	10224.25	1124.666667	20045.66667	127379.3625
Total					
Count	12	12	12	12	
Sum	12717	15235	18023	19810	
Average	1059.75	1269.583333	1501.916667	1650.833333	
Variance	11807.29545	121749.9015	94174.81061	108985.9697	

ANOVA

Source of Variation	SS	df	MS	F	P-value	F crit
Sample	1419238.042	2	709619.0208	32.67190463	0.000000008	3.25944427
Columns	2431282.229	3	810427.4097	37.31327129	0.000000000	2.866265447
Interaction	1502755.958	6	250459.3264	11.53151619	0.000000360	2.363748308
Within	781903.75	36	21719.54861			
Total	6135179.979	47				

The final null hypothesis is that there is no interaction between the two factors as they relate to any differences in *position* and *day*. The researcher can interpret the ANOVA results in two ways. First is the traditional *p*-value approach. Since these are less than the .05 level of confidence, we can reject the null hypotheses. Another way is to compare the F-statistic with the critical value of F. In the past, analysts had to look this up in a table of values for various degrees of freedom and values for the .05 and .01 levels of confidence. This is no longer necessary. The critical value for the data and degrees of freedom are presented alongside the *p*-value. If the F-statistic is smaller than the critical value from the F-table, the null hypothesis is retained. In this example, the F-statistic is larger than the critical F for all three hypotheses. Hence, all three null hypotheses must be rejected. The samples (newspaper locations) are statistically different from one another.

Three-Way ANOVA and More

Three-way designs are very much like two-way ANOVA. The principal effects of each factor are examined to see if it makes a difference between groups. This is followed by tests for interactions among the variables. However, now these interactions are expanded; two-way interactions, three-way interactions, and more are evaluated. The results are interpreted in the same way as one- and two-way analyses.

SUMMARY

This chapter has looked at a number of the ways decision makers test for differences in data sets. With regression and correlation analyses, difference tests are probably the inferential statistical tools used most often by researchers and managers in public administration and nonprofit organizations.

Two broad classes of tests were discussed. First, the various two-sample *t*-tests were examined. Minor variations in portions of the computation formulas are necessary for paired or independent samples. The Microsoft Excel analysis programs Function Wizard and Data Analysis Tools both take these differences into consideration, allowing the researcher to specify which computation procedure to follow. The paired-sample *t*-tests in Microsoft Excel can be used to compare the means for the two variables (pretest and posttest), report the difference in the means, and calculate a *p*-value for the *t*-statistic. The samples may be paired or independent. Independent samples may be from one population with equal variance or from different samples with unequal variance.

Typically, *t*-tests can be used to compare the means of only two groups at a time. They are used with small sample sizes (around a total of thirty cases), and they should be used with groups that are equal in size. Analysis of variance (with the F-test) is used for samples of any size and with any number of groups or subgroups. Three different levels of analysis of variance (ANOVA) tests were discussed.

ADDITIONAL READING

Brightman, Harvey J. 1999. *Data Analysis in Plain English with Microsoft Excel.* Pacific Grove, CA: Duxbury Press.
Levine, David M., Mark L. Berenson, and David Stephan. 1997. *Statistics for Managers Using Microsoft Excel.* Upper Saddle River, NJ: Prentice Hall.
Miller, Gerald J., and Marcia L. Whicker, eds. 1999. *Handbook of Research Methods in Public Administration.* New York: Marcel Dekker.

17

TESTING RELATIONSHIPS WITH CORRELATION AND REGRESSION

Measurements of two or more variables often appear to be related to each other. Measuring the strength of such relationships is, in fact, one of the basic tasks of data analysis in public and non-profit organizations. For example, suppose that public use of a municipal government agency's recycling service has declined each of the past three years. The agency director might suspect that the public's use of the service is directly related to the price charged for that service—the decline began right after a 30 percent increase in the fee. Although the city has been growing rapidly, new residents have not been signing up for the service. Citizens' complaints about the rude behavior and slovenly appearance of the collection staff have increased in number. A group of university students conducted a study of 100 residents to determine the attitudes of citizens toward the service. The findings included a high level of concern that the town's largest employer is considering closing its local factory because of the high cost of dealing with wastes generated by the operations of the plant.

The department director called a meeting of department heads and first-line supervisors. The following conclusions came out of that discussion session:

- Public awareness of environmental issues is related to perceived issue importance.
- Jobs are more important to people than protecting the local environment.
- Maintaining consistent quality of the service is a product of employee satisfaction.
- The level of service provided to citizens by a government agency's staff is related to staff workload.
- Individual employee productivity is related to the amount or type of training received.

A group of administrators looked at the study information and came to these conclusions:

- Public awareness of environmental issues is related to the amount and type of information they receive.
- Program quality is affected by the commitment of staff providers to the program mission.
- Government employees' job satisfaction is related to the announcement of a deferred pay increase.
- Employee productivity varies with changes in the weather (e.g., spring fever).

It was not possible for the director to look at any of these conclusions and determine that a cause-and-effect relationship exists. Without conducting some sort of experiment, all that the director can deduce from the information at hand is that two or more variables might be related in some way.

At first glance there might seem to be intuitively obvious relationships or associations between any two or more variables. However, the relationship is not always what it might appear to be. Variables appear to be associated, but there may be another "confounding" factor affecting the issue.

Obviously, it would be completely irresponsible for the director to make major decisions based on his or her feelings about such relationships. Instead, it is better to assume that associations do not exist until "proven" statistically; that is, until they are shown to be *statistically significant*. The phrase "statistically significant" is a way of stating the researcher's conclusion that the relationship did not occur because of chance alone—some other factor is involved.

Before making an important decision, the department director must look for additional evidence and then weigh how strong that evidence might be. Fortunately, an extensive body of easy-to-use statistical tools exists to help decision makers identify and weigh relationship evidence. The term used to describe relationships between any two or more variables is *correlation,* although words like *relationship* and *association*s are also used interchangeably; they are assumed to have the same meaning.

Correlation can be measured in many ways, depending upon the nature of the measurement data. However, the logic behind correlation tests is similar to that found in hypothesis testing. A null hypothesis states that the variables are independent; they are not related. We use relationship tests for testing these kinds of hypotheses. Public agency administrators first want to know if the variables related; second, in what way they are related; and third, how strong the relationship is.

THE MEANING OF CORRELATION

Association between variables is product of the way they *covary* (that is, the way and amount that they vary *together*). Covariance means that there is some connection between the variables, as seen by the way they variables change together. We cannot conclude that one variable is causing another variable to change with it; relationship is not causation. However, covariance does mean that the two variables are related in some way that results in the two of them "moving" together.

Analysts are interested in three key measurements associated with correlations. First, they want to know the strength of the relationship. Strength is indicated by the size of the *correlation coefficient,* which, except for nominal data, can run from −1.0 to +1.0.

With nominal data, the range of values only runs from 0.0 to 1.0, with no way to determine the direction of the relationship. Plus or minus 1.0 is considered to be a "perfect," or 100 percent, relationship. When the correlation coefficient is squared, it loses its sign, but can then be used as a way of explaining the difference in percentage points. For example, an r^2 of 0.56 is interpreted as variable A (the independent variable) explains 56 percent of the change in variable B (the dependent variable).

Second, researchers want to know the direction of the relationship. That is, is it a positive of negative relationship? Is a positive (or upward) change in one variable reflected by a positive or upward change in the second variable? Or is the relationship the obverse; with a positive change in one variable reflected in a negative or downward change in the other variable?

The third thing that people want to know about a relationship is its *statistical significance.* Statistical significance relates only to interval/ratio data (scale data in SPSS); it is only of interest when dealing with inferential or parametric statistics. Statistical significance is a test of the likelihood that the sample results reflect the total population of interest. It is often described as a *confidence test only.* Statistical significance tells the analyst the likelihood of the sample relationship representing a similar relationship in a larger population. If it is not significant, there is always a greater chance that the relationship does not exist in the larger population and that it occurred only by chance in the sample data.

How does the researcher know for certain that the relationship is "real"? Of course, the researcher can never be 100 percent certain but can put lots of trust in the computation of significance values by modern statistical software. Significance is identified for all correlation coefficients when it is either significant at the .05 or the .01 level of confidence, or both. The indication appears as a single or a double asterisk.

WHAT DOES CORRELATION TELL US?

Although correlation tests are also used for prediction, most of the time the test is used as an explanatory tool. One or more tables of bivariate (two variables at a time), linear relationship can be found in nearly all quantitative study reports. The correlation table should be looked upon as a summary table. Researchers develop descriptive, explanatory statements about the relationships printed in the summary table, highlighting the highest and, often, the lowest bivariate correlation values and their significant level, if available. Some researchers also use the table results to suggest, or make inferences, about causality for higher-level coefficients, although this is not an appropriate use for correlation.

Finally, reporting the tables in the research report when a large number of scale values are compared at once can be extremely confusing. As a result, analysts often make some arbitrary cut in what they report and what they leave out. A typical example is to include all correlation coefficients that exceed ± 0.40 or 0.50, or, if a great many still exist, raise the cutoff to 0.60.

Testing for Relationships

Relationship tests have two broad applications with hypotheses testing: (1) they can be used to examine the way in which variables vary together (*covariation*), or (2) they can be used to suggest whether a *causal* relationship exists.

An example of a *covariational* relationship is the statement that "Wisdom increases with age." The hypothesis is that as people get older, they also get smarter; the two phenomena change together. An example of a *causal* relationship is a prediction that if expenditures on communication are increased, awareness of the service provided by an agency will also increase. The hypothesis in this instance is that communication "causes" public awareness. Researchers and administrators are always on the lookout for these *cause-and-effect* relationships. Because covariational relationships are seldom studied in public administration organizational applications, only causal relationships will be discussed here.

All causal relationships have three key characteristics in common. First, the variables always vary together (either positively or negatively). Second, a time factor is always involved. One variable must change in order to "cause" a commensurate change in the other. The *independent variable* always changes first, followed by the *dependent variable.*

Finally, the relationship is statistically significant; it did not appear through chance alone. In other words, it is not a "fake" or "spurious" relationship. An example of a fake relationship occurred more than fifty years ago when scientists reported an increase in the number of people being diagnosed with cancer. It was also reported elsewhere that more families were cooking with pots and pans made of aluminum. Reporters assumed that a cause-and-effect relationship existed between these two independent social factors. Knowledgeable scientists quickly debunked this spurious relationship. People still cook with aluminum pots and pans, and the incidence of most cancers is declining.

THE LINK BETWEEN REGRESSION AND CORRELATION

The analytical techniques used to test relationships fall into two families of tests: *regression analysis* and *correlation analysis.* Correlation analysis is concerned with providing a mathematical measurement of the *strength* of a relationship between variables. Regression analysis, on the other hand, identifies *the way* in which two or more variables are related. Correlation and regression analyses should only be used with interval- and ratio-level measurements. When dealing with categorical or ranked data, other, somewhat less powerful relationship tests are available.

Regression analysis provides a way to estimate the value of one variable from the value of another, or of determining the way in which two or more variables are associated. Correlation analysis, on the other hand, enables us to measure the degree to which the two variables are related; this is called the "strength" of the relationship. Correlation analysis lets us measure the strength of the relationship and, with data above nominal level, indicates the direction of that association—positive or negative. Correlation analysis should be used instead of regression analysis when the only question the decision maker has is: "How strongly are the two variables related?"

If all the paired points of X and Y lie on a straight line, then the correlation between the variables is said to be "perfect"; the correlation value is 1.0. The value 0.0 is used when there is no association whatsoever between the variables. The value 1.0 represents a perfect *positive* correlation; −1.0 is the value for a perfect *negative* correlation. A negative correlation means that as the values on the x-axis *increase,* y-axis values *decrease;* oppositely, as x-axis values decrease, y-axis values increase.

In correlation analysis, these numerical values serve as a mathematical summary measure of the degree of correlation between the X and Y variables. The summary number is the *correlation coefficient;* it is expressed in statistical notation as the lowercase Greek letter r. For *nominal*-level measurements, the value of any r falls between 0.0 and 1.0 (negative relationships are not noted). For all other measurements (*ordinal, interval,* and *ratio* data), the value falls between −1.0 and +1.0 (negative relationships are noted).

Some writers use the term *agreement* to refer to the relationship between variables. For example, in discussing scores from an evaluative test such as the General Management Aptitude Test (GMAT), separate scores are reported for mathematics and language abilities. If an applicant receives perfect scores in both parts of the examination, the scores are said to be *in perfect agreement.* If, on the other hand, the applicant receives a perfect score on one part and a very low score on the other part of the examination, the scores are said to be in *perfect disagreement.* This is an example of the *covariational* application of correlation discussed at the beginning of this chapter.

THE COEFFICIENT OF DETERMINATION

The coefficient of determination (r^2) is the square of the correlation coefficient value (r); it is probably the most useful measurement in correlation analysis. It provides a clear, easy-to-understand measurement of the *explanatory power* of a correlation coefficient. In addition, r^2 can help show how close the computed r describes the relationship between two variables.

For example, say that a correlation coefficient of 0.667 is found to exist between the variables *awareness* and *communications*. Squaring this value gives an r^2 of 0.44. In this way, the coefficient of determination can be used for an interpretation that everyone can understand. It would be interpreted as follows: 44 percent of the variation in the variable *awareness* is "explained" by variation in spending on *communications,* while 56 percent is "unexplained." That is, it may be due to other, unidentified factors.

An important caveat to keep in mind when making such interpretations of the results of correlation analysis is that it is never possible to say for certain that a dependent variable or variables actually *causes* a change in the independent variable (that "X causes Y"). Instead, the researcher can only report the existence and strength of a statistical relationship.

Calculating and Interpreting Correlation Values

It only takes three quick steps to provide most of the information a researcher needs to have about the potential relationship between a set of values. If Microsoft Excel is used, these steps are:

1. The XY SCATTER PLOT in the Chart Wizard
2. The CORREL command in the Function Wizard
3. The RSQ calculations, also in the Function Wizard

A set of categories has been established for describing correlations (relationships) in terms that have meaning for everyone; they range from 0 to 1, in units of twenty percentage points for each level. The categories, their labels, and their respective values are displayed in Table 17.1. It is important to remember that these are only intuitive interpretations; others use different but similar labels for the correlation values.

Table 17.2 displays another example of a suggested scheme for interpreting correlation coefficients (Miller 1991). Miller adds the following additional interpretation guidelines: (1) the usefulness of a correlation is determined by its size, (2) the sign of the coefficient has no bearing on the strength of the relationship; it determines only the direction of the relationship: positive or negative.

The Coefficient of Determination (r²)

Interpretations of the correlation coefficient (r) and the coefficient of determination (r^2) are slightly different. For example, for two-test score data, an r-value of −0.99 could be interpreted as: "The correlation coefficient of −0.99 suggests that the relationship between the two test scores is very strong; the two variables have a nearly perfect negative relationship." The r^2 of this coefficient (the coefficient of determination) is 0.95. This could be interpreted as: "The r^2 of 0.95 suggests that 95 percent of the movement in the Y variable is explained by movement in the X variable."

REGRESSION ANALYSIS

Regression analysis is a statistical procedure developed to determine whether two or more interval- or ratio-level variables are related and whether the change in one variable is related in any way to movement in the other or others. To put it another way, regression analysis allows the decision maker to determine how different values of one variable (called the *dependent variable*) might or might not help to *explain* variation in another variable (the *independent variable*).

Table 17.1

Interpretation Guidelines for Correlation Values

00.0	=	No relationship
0.01–0.19	=	Weak relationship
0.20–0.39	=	Low but definite relationship
0.40–0.59	=	Moderate relationship
0.60–0.79	=	Strong relationship
0.80–0.99	=	Very strong relationship
± 1.00	=	A perfect positive or negative relationship

Table 17.2

Interpretation Guidelines, Alternate Approach

0.00–0.19	Little or no relationship
0.20–0.39	Some slight relationship
0.40–0.59	Substantial relationship
0.60–0.79	Strong useful relationship
0.80–0.99	High relationship
± 1.00	Perfect relationship

Source: Adapted from Miller 1991.

This is the methodology underlying experiments, which are often specifically designed to determine whether changes in one variable will influence changes in another variable. The testing of the effect of changing state sales tax rates on residential consumption of water is an example of an experiment. In such an experiment, a legislative research team might test different rates for a three-month period in three similar communities in the state. A random sample of water-use records of 100 customers will be selected from each community and a three-month average for the same period for the previous year established as the benchmark against which changes in consumption will be compared. In each test, only one variable—the tax rate—will be changed, with all other variables kept as constant as possible. Different tax rates will be randomly assigned for each community; each community is a *test market*. The test will then run over a three-month period. At the end of the test period, changes in consumption rates in each household in each test market will be compared to see if the tax rate had any impact on demand.

In addition to measuring the way in which variables are related, regression analysis also enables managers to predict responses or reactions to changes in independent variables. Such predictions are often needed before making expenditure decisions. From the above example, a state utility regulator will be able to predict with some degree of certainty citizens' water use at different price levels. This, in turn, will enable the legislature to predict what tax revenue it can expect from utility purchases and help local water distribution utility managers predict how much water they will need. The finance staff will be able to predict how much money to borrow to build new wells, pipelines, or other physical plant facilities to meet growth in demand. In this way, researchers are often able to measure citizen reaction to potential shifts in policies. Prediction is one of the most important (if not *the* most important) uses of regression analysis results.

The Regression Procedure

The regression analysis procedure begins with collecting a data set that includes pairs of observed values or measurements. One set of measurements is needed for each variable to be included in the analysis. The idea of *pairs of measurements* may be somewhat misleading. It does not mean regression analysis is restricted to analyzing just two variables at a time. With multiple regression analysis, which will be discussed later, many variables can be included. The term *pairs* refer instead to measurements for a *dependent* and one or more *independent* variables.

The next step in the procedure is to produce a scatter plot of the measurements. Value pairs should be plotted as points on a *scatter diagram.* A scatter diagram has two axes: a vertical line (the *y-axis),* and a horizontal line (the *x-axis).* The vertical line represents values on the dependent (or changed) variable. Of course, the data points do not need to be plotted by hand; most statistical software programs produce scatter diagrams with little effort by the researcher.

Regression analysis evaluates all recorded data points and computes a regression equation. A *function,* or numerical value, is produced which, when multiplied with independent variable values, lets the decision maker *predict* the value of the independent (Y) variable given a value of the X variable or variables. The final step in the regression analysis procedure is interpretation of the findings.

The Regression Equation

Interpreting the findings of a regression analysis statistical procedure begins with fitting the sample data to a "best-fit" line. The regression analysis procedure does this through a process called the *method of least squares.* This process measures the amount each point varies from a proposed line, squares each deviation, and then sums the squares.

After computing these values, the minimum squared value of all differences establishes the slope of the regression line. At the same time, the regression process determines the point at which the y-axis (the vertical line in the scatter diagram) and the computed regression line would meet. This point is called the *intercept.*

Once this point is known, the regression equation is used to predict additional points along the line, given a value for the x-axis. In statistical notation, the regression equation is expressed thus:

$$Y = a + bX$$

where

$Y =$ the value of Y calculated from the estimated regression equation
$a =$ the point on Y where the regression line intercepts on Y
$b =$ the amount of change in X required for a corresponding change in Y which, when plotted, represents the slope of the line
$X =$ a measured value for X

(Note: In some statistics texts, the statistical symbol for the Y intercept point is given as b_0, and the symbol for the regression slope value as b_1.)

The Linear Regression Equation

The regression equation for straight-line regression (linear) is depicted as:

$$Y_i = b_0 + b_1 X_i$$

where

Y_i = the predicted value of Y for measurement i
X_i = the value of X for measurement i

In general terms, the $Y = a + bX$ equation is interpreted in this way: "As X changes, Y also changes by b times the change in X."

Once the regression equation has been obtained, predictions or estimates of the dependent variable can be made. For example, say that we have computed the following regression equation:

$$Y = 4.0199 + .00896 * X$$

This could be interpreted to mean that the regression line begins at that point on the vertical axis that coincides with the value of 4.0199. Then, any subsequent increase in a value on the x-axis, multiplied by 0.00876 and then added to 4.0199 will equal a corresponding change in Y. By moving along the x-axis and periodically plotting the increases to both X and Y, connecting each point, it is possible to get a graphic impression of the regression line.

The Shape of the Regression Line

The shape of the regression line is an indication of how much of the change in the independent variable is explained by the dependent variable. The regression equation indicates how steep the line must be and whether it slopes to the right or left or is curvilinear. Decision makers look for a *linear* relationship, one that shows a definite relationship between the variables. When very little or no relationship exists, the scatter plot will show the data points distributed haphazardly around the space with no connection visible.

Not all relationships will be linear. Some will be curvilinear; some will be more or less flat, showing no relationship whatsoever; some may be U-shaped; and others take on S-like patterns. Techniques are available for dealing with nonlinear relationships, but are not part of most introductory management statistics texts, and are not discussed here.

An Example of Simple Regression

Colindale River Medical Services is a storefront provider of low-cost health services with fifty-eight branches in a twelve-state area. Although officially a nonprofit organization, the organization must have enough income to pay for operations, such as rents and salaries. Fees for service are charged on a sliding scale of fees based on family income and size, and many patients receive care free of charge. Lately, however, income has not met expenses. The board of directors of the organization is interested in knowing what relationship, if any, is between the number of patients and gross income. The data will be used to show branch clinic supervisors whether they would benefit by increasing the number of patients. Data is collected from a random sample of twenty representative operations. The total number of patients served per week and the gross revenue was collected from each clinic in the sample. The data are shown in Table 17.3.

A regression analysis is then conducted on the data. In this simple example, decision makers may use three Microsoft Excel Wizard applications. First, the Excel Chart Wizard XY SCATTER PLOT program may be used to graphically display the type of relationship that exists between the two variables. If the scatter diagram reveals a linear relationship, the next step is to call up the

Table 17.3

Sample of Patients and Gross Income at 20 Clinics, July 7–14

Sample clinic	Weekly patients	Income (in dollars)
1	853	8,000
2	916	9,534
3	259	4,420
4	372	4,798
5	345	4,740
6	444	5,098
7	431	4,765
8	255	3,623
9	365	3,652
10	320	5,210
11	575	6,132
12	425	4,610
13	358	5,003
14	507	5,876
15	476	6,100
16	380	4,775
17	710	8,733
18	438	5,244
19	972	9,989
20	452	6,340

CORREL (correlations) program under the Function Wizard. The value produced is the correlation coefficient (also referred to as the *Pearson Product Moment Correlation Coefficient* after the statistician who first reported its application).

The third step is to interpret the relationship findings. Using the RSQ (R-square) capability in the Function Wizard makes it much easier to make an interpretation. The r^2 value produced is the *coefficient of determination;* it is used to express the relationship as a *percentage.*

The final step in this process is to compute the slope of the regression line and its intercept with the y-axis. These are two separate steps in Excel: INTERCEPT and SLOPE. The results of these tests are shown under Figure 17.1.

Two Approaches to Regression

When carrying out a regression analysis procedure, two approaches are possible. They differ only in the number of variables used in the regression equation. The first is called "simple regression" and includes just one independent variable to explain one dependent variable. The second approach is known as "multiple regression analysis" and, as its name implies, involves more than one independent variable in the regression equation.

The test statistic in both simple and multiple regression analysis is *Pearson's r,* which ranges in value from −1.0 (a perfect negative relationship) to +1.0 (a perfect positive relationship). The square of Pearson's r (r^2) is the *coefficient of determination.* This value represents the *proportion* of the variation in Y that can be explained by linear regression on X. This makes interpreting the results easy. The researcher simply states the obvious: "An r^2 of .37 means the 37 percent of the variation (or change) in Y can be explained by changes in the combination of variables in X."

Figure 17.1

Results of Excel CORREL and Related Regression Analysis Tests

Test results	
CORREL	0.950299
R^2	0.903069
INTCEPT	$1,725
SLOPE	8.336909

THE STANDARD ERROR OF THE ESTIMATE

One of the key concepts of statistics discussed early in this section on quantitative analysis had to do with measures of variability. These included the range, variance, and standard deviation. Seldom, if ever, do measurements fit neatly into values that researchers would like. Instead, individual measurements almost always vary, positively *and* negatively, around some central point. In our discussion of descriptive statistics, this central point was the mean score. A similar variability applies in regression analysis, although now the central point is the computed best line of regression. Because the observed data points do not all fall on the regression line, the regression equation is never a perfect indicator of association; rather, it is an estimate. How close it comes to estimating can be judged by computing one additional value, the *standard error of the estimate.*

In statistical notation, the standard error of the estimate is indicated by the symbol S_{yx}. When calculated, the standard error of the estimate provides a measure of the variation around the fitted or best line of regression. This value is measured in the same units as the dependent variable (Y) in much the same way that the standard deviation measures variability around the mean.

In application, the standard error of the estimate is used to make inferences about the predicted value of Y. For example, a small standard error suggests that the data points cluster relatively closely to the plotted regression line. In a word, the data are *homogeneous.* A large standard error suggests that data points are widely disbursed on either side of the regression line and that a high degree of variability exists. There are no rules or guidelines to establish what is small and what is large in this case. Instead, the researcher must use judgment based on experience.

A second inference statistic is produced with the standard error of the estimate: a *p*-value. The *p*-value can also be used to make decisions about the statistical significance of the relationship between the two variables. Values less than .05, for example, suggest that the relationship is valid, whereas larger *p*-values lead the researcher to conclude that the results are not significant.

SUMMARY

Several different relationship concepts were discussed in this chapter. The two key concepts are *regression analysis* and *correlation analysis.* Regression tells the decision maker if and how two or more variables are related. Correlation analysis provides information about the strength and direction of the relationship. Typically, correlation and regression tests are done for one of two purposes. First, a decision maker may be interested in seeing how two or more variables vary together. A second application is predicting change in one variable by changes in two or more other variables—measuring "cause and effect." Use of regression analysis as a prediction tool is the most commonly used application in public administration and nonprofit organization research.

Two types of regression analysis are used: *simple regression analysis* and *multiple regression analysis*. Simple regression tests the correlation between just two variables, whereas multiple regression analysis computes a regression equation that incorporates the influence of any number of variables. Microsoft Excel includes programs in its Function Wizard for simple regression and correlation analysis and the capability to compute multiple regression analysis in its Data Analysis Tools.

ADDITIONAL READING

Brightman, Harvey J. 1999. *Data Analysis in Plain English with Microsoft Excel.* Pacific Grove, CA: Duxbury Press.
Neufeld, John L. 1997. *Learning Business Statistics with Microsoft Excel.* Upper Saddle River, NJ: Prentice Hall.

18

EXPERIMENTS AND EXPERIMENTAL DESIGN

Administrators at all levels of government and nonprofit organizations are often faced with the need to determine which of several options is the best course of action to select. One way for the researcher to make this decision is to design and conduct an *experiment* first. In an experiment, the researcher takes an active rather than a passive role in the data-gathering process. Rather than simply collecting data from other sources, in an experiment the researcher purposefully manipulates one or more variables. *Manipulation* simply means changing the variable some way. The purpose for making these changes is to measure what effect, if any, they will have on some other variable. The manipulated or changed variable is called the *independent variable*. The variable that an independent variable may have an impact upon is called the *dependent variable* or *response variable*. Both variables are sometimes referred to as *factors*.

Experimental research is often called *causal research* because researchers are checking if the manipulated variable "causes" a change of any direction in the other variable. The purpose of the experiment is to establish whether the independent variable causes a *predictable* level of change in the dependent variable. When this happens, the administrator can initiate or make changes in a public service while having a strong idea of the public's reaction to the change.

In public administration, the dependent variable is often some measure of the public's acceptance of a proposed program or satisfaction with some level of service. In experimentation, these manipulations are known as *treatments*. Examples include:

1. Different prices for services
2. Different ways of doing things, such as methods of training workers
3. Different variations of something, such as methods of public transportation
4. Different amounts of a product or service, such as several different amounts of fertilizer applied to municipal parks and golf courses

An example of a public administration experiment is testing the effectiveness of different communications methods to inform and educate a sample of high school students about ways to prevent contracting AIDS. One instructional method is distributing brochures in the classroom; another method is requiring attendance at an illustrated lecture given by a health-care professional; and a third is showing a film in a health education class. In this experiment, the researcher would randomly assign students to groups receiving each of the three methods. The different groups' scores on a quiz administered after the three education events would be compared to weigh the relative effectiveness of the methods.

Experiments also play an important role in operations and systems design, management tools that are receiving much attention in today's public administration research. Designed experiments involve testing a planned change made to an independent variable, then comparing the results of the change with results of the independent variable without any change. The objective is to determine and/or measure changes in the process. An example is teaching a group of MPA students in the traditional way with lectures and discussions; this becomes the control group. A second group of students is taught the same material in a new way. This is the experimental group. At the end of the experiment, both groups are then administered the same learning achievement examination, with achievement scores compared. The mean scores can then be tested for statistically significant differences.

KEY CONSIDERATIONS IN EXPERIMENTAL DESIGN

The term *experimental design* is used to refer to a variety of different-but-related approaches to conducting an experiment. The term *design* is used to indicate that the experimental method selected is the researcher's decision. The design selected depends first upon what information the administrator needs and second on the resources available to do the research to acquire that information.

There are six key issues to consider when making decisions about what design to follow in an experiment:

1. What *independent* variable or variables should be used in the experiment?
2. What *manipulations* (changes) in the independent variable are most appropriate?
3. Which variable is the most appropriate *dependent* variable?
4. How should changes in the dependent variable be *measured?*
5. What subjects or elements should be chosen as the *test units?*
6. Which *external variables* should be controlled in the experiment?

Selecting the Independent Variable(s)

An *independent variable* is a variable whose values can be changed or manipulated by the researcher. Using different instructional methods, applying different levels of disinfectant chemicals, selecting different prices for a service, using different formats for reports, and trying different performance measurement methods are all independent variables. The researcher can select any variable that can be changed or altered in some way.

Independent variables are variables that the researcher *suspects* influence changes in the dependent variable. The researcher describes this suspected influence in a *hypothesis*. The object of the experiment, then, is to test how and in what way, if any, the suspected influence occurs.

In simple experiments, only two different values of the same independent variable and one dependent variable are tested. For example, in order to identify more effective delivery of prenatal care to indigent females in a farming community, a researcher designs an experiment to determine which of two prenatal service-delivery approaches results in healthier newborn infants. The researcher randomly assigns subjects seeking care to one of two groups. One group will receive prenatal care at a central hospital emergency facility; the second group will receive care in a storefront clinic near to where most patients live. Care is taken to ensure that the same level and type of patient care are provided at both locations.

The researcher uses the two-category care-location variable as the independent variable. The dependent variable in the study is the measure of birth complications recorded for each independent group. The group receiving prenatal care at the hospital emergency facility, which is the traditional delivery location for care to the indigent, is called the *control group*. A control group is the body of subjects whose treatment is not changed; conditions are said to *remain constant*. The experiment is designed to test the program administrator's idea that a storefront delivery system will encourage more of the target population to take advantage of the service. Therefore, the group receiving care at the storefront facility is the *test group*, while the group receiving care at the emergency facility is the *control group*.

Changes in the Independent Variable

Values of independent variables can be any of the four classes of measurement: *nominal, ordinal, interval,* or *ratio* data. In public administration research, however, independent variables are usually nominal or ordinal. This makes them *categorical* in nature.

In the prenatal care delivery example, the changes are the different locations of the service. In a slightly more complex design, three or more methods could have been included with very little additional effort required for processing the results of the experiment. Additional independent variables could also have been included in the design.

For example, suppose the researcher wants to determine whether women living in rural areas respond differently than do women in either suburban or urban locations. Such a design is a "three-by-two" design—three residence locations and two care delivery locations. The researcher would now have the results of six different groups to compare.

The researcher might also want to know if first-time mothers respond differently than patients giving birth for the second time or more. In this case, the researcher would have a "three-by-two-by-two" design, involving twelve groups instead of six.

Adding too many levels or independent variables to the study can cause problems by raising the complexity of the design and the number of groups to compare. In addition, to make sure that each group is large enough to provide meaningful data, the total sample size must be increased. To avoid such complexity and the added cost of a bigger sample size, most public administration experimental research is done with simple, one-variable, random designs.

Selecting the Dependent Variable

Selecting the right variable to test in an experimental study begins with the first statement of the study problem and its relevant component parts. Other terms to identify these parts of a study problem are *constructs, concepts,* and *component factors*. Next, the researcher must identify the most important *measurable* indicators of each basic construct. For example, in a study designed to measure program performance, indicators might be absenteeism, turnover, or employee morale. Each of these can be measured, and each can be a dependent variable in an experiment.

The next step is to develop a hypothesis for each of the indicators and the variables that the researcher believes can impact upon the indicator—that is, "cause" a change in the dependent variable. Variables that can conceivably "cause" increases or decreases in these indicators are what will be tested in the experiment; they are the independent variables.

To learn as much as possible about the problem and its component factors, a researcher often begins with an exploratory study. A primary activity in exploratory studies is conducting a series of interviews with "key informants." Key informants are persons who are assumed to have a greater than normal familiarity with the problem, its symptoms, and its probable causes. Key informants are typically excellent sources of information about the main components of a problem.

Measuring Changes in the Dependent Variable

To identify appropriate units of measurement for a dependent variable in an experiment, the researcher begins by listing everything that can be considered an indicator of one or more facets of the study problem. As noted, indicators are variables that, first, can be identified and measured, and second, can be influenced by another variable in some way. Examples of measurable indicators for a program are:

- Citizen's ability to recall what a program does
- The number of citizens using the program
- How well people can describe activities of the program
- How much people like the program.
- How much people are willing to invest in the effort to participate
- Their ability to describe the benefits of participating

There is obviously more than one way to measure each of these indicators. The unit selected will depend for the most part on the objectives of the study. Possible units of measurement for indicators include the following:

- A numerical scale of client satisfaction
- Growth in the number of clients served
- The amount clients are willing to pay for the service
- The total number of client complaints received
- The percentage of the target population enrolled in the program
- The number of positive statements in subjects' descriptions of the program
- Numerical values assigned to a quantity of acceptable cost (including social cost)
- Number of subjects who can name program benefits

Selecting Test Units

Test units are the clients, citizens, staff members, cities, towns, counties, or any other entity whose responses to manipulations of the independent variable are to be measured. Individual units should be selected randomly from a list of all population units, where every unit has an equal chance of being selected for the study and of being assigned to any of the groups to be tested. Random samples are also known as *probability samples*. A list of potential study subjects is called a *sampling frame*.

Researchers try to achieve sample groupings with *matching units* wherever possible. When this is a concern, it means that the sample selection process is not entirely random. Rather, this process involves what are called *stratified samples*. Selection of a stratified sample is still a random process, but the units are selected from portions of the population that are more or less the same on the characteristic of interest. The idea is for the samples to match as closely as possible the characteristic distribution of the population.

Controlling External Variables

External variables (also known as *confounding* or *extraneous variables*) are variables that may also affect the dependent variable, but that the researcher feels do not directly cause changes in the outcome variable. They can *influence,* but not *cause,* change. Therefore, the researcher takes special steps in the design of the experiment to control or eliminate the effects of these variables. McDaniel and Gates (1993) identified four approaches that are used to control for the effects of extraneous variables:

1. Randomly assigning subjects to treatment groups
2. Physically controlling factors that might influence the results, such as matching subjects on selected characteristics
3. Controlling the design to ensure that only relevant causal variables are manipulated
4. Using statistical control procedures that can make adjustments for the effects of extraneous variables. Analysis of covariance (ANCOVA), for example, does this by making statistical adjustments in the dependent variable value for each treatment.

In addition to controlling for the effects of external variables that might confound the determination of causation, researchers must also control for a variety of other potential experimental design errors (Zikmund 1994). The two main types of error that the research must consider are random sampling error and constant or systematic error. Another word often used to describe constant error is *bias.*

Adhering to random sample selection procedures can control sampling error. Constant or systematic error occurs when external variables, such as testing conditions, are allowed to creep into the experiment. Constant error will distort the results of an experiment in a particular direction.

TYPES OF EXPERIMENTAL DESIGNS

There are many different types of experimental designs. These can be grouped into two basic types: *preexperimental designs* and *true experimental designs.* The basic difference is the amount of independent variable manipulation that is possible. Figure 18.1 is a graphic classification of the main preexperimental and true experimental designs.

Preexperimental Designs

Preexperimental designs are conducted with the same goal as true experimental designs. This is the determination of the ability of an independent variable (or variables) to influence changes in a dependent variable. However, in preexperimental designs the researcher has little if any control over external factors. These designs are appropriately used in exploratory research for identifying potential hypotheses; they should not be considered as strong tests of existing hypotheses. Their major advantage is that they are simple and inexpensive to conduct. There are three main types of preexperimental designs: one-shot case studies, one-group pretest and posttest studies, and static-group comparisons (McDaniel and Gates 1993).

One-Shot Case Study Designs

One-shot case study designs involve exposing a single group of subjects to a single treatment, then measuring the effect on the dependent variable. Only one treatment is used, no control group is involved, and only an "after" measurement is taken. This makes it impossible to determine whether any "caused" change in the dependent variable has taken place. The design does not control for the effects of external variables. The primary reason to use this design is to identify possible causal hypotheses.

Figure 18.1   **A Classification of Experimental Designs**

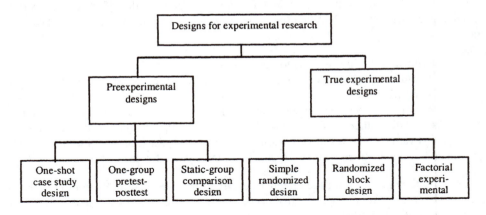

One-Group Pretest–Posttest Designs

This is a very popular design. It allows the researcher to measure change in the dependent variable. Its major drawback is that it does not include a control group, which puts severe limitations on the researcher's ability to control for extraneous variables. Another weakness of the design is that it does not control for any learning or historical effect that might have taken place between the pretest and the posttest. Subjects can often become "test savvy," learning to provide answers that they believe the researcher desires.

Static-Group Comparison Designs

This design is closest to true experimental designs. It involves two samples, a test group and control group. The groups are subjected to different treatments, but no pretesting takes place. Nor are subjects randomly assigned to the different groups.

This design is popular in educational research. In these situations, the test and control groups are two separate classes. Instead of individual subjects being randomly assigned to a group, an entire class is subjectively assigned to either the test or control group. This is done to minimize disruption of normal classroom routine. One instructional method is used with one class, with a different method used in the second class. At the end of the experiment, both groups are tested. Achievement scores are often used as the dependent variable.

True Experimental Designs

The three types of true experimental designs used most often in public administration and nonprofit management research are simple randomized designs, randomized block designs, and factorial designs. A number of variations are possible within each of these categories. Before discussing those possibilities, however, a brief caveat about the results of experiments is in order. It is important for researchers to remember that experimental results will almost always differ from subject to subject, and the effect, if any, of external variables will have greater or lesser impact on individual subjects as well. Therefore, when researchers concern themselves with experimental results for groups, the results should be considered to be only an estimate of the "true" effect.

Table 18.1

A Simple Randomized Two-Group Design

Group	Method of unit selection	Treatment variable	Dependent variable
A. Experimental	Random	X1	O1
B. Control	Random	X2	O2

The only way the "true" effect could ever be determined is if all members of the population were to be included in what is otherwise a perfectly controlled experiment. This never happens in the real world. Therefore, a good experimental design will address this issue by controlling error so that the estimate is as good as possible. An experimental design that achieves this will have the following chief characteristics:

- The design ensures that the observed changes in the dependent variable are unbiased by controlling for randomness error.
- The observed changes (called *treatment effects*) in the dependent variable can be reliably measured, thus controlling for systematic error.
- The effects can be measured with the desired degree of precision (as indicated by the computed confidence level).
- The design will permit an objective test of the null hypothesis; it is an efficient design, one that satisfies all requirements at the "best" cost.

Simple Randomized Designs

Simple randomized experiments test for a causal relationship between just one independent and one dependent variable. These designs are sometimes called *one-factor* designs. In this design, each treatment is independently administered to a different group (not applying or changing a treatment is the same thing as a changed treatment). All sample units are randomly chosen from the parent population and assigned to groups without bias.

The simple randomized design is also known as a *one-way classification* design. This is because only one independent variable is used at a time. However, that variable can have any number of different levels. For example, if the treatment variable in an employee training experiment is training methods, the researcher is not limited to just two different methods; any number of different methods can be included in the same design. As in all true experiments, sample units must be randomly assigned to test and control groups. Graphic representations of two-level and four-level designs are displayed in Table 18.1 and Table 18.2.

While the two-group example in Table 18.1 does not indicate whether a pretest occurred, the design does not preclude that possibility. Conducting a pretest would make it easier to measure effects in the dependent variable and make it possible to be more precise in the final interpretation of the test.

Table 18.2 depicts a simple randomized design with three different treatments and a control group (the control group makes up the fourth treatment group). Test subjects are, again, randomly assigned to each of the four groups.

Randomized Block Designs

In a randomized block design experiment, test units are placed into groups according to selected characteristics of an *external* (extraneous) variable. The purpose of the block design is to make sure

Table 18.2

A Simple Randomized Four-Treatment Design

Group	Method of unit selection	Treatment Variable	Dependent Variable
A. Experimental$_1$	Random	X_1	O_1
B. Experimental$_2$	Random	X_2	O_2
C. Experimental$_3$	Random	X_3	O_3
D. Control$_4$	Random	X_4	O_4

Table 18.3

A Two-Level Randomized Block Design

	Treatments		
Block	Treatment A (brochure)	Treatment B (video)	Treatment C (lecture/discussion)
X (Urban)	X_{1-X}	X_{2-X}	X_{3-X}
Y (Rural)	X_{4-Y}	X_{5-Y}	X_{6-Y}

the test groups are matched as closely as possible on the characteristics of the external variable. This is a method of controlling for any variation "caused" by the extraneous variable.

In the following example, the director of a student club wanted to determine the best way to inform high school students about after-school programs at the club. With the support of school officials and teachers, the director designed an experiment that began by randomly assigning students into three different groups. One group was to learn about the club through a brochure distributed in a classroom. A second group would be shown a short video that described club activities, while a third group would be informed about the club in a classroom presentation given by a club counselor serving as a guest lecturer.

The club director believed that an external factor that could limit club participation was the location of students' residences. Students living in town could travel to and from the club using public transportation. Students residing in rural areas were unable to use city transportation; therefore, she decided to use *residence location* as a blocking variable. This meant that the design now required samples for both urban and rural students. This design is displayed in Table 18.3.

Factorial Designs

Experimental designs that test two or more independent variables at the same time are called "factorial experiments" or "factorial designs" (independent variables are also known as *factors*). In addition to testing for statistically significant differences among individual factors, the procedure also tests whether two or more of the variables working together have an impact on the differences. The term used to describe this combination effect is *interaction effect*.

For an example of a two-factor analysis of variance procedure, a food service manager at a community senior center wants to determine the best day to advertise menu specials in the department's local newspaper. She also wanted to know in which section of the paper the ad should appear. The two factors for this design are *day* and *position*. The design called for ads to run on four different days: Wednesday, Thursday, Friday, and Saturday. Three locations in the paper were to be tested: general news (the first two sections of the paper), the sports section, and the family

Table 18.4

A Two-Factor Experimental Design

Factor I (position)	Factor II (day)			
	Wednesday	Thursday	Friday	Saturday
Position A	A-1	A-2	A-3	A-4
Position B	B-1	B-2	B-3	B-4
Position C	C-1	C-2	C-3	C-4

section (which includes the entertainment pages). Comparisons were to be based on daily sales volume. Table 18.4 displays the design needed for this experiment. Three levels of the *position* variable were included for each of the four levels of the *day* variable, making it necessary to test a total of twelve groups.

Interpreting the Results of Experiments

Various versions of the analysis of variance (ANOVA) statistical procedure are used to interpret the results of experiments. With ANOVA, it is possible to test the role of each of several variables independently and then to determine whether two or more of the variables interact to influence any differences in the dependent variable. ANOVA allows the researcher to test the influence of each factor or variable independently. Then, two or more variables can be tested together to determine if they are interactive in any way in their influence on the result.

SUMMARY

Public administrators and researchers in public administration must often design and carry out laboratory and field experiments. Experiments are used to test hypotheses about the effects of changes in a dependent variable that have been influenced or "caused" by manipulations in an independent variable. Experimental design is the term used to describe a variety of different approaches to experimentation. These can be grouped into two broad categories of experiments, *preexperimental* designs and *true experimental* designs.

Analysis of variance (ANOVA) procedures are used in experimental designs to test for statistically significant differences in the results of two or more groups. These tests use the F-statistic to compare variances between samples or groups. Analysis of variance procedures do not limit the number of groups being compared. Three, four, or more levels or group scores can be compared at the same time. Equally, analysis of variance can test for differences with more than one factor at a time.

One-way analysis of variance tests a single factor for differences. Two-way analysis of variance tests two factors individually and then tests whether the two factors interact in some way to influence the differences. More than two factor analysis of variance procedures, together with tests that permit testing a number of factors with more than one grouping variable (MANOVA), have been developed. Finally, a procedure that combines analysis of variance with regression analysis, ANCOVA, makes it possible to do all these tests at one time.

ADDITIONAL READING

Einspruch, Eric L. 1998. *An Introductory Guide to SPSS for Windows.* Thousand Oaks, CA: Sage.
Montgomery, D.C. 1991. *Design and Analysis of Experiments.* 3rd ed. New York: John Wiley.

19

NONPARAMETRIC STATISTICS

Quantitative data are often grouped into two broad classes of measurements: *parametric* and *nonparametric* statistics. Parametric statistics are measurements about samples and their relationship to populations. Sample measurements are called *statistics;* population measurements are called *parameters.* Parametric statistics are also called *inferential* statistics because the statistical results from the sample are used to make *inferences* about a larger group (a population) from which the sample was drawn. Most quantitative research in public administration and nonprofit management is concerned with parametric statistics.

Measurements can be either *continuous* or *discrete.* Continuous variables can have many different values; they are not restricted to a specific number of categories. *Categorical variables* are variables with specific categories, such as male or female, occupation, and so on. An example of a continuous variable is a test score; an example of a categorical variable is the answer to a yes or no question. Parametric or inferential statistics deal with measurements from *continuous* variables. Nonparametric statistics deal with categorical measurements.

BASIC ASSUMPTIONS FOR STATISTICS

A large collection of nonparametric statistical tests has been developed for use with categorical variables. In fact, Lapin (1993, 605) considered the many choices to be one of the major *disadvantages* of the body of nonparametric test; almost too many choices exist. It is hard to be sure what the best test is for the data set being investigated.

Assumptions for Parametric Statistics

Parametric statistics must meet several basic assumptions: (1) the samples are randomly selected, (2) the data are from samples with equal variances, (3) the responses are normally distributed, and (4) the samples are independent from one another. Another common assumption is that researchers must be able to replicate the results with other studies. In most parametric statistics, the measurements must be *interval-* or *ratio-level* data; they use *mean* scores in their computations. Nonparametric statistics, on the other hand, use *rank* and *frequency* distribution information (Lehmkuhl 1996). Means are not appropriate for these data. Instead, measures of central tendency are likely to be either the median or the mode.

These required assumptions cannot always be met. Distributions are often not normal; they may all be gathered around one value, becoming what is known as "positively or negatively skewed." They may be bipolar or evenly distributed across all possible scores. When only two answers are possible, it is meaningless to talk about a "normal distribution" or a "bell-shaped curve." In addition, researchers often draw samples from two or more very different populations. Therefore, no assumptions can be made about the population parameters. When this happens, there is no way of assuring that the samples have equal variances. In all these cases, nonparametric statistics may be more appropriate for analyzing research results.

Assumptions for Nonparametric Statistics

Parametric statistics are used for making inferences about some population parameters. With nonparametric statistics, however, the assumption of a normal distribution does not apply; that is, nonparametric statistics are those that are considered to be "distribution free." In a dichotomous variable, for example, the distribution can only be binomial (only two answers); this is the same type of data created by flipping a coin.

Nonparametric statistical tests can be used with all levels of data, but are not because they typically provide less information than parametric statistics. They are sometimes described as less powerful or not as robust as parametric tests. However, there are times when nonparametric statistics are the only appropriate choice. Lehmkuhl (1996, 106) summarized when parametric statistics should and should not be used in the following way:

> Nonparametric tests should not be substituted for parametric tests when parametric tests are more appropriate. Nonparametric tests should be used when the assumptions of parametric tests cannot be met, when very small numbers of data are used, and when no basis exist for assuming certain types of shapes of distributions.

Nonparametric statistics are entirely appropriate for use when the researcher cannot make any assumptions about distributions, when the sample size is small (less than 100), and measurements are nominal or ordinal level. Such applications occur when the data are categorical (nominal level) or ranked or ordered (ordinal level). An example of an appropriate application is the chi-square-based *Cramer's V* test for relationships between nominal level variables. This statistic provides an index of the strength of a relationship, although it does not tell the direction of that relationship. While nonparametric tests for differences will provide information about differences in measurements between two or more groups, they are unable to include information about possible interactions between two or more influencing variables.

NONPARAMETRIC VERSIONS OF PARAMETRIC TESTS

At least one nonparametric equivalent test exists for each type of basic parametric statistical test (StatSoft 2002):

- Tests for location (i.e., central tendency)
- Tests for statistically significant differences between groups (independent samples)
- Tests for differences between variables (dependent samples)
- Tests for associations between all types of variables

The most common statistical tests used with parametric statistics and interval and/or ratio-scale data are: (1) the single-sample *t*- or *z*-tests, (2) the two-sample *t*-test for independent samples and

Table 19.1

Selected Nonparametric Analogues to Parametric Statistical Tests

Test Type	Nonparametric Analogue	Parametric Tests
Tests for location	Chi-square one-sample tests Kolmogorov-Smirnov one-sample test	t-test for small samples z-test for samples of 30 or more
Differences tests with independent samples	Mann-Whitney U-test Kolmogorov-Smirnov two-sample test Kruskal-Wallis H-test Kruskal-Wallis ANOVA	t-test for independent samples F-test of variance (ANOVA)
Differences tests with dependent samples	Friedman's two-way analysis of variance test McNemar's chi-square test	t-test for dependent [paired] samples ANOVA
Tests for association between two or more variables	Spearman's R, X^2, Phi, and Cramer's V	Pearson's correlation coefficient

the analysis of variance test for two or more samples, (3) the two-sample t-test for differences in the means of dependent samples, such as with pre- and post-same-group testing and paired-sample testing, and (4) the Pearson's correlation coefficient statistic for associations. Table 19.1 displays a variety of the available nonparametric analogs of these tests. Only some of the nonparametric tests listed in Table 19.1 are included in Microsoft Excel. The majority of the nonparametric relationship and differences tests are included in the more comprehensive and powerful statistical software package, SPSS.

Nonparametric Tests of Location

Tests of location are designed to determine whether a sample could have come from a known population (Siegel 1956). The procedure is to compare a sample's measurement of central tendency with a known or hypothesized parameter. The one-sample t-test and z-test are the preferred procedures for dealing with parametric data. The t-test compares the mean score of a sample with a hypothesized population mean; the z-test is used with large samples, and the unknown population standard is replaced by the sample standard deviation. In both applications, the scores are assumed to have come from a population with a normal distribution. Because both tests compare means, the data must be either interval or ratio. When these assumptions cannot be met, the nonparametric chi-square test of location may be substituted for the t-test or the z-test.

In general, nonparametric tests of location are very similar to the chi-square goodness-of-fit procedure. Both one-sample and two-sample models compare the actual distribution with an expected distribution. In the one-sample test, the researcher draws a sample and then attempts to determine if there is any significant difference in the location (central tendency) between the sample and the population. Because the data are nominal or ordinal, the median is used as a central tendency measurement. In a two (or more) sample test, the researcher wants to know if there is a statistically significant difference between the actual (observed) distribution of responses and an expected distribution. Modified versions of the chi-square test are appropriate for one, two, and three or more samples.

Tests based on the chi-square statistic (X^2) are extremely versatile statistical tools. Greek letters are used throughout statistics and mathematics. The Greek letter X is "chi," pronounced with a hard "k" as in "ki." Because it is a squared value, the test, the statistic, and the distribution are all called *chi-square* (or chi-squared) and written as X^2.

Chi-square has important applications for both parametric and nonparametric statistical tests. The statistic is based on the X^2 distribution, which was originally developed for use with small samples where the assumptions of normality could not be upheld. Small sample results seldom resemble a normal distribution because of the limited number of available responses. The one-sample location test is just one of many tests based on the X^2 distribution.

This simple-to-use and easy-to-understand test is popular for making decisions about the distribution of responses in one-sample situations. The inclusion of this test in the majority of statistical software packages has increased its popularity so much that it has replaced other tests, such as the *one-sample sign test,* in many empirical research applications. Although it is used with all types of measurements, the test is best with all types of *categorical* measurements, such as gender, occupation, yes-no, and others.

ONE-SAMPLE NONPARAMETRIC TESTS

Of the many statistical tests that available for testing hypotheses about a single sample, two of the most popular are the chi-square test for use with nominal data and the Kolmogorov-Smirnov one sample test for ordinal data. One-sample tests are conducted to test hypotheses that the sample in question could come from an identified population. One-sample tests use a goodness-of-fit model, in which they test for a disproportionate or unexpected distribution of scores across the various categories of a variable.

The One-Sample Chi-square Test

The X^2 one sample-test should be used when a researcher has questions about how the distribution of responses falls into the spread of possible responses. For example, say that the county clerk of a small rural county reports that for the past decade, the number of registered voters in the county has remained stable. County records reveal that 45 percent of residents are registered Democrats, 38 percent are Republican, 12 percent are Independent, and 5 percent are members of the Socialist Labor Party (Table 19.2). In these applications, the one-sample test is similar to the *goodness-of-fit test* because it compares the set of *observed* cases against an *expected* distribution (Siegel 1956).

The null hypothesis for this test is that the proportion of cases that make up a sample of county voters will not differ from the known distribution. The alternate hypothesis is that the distribution does mirror the known distribution of responses.

The Excel chi-square test (CHITEST) in the Function Wizard looks at differences within the sample, computes a chi-square distribution, and compares the actual distribution of responses with a hypothetical expected distribution. The only required assumptions for the X^2 test are (1) that the sample is randomly selected, and (2) each observation must fit into one and only one class or category. CHITEST only returns the two-tailed *probability* for an X^2 statistic with the appropriate degrees of freedom (rows − 1); it does not return a calculated chi-square value.

The syntax for this test is CHITEST = (actual range, expected range). Expected results are established on the basis of totals for rows and columns as shown in Table 19.2, or as an estimate of what the expected results should be based on a researcher-established null hypothesis. The estimated results are then inserted in the expected cases column. The null hypothesis for this test is, "The distribution of responses for the sample is not representative of the population from which the sample was drawn."

For the data in Table 19.2, Excel returned the probability of .23 that the actual proportion of

Table 19.2

Distribution of Registered Voters in a Population and a Sample

Party affiliation	Number of Registered voters (N = 131,687)	Expected percentage	Number in sample (n = 250)	Observed percentage
Democrat	59,260	45	128	51
Republican	50,041	38	80	32
Independent	15,802	12	37	15
Socialist Labor	6,584	5	5	2
Total	131,687	100.0	250	100.0

Table 19.3

Frequencies for Wednesday–Thursday Preferred Television Programs

Program type	Program code	Observed cases	Expected cases	Percent
Situation comedy	1	22	25	12.5
Medical drama	2	28	25	12.5
News magazine	3	14	25	12.5
Sports show	4	30	25	12.5
Variety musical	5	22	25	12.5
Slice-of-life	6	30	25	12.5
Ethnic comedy	7	26	25	12.5
Children's omnibus	8	28	25	12.5
Total		200	200	100.0

voters in the four categories is representative of the known population parameter distribution. As with the parametric tests discussed earlier, decisions regarding nonparametric hypotheses are made based on the size of the *p-value*. If the researcher elects to use a .05 confidence level for the test, the *null hypothesis* cannot be rejected; the computed *p-value* of .23 is greater than .05. The researcher must conclude that the sample is not representative of the population.

When a computer statistical program is not available, the chi-square test can be conducted using the actual responses, calculated expected responses, and a standard chi-square table found in almost all statistics texts. Table 19.4 illustrates how this chi-square test is done. The calculated chi-square value is compared with a chi-square value for the appropriate degrees of freedom and alpha (.05 or .10).

The Logic behind the Chi-square Test of Location

In the following one-sample example, a media buyer planning a political advertising campaign wants to know which Wednesday and Thursday prime time television programs are adult registered voters prefer. The media buyer will use this information to place advertisements for her candidate. Data are gathered from a sample of 200 subjects. Local advertising can be purchased on eight programs over the two evenings. The variable of interests is *preferred television program*. The null hypothesis is that the distribution of preferred programs is equal; no one program is preferred above any other program. The data are *categorical* (preferred, not preferred).

The data are presented in Tables 19.3 and 19.4. The number of *expected* cases was determined

Table 19.4

Calculations for a Chi-square Test

Code	Actual count (A)	Actual percent	Expected count (B)	Expected percent	Actual minus Expected (A − B)	(A − B)/25
1	22	0.110	25	0.125	−3	0.36
2	35	0.175	25	0.125	10	4
3	28	0.140	25	0.125	3	0.36
4	18	0.090	25	0.125	−7	1.96
5	32	0.160	25	0.125	7	1.96
6	25	0.125	25	0.125	0	0
7	21	0.105	25	0.125	−4	0.64
8	19	0.095	25	0.125	−6	1.44
	200	1.00	200	1.00	0	10.72
					X^2 (table)	14.067

Source: Sample data from Table 19.3.
Computed Chi-square = 10.72
Degrees of freedom (r − 1) = 7
Table X^2 value = 14.067

by dividing the total number of cases by the number of classes or categories (100/8 = 12.5); degrees of freedom refers to the number of categories (rows) minus 1 (8 − 1 = 7).

Using the chi-square distribution (CHIDIST) capability in the Excel Function Wizard, a one-tailed *p*-value of .0853 is found for the distribution of 12.5 observed cases per cell and 7 (*n*–1) degrees of freedom. Since this is a two-tailed test, the one-tailed probability of .0853 must be doubled, for a final value of .1706. The null hypothesis cannot be rejected; the distribution of responses is statistically disproportionate. The null hypothesis for both a one-tailed and a two-tailed test would be rejected at the .05 level of confidence. The alternate hypothesis is retained for both (or accepted).

The K-S One-Sample Test for Ordinal Data

The Kolmogorov-Smirnov (K-S) one-sample test for ordinal-level data is different in concept than the nominal-data test for location. Instead of comparing a sample median with a population median, it compares the distribution of a sample data set with a theoretical *expected distribution*. The K-S test is used to determine whether the sample rankings can be assumed to be from a population with those theoretical rankings.

The K-S one-sample test is an efficient statistical procedure for testing for differences among the rankings of classes within one sample. The only two assumptions that must be met are the test requires that the data are at least ordinal level (rankings) and that they are from a randomly selected sample. A null hypothesis for this test is that there is no difference in the way groups in the sample rank a given set of objects. Therefore, the K-S one-sample test may be said to be a test that follows the *goodness-of-fit* model (Seigel 1956).

The K-S test is included in the SPSS Nonparametric Tests group, listed as "1-sample K-S"; it is not available in Excel. The test computes a mean rank for each group, a *z*-score and a two-tailed probability. It requires selection of a test distribution (Normal, Uniform, or Poisson). In almost all cases (unless the manager knows specifically that another distribution is present), the

Table 19.5

A Partial List of Nonparametric Tests for Significant Differences

	Independent Samples		Related Samples	
	2-Sample Tests	3-or-more Sample Tests	2-Sample Tests	3-or-more Sample Tests
Nominal data	Kolmogorov-Smirnov Test	X^2 Test for Independent Samples	McNemar Test	Cochran's Q Test
Ordinal data	Mann-Whitney U-Test	Kruskal-Wallis One-Way ANOVA	Wilcoxon Rank Sum Test	Friedman Analysis of Variance Test

Source: Siegel 1956.

Normal distribution option is selected even though this is a distribution-free test. The test results are interpreted by comparing the two-tailed probability value with the desired confidence level. The null hypothesis is retained if the *p*-value is greater than the chosen alpha result.

NONPARAMETRIC TESTS FOR DIFFERENCES

A number of nonparametric statistical tests have been developed to measure the significance of differences in variables in nominal- or ordinal-level data. Table 19.5 displays a small sample of the better-known nonparametric differences tests, including one-sample tests. The table lists dependent and independent group nonparametric tests that have been developed for one, two, and more than two samples comparisons.

Not all of the differences tests identified in Table 19.5 are regularly used in standard public administration research situations. The following discussion looks at only those tests that might be seen in political science, administrative science, and public administration journals, and which are easy to employ and interpret.

Two Independent-Sample Tests

SPSS includes four two-independent-sample test procedures in its powerful Nonparametric Tests subprogram. Two of these independent sample tests are often used in public administration research—the Kolmogorov-Smirnov Z-test (K-S), which is used with categorical (nominal-level) data, and the Mann-Whitney U-test (M-W), which should be used with ordinal-level data.

The nominal-data K-S Z-test compares the observed distribution counts of numeric variables across categories for two samples or groups. A Z-value and a two-tailed probability value are produced. The test results are interpreted by comparing the *p*-value with the desired confidence level (.01, .05, or .10). The only required assumption is that the samples are randomly selected.

The Mann-Whitney U-test ranks all responses to an ordinal-level variable and computes a U-score and its significance level, which is used for interpreting the results of this test. It tests the hypothesis that two independent samples come from populations having the same distribution. The Mann Whitney U-test requires that the samples are randomly selected and that data are ordinal level. The U-test converts the observed data to ranks and compares the differences.

For example, suppose that a state elections board is evaluating the effectiveness of two different vote-recording systems. The existing system is a manual process that requires voters to use a small

Table 19.6

Time and Rank Order for Two Voting Procedures

Sample No.	Control Group		Experimental Group	
	Time (seconds)	Rank order	Time (seconds)	Rank order
1	217	20	239	22
2	256	24	198	12
3	285	27	201	14
4	192	10	204	15
5	191	9	187	7
6	175	2	162	1
7	268	26	211	18
8	261	25	213	19
9	380	30	183	6
10	292	28	176	3
11	189	8	207	16
12	210	17	182	5
13	244	23	177	4
14	220	21	200	13
15	360	29	195	11

metal stylus to punch out partially perforated windows in card-like ballots. The finished ballots are then counted at the end of the day by equipment resembling old IBM punch-card readers. The second system is an electronic touch-screen that records votes, allows voters to erase or change any mistakes, and electronically counts all ballots as they are completed. A random sample of thirty voters is selected to test both systems, with the time to complete the voting in seconds recorded for each voter. Half of the sample is randomly assigned to the existing system (the *control group*) and half is randomly assigned to the new electronic system (the *experimental group*). The time (in seconds) for each sample member to complete the voting process is displayed in Table 19.6.

Two Related-Sample Tests

A large majority of the applications of differences tests involve independent samples. Tests with related samples are primarily used in laboratory-based experimental research. The setups and test results for dependent sample tests are nearly identical to those for independent tests. In the SPSS Nonparametric Tests statistical program, four types of related-sample tests are grouped under the "two-related-samples tests" set of procedures. Two of these tests for related samples are the McNemar test for dichotomous (nominal) data, and the Wilcoxon rank-sum test for ordinal data. The McNemar test is designed to test hypotheses about pairs of variables, such as spouses or in before-and-after designs. Norušis (2000, 344) defined the McNemar procedure as one that "tests whether the two possible combinations of unlike values for the variables are likely." In a before-and-after experiment, subjects are tested before a treatment, such as being exposed to a communication, and again after the treatment.

The Wilcoxon rank-sum test performs a similar function for data at the ordinal level, but that data does not have to be dichotomous. The test computes differences between pairs of variables, ranks the differences, and computes a Z-statistic and significance level for interpretation. The null hypothesis for this test is that there is no difference in the way the related samples ranked the variables. It is interpreted using the *p*-value approach.

Table 19.7

Data Distribution for a Survey of Attitudes Regarding Cuba

15–29 years of age	30–44 years of age	45–59 years of age	60 years of age or older
1	1	2	2
1	2	2	1
2	1	2	1
2	1	2	2
1	2	1	2
1	1	2	2
1	1	2	2
2	2	2	2
1	1		2
	2		

Key: 1 = Yes; 2 = No

Tests for Three or More Independent Samples

Nonparametric tests are also available to test for differences in more than two independent samples. A procedure for three or more sample tests is also included in the SPSS Tests for Several Independent Samples capability (called K Independent Samples in the dialog box menu).

The X^2 K-Independent Samples and Fisher's Exact Probability Tests

The K-sample X^2 test for three or more independent samples compares the medians of three or more independent samples, computes a chi-square and a significance value (p-value). This test is included in the SPSS Crosstabs procedure in the Descriptive Statistics section. According to Siegel (1956, 175):

> When frequencies in discrete categories constitute the data of research, the X^2 test may be used to determine the significance of the differences among (3 or more) independent groups. The X^2 test for k independent samples is a straightforward extension of the X^2 test for two independent samples. . . . In general, the test is the same for both two and k independent samples.

In the following example, a researcher is interested in determining whether Cuban Americans in four age categories support normalizing relations with Cuba. The age-group categories are 15 to 29 years, 30 to 44 years, 45 to 59 years, and 60 years and older. Subjects were asked to answer "yes" or "no" to the question "Should the United States normalize diplomatic relations with Cuba as long as Castro still leads the country?" The data from a small-sample attitude survey are displayed in Table 19.7. Table 19.8 is a crosstabulation table produced by the SPSS Descriptive Statistics procedure. Table 19.9 displays a table of the results of the chi-square test.

Two results of interest are presented in Table 19.9. One is the result of the X^2 test. The calculated X^2 value is 7.897, with 3 degrees of freedom (rows − 1). A two-tailed probability of .048 indicates that at the .05 level of confidence, the hypothesis that the age groups are not from the same population must be rejected.

Table 19.8

Should U.S. Normalize Relations with Cuba? Crosstabulation of Age-Group Data

	Should U.S. Normalize?		
Age group	Yes	No	Totals
15–29	6	3	9
30–44	6	4	10
45–59	1	7	8
60 or older	2	7	9
Totals	15	21	36

Table 19.9

Chi-square Test Results, Age-Group Membership: Should U.S. Normalize?

	Value	df	Asym. Sig. (2-sided)
Pearson Chi-Square	7.897	3	.048
Likelihood Ratio	8.421	3	.038
Linear-by-Linear Association	5.812	1	.016
N of Valid Cases	36		

5 cells (62.5%) have expected count less than 5. The minimum expected count is 3.33.

Kruskal-Wallis Analysis of Variance Test

The Kruskal-Wallis analysis of variance test examines differences in the ways that three or more groups respond to one or more ordinal-level variable, such as the way subjects rank a set of statements in order of importance. The test computes an H-statistic similar to a chi-square distribution (a chi-square value is also printed as the default). This test also provides a significance value that can be used in the same way as a p-value for interpreting the results. If there are a large number of ties in raw data, a second chi-square and significance value corrected for ties are also computed.

The Kruskal-Wallis procedure tests for differences in the way that three or more independent groups or samples rank a variable in order to establish whether they are from the same population. In much the same way as the Kruskal-Wallis H-test, it computes a chi-square and a significance value, then repeats these results corrected for ties in the data. This test is also included in SPSS Nonparametric Tests.

In the following example, a researcher is interested in determining the best appeal to influence citizens' attitudes about constructing a new wastewater treatment facility in the community. The city and county must float a bond issue in order to pay for the facility; property taxes are expected to increase if the bond issue passes. Table 19.10 displays the data for three independent groups exposed to different advertising appeals and a control group that does not get the treatment. All subjects were asked to rank the importance of a proposed community bond issue by awarding up to 100 points; the more points, the greater the perceived importance.

To prepare the data for an SPSS K-W analysis of variance test, the data in Table 19.10 must be rearranged into three columns, as displayed in Table 19.11. Column 1 is the subject number variable, with subjects numbered sequentially from 1 to 21. Column 2 is the grouping variable.

Table 19.10

Data for Kruskal-Wallis ANOVA Test

| | Importance Rankings | | |
Group 1	Group 2	Group 3	Group 4
20	25	65	30
25	10	40	70
60	40	15	70
80	30	25	40
50	90	35	95
40	20	75	100
45	50		20
	50		15

Table 19.11

Importance Data Reformatted into SPSS Columnar Form

Subject	Group	Importance Score
1	1	20
2	1	25
3	1	60
4	1	80
5	1	50
6	1	40
7	1	45
8	2	25
9	2	10
10	2	40
11	2	30
12	2	90
13	2	20
14	2	50
15	2	50
16	3	65
17	3	40
18	3	15
19	3	25
20	3	35
21	3	75
22	4	30
23	4	70
24	4	70
25	4	40
26	4	95
27	4	100
28	4	20
29	4	15

Groups are numbered from 1 to 4, with 1 assigned to the control group, 2 to the reason group, 3 to the emotion group, and 4 to the financial appeal group.

The third column is each subject's rank value. The SPSS procedure requires entry of the rank variable as the test variable and the group assignment variable as the grouping variable. The default selection for the test is the K-W H-test, so this box should already be checked.

Table 19.12

Mean Rank Calculations for SPSS Kruskal-Wallis *H*-test

Ranks

Group (IMPRANK)	N	Mean Rank
Control group	7	7.93
Appeal to reason	8	13.38
Appeal to emotion	6	14.50
Financial appeal	8	23.19

Table 19.13

Chi-square, Degrees of Freedom (df), and *p*-Value for K-W *H*-Test

Test Statistics	IMPRANK
Chi-square	12.602
df	3
Asymp. Sig.	.006

Kruskal-Wallis Test
Grouping Variable: Group

The SPSS procedure produces a summary table in which the calculated mean rankings for each group are displayed, and a test statistics result for the test (Table 19.13). In this example, the computed chi-square is 12.602, with three degrees of freedom and a significance of .006. There are only six chances in 1,000 that a Type I error will occur. The null—the distribution of rankings is not the same in all groups—must be rejected and the alternate hypothesis, the distribution is similar in all groups, accepted.

Tests for Three or More Independent Samples

The nonparametric test for differences in three or more related samples is the Cochran Q test for nominal data. For differences between three or more related samples with ordinal data, the Friedman analysis of variance test may be used. Neither of these tests is included in the standard edition of SPSS for Windows, Version 10.0 and below. Readers are encouraged to consult a standard nonparametric statistics text for instruction on the manual methods for conducting these two tests. The tests are included in more powerful editions of earlier desktop and mainframe versions of the software.

NONPARAMETRIC RELATIONSHIP TESTS

As previously discussed, two different statistical techniques are needed to know whether a significant relationship existed and the strength and direction of the relationship. Regression analysis measures the way in which variables might be related; correlation analysis provides a numerical measure or index of the strength of the relationship. These tests for nonparametric statistics are displayed in Table 19.14.

Table 19.14

Some Nonparametric Relationship Tests

Nominal Data Tests	Ordinal Data Tests
X^2 test for independence	Spearman's rank order coefficient R (rho)
Cramer's *V* test (for square tables)	Kendall's tau-b (for square tables)
Phi statistic (for rectangular tables)	Kendall's tau-c (for rectangular tables)

Tests for Nominal-Level Data

Often, the first step to test for associations between nominal-level data is the chi-square test for independence. This test provides a coarse measurement of association that allows the manager to test a null hypothesis that the two categorical variables are independent (that is, they are not related). The chi-square test is included in two separate categories of statistical tests in SPSS for Windows: *Crosstabulations* and *Nonparametric Tests.*

Crosstabulations, which are two-way frequency distribution tables, include a number of other relationship or association tests for categorical data. Two of the most useful are tests for the *phi* statistic and Cramer's *V.* Both of these tests compute a nonparametric correlation coefficient index number that ranges from 0 (no relationship) to 1.0 (a perfect relationship). This means they can only provide a one-directional measure of relationship; it is impossible to determine whether the relationship is positive or negative. Either test can be used with any size sample.

The only difference between these two tests is the way they are structured for comparing responses to different numbers of categories. The phi statistic is used with tables that are "square"; that is, tables with the same number of categories in both rows and columns. For example, a two-by-two table is one with just two possible classes for each variable. Examples include such dichotomous variables as gender, yes or no, read or don't read, member or nonmember, use or don't use. Cramer's *V* test, on the other hand, measures association for all tables that are rectangular in shape; when there is not the same number of rows and columns. Both tests are included under the same statistics option in the SPSS Crosstabs procedure.

The Crosstabs procedure prepares tables and measures of association for two or more nonscale-level variables. Crosstabs may be prepared with any level of data, but are particularly appropriate for categorical data. The association measures are grouped in three categories: nominal data, ordinal data, and tables where one variable is nominal and the other is interval level. The options for the table are rows percentages, column percentages, and the percentages of the total represented by each cell count. Counts (or "observed" frequencies) for each category are always printed. It is also possible to have the expected frequencies counted for goodness-of-fit applications.

The data dictate which test the statistical software carries out (they are included in the same selection option). Interpretation of these chi-square-based tests is identical. Each produces a relationship value (correlation coefficient) ranging from 0 to 1.0. This can be interpreted in the same way as the parametric coefficient of determination's percentage of association.

Ordinal Data Association Tests

Even though they use ranked data, ordinal-level measurements, like nominal data, are considered to be measures of *category* rather than quantity (remember the rule for ordinal data that the differences between rank levels need not be equal). With nominal data, the numbers mean how many cases fall into each specific and discrete category, such as "male" or "female" in the variable "gender." With ordinal data, the numbers also refer to how many observations fall into each of the descriptive categories, but now they also mean that the various categories may be placed in some kind of *order*. Examples included voters' preferred presidential candidates, the perceived importance of how a set of factors influence determination of public policy, or the possession of more or less of a characteristic, such as a "liberal attitude." Each level in ordinal measurement is a statement of order for the category. It is not possible to tell from the rankings how far apart the levels are, simply that one level is higher (or lower) than others.

Researchers often want to know how ordinal-level variables are related to one another, if at all. For example, a public administrator wants to know if there is any relationship between the importance that citizens place on a civic service and how the public perceives the quality of the service.

When at least one of the variables in a crosstabulation test is ordinal level, the SPSS Crosstabs procedure allows a choice of several different tests. These include the Spearman correlation coefficient (Spearman's rho), zero-order gammas, Somer's *d*, and Kendall's tau-b and tau-c tests. Spearman's rho is the most-used measure of correlation between two ordinal-level variables. It is the nonparametric analogue of the parametric *product moment correlation coefficient* (Pearson's *r*) and is interpreted in the same way as the interval-level test. It also identifies whether the relationship is positive or negative. Spearman's rho can be used with samples of any size, with equal or unequal size groups, and with any table shape.

The Kendall tests are also simple to use and interpret; each is appropriate for slightly different situations. Tau-b is used for square tables (when the number of columns equals the number of rows in the Crosstabs table); a tau-b "corrected for ties" test is also computed. Tau-c is used when the tables are rectangular rather than square.

Nominal Data Association Tests

Among other applications, the X^2 statistic is used as a test for independence between variables, as a test for *normality* (normal distribution), or as a *one-sample relationship test*. Another important use for the chi-square statistic is the X^2 *goodness-of-fit test*, which is a nonparametric test evaluating the distribution of responses for a categorical variable. It is called a *goodness-of-fit* test because it looks at the data to determine whether the distribution of responses "fits" the allowable distribution of categories or if it is *disproportionate*. The idea of the goodness-of-fit test is to compare the actual frequency results against a hypothetical distribution, known as an "expected distribution." While most nonparametric tests were developed for nominal- and ordinal-level data, the X^2 goodness-of-fit test can be used with interval and ratio data as well, although other, more powerful tests are used for the higher-level measurements.

The goodness-of-fit test compares two sets of data. One set is the actual collected data (called the *observed data*); the second is a hypothetical data set (called the *expected data*). The hypothetical data represents what the data would be if the null hypothesis of *no difference* were really true. For a goodness-of-fit test, the null hypothesis might be "the distribution of responses found in the collected data is not different from the expected distribution." If the collected data differs significantly from the expected distribution, the null hypothesis is rejected.

The researcher or statistical program may establish the expected distribution. Statistical software packages calculate a chi-square, the degrees of freedom, and a *p*-value—the significance level. Large chi-square values suggest that the null hypothesis must be retained. Small chi-square values mean the null hypothesis must be rejected. A computed p-value is used to make the final decision. Any p-values the same as or less than the selected significance value (typically 05, although .01 and .10 levels are also used) call for rejecting the null hypothesis.

Finally, when carrying out a goodness-of-fit test, it is important that there be at least five responses in each category or cell; if not, the results of the test are considered to be *spurious,* that is, they are considered more likely to have occurred by chance.

SUMMARY

A number of nonparametric statistics procedures are included in Microsoft Excel, and all are included in SPSS and SPSS for Windows software. Nonparametric tests, which are also known as *distribution-free* tests, are appropriate when a researcher deals with categorical or ranked data. Nonparametric statistics are used when the researcher cannot make any assumptions about distributions, when the sample size is small (less than 100), and measurements are nominal or ordinal level. Such applications occur when the data are categorical (nominal level) or ranked or ordered (ordinal level).

There are many different uses for nonparametric tests. They begin with several different versions of chi-square tests and extend across a variety of independent- and paired-sample applications for one, two, and three or more samples or groups. They include tests for differences and tests for relationships.

At least one nonparametric equivalent test exists for each type of basic parametric statistical test. Nonparametric statistical tests have been developed for each of the general categories of statistical analysis: tests for location, tests for statistically significant differences between independent and related samples, and tests for associations between variables.

Two of the most popular one-sample nonparametric tests are the chi-square test for use with nominal data and the Kolmogorov-Smirnov one sample test for ordinal data. One-sample tests are conducted to test hypotheses that the sample in question could come from an identified population.

Two of the independent sample tests in SPSS are often used in political science and public administration. They are the *Kolmogorov-Smirnov Z-test* (K-S), which is used with nominal-level data, and the *Mann-Whitney U-test* (M-W), which should be used with ordinal-level data. For two related-samples, the McNemar Test for dichotomous (nominal) data, and the Wilcoxon rank-sum test for ordinal data should be used.

The SPSS Crosstabs procedure prepares tables and measures of association for two or more nonscale-level variables. When at least one of the variables in a crosstabulation test is ordinal level, Spearman's rho is the most appropriate measure of correlation.

ADDITIONAL READING

McCall, Robert B. 1986. *Fundamental Statistics for the Behavioral Sciences.* San Diego: Harcourt Brace Jovanovich.

Neufeld, John L. 1997. *Learning Statistics with Microsoft Excel.* Upper Saddle River, NJ: Prentice Hall.

Norušis, Marija. 2005. *SPSS 14.0 Statistical Procedures Companion.* Upper Saddle River, NJ: Prentice Hall.

Sincich, Terry. 1996. *Business Statistics by Example.* 4th ed. Upper Saddle River, NJ: Prentice Hall.

20

EXPLORING MULTIVARIATE STATISTICS

This chapter explores four sets of statistical tests that fall under the category of *multivariate statistics*. A common goal of multivariate statistical analysis is to determine and explain how groups of variables are related, and ultimately to develop theories of causation that can be traced to those relationships (Bernard 2000). Among the many multivariate procedures developed for data analysis are multiple regression analysis, partial regression, path analysis, multiple dimensional scaling, multiple analyses of variance and covariance, multiple discriminant analysis, factor and cluster analysis, and more. We will explore the three major families of multivariate statistics: (1) multiple regression analysis, (2) the group–membership prediction and classification tool, Multiple Discriminant Analysis (MDS), and (3) factor analysis and cluster analysis for data reduction and statistically summarizing data sets.

MULTIPLE REGRESSION ANALYSIS

Multiple regression analysis, a popular multivariate statistical method, has wide application in political, economic, social, and educational research (Kerlinger and Pedhazur 1973). An extremely robust procedure, it can be used with either continuous (interval and ratio) measurements or categorical (nominal and ordinal) data. In addition, *theoretically* there is no limit to the number of independent variables it can handle.

Multiple regression analysis (MRA) is an extension of the simple regression procedure described in chapter 17. In multiple regression, instead of one predictor variable, several are used. Analyzing the contribution that more than one independent variable makes to the relative change in a dependent variable makes it possible to explain and/or predict future events from measurements of a variety of independent variables. Analyzing several variables in place of one holds the promise of explaining more of the variation in the dependent (Y) variable, thus making it possible for the prediction to be more precise.

Public administration researchers use multiple regression analysis to study how such phenomena as gender, age, education, party affiliation, ethnic status, income level and occupation, place and type of residence, and similar characteristics influence behavior. University admissions personnel use MRA to predict successful completion of advanced degree programs from such independent variables as graduate aptitude tests and college grade point averages. Medical personnel use MRA to predict the likelihood of contracting a disease from such factors as weight, exercise, and diet.

In an example of a typical use of the method, say that the manager of the copy center in a

Table 20.1

Variables with Potential Impact on Gross Revenue

Rows			Columns		
Job number	# of copies	Time (minutes)	Cost (dollars)	Errors	Gross revenue
1	150	4.0	1.75	2	1.50
2	310	15.5	1.35	5	1.00
3	450	11.0	1.10	6	0.90
4	1,150	19.5	0.80	9	1.20
5	800	16.0	0.99	3	0.80
6	200	6.0	1.30	2	1.00
7	300	8.5	1.35	4	1.10
8	250	6.0	1.30	2	0.80
9	910	14.5	1.05	3	1.20
10	100	14.0	2.00	5	1.10
11	500	14.0	0.95	2	0.20
12	225	10.0	1.30	1	0.50
13	50	4.0	1.75	0	0.60
14	920	17.0	0.90	5	1.50
15	5,000	49.0	0.70	10	1.25
16	600	13.0	1.10	2	1.50
17	1,400	22.5	0.95	6	1.00
18	2,750	28.0	0.90	2	1.25
19	410	12.5	1.25	1	1.00
20	2,500	29.0	0.95	2	1.50

government agency is interested in determining whether existing cost controls are effective at lowering costs and improving productivity. She elects to measure productivity by the gross revenue earned per individual copy made. Records are kept of each copying order, including the time to produce each copy in seconds, the labor cost per sheet, the number of bad copies in each order, and a measure of gross profit per sheet in cents per sheet. The manager randomly selects a sample of twenty jobs and comes up with the data presented in Table 20.1.

The independent variables in this example include the *number of copies, time to produce each copy, cost per copy,* and the *number of errors.* The number of errors is particularly important because the manager has just completed a development program designed to improve productivity by eliminating waste caused by copying errors. A simple regression analysis procedure can be conducted on the each independent variable to establish what impact it has on gross revenue. However, the more appropriate statistical test to use for evaluating the relationships between these values is *multiple regression analysis.*

The multiple regression programs in SPSS and Microsoft Excel allow the researcher to conduct both linear and curvilinear regression analyses and to produce several different statistical-test results. Options in SPSS include a table of descriptive statistics for all variables in the analysis. These statistics (the mean and standard deviation) are displayed in Table 20.2.

Both programs produce a correlation table for the variables included in the equation. Table 20.3 is a *correlation matrix* produced by Excel. The most relevant information are the moderate and low correlations for each of the independent variables and the dependent variable, Gross Revenue: .35 for Copies, .32 for Time, –.13 for Cost, and .27 for Errors.

Correlations measure the strength and direction of the relationship between any two pairs of interval or ratio-scale variables. Other relationship tests, such as Spearman's rank order correla-

Table 20.2

Descriptive Statistics for the Variables in Table 20.1

	Descriptive Statistics		
	Mean	Std. Dev.	N
Gross revenue	1.05	.350	20
n of Copies	948.75	1208.779	20
Time in minutes	15.70	10.495	20
Cost in dollars	1.19	.339	20
n of errors	3.60	2.644	20

Table 20.3

A Correlation Matrix for the Independent Variables in Table 20.1

	Copies	Time	Cost	Errors	Revenue
Copies	1				
Time	0.96058259	1			
Cost	-0.63637334	-0.650999	1		
Errors	0.50486879	0.600563	-0.41956	1	
Revenue	0.35267705	0.320736	-0.12931	0.276613	1

tion, are available for ordinal- and nominal-level data. Excel produces a lower-half correlation table, not repeating the same table on the upper half.

The values printed in a correlation table are correlation coefficients, which indicate the strength and direction of the relationship between variable pairs. For example, the coefficient for the variables *errors* and *time* is 0.60, and the variables are positively related. *Errors* and *cost* display a negative correlation of –0.42. The strongest relationship in the table is the nearly perfect positive (0.96) between the variables *time* and *number of copies*.

Excel regression program results are displayed in Figure 20.1. They include summary output for the regression analysis procedure and significance tests for the full regression equation individual variables in the equation.

The regression analysis procedure produces summary regression statistics, an ANOVA table with the results of an F-test, and a *t*-test for each independent variable. Summary regression statistics include a solution for the regression equation and a regression coefficient [r], a regression coefficient of determination [r^2], and an adjusted r^2.

The three sets of statistics displayed in Figure 20.1 are: (1) the set of regression statistics, (2) an ANOVA table, and (3) the coefficients, standard error, *t*-statistic and its value, and the confidence intervals for the coefficients. The coefficients are the calculated values that, with the computed calculated values and the computed Y-axis intercept value, are values included in the computed regression correlation. These values are the data needed to calculate a future value for Y given new values for the independent variables.

The model summary produced by SPSS displayed in Table 20.4 includes (1) the regression coefficient [r], (2) a regression coefficient of determination [r^2], (3) an adjusted r^2, and (4) the standard error value. The strength of the computed r^2 shows how effective the set of independent variables are at "explaining" the variation in the dependent variable Y. In the copy center example

Figure 20.1   **Regression Analysis Output Produced by Microsoft Excel**

SUMMARY OUTPUT

Regression

	Statistics
Multiple R	0.41
R square	0.17
Adjusted R square	−0.05
Standard error	0.36
Observations	20

ANOVA

	df	SS	MS	F	Significance F
Regression	4	0.399141	0.09978	0.777402	0.55692
Residual	15	1.925359	0.12835		
Total	19	2.3245			

	Coef-ficients	Standard error	t Stat	P-value	Lower 95%	Upper 95%	Lower 95%	Upper 95%
Intercept	0.7675	0.5336	1.4381	0.1709	−0.36998	1.90492	−0.36998	1.90492
Copies	0.0002	0.0003	0.9102	0.3771	−0.00032	0.00079	−0.00032	0.00079
Time	−0.0164	0.0324	−0.5072	0.6194	−0.08557	0.05267	−0.08557	0.05267

Table 20.4

Model Summary Produced by the SPSS Regression Procedure

	Model Summary			
Model	R	R^2	Adjusted R^2	Std. error of the estimate
1	.414	.172	−.049	.358

Predictors: (Constant), n of errors, cost in dollars, n of copies, time in minutes.

data, the r^2 of 0.17 suggests that the model is only marginally successful at explaining the variation in gross revenue. The adjusted r^2 is an estimate of how well the model would fit a different data set from the same population; the adjusted r^2 is always less than the r^2. The standard error of the estimate is a measure of the variability of the distribution of values of the dependent variable. The smaller this value is in real terms, the less variability in the Y values. Normally, close to 95 percent of all Y values will fall within two standard errors of the estimate.

The ANOVA table is a hypothesis test on the regression equation. The purpose of the test is to determine whether a linear relationship exists between the set of independent variables and the dependent variable. The null hypothesis for this test is that the set of independent variables cannot predict Y.

Table 20.5 displays the results of an ANOVA test on the data in Table 20.1. The large significance (0.557) and the small F of 0.777 indicate that this regression model is clearly not a good predictor. There is a probability of more than 55 percent that the variables cannot predict changes in Y any better than could random prediction.

Table 20.5

ANOVA Table for SPSS Regression Analysis

ANOVA

Model		Sum of squares	df	Mean square	F	Sig.
1	Regression	.399	4	.100	.777	.557
	Residual	1.925	15	.128		
	Total	2.325	19			

Predictors: (Constant), n of errors, cost in dollars, n of copies, time in minutes.
Dependent Variable: gross revenue.

Table 20.6

Regression Coefficients Produced by the SPSS Regression Procedure

Coefficients

Model		Unstandardized Coefficients B	Std. Error	Standardized Coefficients Beta	t	Sig.
1	(Constant)	.767	.534	1.438	.171	
	n of copies	2.359E-04	.000	.815	.910	.377
	Time in minutes	−1.645E-02	.032	−.494	−.507	.619
	Cost in dollars	.170	.321	.165	.531	.603
	n of errors	3.051E-02	.041	.231	.741	.470

Dependent Variable: gross revenue

In the equation, the value for the slope (a) plus the measurements for each of the X variables multiplied by their corresponding coefficients are necessary to compute future values of Y. Results of the corresponding t-tests are significant tests for each of the independent variables. Since all significance values are greater than the normal cutoff of .05, none of the variables are significant. The overall conclusion is that the four independent variables of number of copies, cost, time, and number of errors are not good predictors of gross revenue. Table 20.6 displays the individual coefficients for each of the independent variables in the regression equations.

Multiple Regression with Dummy Variables

Multiple regression analysis is generally employed with continuous independent and independent variables. However, it is also possible to use categorical data for either the dependent or independent variable, or both. This requires creating what is called an *indicator*, or *dummy*, variable out of the categorical variable (Siegel 2002). For example, say that the variable *gender*—with two categories, female and male—is an important factor in a regression equation. To create a dummy variable, the research simply assigns a value of zero to the first category of *gender* and a value of 1 for the other category. The multiple regression equation uses one category as the baseline, against which to compare the presence of the second category. Dummy variables can be used by themselves in a regression equation, or in conjunction with continuous variables.

Values for dummy variables are assigned according to the number of alternative categories named for a variable. The general rule is to assign one fewer categories than the total number of values. Thus, for a two-category variable such as *gender*, dummy variables of 0 and 1 are assigned. For a three-category variable, dummy variables are 0, 1, and 2.

Multiple regression models have also been developed for when the researcher wants a categorical variable for the dependent or *Y*-axis variable. If the categorical dependent variable has only two categories, either a *multiple logit regression* or a *probit regression* model can be used. If the dependent variable has more than two values—for example, *yes, no,* and *maybe*—then the *multinomial* logit or *multinomial* probit model should be used. None of these four models is available in the standard Excel or SPSS software packages, but may be found in later, additional extensions of the software programs.

The probit model is used extensively in public administration and political science research. According to the Norušis (2000), probit analysis should be used when the researcher wants to estimate the *strength of a stimulus variable* or set of variables that are needed to produce a certain proportion of dichotomous responses (such as "vote" or "not vote"). Examples of stimulus variables are television advertising, newspaper advertising, voters' perceptions of a candidate's performance during a televised debate, and political party affiliation. An example of a response that these stimuli might influence is the proportion of voters who are likely to vote for a particular candidate. In a logit analysis procedure, the dependent variables are *always categorical,* while the independent variables can be factor scores. Factors are composite variables that are composed of one or more individual items or variables. The program allows the researcher to use from one to ten dependent and factor variables combined.

PREDICTING WITH DISCRIMINANT ANALYSIS

Discriminant analysis, another in the family of multivariate tests, is one of a series of statistical techniques designed to analyze relationships among two or more variables (Bennett and Bowers 1976; Maxwell 1977; Klecka 1980). Discriminant analysis has been defined as *a mathematical technique that weighs and combines a set of measurements in a way that their ability to discriminate between two or more groups is maximized* (Cooper 1987). When more than two grouping variables are used in the design, the discriminant process is considered to be *multiple discriminant analysis* (MDA).

Classifying groups with cluster analysis is done with a set of *classification correlations* that are mathematically generated between each scale item and the composite functions. Contribution is measured by the size of correlation value; higher correlation coefficients mean greater contribution (Dalgleish and Chant 1995). The functions are then interpreted by the strength of the individual items that contribute most to the function. While several authors have examined mathematical rules for determining cutoff points for including an item in the interpretation (see, for example, Glorfeld 1995), most analysts leave coefficients of less than 0.40 or 0.50 out of the analysis, but this is only a subjective decision. Too many retained items make it much more difficult to subjectively interpret functions; too few and the function lacks intuitive sense.

The underlying research problem in discriminant analysis is how to establish a decision rule that enables assigning (or predicting) a subject whose group membership is not known to only one of the categories that make up a complete group. Although assigning is done on the basis of measurements on a set of descriptor variables, the researcher must select these loading items. Thus, it is difficult if not impossible to know if the selected items constitute the best combination of items.

A *set of measurements* can be any number of different types of descriptive variables, such as demographics, attitude scales, lifestyle characteristics, behavioral measurements, and preferences.

Group assignment or prediction is made upon the basis of subjects' scores on these characteristics. A group can be any two or more distinct sets in a sample. Examples of two-group sets include Republican/Democrat, committed/noncommitted voters; legislators who traditionally vote for legislation on social issues and those who vote against such legislation; nonprofit organizations that either support or ignore environmental issues; patients with one or more symptoms who are likely to develop or not develop a disease.

Regardless of the application, discriminant analysis requires that several important assumptions be met. First, the distribution of measurements for the descriptive (independent) variables must be approximately normal. Second, the sample must be relatively large; samples in the range of 250 to 300 are considered to be of minimum size, although the process works with even smaller samples. Third, independent variable measurements must be at least nominal level (or transformed into dummy variables). Fourth, it must be possible to distinguish between two or more known categories among the sample. And fifth, there should be no missing values on either the dependent or independent variables for any subject included in the analysis; most statistical packages provide for elimination of cases with missing data with a simple checked instruction.

Purposes for Discriminant Analysis

In practice, discriminant analysis can be used in at least five different types of applications. First, the technique can *classify* and *describe* subjects in two or more respective relevant groups at the same time. Second, public administrators use discriminant analysis as a tool for improving the quality of their *predictions* about which subject is most likely to belong with which citizen group and why. Third, researchers use the technique to determine which descriptive variables have the greatest *power to discriminate* between two or more groups of people. Fourth, the method may be a *post hoc* test, a check for diagnoses or predictions made on the bases of other types of evaluations. Fifth, discriminant analysis may gauge how far apart groups are located on a set of descriptive characteristics. In this application, which is somewhat similar to the discrimination test, the distance between groups is based upon the location of the central tendency values (called *centroids*) for each group in two-dimensional space established by computer-generated functions.

The Descriptive Discriminant Analysis Model

In their review of the capacity of discriminant analysis procedures contained in three different statistical software packages, Huberty and Lowman (1997) distinguished between two fundamental types of discriminant analysis: descriptive discriminant analysis (DDA) and predictive discriminant (PDA). In the DDA model, the *grouping variable* serves as the predictor variable, with the responses on the descriptive characteristics variables taking on the role of outcome variables.

The research question in descriptive designs is centered not on the differences themselves, but instead on *how* the groups differ on some set of descriptors. For example, discriminant analysis may be used to test whether voters and nonvoters have the same lifestyle characteristics. The same model could develop descriptive profiles of several candidates for political office, or between adults who are politically active or politically inactive. The DDA method tests the power of the grouping variable to differentiate among the characteristics of group members.

DDA was used in a study conducted to test methodology for segmenting students' preferences for various types of postsecondary education (McNabb 1980). This study compared different scales of measurement on the basis of their power to discriminate between preidentified segments. The study first grouped a sample of 195 secondary school students into different groups according their stated intent to attend one of five different types of postsecondary institutions. A sixth group that did not plan to continue their education immediately after high school was also tested. This enabled the researcher to determine which of the demographic, social, economic, and attitudinal scales had the greatest power to classify subjects into their preidentified choice-groups.

The Predictive Discriminant Analysis Model

Most applications of discriminant analysis in public administration research use the predictive approach. In predictive applications, the grouping variable is the categorical variable that signifies group membership; in these circumstances, the set of characteristics variables serve as the predictor variables. In an example of the predictive (PDA) application, Cooper (1987) first used cluster analysis to group nations according to the type and size of their debt to foreign banks. After developing a profile of nations that had failed in the past, he then used discriminant analysis to predict which debtor nations were most likely to fail in their debt repayments.

Roberts (1992) used the PDA model in a voter prediction study. She employed panel information gathered in three waves leading up to the 1990 Texas gubernatorial elections. The data were measurements of subjects' attitude changes over time. Her sample of 283 subjects was 52.5 percent male and 47.5 percent female; 49.6 percent were registered Republicans and 50.4 percent registered Democrats. The dependent variable in the study was exit interviews in which subjects reported which candidate they voted. Independent variables—the descriptive scales—consisted of multi-item variables measuring partisanship, gender, degree of media reliance, and how closely they were following the race. After editing for missing data, Roberts had a database of 160 valid cases. Using the set of independent variable demographic measurements, predictive discriminant analysis revealed that they correctly grouped 84 percent of the male voters and 91 percent of the female voters.

In another example of a predictive application, Kim (1995) conducted a comparative study of the power of selected scales to predict the voting behavior of uncommitted voters in 1992 presidential elections. He tested his model on samples in North Carolina and in the Republic of South Korea. Kim then used the same scales to predict how voter behavior would change if a third or minority party dropped from the race late in the campaign period. Kim found that in political polls, analysts are often uncertain as to how to treat uncommitted voters. That uncertainty has resulted in at least four different ways of looking at uncommitted voter data:

1. Eliminate the group from the analysis entirely.
2. Assign the uncommitted group on the basis of another discrete descriptive variable, such as the party affiliation of the respondent.
3. Predict the group assignments on the basis of an attitudinal variable, such as the respondent's attitude towards candidates, parties, and/or their position of key political issues in the campaign.
4. Use qualitative information gathered from intensive personal interviews with a small sample of respondents, then classify the uncommitted group according to similarities to the interviewed sample.

Kim was convinced that none of the four approaches took full advantage of the collected information. Also, they often resulted in grossly inadequate prediction results—a fact that could have serious effects on a political campaign strategy. Kim proposed using a discriminant analysis design upon which to base the uncommitted voter classifications. Kim concluded that discrimi-

Table 20.7

Example of Discriminant Results for a Prediction Application

Country Sample	Prediction Power with 3rd-Party Candidate in the Race	Prediction Power with 3rd-Party Candidate out of the Race
United States	73.0% of grouped cases correctly classified	87.0% of grouped cases correctly classified
Korea	82.9% of grouped cases correctly classified	87.2% of grouped cases correctly classified

nant analysis is particularly useful for the following purposes: (1) to identify the election issues and demographic variables with the greatest power to discriminate between groups, (2) to predict how the uncommitted voters would vote, and (3) to judge the effect one candidate withdrawing from a race with more than two candidates will have on the distribution of votes for the remaining candidates.

Kim's comparison of possible Korean voter reaction with third-party candidates in a race and their reaction when the third-party candidate withdraws was particularly insightful. The results of his analysis with seventeen predictor variables are displayed in Table 20.7.

GROUP-CLASSIFICATION APPLICATIONS

The group-classification process works in much the same way that Kim used the PDA model. Consider the following example: Suppose that a researcher is working with two equal-size groups of politically aware people, of which 160 consider themselves to be liberals at heart and 160 say they are conservatives. Each of the 320 subjects is measured on several describing characteristics. The researcher wants to know whether the variables can be used as a tool for distinguishing between the two political groups. Discrimination analysis that compares known with predicted group membership gives a numeric measure of the prediction effectiveness of the scale. Using MDA can give the researcher indispensable evidence for supporting a conclusion.

As a Post Hoc Validation of Other Prediction Methods

Runyon, Faust, and Orvaschel (2002) used discriminant analysis to determine whether two scales developed to diagnose children with post-traumatic stress disorder (PTSD) could distinguish whether children were suffering current depression. The researchers tested the Kiddie-Schedule of Affective Disorders and Schizophrenia (K-SDAS) and the Children's Depression Inventory (CDI) on a sample of 96 children ages five to seventeen years. Their discriminant analysis found that, overall, the items they selected after analysis of variance for statistically significant differences were able to successfully classify children with both disorders 81.8 percent of the time.

Using Discriminant Analysis Software

The Statistical Package for the Social Sciences (SPSS) contains a discriminant analysis capability. Discriminant analysis predicts which individuals will fall into two or more separate groups based upon the measurements taken from a similar sample of subjects. This is the method that SPSS defines in the Version 11 (2001) of the package: "Discriminant analysis is useful for situations where you want to build a predictive model of group membership based on observed characteristics of each case. The procedure generates a discriminant function (or, for more than two groups, a set of discriminant functions) based on linear combinations of the predictor variables that provide the best discrimination between the groups."

According to information in the "Help" section of the program, on average, people in temperate zone countries consume more calories per day than those in the tropics, and a greater proportion of the people in the temperate zones are city dwellers. A researcher wants to combine this information in a function to determine how well an individual can discriminate between the two groups of countries. The researcher thinks that population size and economic information may also be important. If these variables are useful for discriminating between the two climate zones, the values of D will differ for the temperate and tropic countries. If you use a stepwise variable selection method, you may find that you do not need to include all four variables in the function.

FACTOR AND CLUSTER ANALYSIS

Many multivariate analysis techniques or methods were developed specifically to assist in the management and analysis of large databases. Large databases are those data sets with 300 or more subjects and/or 100 or more variables. Some techniques to analyze these data sets are *principal component analysis, standard factor analysis,* and *cluster analysis.* Principal component analysis (PCA) is similar to standard factor analysis (SFA) in concept and application. In fact, it is just one of several ways that SPSS provides for extracting the factors that underlie a set of measurements. However, the principle component model does not result in a direct reduction in the number of variables. Instead, the model lists components in the order of the amount of variation they explain in all the variables (Cattell 1978; Goddard and Kirby 1976). Principal component analysis transforms an original data set of variables into a set of uncorrelated variables. The new composite variables (components) include most of the information in the original data set, but are fewer in number (Dunteman 1994, 157).

Factor analysis serves many different purposes, the most important of which are the reducing the number of variables and testing hypotheses. The SFA model, which is also known as *common factor analysis,* is used more often than principal component analysis. With SFA, the observed variables are causal influences on the underlying factors as well as influences on factors that are unique to each observed variable (Lance and Vandenberg 2002).

Cluster analysis also results in a reduction in the amount of data with which the researcher must work, but involves more subjective decision making than factor analysis. However, cluster analysis is a popular tool for grouping people into similar categories or classifications; it has become an important statistical tool to identify and describe voter segments in political campaigning, and even more important as a tool for segmenting markets for products and services.

Factor Analysis

Factor analysis is one of a family of statistical techniques for summarizing interrelationships among a set of variable measurements, identifying underlying structure in a data set, and reducing the number of variables to work with. The techniques all produce a smaller number of artificial variables, called *factors* or *components.* Factors are artificial constructs generated by the statistical program that are based on inter-correlations; they represent what is common among the original variables (Babbie 2001; Cattell 1978; Lance and Vandenberg 2002). Bernard called these underlying constructs "super variables" because they are made up of more than one initial variable. The initial variables make up the factors on the basis of the strength of their *similarity correlation* with the factor. The variables included in the factor, in turn, help the researcher find meaning in and subjectively explain the composition of each factor.

A *factor* is a new variable that is a composite of other variables. By examining the commonality of the initial variables and the strength of their factor correlations (called *factor loadings*), factor analysis helps make it possible to explain portions of the variance in a dependent variable. An arbitrary number of important variables (importance is determined by the size of the factor loadings) are determined to make up the composite factor. Interpretation of the factor and the cutoff point in the number of variables loading on a factor are at the discretion of the researcher. Traditionally, only variables with correlation values of 0.60 or greater are always included, and loadings from 0.30 to 0.59 are considered as possible contributors. According to Bernard (2000), however, some researchers use 0.50 as the cutoff point in factor loadings, with values from 0.30 to 0.49 considered as possibly worth including.

One of the greatest advantages of factor analysis is the subjective interpretation of factors. Subjective interpretation interjects an aspect of reality into the process; it is an attempt to decipher meaning from simple numerical description. However, Babbie (2001) saw this subjectivity as the root cause of several disadvantages of the technique, including the following:

- The factors themselves are generated mathematically, with no meaningful assistance of the researcher; interpretation occurs *after* establishment of the factors and factor loadings of the individual variables.
- Factor analysis does not provide a means for disproving a hypothesis; therefore, it is more a qualitative analysis technique than a scientific, positivist research approach.
- No matter what data the researcher includes in the analysis matrix, factor analysis will generate a factor solution. The algorithm ignores the form and content of the initial variables. Therefore, the factor result may be nonsense.

Factor analysis requires that the data meet a few simple assumptions: a normal distribution, a large sample size (an *n* of at least 300, although some researchers reduce this to a minimum of 150 cases), at least nominal-level (or standardized) data, a linear relationship, and outliers screened and omitted.

Applications of Standard Factor Analysis

Factor analysis is used in two major applications. One, *exploratory factor analysis* (EFA), identifies relationships among variables. The relationships are not always obvious in the data, but show up as a pattern of correlations with artificial factors. EFA summarizes, groups, and explains the data. The researcher interprets the meaning of the factor according to its correlated items. The second chief application for factor analysis is *confirmatory factor analysis* (CFA). CFA is the newer of the two uses and is rapidly gaining acceptance in research.

Exploratory Factor Analysis

In exploratory factor analysis, the researcher uses the method to determine the minimum number of hypothetical factors or components that account for the variance between the variables; it also is used to *explore* the data for ways to reduce the number of active variables. Well into the 1990s, exploratory models have remained the chief factor analysis application in the social sciences (Kim and Mueller 1994). The following steps are presented to guide the researcher through the EFA process:

1. Collect the data from a representative sample.
2. Determine which of the observed variables should be included in the analysis.
3. Determine which method of extraction to use in the analysis.
4. Specify how many factors to include in the solution.
5. Interpret the patterns of factor loadings, variances, and covariances.
6. Rotate the matrix to test for alternative factor structures.
7. Interpret the final EFA solution.

In an example of an exploratory factor analysis, data collected by Lee, Barnowe and McNabb (2001) was subjected to an EFA to identify the underlying structure of an international environmental awareness database. The study assessed awareness and perceived importance of risk associated with a number of environmental and social concerns among a sample of 295 university students in the United States and Taiwan. The researchers combined portions of several instruments available in the research literature to produce a topical and comprehensive instrument. The final instrument was pretested in several undergraduate and graduate classes in private and public universities. Pretesting led to a revision to the response scales: a sixth response, *"Not familiar with this issue,"* was added for all items.

The instrument contained a list of forty-five issues that the researchers believed were naturally classified into three broad groups: natural environment issues, social environment issues, and technological environment issues. The natural environment scale consisted of twenty-four items often cited as pressing environmental problems. These ranged from ozone depletion and acid rain to the Ebola virus and dioxins. The scale was developed from items focusing on five broad categories of environmental problems:

- Air Pollution (5 items): Outdoor pollution, chemical pollution, radon gas, indoor air pollution, and ozone depletion,
- Water Pollution (3 items): Acid rain, tap water pollution, and chemical spills.
- Solid and Toxic Waste (3 items): Solid waste, toxic waste, and waste incineration.
- Climate and Nature, including species loss (6 items): Climate change, forest fires, rain forest destruction, depletion of fish stocks, species loss, and wetlands loss.
- Disease and Health Concerns (7 items): Ebola, food bacteria, lead, cancer, food additives, dioxins, and pesticides.

The social environment issues scale contained thirteen items associated with the quality of life and health and welfare in modern society. Example items range from tobacco and drug use to AIDS and crime and violence. The scale was constructed from six items in each of two subscale categories:

- Social Issues (6 items): Abortion, crime, street gangs, overpopulation, road rage and traffic congestion.
- Health-Related Issues (7 items): Alcoholism, drug addiction, asbestos, AIDS, venereal disease, tobacco and motor vehicle accidents.

The technological environment scale contained eight items that ranged from nuclear waste to cloning and irradiation of food. These items were subjectively assigned to the technology scale.

The scale was constructed from four items each in of two subscale categories:

1. Technological Dangers (4 items): Tainted blood supply, food irradiation, high voltage power, and medical x-rays.
2. Science and Energy (4 items): Nuclear reactors, genetic engineering, cloning, and nuclear waste.

The revised instrument was administered to a sample of 192 undergraduate and graduate-school students at three U.S. universities, with a translated version administered to 103 students at the National University of Taiwan. Responses were made using five-point scales ranging from Not-at-all-Important to Absolutely Critical. A set of demographic classification items was also included.

Confirmatory Factor Analysis

The purpose of the confirmatory factor analysis model is to test hypotheses, either about the number of underlying factors or the variables or items that load on any single factor or component. Having made the assertion in advance which items belong to which factor, the researcher can test his assertion (hypothesis) by examining factor loadings. While describing the difference between the two approaches is relatively simple, Kim and Mueller (1994) point out that in practice, the distinction is not always this clear; some of both models are found in many studies.

Factor analysis methods trace back to 1904 and Charles Spearman's principal components model. Through the 1970s, nearly all factor analysis literature was concerned with exploratory applications. However, from the 1980s onward, there has been significantly more interest in the CFA model. The objective of confirmatory factor analysis is related to hypothesis testing. The researcher hypothesizes that a number of items or variables are collectively related. He or she can run a factor analysis on the data to test whether the relationships exist as they were hypothesized.

In his monograph on confirmatory factor analysis, Long (1983) identified a number hypotheses that may be established for a CFA analysis. These include (1) specifying the number of factors to be included in the solution, (2) deciding what variables to include, (3) deciding what variances and covariances to expect among both common and unique factors, and (4) establishing what relationships between variables and underlying factors and/or between unique factors and initial variables to expect.

Lance and Vandenberg (2002, 223) developed the data in Table 20.8 to illustrate the major differences between the EFA and CFA approaches. They added that the CFA should be considered a tool for testing the *validity* of an underlying structure using prior-identified variables, whereas EFA should be a technique for identifying which variables are related with which other variables. The following seven steps were proposed by Lance and Vandenberg (2002, 221) to lead the researcher through the process of conducting a confirmatory factor analysis:

1. Define the theoretical factors or components to be used in the CFA.
2. Determine what observed variables should load on each theoretical factor.
3. Collect the data from a representative sample.
4. Specify in advance the patterns of factor loadings (which variables should have higher loadings) together with amounts variances and covariances (which factors ought to account for the greatest amount of variance).

Table 20.8

A Comparison of EFA and CFA Factor Analysis Approaches

Issue	EFA	CFA
Mathematical model	Either standard factor or principal components	Standard factor model
Selection of measures	Wide variation	Determined by hypothesized factor format
Number of factors	Determined from the data	Specified before the analysis
Interpretation of factors	Interpreted from items loading on each factor	Specified before the analysis
Factor pattern matrix	Fully free; no constraints	Constrained; a fixed set of elements
Factor correlations	Established after rotation	Estimated before the analysis
Goodness of fit	Not an issue	A key, controversial issue

Source: C.E. Lance and R.J. Vandenberg 2002.

5. Propose alternative, competing theoretical factor structures.
6. Estimate model parameters and assess goodness of fit.
7. Interpret the CFA solution.

Conducting a Factor Analysis with SPSS

The SPSS factor analysis program procedure is highly flexible: it provides seven methods of factor extraction and five methods of rotation. Three methods of computing factor scores are included, and factor scores can be saved as variables for additional analysis. The following example is contained in the Help file of SPSS for Windows under "Factor Analysis":

> What underlying attitudes lead people to respond to the questions on a political survey as they do? Examining the correlations among the survey items reveals that there is significant overlap among various subgroups of items—questions about taxes tend to correlate with each other, questions about military issues correlate with each other, and so on. With factor analysis, you can investigate the number of underlying factors and, in many cases, you can identify what the factors represent conceptually. Additionally, you can compute factor scores for each respondent, which can then be used in subsequent analyses.

For each variable, SPSS produces the number of valid cases, the mean, and standard deviation. The SPSS factor analysis program also produces a correlation matrix of variables, including their significance levels; an initial solution, with communalities, eigenvalues, and percentage of variance explained; an unrotated solution, including factor loadings, communalities, and eigenvalues; a rotated solution, including rotated pattern matrix and transformation matrix; and a factor score coefficient matrix and factor covariance matrix.

In addition, the SPSS factor analysis program produces two plots: a "scree plot" of eigenvalues and a loading plot of the first two or three factors. The scree plot shown in Figure 20.2 was

Figure 20.2 **An Example of a Scree Plot Showing Eigenvalues for Five Components**

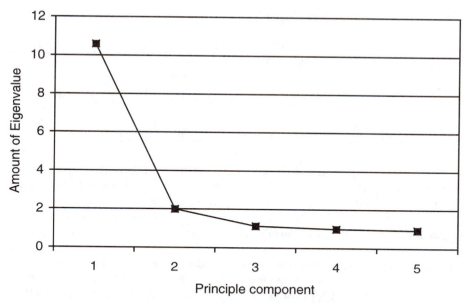

Source: From material in the *London Index of Deprivation.* Greater London Council, 2002.

produced from the principal component analysis results in *The London Deprivation Index* published in 2002 by the Greater London Council. The data are summary data are displayed in Table 20.3. Scree plots are simply the value of the eigenvalue plotted on a y-axis (vertical), with the number of the factor (the composite variable) plotted on the x-axis (horizontal). The term "scree" is a geological term for the rubble and other debris that collects at the bottom of a rocky slope (Child 1990). The SPSS-produced table in which eigenvalues and amount of explained variance are displayed serves as a visual cue for deciding which factors to include and which to omit. There are no set rules for establishing the optimum number of factors in the final solution, but several different methods are used for making this decision. One is the scree plot discussed earlier; another is the Kaiser-Guttman rule of thumb, which specifies that only factors with an eigenvalue larger than 1.0 should be retained (Cattell 1978; Hutcheson and Sofroniou 1999).

To determine how many factors or components to include in the final analysis using the scree method, simply use the point where the curve straightens out as the maximum number of factors to include. In the example in Figure 20.2, the curve begins to flatten out convincingly at the third component. Therefore, the London Index included three components in its principal components analysis. As can be seen in Table 20.9, three components account for more than 65 percent of the variance in the model.

The term e*igenvalue* (also known as *characteristic root* and other names) is an important mathematical concept in factor analysis; it is particularly important as a component in deciding how many factors or components to retain in the final analysis (Kim and Mueller 1994), and for determining how much variance is explained by each factor.

Eigenvalues are simply *the sum of the squares of the factor loadings on each independent factor.* This is the total amount of variance for that factor. A glance at the computed factor-loading matrix

Table 20.9

Summary Data for London Deprivation Index

Component	Eigenvalue	Percent of Variance	Cumulative Percent
1	10.587	50.414	50.414
2	1.991	9.48	59.894
3	1.121	5.339	65.223
4	0.983	4.681	69.914
5	0.934	4.446	74.36

Source: London Index of Deprivation. Greater London Council, 2002.

reveals that variables load on more than one variable at the same time. This is not a problem, for it is the sum of all (squared) loadings—the similarity coefficients—that are of interest. The larger the eigenvalue, the more variance is explained by the factor.

Using Cluster Analysis to Group Variables

Cluster analysis is a generic label for a number of statistical processes used to group objects, people, variables, or concepts into more or less homogeneous groups on the basis of their similarities (Loor 1983). Bernard (2000, 646) defined the cluster statistical technique as "a descriptive tool for exploring relations among items—for finding what goes with what." The result of a cluster analysis is a set of classes, types, categories, or some other type of group. One of the difficulties researchers have with using cluster analysis is the lack of consensus on the terms used for cluster parts and processes. For example, some of the names used for cluster techniques include *typological analysis, numerical taxonomy, pattern recognition,* and *classification analysis.*

Other terms that are used interchangeably in applications of cluster analysis to mean the "things" being classified are subject, case, entity, object, pattern, and operational taxonomic units. "Entity" seems to be used most often, but certainly not by any meaningful majority. Terms used to mean the "things" that are used to assess the similarities between entities include variable, attribute, character or characteristic, and features. Finally, the following terms are used interchangeably to mean similarities: resemblance, proximity, and association (Aldenderfer and Blashfield 1984).

Cluster analysis can be used for many different tasks, including but not limited to data reduction, identification of natural groupings or types, development of classifications systems, and the testing of hypotheses. A cluster analysis process can be used to (Loor 1983, 3–4):

1. Identify natural clusters of independent variables.
2. Identify distinguishable groups or clusters of cases.
3. Construct a rationale for classifying subjects or items into groups.
4. Generate hypotheses within the data by uncovering unexpected clusters.
5. Test hypothesized groupings that the researcher believes are present in a larger group of cases.
6. Identify homogeneous subgroups that are characterized by the patterns of variables the classification reveals.

Cluster analysis is not without its disadvantages, a number of which were pointed out by Aldenderfer and Blashfield (1984). Cluster analysis, unlike much of our statistical knowledge, is constructed upon rather simple mathematical procedures; the techniques are not yet supported by a large body of statistical reasoning. As a result, a great deal of subjective interpretation is required in the underlying structure and the selection of distinct clusters from the output. A second problem is that cluster analysis methods have been developed in many different disciplines, including anthropology, sociology, psychology, and political science. Thus, the conventions that have been built up over the years reflect the biases extant in those disciplines. Furthermore, as more applications occur, new users seem intent upon adding their own contributions to the process, as is evidenced by the lack of even a standard terminology.

A third disadvantage of cluster analysis is the problematic nature of replication—a key requirement for scientific analysis. Different cluster methods regularly result in different cluster solutions from the same data set. A fourth disadvantage has to do with the strategic rationale for grouping in the first place: the reason for doing a cluster analysis is to identify the structure within a data set, whereas the technique itself imposes a structure upon the data.

Like all statistical processes, the cluster analysis procedure progresses through a logical series of steps, which are presented in Figure 20.3. Not included in the chart but also a vital preliminary step is the establishment of *objectives* for the research. The researcher must always determine in advance what outcome of the statistical procedure is desired. Once this is established, the researcher then develops or selects an appropriate data-gathering instrument, for which an adequately large sample of subjects and a representative set of attributes or characteristics for collecting measurements exists.

Cluster analysis works with all types and levels of data, but it is usually best to standardize the scores so that a common measurement is used in the final analysis. If the database is too large, if there are too many variables and too many branches in the cluster tree for logical interpretation, the researcher may wish to reduce the number of active variables. One way to do this is by conducting either a standard factor analysis or principal component analyses first, and then use the results as input for the cluster analysis procedure. Selecting the right algorithm refers to the many different types of clustering methods that are available. Alderndefer and Blashfield (1984) identified seven different clustering methods: hierarchical-agglomerative, iterative, and factor analytic are three most popular methods used in social science research, including public administration.

Of these, hierarchical-agglomerative cluster analysis is most common. Other types of cluster algorithms include hierarchical divisive, density search, clumping, and graph theoretic. Researchers interested in knowing more about these models should consult one of the many books written specifically on the cluster analysis method.

Within the hierarchical agglomerative model, researchers can chose from several different linkage models—linkage refers to the way that *dendograms* (cluster analysis trees) are used to identify groupings—single linkage, complete linkage, and average linkage. Because of its simplicity and ease of interpretation, single linkage may be the more popular model.

Cluster analysis may have any combination of the following goals: (1) to develop a typology or classification system, (2) to investigate methods for grouping subjects, (3) to generate hypotheses through data exploration, and (4) to test hypotheses by comparing cluster analysis groupings with groups identified another way. Of these uses, the creation of classifications is by far the most common use for cluster analysis. However, in applied cluster analysis, two or more of these uses are likely to be combined in the study.

MULTIPLE ANALYSIS OF VARIANCE (MANOVA)

Statistical procedures have been developed to test the impact on differences of more than two sets of groups at the same time. These tests compare all factors against each grouping variable

Figure 20.3 **A Flowchart of the Steps Involved in a Cluster Analysis Procedure**

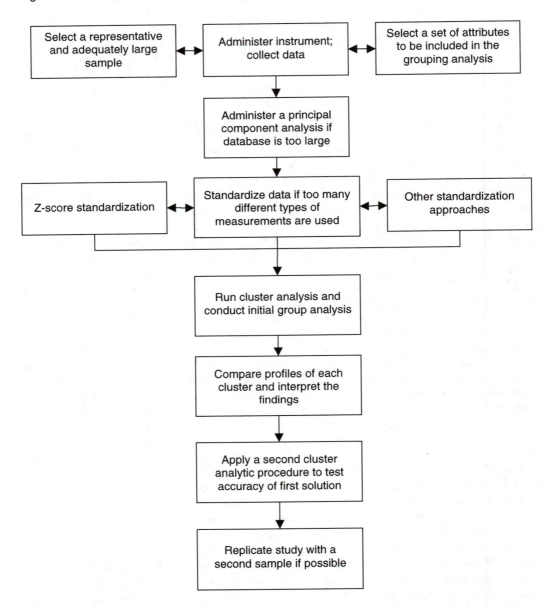

at the same time, then test for interaction, and then test again for combinations of groups. These procedures are known as *Multivariate Analysis of Variance* (MANOVA). In addition, a procedure called ANCOVA has been developed that combines a regression analysis with ANOVA. Neither MANOVA nor ANCOVA are employed sufficiently to warrant a more detailed discussion here. However, since they are based on the same concepts underlying analysis of variance procedures used in experimental research designs, they are not difficult to learn and use. Additional information about these two procedures is available in most advanced statistical methods textbooks.

SUMMARY

This chapter looked at several popular multivariate statistical procedures: multiple regression analysis, factor and cluster analysis, and multiple discriminant analysis. In multiple regression analysis, two or more independent predictor variables are used to explain the variance in the dependent variable. Multiple regression analysis requires continuous independent and dependent variables, although it is also possible to use categorical data for either the dependent or independent variable, or both, by creating *indicator,* or *dummy,* variables.

Discriminant analysis is one of a series of statistical techniques designed to analyze relationships among two or more variables. Discriminant analysis is a mathematical technique that weighs and combines a set of measurements in a way that their ability to discriminate between two or more groups is maximized. When more than two grouping variables are used in the design, the discriminant process is considered to be multiple discriminant analysis (MDA).

The underlying research problem in discriminant analysis is how to establish a decision rule that enables assigning (or predicting) a subject whose group membership is not known to only one of the categories that make up a complete group. Although assigning is done on the basis of measurements on a set of descriptor variables, selection of these loading items is the province of the researcher.

Discriminant analysis can be used for at least five different purposes: (1) as a way of classifying and describing subjects in two or more groups at the same time; (2) as a tool for improving the quality of predictions about which subject belongs with which group and why; (3) to determine which descriptive variables have the greatest power to discriminate between two or more groups of people; (4) as a *post hoc* test, in which it serves as a check for diagnoses or predictions made on the basis of other types of evaluations; and (5) to gauge how far apart the groups are located on a set of descriptive characteristics.

A number of multivariate analysis procedures have been developed to help researchers manage large databases—that is, data sets that consist of measurements in the neighborhood of 300 or more subjects and/or more than 100 variables. These tools include principal component analysis, standard factor analysis, and cluster analysis. Principal component analysis (PCA) is similar to standard factor analysis (SFA) in concept and application; it is one of seven different ways that SPSS provides for extracting the factors that underlie a set of measurements.

Factor analysis serves many different purposes, the most important of which are reducing the number of variables and hypothesis testing. Factor analysis requires the researcher to subjectively interpret each factor based on the variables that load on the factor—which some believe to be one of the greatest advantages of factor analysis. Subjective interpretation makes it possible to attempt to decipher meaning from what is otherwise a simple numerical description.

Cluster analysis also results in a reduction in the amount of data with which the researcher must work, but involves more subjective decision making than factor analysis. However, cluster analysis is a popular tool for grouping people into similar categories. It has become an important statistical tool for identifying and describing voter segments in political campaigning, and even more important as a tool for segmenting groups of citizens with needs for various public services.

ADDITIONAL READING

Huberty, Carl J. 1994. *Applied Discriminant Analysis.* New York: John Wiley.
Norušis, Marija J. 2007. *SPSS 15.0: Advanced Statistical Procedures Companion.* Upper Saddle River, NJ: Prentice Hall.

CONDUCTING STATISTICAL TESTS WITH SPSS

SPSS (Statistical Package for the Social Sciences) is a powerful software package that performs statistical analyses of quantitative data. The program enables users to create, modify, and analyze very large sets of data. It can also produce such graphic displays as tables, charts, and graphs. Data entry is facilitated by the use of a standard spreadsheet format; cases are in rows and variables are in columns. A *case* is the responses or measurements of a single subject or study element. A *variable* is something that the researcher is able to measure or count in some way.

HOW DO I START USING SPSS?

SPSS is loaded on many but not all of the personal computers (PCs) in college and university computer labs and, increasingly, many public offices. When it is available, it is a relatively easy and powerful way of processing large-sample databases; it is essentially unlimited in the number of either subjects or variables it can process at any one time.

The process of launching SPSS software is the same as any other frequently used software. At the initial window, double-click on the SPSS icon. The Data Editor window will appear on the screen. (If the SPSS shortcut icon does not appear on the main Windows screen, click on Start, then Programs, then select SPSS. The opening SPSS screen should appear.) Superimposed on this opening screen may be a dialog window that asks "What would you like to do?" Available options include:

- Run the tutorial
- Type in data
- Run an existing query
- Create a new using the Database Capture Wizard
- Open an existing file.

If you have a database loaded on the hard drive or on an inserted floppy disc, you may call up that file for immediate activity. Or, you may select Cancel, which opens the Data Editor for data entry. You must enter data in the Data Editor before SPSS can perform any operations. Data can be entered directly or imported from an existing file, such as an Excel spreadsheet or a word-processing program.

THE SPSS OPENING SCREEN

The SPSS opening screen will show two toolbars at the top of the screen and a full-screen spreadsheet (with grid lines). Along the left side of the screen are row numbers. At the top of the spreadsheet is a row for you to indicate the names of the variables in your study.

Above the spreadsheet is the Main Menu Bar or for versions lower than Version 10, the SPSS Data Editor Toolbar. Menus are named; tools are displayed as icons.

Main Menu Bar

Look at the top line on the SPSS screen. Running across the screen are the names for ten file menus. These menus allow you to access every process, tool, and feature contained in SPSS. Beginning at the left and running across the screen, these file menus are:

- *File* menu: This allows you to open, close, save, and otherwise work with all types of SPSS files.
- *Edit* menu: This allows you to cut and paste, move files, and find elements in a file or record (a *record* is all the data for a single case).
- *View* menu: This allows you to turn on or off visible features, change fonts, and show grid lines.
- *Data* menu: A key option, this allows you to define variables, indicate the type of measurements used, and assign labels to variables and values.
- *Transform* menu: This feature allows you to convert or change variable values, count responses, recode values, and so on.
- *Analyze* menu: Along with the Data menu, this is the option you will use most often; it can be considered to be the heart of SPSS. It allows you to name any type of analysis you want to carry out.
- *Graphs* menu: This feature allows you to select from fifteen different ways to graphically display data, including tables, graphs, and charts.
- *Utilities* menu: This allows you to call up information about your variables and your data file.
- *Windows* menu: Allows you to switch from one window to another, and back.
- *Help* menu: The standard online help feature that explains all features and tools needed by the analyst.

ENTERING AND NAMING VARIABLES AND VALUES: SPSS VERSION 10 AND ABOVE

Versions 10 and above of SPSS employ a slightly different system for identifying variable labels in a data set. Rather than simply clicking on the first cell under the column indicator, you must now go to a separate file. When you are in this file, it is possible to define all variables in a data set at one time. This should be done before any data are entered.

How to Define Variables and Assign Value Labels

Look at the bottom left-hand corner of the SPSS Data Editor dialog box. You should see two file tabs: One says Data View, and the other says Variable View. Click on the Variable View tab. You are now ready to define your variables and their values. In this file, all information about each variable is entered in *row* format, going across the page (this is an important distinction because data for each variable will later be entered in *column* format). The first row will hold all the information for your first variable; row two will hold all information about your second variable, and so on. SPSS will *automatically* move this information into the appropriate column for the variable.

You will have ten decisions to make about each variable in your data set, although several will be made for you (in what is called the *default* mode). These choices are in ten columns. To enter defining information, click on the cell in the appropriate column, as follows.

Column 1: This is where you enter the name of the variable. Names can be no longer than eight characters in length and must start with a letter of the alphabet. On the screen, variable names appear in lowercase type.

Column 2: This permits you to change the form of the variable data. The default is "numeric," which is the form you will almost always use. Make sure that is what appears in the cell.

Column 3: This establishes the width of the cell. The default is eight spaces. You can widen or narrow it, or leave the default width of eight spaces. The defining characteristic is the number of characters you use for the variable name *or* the number of characters in a value for that variable. For example, a variable name that is six characters wide (such as *gender*) might have values that are one character wide (such as the number 1 for female and 2 for male), the cell will require a column width of six characters—the length of the *variable* name. If, however, the variable length is only three characters wide (such as *Inc* for *Income*) but the values might require five characters for an income amount (such as 45000), then the column width for this variable will be based on the number of characters required for the largest value, not on the three-character-wide variable name.

Column 4: This changes the number of decimals you want to use for each variable. The *default* is two decimal points. It can be raised or lowered or left as it is. For categorical data, it is usually best to make this number zero (0).

Column 5: This is where you may enter a longer label for the short variable name you entered in column 1. The longer variable label will then appear along with the shorter variable name in all printouts, making it easier for you to later remember what the statistical results apply to; this is very important with databases with many variables. Variable labels can be up to forty characters in length, including spaces and symbols.

Column 6: This opens the box for providing definitions to the values of a variable. Value labels can be up to twenty characters in length, including spaces and symbols. Follow this five-step procedure to input these value labels into your data dictionary:

Step 1: Click on the blank cell in this column. Then, click on the small three-dot box that will appear at the right-hand side of the cell. This will bring up the Values dialog box.

Step 2: Enter a number you have assigned for the value in the Values window.

Step 3. Enter a label (less than twenty characters in length) for the value in the Value Labels window.

Step 4: Click on the Add button. This is a critical step; you must do this after entering each value and value label!

Step 5. Repeat the process for each value of the variable. Click on OK.

Column 7:   This is where you assign a value for any data missing for this variable. Follow this procedure:

    Step 1: Click on the three-dot button.
    Step 2: Click on the Discrete Missing Values button.
    Step 3: Enter the number you want to use to signify missing data for this variable.
    Step 4: Click OK. You can use any number or numbers that are not actual values for the variable. For most variables, the value 9 is used. This is an important step. If you leave a cell blank, it will still be counted and used in the divisor when calculating statistics.

    TIP: *Never* leave a cell blank; *never* leave a row blank! You will know if it is blank because a faint period (dot) will show in the cell when you are in the Data View file.

Column 8:   This column allows you to specify how wide the variable name will be. The *default* is the exact width of the name as it appears. If you want to change the default, change the width to match the number of characters taken by the name, but no more than eight. Most of the time, you will not need to change this value.

Column 9:   This column allows you to specify the alignment you want for the data in each cell—flush right, left, or centered.

Column 10:   In this column you may tell the computer the type of measurement for the variable. You can choose from Scale, Ordinal, or Nominal.

When you have identified all variables, values, and data types, click on the Data View tab at the lower left-hand corner of the screen. All the information you entered for each variable will be inserted in its proper location, with each variable and value now defined. Remember, you can always go back and change anything by clicking on the Variable View tab and moving your cursor to the proper cell. You are now ready to enter data. All data for any one case *must* be entered in rows and inserted in the correct columns for that variable. Remember to regularly save the data.

Data Editor Toolbar for SPSS Version 9 and Lower

For SPSS Version 9 and lower, the Data Editor Toolbar allows quick access to commands dealing with data and data files. A string of sixteen different icons is displayed on the toolbar, running across the screen just under the Main Menu bar. These icons are shortcuts to a variety of SPSS commands, most of which are also embedded within the main menus. Using the icons just makes it easier and quicker to do your analyses. Beginning at the left of the toolbar, the icons represent the following actions:

- *Open* a file.
- *Save* the file you are working on.
- *Print* a file or output from a statistical process.
- *Recall* the last dialog box you used.
- *Undo* reverses the last process.
- *Go to* a named chart in the file.
- *Go to* a named case in the file.
- *Access* information about variables.
- *Find* a record in a file.

- *Insert* a case (record) into a file (cases are *rows*).
- *Insert* a variable into a file (variables are *columns*).
- *Split* a file on some dimension of a variable.
- *Weight* allows you to assign weights to variables.
- *Selects* cases according to a user-selected dimension or measurement.
- *Turn value labels* on or off in the visual display.
- *Create* a set of variables to use as an index.

ENTERING DATA

SPSS has a few limitations in what it accepts as "data." The easiest way to deal with these limits is to treat all information that is going to be processed in an SPSS analysis as *numeric data.* Other than names developed for *variables* and measured or assigned *values* of those variables, only numbers should be entered for processing. Thus, SPSS data are numbers used to signify a set of measurements or labels for a specific set of cases.

The term *case* is used to mean a single entity in a data set. Examples include one person among a group of people studied (i.e., in a *sample*), one city in an investigation of a group of cities, or one household in a group of political precincts examined for voting results. Whatever the element included in the study, the collective group of cases is usually referred to as a *sample*.

Cases are always listed in *rows* in an SPSS data file. Each case in the sample is assigned its own identifying number (1, 2, 3 . . .). Each case contains a set of features that are identified and recorded as numbers. These features are the values assigned to each of the *variables*. Examples of variables include the *gender* of a subject (*subject* is another word for a case), the number of school-aged children in a community, or the number of citizens in a precinct who voted in the last election. A more formal definition of a *variable* is any feature or concept that can be measured or assigned a value on any one of the four measurement scales (nominal, ordinal, interval, and ratio).

Variables are always listed in columns in an SPSS data file. The measurements or values for each variable must always be placed in the data file in the same reference order. For example, if the values assigned to the variable *gender* follow the values assigned to the variable *age* in the first case entries, they must always be entered in that same order. In an SPSS data file, a complete row for an individual case is called a *record*.

It is possible to enter data in an SPSS data file in two different ways. The one used most often is called the *fixed format;* the other is *free format*. In a fixed format file, every value for every variable is always entered in exactly the same column in the data file. Thus, every line of the data file will have the same number of columns, with the data for a variable always in the same place in the file. This is the format used by most researchers because it allows for easier editing and proofreading of a file; it is the only format discussed here.

If desired, empty spaces may be left between each variable, as in the fixed format example in Table 21.1; cases 4 through 9 are omitted for this example only.

If empty spaces are not used, the file would look like this: 011191215015, 022181114825, 032171113214, and so on. In this data file, 1 and 2 were used as database values for the two possible genders, female and male. Education is indicated by the number of years of school completed; "MS" refers to number of parents at home. "State" refers to place of birth with each state assigned a numerical value; and different values distinguish the occupations of the primary wage earners.

Data (the numerical values you collect and/or assign to values) is entered into a file using the SPSS data editor capability. This can be done in several different ways. The most common way is to type the data directly into the appropriate columns in the Data Editor window. However, to do it

Table 21.1

A Sample SPSS Database with Variable Labels

SNO	Gender	Age	Educa	MS	State	UrbSub	Occupa
01	1	19	12	1	50	1	5
02	2	18	11	1	48	2	5
03	2	17	11	1	32	1	4
04–09 are omitted for this example.							
10	1	20	13	2	47	2	4
11	1	22	10	1	33	1	3

this way, you must first define your variables and assign labels to all possible values of each variable. It is also possible to enter your data in a spreadsheet and then transport the file to SPSS.

Variables and Values in SPSS

As previously stated, a variable is a characteristic, a concept, or a descriptive property that can take on different values or categories. Another way to say this is that a variable is something that can vary. Research deals with four broad classes of variables:

- Independent variable: The characteristic that is supposed to be responsible for bringing about some change in another variable. It is sometimes called a "cause" variable.
- Dependent variable: The characteristic that is altered or otherwise affected by the changes in an independent variable. It is sometimes called an "outcome" variable.
- Extraneous variable: A characteristic or factor that is not part of the independent/dependent variable relationship. It may increase or decrease the strength of the relationship between two variables, but has no part in whatever "causation" might be present.
- Intervening variable: Sometimes called a "confounding variable," serves as a link between the independent and dependent variables. Often, the relationship between the independent and dependent variable cannot occur without the presence of an intervening variable; that is, the "cause" variable will only work in the presence of an intervening variable.

Naming Variables (Version 9 or Lower)

When you first open SPSS, the Data Entry Window automatically appears. The first cell in the upper left-hand corner of the spreadsheet will have a dark line around it. This signifies the location of the cursor. You must now click on the Data selection on the menu bar. This should bring up a gray box in the middle of the spreadsheet. This is the Define Variables dialogue box. Now, type the name of the first variable in the open box just to the right of the Variable Name prompt. Here are some tips to help you with defining your variables.

- Variable names must be no longer than eight characters; they can be less than eight; spaces cannot be used in the name.
- Variable names must always *start* with a letter of the alphabet, but can include some numbers and symbols among the eight characters. For example, you can name variables *var1* or *var2* but not *1var* or *2var*.

- Every variable must have its own distinct name; never repeat a variable name.
- Use names for variables that have some meaning to you and that are easy to remember. For example, instead of *plofbrth* for the variable *place of birth*, you might want to instead use the full word *state*, or *birth*, or *place*. It is always your choice!
- Some words cannot be used as variable names. These are words used in computational syntax, such as AND, OR, BUT, LESS, and MORE.
- All variables will be entered in *lowercase* type, so forget about using capital letters. For example, you might type in *Gender* or GENDER for a variable name, but it will always be displayed as "gender" on the screen and in all statistical output.
- Always remember to also enter longer variable labels when there is a possibility of confusion or misunderstanding. These labels can be as long as forty characters (including spaces). They will always be printed along with the shorter variable names in statistical output.

Variable Labels

It is typical to have a longer, more meaningful statement or label for the variable name spelled out in all SPSS statistical output. This is particularly important if the name assigned to a variable is an abbreviation of two or more words or an acronym. SPSS makes this possible by allowing you to add a longer name once during the Define Variables phase of the data entry. You can then continue to use the shorter variable name in your processing commands. The variable label can be as long as forty characters. For example, you might select the three-character name DOB for a variable referring to subjects' date of birth. You could add the longer variable label *Subjects' date of birth* to avoid any confusion. Follow this brief procedure to add longer labels into your program file:

1. Click on the Data box in the dialog line. The Define Variables dialog box should appear.
2. If you have not done it previously, type in the variable name *DOB* in the appropriate location.
3. Now, look at the area in the center of the dialogue box that is titled Change Settings. There should be four different choices under this heading: Type, Missing Values, Labels, and Column Format.
4. Click on the Labels box. This should bring up a new dialog box, one that permits you to enter the longer name for the variable—and to assign labels for each of the values you must assign to variables.
5. If you do not wish to add labels for the different values possible for each variable, click on OK. You have now added a longer label for the variable name.
6. Repeat this process for each variable in your data set. Remember: Variable names must be *eight characters or less* in length; variable labels can be up to forty characters long (including spaces and/or symbols).

Value Labels

Most of the time, adding a longer name for each variable is not enough. You will also want a name printed out for each value of your variables. For example, if the variable is gender, you will have two possible values, one for female and one for male (and possibly a third value for a category where subjects did not respond to the question). If you only enter the numeric values, when the data are processed you will get results for each numeric value, but your reader will not know that you meant 1 to signify females and 2 for males. If you add labels for each value, they will always appear with the results of any statistical analysis carried out with that variable.

Entering value labels is as easy as entering labels for variables. It is also possible to go back later and add, change, or remove values and their labels. To add labels in a new data set, follow this simple procedure:

1. Click on the Data box in the dialog line. The Define Variables dialog box should appear.
2. If you have not done it previously, type in the variable name *DOB* in the appropriate location. Do the same for adding longer variable labels.
3. In the dialog box titled Change Settings, select the Labels option. This should bring up a new dialog box that permits you to enter the longer name for the variable—and to assign labels for each of the values you must assign to variables.
4. In the Value Label section of this dialog box, enter the number for the first value for this variable. To return to the *gender* example, enter the number 1.
5. Now click on the Value Label box beneath this value and enter the label you wish to use. Value labels can be twenty characters or less in length.
6. Click on the Add box. The value and label assigned should appear in the larger white area alongside the Add button.
7. Click on the Value Label box again to add the next value and its label. Be sure to click on the Add button after entering every value and its label.
8. When you have entered all values and their labels for a variable, click on the Continue button; this brings you back to the Define Variable dialog box. If you are finished, click on the OK button. However, you may also wish to add values for missing values. That procedure is discussed in the next section.
9. Repeat this process for each value of each variable in your data set. Remember: Variable names must be eight characters or less in length; variable labels can be up to forty characters long (including spaces and/or symbols) and value labels can be up to twenty characters in length.
10. To change or remove values and/or their labels, as would be necessary if you were to combine two or more values into one, click on the Change or Remove buttons in the Define Labels dialog box and follow instructions. Length limitations still apply,

Missing Values

SPSS considers *every* cell in a data set to have some numeric value entered—even if it is left blank. Typically, a blank cell is read as a 0. Therefore, when entering data it is a good idea to not leave any cells blank. However, you do not always have data for every cell; often subjects will intentionally or accidentally omit a response to a variable. When this happens, researchers using SPSS usually enter a value to indicate that data are missing. These values are counted separately and not included in analysis requiring a mean (average) of the data. An example of a missing value is the number 9 entered when subjects fail to indicate their gender on a self-administered questionnaire. The number used to indicate missing data is only valid for a single variable, although the same valid number can be used for as many variables as desired. Any number other than those values specifically assigned in the data set can be used; however, the values 9 and 0 are usually used.

Whatever value is assigned to represent missing data, that same number must not be used for another response in the same question. For example, if subjects are asked to indicate their rank order preference for a set of 9 or 10 items, neither 9 nor 10 can be used to signify "missing data" in the data file. To add labels in a new data set, follow this simple procedure:

1. Click on the Data box in the dialog line. The Define Variables dialog box should appear. Choose the Change Settings option.
2. In the dialog box titled Change Settings, select the Missing Values option.
3. This should bring up a new dialog box, Missing Values. Two buttons appear at the top of the box. One is titled No Missing Values; if you have not already assigned a value, this button will display a small black dot. The second option is for Discrete Missing Values. Click on this second button.
4. Enter the number you wish to use to signify missing data in the first of three small boxes below the Discrete Missing Values button.
5. When you have entered the missing value for a variable, click on the Continue button; this brings you back to the Define Variables dialog box.
6. You may now select the Value Labels option to add a label for number you want to use to signify a missing value. This is done in the same way as adding all value labels. First enter the value, then enter the label Missing Values, No Response, or any label you want to use. Remember to click on the Add button when you have entered the value and its label.
7. If you are finished, click on the OK button. Repeat this process for each missing value of each variable in your data set. As always, remember that variable names must be eight characters or less in length; variable labels can be up to forty characters long (including spaces and/or symbols); and value labels can be up to twenty characters in length.

DATA IN SPSS

The final option in the Define Variables dialog box is Measurement. This box has three options: Scale, Ordinal, and Nominal. These tell the statistical processor what type of data it has for each variable. Different types of data (or measurements) require different types of statistical analyses. When you indicate to the data file editor the type of data represented by each variable, it will automatically select the correct analysis technique for each test you ask it to do.

Types of Data

Scale data consist of measurements that are considered to be at least *equidistant interval* (usually simply identified as *interval*). Statistical analyses conducted on these data types usually provide the researcher with the greatest amount of information possible. Examples are comparative rating scales, attitude scales, awareness scales and similar types of questions. The key to understanding this type of measurement is that the intervals between the various points on the scale are (or are considered to be) exactly the same size; they are equidistant from one another. They are the closest things to a "ruler" that we have available in the social sciences.

A second variety of scale data encountered in statistical texts is called *ratio* data. In these measurements, an equal difference remains between points on the scale, but the *ratio scale* has a "fixed" or absolute zero point. The same statistical analyses are used for both variations of scale data.

Another way of defining scale measurements is that the data produced are considered to be *continuous* rather than *discrete*. Continuous data (or data from continuous variables) are data that can be any value on the scale. For example, an "average" or mean score on a five-point attitude scale can be 2.0, 3.4, 1.7, or 4.3.

Table 21.2

SPSS Data Types and Their Applicable Rules

Data type	Applicable rules for differentiation
Nominal	Different numbers always refer to different things.
Ordinal	The numbers can be ranked or ordered on some dimension.
Scale (Interval and Ratio)	The different points on the scale are equidistant (i.e., equal), and the scale must have a fixed or absolute zero

The second option in this question about the type of measurement data gathered for a question is what is called *ordinal scale data*. The easiest way to differentiate ordinal data from scale or nominal measurements is that these measurements are *ranked* or *ordered* on some set of characteristics, but that the differences between rankings are not known or considered to be equidistant. All rank order *preference scales* are ordinal measurements.

Discrete data are data taken from *nominal scale* measurements. An example of discrete data is the values assigned to a dichotomous question such as "What is your gender?" The answer could only be female or male (i.e., 1 or 2). No mean can be calculated. Another example is a list of eight different types of occupations from which subjects select the one that applies to them. Frequency distributions of all responses for a sample would result in a distribution of responses across the eight options; no mean can be calculated. The set of rules in Table 21.2 differentiates between the different types of measurements. Remember: prior rules also apply to higher-level data.

Entering Data

Once you have indicated the type of measurement data used for that variable in the small circle alongside the data type, click on the OK button on the Define Variables dialog box. You are now ready to begin entering data into your data file. This is a very simple process, much like all other spreadsheet programs. Data are usually entered across the page in rows that correspond to an individual case or subject. You can move from cell to cell using either the tab or arrow keys.

Figure 21.1 is a classification of some of the key layers of statistical analysis seen in public administration research reports, together with the statistical analysis tools in SPSS and the commands for conducting those analyses. When all the variables and values are defined and all the data have been entered into your data file, it is time to save this information into an SPSS Save file.

PUTTING SPSS TO WORK

Assuming that you have successfully entered data to a data file, defined all the variables in that file, and established labels for variables and values of those variables, you have completed the setup phase of SPSS. You can begin to use this powerful software to manipulate and analyze the data set. The remainder of this chapter will focus on four analytic processes: (1) developing descriptive statistics for the data set, (2) designing and preparing graphic displays of the data, (3) transforming and recoding the raw data for refined analysis, and (4) performing some simple inferential statistical analysis on the data.

Developing Descriptive Statistics

SPSS calculates descriptive statistics for three types of measurements: scale, ordinal, and nominal. *Scale* is the label SPSS uses to identify both interval and ratio data. Measurement data are often

Figure 21.1   **A Classification of Some Key Statistical Analysis Procedures in SPSS**

Analysis Level	Analysis Process	Data Type	Available Statistics	SPSS Commands
Level 1-A (Descriptive)	Univariate frequency distributions	Any data	Counts, percentages, chi-square	Frequencies, Explore, Descriptives
Level 1-B	Bivariate frequency distributions	Any data	Counts, percentages, chi-square, phi, Cramer's V	Crosstabs, Multiple Response
Level 2-A	Bivariate relationship tests	Nonparametric (nominal and ordinal data)	Phi and Cramer's V Spearman's rho	Crosstabs
Level 2-B	Bivariate relationship tests	Parametric (interval and ratio data)	Pearson's r	Correlation, Simple Regression
Level 3-A	Bivariate differences tests	Nonparametric (nominal and ordinal data)	Chi-square Mann-Whitney U or Wald-Wolfowitz runs test	Nonparametric Statistics: Chi-square, M-W U, W-W runs
Level 3-B	Bivariate differences tests	Parametric	T-test F-test (ANOVA)	Compare Means: T-Test One-way ANOVA
Level 4-A (Relationships)	Multivariate association tests	Parametric (and nonparametric with data transformations)	Multiple regression analysis, multiple discriminant analysis, time series	General Linear Model: Multivariate Classify: Discriminant Time Series
Level 4-B (Differences)	Multivariate differences tests	Parametric (and nonparametric with data	Multiple analysis of variance	Compare Means: Means
Level 5 (Data Reductions)	Multivariate statistics	Parametric	Cluster analysis, factor analysis	Classify: Hierarchical Cluster Analysis Data Reduction: Factor

described in at least two additional ways. First, data may be *discrete* or *continuous*. Second, data may be described to as *qualitative* or *quantitative*.

Discrete data consist of numbers used to identify specific groups or categories, such as female and male, or undergraduate and graduate student. They are sometimes described as *categorical* data. Researchers are concerned with how many subjects fall into each category; this information can be presented either as a simple count or as a percentage of the total. Nominal data is always discrete (or categorical). Because of the nature of the data, they are also considered to be *qualitative*.

Continuous data, on the other hand, are considered to be *quantitative* because they can consist of any value within a specified or possible continuum. Values are not restricted to whole numbers. While the number of children in a family is *discrete* data because the count must be a whole number, the annual income of a sample of families is *continuous* because it can be any amount. Another example of a continuous variable is the amount of electrical energy consumed each year by households in Shelton, Washington. SPSS considers all data from *scales* (such as questions about attitudes and beliefs) as continuous data. Ordinal data are categorical data, but in social science usage, it is often treated as continuous data.

Univariate Descriptive Statistics and Categorical Measurements

Qualitative measurements are numbers that are applied to categorical variables. The values assigned to categorical variables refer to mutually exclusive groups, categories, or classes within a variable and have no quantitative reference. Examples include the categories used to differentiate subjects by gender, race, political party affiliation, and voting behavior (did vote vs. did not vote). Researchers want to know how many cases fit into each category. The statistics used for these measurements are called *nonparametric*.

The SPSS procedure used to develop descriptive statistics for categorical variables is called Frequencies. This procedure counts the number of cases in each designated category and identifies the *mode* for the variable (the mode is the category with the most cases). The mode is one type of "average" (or *measure of central tendency*); it is the only average to use with this kind of data.

SPSS Frequencies produces its results in the form of a table—sometimes referred to as a *frequency distribution* table. Within each Frequencies table are five columns of information; moving from left to right, these are:

1. User-assigned Value Labels (such as female, male, yes, no, etc.)
2. The Frequency (i.e., the count) with which this category occurs.
3. The Percent of the total that each row represents. If any data are missing, a row will indicate what percentage of the total the missing cases represent.
4. A Valid Percent column, in which are displayed the percentages of the total minus any missing cases that are accounted for by the counts for each category. If there are no missing cases, this column will be a repetition of the third (Percent) column.
5. Finally, a Cumulative Percent column, which totals the percentages of each row plus all rows preceding this row. For example, if the percent of responses for the first category on a five-point rating scale is 13, and the percent of the second category is 12, the cumulative percent for the first category is 13 and the cumulative percent for the second category is 25. If the percent for the third category is 10, the cumulative percent for this third row is 35. The cumulative percent column has no statistical relevance to qualitative variables, however, and should be ignored when processing this kind of data.

Using the Frequencies Dialog Box

To carryout the SPSS Frequencies procedure on data entered into a data file, first click on the Analyze option on the main toolbar. Then click on the second option from the list that appears: Descriptive Statistics. You will then have four options from which to choose: (1) Frequencies, (2) Descriptives, (3) Explore, or (4) Crosstabs. Click on the Frequencies button.

The Frequencies dialog box contains two large windows and several different command options. All variables in the data file will appear in the large window at the left side of the box. Highlight the variable you wish to analyze by clicking on it in the list. Then click on the small arrow between the two large windows. The selected variable will now appear in the right window. To remove it, simply reverse the process. It is possible to highlight as many variables as you want to at the same time. One click on the center arrow will move all variables you select to the Analyze window.

Now click on the small window that reads Display Frequency Tables—it appears just beneath the main variable list. A check mark showing in the small window means that a table will be produced.

Now go to the Statistics button located near the bottom of the gray dialog box. This will bring up the Frequencies: Statistics dialog box. You may request percentile information, measures of dispersion (such as the standard deviation), measures of central tendency, or measures of distribution. Go to the Central Tendency section and click on the small window alongside the Mode.

All you need to do to have SPSS process your request is to click on Continue in this dialog box and then click on OK in the Frequencies dialog box that reappears.

Univariate Descriptive Statistics for Quantitative (Continuous) Measurements

Statistical analysis of *quantitative (numerical)* measurements can be said to take place on two fundamental levels: *descriptive* statistics and *inferential* statistics. There are, of course, statistical tools that do not fall into either of these categories; learning about them is best left to a course in quantitative methods. The statistics used with these types of measurements are called *parametric*.

Descriptive statistics are used to summarize the numerical information in a data set, to numerically describe the cases in a data set, and to provide some sort of structure to the data. *Univariate* descriptive statistics do this one variable at a time. However, it is also possible to develop descriptive statistics for two variables at the same time; this is called *bivariate* statistical analysis. It is also possible to analyze more than two variables at once in what is called *multivariate* statistical analysis, but these processes are not discussed here.

Three SPSS processes can be used to produce univariate statistics for quantitative variables (i.e., variables with ordinal, interval, or ratio data). These procedures are (1) Frequencies, (2) Explore, and (3) Descriptives.

How to Use the Frequencies Command

The use of Frequencies with quantitative—nominal—data is the same as it is for qualitative data, except for the selection of the appropriate measure of central tendency. For quantitative variables, the mean and median are also calculated. The mean is the arithmetic average; the median is the midpoint in the range of possible values. Also important for quantitative measurements are measures of variation and of dispersion. To employ the Frequencies procedure, follow this set of steps:

1. Select Analyze $\Rightarrow$ Descriptive Statistics $\Rightarrow$ Frequencies.
2. Select the variable or variables desired; move them into the Variables window.
3. Click on the Display Frequency Tables button.
4. Select Statistics $\Rightarrow$ Central tendency $\Rightarrow$ Mean, Median, and Mode.
5. Next, in the Dispersion box of the Statistics dialog box, select Standard Deviation, Range, Minimum, and Maximum.
6. Select Continue.
7. Select OK.

How to Use the Explore Command

To calculate descriptive statistics for a variable using the SPSS Explore process, begin by clicking on the Analyze command on the Main Menu bar. From the list of available statistical processes, select Descriptive Statistics. Then select Explore. This will bring up the Explore dialog box. This box has four windows. The largest box displays the names of all the variables in your data set. Highlight the variable or variables you want to analyze. Then click on the small arrow alongside this box; the variables will be moved to the window labeled Dependent List. When you want complete analysis for one variable at a time, ignore the other two windows (i.e., Factor List, and Label Cases By). Click on OK and complete descriptive statistics will be produced for each variable named.

The Explore process can also be used to develop descriptive statistics for different levels of a variable. The phrase "different levels" means the different categories represented in the variable. For example, the variable *gender* has two levels (also referred to as *categories* or *groups*): female and male. The variable *political party* might have three levels: Democrat, Republican, and Independent. The variable *class standing* might have five levels: Freshman, Sophomore, Junior, Senior, and Graduate. The Explore command will quickly and easily produce descriptive statistics for each subgroup in the variable. Follow these steps:

1. Select Analyze $\Rightarrow$ Descriptive Statistics $\Rightarrow$ Explore.
2. Select the variable or variables desired; move them into the Dependent Variables window.
3. Select the grouping variable for which you want the statistical breakdown and move it into the Factor List window.
4. Click on the Display Frequency Tables button.
5. Click on the Statistics button.
6. Select Continue.
7. Select OK.

How to Use the Descriptives Tool

Descriptives is the third way to produce descriptive statistics for numeric data with SPSS; it provides a quick list of each variable, the number of valid responses for each variable, and selected descriptive statistics. To access the program, follow these steps:

1. Select Analyze $\Rightarrow$ Descriptive Statistics $\Rightarrow$ Descriptives.
2. Select the variable or variables desired; move them into the Variables window (remember to *not* include qualitative variables).

3. Select Options. For quantitative data, click on Mean, Standard Deviation, and if desired, Minimum and Maximum.
4. You can choose to have the data presented in any one of four different ways:

> By the way the variables appear in your variable list
> In alphabetic order
> By ascending value of their means
> By descending order of their means

Bivariate Descriptive Statistics

Known as two-way frequency distribution tables, the results of a crosstabulations table present the distribution of responses, with percentages, of two or more variables at the same time. In addition, a wide variety of statistical analyses are included in the Crosstabs procedure. All types of data can be used analyzed in a Crosstabs table.

The SPSS Crosstabs procedure is a tool for displaying the data from one variable against that of another variable or variables. The rows of a crosstabulation table (called a Crosstab by SPSS) represent the different values or levels of one variable, while the columns of the table represent the values of a second variable. A simple 2 × 2 Crosstab will look something like Figure 21.2; Table 21.3 is a 3 × 5 table.

Convention requires that each box in a table (except for those with labels) be called a *cell*. Thus, in Figure 21.2, the data for females who answered yes will fall in cell 1, data for females/no in cell 2, males/yes in cell 3, and males/no in cell 4.

Crosstab tables can have as many rows and columns as required. However, a table with more than five or six rows or columns can become cumbersome to read and difficult to interpret. Crosstabs produces statistical tests for use with interval, ordinal, and nominal (i.e., categorical) data.

SPSS permits up to four bits of information to be displayed in each cell. These include: (1) the count of occurrences, (2) the percentage of the row total represented by the count in a cell, (3) the percentage of the column total in the cell, and (4) the percentage of the total number of counts for the variable. Row and column total counts and percentages are displayed in the table margins.

Crosstabs tables are most appropriately used when both variables are categorical (i.e., nominal data). However, there are times when a researcher wishes to display the distribution of ordinal- or interval-level responses across the entire range of cells. In such cases, the categorical variable is often referred to as a *grouping variable,* and its values are placed as rows. The scale data is displayed in columns. The following example uses party affiliation data as its row variable and the responses of a sample of subjects to a five-point rating scale. Rating scale values in columns are *Strongly Agree, Agree, Neither Agree nor Disagree, Disagree,* and *Strongly Disagree.*

From the information in Table 21.3, it is obvious that this is a relatively cumbersome way to present data; the table is complex and "busy." Possibly a more meaningful way to present and analyze the information in the table would be a simple 3 × 1 table, with the means scores on the scale shown for each of the three categories of party affiliation. A one-way analysis of variance test could then be conducted to test for statistically significant different attitudes among the three party affiliation groups.

How to Use Crosstabs

The *Crosstabs* procedure is bundled into the same Summarize statistics package along with Frequencies, Explore, and Descriptives. In addition to this summary table, another key feature of Crosstabs is its ability to produce both association and differences test statistics for nominal, ordinal, and scale data.

Figure 21.2   **A Typical 2 x 2 Crosstabulation with Cells Numbered**

	Response	
Gender	Yes	No
Female	(Cell 1)	(Cell 2)
Male	(Cell 3)	(Cell 4)

Table 21.3

An Example 3 x 5 Crosstabulation Table with Counts and Totals

	Response					
Political Party Affiliation	Strongly Agree	Agree	Neither Agree nor Disagree	Disagree	Strongly Disagree	Totals
Democrat	38	27	15	9	7	96
Republican	7	10	12	22	30	81
Independent	10	11	7	8	10	46
Totals	55	48	34	39	47	223

Tests for Independence

The *chi-square test of independence* can be used with all data types. Its purpose is to test whether the row subgroups are independent from each other. The chi-square test is interpreted by examining the probability value produced with the chi-square value. When using a 95 percent confidence level, if this p-value is .05 or less, the null can be rejected and the alternative hypothesis is retained (that is, if the p-value is .05 or less, the responses of the groups can be assumed to be statistically different).

Measures of Association

Statistics for Nominal Data. There are four categories of statistical tests from which to select for nominal data: the contingency coefficient, phi and Cramer's V, lambda, and the uncertainty coefficient. Of these, the two easiest statistical tests to use for testing for association are the phi statistic and Cramer's V. Both the phi and Cramer's V statistic measure association in one direction; the values produced can range from 0.0 to 1.0. Therefore, while they indicate the strength of an association, they do not indicate the direction of that association (i.e., positive or negative). The phi statistic should be consulted for 2 x 2 tables only; Cramer's V is applicable for all rectangular tables. These are accessed through the same selection in the Nominal Data section of the Crosstabs $\Rightarrow$ Statistics dialog base.

Statistics for Ordinal Data. SPSS Crosstabs statistics provide a variety of optional association tests for use with ordinal data. The first of these, and the one that is often considered to be most appropriate, is the Spearman correlation coefficient, called *Spearman's rho*. This test is accessed through the Correlations button on the Crosstabs $\Rightarrow$ Statistics dialog box. The program produces both a Pearson's r correlation coefficient for use when the column variable is interval or ratio level, and the Spearman's rho when the column data are ordinal. Care must be taken in selecting the correct statistic, since the values appear in the same output box.

Both r and *rho* are interpreted in the same way—as indicators of the relative strength of an association. They should not be interpreted as measures of causation. Their values can range from –0.1 to +0.1.

Other ordinal-level statistical tests available in Crosstabs include gamma, Somers' *d*, Kendall's tau-b and Kendall's tau-c. To determine what they do and when to use them, consult Marija J. Norušis' (2005b) *SPSS 14.0 Guide to Data Analysis* or her (2007) *SPSS 15.0 Guide to Data Analysis*.

Statistics Involving Interval Data. A test for association is also possible when one of the variables in a Crosstab is interval (or ratio) level and the other variable is nominal level. This is the *eta coefficient. Eta* is interpreted in the same way as Pearson's correlation coefficient. *Eta* does not assume a linear relationship exists between the two variables. When squared, the value of *eta* can also be interpreted as a measure of the proportion of the total variability in the interval-level variable that can be known when the values of the nominal-level variable (gender, for example) are known.

SUMMARY

SPSS and other spreadsheet-based statistical software packages have revolutionized the use of statistics in all branches of the social sciences, including public administration and political science. Statistics is no longer the exclusive territory of a small cadre of mathematically trained specialists. Rather, the new statistical software packages such as SPSS have made the task of learning how to use and interpret statistical tests accessible to everyone with a desktop or notebook computer.

SPSS allows researchers to quickly define the variables and the values assigned to different levels of each variable. Through this process of data definition, the researcher must make these definitions just once, at the beginning of the analysis process. All subsequent tests and their results will automatically display the researcher's assigned definitions and labels.

In addition, SPSS also allows the researcher to quickly and easily compute new variables from combinations of old variables, edit a data set, and recode or transform mathematical measurements with mathematical operations and functions. The researcher can save all calculations and operations in various output files on either a hard drive or a portable disk at any time during a data processing session. And, perhaps most importantly, SPSS statistical test results can be exported directly into reports prepared in most word processing programs.

The basic SPSS software package will allow the researcher to calculate and display all commonly used descriptive statistics. The package also makes it possible to display descriptive statistics in a variety of tables, charts, and graphs. Finally, SPSS has the capability to carry out an extensive array of one- and two-variable hypothesis tests, association (correlation) tests, and single and multiple regression analyses. Finally, the basic package contains provisions for data reduction with factor analysis and classification process with cluster and discriminant analyses, as well as provisions to conduct many nonparametric statistical tests.

ADDITIONAL READING

Einspruch, Eric L. 1998. *An Introductory Guide to SPSS for Windows.* Thousand Oaks, CA: Sage.

Morgan, George A., Karen C. Barrett, Nancy L. Leech, and Gene W. Glolekner. 2006. *SPSS for Introductory Statistics: Use and Interpretation.* 3rd ed. Mahwah, NJ: Lawrence Erlbaum.

Norušis, Marija J. 1998. *SPSS For Windows Base System User's Guide* (Version 9.0). Chicago: SPSS.

———. 2000. *SPSS For Windows Base System User's Guide* (Version 10.0). Chicago: SPSS.

PART 5

QUALITATIVE RESEARCH STRATEGIES AND METHODS

INTRODUCTION TO QUALITATIVE RESEARCH

The term *qualitative research* describes a set of nonstatistical inquiry techniques and processes used to gather data about social phenomena. *Qualitative data* refers to some collection of words, symbols, pictures, or other nonnumeric records, materials, or artifacts that are collected by a researcher and have relevance to the social group under study. The uses for these data go beyond simple description of events and phenomena; rather, they are used for creating understanding, subjective interpretation, and critical analysis.

Qualitative research differs from quantitative research in several fundamental ways. For example, qualitative research studies typically involve what has been described as "inductive, theory-generating, subjective, and nonpositivist processes." In contrast, quantitative research involves "deductive, theory-testing, objective, and positivist processes" (Lee 1999, 10).

Creswell (1994) identified five ways these two approaches differ, based upon these philosophical foundations: *ontology* (researchers' perceptions of reality); *epistemology* (the role or roles taken by researchers); *axiological assumptions* (researchers' values); *rhetorical traditions* (the style of language used by researchers); and *methodological approaches* (approaches taken by researchers). The differences identified by Creswell are displayed in Figure 22.1.

A key difference lies in the *epistemology* of the two approaches. In qualitative research designs, researchers must often interact with individuals in the groups they are studying. Researchers record not only what they see, but also their interpretations of the meaning inherent in the interactions that take place in the groups. Quantitative researchers, on the other hand, maintain a deliberate distance and objectivity from the study group. They are careful to avoid making judgments about attitudes, perceptions, values, interactions, or predispositions.

Another way to describe the differences between qualitative and quantitative research methods has been proposed by Cassell and Symon (1997). The most fundamental of these differences is a bias against using numbers for qualitative research, whereas quantitative research is biased heavily toward numeric measurements and statistical analysis—the *positivist* approach to scientific analysis (White 1999). The objective of this positive approach to research is to control events through a process of *prediction* that is based on explanation; it employs inferential statistical methods (White and Adams 1994).

The second difference is what is referred to as the *subjective-objective dichotomy*. Qualitative researchers "explicitly and overtly apply" (Lee 1999, 7) their own subjective interpretations of what they see and hear—often, they are active participants in the phenomenon under study. On the other hand, a foundation stone of the quantitative, positivist research approach is researcher

Five Differences Between Qualitative Research and Quantitative Research

Philosophical Foundations	Research Strategies	
	Qualitative Research Designs	Quantitative Research Designs
Ontology *(Perceptions of reality)*	Researchers assume that multiple, subjectively derived realities can coexist.	Researchers assume that a single, objective world exists.
Epistemology *(Roles for the researcher)*	Researchers commonly assume that they must interact with their studied phenomena.	Researchers assume that they are independent from the variables under study.
Axiology *(Researchers' values)*	Researchers overtly act in a value-laden and biased fashion.	Researchers overtly act in a value-free and unbiased manner.
Rhetoric *(Language styles)*	Researchers often use personalized, informal, and context-laden language.	Researchers most often use impersonal, formal, and rule-based text.
Methodology *(Approaches to research)*	Researchers tend to apply induction, multivariate, and multiprocess interactions, following context-laden methods.	Researchers tend to apply deduction and limited cause-and-effect relationships, with context-free methods.

Source: Creswell 1994.

objectivity. The researcher is expected to function as an unbiased, unobtrusive observer, reporting only what happens or what can be measured.

These two approaches also differ in a third way: qualitative researchers tend to approach the research process with a willingness to be flexible, to follow where the data lead them. Qualitative researchers approach a topic with few or no preconceived assumptions; conclusions are expected to appear out of the data as they are collected and studied. Quantitative research, on the other hand, tends to be guided by a strict set of rules and formal processes. Typically, specific hypotheses are established prior to the data gathering and tested during the analysis. Variables are identified and explicitly defined beforehand. Searching for cause-and-effect relationships between defined variables that can be measured is a hallmark of quantitative research studies.

A fourth way that the two approaches differ has to do with the aim of the study. Qualitative researchers seek understanding of social interactions and processes in organizations, whereas quantitative studies are more often concerned with predicting future events and behaviors. To make these predictions, they often apply inferential statistical analyses to measurements taken from representative samples drawn from a population of interest.

Another difference is associated with the context of the study. Qualitative research is usually concerned with a situation or event that takes place within a single organizational context. A major goal of much quantitative research is to apply the study results to other situations; thus, quantitative research is what Lee (1999) termed "more generalizable."

A sixth way that these two approaches to research differ is the emphasis that qualitative researchers assign to the research process. The way that subjects interact with, and react to, the researcher during the qualitative study is of as much interest as the original phenomenon of interest. Quantitative researchers tend to take great pains to avoid introducing extraneous influences into the study and seek to isolate subjects from the process as much as possible by controlling for process effects.

Figure 22.2   **Qualitative Strategies and Approaches in Public Administration Research**

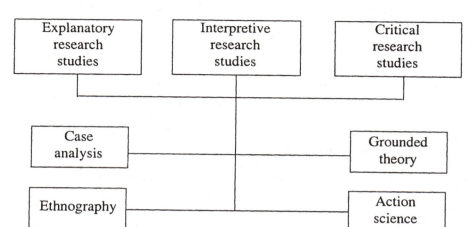

CLASSES OF QUALITATIVE RESEARCH STRATEGIES

Qualitative research strategies can be grouped into three broad strategic classes: (1) *explanatory research studies*, (2) *interpretive research studies,* and (3) *critical research studies.* These strategies and the four key approaches that are followed in most public administration research are displayed in Figure 22.2. These roughly correspond to the exploratory-descriptive-causal categories of quantitative research designs.

Explanatory Research

In his dictionary of research terms and concepts, Thomas Schwandt (1997) defined explanatory research as studies that are conducted to develop a causal explanation of some social phenomenon. The researcher identifies a specific social event or circumstance (a *consequence*)—such as crime in the inner city—that he or she wants to investigate. The researcher then seeks to identify the social, economic, climate, practice, or other such characteristic (variable) in the social environment that can be explained as a *cause* of the consequence of interest.

One of the major objectives of explanatory research is to build *theories* that researchers can then use to explain a phenomenon and then to predict future behavior or events in similar circumstances. The ability to predict responses allows investigators a measure of control over events. Therefore, the ultimate goal of all explanatory research is the control of natural and social events (White 1999). Explanatory research is the easiest approach to understand and apply, and is often used simply for this reason.

Explanatory research is seen as the fastest way to produce a cumulative stream of knowledge in a field or discipline. Possibly because of this trait and the control factor, studies that are designed to explain a phenomenon are most common in public administration research.

Explanatory strategies fulfill much the same role in qualitative research that exploratory research does in quantitative research; they are used as a means of gathering fundamental information about the topic, its contributing factors, and the influences a phenomenon might have on various outcomes. This process can be described as *gaining insights and ideas* about a study problem. These studies are seldom complete in themselves; they are conducted as preliminaries to additional follow-up research.

Interpretive Research

Not all research theorists agree that human events or actions can be defined by the causal explanations that are part and parcel of explanatory research. Instead, these critics argue that human action can never be explained this way. It can only be understood by studies that follow the second approach in the triad of qualitative approaches, which is interpretation. The researcher arrives as an interpretation of a phenomenon by developing (subjective) meanings of social events or actions.

According to White (1999), interpretive research helps us achieve understanding of actions of people in social circumstances and situations. He cites as an example the way an interpretive researcher goes beyond describing why a job-enrichment program is not working, using established hypotheses of motivation and job design. Instead, the interpretive researcher might circulate among employees in their job setting, asking them what they think about the program, the meaning it has for them, and how it conflicts or reinforces their existing attitudes, opinions, and behaviors. In this way, the researcher seeks to "discover the meaning of the program; how it fits with [the workers'] prior norms, rules, values, and social practice" (p. 45).

Schwandt (1997, 73) offered this definition of *interpretation:* "A classification, explication, or explanation of the meaning of some phenomenon." Interpretive studies require the researcher to go beyond simply describing or explaining what a phenomenon is to also interpret the phenomenon for the reader. This entails providing an interpretation of what the phenomenon *means,* as well as what it *is.* Schwandt concluded that the term *interpretation* is used as a synonym for *hermeneutics* or *Verstehen* (the latter term defines an approach to the social sciences that is committed to providing *understanding* of human actions).

Research can be classified as *interpretive* when it builds on the assumption that humans learn about reality from the meanings they assign to social phenomena such as language, consciousness, shared experiences, publications, tools, and other artifacts. The task is made difficult because a fundamental tenet of interpretive theory is that social phenomena are constantly changing. Thus, the meanings that people assign are in constant flux. At the same time, interpretive research is always *context-laden.* Thus, interpretation is like shooting at a constantly moving target.

A primary goal of the interpretive research approach is to provide many-layered descriptions and interpretations of human experiences (Meacham 1998). To achieve this goal, interpretive research looks at the way humans make sense out of events in their lives—as they happen, not as they are planned. Therefore, to thoroughly understand an event or an organization, the researcher must also understand its historical context.

Interpretive research is important for the study of government organizations and agencies (White 1999, 45). The fundamental objective for interpretive research makes this approach particularly relevant in applications such as these:

> The basic aim of the interpretive model is to develop a more complete understanding of social relationships and to discover human possibilities. Recent studies of organizational culture demonstrate the importance of interpretive methods for properly understanding norms, values, and belief systems in organizations.

Seven Principles of Interpretive Research

Klein and Meyers (1999) developed a set of seven fundamental principles to help researchers conduct and evaluate interpretive research studies. The first and most fundamental of these principles is the *hermeneutic circle*, which is derived from document and literary analysis. The hermeneutic circle was devised to illustrate a phenomenon of the learning/understanding process. People develop understanding about complex concepts from the meanings they bring to its parts, such as words, and the way that these parts relate to one another. Interpretation of the larger whole moves from a preliminary understanding of the parts to understanding the whole, then back again to a better understanding of the parts, and on and on. The process of understanding thus moves continuously in an expanding circle of greater and greater understanding.

The second principle of interpretive research, mentioned earlier, is the importance of the *contextual nature* of the studied phenomenon or organization. The researcher's meaning is derived out of the particular social and historical context in which the phenomenon is embedded; at the same time, all patterns that can be discovered within this embedded context are constantly changing. The organization that is interpreted is thus time and situation specific.

The third of the seven principles of interpretive research is *interaction between researchers and the subjects they study*. The information is not something inherent in the phenomenon; rather, it is developed as a result of the social interrelations of both subjects and researcher. Gummesson (1991) likened this relationship to the interaction that often results in the researcher metamorphosing into an "internal consultant" during case study research. The researcher, by interacting with participants, becomes one with the members of the group under study.

Abstraction and *generalization* together make up the fourth principle of interpretive research. Such research deals with abstractions as it attempts to bring order to disunited parts by categorizing them into generalizations and concepts with wider application. The inferences that are based on the researcher's subjective interpretation of the single case must be seen as theoretical generalizations.

The fifth principle of interpretive research is *dialogical reasoning.* In this intellectual process, the researcher explicitly weighs all preconceptions and/or biases brought to the planned research activity against the information that actually emerges from the actual research process. This principle forces the researcher to begin by defining the underlying assumptions that guide the research and the research paradigm upon which the study is based. By a process of dialogue with participant actors, the researcher defines and redefines the assumptions and research questions in light of the data that emerges.

The *principle of multiple interpretations* demands that researchers aggressively compare their historical and contextual interpretation of the phenomenon against all other available interpretations and the reasons offered for them. Thus, the researcher subjects his or her own preconceptions and biases to comparison against competing interpretations, including those of the participants in the organization under study. Even if no conflicting interpretations are found during the study, the researcher is expected to probe for them, and to document the fruitless process. In this way, the researcher strengthens the conclusions and interpretations derived from the analysis.

The final principle of interpretive research is *suspicion*. This requires the researcher to not accept an interpretation at face value. To avoid making false interpretations, the researcher must examine every personal preconception, conclusion, definition, and derived meaning with a healthy dose of skepticism.

Critical Research

Critical qualitative research is a third approach to investigations of social phenomena adopted by the public administration researchers. Critical research in public administration has evolved from approaches exemplified in Marxian critical sociology and Freudian psychotherapy traditions (Argyris, Putnam, and Smith 1985). According to Klein and Meyers (1999), a study can be considered *critical* in nature if it is a social critique that exposes harmful or alienating social conditions. Furthermore, the purpose of the critique should be to emancipate members of the society from the harmful conditions, thus eliminating the causes of the alienation. Members of the society are not told how to change their conditions, but are instead helped to identify on their own alternative ways of defining their society and for achieving human potential.

The primary objective of critical research is to help people *change* their beliefs and actions as part of a process of helping them become aware of the often-unconscious bases for their actions or beliefs. According to White (1999, 46), by becoming aware of *why* they live and think the way they do, critical research "points out inconsistencies between what is true and false, good and bad; it compels [people] to act in accordance with truth and goodness."

Critical public administration research begins with the assumption that a crisis exists in some aspect of society. The researcher approaches the study of this crisis from a deeply personal and involved commitment to help the people involved. Recognition of a crisis, then, is one of the key concepts of the approach. Hansen and Muszynski (1990, 2) explain the role of critical research in these circumstances:

> From (the crisis) perspective, society is seen as (torn) by social and political divisions which make the process of social reproduction . . . prone to actual or incipient breakdown. Society [is not] a harmonious, self-regulating system. Rather, it must be seen as a field of complex and contradictory possibilities for social actors who would . . . assume command of these possibilities and produce new social realities which would express their ability to act as empowered, autonomous agents. The task of critical research involves identifying these possibilities and suggesting what social actors might do to bring their lives under their conscious direction.

Schwandt (1997, 24–25) identified a number of structural themes that characterize critical research. The two that seem to appear most regularly in the literature of critical research methodology are distortion in the perceptions held by members of a group, and rejection of the idea of the disinterested scientist. With the first theme, the goal of critical research is to integrate social theory and application or practice in such a way that the members of social groups become cognizant of distortions and other problems in their society or their value systems. Then, the group members are encouraged to propose ways to change their social and value systems in ways that improve their quality of life.

The second key theme in critical research is the refusal to accept the traditional idea of the social scientist's role as objective or disinterested, replacing this with the concept of the active, change-oriented researcher whose emphasis is on motivating change processes in social groups and individuals. Blyler (1998, 33) addressed the issue of adopting a critical perspective in professional communication in general, defining the technique thus:

> The critical perspective aims at empowerment and emancipation. It reinterprets the relationship between researcher and participants as one of collaboration, where participants define research questions that matter to them and where social action is the desired goal.

WHICH STRATEGY IS BEST?

There is no one best qualitative research strategy. The choice of which strategy to adopt when designing a qualitative study will depend upon the objectives the researcher has identified for the study. These must be clearly stated prior to going into the field to embark on the collection of data.

Possibly because it is often considered the easiest of the three strategies to carry out, most public administration research studies follow an *explanatory* design. However, according to White (1999) and others, there is a strong movement in all the social and administrative sciences to go beyond a simple descriptive explanation of a phenomenon to also explore whatever meaning underlies the behavior, event, or circumstance. Professionals, administrators, sponsoring agencies, and the public at large are asking researchers to explain what things *mean,* rather than simply describing them as they appear.

A small number of researchers are extending the range of research even further by designing studies that begin with a critique of a social phenomenon and end with the design and introduction of subject-sponsored new ways of addressing old problems (Robinson 1994). The critical approach in public administration is still in its infancy (White 1999). The critical approach has been employed often enough, however, to result in a reputation for making it difficult to transform research results into meaningful program applications. The method requires subjects to form alternative concepts or courses of action; the role of the researcher is to assist the group to first identify and to then resolve their social problems themselves. Despite this difficulty, the critical approach is seen as an important way of addressing single-case studies.

THE CHANGING PARADIGM

One important consequence of this push to extend the scope of research has been a widespread increase in the use of subjective qualitative methods to augment, if not replace, the once-prevalent emphasis on objective, positivist research principles. Lan and Anders (2000) have described this change in emphasis as a major paradigm shift. Building their argument on the seminal work of Thomas S. Kuhn (*The Structure of Scientific Revolutions,* 1970), Lan and Anders concluded that more than one approach to research is not only possible, it is desirable. If science does progress by shifts in paradigms, as their interpretation of Kuhn's work suggests, and if it is indeed true that more than one paradigm can exist within a single discipline, then the question of which research approach to take is moot. Researchers are not required to follow the same set of rules. White and Adams (1994, 19–20) summarized this point with this conclusion:

> We are persuaded by the weight of historical and epistemological evidence that no single approach—even if accorded the highly positive label *science*—is adequate for the conduct of research in public administration. If research is to be guided by reason, a diversity of approaches, honoring both practical and theoretical reasons, seems necessary.

RESEARCH WITHOUT LIMITS

There are no limits to what may be researched or how researchers go about conducting their research activities. Nor are researchers limited to one or even a few different approaches to their scientific investigations; many different types of qualitative research strategies can be followed.

Just as there are no restrictions on research topics, there is no set rule that limits any researchers pplication focus, although case studies or ethnography may be more appropriate for research n exploratory focus. Grounded theory and hermeneutics, on the other hand, are approaches are typically employed in interpretive research strategies; phenomenology, hermeneutics, and on science are most applicable for research that follows the critical model. Clearly, these approaches and applications often overlap, just as different observers may see different approaches taken in any individual research study.

QUALITATIVE RESEARCH IN PUBLIC ADMINISTRATION

Many different types of research approaches are employed for conducting qualitative research in public administration. The four research approaches most often followed in public administration are case studies, grounded theory, ethnography, and action science. Other less commonly used research approaches include phenomenology, hermeneutics, ethnomethodolgy, atmospherics, systems theory, chaos theory, nonlinear dynamics, symbolic interactionism, ecological psychology, cognitive anthropology, human ethnology, and holistic ethnography (Patton 1990; Denzin and Lincoln 1994; Morse 1994; Marshall and Rossman 1999).

Figure 22.3 displays six popular research approaches, their disciplinary traditions, some ways data are gathered, and a suggestion of some of the types of research questions addressed. The approaches compared include: (1) *ethnography,* (2) *phenomenology,* (3) *case studies,* (4) *hermeneutics,* (5) *grounded theory,* and (6) *action science.*

Ethnography

Anthropologists developed the approach to research known as ethnography as a method for studying different cultures and how members of different societies develop and employ coping mechanisms for social phenomena. A differentiating characteristic of this approach is its emphasis on specific ways to prepare field notes and rules for writing about cultural events.

The primary data-gathering technique used in ethnography is *participant observation.* Ethnographers often live, work, and play for long periods of time with the members of the group under study. Their aim is to be absorbed into the group, with the underlying objective of becoming accepted as a nonthreatening or nonintrusive member of the groups so that events and interrelationships unfold as they would naturally, as if the observer were not in attendance.

Ethnography methods are used in the administrative sciences to analyze and diagnose organizational cultures (Wilson 1989; Schein 1992; McNabb and Sepic 1995). However, the rules for conducting fieldwork and preparing field notes tend to be less rigorously applied than is the case in anthropology research.

Phenomenology

The phenomenological approach to qualitative research has its roots in such traditions of philosophy as existentialism and the study of the meaning of language and other symbolic behaviors. In public administration research, it is used to establish "meanings" social actors apply to events, works, symbols, and the like. Researchers gather data through narratives, personal experiences, and in-depth personal interviews.

The underlying concept of interest is the *life history* of individual persons. Researchers often employ taped discussions and other narrative recording tools to study subjects' everyday experiences, which often feature socially aberrant behavior. Examples include the narrative personal

Figure 22.3 **Various Approaches to Qualitative Research and Typical Focus**

Qualitative Research Approach	Disciplinary Traditions	Typical Data-Gathering Methods	Types of Research Questions
Ethnography	Anthropology	Participant observation, unstructured interviews, analysis of cultural artifacts	"Culture" questions: What are the values of this group? What is accepted behavior? What is not acceptable?
Phenomenology	Philosophy	Personal experience narratives, video or audiotaped discussions, in-depth interviews	"Meaning" questions: What is the meaning of a person's experience? How do group members cope with various phenomena?
Case studies	Psychology, public administration	Observation, personal interviews, organizational studies	"Explanatory" questions: What is distinct about this group?
Hermeneutics	Biblical studies, literary (text) analysis	Content analysis, narrative and discourse analysis	"Interpretation" questions: What meaning does this text hold?
Grounded theory	Sociology, social psychology	Personal interviews, diaries, participant observation	"Process" questions: What theory is embedded in the relationships between variables? Is there a theory of change?
Action science	Social psychology, education	Discourse analysis, intervention studies	"Critique" questions: How can we emancipate group members? What inhibits change?

histories of gang members and of participants in the drug culture. The goal of the researcher is for the subject to define the meaning of the behavior.

The Case Study Approach

The case study approach to research in the social and administrative sciences focuses on the agency, organization, person, or group under study, rather than dealing with variables (Schwandt 1997). The objective of the case is to serve as a defining description of the organization. In this way, the case description serves as an example of similar groups.

Today, case studies are used extensively in education and public administration, although their disciplinary roots are centered in psychology. They are one of the most often used approaches to conducting research in public administration. The following examples are taken from a single issue of the public administration journal *Public Productivity & Management Review* (March 2000):

- "The dual potentialities of performance measurement: The Case of the Social Security Administration."
- "Organizational Change Issues in Performance Government: The Case of Contracting."
- "Comprehensive Management and Budgeting Reform in Local Government: The Case of Milwaukee."
- "Implementing Performance Accountability in Florida: What Changed, What Mattered, and What Resulted."

Each of these articles describes in some detail the organization and its experiences with some aspect of administration. They are intended to serve as examples for other administrators or agencies to follow.

Hermeneutics

Hermeneutics is an approach to qualitative research that focuses on the *interpretation* of such social phenomena as tools, objects, works of art, texts, statements of other people, and particularly, the actions of human in social environments. Developed at the end of the eighteenth century, it was originally concerned with interpreting classical, legal, and biblical texts. Today, however, it is often used as an approach in investigating social phenomena, such as statements and behaviors in public administration groups and agency settings.

Researchers in many different disciplines have discovered that they use a number of similar hermeneutic techniques, methods, and principles in arriving at their interpretations. According to White (1999, 130), this type of interpretation can be applied to the study of social action because of an "assumption that social situations display some of the features of a text and that the methodology for interpreting social action develops some of the same procedures of text interpretation."

The principal analysis technique in these studies involves what is called *the hermeneutic circle*. As previously mentioned, this describes the method of relating parts of the text or conversation to the whole, then back again to the parts. Analysis proceeds in this circular way until the entire text is interpreted. Furthermore, every interpretation is connected to earlier interpretations and understandings; nothing exists outside to interpretation.

The following four laws guide all hermeneutic interpretation processes (White 1999, 143–145): (1) social actors and their beliefs and actions must be understood on their own terms and not be imposed by the investigator; (2) the interactions of all actors in the social setting must be understood within their own context; (3) the researcher must have some preexisting experience with the group members—some common experience must bind them together, and (4) the interpretation arrived at by the investigator must conform to the intentions of the actors.

Grounded Theory

The *grounded theory* approach to research in the administrative and social sciences has its roots in sociology and social psychology. According to Strauss and Corbin (1998), this approach to research has as its primary objective to develop theory out of the information gathered, rather than the testing of predetermined theories through a process of experimentation. Ground theory researchers approach their study organization by gathering all possible facts pertaining to the problem through personal interviews, analyses of participants' diaries, and participant observation. Once the data are collected, they are analyzed and interpreted by the investigator, who finally develops a theory from that analysis and interpretation.

As developed by Strauss, grounded theory employs a detailed list of rigorous steps and processes for developing theory out of social situations. Insights and ideas are generated only after in-depth analysis of the data, during which the analyst searches for commonalties and differences. These are compared and contrasted as the analyst weighs possible theories against opposing interpretations. Ultimately, a theory that is grounded in the data emerges.

The Action Science Approach

The *action science* approach has been defined as a way of changing social systems by studying the way they function It has also been described as "an informal, qualitative, formative, subjective, interpretive, reflective, and experimental model of inquiry in which all individuals involved in the study are knowing and contributing participants" (Gabel 1994, 1).

Argyris, Putnam, and Smith developed this approach from the earlier contributions of John Dewey—who proposed separating science and practice—and Kurt Lewin in field group dynamics, an area of study in social psychology. Dewey's contribution led to Lewin's separation of the idea of *diagnosis* of an organization or other social group and the idea of *intervention,* which is the concept of working to bring about change (Argyris, Putnam, and Smith 1985; Schein 1996). Although Lewin never explicitly defined the action science method as such, his early work in developing approaches to interventions and change in social organizations led Argyris, Putnam, and Smith to give him credit for developing most of the techniques involved in the approach.

Themes in Action Research

The following five themes in action research were developed by Lewin and used by Argyris, Putnam, and Smith in developing the approach as it is used today: First, the approach entails applying change experiments to real problems in existing social systems, with the goal of helping the organization or system resolve the problem. Second, the research method involves a cyclical process of problem identification, planning, acting, and evaluating—over and over again. Third, a major component of the proposed change is reeducation to change the way group members think and act. The fourth theme is an emphasis on participation and free choice in problem resolution—a reflection of Lewin's emphasis on democratic values. Finally, there is a dual purpose or goal to action research; research results should contribute to basic social science knowledge, while also improving everyday life in social groups (Argyris, Putnam, and Smith 1985, 8–9).

Action research can be used to test two kinds of statements: *dispositional attributions* and *theories of causal responsibility.* The first of these is an assertion by an actor in the social group about the perceived mental outlook, tendency, or characteristic of another actor in the group. Examples of a dispositional attribution are the statements "John is insensitive (to my feelings)" and "Mary is a thoughtful, caring supervisor." An example of a theory of causal responsibility is "Our supervisor's insensitivity to minorities is causing discomfort and dissatisfaction in our work group."

Two additional important points about action research are what has been termed the *domain of action research* and the *data of action research.* "Domain" is another way of describing the appropriate area of application for the approach, whereas "data" refers to the type or form of information gathered. Action science should be used when the researcher is concerned with *actions* and *interpretive understandings.* Argyris, Putnam, and Smith (1985, 54–57) explained that the data of action research are *actions* that are taken by members of the social group under study; the most important of these actions is *talk.*

> The first point to note is that talk *is* action . . . talk is meaningful. . . . When people talk they are performing such actions as promising, justifying, ordering, conceding, and so forth. Using talk as data for the empirical testing of theory forces us to deal with the issues raised by interpretation.

In practice, action research activities should follow a circular process (Gabel 1995). The process begins with observation and/or reconnaissance, which in turn leads to the developing a thorough understanding of the problem affecting the organization. The second step is developing a general plan that spells out how a proposed intervention will resolve the problem. The third step implements the intervention and then monitors the processes of change (or lack of change) that occur. In the fourth step, researchers reflect upon the progress of the intervention and then follow with revisions or new interventions, if necessary. The cycle then begins anew; it is continued in this way until a satisfactory understanding or desired change is achieved.

COLLECTING, ANALYZING, AND INTERPRETING QUALITATIVE DATA

All qualitative research strategies and approaches involve three basic components: (1) collection of data, (2) analysis and interpretation of that data, and (3) communicating research findings in one or more communications media, such as producing a written report (Strauss and Corbin 1998).

Collecting Qualitative Data

The major methods used to collect qualitative data include: (1) participation in the group setting or activity, (2) personal and group interviewing, (3) observation, and (4) document and cultural artifact analysis. There are also many secondary methods of collecting information (Marshall and Rossman 1999). These include historical analysis, recording and analysis of live histories and narratives, films, videos and photographs, kinesics, proxemics, unobtrusive measures, surveys, and projective techniques.

Some researchers collect qualitative data by actually participating in a social situation and writing down what they see, while others do so by unobtrusively observing social interrelationships and behaviors. Researchers also gather qualitative data for analysis by video- or audiotape recordings of narrative accounts of life histories, events, perceptions, or personal values; they question subjects using structured or unstructured personal or group interviews. Still others collect qualitative data by examining collections of printed documents, past and present artifacts, or cultural or artistic creations, including the media. Some use a combination of these and other methods.

Analyzing Qualitative Data

The analysis and interpretation of qualitative data begins with bringing the raw data into some level of order. First, the researcher identifies and selects a set of relevant *categories* or *classes* in which to sort the data. Comparing the data across categories—a step that is typically used in the testing of hypotheses—often follows the initial comparing phase of the analysis. Strauss and Corbin (1998) call this a process of *conceptualizing*. Conceptualizing means reducing often-bulky amounts of raw data into workable, ordered bits of information that the researcher can manage with confidence. Kvale (1996) described this act of data categorization as a key qualitative research activity, and one that most distinguishes qualitative strategies from quantitative research.

Another procedure sometimes used for this purpose is what is known as *power* or *influence analysis.* In this process, the researcher first collects data through observing the way people interact or by questioning them on their perceptions of such factors as power or influence in the organization. The researcher can then draw a diagram or chart to illustrate the interactions and responses to others within the group. Examples of graphic displays of this type include context charts, linkage patterns and knowledge flowcharts, and role and power charts (Miles and Huberman 1984).

Interpreting Qualitative Data

The next step in analysis of qualitative data is *interpreting the patterns and connections* that are revealed or hidden by bringing the data into order. Interpretation occurs when the researcher draws conclusions from whatever structure is revealed in the data. If graphic diagrams are used, the researcher must examine and describe the personal connections, misconnections, interfaces, relationships, and interplay of behaviors. These explanations become the gist of a cogent and meaningful report, the production of which is the third step in the process.

These three steps must be followed in all qualitative research studies, regardless of which approach the researcher follows or which technique is used to gather and analyze the data.

SUMMARY

Qualitative research describes a set of nonstatistical inquiry techniques for gathering data about social phenomena. *Qualitative data* are words, symbols, pictures, or other nonnumeric records, materials, or artifacts collected by a researcher. The uses for these data go beyond simple description of events and phenomena; they are used for creating understanding, for subjective interpretation, and for critical analysis as well.

Qualitative research differs from quantitative research in several fundamental ways. Qualitative research studies employ inductive, theory-generating, subjective, and nonpositivist processes, while quantitative research uses deductive, theory-testing, objective, and positivist processes. Creswell (1994) identified five ways these two approaches differ, based upon these philosophical foundations: *ontology, epistemology, axiological assumptions, rhetorical traditions,* and *methodological approaches.*

Qualitative research strategies can be grouped into three broad classes: (1) *explanatory research studies*, (2) *interpretive research studies*, and (3) *critical research studies.* These roughly correspond to the exploratory-descriptive-causal categories of quantitative research designs. The choice of which strategy to adopt when designing a qualitative study will depend upon the objectives set for the study. These must be clearly stated prior to going into the field to embark on the collection of data.

Many different types of research approaches are employed for conducting qualitative research in public administration. Among the disciplinary approaches often followed in public administration are *ethnography, phenomenology, case studies, hermeneutics, grounded theory,* and *action science.*

All qualitative research strategies and approaches involve three basic components: (1) collection of data, (2) analysis and interpretation of that data, and (3) communicating research findings in one or more communications media, such as producing a written report.

The major methods used to collect qualitative data include: (1) participation in the group setting or activity, (2) personal and/or group interviewing, (3) observation, and (4) document and cultural artifact analysis. There are also many secondary methods of collecting information, including historical analysis, live histories and narratives, films, videos and photographs, kinesics, proxemics, unobtrusive measures, surveys, and projective techniques.

ADDITIONAL READING

Cassell, Catherine, and Gillian Symon, eds. 1997. *Qualitative Methods in Organizational Research.* Thousand Oaks, CA: Sage.

Creswell, John W. 1994. *Research Design.* Thousand Oaks, CA: Sage.

Lee, Thomas W. 1999. *Using Qualitative Methods in Organizational Research.* Thousand Oaks, CA: Sage.

Marshall, Catherine, and Gretchen B. Rossman. 1999. *Designing Qualitative Research.* 3rd ed. Thousand Oaks, CA: Sage.

Strauss, Anselm, and Juliet Corbin. 1998. *Basics of Qualitative Research: Techniques and Procedures for Developing Grounded Theory.* 2nd ed. Thousand Oaks, CA: Sage.

23

RESEARCH USING THE CASE STUDY APPROACH

The case method has long been one of the most popular approaches followed in public administration research. Whelan (1989) traced the approach back to 1948, when a planning committee was formed at Harvard University to develop guidelines for applying the method to research in public administration. Under the leadership of Harold Stein, the original committee was renamed the *Inter-University Case Program* (IUCP) in 1951. The IUCP published a text with twenty-six cases just a year later. In the introduction to that casebook, Stein (1952, xxvii) defined the public administration case as "a narrative of the events that constitute or lead to a decision or group of related decisions by a public administrator or group of public administrators."

A number of now-classic case studies were published beginning about the same time as the method was evolving at Harvard. Philip Selznick's *TVA and the Grass Roots* appeared in 1949; Herbert Kaufman's study of the forest service, *The Forest Ranger,* was published in 1960. A third classic case study, Michael Lipsky's (1980) study of city bureaucracies, *Street-Level Bureaucracy,* has helped the case approach to achieve recognition as a valid and important research methodology.

These larger case studies were mirrored in miniature by acceptance of the approach in the discipline's professional literature. In his detailed overview of the state of public administration research methods, Yeager (1989) found that one or more case studies appeared in every issue of *Public Administration Review* (PAR) for more than forty years. If their continuing appearance in *PAR*—the discipline's leading publication—and other public administration journals is any indication, case studies are just as popular today as they were when Yeager examined the field in the late 1980s.

The popularity of the case study approach lies in its great flexibility. Case studies can serve as examples of what a public administrator ought not to do, as well as what should be done. However, their primary purpose is to instruct public administrators in what other administrators are doing—to inform administrators about what is going on in their field. Today, this means that administrators are able to learn about managerial and administrative experiences from agencies, locations, and levels of government around the globe.

DEFINING THE CASE STUDY APPROACH

Many different definitions for case studies have been proposed. Yeager traced most of them to Harold Stein who, in an article published in 1952, was one of the first to promote the method as a way to do public administration research. While crediting Stein, Yeager (p. 685) offered this definition: "A public administration case (is) a narrative of the events that lead to a decision or group of related decisions by a public administrator or group of public administrators."

Another definition of the case study referred to by Yeager (1989, 685) was that proposed by the marketing scholar T.V. Bonoma in a 1985 *Journal of Marketing Research* article. Bonoma's definition had a general management focus:

> A case is a description of a management situation based on interview, archives, naturalistic observation, and other data, constructed to be sensitive to the context in which management behavior takes place and to its temporal restraints. These are characteristics shared by all cases.

In the first edition of his important book on the case research method, Robert K. Yin (1984, 13) stated that the distinguishing characteristic of the case is that it attempts to examine a phenomenon in its real-life context when the boundaries between phenomenon and its context are not clear. In the 1994 edition, Yin added that the case study as "an empirical inquiry" that investigates a contemporary phenomenon within its real-life context, and particularly when "the boundaries between phenomenon and context are not clearly evident" (p. 13).

Case studies are often intensive studies of one or a few exemplary individuals, families, event, time periods, decision or set of decisions, processes, programs, institutions, organizations, groups, or even entire communities (Lang and Heiss 1994; Arneson 1993). Discussing the case method as one of three qualitative approaches for research in organizational communications, Arneson (1993, 164) saw it as an appropriate research method when a case involves some noteworthy success or failure, adding, "Qualitative case studies most appropriately address programs directed toward *individualized* outcomes."

The subject selected as a case example typically is chosen for study because it points out some underlying problem or because it represents a successful solution to a problem. It is hoped that publishing the successful experience can provide model for others to emulate.

When the Case Study Approach Is Appropriate

Because public administration researchers have used the case study for so long and in so many different ways, it is not surprising that so many different purposes for the method have surfaced. However, most authors agree with Lang and Heiss (1994, 86) that one fundamental principle underlies all case studies:

> The basic rationale for a case study is that there are processes and interactions . . . which cannot be studied effectively except as they interact and function within the entity itself. Thus, if we learn how these processes interact in one person or organization, we will know more about how the processes as factors in themselves and perhaps apply these (what we have learned) to other similar type persons or organizations.

PURPOSES FOR CASE STUDIES

Stake (1994) grouped case studies into three categories: (1) intrinsic case studies, (2) instrumental studies, and (3) collective studies.

Intrinsic case studies are done when the researcher wants to provide a better understanding of the subject case itself. This type of case is not selected because it is representative of a larger genre or because it serves as an illustrative example of something. Nor is it selected because the researcher plans to build a theory upon what is found in the analysis of the case. Rather, the case is studied simply because the researcher is interested in it for some reason.

Instrumental case studies, on the other hand, are used when the public administration researcher wants to gain greater insight into a specific issue. In these situations, the subject case is expected to contribute to a greater understanding of a topic of interest, such as performance measurement. The subject case itself is of secondary interest; examining the case improves understanding of the phenomenon, not the case.

The third type of case study is what Stake called the *collective case*. This is a multiple-case design. A group of individual cases are studied together because they contribute to greater understanding of a phenomenon, a population, or some general organizational condition. Another name for this type of case is *multisite qualitative research* (Yeager 1989).

Others have proposed a number of different scenarios for when the case study method is a particularly appropriate design. Van Evera (1997), for example, identified these five purposes for case studies: (1) to establish a theory or theories, (2) to test theories that already exist, (3) to identify a previous condition or conditions that lead or contribute to a phenomenon (what Van Evera called *antecedents*), (4) to establish the relative importance of such contributing conditions, and (5) to establish the fundamental importance of the case with regard to other potential examples.

Establishing a theory upon which to base predictions of future events is an important reason for much of the published research in the administrative sciences. In his review of works that used the case study method to examine city planning and planners, Fischler (2000) noted that case studies are uniquely suited for exploring the interaction of personal behavior and collective institutions, and the interplay of agency and structure. Fischler saw the planning cases as contributing to the development of a theory of government planning practices.

Fischler called cases the "most essential tools" in theory development. In the Fischler approach, developing theory from case studies occurs through a four-phase process: (1) formulation of research questions and hypotheses, (2) selection of the case and definition of units of analysis, (3) data gathering and presentation, and (4) analysis and theory building. Finally, he concluded that case studies should remain an important study approach: "Case studies that explore the behavior and experience of innovative practitioners and innovative organizations, be they public, private, or not-for-profit, should therefore be placed high on our agenda" (p. 194).

Bailey (1994) also identified a variety of purposes for the case study in public administration. They can be descriptive, interpretive, or critical; they can be used for solving administrative problems or for forming a theory. They can have a purely practitioner-oriented focus, or they can be esoteric scholarly studies. For maximum value, however, Bailey concluded that the ideal case study was one that had value for *both* practitioners and academics.

DESIGNING CASE STUDIES

Case studies can be single-case or multicase designs. Designs that compare one case against other are called either multicase or cross-case designs. For both the single and multicase approaches, the purpose of the study is never to be a representative picture of the world, but simply to represent the specific case or cases (Stake 1994). While this is certainly true, it is also true that good case studies do include features of the case or set of cases that are uniform and generalizable, as well as those that are relatively unique to the case under study (Bailey 1994, 192).

Single-Case Study Designs

Most case studies that are conducted in public administration are single-case studies; they are found in all the social and administrative sciences, making them what Miles and Huberman (1998, 193) called the *traditional mode of qualitative analysis.*

An early example of the single case study is the 1951 analysis of the Glacier Metal Company in London by a team of researchers led by Elliott Jacques. Jacques explained the report as a case study of developments in the social life of one industrial community; as a case study, the report was not intended to serve as a statement of precise and definite conclusions. Rather, it was written to show how managers and employees in one company deal with change.

An example of a public administration single-case study is Soni's (2000) study of a regional office of the U.S. Environmental Protection Agency. The study focused on workplace diversity and the attitudes of agency personnel toward mandated awareness initiatives. Soni first determined how employees valued workplace diversity and then looked at whether the staff supported the agency management-development program. That program was designed to enhance worker acceptance of racial, age, and gender diversity in the organization. This included requirements for diversity-management initiatives in five-year strategic plans and diversity goals at the local or agency group level.

Analysis of this single case led Soni to conclude that workers accept and support diversity to a far lesser extent than the ideal published in the literature. In addition, diversity-management programs appeared to have only minimal effects in changing workers' sensitivity to differences, increasing their acceptance and valuing of diversity, reducing stereotyping and prejudice, or any of the other goals established for the program.

Case studies such as that carried out by Soni should not be used to infer similar behaviors or conditions in other or related organizations. The results of a case study are applicable only to the organization or group examined. No inferences can nor should be made from the results. Soni (2000, 407) reflected this possible limitation of the method by adding the following caveat at the conclusion of the paper: "The racial and gender effects found in this case study may be a consequence of the many specific organizational characteristics and cannot be assumed to be representative of other organizations."

In another example of a single case study in the public administration literature, Poister and Harris (2000) examined a "mature" total quality management program in the Pennsylvania Department of Transportation. The program began in 1982 with the introduction of quality circles and evolved into a major strategic force in the department, with quality concepts incorporated into all levels of the culture of the organization. Poister and Harris (p. 175) point to the experience of this department as an example for other agencies to emulate—one of the key purposes of the case study. They concluded their study with the statement that the department "has indeed transformed itself over the past 15 years around core values of quality and customer service. Hopefully, its experience along these lines will be helpful to other public agencies that have embarked on this journey more recently."

Multicase Study Designs

Ammons, Coe, and Lombardo (2001) used a multicase approach to compare the performance of three public sector benchmarking projects. Two of the projects were national in scope, while the third was a single-state program.

The first project was a 1991 program sponsored by the Innovation Groups to collect performance measurement information from cities and counties across the country. This information was eventually incorporated into a national performance-benchmarking information network, eventually named the PBCenter. Participants were charged a $750 fee to join the project. Although the effort started aggressively by measuring forty-three programs, ultimately both participation and enthusiasm among potential users of the information were disappointing.

The second case in this multicase study, the Center for Performance Measurement, was a national program sponsored by the International City/County Management Association (ICMA). This program was established in 1994 by a consortium of thirty-four cities and counties with populations over 200,000. Performance measurements were collected and shared in these four core service areas: police services, fire services, neighborhood services, and support services. Neighborhood services included code enforcement, housing, libraries, parks and recreation, road maintenance, garbage collection, and street lighting.

The third case examined in the study was a state project that began in North Carolina in 1994; its purpose was to provide performance statistics to the state's city managers. By 1995, it had evolved into the North Carolina Local Government Performance Management Project and was run by the Institute of Government at the University of North Carolina-Chapel Hill. By 1997, thirty-five cities and counties were participating. The Ammons, Coe, and Lombardo study concluded that all three programs failed to deliver results that even approached the expectations of their participants, many of whom felt that program costs exceeded any benefits. On the basis of their comparative analysis of the three cases, the authors recommended that administrators of similar projects in the future should make sure that participants have realistic expectations for benchmarking before they buy into their programs.

In another multicase design, Fernandez and Fabricant (2000) examined two cases from Florida's experience with privatization of child support programs in an effort to compare the effectiveness of public and private service providers. Their analysis concluded with recommendations on ways to avoid problems encountered in the evaluation process.

The primary objective of this study was to determine whether research methodology used by the state of Florida was accurate. The topic was collection of delinquent child support payments from an absent parent. The initial report issued by the state indicated that in one case, the state agency produced a collection rate that was 307 percent greater than that of the private or contracted group. The authors revealed that Florida's study design was fatally flawed. The agency success report was based on a sample that represented the total population of cases, whereas the sample worked on by the private firm represented only those cases that had been delinquent for longer than six months and that the state agency had been working on unsuccessfully for the six-month period. The authors suggested that a negative correlation probably existed for the period of time a case is delinquent and the probability of collecting owed child support. Had similar samples been used, the researchers would not have replicated the heavily biased results produced with the faulty design.

STEPS IN THE CASE STUDY METHOD

Figure 23.1 illustrates various steps in the selection and preparation of a case study displayed as a flowchart; case study activities begin at the top and proceed downward. The concepts included in the model owe much to Robert Stake's 1994 synopsis of the case method. Additional contribution to the model came from the five components of a case study design identified by Yin (1994, 20).

Figure 23.1 Steps in Planning, Analysis, and Presentation of Case Studies

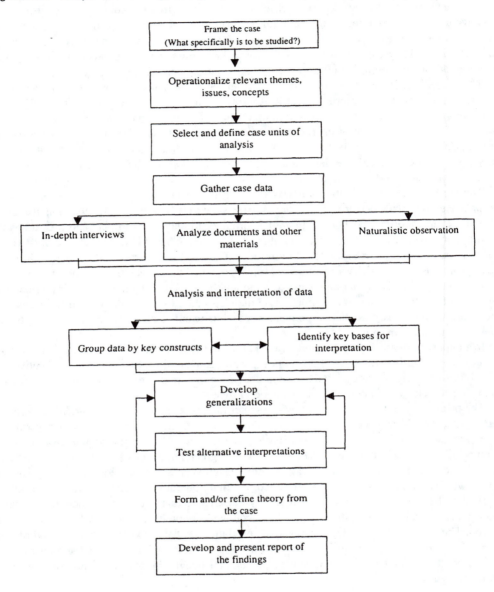

Step 1: Frame the Case

Framing means placing the case in a frame of reference, deciding what specifically about the case is to be studied, analyzed, and communicated. The researcher must study some managerial or delivery aspect of the case that will bring to light concepts that have greater applicability.

Step 2: Operationalize Key Constructs

Operationalizing relevant themes, issues, research questions, and variables is the second step in the process. Operationalizing describes the process of *defining* or *conceptualizing* the key constructs or themes that form and shape the research. Operationalizing also requires the researcher to identify any limitations and assumptions for the research. The purpose is to impose *order and structure* on the data to ensure that the needed data will be collected during case interviews and observations. Finally, when a researcher operationalizes the salient themes or constructs for a case study, it is much easier to organize the data as it is collected.

Depending upon the research approach followed, operationalizing activities can take place before or after the data are collected. The process occurs before data collection in the case study approach. However, when it is done after the data are collected, the study is called a *grounded theory study*. In the grounded theory approach, the structure and order emerges from the collected data; in these studies *all* data are "right."

Defining the categories also involves providing some amount of descriptive information in any number of ways. Strauss and Corbin (1998) defined this as the process of applying order to collected data by placing them in discrete categories, adding that researchers are almost certain to include descriptive material along with the code descriptions and category definitions.

Gathered information must be coded and assigned to its proper category. Coding is based on a researcher-selected set of general properties, characteristics, or dimensions. In their discussion on coding of qualitative data, Strauss and Corbin added that conceptualizing is also the first step in theory building. A concept is the researcher's description of a significant event, object, or action-interaction. The researched phenomena must be named in order to be organized into logical groupings, classifications, or categories that share some common characteristic or meaning. Thus, "a labeled thing" is something that can be located, placed in a class of similar objects, or *classified* in some way (p. 103).

Step 3: Define Units of Analysis

The third step in case study analysis is defining the *units of analysis*. This critical step hinges upon how the researcher has defined the problem to be studied. As noted earlier, case studies can focus on many different types or amounts of phenomena; they can be either single-case or multicase studies. While most case studies typically focus on individuals, pairs (dyads), small or large groups, processes, or organizations (Marshall and Rossman 1999), they can also be about decisions made by administrators, supervisors, or work teams. They can focus on programs, agencies, small subunits of agencies, or groups of agencies that address a similar problem or service. They can even be about entire communities.

All of these are what is meant by *unit of analysis*. Deciding on the unit of analysis is what Yin (1994) called *a narrowing of the relevant data*. Narrowing the data allows the researcher to focus the study on topics identified in the research objectives.

Taking the unit-of-analysis decision to the next level depends first on the way the researcher has defined the study question. For example, a study designed to bring to light the effects of a reduction in the number of beds available at a state mental health hospital could be addressed from several points of view. First, the study could chronicle the effects that inability to access treatment might have on one or a group of patients. Another study might focus on the impact the closures will have on community-based treatment centers. An even more focused study could limit the investigation to locally funded charitable organizations treating the client base.

A broader view might look at the economic impact that funding the services locally will have on other community-based programs competing for shares of the same funding pool. Clearly, defining the unit of analysis is a critical first step that must take place before moving to the next step, collecting information.

Finally, operationalization requires that the researcher identify each of the procedures that will be followed, both in data collection and analysis; identify the coding plans and methods that will be used; and prepare a preliminary list of categories for the analysis.

Step 4: Collect the Data

The fourth step, *data collection*, can take place in a variety of ways. The techniques used most often in public administration research include (1) interviews, (2) simple observation (also called naturalistic observation), and (3) analysis of internal and external documents. One of the hallmarks of a good case study is the selection of two or more of these methods (Arneson 1993). As well as providing a means for *triangulation* (studying a phenomenon in two or more ways to substantiate the *validity* of the study findings), the use of more than one approach helps ensure that relevant data is not missed.

Interviews

Gathering data by interview may take one of several different forms. The method used most often in public administration research is the in-depth personal interview. Individual interviews occur as conversations between a researcher and a subject or respondent. To keep the conversation focused, the research uses a conversation guide in which key points to be covered in the interview are listed. The respondent is free to provide any answer that comes to mind. Another type of interview is more structured, requiring respondents to reply to specific open-ended questions. An approach that is often used in public administration research is the *focus group interview*. A focus group consists of six to twelve subjects who meet as a group to discuss a topic or issue.

Observation

Naturalistic or simple observation is another way data are gathered for case studies. Marshall and Rossman (1999, 107) described this method as "the systematic noting and recording of events, behaviors, and artifacts in the social setting chosen for study." The researcher records events and behaviors as they happen, collecting the written records into compilations of impressions that are similar if not identical to the field notes that characterize data collection in ethnographic studies. In this type of observation, however, the researcher does not seek to be accepted as a member of the group, staying, instead, an outsider.

It is a toss-up which is more important in the case study approach to research: personal interviewing or simple observation. Each has its own advantages and disadvantages. Interviews, for example, allow researchers to delve deeply into a subject, encouraging respondents to provide reasons for their behavior or opinions. Interviews are time-consuming, however, and require interviewers with special questioning and listening skills.

Observation has long been an important data-gathering technique used in social science research. While it may be called "simple observation," it is not an easy process to employ. According to Marshall and Rossman (1999, 107):

Observation is a fundamental and highly important method in all qualitative inquiry: it is used to discover complex interactions in natural social settings. . . . It is, however, a method that requires a great deal of the researcher. Discomfort, uncomfortable ethical dilemmas and even danger, the difficulty of managing a relatively unobtrusive role, and the challenge of managing a relatively unobtrusive role, and the challenge of identifying the "big picture" while finely observing huge amounts of fast-moving and complex behavior are just a few of the challenges.

One way that researchers try to get around the time and skills limitations of in-depth interviewing is with the use of focus group interviewing. Researchers use these *focus groups* because they make it possible to investigate in depth one or a few issues or concepts. Focus groups consist of six to a dozen individuals with similar interests or characteristics who are interviewed together in the same room. The researcher functions as a moderator, keeping any one participant from monopolizing the conversation or intimidating other group members. Each participant is called upon to contribute and others comment on the contribution. In this way, group interaction often occurs, providing a richer, more meaningful discussion of the topic.

Document and Other Evidence Analysis

The study of documents and archival data is usually undertaken to supplement the information the case study researcher acquires by interview or by observing in a situation. These may be official government records, internal organization reports or memos, or external reports or articles about a case subject. The technique that is usually used in document analysis is content analysis, which may be qualitative, quantitative, or both. One of the key advantages of document analysis is that it does not interfere with or disturb the case setting in any way. According to Marshall and Rossman (1999), the fact that document and archival analysis is unobtrusive and nonreactive is probably its greatest strength.

Step 5: Analyze the Data

The *analysis* of all qualitative data analysis takes place in a progression of six separate phases. Figure 23.2 displays a slightly different version of the progression of analysis steps. An important requirement inherent in all data analysis is that the data be reduced in volume at each stage. Unless this occurs, the researcher may be inundated with reams of unrelated information that make logical interpretation impossible. Organizing the data into sets of mutually exclusive categories is one way to reduce the volume of data.

Raw data in the case study method can be any or all of the collected information. The primary responsibility of the analyst is to remain focused on information that sheds light on the study question. This may mean ignoring or leaving to a later review highly interesting but extraneous data. Analysis of case data involves looking at and weighing the collected data from a number of different viewpoints before writing the final case narrative.

In Figure 23.1, these analysis steps were broken down into five separate steps:

(1)   Grouping the data according to key constructs
(2)   Identifying bases for interpretation
(3)   Developing generalizations from the data
(4)   Testing alternative interpretations, and
(5)   Forming and/or refining generalizable theory from the case study.

Figure 23.2   **A Procedure for Data Analysis**

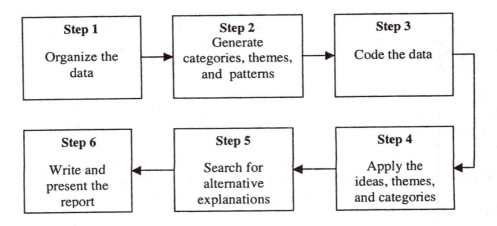

Data analysis does not always take place in the logical sequence illustrated in Figure 23.2. Rather, two or more of the activities may occur at the same time. In addition, data analysis does not simply end with the first set of conclusions; it is a *circular* process. Parts of the analysis may be moved forward to the next step, while other parts, even whole sections, may butt up against conclusions with dead ends. When this happens, the researcher must search for alternative explanations, test these against the themes that evolved in the operationalization phase, and then either reach new and different conclusions or adjust the themes and categories to reflect the reality of the data.

Step 6: Prepare and Present a Report of the Findings

The final step in the process is producing a comprehensive narrative of the case, in which the connections between key concepts and study objectives are addressed. The *narrative* is a descriptive account of the program, person, organization, office, or agency under study. All the information necessary to understand the case must be included in the narrative. It typically revolves around the researcher's *interpretation* of the behaviors and events observed in the case during the study period.

Patton (1980, 304) referred to the final case narrative as "the descriptive, analytic, interpretive, and evaluative treatment of the more comprehensive descriptive data" collected by the researcher. Patton saw the report-writing phase taking place in a series of three distinct steps:

1. Collect and categorize the raw case data. This is all the information that can be gathered by interviews, by observing, and by reviewing any relevant documents and/or literature.
2. Construct a preliminary record of the case. A case record is the researcher's coding and subsequent distillation of the mass of raw case data. It involves establishing categories and assigning the data to them in a logical order. A draft of the report eventually emerges from completion of this and the first step.
3. Produce a case study narrative. This is the final written narrative (or other presentation form) that presents in a readable, informative, and evaluative way how the case meets the original objectives for the research. It includes all the information that readers need to fully understand the subject. It can be presented as a chronological record of events or according to a set of themes—or both.

The case study report must clearly explain what the researcher perceives to be the "facts." In addition, it must discuss relevant alternative interpretations and explain why the researcher chose not to accept those alternatives. Finally, the case study should end with a conclusion that is soundly based in the researcher's interpretation (Yeager 1989).

GUIDELINES FOR PREPARING CASE STUDIES

A number of guidelines have been offered for preparing case study reports. Yin (1994) identified five key characteristics of the best, most informative case studies.

The Case Study Must Be Significant

Cases that are "significant" stand out as superior examples of research. They illustrate a particular point in a better or more succinct way than others that could have been chosen. The researcher indicates not only that selection of the case or cases was appropriate, but that the study adds to the body of knowledge about the topic or issue; the study makes a significant contribution. Research problems that are trivial do not make good case studies. Yin (1994, 147) concluded that the best case studies are those in which:

- The single case or sets of cases are unusual and not "mundane."
- The case or cases are interesting to the public.
- The fundamental issues brought to light in the case have wide appeal—they are "nationally important" either as theory, as policy, or in practical application.

The Case Study Must Be Complete

Cases that are "complete" leave the reader with the feeling that all relevant evidence has been collected, evaluated, interpreted, and either accepted or rejected. The operative word here, of course, is *relevant*. According to Yin (1994), a case study is not absolutely complete unless it is complete on three distinct dimensions. First, in a complete case the phenomenon of interest is explicitly addressed. Second, all the relevant information is collected; no information that relates to a dimension should be left ungathered or, if collected, left uninterpreted and discussed in the final narrative. Third, the researcher must not impose any artificial conditions during the analysis or evaluation of the collected data. This means, for example, that the researcher must not stop collecting relevant information because he or she ran out of money or time, or for any other nonresearch constraint.

The Case Study Must Consider Alternative Perspectives

It is important that the researcher not limit the analysis of case data to a single point of view. Alternative explanations for a social phenomenon *always* exist (Marshall and Rossman 1999). Throughout the analysis of the case data, the researcher is obligated to identify alternative explanations or interpretations of the raw data and to show why these are rejected in favor of the adopted explanation. Evidence that supports the selected interpretation must also be presented.

The Case Study Must Display Sufficient Evidence

Data reduction solely for the sake of brevity in a case analysis is not desirable. All the relevant evidence must appear in the final narrative. Certainly, the researcher must condense, distill, and combine data at each step of the analysis; otherwise, the final report would be little more than a collection of unrelated, disjointed, raw data. However, the researcher should probably err on side of including *too much* material rather than finding out later that he or she has omitted important evidence from the final case report.

The Case Study Must Be Composed in an Engaging Manner

While this does not apply directly to the concept of completeness in a case report, it is relevant because it has a great influence on whether the case will ultimately be read, understood, and, where appropriate, used in policy development. It is a question of *style*. According to Yin (1994), complaints that are often heard about case studies are that they are too long, cumbersome to read and interpret, and simply boring. He suggested that the writers of case studies strive to engage readers' intelligence, entice their interest by hinting at exciting information to come, and seduce readers into accepting the underlying premise.

SUMMARY

The case method has long been one of the most popular approaches followed in public administration research. The popularity of this approach lies in its great flexibility. Case studies can be written to serve as examples of what a public administrator ought not to do, as well as what should be done. However, their primary purpose is to instruct public administrators in what other administrators are doing.

Case studies are often intensive studies of one or a few exemplary individuals, families, event, time periods, decisions or sets of decisions, processes, programs, institutions, organizations, groups, or even entire communities. Discussing the case method as one of three qualitative approaches for research in organizational communications, Arneson (1993) described it as an appropriate research method when a case involves some noteworthy success or failure.

There are three types of case studies: (1) intrinsic case studies, (2) instrumental studies, and (3) collective studies. *Intrinsic* case studies are done when the researcher wants to provide a better understanding of the subject case itself. *Instrumental* case studies are used when the public administration researcher wants to gain greater insight into a specific issue. The *collective* case study is a multiple-case design; a group of individual cases studied together because they can contribute to greater understanding of a phenomenon, a population, or some general organizational condition. Another name for this type of case is *multisite qualitative research*.

Five purposes for case studies have been identified: (1) to establish a theory or theories, (2) to test theories that already exist, (3) to identify a previous condition or conditions that lead or contribute to a phenomenon, (4) to establish the relative importance of those contributing conditions, and (5) to establish the fundamental importance of the case with regard to other potential examples.

Case studies can be single-case or multicase designs. Most case studies that are conducted in the behavioral and administrative sciences are single case studies. Multicase designs can be used to compare two or more cases or to gather extended evidence across a group of like cases.

A case study is designed and prepared through a series of interlocking steps. In step 1, the case must be *framed*, which means that the researcher must determine what should be studied in what case, and why. In step 2, key constructs, variables, terms, and so on are operationalized so that no confusion occurs later in the analysis process. In step 3, the researcher selects and defines the unit(s) of analysis—individuals, groups, neighborhoods, or other entities. The researcher collects data in step 4. This usually involves conducting in-depth interviews, performing naturalistic or simple observation, and examining any relevant documentation. The data are analyzed in step 5, and a final case report is produced during step 6.

ADDITIONAL READING

Lincoln, Norman K., and Yvonna S. Lincoln. 1998. *Collecting and Interpreting Qualitative Materials.* Thousand Oaks, CA: Sage.

Marshall, Catherine, and Gretchen B. Rossman. 1999. *Designing Qualitative Research.* 3rd ed. Thousand Oaks, CA: Sage.

Stake, Robert E. 1994. "Case Studies." In *Handbook of Qualitative Research,* ed. N.K. Denzin and Y.S. Lincoln, 236–47. Thousand Oaks, CA: Sage.

Yin, Robert K. 1994. *Case Study Research: Design and Methods.* 2nd ed. Thousand Oaks, CA: Sage.

24

RESEARCH USING THE GROUNDED THEORY APPROACH

Since its introduction in the late 1960s, the *grounded theory* approach to research has captured the methodological interest and imagination of researchers in all the social and administrative sciences. One of its principal inventors, Barney G. Glaser (1992, 842), described it as a methodology for getting from the systematic collection of data to production of a multivariate conceptual theory.

The grounded theory method has been used successfully in many different circumstances, disciplines, and cultures. The fact that it is easily generalizable to many different disciplines and research topics has contributed to its increasing acceptance worldwide. As Glaser (1992, 842) noted:

> Grounded theory is a general method. It can be used on any data or combination of data. It was developed partially by me with quantitative data (which) is expensive and somewhat hard to obtain. . . . Qualitative data are inexpensive to collect, very rich in meaning and observation, and rewarding to collect and analyze. So . . . grounded theory is being linked to qualitative data and is seen as a qualitative method, using symbolic interaction, by many. Qualitative grounded theory accounts for the global spread of its use.

THE BEGINNINGS OF GROUNDED THEORY

The grounded theory method evolved from roots in the *symbolic interactionism* theoretical research of social psychologist George H. Mead at the University of Chicago, his one-time student Herbert Blumer, and others (Robrecht 1995). Mead believed that people define themselves through the social roles, expectations, and perspectives they acquire from society and through the processes of socialization and social interactions. Blumer added three concepts to Mead's thesis: (1) the meanings that people have for things will determine the way they behave toward them, (2) these meanings come from people's social interactions, and (3) to deal with these meanings, people undergo a process of constant interpretation (Annells 1996). Grounded theory was created by Glaser and Strauss (1967) as a way to develop explanatory and predictive theory about the social life, roles, and expected behaviors of people.

From its early roots in sociology and social psychology, the method has evolved and grown in importance to become what has been described as the most comprehensive qualitative research methodology available (Haig 1995). Also noting this increased acceptance, Denzin and Lincoln

(1994a, 204) called it "the most widely used interpretive strategy in the social sciences today." Recently, this method has also become an increasingly important research approach in public administration.

"Grounded theory has gone global, seriously global among the disciplines of nursing, business, and education and less so among other social-psychological-oriented disciplines such as social welfare, psychology, sociology, and art," according to Glaser (1999, 841). Miller and Fredericks (1999, 538) have also commented on this growth:

> It is increasingly apparent that the grounded theory approach has become a paradigm of choice in much of the qualitatively oriented research in nursing, education, and other disciplines. Grounded theory has become a type of central organizing concept that serves to both direct the research process as well as provide a heuristic for data analysis and interpretation.

Grounded theory was first proposed as a reaction against the restrictions that its developers saw in positivist research methodology. Chief among those perceived restrictions was the requirement to conduct research for the purpose of testing preconceived theoretical hypotheses. Today, the primary objective of all grounded theory research is to develop theory out of the information gathered, rather than testing predetermined theories through a process of experimentation.

The process begins with the researcher focusing on some area of study. This could be any phenomenon, circumstance, trend, or behavior in any of the social or administrative sciences. Using such tools as observation and interviewing, among others, the researcher gathers relevant data from as many different sources as are available. Analysis of the data begins with grouping it into categories and assigning codes. Through a process of continually comparing data in various categories, the researcher may generate theory.

Grounded theory requires the researcher to organize and apply *structure* to the data according to an eclectic set of researcher-determined groupings or *categories*. As the researcher forms categories, new data are compared across the formed categories. Linkages between categories and characteristics are also identified. The data and their linkages are assigned discrete codes that enable the researcher to identify them with their specific groupings. Similar codes are in turn assigned to other data that fit a broader category or categories. As the process continues, categories are constantly reevaluated and changed when necessary. Only when no additional revisions are intuitively possible does the analyst form a *theory* from the collected and analyzed data. Figure 24.1 illustrates the constant comparative method of data analysis.

THE IMPORTANCE OF GROUPING AND CODING

Rather than functioning only as a matter of convenience for later reference, the actual assigning of data to their formed groupings is a critical early step in the analysis process. Strauss and Corbin (1998, 3) defined the coding process as the "analytical process through which data are fractured, conceptualized, and integrated to form theory." It is the key activity in the *microanalysis* stage of the data; it includes both the first and the second stages of coding.

The researcher applies a rigorous analytical process in order to develop theory out of the investigated social situation(s) *after* several runs through the raw data and coded categories. Thus, a key concept in grounded theory is the *continual analysis* of the data while and after they are collected.

Insights and ideas are also generated after in-depth analysis of the data. The analyst searches for commonalties and differences in the data. New data are fitted into the constructs or categories that

Figure 24.1   **Constant Comparative Method of Data Analysis**

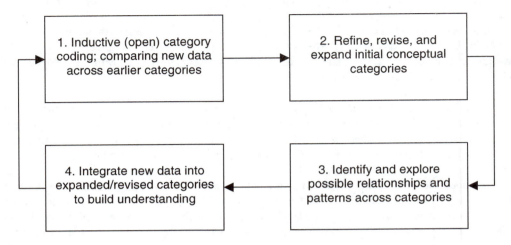

Source: Maykut and Morehouse 1994, 135.

are seen as pivotal in the data. Commonalities are compared and contrasted as the analyst weighs possible theories against other possible interpretations. Ultimately, a theory that is "grounded" in the data will emerge from the analysis.

Grounded theory researchers conduct their studies by gathering all possible facts that pertain to a problem through personal interviews, analyses of participants' diaries, and participant observation. The data are analyzed and given an initial interpretation as they are collected by the researcher (Strauss and Corbin 1998). This initial interpretation is called *open* or *substantive* coding.

TWO APPROACHES TO GROUNDED THEORY

The analysis process identified by Glaser and Strauss in 1967 has been modified over time, so today there are at least two approaches to grounded theory. Locke (1996) identified the two approaches as the *Straussian*—after Anselm Strauss—and the *Glaserian*—after Barney Glaser. Strauss and Corbin (1990), reporting that their graduate students had great difficulty organizing, coding, and analyzing their data, proposed that an additional step be added to the process. Glaser responded in 1992, taking issue with Strauss and Corbin for straying from the original emphasis on developing theory and adopting instead a process that he believed emphasized conceptual description over theory generation.

Both approaches are fundamentally similar, but the controversy focuses on the addition of a third level of coding proposed by Strauss and Corbin. Glaser (1992) advocates sticking to the two steps in the coding process introduced in the original work. Both approaches emphasize the importance of coding as a key concept in the analysis.

Glaser's two coding processes are *open* (substantive) and *theoretical*. During the first phase, coding can be relatively freewheeling, open to continuous revision, compression, and merging. During the final, theoretical, phase of the analysis, the researcher is advised to rework the groupings as required to bring substance to any emerging theoretical conclusions.

Strauss and Corbin (1990) reported that the grounded theory process as originally proposed in 1967 made it difficult for beginning researchers to produce clear and cogent theory from the data.

Figure 24.2   **The Strauss and Corbin Paradigm Model for Axial Coding of Data**

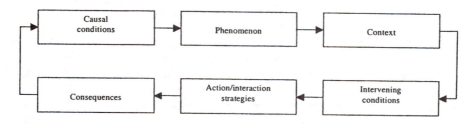

Source: Adapted from Glaser and Strauss 1967.

Retaining the open and substantive coding levels, they proposed adding a third, intermediate step in the coding/analysis process. They called this intermediate step "*axial coding*" (Glaser 1992; Kendall 1999). This step—proposed as a way to "demystify" the grounded theory process—requires the researcher to place all the initially "open-coded" data into six categories specified by Strauss and Corbin. The six predetermined categories are (1) *causal conditions,* (2) *phenomena,* (3) *context,* (4) *intervening conditions,* (5) *actions/strategies,* and (6) *consequences* (Figure 24.2).

A number of authors have objected to what they see as an artificial restriction that axial coding forces upon the researcher. Hall and Callery (2001), for example, concluded that the intermediary six steps resulted in a "mechanical approach" to data analysis that limited theory building. Kendall (1999) saw that axial coding could be advantageous for beginning researchers, but added that it forced her from her original research question when she used it in her dissertation. After several years of working with her data, she found herself spending so much time trying to fit the data to the Strauss and Corbin "paradigm model" that she stopped thinking about what the data was communicating about the original study question. She felt that using predetermined categories directed her analysis artificially by limiting her thinking to only the six categories.

The important thing to remember about the two different approaches is not that the two creators of the grounded theory method disagree on how many steps there should be in the coding process, but rather that they agree on almost all other aspects of the process. Data should be continually compared with new data, coded, and placed in categories for interpretation. The researcher selects both the code and category in the first and the last steps in the analysis.

The Key Actions in Action Research

Lee (1999) proposed eight key activities when conducting a grounded theory study (Box 24.1). Lee emphasized the importance of continuous comparisons of categories in his list of actions, but did not include the Strauss and Corbin axial coding process. In this way it is very similar to the original Glaser and Strauss proposal.

THE SEVEN STAGES OF ACTION RESEARCH

Figure 24.3 (p. 305) is a model of the grounded theory research process that was developed to illustrate the sequential nature of the method. Glaser and Strauss described the seven key steps in this process in detail in their 1967 narrative on how the method was developed, and reiterated elsewhere (e.g., Glaser 1992; Strauss and Corbin 1998).

Box 24.1
The Eight Key Actions in Grounded Theory Research

Action 1. The researcher comes up with some ideas, questions, or concepts about some area of interest. These ideas can come from the researcher's own experience in the field, from a few key interviews, or from an analysis of the published literature.

Action 2. By creatively looking at the ideas, questions, or concepts, the researcher proposes some possible underlying concepts for the phenomenon and their relationships (linkages).

Action 3. The researcher now tests these initial linkages by comparing them with real-world data.

Action 4. By continually comparing the concepts to the objective world phenomena, the first steps in testing a theory take place.

Action 5. By continually analyzing the data and comparing new data against the concepts, the researcher works to integrate, simplify, and reduce the concepts, seeking to establish core concepts.

Action 6. The researcher prepares 'theoretical memos' (these are simply preliminary attempts to spell-out possible connections and/or theoretical explanations). This is now a continuing process, requiring the researcher to continually test and revise possible theory.

Action 7. The researcher continues to collect data and to code data by categories and or characteristics, while also producing theoretical interpretations of the material; this often requires the researcher to go back and repeat earlier steps in the process.

Action 8. The researcher prepares a final research report. In grounded theory research, this is not simply a 'detached, mechanical process;' it is instead a key part of the research process.

Source: Lee 1999.

Stage 1: Select a Topic of Interest

In public administration, theories explain and predict human behavior among public employees, the citizenry, or organizations that are in some way acted upon or that influence public decisions. "Theory is a strategy for handling data in research, providing modes of conceptualization for describing and explaining" (Glaser and Strauss 1967, 3).

Research topics—areas of interest to study—are not hard to find. They are everywhere in the researcher's field of interest, career field, and the practice of administrating for the public good. The key thing to avoid in grounded theory is approaching a study area with a preconceived hypothesis. The hypothesis must come from the data. Glaser (1992, 23), warning budding researchers to avoid the advice of others, cautioned:

> When a research problem is elusive or hard to come by a lot of people tend to give advice . . . the researcher's search for the preconceived problem is subject to the whims and wisdoms

Figure 24.3   **A Model of the Grounded Theory Data Collection and Coding Processes**

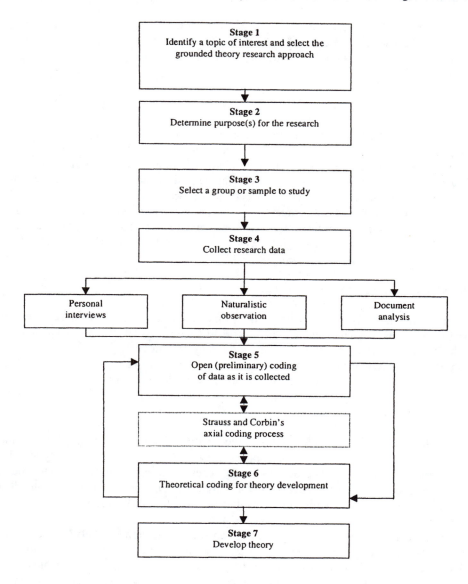

of advisors with much experience and of colleagues. He should be careful as he may just end up studying his advisor's pet problem with no yield for him and data for the advisor. And he will likely miss the relevance in the data.

It is important to remember that the identification of a research question is not a statement that clearly and succinctly identifies the topic that is going to be studied. Rather, the problem emerges from the data as it is collected. Open coding, selective (theoretical) sampling, and constant analysis of this information form a focus for the research study.

Stage 2: Determine a Purpose for the Research

Glaser and Strauss (1967) identified five main purposes or uses for grounded theory: (1) to evaluate accuracy of earlier evidence, (2) to make generalizations based on experience, (3) to identify a unit of measurement for a one-case study, (4) to verify an existing theory, and (5) to generate a theory.

Evaluating Evidence

Data from additional groups are collected to compare with data that has already been collected for the purpose of evaluating whether the first evidence was correct. This often serves as a test for replicability and can be applied for validating both internal evidence (from within the study group) and external evidence (data from sources other than the study group). This can be a powerful and important use for grounded theory because a study's categories and properties are generated from collected evidence. Collected and compared evidence is used as a defining illustration of the conceptual category. Glaser and Strauss (1967, 23) considered these categories to be the fundamental building blocks of theory: "In generating theory, it is not the fact upon which we stand but the conceptual category that was generated from it."

Establishing Generalizations from the Data

If a theory is to emerge from the collected "facts," they must be generalizable to other situations, otherwise they remain isolated bits of data—interesting but irrelevant. If they are applicable only to a single case, group, circumstance, or situation, they remain descriptors of only that specific phenomenon. In searching for generalizations, or *universals,* the researcher establishes boundaries of applicability while at the same time attempting to broaden the theory.

Specifying a Concept

This is the first step in a design requiring specific identification of a study sample or population for a one-case study. Grounded theory's comparative evaluations are used to clearly identify the key concept that makes the study group distinctive. These concepts tell the reader why you chose to study one group and not another. They involve comparing the unit of analysis (individuals or groups) selected for the study with other units that are not selected. This comparison often brings to light the distinctive properties of the selected unit.

For example, a study of homeless women—such Alice Waterston's (1999) *Love, Sorrow, and Rage: Destitute Women in a Manhattan Residence*—has many different categories of subjects from which to select a sample. Waterston chose to study a group of HIV-positive or possibly HIV-positive homeless women residing at a shelter in a metropolitan area. Her data analysis began with a comparison of the characteristics of this study group with other similar groups of at-risk women. By revealing the specific characteristics of the study group that are of interest, she distinguished the study group from other groups that were not included.

Verifying a Theory

When conducting a grounded theory research study for the purpose of verifying an existing theory, the researcher focuses on finding information that corroborates the existing concept. In the process, the researcher generates new theories only for the purpose of adjusting or modifying the original theory. No new theories are sought. Neither Glaser nor Strauss says much about this potential use for the grounded theory method, emphasizing instead its role in generating new theory.

Generating Theory

This is the primary purpose of grounded theory research; the researcher's main goal is the systematic generation of new theories from the data collected. There are two broad types of theory that can be generated through this process: substantive theory and formal theory. *Substantive* theory addresses specific empirical or applied tasks in public administration, such as police and fire department community relations, management development programs and employee training, solid waste disposal, water purity, road construction, and city planning. *Formal* theory, on the other hand, deals with broader, often philosophical issues, such as public participation in the democratic process, authority and power in management situations, and reward systems.

Both of these applications are what Glaser and Strauss (1967, 32–33) identified as "middle-range," meaning they fall somewhere between practical working hypotheses in the everyday conduct of an administrator's job and all-inclusive "grand theories," such as global warming. It is important to note that both of these types of theories must be grounded in data if they are to be accepted as relevant.

Stage 3: Select a Group to Study

Determining where to go to get the data needed for a research study remains one of the major issues that confront grounded theory researchers. Researchers need to know who can provide the information that illustrates the central or core concept in the study. Strauss and Corbin call this the *theoretical sampling* problem and define it as the process of picking the sources that can provide the most information about the research topic. The aim of theoretical sampling is "to maximize opportunities to compare events, incidents, or happenings to determine how a category varies in terms of its properties and dimensions" (202). This suggests that the researcher must be more concerned with ensuring the representativeness of the sample than in the concept of randomness. Researchers are encouraged to carefully select the subjects from whom information will be acquired. This becomes even more important as the study progresses. Sampling must become more specific with time because the theory that is emerging must eventually control the sample selection. Once some categories are established, all further sampling must be focused on developing, solidifying, and enriching the formed categories. Glaser and Strauss (1967, 47) stated it this way in their description of their development of the technique:

> The basic question in theoretical sampling is: what groups or subgroups does one turn to next in data collections. And for what theoretical purpose? In short, how does the [researcher] select multiple comparison groups? The possibilities of multiple comparisons are infinite, and so groups must be chosen according to theoretical criteria.

Stage 4: Collect Research Data

There are no restrictions to how data are collected in a grounded theory design. However, most researchers use personal interviews, simple or naturalistic observation, narratives, and document or artifact analysis. One of the distinctive characteristics of the grounded theory method is that the data collection, coding, and interpretation stages of the research are carried out in concert, not as individual activities. One leads to the other, then on to the next, and back again. These steps "should blur and intertwine continually, from the beginning of an investigation to its end" (Glaser and Strauss 1967, 43).

Grounded theory methodology can be used for arriving at theories from data that are collected in any type of social research—quantitative and qualitative. All theories are developed for one or both of two fundamental purposes: to explain or to predict.

Stage 5: Open Coding of Data

Coding is the process of applying some conceptually meaningful set of identifiers to the concepts, categories, and characteristics. The key things to remember about open coding are that it is always the *initial* step in data analysis and that its purpose is to establish (or discover) categories and their properties.

Open coding is the free assignment of data to what the researcher sees as the naturally appearing groupings of ideas in the data (Lee 1999). The researcher creates as many categories as needed. These can be looked upon as the fundamental, explanatory factors that identify the central research concept. Each category contains as many bits of data as are found to fit in that category. Data bits are more or less indivisible, and intuitively fit into just one category.

The open coding process continues until one or more "core categories" are established (Strauss 1992). Then, the coding process turns either to Strauss and Corbin's axial coding, using preconceived categories, or proceeds directly to the theoretical coding identified by Glaser and Strauss (1967) or Glaser (1992). *Axial coding* is the process of assigning categories into more-inclusive groupings. Strauss and Corbin urged the researcher to use the six second-level classifications they proposed. Lee (1999), on the other hand, following the original Glaser and Strauss (1967) model, called for the researcher to propose the axial categories.

The researcher first comes up with several categories that seem to bridge all the open-coded categories. Second, the researcher examines all the open categories to see which fit within the selected second-level category. The remaining data are then compared across the second researcher-selected broader category; those categories that belong are assigned. The process continues until all the data have been compared against all the second-level categories and classified. Additional axial categories might have to be added to encompass all the data.

How to Determine Categories from Data

There are no hard and fast rules for grounded theory research (Lee 1999). Even the inventors of the method disagree about how to go about coding and categorizing collected data. There are also many different ways to discover or establish meaningful categorical distinctions in data. Miles and Huberman (1984), for example, discuss twelve different ways to go about developing codes for raw data (Table 24.1).

An example of a code set developed for an educational site study can be found in Miles and Huberman (1984, 58–59). These five broad constructs (categories) and their codes were proposed in the preliminary coding: Innovation Properties (IP), External Context (EC), Internal Context (IC), Adoption Process (AP), Site Dynamics and Transformations (TR). These five constructs are the "core categories" of this study.

A different number of characteristics or dimensions were identified for each of the categories.

Table 24.1

Tactics for Generating Meaning in Conceptual Categories

1. Counting	7. Particular to general
2. Noting patterns, themes	8. Factoring
3. Seeing plausibility	9. Relationships
4. Clustering	10. Finding intervening variables
5. Making metaphors	11. Chain of evidence
6. Splitting variables	12. Theoretical coherence

Source: Adapted from Miles and Huberman 1984, 215.

Five of the characteristics that were determined to contribute to the Innovation Properties category were Objectives, Organization, Implied Changes–Classroom, Implied Changes–Organization, and User Salience.

A complete set of definitions was developed for each of the categories and the specific characteristic associated with the category. For example, in the Site Dynamics and Transformations (TR) category, the code TR-START was assigned to data that fell into the Initial User Experience category and dimension. The definition for this code was: "Emotions, events, problems or concerns, assessments, made by teachers and administrators during the first six months of implementation" (p. 62). Similar definitions are produced for every category/characteristic in the study.

Glaser was adamant that open coding and category building *not* be forced into any preconceived second-level (axial) groupings. Strauss and Corbin, on the other hand, give the researcher more leeway in this decision. As a result, both approaches to grounded theory coding are found in the research literature. There is no disagreement regarding the third (and final) coding process: selective (or *theoretical*) coding.

Stage 6: Selective (or Theoretical) Coding of Data

Selective or theoretical coding is the name given to the process of imposing a final structure on the data and establishing rank-order importance of the conceptual categories (Lee 1999). Just as in the second-level coding process, the researcher proposes a small number of overarching categories. Next, these categories are ordered according to how the researcher sees their potential to contain or explain the collected data. In the third step, the researcher picks which is the most powerful or important category; all of the data is then judged for their fit in that theoretical category. The researcher then repeats the process, picking a second most important category and all remaining data that fit in this category. The process continues until all data are categorized. The researcher is then ready to develop theory about the phenomenon.

From Core Categories to Grounded Theory

The underlying purpose of all theory is to explain and/or predict. Theories are built in a process that moves from the *specific* (individual examples, incidences, or cases, for example) to the general. In this way, the researcher develops a *theory* that is applicable (explains and/or predicts) to more than the individual example, incidence, or case. The purpose of the theoretical coding stage is to identify the relationships between categories and their properties as they are found in the data.

The process occurs in the following six stages (Miller and Fredericks 1999):

1. Preliminary (open) categories are formed from the first data collected.
2. More general or broad categories that include preliminary groupings are formed from this and new data as they are added to the analysis.
3. Categories are further refined and defined.
4. A set of *core* categories is finally accepted.
5. As data are analyzed, they are assigned as characteristics or dimensions of these core categories.
6. Continual comparison may produce a revised coding scheme, which in turn may require revisions to the characteristics/dimensions of the codes.

Stage 7: Develop a Theory

This is the culmination of all preceding activities in the process: forming a theory that is grounded in the data. Although it is last in this process model, theory development is not saved for last. Rather, at each stage in the process of grounded theory the researcher prepares *theoretical memos* in which to record ideas, conclusions, propositions, and theoretical explanations of the phenomena under study. These memos summarize the researcher's conclusions—recorded as they are being formed—and are the gist from which a *theory* or set of hypotheses are developed.

To qualify as a *grounded theory,* it must exhibit these key characteristics (Locke 1996):

1. The theory must closely fit the topic and disciplinary area studied.
2. The theory must be understandable and useful to the actors in the studied situation.
3. The theory must be complex enough to account for a large portion, if not most, of the variation in the area studied.

Often, grounded theory researchers neglect to address the issue of theory in the presentation of their findings. This does not take anything away from the process, however, because in describing what was discovered from the research and in the specific recommendations, some *derived theory* must underlie the conclusions. It is just a matter of putting it into words. The researcher would not have the confidence necessary to make recommendations regarding the findings unless he or she was sufficiently confident in the theoretical conclusions derived from the data.

A Not-So-Subtle Reminder

One of the reasons that Strauss and Corbin proposed their six preconceived categories for the second-level or axial coding step was that their graduate students were having great difficulty in conceptualizing the necessary categories for collected data. Lee (1999, 50) also commented on the difficulty of the method:

> Grounded theory is a long-term, labor-intensive, and time-consuming process. It requires multiple waves of data collection, with each wave of data based on theoretical sampling. In addition, the iterative process should continue until a theoretical saturation is achieved. Given all this, researchers should avoid grounded theory approaches unless they can commit substantial resources to a study.

GROUNDED THEORY RESEARCH IN PRACTICE

King, Felty, and Susel (1998) used grounded theory methodology in their study of the underlying causes of public antipathy in the political process and ways to improve participation in public administration policy-making decisions. Using personal interviews and focus group discussions, they gathered data from private citizens and public administrators from several communities in Ohio. Focus-group participants were asked to respond freely to four broad questions: (1) how can more effective public participation be achieved; (2) what public participation means to the participant; (3) what are the barriers to participation; and (4) what advice did they have for people trying to bring about more—and more diverse—participation.

The analysis occurred in two stages. First, in the open stage of their coding, the transcribed interviews were coded by each researcher working independently and using a qualitative form of content analysis. Second, the researchers synthesized the individually coded responses to come up with a set of categories and themes. These were discussed in detail in their report. Specific quotations from respondents were woven throughout their final narrative, thus providing insightful reinforcement of the thematic concepts they drew from the data.

King, Felty and Susel identified three categories of barriers to effective public participation: contemporary lifestyles, existing administrative practices, and current techniques for participation. The pressures and complexity of daily life, together with certain demographic factors such as class, income, education, and family size, and a breakdown in traditional neighborhood ties were identified as probable causes for the lack of public participation in the communities studied. Existing administrative practices, such as abbreviated time allowed for public contribution, waiting too long to call for public input in the policy development process, and some administrators' perception of participation as a threat also hindered the amount and quality of participation. Finally, there was widespread agreement that current techniques used to gain public participation—such as the public meeting—were inadequate and, often, entirely ineffective.

The theory generated from this research included a three-part proposal for dealing with the three sets of barriers to participation. First, citizens within the community must be empowered and, at the same time, educated in ways to organize and research issues and policies. Second, public administrators must be reeducated; their traditional role of "expert manager" must be replaced with one of "cooperative participant" or "partner." Administrators must also develop their interpersonal skills, including listening, team building, and the like. Finally, the structures and processes of administration must be changed to make it easier for the public to become involved and contribute to the policy formation process.

Additional Examples

Strauss and Corbin have edited a volume of research studies—*Grounded Theory in Practice* (1997)—that illustrate a variety of applications of the grounded theory approach to research in the fields of health, sociology, business and public administration, and social psychology. Konecki's study of the recruiting process was done while he was enrolled in Anselm Strauss' grounded theory seminar at the University of California. Konecki conducted a series of twenty intensive interviews with employment recruiters, one with a client employment candidate, and one with a firm that used executive search firms. He also included previously published case study descriptions of the search process.

The Konecki study is noteworthy primarily for its clear, detailed description of his application of the Strauss and Corbin third-level axial coding of the collected data. He compared the data from different types and sizes of search firms and wrote a number of theoretical memos to himself about the collected material. He then developed a conceptual matrix, subjecting the open-coded ideas to Strauss and Corbin's six established conditional categories of causal conditions, phenomena, context, intervening conditions, actions/strategies, and consequences.

Konecki (1997, 143–144) theorized that the effectiveness of an employment search process is affected by five conditions: internal search-work circumstances, and organization, interactional, market, and cultural conditions. He closed with the conclusion that grounded theory methodology is "a very useful tool for the reconstruction of conditions and combinations of the conditions of a category."

Other papers in the Strauss and Corbin book of example applications include studies on identity, physicians' interpretations of patient pain, abused women's self-definition, scientific knowledge about cancer, reproductive science, the evolution of medical technology, tuberculosis, and collective identity.

GROUNDED THEORY AND PUBLIC POLICY

Cook and Barry (1995) used the grounded theory method to research the public policy interactions of managers and owners of small businesses. They chose the grounded theory method because of what they termed the "paucity of work" in the area and because of a desire to build a rich description of the business owners' ideas and beliefs about public policy and their ability to help shape it. Over the two-year study, Cook and Barry conducted thirty-one in-depth interviews with the owners of twenty-seven firms and with four government administrators. In addition to these in-depth interviews, Cook and Barry also attended nine trade association meetings with a government-relations focus; more than fifty additional executives participated in the meetings. Concluding their data-gathering process, they examined more than 150 public documents, papers, memos, and newspaper stories.

In what is clearly one of the major disadvantages of the method—an overabundance of raw data—Cook and Barry reported that their initial transcripts produced more than 700 pages of data. Before they could code and analyze the data, they were forced to produce detailed abstracts of each transcript, thus eliminating some 60 percent of the original data.

Two levels of coding were then used on the remaining data: "received" coding and "emergent" coding. The first level was derived from their review of the literature in the field, their prior learning and biases, and from categories that the interviewees themselves used. These were primarily descriptive and definitional in nature. These codes were then merged into broader codes—called *overarching dimensions*—that related to issues, issue characteristics, and the influence process.

In the sense of *theory,* Cook and Barry found it "evident" that interactions between owners of small firms and policy makers helped to create a system for interpreting and making sense of the process. These interactions determined (1) whether a small business executive would commit to working on a policy issue, and (2) how he or she would carry out that work. Executives tended to agree to work on issues that they believed they had some possibility of influencing and to ignore policy questions that they felt were beyond their reach.

SUMMARY

Grounded theory is a general qualitative research method that can be used on any data or combination of data. It was developed initially for use with quantitative and/or qualitative data. However, quantitative data often is expensive and difficult to obtain. On the other hand, qualitative data are inexpensive to collect; they can be very rich in meaning and observation; and are often rewarding to collect and analyze. Grounded theory research today is classified as a qualitative method that uses symbolic interaction.

The grounded theory research process begins with focusing on some area of study—a phenomenon, circumstance, trend, behavior, etc., in any of the social or administrative science areas. Using observation and interviewing, among others, researchers gather relevant data from as many different sources as are available. Analysis of the data begins with grouping it into categories and assigning codes. Through a process of continually comparing data with other categories, theory may be generated.

Completion of a grounded theory research project results in the researcher identifying one or more core concepts that relate to the issue of interest, example or *empirical,* examples in the data that are representative of each core concept, and an indication of a set of relationships between the core concepts and their example indicators. These relationships may be illustrated in what are called *concept maps,* which are graphic depictions of each concept category and their characteristics or indicators. The conceptual depiction also shows how, and it what direction, larger categories are influenced by or related to (1) each other, (2) lower to upper or broader-level concepts, and (3) higher level to lower level. This process is similar to the "bathtubs and beer-barrels" method of showing relationships developed by Kurt Lewin.

It is important to remember, however, that grounded theory is a long-term, laborious, and time-consuming process. The researcher should have a substantial grounding in the area of interest, and the ability to formulate a broad, meaningful conceptual interest area. This does not mean that a 'study problem' must be identified in advance but rather, that the researcher be conversant enough with a phenomenon to justify an open research project in the area. Furthermore, grounded theory research requires multiple levels of data collection, each based on theoretical sampling and continual comparisons. In addition, the coding and classifying process should continue until a theoretical saturation is achieved. Researchers are advised to avoid grounded theory approaches unless they can commit substantial resources to a study.

EXERCISES

Exercise 24.1

Your agency has been given the task of determining how *information technology* can be used to improve interagency [interorganizational] learning (IOL) across state government. As you and your staff plan a research study, two of the questions that come to your mind are (1) does information technology's contribution to learning differ among lower and higher levels of management, and (2) does the traditional turf-protection nature of bureaucratic organizations preclude the development of trust that is essential for interagency learning to occur? Scott (2000) defined mutual trust as "the expectation shared by [participants] that they will meet their commitments to one another." When mutual trust is present, cooperating agencies are more likely to remain open and willing to share information and knowledge over time and are less likely to worry about how much, if any, information leaks to other agencies, the press, and the public.

In discussions with your supervisor, you agree that the primary unit of analysis for the proposed study is the collection of agencies/departments that operate in your state. Smaller units in the study are the individual agencies themselves. Examples of embedded units in the state government are the Department of Corrections, the Department of Social and Health Services, and the Department of Natural Resources. Selecting sites for data collection depends on your ability to identify representative examples within the larger context of the entire state government.

From your background in information technology and what you have read about the topic in professional journals, you and your team come up with four objectives for your study. These are:

1. Find out as much as you can about the phenomenon of interorganizational learning
2. Explain how and why information technology facilitates interagency learning
3. Develop a rich, descriptive narrative that describes interagency developments, trends, and successes
4. Produce an empirically based theory of information technology's ability to enhance interagency learning and trust

Source: This case is based on a paper by Judy E. Scott, "Facilitating Interorganizational Learning with Information Technology." *Journal of Management Information Systems* 17:2 (Fall 2000), 81–114.

Questions

1. Is the grounded theory method appropriate for conducting this research study? Explain why or why not.
2. Explain how you would collect data to accomplish the four research objectives.
3. Briefly, name several potential broad conceptual factors or categories that you might use to organize your collected data.

Exercise 24.2

You are a student in your university's Master's degree in Public Administration program. You are asked to work with a team of three other students in the program to design and conduct a research study dealing with a consortium of eleven public schools that intend to introduce global education into their curricula.

According to the National Council for the Social Studies, the purpose of global education is to help students develop the knowledge, skills, and attitudes needed to live in a world of limited natural resources and wide ethnic diversity, cultural pluralism, and growing interdependence abound nations and people.

The university's School of Education has received a grant to fund a project that will involve working with and studying elementary and secondary school teachers. The objective of the grant is to improve education by widening the vision of teachers and students through instruction in global education. The objective of your study is to develop theory on the factors that influence the spread of global perspectives and actions in educational institutions. Specifically, in order to facilitate infusion of global thinking and acting, your team needs to understand how successful teachers go about adopting global thinking, introducing global educational materials and methods, and, in the broadest sense, functioning as change agents in their schools.

Source: This case is loosely based on an article by Roberta Lessor, "Using the Team Approach of Anselm Strauss in Action Research: Consulting on a Project in Global Education." *Sociological Perspectives* 43:4 (Winter 2000), S133–148.

Questions

1. Do you believe that the grounded theory method is an appropriate design in this research situation? Why or why not?

2. How would go about conducting field research for gathering the data necessary to accomplish your team's research objectives?

3. Would you begin your research by developing one or more hypotheses beforehand, then using your interpretations of the data to test the hypotheses? Why or why not?

Exercise 24.3

You have been assigned the task of designing and carrying out a research study to establish how life situations and extraneous events influence the onset of drug use and drug-using behaviors among an inner-city population of women. You are convinced that the personal and private nature of the issue, together with the lack of formal structure or cohesiveness in the sample, justifies your adopting a grounded theory approach to conducting the research.

Prior to beginning your study, you sought and were granted approval from the university's ethics committee for research with human subjects. You then concluded that the best way to capture the subtleties of people's reactions to the study topic was to tape-record a series of personal, in-depth interviews with a cross-section of participants who fit the defined sample profile. You select subjects from a list of women receiving subsidized medical care at the university's medical school. To ensure that participants show up for their interviews, you have received permission to pay all subjects $15 for each one-hour interview. To guarantee anonymity, you will ask all subjects to use fictitious names.

Although the grounded theory method calls for interviews to be unstructured with no preconceived topics to cover, you elect to develop and follow a loosely structured schedule of topics in order to ensure the interviews will focus on the events that surround the phenomenon of interest: illicit drug use and social conditions affecting its onset. You begin open coding of the information during and after the first interview, and continue until all interviews are completed. You are unsure whether to use the intermediate step of axial coding or if you should move directly to theoretical coding and theory development.

Source: This case is loosely based on an article by Carol A. Roberts, "Drug Use Among Inner-City African American Women: The Process of Managing Loss." *Qualitative Health Research* 9:5 (September 1999), 620–639.

Questions

1. Do you feel that the axial coding paradigm, using the six categories proposed by Strauss and Corbin (1990), will be an asset in arriving at conceptual understanding of the data in this study? Why or why not?

2. Do you feel that writing conceptual memos to yourself as you code and categorize data would help you to develop a theoretical understanding of the phenomena surrounding drug addiction?

3. How would you handle the situation if a subject refused to be tape-recorded during her interview?

ADDITIONAL READING

Glaser, Barney G. 1992. *Emergence vs. Forcing: Basics of Grounded Theory Analysis.* Mill Valley, CA: Sociology Press.

Lee, Thomas W. 1999. *Using Qualitative Methods in Organizational Research.* Thousand Oaks, CA: Sage.

25

RESEARCH USING THE ETHNOGRAPHIC APPROACH

Ethnographic methods are not employed as often in public administration research, but when they are they can provide great quantities of important information. These study designs typically require more time to conduct than public administrators are able to devote to their research projects. In the parent disciplines of anthropology and sociology, ethnographic studies may take six months to a year or more to complete. When they can be used in public administration research, however, they have the capacity to produce powerful narratives that provide deep insight to the needs of society.

A hallmark of all ethnographic research is the practice of producing reports with "thick description." *Thick description* refers to research notes that exhibit great depth and detailed complexity. An example cited by Neuman (2000) is the description of a social event that might last three minutes or less, but which takes up many pages of descriptive narrative. This use of detailed description means that ethnographic methods can be an excellent design choice when the study objective is to provide deep background information for the formation of long-term, strategic public policy. On the other hand, ethnographic methods are generally not appropriate when a management decision must be made immediately on the basis of the findings of the research.

A BRIEF HISTORY OF ETHNOGRAPHY

Despite their drawbacks, ethnographic methods have a long and important history in research in the social and human sciences. They can be traced at least as far back as the Industrial Revolution, if not longer (Neuman 2000).

Industrialization and the Social Sciences

A by-product of the industrialization of Western society was the belief of some observers that factory labor was dehumanizing society; unskilled workers were often seen as just another easily replaceable component in the production process. Beginning in the nineteenth century, however, concern over the deteriorating human condition in tenements and factories resulted in calls for changes in the way society treated its citizens. An increasingly educated public, the clergy, and a few in the governing elite came to recognize that the deterioration in social conditions needed to be stopped and, if possible, reversed. These early critics looked to *science* for solutions to the problems of the new industrialized society.

This faith in the power of science to produce answers to society's problems encouraged adoption of a scientific approach to the study of the social problems and needed changes. If advances in the natural sciences and technology could be *profitably* applied to problems in industrial invention and innovation, these critics reasoned, why couldn't they also be applied to solving social problems? If science could be used to improve production, why couldn't it also be used to improve everyone's quality of life?

The new *social,* or *human* sciences that emerged out of the intellectual vitality that characterized the nineteenth century included sociology, psychology, and anthropology. Sociology emerged from early studies of the social ills that were identified as unwanted by-products of the industrialization process. At about the same time, early attempts at establishing a systematic way of explaining human behavior and mental aberrations resulted in the modern science of psychology. The tradition born in early travel stories ultimately forged a scientific way of studying indigenous cultures; this social science was called *anthropology.*

In each of these new scientific disciplines, curiosity about what was happening to society resulted in research that had the objective of understanding (1) why social problems occurred, and (2) what could (or *should*) be done to change society in order to improve the lot of the aged, children, the working poor, and the otherwise disenfranchised.

Early Field Research

The early missionaries and adventurers who traveled with European traders and explorers on voyages to new lands encountered new and, to them, strange cultures. Early reports of these encounters became extremely popular. Often, however, they were little more than lurid or bizarre tales of fancy, with little basis in reality. Despite their limited basis in fact—or possibly because of it—the tales often gained widespread distribution in books and the popular press of the time. Before long, these new social scientists were permitted to join in on the many voyages of discovery that were taking place. Some of these scientific expeditions were carried out specifically to study primitive cultures before they disappeared, were eradicated by disease, or were subsumed into the Western economic tradition.

Early researchers wanted to understand how these different primitive societies developed and their unique ways of coping with social phenomena. The result was a body of descriptive literature.

As reports of these encounters circulated in Europe and the Americas, a few of the early social scientists saw a need to apply what they called "scientific rigor" to the research that was being done. They turned to research methodologies similar to those that had been emerging in the natural sciences, adopting the positivist model with its quantitative emphasis and causal focus. However, interpreting the coping behaviors, attitudes, and other cultural phenomena of primitive peoples was difficult, if not impossible, with the traditional positivist methodology that was applied. The researchers then modified the positivist (quantitative) approach by adding more verbal description and explanation to their investigations and reports. This new way of doing science became what we now call fieldwork, and the scientific disciplines they followed became the social sciences of anthropology and sociology.

Themes of Anthropology

Today, anthropology is divided into three main types: *cultural anthropology, physical anthropology,* and *archeology.* Of the three, only cultural anthropology has found a significant place in the research conducted in public administration.

Cultural Anthropology

What was traditional anthropology has become what is now called *cultural anthropology*. The *culturalists* concentrate on describing existing social cultures, no matter how small, distant, or foreign. The research method they use most often is called *ethnography*. Ethnographers often live with the groups they study for long periods of time.

Cultural anthropology, originally devoted almost exclusively to the study of distant, often primitive cultures, was soon found to be an appropriate way of studying less complex but still modern world societies that had remained in relative isolation from the emerging industrialized world (Alasuutari 1995). From that expanded application it was not long before anthropology and its research tool, ethnography, were seen to have a place in the study of modern cultures and subcultures.

Physical Anthropology

The physical anthropologists followed Darwin's lead in studying the evolution of humankind. Physical anthropologists are concerned with determining the earliest primate ancestors of humans, the physical characteristics of ethnic groups, and so on. Physical anthropologists are sometimes called in to assist forensic scientists in the identification of crime and accident victims or to aid in the design of living and work spaces, including furniture and tools.

Archaeology

Archeologists were at one time included under the cultural anthropology umbrella, but found their own niche by focusing on studies of ancient and unknown material cultures. Today, however, modern anthropologists can be found conducting analyses of relatively recently deposited cultural artifacts. An example is the archeological study of garbage dumps in order to analyze trends in fashion, invention, and other cultural phenomena.

The Evolving Focus of Sociology

The traditional focus of sociology—another discipline that uses ethnographic methods in research —has also changed. Initially, the purpose of sociological research was to identify cause-and-effect relationships between the perceived ills and abuses of the new industrial society and the lives of adults and children forced to live and work in crowded, dangerous, and often unsanitary conditions. Sociology worked closely with the earliest social workers to discover how modern industrial society functioned and how to resolve social ills. However, as Alasuutari (1995, 24) noted, "many of the post-war [i.e., World War II], 'post-industrial' developments have evaded the conceptual net provided by established academic sociology, which in many countries became a tool for social engineering and social statistics." As a result, the rationale behind traditional sociological research is no longer the only purpose behind such research.

Because of the continually evolving nature of the focus of study for the social sciences, a new direction for ethnographic research emerged. Today, ethnographic studies are carried out in the inner cities of modern societies, in suburban and rural settings, in cross-cultural designs, and in large and small organizations; the purpose is to investigate the ways that the social forces of culture and subculture impact people. More important, however, is the emphasis on *interpreting* social behavior that has replaced the earlier model of simply *describing* a society.

The role of the ethnographer has taken on the important task of contributing to the formation of public policy.

There is a fine line dividing sociological and anthropological ethnographic studies. Probably the easiest way to distinguish the two is to remember that sociologists are concerned with the impact of social circumstances and situations on people, whereas anthropologists tend to place greater attention of the role of culture and/or subculture on the behaviors of people. There is a place for both emphases in public administration research.

Through an eclectic process of trial and error, anthropologists and sociologists developed a way of conducting research that allowed them to meet their study objectives in all kinds of social and cultural settings. The name given to this method was *ethnography*. Researchers in public administration have also adopted this method of research. Ethnography is one of several important approaches for the study of *culture* as and the act of governance, the formation of public policy, and the administration of diverse agencies and functions of government. The research conducted in these disciplines has often had a great influence on public policy.

ETHNOGRAPHIC RESEARCH

The practice of anthropology—and its principal research method, ethnography—evolved and expanded its focus over the last several centuries. Traditional positivist methods used to study primitive cultures and societies were found to be inappropriate for developing understanding of modern cultures and behaviors. Anthropologists in Europe and the United States eventually supplemented traditional research methods with a new approach to the study of primitive cultures and societies that was designed to improve the way of studying humans in social settings. A key element of this new approach was its emphasis on specific ways to prepare field notes and rules for writing about cultural events. The name of this new research approach was *ethnography*—which means graphically describing a society or social group. The new data-gathering process was called *fieldwork*.

Ethnography, Ethnology, or Ethology?

Several different terms are used in reports of ethnographic research. Among these are ethnography, ethnology, and ethology. *Ethnography* means the descriptive study of living cultures, while *ethnology* refers to the activity of *using* the information gathered by ethnography. Thus, a public administrator might use an ethnological report in the process of framing public policy. *Ethology* is simply a somewhat different approach to the research process; it refers to the less-intense practice of simple observation (Jones 1996). The model presented in Figure 25.1 illustrates how anthropology, sociology, and psychology, with their different but related research focuses, have each contributed to the development of ethnographic research in public administration.

The science of ethology is most commonly encountered in the context of the study of animal behavior, although a branch seeks to apply ethological principles to human behavior as well. Ethnography involves actively observing, recording, and explaining why a culture is described in the way it is by the ethnographer; it is sometimes used as a synonym for "participant observation." Ethology is used as a synonym for "simple" or unobtrusive observation.

Ethnographers immerse themselves in the day-to-day activities of the group they are studying in order to (1) describe the setting in as much detail as possible (a process called *thick description*), and (2) to come up with some theoretical ideas that allow them to interpret and explain what they have seen and heard. The goal is to learn as much as possible about the behaviors and social processes taking place in the culture.

Figure 25.1 **A Model of the Relationships Between Social Sciences, Ethnography, Public Administration Research, and Public Policy**

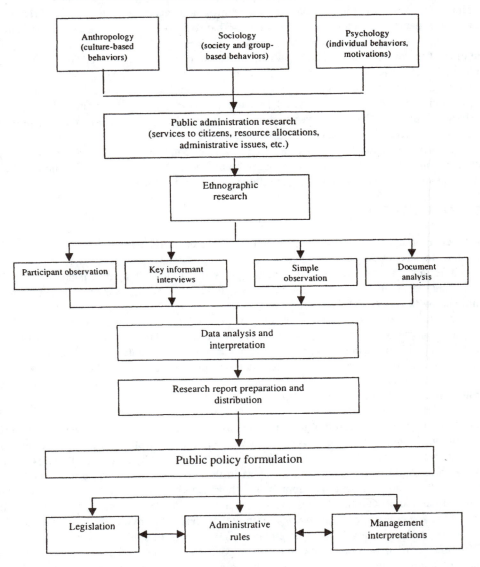

Terry Williams (1996, 31–32), writing about his ethnographic study of the cocaine subculture in New York after-hours clubs during the 1970s and 1980s, defined ethnography as:

> a science of cultural description; more than that, it is a methodology. It is a way of looking at people, a way of looking at a culture. It is recording how people perceive, construct and interact in their own private world. It embraces the subjective realm of the individuals it seeks to understand. It defines the group the way the group defines itself.

Ethnographers live, work, and play with their study populations for long periods of time. Their aim is to be absorbed into the group and accepted as a nonthreatening, nonintrusive member. Then, events and interrelationships will unfold as they would naturally, as if the observer were not in attendance. This process is called "gaining entry," and is the key to a successful research project. Without acceptance, without entry into the inner workings of the group, the researcher remains an outsider—perceived as a threat and subsequently either shunned or lied to, at best.

The process of living with a social group (*doing fieldwork*) involves observing and recording individuals' behaviors. The ethnographer summarizes these field notes into a larger descriptive generalization that purports to describe the behavior of the larger society. The researcher must then develop *subjective descriptions* that are based on a large number of *generalizations*. In making these generalizations, the ethnographer moves from the *specific* to the *general*. That is, the behaviors of one or a small group are used to infer that those behaviors are also those of the larger groups in similar circumstances. The ethnographer should also develop *interpretations* of the observed behaviors; the question "why" should be answered to the best of the ethnographer's ability.

According to Jones (1996), one of the major attractions of ethnography for field researchers is it permits them to develop meaningful, coherent pictures of the social group and setting. Researchers get to see the phenomenon as a whole, in all of its complexity, and not just bits and pieces.

Jones also suggested a way to differentiate between ethnological and ethological research involving human behavior. The key differentiating characteristic is whether the research is conducted to develop a theory or to provide background information needed to make a management decision. Figure 25.2 illustrates the point that, despite the different steps involved in the two approaches, they are very similar.

Modern Ethnography and Ethology

For most of the early history of ethnography, study results were often little more than simple descriptions; interpretation of the event, setting, or behavior was left to the reader. This often resulted in doubts about the *validity* of ethnographic generalizations. The following statement illustrates the older paradigm: "Ethnographic generalizations are by themselves only best fit statements about the incidence or frequency of occurrences in the society. By themselves they say little or nothing about what goes with what" (Cohen 1973, 37–38). Cohen's solution to this problem was to call for more correlational or *causal* research into ethnography. This, he believed, would improve validity by improving interpretation.

In its earliest applications, *doing ethnography* meant studying isolated, primitive cultures to develop a descriptive profile or summary of the social practices of the group of people (Naroll and Cohen 1973). Today, however, ethnographers are not required to seek out isolated, primitive groups for their research; rather, there are no limits to how and where ethnographic field research can be applied. Ethnography, like its parent discipline anthropology, is not restricted to the study of distant or nonliterate cultures. One reason for this is that there are few if any societies left untouched anywhere in the world. Most have been studied and restudied to the point that little new about their "primitiveness" can be learned. The world has become smaller, and distant, diverse societies no longer live in "glorious isolation." As Alasuutari (1995, 24) noted, "the 'Other' have moved next door, and 'Western' artifacts, television programmes, and economic networks have invaded practically the entire globe."

Figure 25.2   **Fieldwork Processes for Ethnography and Ethology**

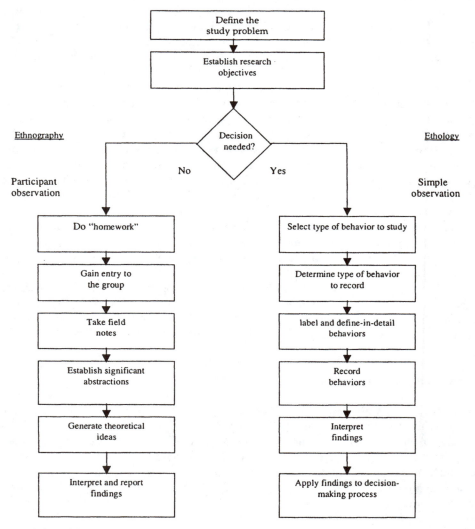

Source: Adapted from Jones 1996, chapter 3.

THE ACTIVITIES OF MODERN ETHNOGRAPHERS

According to Whiting and Whiting (1973), ethnographers collect samples of types of behavior in order to understand the cognitive and social-structure *regularities* in a society. Ethnographers study the roles people adopt, economic systems, political systems, religious systems, personality, and many other aspects of any or all types of social organizations and systems.

Duveen (2000) has described the work that ethnographers do as the production of thick description, a two-part process. First, the researcher writes down everything that he or she sees.

Figure 25.3   **Ethnographic Fieldwork, Analysis, and Presentation Processes**

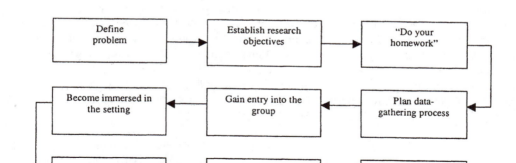

Duveen referred to this thick description of events, settings, and behaviors as capturing the sense of the social actors, groups, and institutions being described. Second, the researcher's own interpretation of what is recorded influences the final description. Together, the two-part process of observation-interpretation moves from one activity to the other, then backward to repeat itself again and again.

Figure 25.3 illustrates the key processes involved in conducting and presenting the results of an ethnographic study. It illustrates several different layers of observation-interpretation that characterize good ethnographic fieldwork, field notes, and final report preparation.

Ethnographic methods are employed in a number of different forms. Examples of these variations are *ethnomethodolgy, community-based ethnography,* and *ethology.* Each of these research approaches has its advocates and detractors, but all are considered to fall under the larger category of *field research.*

Ethnomethodolgy

Ethnomethodolgy has been defined by Neuman (2000, 348) as "the study of commonsense knowledge." It combines themes from sociology and philosophy, and is usually seen as an application of *phenomenology* (Adler and Adler 1998). Researchers who follow this approach focus their concern on how people go about living their everyday lives. Ethnomethodologists study mundane, everyday behaviors in exceptionally close detail. They often use mechanical and electronic methods of recording the behavior of people. They then analyze in minute detail these audio- and videotapes, films, and other records, using what Adler and Adler (1998, 99) have described as "an intricate notational system that allows (them) to view the conversational overlaps, pauses, and intonations to within one-tenth of a second . . . they have directed a particular emphasis toward conversation analysis."

Community-Based Ethnography

Community-based ethnography, also known as community-based research (CBR), is closely associated with the critical approach known as *action research* (Stringer 1997) and has been used primarily in research in education. Stringer described the purpose of community-based research as a way of providing workers in professional and community groups with knowledge that is normally available only to academic researchers. As with all action research, CBR is designed to help people expand their knowledge and understanding of a situation so they can come up with effective solutions to the problems they face. Everyone—researcher and researched—are involved in the process. Stringer (1997, 17–18) describes CBR as:

> [I]ntrinsically participatory; its products are not outsider accounts, portrayals, or reports, but collaborative accounts written from the emic—or insider—perspective of the group. Such accounts, grounded in hermeneutic, meaning-making processes of dialogue, negotiation, and consensus, provide the basis for group, community, or organization action. People can review their activities, develop plans, and resolve problems, initiate projects, or restructure an organization.

Ethological Methodology

Ethological research addresses many of the same issues addressed by traditional ethnography. Initially, the method focused primarily on animal behavior—Charles Darwin, for example, is considered one of the pioneers in this field of research. Today, however, this approach is often used in organizational research, where it is employed for identifying and describing behavior in social settings.

The approach taken in an ethology study involves *simple observation,* which can be either visible or hidden (unobtrusive). Organ and Bateman (1991), discussing etholic observation in the context of organizational behavior research, referred to the method as *naturalistic observation.* They identified a number of appealing characteristics, as well as some of the shortcomings, for this approach. Possibly the most important advantage is what Organ and Bateman called the *contextual richness* that is possible with observation (p. 36). This includes more than the thick description that characterizes ethnographic field notes. It also refers to the fact that this type of research has enjoyed wide acceptance over the years, with results published in many articles, books, autobiographies, newspaper stores, conversations, and speeches.

In addition to this extensive body of available literature, the natural experience that researchers gain from working in and dealing with organizations of all types, sizes, and purposes is also an advantage. This is what is referred to as the *richness in personal insight* of naturalistic observation in organizational research. Organ and Bateman (1991, 37) concluded their critique of the method this way:

> [Simple] observation is an attractive method of research because it confronts its subject head-on. It deals with raw, real-world behavior. Because the data are rich with the drama of human existence, it is easy to relate to accounts of these studies.

The major disadvantage of observation is that it often results in a report bias that is traceable to people's natural tendency to exercise *selective perception* and *selective retention.* Selective perception means that from all the myriad stimuli that people encounter, they see what they want to see, what they are interested in, what they think is important. Whether they do so consciously or unconsciously, people ignore much of what else goes on.

This idea has been suggested by a number of different investigators. John Dewey, for example, noted that human perception is never "neutral." Rather, human knowledge and intelligence, what we think of as *past experience,* always influences perception. Furthermore, judgment is involved in all perception. Otherwise, the perception is nothing more than a form of what Dewey called *sensory excitation* (Phillips 1987, 9).

According to Hanson (1958), the theories, hypotheses, frameworks, and background knowledge held by researchers have the power to unconsciously influence everything that is observed. Therefore, observation cannot have a neutral foundation. *Selective retention* means that people usually remember what they *think* was said, what they *wanted* to hear, what they *believe* occurred, or what fits within their personal framing of the issue. Hence, what is remembered is inherently subjective; it can never be considered the "truth."

Because observation is recorded as the field notes of one or more researchers, it will always contain what the researcher *feels* is important. Field notes will often omit what the researcher believes to be trivial or unimportant. We are all drawn to the dramatic or exciting in situations—it makes for interesting reading, even when it has little or no bearing on the central issue. Both field notes and the material that is eventually included in a report pass through a filter formed from the perceptions and memory of events held by the researcher. Therefore, researchers must always struggle with the answerable question: Would another observer have drawn the same conclusion from these events? Researchers use thick description in an attempt to provide an answer.

Ethology and Simple Observation

A key objective for all research in ethnography and ethology is the study of behavior in social groups. Ethnography involves participant observation, where the researcher becomes immersed in the group under study. For the ethologist, however, the process is not participatory. Rather, the researcher simply observes and records what is taking place. As noted earlier, while ethology is primarily concerned with the study of the behavior of animals in their natural and manipulated environments, it often deals with the behavior of humans.

Ethologists often conduct controlled behavioral experiments with animals and human beings. As a nonparticipating observer, the researcher is always an outsider, on hand simply to record what is seen and never becoming a member of the group under study. The reports of ethologists tend to be primarily descriptive or explanatory, and do not involve interpretation of the observed social setting.

DOING FIELDWORK

All variations of ethnography involve fieldwork. *Ethnographic fieldwork* includes such activities as (1) engaging in participant observation, (2) collecting genealogies, (3) recording conversations, (4) writing field notes, (5) interpreting the findings, and (6) writing up the field notes and interpretations as reports. Field notes describe events, incidents that catch the researcher's eye, in addition to anything and everything that is deemed relevant to the study at hand at the moment it occurs.

According to Fetterman (1989), fieldwork is the key activity in all ethnographic research designs. The basic concepts of anthropology, the methods and techniques of collecting data, and data analysis are the fundamental elements of "doing ethnography." The selection of methods and equipment to use—including tape recorders, videotaping, and actual interviewing—is a major decision in fieldwork. "This process becomes product through analysis at various stages in ethnographic work—in field notes, memoranda, and interim reports, but most dramatically in the published report, article, or book" (p. 12).

Anthropologists and sociologists who study cultures firsthand have determined that the best way to do their fieldwork is with the process of participant observation. The early ethnographic researchers chose this method for their preferred way to function in the field for many reasons. One was the great distances they often had to travel to reach the study society. They were therefore forced to spend longer periods with the groups under study simply to justify the cost of the trip and the physical hardship they endured. Living for long periods of time in the primitive community, sometimes in the same huts or shelters of the members of the society under study, they were forced into being participants in order to survive—let alone understand what they were observing.

Bernard (1994) pointed out that participant observation requires researchers to get close to people, making them comfortable enough to permit the researcher to observe and record observations about their lives. Establishing rapport with people in the new community means learning how to act in such a way the people go about their day-to-day business when the researcher appears. Possibly most important, it means being able to retreat from the group-member role to think about what has been learned and write about it convincingly.

A reason for the evolution of ethnography from its former exclusive application to primitive cultures to now include research in today's settings was simply the long period of time needed to manually collect ethnographic information. Ethnographies are built on a combination of observations and extensive interviewing (Whiting and Whiting 1973), and these take time. Observation, regardless of the society or culture upon which it is focused, can be directed toward many different topics of investigation.

Whiting and Whiting have identified six subjects of potential focus for research: (1) an activity of some kind, (2) a larger category of acts, such as gang behavior, (3) an object or person that is the center of attention for a larger group of persons, (4) a person that functions as a representative of a status category, (5) a pair of individuals (a *dyad*), or (6) a setting for a social event.

ETHNOGRAPHY IN PUBLIC ADMINISTRATION RESEARCH

When public administration evolved into an academic discipline during the early decades of the twentieth century, its own journals, professional associations, conferences, and academic departments soon followed. Bits and pieces from all the social and behavioral sciences were incorporated into its structure—and its research methodology. It is important to remember that *all* the tools and methods used in public administration research were invented for other purposes. Sociology, anthropology, archeology, philosophy, economics, and business administration all have contributed to the lexicon of PA research method.

Ethnography has become one of the most widely applied qualitative research methods in public administration (PA). It has been shown to be a valuable tool for gathering information about behaviors embedded in, and specific to, cultures and subcultures. It was often used to identify administrative options for making decisions on matters of public policy. Fetterman (1989, 11) defined the method and its focus this way:

> Ethnography is the art and science of describing a group or culture. The description may be of a small tribal group in some exotic land or a classroom in middle-class suburbia. [The] ethnographer writes about the routine, daily lives of people. The more predictable patterns of human thought and behavior are the focus of inquiry.

Ethnographic methods are used in public administration to analyze and diagnose the *culture* and *operating climate* of organizations (Wilson 1989; Schein 1992). In this application, the purpose of the research is to improve the *practice* of administration in the public sector, while ethnographic research is a way of acquiring the information that makes such improvement possible.

Yeager (1989, 726) has described participant observation as an "old and widely used research method both in public administration and in other fields of study." In public administration use today, it incorporates many different techniques, including simple, group, and unobtrusive observations, depth-interviewing key informants, ethnography, and controlled observation techniques.

> Participant observation includes material that the observer gains directly from personally seeing or hearing an event occur. Often the participant observer establishes personal relationships with subjects and maintains those relationships over a period of time. . . . Rapport and trust are established with subjects to a far greater extent than in other methods. Typically, more exhaustive data are gathered on fewer subjects using participant observation that with other methods.

In public administration, the once-traditional activity of spending long periods in the field is neither possible nor desirable because it is not considered to be worth the cost. Rather, the most important part of fieldwork is simply "being there" to observe, ask questions, and write down what is heard and seen (Fetterman 1989). Participant observation, like ethnography, has changed from its original concept of total immersion in a society under study to include new and different topics and locations of study, in addition to a wide variety of data-gathering tools and techniques.

Ethnographic field research requires the most intense connection between the researcher and the subjects of the study (Kornblum 1996); it is not unusual to see ethnographers who have lived and worked within a group for many years to begin to take on a self-identity that places loyalty and connection to the study group above the researcher's prior connections.

While similar in method and analysis, ethnography as it is applied today is far different from the ethnography that evolved with the social sciences more than a century ago. "Ethnography is no longer a method used only to study foreign cultures; it has also become a method to study what is foreign or strange in our society and how social subcultures or subworlds are constructed—the adventure that begins just around the corner" (Flick 1999a, 641).

As ethnography moved beyond its original focus on describing small, distant, and primitive societies or examining the social disruption that was rooted in communities undergoing industrialization, it was used to study groups in locations that its founders would never have considered. One of these is the modern city.

All facets of urban life are now considered to be legitimate targets of ethnographic research for contributing to the establishment of public policy. Studies have ranged from the public behaviors of homosexuals, ghetto dwellers, drug cultures, the urban poor and homeless, schoolchildren, and many other subjects. There is apparently no limit to what studies can or should be carried out using an ethnographic approach.

According to Fox (1977, 9), urban anthropologists take several different directions: the anthropology of *urbanism,* the anthropology of *poverty in urban settings,* and the anthropology of *urbanization.* Despite their differences, they all appear to have the following principals in common: First, there is near-unanimous agreement among urban anthropologists that cities are important locations for research. Second, they are convinced that anthropology can make "important methodological and theoretical contributions to the study of urban place."

Urbanism Studies

Studies in the ethnology of *urbanism* are concerned with how movement from rural to urban locations has affected individuals, families, and larger groups. These major social movements are seldom seen in the industrialized West; researchers studying the rural-urban phenomenon today are more likely to focus their attentions on such locations as India, Southeast Asia, South and Central America, and other third world regions.

An example of this type of modern ethnographic study is Narotzky's (2000) research with a small population in the rural Vega Baja del Segura district of Valencia in Spain. Narotzky conducted intensive fieldwork in a town of about 5,000 residents. The region is an irrigated plain with a mix of agricultural and industrial economic activities, with the greater contribution now coming from the shoemaking industry. Large shoe factories were established in the region during the 1960s and 1970s. During this period, many single men and women and young families migrated from small farms to the towns where the factories were located. Other families did piecework in their homes. Other people work in small sweatshops that produce shoe parts and components for larger jobbers and finish factories.

By the year 2000, a mix of large factories, small family farms, unregulated workshops, jobbers, home-based workers, and migrant farm workers characterized the economy of the region. Narotzky was interested in how the local population has come to grips with a local, specialized industrial economy that was suffering shocks due to increased global competition. She described the region as one in which production processes are structured in diverse ways and where people tend to shift between different labor relations that vary greatly in their stability. Some people have stable work opportunities, while others do not. A major social problem that arises from the changing character of the workforce is that many workers are unable to gain access to unemployment benefits and other welfare programs.

Urban Poverty Studies

Urban poverty is a global phenomenon; organizations as disparate as the United Nations, private foundations, universities, governments, and the World Bank either fund or participate in studies of its causes and effects. Ethnographers study social groups and populations in urban settings such as the ghetto and barrio. They also focus their attention on the homeless, alcoholics and other substance abusers, Native American populations, at-risk youth, and others whom Fox (1977) has identified as social groups "whose lifestyles are described as being at the furthest cultural remove from the mainstream world."

Carol Stack (1996) is an example of an ethnographer conducting modern urban poverty studies. Over a three-year period she carried out participant observation in one of the poorest sections of a minority community in a large city in the American Midwest. Most of the residents of the area were unemployed; those who worked did so in low-paying service jobs that left them little better off than those eligible for welfare. One of the key findings of her study was that families developed large kinship-based exchange networks that included many nonrelated individuals and family units. These networks provided extensive support for other members of the network, helping the residents of the area adapt to a life of poverty, unemployment or underemployment, and welfare dependency.

Another recent example of ethnographic research in the realm of urban poverty is the 1999 work of urban anthropologist Alice Waterston. Waterston spent two years studying the residents of a shelter for at-risk women in New York City. She employed what she described as a "more interactive approach to data gathering," a practice that is common among qualitative researchers. Her primary method was participant observation, although she also used informal chats and formal tape-recorded, open-ended interviews with both the staff and the residents of the shelter.

Waterston developed the data for her study and final report from themes that emerged from her observation and extensive interviews. Among the themes she included in her study were poverty, homelessness, work, substance abuse, sexual violence, mental illness, AIDS, family and interpersonal relationships, sexuality, race, gender, and food. She found food and preparing meals to be a unifying concept around which many of the other themes were discussed.

Research on Urbanization Issues

Ethnographic research in the anthropology of *urbanization,* while similar to that of urbanism, focuses instead on the larger, evolutional *process* of urbanization that characterizes most modern industrial societies. How societies deal with health and safety concerns, waste management, work, play, and the many other difficult social issues associated with urban living are the study topics addressed by these social scientists. The nature of the urban locale, cultural roles in society, demography, class organization, and government are all part of the greater area of interest.

Lynne Nakano's 2000 study of volunteerism in modern Japan is an example of an ethnographic study on urbanization's effect on a society. Her study focused on the way modern some modern Japanese are achieving their self-identity by volunteering to help in the operations of government, nonprofit organizations, schools, corporations, community groups, and other social groupings. This type of study can have great impact upon public policy making, as well as providing significant direction for managers of nonprofit organizations in a community.

In the past, Japanese society held two distinct views. The more recent view is that people must develop themselves through self-expression, while the older, traditionalist view was that individuals must connect themselves to a social group, such as a firm or school, and define themselves through their commitment to that group. Since the 1990s, however, proponents of a third view—volunteerism—have proposed that *both* camps can be satisfied because volunteerism straddles the divide; it develops the self and contributes to society at the same time.

Nakano analyzed volunteering in a densely populated middle- to lower-middle-class residential neighborhood on the outskirts of Yokohama. The community contained a variety of housing types that reflected a mix of socioeconomic lifestyles. On one end of the scale was a 1,040-household public housing project for low-income citizens. Other types ranged from rental apartments and privately owned condominium apartments to single-family detached homes at the top of the scale.

The practice of using volunteer activity for self-identity flourished in the area for several reasons. First, the neighborhood was aging, a trend led by the people residing in the large public housing project, where one in four residents was sixty-five years old or older—nearly twice the average in Japan today. These older residents were both potential volunteers and the recipients of voluntary services.

Second, identifying oneself as a volunteer served as *symbolic leverage* for neighborhood newcomers. A "newcomer" was defined in the largest sense of the word; barely one percent of the population of the region were descendents of the original landowning and farming families. Yet they remained as leaders of many social groupings in the region. Some "newcomers" had lived in the community for more than twenty years.

Third, volunteerism was seen as a socially recognized activity that was particularly acceptable for middle-aged women and retired former "salary men," though volunteering was more of a social risk for men than for women. Becoming a volunteer, in fact, often resulted in a *promotion* in status for female homemakers, who became quasi-public figures in their volunteer roles.

An earlier example of an urban ethnographic study is the research carried out by Ulf Hannerz (1969) among urban blacks on Winston Street in Washington, DC, and described by Fox in his 1977 monograph on urban anthropology. Hannerz's study objective was to identify and describe ways in which ghetto lifestyles and social behavior differed from those in what he called "mainstream America." Hannerz identified four prototypical ghetto lifestyles: mainstreamers, swingers, street families, and street corner men.

An example of sociological ethnographic research is Alasuutari's (1995) report of his research involving long hours over a period of several months socializing with drinkers in a bar in Finland. He described the role that drinking and playing darts had for regular patrons of the bar. Alasuutari's study constituted a social commentary of a pattern of behavior that was thought to contribute heavily to illness, accidents, and suicide among Finnish males—all issues with major resource demands on government agencies. Alasuutari included some historical explanation of why Finnish males spent time in bars, tracing the practice to the erosion of Finnish traditional rural society and the immigration of farmworkers to urban centers. These were explained as significant contributors to the role that alcohol consumption plays in certain segments of Finnish society.

RESEARCHING THE CULTURE OF PUBLIC ORGANIZATIONS

Every organization, whether in the public or private sector, has its own distinctive culture and operating climate. Culture and climate have tremendous influence on the effectiveness and efficiency of government agencies and are closely monitored by public administrators. The study of organizational culture owes much of its method and underlying principles to ideas produced through ethnographic research. Change-agent consultants working on organizational development projects are very likely to use either ethnography or ethology methods for their data gathering.

Organizational culture has been defined in many different ways, but most definitions are similar to that offered by Schein (1985, 229): "Organizational culture is the shared and implicit assumptions held by a group and that determines how members of the group perceive, think about, and react to its various environments." Other definitions include those of Margulies and Wallace (1973), who defined organizational culture as the learned beliefs, values, and patterns of behavior that characterize an organization; and Peters and Waterman (1982), who saw culture as the shared system of values that manifests itself through different cultural artifacts.

In addition to its culture, organizations can also be said to have a distinct operating climate that results from the interaction of employees, administrators, and managers functioning within that culture. *Operating climate* reflects the content and strength of the salient values, attitudes, behaviors, and feelings of the people working in an organization (Payne 1971). Lewicki et al. (1988) saw operating climate as the level and form of organizational support, openness, style of supervision, conflict and conflict resolution, autonomy, and the existing quality of relationships that exist within the organization. Dastmalchian, Blyton, and Adamson (1991) were more succinct, terming operating climate as simply the atmosphere prevailing in an organization.

The study of culture in organizations is approached from two broad perspectives: (1) studies that follow a traditional, positivist approach, and (2) studies that adopt a postpositivist approach. Researchers who study organizational cultures from a positivist viewpoint hold the opinion that there are clear, easily identified dimensions of culture that can be measured (usually with a questionnaire). McNabb and Sepic (1995), for example, developed a scale for diagnosing the organizational culture of an agency of the federal government. They used employees' attitudes and opinions on nine dimensions of culture and climate: (1) organizational structure, (2) responsibility, (3) risk and challenge, (4) rewards, (5) warmth and support, (6) conflict, (7) organizational identity, (8) ethics, and (9) approved practices. The descriptive profiles developed with such studies of an organization can then be compared with the cultures of other groups. Organizational culture is something that can be reinforced or *changed*—the fundamental goal of an organizational development initiative.

The second school of thought follows an interpretist view. To these investigators, it is impossible to measure culture because it changes form with each attempt to pin it down; each observer comes away with a different interpretation based upon their personal values and experiences. Culture is, therefore, extremely difficult to manage; efforts to initiate a desired change may be fruitless—a mindless task with no hope of a concrete, lasting result.

One of the principal investigators in the field of organizational studies is Edgar H. Schein, who helped to establish the field of organizational studies at the Massachusetts Institute of Technology. Building on earlier work by such pioneers in social psychology as Kurt Lewin and Rensis Likert, Schein believed that the innate culture of an organization often serves as a barrier to planned change. Schein (1996) noted that when organizations try to alter and improve their operations, they often run into resistance that is based in the culture and/or subcultures that exist within all groups. This culture exists whether it is recognized or not. Members of the group are often not even aware of the culture of their group until they are faced with replacing it with something new and different.

Schein is critical of the positivist approach to the study of organizational culture. Traditional research has often resulted in a dependence upon abstractions about organizations and human behaviors in groups that are developed exclusively from a limited number of answers to questionnaires. These questionnaire-developed abstractions have created an artificial fabrication of reality. This has resulted in what Schein called *fuzzy theory*—research findings that depend upon "massaging the data" statistically to establish significant results. His solution to this problem involves taking an interdisciplinary approach that includes ethnographic involvement in the research process. "Concepts for understanding culture in organizations have value only when they derive from observation of real behavior in organizations, when they are definable enough to generate further study" (p. 229).

EXERCISES

Exercise 25.1: Trouble in the Projects

For many reasons, funding for welfare programs at both the national and state levels has declined greatly. Whether you feel this is just or unjust, you and your agency have no alternative but to act within the policy mandates and regulations handed down by the governor, the legislature, and the director of your agency.

One of the most controversial proposals circulating among state legislators is a plan to do away with all programs to ease the plight of indigent patients in the AIDS wards of public hospitals. Also to be eliminated are programs to aid homeless drug addicts; in the future, no state Medicaid funds are to be used for these patients. As part of a multiagency effort, the director of the Department of Social and Health Services has appointed a research team to gather information about current and potential recipients of public assistance. This information will be used by the legislative committee charged with developing a new program that will set public policy for the next ten years.

The team will begin its research in the section of the state's largest city known as the Portland Street Shipyard Projects. The Projects is a community of mixed ethnic background; the housing units were hastily constructed during World War II to house families of a since-closed naval shipyard. The units are small and often in need of extensive repairs. Today, the fastest-growing ethnic groups in the section are newly arrived immigrants from Latin America, the Ukraine, and Southeast Asia. Many of the residents of the Projects are unemployed, and most of those who are employed have low-paying service jobs that leave them not much better off than those who are eligible for welfare benefits.

Questions

1. Do you feel that an ethnographic research design is appropriate? Why or why not?
2. Describe in some detail how you propose to conduct your research in the region, making sure you begin with a clear statement of your research objective(s).

Exercise 25.2: Ethnic Problems in the West

Over the past several decades, the economy of a Western state has undergone a series of severe shocks, the most telling of which has been the closing of sawmills and the resulting elimination of most its employment base. The population of the region includes members of almost every major ethnic and racial group that has settled in the American West over the last century—Europeans, Latinos, Asians—but few African Americans. Only a small number of Native Americans remain in the area.

In the past, the region evidenced strong worker solidarity, with widespread trade union activity and one-party political loyalty. Few cultural antagonisms between the different groups have been encountered—until recently. With an increasing rate of migration of Latinos and Asians into the region has come an increase in the rate and severity of hate crimes.

As the strong labor union activity of the past has faded with the decline in the number of operating mills left in the region, new social organizations have filled the void. Many of these groups have white supremacist foundations. Others have strong ties to fundamentalist religious sects. Most have an "America First" clause in their platform, and most reject the idea of diversity. Clearly, there is strong potential for severe damage to the social and economic climate of the region.

The governor of the state has formed a blue-ribbon panel of university people, members of the clergy, local elected officials, business leaders, and state agency people to conduct research in the region before developing a broad policy statement for dealing with the many issues facing the region. The panel has contracted your group to conduct that research.

Questions

1. Is an ethnographic research approach appropriate? Defend your answer.
2. Describe in some detail how you propose to conduct your research, making sure you begin with a clear statement of your research objective(s).

Exercise 25.3: Problems Recruiting Law Enforcement Officers

The newly appointed director of a local law enforcement agency is concerned over the apparent low morale and lack of commitment among the rank-and-file officers and staff. Not only are officers with high seniority leaving the force, the director is finding it increasingly difficult to recruit the educated personnel dedicated to public service that he is convinced are necessary for the agency to maintain its high professional standards.

The agency is divided into five major arms or administrative sections, each with its own chief officer and promotion structure: (1) county law enforcement; (2) contract law enforcement, with personnel more or less permanently serving as law enforcement officers of the several municipalities that contract for these services; (3) corrections officers, who run the county jail; (4) service bureau staff, who provide law enforcement services such as forensics to all law enforcement agencies in the county; and (5) administrative staff personnel. Several different unions represent the various sections in contract negotiations and grievance resolution. Each section operates semi-independently; there is considerable infighting for resources and recognition; and the entire department is rife with bickering, charges of sexual harassment, and favoritism.

Two recent events have brought the unrest in the department to the boiling point. A female patrol officer involved in a high-speed chase collided with a family minivan, resulting in the death of one child and crippling injuries to other family members. In a second incident, an officer on patrol in an area of high crime and drug activity shot and killed a popular minority teenage athlete who, it turned out later, was not engaging in any criminal activity but was simply jogging home from a friend's house.

Both events received extensive regional press coverage. Community leaders were highly vocal in their demands for retribution against the two officers, both of whom had been placed on paid administrative leave. Union leaders of the police officers' union were demanding that the department not punish the officers and threatened to call a district-wide strike if both officers were not immediately reinstated. The department was in the middle of labor negotiations with the staff of the local corrections facility; their union was demanding equal pay and benefits with those of serving patrol officers. They threatened a strike if their demands were not met. The chief of the agency resigned his office.

The new director of the agency wondered if an organizational development program, including team building and staff cross-training and employee empowerment, might ease tensions, renew employee commitment, and help in staff retention. Before he could begin such a program, however, he needed a better picture of the culture and operating climate of the organization. He has contracted with your research team to conduct the study.

Questions

1. Is an ethnographic research design appropriate here? Why or why not?
2. Describe in some detail how you propose to conduct your research, making sure you begin with a clear statement of your research objective(s).
3. What would you do if you wanted information about trends in public service employee retirement?

SUMMARY

The new social scientists that emerged in the eighteenth and nineteenth centuries were curious about primitive societies and the effects of industrialization on children, families, and the working poor. This resulted in research efforts to understand why social problems occurred and what could (or *ought* to) be done to change society in order to improve the lot of the poor and disenfranchised. Adding to this curiosity was news about many strange and unknown societies and cultures.

Sociology evolved as a way to conduct systematic investigations into the newly emerging industrial society and the litany of social ills that was seen as an unwanted by-product of the industrialization process. Early attempts at establishing a systematic way of explaining human behavior and mental aberrations resulted in the creation of the science of psychology. Building on a tradition born from early travel stories and a scientific way of looking at indigenous cultures, another group of scholars forged the new social science of anthropology.

Through an eclectic process of trial and error, anthropologists and sociologists developed a way of conducting research that allowed them to meet their study objectives in all kinds of social and cultural settings. The name given to this method was *ethnography.* Researchers in public administration have also adopted this method of research.

Ethnographers often live, work, and play for long periods of time with the members of the group under study. Their aim is to be absorbed into the group, with the underlying objective of becoming accepted as a nonthreatening or nonintrusive member of the group so that events and interrelationships unfold as if the observer were not in attendance. This process, called "gaining entry," is the key to a successful research project.

The process of living with a social group during fieldwork involves observing and recording individuals' behaviors. The ethnographer summarizes these field notes into a larger descriptive generalization that purports to describe the behavior of the larger society. The researcher must then develop *subjective descriptions* that are based on a large number of *generalizations.* In making these generalizations, the ethnographer moves from the *specific* to the *general.* That is, the behaviors of one or a small group are used to infer that those behaviors are also those of larger groups in similar circumstances. The ethnographer should also develops *interpretations* of the observed behaviors; the question "why" should be answered to the best of the ethnographer's ability.

SUGGESTED READING

Alasuutari, Pertti. 1995. *Researching Culture: Qualitative Method and Cultural Studies.* London: Sage.
Bernard, H. Russell. 1995. *Research Methods in Anthropology.* 2nd ed. Walnut Creek, CA: Alta Mira Press.
Fetterman, David M. 1989. *Ethnography: Step by Step.* Newbury Park, CA: Sage.
Fox, Richard G. 1977. *Urban Anthropology: Cities in Their Cultural Settings.* Englewood Cliffs, NJ: Prentice Hall.
Gray, Ann. 2003. *Research Practice for Cultural Studies: Ethnographic Methods and Lived Cultures.* London: Sage.

26

CRITICAL RESEARCH:
ACTION RESEARCH APPROACHES

Action research is a way of initiating *change* in social systems—societies, communities, organizations, or groups—by involving members of the group in on the research process. The researcher first examines the way the group functions and the problems affecting the group, and then helps members of the group bring about the needed change that they perceive is right for them.

THE CONTRIBUTIONS OF LEWIN AND DEWEY

The term "action research" was first used in 1948 by Kurt Lewin to describe an approach to solving practical problems in social groups. He described action research as taking place over four distinct steps: planning, executing, reconnaissance, and evaluating (Kuhne and Quigley 1997; Lewin 1948). His approach was characterized by a combination of research and theory building (Cunningham 1995). Lewin's perception of the change process included collaborative research between the social science researcher and the client. Lewin saw the method as *empirical research*—that is, an *applied* approach to social research, as opposed to a pure science or purely theoretical approach.

Lewin and his team of researchers at the University of Iowa and later at the Massachusetts Institute of Technology maintained a practical, participatory democracy focus in their research by studying citizens' participation in solving community problems. For example, early in the United States' participation in World War II, anthropologist Margaret Mead invited him to do research with her for the Committee on Food Habits of the National Research Council. Lewin and his team began a series of studies to determine (1) the food consumption habits of Americans at the time, and (2) the best way to get people to change their eating habits in order to improve nutrition and to make up for widespread food shortages. Working under Lewin's direction, researchers at Iowa had recently completed a set of behavioral studies in autocratic and democratic situations, mostly through a series of experiments with preteenage boys. Applying that methodology to the food studies, Lewin took the early steps in what he was to call *action research*—the experimental application of social science to advancing democratic processes (Marrow 1997).

One of the most important conclusions to emerge from this research was that groups of people can do a thing better when they themselves decide to do it and when they also decide how they themselves will reduce the gap between their attitudes and actions (Marrow 1997, 130–131).

This emphasis on encouraging citizen participation is one of the reasons that action research is interesting to public administrators. Despite this interest, however, very little pure action research is conducted directly by or for public administrators. However, the action research approach has become widely accepted among social psychologists, sociologists, social workers, and educators, many of whom plan and conduct research on topics of interest to public administrators and managers of nonprofit organizations.

To summarize, action research is a form of inductive, practical research that focuses on improving understanding of a social problem and on achieving a real change or improvement in the way people function in groups through a collaborative effort (Kuhne and Quigley 1997).

John Dewey was another early contributor to the development of action research. However, rather than focusing on social organizations, Dewey was primarily concerned with the role of education in the process of becoming socialized. Born in 1859 and both a high school and university teacher, Dewey wanted to improve educational processes as a tool for teaching democracy and participation in democratic living. Lewin drew upon Dewey's philosophical writings in coming up with the action research approach that is now used for research in education, psychology, sociology, and other related disciplines.

Dewey was interested in developing theory, but theory that guided the *practice* of education and learning. Dewey also believed that by participating in democratic activities in classrooms, the large number of children of immigrant families flooding public schools in the early 1900s could learn concepts, ideas, and skills needed for cooperative living (Schmuck 1997). The work of Dewey sparked an interest in action research among educators in the 1950s. That interest quickly waned, however, and did not reemerge until publication in 1967 of Robert Schefer's *The School as a Center of Inquiry,* in which Schefer recommended use of action-oriented collaborative research by teachers (Quigley 1997). Today, because of its focus on early intervention and process improvement, action research has become one of the most popular qualitative research methods used in education. According to Quigley, "[T]he movement has . . . grown to form a growing counterhegemony to traditional teacher preparation programs in public education and, more important . . . to traditional scientific positivism and the academic control of knowledge" (p. 10).

Action research in education is conducted in the same way as it is in other fields of study. For example, in their *Guide to Research for Educators,* Merriam and Simpson (1984) identified a six-step process for conducting action research projects: analyzing the situation, getting the facts, identifying the problem, planning an intervention process, taking action on the problem, then repeating the cycle as new concepts and information emerge from the process.

FIVE MODELS OF ACTION RESEARCH

Today, at least five different models of action research are used by researchers in the human and administrative sciences. Small (1995) identified four of the models: (1) traditional action research, (2) participatory action research, (3) empowerment research, and (4) feminist research. Although not discussed by Small, *action science* is a fifth model used in action-based research. Each of these models is discussed in this chapter. These models and their relationships are displayed in Figure 26.1. Traditional action research, participatory research, and action science will be discussed in this chapter; empowerment and feminist research will be discussed in chapter 27.

Traditional Action Research

The *action research* model developed from the work of Lewin and others. This model took shape during the 1930s and 1940s. A victim of Nazi discrimination that ended his opportunity to participate fully in an academic career in Germany, Kurt Lewin immigrated to the United States

Figure 26.1   **A Schematic Display of Five Models of Action Research**

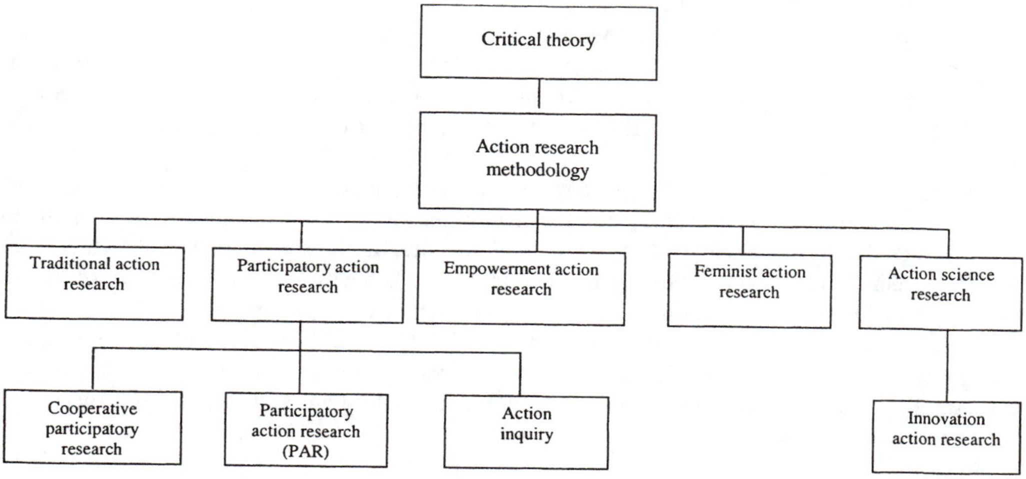

```
                              ┌─────────────────┐
                              │ Critical theory │
                              └────────┬────────┘
                                       │
                              ┌────────┴────────┐
                              │ Action research │
                              │   methodology   │
                              └────────┬────────┘
      ┌───────────┬───────────┬────────┴────────┬───────────┬───────────┐
┌───────────┐ ┌───────────┐ ┌───────────┐ ┌───────────┐ ┌───────────┐
│Traditional│ │Participat-│ │Empowerment│ │ Feminist  │ │  Action   │
│  action   │ │ory action │ │  action   │ │  action   │ │  science  │
│ research  │ │ research  │ │ research  │ │ research  │ │ research  │
└───────────┘ └─────┬─────┘ └───────────┘ └───────────┘ └─────┬─────┘
      ┌─────────────┼──────────────┐                          │
┌───────────┐ ┌───────────┐ ┌───────────┐              ┌───────────┐
│Cooperative│ │Participat-│ │  Action   │              │Innovation │
│participat-│ │ory action │ │  inquiry  │              │  action   │
│    ory    │ │ research  │ │           │              │ research  │
│ research  │ │   (PAR)   │ │           │              │           │
└───────────┘ └───────────┘ └───────────┘              └───────────┘
```

in 1933. Reflecting on his experiences in Europe, he designed a field of research that looked at how democracy can disappear under the influence of a powerful, charismatic leader. Lewin was convinced that social science could strengthen democracy, and searching for ways to make that happen became his life's work.

In the traditional action research approach established by Lewin and his followers, the researcher's primary objective is to help change dysfunctional social institutions, such as communities, while also contributing to the general fund of theory and knowledge. Lewin was convinced that researchers should be concerned with two kinds of knowing: (1) general laws of human and organizational behavior, and (2) specific information about the institution or system that is the focus of the change effort.

Gabel (1995, 1), building upon Lewin, Dewey, and other early contributors to the action research approach, described traditional action research as "an informal, qualitative, formative, subjective, interpretive, reflective, and experimental model of inquiry in which all individuals involved in the study are knowing and contributing participants." He saw subject involvement in the process as a key characteristic of the research approach.

Although it is usually considered to fall into a postpositivist tradition, no specific methodology is associated with action research; both quantitative and qualitative data are relevant for action research. However, the approach may be characterized by the following traditional practices.

First, data gathered in an action research study may be of any type and can be gathered by such different methods as structured survey questionnaires, simple observation, or unstructured personal or focus group interviews. Second, because of its interventionist nature, action research is always conducted in the location or setting of the social problem and usually involves the entire group (a universe) rather than a sample. Third, it usually focuses on a single case or organizational unit. Fourth, the researcher collaborates with subjects who are members of the group under study. The researcher brings scientific and theoretical knowledge and skills to the project, while group members add important practical knowledge and experience with the situations that frame the study. Both parts of this knowledge picture are deemed essential for the action research process to work.

Participatory Action Research

Participatory action research is the second model described by Small (1995). Researchers employing this approach are typically concerned with three activities: research, education, and action. It owes much to the emergence of critical theory, in that a primary goal of participatory research is to effect a fundamental, emancipating change in a society. Participatory research developed from social movements among oppressed societies in the Third World, including Africa, Asia, and Latin America.

Participatory research has also gained a strong foothold in North America. For example, a four-year study participatory research study with residents of the town of North Bonneville in Washington was conducted in the early 1970s (Comstock and Fox 1993). Groups of students and faculty from The Evergreen State College in Olympia, Washington, worked with some 450 residents of a town that was scheduled for demolition to make room for a new dam spillway and power plant.

During initial meetings with town residents, the U.S. Corps of Engineers refused to consider moving the town, and instead offered payments for residents to move to other areas. Comstock and Fox described how residents overcame a critical hurtle in their path to achieving success in their dealings with the Corps:

> Very early in the struggle, the residents discovered the contradiction between the Corps's meaning of community and their own. To the Corps the community was individuals and physical structures. This ignored the reality of community values, attachments to the land, and social networks. Through a careful description of their community, the residents gained a more articulate description of their community and vitality as a community. (p. 121)

Once residents learned how the Corps perceived the community and its residents and how Corps agents were using the agency's control of information as a wedge to divide citizen opinion, they moved to acquire technical information on their own. They then provided that technical information to everyone in a way that could be understood, thus breaking down the Corps' monopoly of ideas. The town eventually won its fight to survive; the Corps of Engineers did build a new town in the location wanted by residents of the old town. The new city of North Bonneville was officially dedicated in July 1976.

Researchers using the participatory action model believe that if, through education, members of a society become aware of better ways to function, they will bring about the change themselves. Thus, a key part of the research process is helping community members become active participants in their study and its action aftermath. Participants are expected to take primary responsibility for the study, including its overall design, data gathering and analysis, and eventual distribution of the findings.

Small (1995, 943) made the following special note of the part that political activity plays in the participatory action approach:

> Participatory researchers are openly and explicitly political. Their ideology emphasizes large-scale structural forces, conflicts of interest, and the need to overcome oppression and inequality through transforming the existing social order. The lack of access to useful and valued forms of knowledge by oppressed or disenfranchised peoples is viewed as a major problem that can be overcome through the research process.

Comstock and Fox (1993, 123) also noted the political nature of the participatory action approach in their conclusions about how the people of North Bonneville were changed by the experience:

Perhaps the most striking result of the North Bonneville experience has been the degree to which a self-sustaining political process was initiated. . . . The growth of self-direction continued as residents, no longer content with their original demand that a new town be planned and built for them, demanded (and got) control over the design of their own community.

Finally, a key distinguishing characteristic of this approach is an emphasis upon empowering the people within the group or community, making it possible for them to take control of their study. In time, the researchers are expected to back away in order to follow the lead of the participants, rather than the reverse.

Action Science

Action science is the model of action research used most often in public administration and other organizational settings. While it was not discussed in Small's overview, this approach clearly deserves an equal place alongside all other action research models. Chris Argyris and others developed the action science approach from the earlier contributions of Kurt Lewin, who contributed greatly to the field of group dynamics (an area of study in social psychology), and of John Dewey, who proposed separating science and practice in education. The contributions of Dewey and Lewin on the separation of diagnosis of an organization from practioner intervention became the concept of using research to bring about change (Argyris, Putnam, and Smith 1985; Schein 1996). In this model, diagnosis of a problem by research is always followed by participant-led intervention (change).

Action science has been described specifically as an *intervention method* that is based on the idea that people can improve their interpersonal and organizational effectiveness by examining the underlying beliefs that guide their actions (Raelin 1997). As White (1999, 142) and others have noted, this phase may also take the form of *evaluation:* "The evaluation of social situations is the point of any action theory, which strives to help actors understand their situations in a different light and to make value judgments about whether or not their situations should be changed."

Lewin never explicitly defined an action science method as such—he retained instead the label *action research.* However, his early work in developing approaches to interventions and change in social organizations led subsequent researchers to give him credit for development of most of the techniques involved in the approach (Argyris, Putnam and Smith 1985; Schein 1995). Argyris proposed the action science concept because: (1) then-current applications of action research were ignoring the theory-building element of the original approach, and (2) he believed that the practice of following traditional, positivist approaches to research was self-limiting and harmful to the growth of knowledge. Today, the two terms are usually used synonymously, together with other closely related variations such as "action learning" (Raelin 1997), "action inquiry"(Reason 1998), and "innovation action research" (Kaplan 1998), to name just a few.

ACTION RESEARCH AND CRITICAL THEORY

Philosophically, action research is closely related to the *critical theory* approach to research; both seek intervention in social organizations for the purpose of helping people (clients) find better ways of living, socializing, and functioning in groups. Argyris, Putnam, and Smith (1985, 234) even go so far as to consider this approach a kind of critical theory. However, despite their similar roots, they are not the same. Critical theory and research evolved from the emancipatory tradition of Marx and Freud. It was ultimately refined in the 1920s by Habermas and others of the Frankfurt School. Action research, on the other hand, has its roots in Kurt Lewin's work in participatory democracy and the education systems research of John Dewey.

The *Frankfurt School* is the name given to a group of philosophers who expressed their dissatisfaction with traditional epistemology and its positivist theory by constructing a new philosophy of social science. Today, that new philosophy of science is called *postpositivism*. The name given to the new type of theory associated with the new postpositivist realm is *critical theory*. The Frankfurt School believed that critical theory has three fundamental characteristics that distinguish it from traditional positivist theory (Geuss 1981, 1–2):

1. Critical theories guide human action in two ways:

    a. They enlighten the people who have them, enabling these agents to determine for themselves what their true interests are.
    b. They are inherently emancipatory; they free people from coercion, which may be partially self-imposed and based in ignorance of better ways to exist.

2. Critical theories are forms of knowledge. Hence, *education* precedes emancipation.
3. Critical theories have a different epistemological basis from the theories that exist in the natural sciences: critical theories are "reflective," whereas theories in the natural sciences are "objective."

To summarize, a critical theory is a reflective theory that gives people ("agents") a knowledge that is inherently enlightening and emancipating. Critical researchers help humans in social systems discover their own ways to change their world—that is, to become *emancipated*—whereas action researchers participate with groups to bring about improvement in the way the group functions. What brings the two approaches near to one another is their focus on bringing about social change.

Despite their differences, the two concepts are often combined into a single research design. DePoy and Hartman (1999, 560), for example, developed what they called a "model for social work knowing founded on the tenets of critical theory synthesized with principles and practices from action research." They applied the model to a case analysis of the Maine Adolescent Transition (MAT) project. The objective of the MAT was to provide at-risk adolescents access to vital health care services. The model identifies a twelve-step process, as follows:

1. Identify a social problem.
2. Convene a steering committee with representation from all stakeholder groups.
3. Identify [delimit] the scope of the research.
4. Select a specific set of research questions to guide conduct of the study.
5. Determine specific change objectives for the study group.
6. Select a collaborative research team (including lay and professional researcher membership).
7. Train nonprofessional researchers in designing, conducting, and using inquiry.
8. Design the inquiry, with specific research questions and analysis strategy.
9. Conduct inquiry and analysis.
10. Report findings in accessible formats to all stakeholder groups.
11. Submit findings.
12. Identify further areas for inquiry.

The Glanz Action Research Primer

Jeffrey Glanz (1999) prepared a small but informative "primer" on action research for adminis-trators, in which he identified just four steps for the process. The first step is to select a focus for the study by knowing what to investigate, developing questions to ask, and establishing a plan to acquire answers to the questions. The second step is to collect some data, but only after you narrow your focus to a specific area of concern; data may be collected using either quantitative or qualitative approaches, or both. A key part of this step is to organize the data so that they can be shared with other readers after the study is completed. The third step is to analyze and interpret the data in order to arrive at some decision. Making a decision is preliminary to the fourth and final step, initiating some action. The project is not complete until this occurs; *corrective action* is fundamental to the idea of action research.

KEY THEMES IN ACTION RESEARCH

In their important work on the philosophical underpinnings of action science, Argyris, Putnam, and Smith (1985, 8–9) identified five key themes of the process from the writings of Kurt Lewin and others. While these themes were applied specifically to the action science model, they are clearly applicable to the other action research models as well. The themes are:

1. *Collaboration in resolution of the problem.* Action science (research) deals with processes and efforts to bring about *change* in real social systems. It targets a specific problem and then provides assistance to the client organization in resolving the problem.
2. *Problem identification, planning, and acting.* Action research proceeds through repetitive cycles of problem identification, planning, acting, and evaluation.
3. *Educating and reeducating.* Change in the social group or organization involves a pro-cess of *educating* and/or *re-educating* group members. This means changing the way people in the group think and act. Thus, the process works at reforming organizational culture. For reeducation to work, all actors in the organization must participate in the diagnosis and fact-finding stage of the process and contribute to identification of new ways of acting.
4. *Democratic participation and action.* Action research maintains a strong commitment to the idea of *democratic* action in improving group behavior and effectiveness. Thus, the method involves questioning the status quo from the perspective of democratic values.
5. *Theory-building and practical application.* Two key objectives of all action research are to contribute to basic knowledge in social science by developing theory and to improve action in social organizations.

PHASES OF PLANNED CHANGE

Ronald Lippitt, a student of Lewin and collaborator on much of his research, published *The Dynam-ics of Planned Change* in 1958, six years after Lewin's death. In that work Lippitt and colleagues identified seven phases of planned change (Figure 26.2).

In *Phase 1,* someone associated with the social group recognizes that a problem of some type exists. This could be anything from an external threat to the organization's existence to a func-tional barrier that hinders effectiveness and fosters frustration. An example is the diagnostic action research study for a federal supply service office conducted by McNabb and Sepic in 1995. The unit had been required to reorganize for implementation of a total quality management program.

Figure 26.2 **Seven Phases of Planned Change**

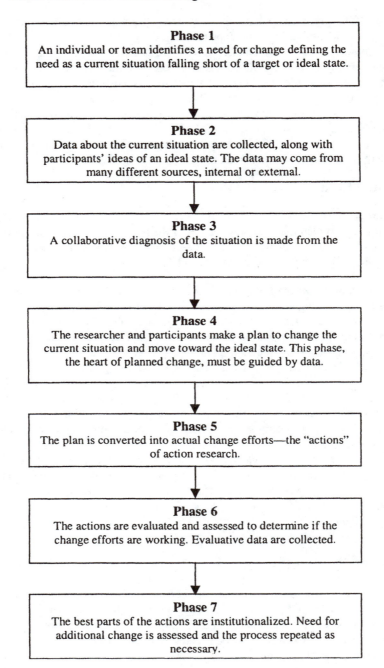

Source: Adapted from R.A. Schmuck 1997, 143.

Five very different functions, with different organizational cultures and traditions, were to merge into one functioning department. Unit leaders and long-term employees were balking at making the change. The leader of one unit refused to accept the stalemate and called the researchers in to help the group find a common ground for problem resolution.

In *Phase 2,* data about the situation are collected. In the federal supply office example, this phase began with a series of meetings, with representatives from all five units present at all sessions. This group became an ad hoc research advisory team, with membership remaining constant throughout the length of the project.

These sessions were tape-recorded, with transcripts circulated to all members for their concurrence and approval before moving on to other problem areas. The group then agreed upon a set of nine problem areas common to the majority of the units that needed to be addressed. These problem areas served as constructs for the collaborative development of a comprehensive survey instrument. Unit leaders then administered the instrument to their own staffs.

In *Phase 3,* a diagnosis of the situation is made from the collected data. In this example, the research team conducted a preliminary analysis of the combined group discussion and questionnaire data. This was shared with members of the ad hoc advisory committee, with their interpretations solicited. With all data collected and both the research team and group participants in general agreement, a composite diagnostic report was prepared. Copies were distributed downward through the organization and upward to the organization's management personnel.

In *Phase 4,* both the researchers and the participants collaborate on a plan that outlines the action steps to be taken to resolve organizational issues and remove barriers to change. This step is considered to be the "heart" of the action research effort. Only action steps that address problems specifically identified in the diagnostic phase should be included in the plan. Once a set of proposed steps is agreed upon, everyone collaborates in setting priorities.

Phase 5 is the action phase in the action research process. Plans must be converted into actual change actions. In this example, the agency's dismal record in two broad areas of organizational climate was a barrier to improving employees' commitment and their willingness to accept a mandated change for which they had not been consulted. The change actions the agency followed to remove the barriers were making substantial improvements to its Rewards and Recognition program, and to work with department administrators to discover and implement improvements in the perceived human resource areas of Warmth and Support (McNabb and Sepic 1995). It is important to remember that neither the researcher nor the agency's senior management should be the ones to suggest specific changes. Rather, in order to succeed, these suggestions must come from the entire organization staff. The researcher's role from this phase on is to function only as a catalyst for internally generated change.

Phase 6 is the evaluation state; it begins with implementation of the change initiatives and continues through their complete acceptance or rejection into the organization. This often requires conducting additional research. Suchman (1967, 31) identified the following six ingredients as essential for an evaluation to be successful:

1. Clear identification of the change goals that are being evaluated
2. Analysis of the organizational or societal problem with which the activity was designed to cope
3. Thorough description and definition of the change activities
4. Measurement of the degree of change that took place
5. Determination of whether the observed change is due to the activity or to some other cause
6. Some indication of the durability of the effects

In *Phase 7,* the best parts of the change actions are made part of the continuing operating climate of the group. Those actions that meet with majority acceptance and approval can be expected to eventually become part of the long-term culture of the organization, accepted as "part of the way we do things around here" and passed on the new members of the group. Where actions result in only superficial or cosmetic change, the members of the group must devise and try new change initiatives in a dynamic process of continuous evolution.

GOALS OF ACTION RESEARCH

The primary goal of all action research in public administration is to come up with the information that is needed for government action. This information is often called "practical" or "everyday" knowledge. Action research has particular value in the following four public administration applications:

1. Action research is well suited as a method of *identifying citizens' needs* in a community, with the added benefit of producing potential solutions for attaining the resources necessary to meet those needs.
2. Through its ability to generate knowledge, it is an excellent way of gaining the guidance necessary to *design the most effective programs* to meet citizens' needs.
3. Action research, because of its interventionist nature, is a highly appropriate means of carrying out *organizational development* activities and programs.
4. Finally, following in the tradition of early emancipatory theory, action research can play a very important role in *community development and redevelopment efforts.*

Achieving the Action Goal

To achieve their goal, action researchers gather data in many different ways. Among the most commonly used tools are group discussions, role-playing, unstructured interviews, and case discussions. A list of data-gathering methods identified by Argyris, Putnam, and Smith (1985) identified the following tools:

1. Observations accompanied by audio taping,
2. Interviews,
3. Action experiments, and
4. Participant-written cases.

They also noted that action researchers often rely on all four methods, but may have different purposes in mind when they select one over another. Common to all of these and other data-gathering methods used in action research are the following three critical characteristics:

1. The data must be generated in a way that makes participants feel causally responsible for them
2. Each method is structured to elicit data on how participants actually act and what they are thinking and feeling at the time
3. Action experiments (such as role-playing) should be used to "unfreeze" people's reasoning and reactions. (p. 239–241)

In all of the ways that data are gathered in an action research or action science project, the key to gathering the needed data is to *engage participants in free and open narrative discussions.* When people are discussing the problems of their organization, they are engaging in a cathartic activity. In this way, "talk *is* action" (Argyris, Putnam, and Smith 1985, 57).

SUMMARY

Action research is a way of initiating *change* in social systems—societies, communities, organizations, or groups—by involving members of the group in the research process. The researcher studies the way the group functions, identifies the problem, and helps members of the group bring about the needed change that they perceive is right for them.

An emphasis on encouraging citizen participation is one of the reasons that action research is interesting to public administrators. Despite this interest, however, very little pure action research is conducted directly by or for public administrators. However, the action research approach has become widely accepted among social psychologists, sociologists, social workers, and educators, many of whom plan and conduct research on topics of interest to public administrators and managers of nonprofit organizations.

Today, researchers use at least five different models of action research in the human and administrative sciences: (1) traditional action research, (2) participatory action research, (3) empowerment research, (4) feminist research, and (5) action science or action inquiry.

EXERCISES

Exercise 26.1: Learner Participation in a Homeless Shelter

You have been employed as a literacy instructor at a long-term homeless shelter for women in a town on the outskirts of a large Midwestern city. Residents have their own bedrooms, but share all other common areas. Residents prepare their own meals. After several weeks on your new job, you realize that many of the residents are reluctant to leave their rooms to attend your classes. The literacy program—called *Getting Active*—includes instruction on life-skill building and can lead to a GED certificate (Kalinosky 1997).

You decide to meet with the director of the center to discuss the problems you are having in reaching all the residents who might benefit from your efforts. With her support, you decide that a research project is needed to determine why some residents are not participating.

To begin, you enlist several former participants who successfully completed the program to form the nucleus of a research advisory committee. These members recruit several nonparticipants to join them in designing a research project. The new advisory committee is scheduled to hold its first meeting tonight.

Questions

1. Prepare an agenda of the items you plan to go over at the first meeting of the advisory committee.
2. State your research question and outline several objectives for your research.
3. Is an action research project an appropriate research methodology for meeting these research objectives?

Exercise 26.2: Introducing Innovation

The manager of the city's Office of Budgets and Planning has expressed frustration with the existing cost and performance measurement systems used in this West Coast town of 250,000 residents (Kaplan 1998). For as long as can be remembered, department managers have been using traditional, standard, direct labor-based costing standards in forecasting project costs. They also use a monthly system of financial variance reporting. According to the budget director, the apparent driving force in the city has been: Keep doing things we have always done them, and stay on budget!

The manager recently attended a weeklong seminar and workshop on activity-based accounting and balanced scorecard evaluation systems (Kaplan and Norton 1996). At the seminar, participants received a copy of a 1998 article by Kaplan, "Innovation Action Research: Creating New Management Theory and Practice." The manager wonders if an action research project can be used to help the city's department managers accept and adopt innovative costing and performance measurements.

Questions

1. How can action research play a role in helping the budget director introduce innovation and change into the city administration—and make sure that it lasts?
2. Who should participate in a collaborative action research project in the city?

ADDITIONAL READING

Argyris, Chris, Robert Putnam, and Diana McLain Smith. 1985. *Action Science*. San Francisco: Jossey-Bass.
Geuss, Raymond. 1981. *The Idea of a Critical Theory: Habermas and the Frankfurt School*. Cambridge: Cambridge University Press.

27

CRITICAL RESEARCH:
EMPOWERMENT AND FEMINIST MODELS

This chapter addresses two critical quantitative research approaches outlined earlier: empowerment and feminist research. Empowerment research is concerned with helping subservient groups break the chain of exploitation and take action to help themselves. This model has its foundations in the research on the psychology of communities carried out by Lewin and other social psychologists. Feminist research was identified by Small (1995) as one of the four types of action-oriented research as first proposed by Kurt Lewin in the 1940s. Its underlying goal is to conduct research without a gender bias. Both of these approaches are associated with interpretive research methods, with some advocates stressing a complete break with positivist, quantitative methods (Sarantakos 2004; Westmarland 2001). This chapter begins with a brief review of the empowerment model and concludes with a more detailed examination of the feminist approach.

Before proceeding with this discussion, however, it should be pointed out that most research in public administration and nonprofit operations still follows a positivist model. Nontraditional approaches such as these types of critical research are still somewhat exploratory, although the feminist approach has made substantial strides toward becoming "mainstream." Schulz and Mullings commented on this state of affairs in *Gender, Race, Class, and Health* (2006, 22):

> At this time in the United States [2005], traditional methodologies remain highly valued, while many other countries rely more on qualitative and consensus studies in setting their public policy agendas and enacting corresponding legislation. The current U.S. Congress is calling for, and in some cases requiring, very narrow "scientific" research designs and protocols that focus on "proving" cause and effect—a troubling and obviously political move.

EMPOWERMENT RESEARCH

Empowerment research is a tool to aid people in gaining mastery over their own affairs. Small (1995) defined *empowerment* as being concerned with individuals and groups who are excluded by the majority on the basis of their demographic characteristics or their physical or emotional difficulties.

Empowerment research may be a particularly relevant model for research in the nonprofit sector. Because the focus of many nonprofits is on aiding minorities and society's less-advantaged citizens, successful empowerment research may help managers of these organizations significantly improve the conditions of their clients.

The selective focus of most empowerment research that has been published thus far supports this conclusion. Empowerment research typically addresses issues of mental health, citizen involvement, sexuality, and community health problems. Certainly these topics are of interest to public administrators, but declining resources coupled with greater demands on their efforts have led to the private and nonprofit sectors handling much of the service load in these areas. As a result, managers at nonprofit organizations have had to adopt many of the research methods first developed in the social sciences—if not to conduct the research themselves, then to know how to purchase and evaluate research conducted by private contractors.

How Empowerment Research Works

The empowerment research approach begins with the researcher identifying or creating situations in which a group has been silent and/or isolated—the "outsiders" of a society, an organization, or a community. As the researcher helps these outsiders understand the underlying issues, they gain a voice in and power over the decisions that affect them. The process is designed to *empower* people.

Page and Czuba (1999, 3) addressed this issue from the perspective of using extension education to empower citizens. They defined the process of empowerment thus:

> [Empowerment is a] multi-dimensional social process that helps people gain control over their own lives. It is a process that fosters power (that is, the capacity to implement) in people, for use in their own lives, their communities, and in their society, by acting on issues that they define as important.

Page and Czuba defined empowerment as multidimensional, socially embedded, and a continuing process. According to Page and Czuba, *multidimensionality* means that the process involves elements of sociology, psychology, the economy, and other components that shape a society. They also noted that the empowerment process occurs at the individual, group, and community levels, often concurrently. Empowerment is a social process because it takes place with individuals acting and reacting with one another; it cannot occur in isolation. The process begins at a starting point and works through a series of phases toward accomplishing an identified goal. Finally, they emphasized that the fundamental tenet of empowerment is the collaborative activity between individuals and a community or group.

The Collaborative Nature of Empowerment Research

Empowerment research is necessarily collaborative in nature. Researchers work with members of the group to identify group strengths and resources that may have not been recognized. As they become empowered, group members achieve control over the internal and external forces that affect them. The process focuses on bringing out the natural abilities and skills of the members of the group under study. Rather than focusing on group members' weaknesses, empowerment research aims at bringing their strengths to the fore and provides guidance in putting those strengths to work.

For the empowerment research team, the process is often long and time-consuming but is personally rewarding. Disenfranchised citizens or those under pressure are often loath to take up the fight again after having failed in previous efforts. The outside research team can turn those attitudes around. When the outsiders see that there is someone with a genuine and lasting interest in helping them to help themselves, their world can be turned upside down. However, the individuals make the transition from subjugation to empowerment on their own. As Page and Czuba concluded, the researchers "cannot give people power and . . . cannot make them empowered." The researchers can only supply the resources, opportunities, encouragement, and support—people need to make the change on their own.

Empowerment research is not without its problems and potential pitfalls. Myron Glazer (1972, 59) discussed one of the most damaging of these pitfalls in his volume on field research:

> Field workers often immerse themselves in societies characterized by deeply rooted social inequality. Indeed, this problem and its solution have long captured the imagination and dedication of social [and administrative] scientists, yet the analysis of human suffering places a special burden on researchers. They are constantly plagued by their own feelings of bitterness and anger. Their very scholarly detachment and struggles for objectivity often lead to a profound sense of guild and impotence. Some field workers hope to strike back through their writing. Others, less patient, more action oriented, join the downtrodden and suffer their fate.

THE EMPOWERMENT RESEARCH PROCESS

Critical research, including empowerment research, takes place in a series of six steps (Kuhne and Quigley 1997). These steps are further grouped into three distinct phases. The first phase, *planning,* includes steps one, two and three. Phase two, *action,* involves implementation of an intervention or program and is the single most critical step in this phase. Finally, the third phase, *reflection,* covers steps five and six. In step five, the researchers and community or group engage in an evaluation of their progress. The last step in this process involves implementing any changes that emerge after evaluation of the activities conducted to that point. The relationship between these six steps and three phases is displayed in Figure 27.1.

First Phase Actions

The first phase in the empowerment approach to critical research involves three key foundational steps. The first step is observing and working with the community to develop an understanding of the problem that includes many possible causes and solutions. This step may result in proposals that are completely unrealistic or even impossible in terms of time, resources, or objectives. The research team will need to help community participants focus their efforts on resolving the most onerous policies and practices they face. This task requires setting and agreeing upon priorities.

Developing an understanding of the problem involves conducting extensive interviews with group members to bring out the subjects' perceptions of the problem and its possible causes. The research team then arranges for community participants to discuss these perceptions in order to arrive at a group consensus.

In collaborative transformation actions such as empowerment research, the researcher's perception of the problem is not nearly as important as how the participants view it. If the study group does not agree on a problem and the action to take for solution, the researcher may become a part of the problem rather than a contributor to a solution. Gathering the benchmark information may involve brainstorming with participants and other researchers, exploring the published professional literature, and often, simple observation of the group. Finally, the researcher and group participants must decide together whether the problem is significant enough to warrant the study.

Figure 27.1   **Phases and Steps of Critical Research**

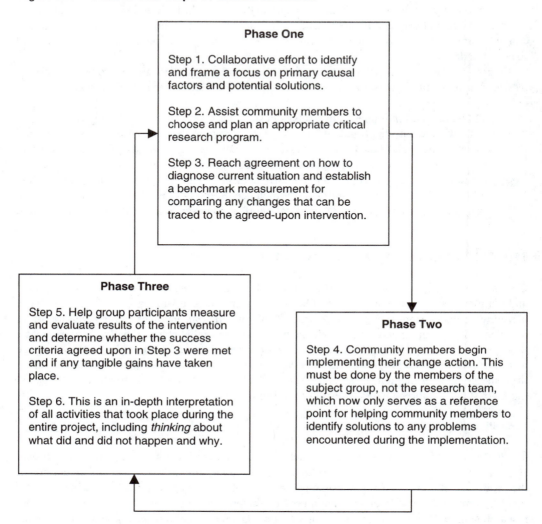

Phase One

Step 1. Collaborative effort to identify and frame a focus on primary causal factors and potential solutions.

Step 2. Assist community members to choose and plan an appropriate critical research program.

Step 3. Reach agreement on how to diagnose current situation and establish a benchmark measurement for comparing any changes that can be traced to the agreed-upon intervention.

Phase Three

Step 5. Help group participants measure and evaluate results of the intervention and determine whether the success criteria agreed upon in Step 3 were met and if any tangible gains have taken place.

Step 6. This is an in-depth interpretation of all activities that took place during the entire project, including *thinking* about what did and did not happen and why.

Phase Two

Step 4. Community members begin implementing their change action. This must be done by the members of the subject group, not the research team, which now only serves as a reference point for helping community members to identify solutions to any problems encountered during the implementation.

Source: Includes elements from Kuhne and Quigley 1997, 28.

Defining and planning the project is the second step in the first phase of the empowerment research process. The most important part of this planning activity is deciding how to deal with the problem at hand. In a collaborative research activity, this means getting the participants to agree on the intervention program they want to implement and then organizing the group for action. The end result of this step should be getting group members ready to not only put in the required effort, but also to accept change of any kind. Finally, it also entails agreeing on how individual participants will be involved in the action phase of the process and what action will be taken in the event of the program's failure to achieve the desired results.

Determining the measurements is the third step in the first phase. This step is the diagnostic stage of critical research. In order to know if something has been improved, if it is "better" in some way, the researcher must have a *benchmark* against which to measure any change. A benchmark is a clear, comprehensive description of the way things were prior to an intervention. This process includes specifying what will be measured during the evaluation stage of the research program. In addition to knowing what to measure, it will also be necessary to determine *when* to measure and how long the intervention should run before an evaluation occurs. There is no set answer to these questions; timing is a function of the severity of the problem and the degree of participatory involvement. Lewin described this process in his 1947 paper on *Frontiers in Group Dynamics* (in Cartwright 1951, 224): "In discussing the means of bringing about a desired state of affairs one should not think in terms of the 'goal to be reached' but rather in terms of a change 'from the present level to the desired one'."

Second Phase Activity

The *action phase* is the only step in the second phase of the research program. Group members must implement the emancipation task, not the research team. The researcher's role is to function as a reference point, providing methodological advice if asked, but not leading or instigating the action. As in other action research, empowerment research involves collaboration and direct participation of the research subjects.

During this phase, it is important that the research team keep the group moving according to their initial plan. If in the opinion of the researchers, the plan will not generate an appropriate intervention or produce the desired change, the team can help the community group plan and initiate a second version of the activity—a contingency plan. Finally, to keep the research program focused on meeting the group's objectives, the research team must maintain good records of the intervention implementation, its effects, and how and in what form changes are generated.

Third Phase Activities

The third phase is the *reflection* part of the emancipatory research project. It includes the last two steps: *evaluating results* and *transitioning the change into the group or organization*. Evaluating the results of the change may take as long as or longer than the team's action. All aspects of the data collected before and during the action phase must be collected and studied. The research team must work closely with group participants to evaluate what the data reveal about the problem and results of the intervention. This includes determining whether the success criteria agreed upon in the third step of the second phase was met and then spelling out whatever tangible gains may have occurred, regardless of how small or great. If the problem is resolved, the project ends. If not, then the cycle is repeated at least once more. Action research cycles should continue until the desired change is accepted and functioning. Suchman (1967, 177) described what is involved in the evaluation process this way:

> What we evaluate is the action hypothesis that defined program activities will achieve specified, desired objectives through their ability to influence those intervening processes that affect the occurrence of these objectives. . . . An understanding of all three factors—program, objective, and intervening process—is essential to the conduct of (evaluation).

The last step in the third phase of the process is causing actual changes in the behavior and attitudes of the oppressor and oppressed groups or organizations. During this stage of the research, the research team and subjects also begin planning to carry the change initiative to the next level. The research team assists the community to think about what happened and didn't while preparing the group to continue on the path to emancipation after the research team has departed. This step includes answering such questions as: Did the project produce promising results? Do the promised changes reflect what is actually happening? Should another cycle of action research be initiated? Kuhne and Quigley (1997, 34) described this step as a process of "analyzing outcomes and revising plans for another cycle of acting."

The sixth step also involves putting together a final report of the entire process. This benefits group participants and any other researcher/participant team planning for a similar intervention. The report must be complete and in a format that everyone can understand. It should add to theoretical knowledge of change in groups and organizations and the action research process in general.

THE FEMINIST RESEARCH MODEL

The feminist approach has made significant contributions to our understanding of both public administration and nonprofit organizations. Feminist issues took center stage in many political theory studies during the turbulent 1970s. An initial goal of feminist research was to "document the dreadful history of misogynist statements" by male authors—statements that were considered to have justified the exclusion of women from the political realm and confined them to their homes (Saxonhouse 1993, 15–16). The feminist approach took on greater importance during the decade of 1980s, when it became the perspective of choice in many research studies on political theory. Galston (1993, 31) chronicled this phenomenon:

[No] story of political theory in the 1980s would be complete without stressing the extraordinary development and vitality of feminist thought. Its explorations ramified into all aspects of politics, society, personality, and inquiry; the constitution and construction of gender differences; the retrieval of neglected writers, agents, and questions, and the corresponding expansion or reconstitution of political theory theorizes about; the exploration of covert gender assumptions in theoretical categories such as the public/private distinction, rights, and justice; the examination of bias and discrimination in practical spheres structured by such categories; and the questioning of entire modes of philosophy and social inquiry . . . as gender-based and partial.

Research for Women by Women

Feminist research, according to Small (1995, 5), has as its primary goal "the promotion of the feminist agenda by challenging the male dominance and advocating the social, political, and economic equality of men and women." It has also been described as "research for women rather than about women" (Allen and Baber 1992).

Feminist researchers share with their fellow social scientists a concern for ethical issues, a belief in social justice, an ethic of compassion, and an awareness of the power of language to distort research subjects' experiences (Small 1995). Typical themes in feminist research are these papers from the April 2002 issue of the *International Feminist Journal of Politics:* Elisabeth Prügl's "Toward a Feminist Political Economics;" "Rewriting (Global) Political Economy as Reproductive, Productive, and Virtual (Foucauldian) Economics" by Peterson; and "The UN Approach to Harmful Traditional Practices" by Winter, Thompson, and Jeffreys.

Feminist research methodology is also common in public administration research. For example, two papers with feminist research foundations were published in the July/August 2002 issue of *Public Administration Review:* "Gender Differences in Agency Head Salaries: The Case of Public

Education," by Meier and Wilkins, and "Sex-Based Occupational Segregation in U.S. State Bureaucracies, 1987–97," by Kerr, Miller, and Reid. Six more papers with a feminist research approach can be found in this Winter/Spring issue of *The Brown Journal of World Affairs.*

A Feminist Research Focus

Small described the focus of feminist research as promoting the feminist agenda by challenging male dominance and advocating female and male social, political, and economic equality. As with all other models of action research, feminist research seeks to (1) bring about social change, (2) emancipate participants (i.e., women), and (3) enhance participants' lives. Sandra Harding (2006, 68) described how this multipart focus translates into actual research topics in more specific terms:

> Indeed many feminist research projects are "mission directed," that is, they are designed to produce solutions to pressing economic, legal, medical and health, political, or other problems that women encounter in some particular social context. Thus, these projects do not aim to discover value-neutral, transcendental truths. Yet, they do produce theoretical knowledge through such research. Indeed, for feminism, theoretical knowledge is also action in the world; how we conceptualize the world around us changes how we will interact with it and how others will interact with us.

Feminist researchers are more likely to adopt a postpositivist approach to their work, although there are no rules that make it the required epistemology. While some believe that a distinctive set of feminist methods should exist, others are less convinced that a purely feminist methodology is possible. According to Small, a third group argues that although no special feminist methodology currently exists, one is slowly being formed as more feminist research appears. Summarizing the feminist model, Small (1995, 947) concluded with the following statement:

> Feminist researchers share the values of overcoming oppression, empowering women, and transforming society so that equality between men and women can be achieved. The purpose of knowledge is to change or transform what is considered the patriarchal nature of society.

Arriving at the current focus of the feminist research perspective has been an evolutionary process, including contributions from liberal, Marxist, and radical political philosophies and the ideas of women of color and lesbians. Harding (2006, 66) described the almost mainstream status of feminist research in the middle of the first decade of the twenty-first century:

> In this heady context, feminist science studies projects headed off in different and sometimes conflicting directions . . . today, [however] the field can seem to have settled into the kind of more sedate mopping-up projects characteristic of mature intellectual and social movements.

Feminist Research Methodologies

The debate on whether distinctive feminist research methodologies exist is still a divisive issue among some advocates of the feminist research model (Harding 1987; Ironstone-Catterall 2006; Waller 2005; Westmarland 2001). The consensus appears to be that while no unique methods have been identified, feminist researchers do apply existing quantitative and qualitative methods in a distinctly feminist way. As a consequence, it is common to find feminist survey research, feminist experimental research, and feminist field research being used when they are consistent with feminist principles. However, it is more common to find feminist researchers using such qualitative methods as in-depth interviews, participant observation, document analysis, and ethnographic studies. Sarantakos (2004, 63) describes how feminist researchers typically adjust these methods to meet their specific perspectives:

> It must be kept in mind that when feminist researchers employ methods that were developed for and by other groups of researchers, they adjust them so that they fit within the critical and emancipatory stance of feminism, and they are directed towards breaking down taken-for-granted concepts and rebuilding them into new entities. In doing so, they lay bare the essential concepts of research and use this as the basis for revealing what is really going on.

If no feminist research methods exist, what then makes this approach different from other research methods? According to analyses of the various branches of feminist research, the following points are common to this approach (Harding 1987; Ironstone-Catterall 2006; Sarantakos 2004; Waller 2005; Westmarland 2001).

- Feminist researchers focus their attention upon marginalized people in a social context. Their objective is to ensure that everyone is heard or represented. Since most research has focused on men, women's voices have not been heard.
- In the belief that action in social settings is subjective and political, feminist researchers often substitute subjectivity for the strict objectivity of the positivist tradition. This is often manifested in a strongly anti-positivistic orientation.
- Feminist researchers study the social conditions of women in a sexist and patriarchal society in order to enlighten citizens about practices that have produced unequal and discriminating social environments.
- Because society is organized in ways that overtly and covertly support sexism, feminist research typically exhibits an explicit focus on change in these social settings, structures, and cultures.
- Feminist research is not exclusively about women, but it is often done—with an emancipatory emphasis—for women. This research tends to emphasize women's experiences.
- Published feminist research is often critical of nonfeminist scholarship, is based on feminist theory, may be multidisciplinary, focuses on social change, and seeks to ensure equal concern for all humanity.
- Because feminist researchers often develop a special relationship with subjects in their studies, published feminist research often includes the researcher's story.

SUMMARY

This chapter has addressed two related critical research approaches: empowerment research and feminist research. Empowerment research helps people find ways to gain mastery over their own affairs. Empowerment researchers help individuals and groups who are excluded from mainstream society because of demographics or some other physical or emotional characteristics. Empowerment research may be particularly relevant for nonprofit sector research.

Empowerment research takes place in a series of six steps, which are grouped into three distinct phases. The *planning* phase includes the first three steps. The second phase, *action,* involves implementation of an intervention or program. During the third phase, *reflection,* changes that have been made are evaluated.

The feminist approach to research and to science in general emphasizes that women see things differently then men; that they have different ways of learning and different ways of describing meaning. Feminist research promotes the feminist agenda by challenging male dominance and advocating social, political, and economic equality. This research seeks to (1) bring about social change, (2) emancipate participants (i.e., women), and (3) enhance participants' lives.

While no uniquely feminist methods appear to exist, feminist researchers use existing quantitative and qualitative methods in a distinctly feminist way. It is common to find feminist survey research, feminist experimental research, and feminist field research used in ways consistent with feminist principles. Feminist researchers use such qualitative methods as in-depth interviews, participant observation, document analysis, and ethnographic studies.

EXERCISES

Exercise 27.1: Research to Shape Crime Victim Empowerment Initiatives

You are an MPA graduate student intern working with the South African Department of Welfare. Your department has been assigned the task of conducting a research project to identify critical success factors in victim empowerment initiatives currently being implemented at the local level in four South African provinces. Recipients of the services include victims of rape and/or child abuse. Your research team developed a two-part study to improve reliability of findings through triangulation. The first component of the study will be to conduct a self-administered survey. The sample of around 100 subjects will be drawn from (1) members of the National Crime Prevention Strategy Victim Empowerment Program Management and Reference teams; (2) appropriate provisional project leaders at the Department of Welfare; and (3) agency personnel attending a course in victim empowerment. The questionnaire includes open- and closed-ended questions focusing on key victim empowerment concepts and measures the level of awareness and attitudes toward the victim empowerment program. The study's triangulation component is series of focus group interviews with a similar sample of service providers and other concerned personnel.

When discussing the planned research with a fellow graduate student, you question whether it will reduce the crime rate in the provinces. Victims are almost exclusively females, many of whom are subjected to sexual discrimination, widespread abuse, and lack of power in their local communities. The department's current programs are almost exclusively reactive in nature, with services following victimization. You are convinced that stronger proactive programs are needed to prevent victimization before it takes place.

Because many women and children in the provinces lack education, they are unaware of the support services in their communities (Nel and Kruger 1999). More importantly, in societies with strong male dominance, the women are traditionally unwilling or unable to bring about changes in their living environments. As a result, they remain victims.

You and your fellow graduate student decide to use this opportunity to conduct the research needed for your graduate thesis. You have recently learned about empowerment research and wonder if your degree committee supervisor will authorize such a study for a two- or three-person team.

Questions

1. Are programs designed for citizens by government agencies without the contribution and collaborative effort of society's victims an effective way to end victimization?
2. What value will a survey of agency service providers and program managers have for administrators of the National Crime Prevention Strategy Victim Empowerment Program?

3. How would you go about planning and carrying out an empowerment research study with a social group in the provinces? Assuming that you receive approval for the study, what is the first thing you must do?

Exercise 27.2: Trouble at the Corrections Department

You are a case manager in a state corrections program, attending graduate school at night to earn your Master's in Public Administration. For some time, you and your fellow caseworkers have been dissatisfied with your working conditions and the lack of focus in agency operations. When you mentioned this dissatisfaction to your supervisor, you were transferred to the female inmate section. This position is considered to be a dead end where nothing happens and with little opportunity to provide proper service to clients.

The former department director kept formal managerial involvement and direction to a minimum, believing that casework required the operating staff to be flexible. The only formal operational directive governing caseworker activity was: "Case managers are to work with each inmate to implement a correctional and rehabilitation plan that has been developed by staff for the inmate" (Gottfredson 1996).

Departmental policy dictates that all male inmates at each state correctional institution receive equal attention from agency caseworkers. Because of heavy workloads and staff limitations, this has not occurred. Correctional plans have not been prepared for the entire male resident population; a recent court ruling ordered deficiencies in serving male inmates be rectified immediately. The only case management research conducted for female inmates was extremely general and offered little or no guidance.

Female inmates express their feelings of powerlessness to rectify what they see as unfair treatment. They feel no one is interested in hearing their concerns. However, your new agency director has proposed a research project involving a group of caseworkers and correctional departmental representatives to produce a set of operational expectations and performance standards for the two departments. As a representative for the female inmate population, you have been asked to be a member of this group.

Questions

1. Is a feminist critical research project appropriate for this situation? Why or why not?
2. Outline the steps you and your team will take if the department elects to follow an action research project plan that does not include the female inmate population.
3. How might you and your team recommend that any changes in your organization's future research program emphasis be implemented?

ADDITIONAL READING

Freire, Paolo. 1970. *Pedagogy of the Oppressed.* New York: The Seabury Press.

Gottfried, Heidi, ed. 1996. *Feminism and Social Change: Bridging Theory and Practice.* Urbana: University of Illinois Press.

Harding, Sandra, ed. 2004. *The Feminist Standpoint Theory Reader: Intellectual and Political Controversies.* New York: Routledge.

Ramazanoğlu, Caroline, and Janet Holland. 2002. *Feminist Methodology: Challenges and Choices.* Thousand Oaks, CA: Sage.

Reinharz, Shalamit. 1992. *Feminist Research Methods in Social Research.* Oxford: Oxford University Press.

PART 6

ANALYSIS AND INTERPRETATION OF
QUALITATIVE DATA

28

ANALYZING QUALITATIVE DATA

The primary building block of all research is *data*. Data can take many different forms and can be gathered in at least five different ways. In their most irreducible forms, they can be quantitative or qualitative. Increasingly, and in more and more disciplines, data exist in *qualitative* form.

Data in any form can be gathered by interviews, questionnaires, overt or covert observation, analysis of documents or artifacts, or by the subjective experiences of the researcher (Martin 2000). Regardless of the form they take or how they are gathered, in its raw state data have little or no intrinsic meaning. Data must be *processed, analyzed,* and *interpreted* by a researcher before they take on any rational meaning.

The *analysis* processes for quantitative and qualitative research data are similar in some ways, but different in others. Similarities include (1) data are not just *there;* they must be collected in some way by a researcher; (2) when processed, both quantitative and qualitative data can be used for inference; (3) comparative analyses are used with both data types; and (4) researchers are concerned with both the reliability and validity of all data.

Quantitative data differ from qualitative data primarily in the way they are tabulated, collated, and processed. Quantitative data are typically computer processed and analyzed with a variety of standard statistical tests. These tests are applied for one or more of the following purposes: (1) to describe a data set, (2) to generate hypotheses through a process of association testing, and (3) to test hypotheses (Fitz-Gibbon and Morris 1987).

Qualitative data, on the other hand, exhibit variety both in form and context. They can also be evaluated and interpreted in a variety of ways. Qualitative data can be words, pictures, artifacts, music scores, and so on. Furthermore, each of the analysis approaches has its own underlying purpose, and each often produces a different outcome. This chapter discusses a few of the more prevalent ways of analyzing qualitative data, and includes two separate but similar processing models.

WHAT ARE QUALITATIVE DATA?

Qualitative data are data that have been gathered during the conduct of interpretive or post-positivist research studies. They exist most often as some sort of narrative. Thus, they can be written text, transcripts of conversations or interviews, transcripts of therapeutic or consultive interviews, records of legal trials, or transcripts of focus group discussions. They can exist as historical or literary documents, ethnographic field notes, diaries, newspaper clippings, or magazine and journal articles. They can also be in the form of photographs, maps, illustrations, paintings, musical scores, tape recordings, films, or any other nonquantitative or quantitative source. Most of the time, however, qualitative research data exist as collections of rough field notes.

Miles and Huberman (1998, 182) suggested that qualitative data exist as "the essences of people, objects, and situations." In their discussion, *essences* refer to the reactions and interpretations that researchers take away from the raw experiences of a research encounter or situation. A researcher must process, analyze, and interpret these essences in order transform them into a meaningful conclusion.

The following brief statement bears emphasizing: *All data must be analyzed and interpreted before they are meaningful.* All unprocessed and uninterrupted data are usually called *raw data.* Raw quantitative data is the compilation of a set of numbers arranged according to values assigned by a researcher to optional responses to questions or as counts of event occurrences. Raw qualitative data exist most often as a body of unorganized, unstructured field notes or narrative—that is, in the form of words, not numbers.

COMPONENTS OF QUALITATIVE DATA ANALYSIS

There are two parts to the interpretation and analysis of qualitative data. The first is *data management;* the second is *data analysis* (Miles and Huberman 1998). Data management includes three important steps. First, managing data begins with organizing the collection process. This includes preplanning, careful selection of the sample or situation to be included in the study, and achieving entry into and acceptance by the study group. The researcher must maintain a concise record of the steps and processes taken throughout the study. A précis of this record must be included in the final research report under the heading of *methodology.*

The second step in this process is designing a system for storage of the collected data. In the past, this meant devising a system of index cards, preparing analytical memorandums, and careful categorical coding—in what some analysts referred to as the *clerical* portion of qualitative research. It was laborious and time-consuming. Today, however, computer software programs are increasingly taking the place of this unappealing activity. The third action in this half of the management/analysis process is devising a system for retrieving data for comparative analyses and other interpretive activities. It is important to review the manual process because some researchers still work this way (Este, Sieppert, and Barsky 1998, 138):

> Only a few short decades ago, QDA [qualitative data analysis] was purely a manual process. Bits of data were copied onto cards, using the traditional technique of cutting and pasting. These cards were filed under appropriate categories generated by the researcher . . . [who] then strove to link the data and connect categories through these physical materials and manipulations, to produce meaningful reflections of the phenomena being studied. The process was a daunting one for researchers. Researchers had to manage overwhelming compilations of material, make analytical decisions that were rarely clear or simple, and work through the tedious and frustrating processes of coding, deriving themes, and building theories.

The second half of the process is the actual analysis of data. This phase of the interpretation process also includes three activities: (1) data reduction, (2) data display, and (3) drawing conclusions from the data. Data reduction is almost always a crucial stage in the interpretation process.

It involves selecting the most salient themes and constructs that emerge from the data. Not every bit of data can be its own category; if this were true, the research report would never be written. Qualitative investigations have been known to generate thousands of pages of records. From out of that mass of unconnected narrative, the researcher must choose a conceptual framework. This framework will be constructed of themes, clusters, and summaries.

The second part of the analysis phase is data display. In the chapters on quantitative research methods, this was discussed as the use of descriptive and summary statistics and of charts, graphs, and tables to present information. These same graphic displays are often used to present qualitative data. Whatever research approach is followed, the objective is to be able to present findings as an organized, focused collection of pertinent information, out of which a researcher—and a reader—can draw relevant conclusions.

Finally, drawing conclusions forces the researcher to *interpret* the results of the study. It is not enough simply to present the data as they appear, even if they have been effectively organized, categorized, and structured. The researcher must explain what the data *mean* in relation to the study design and objectives and in terms of their contribution to theory.

BRINGING ORDER TO QUALITATIVE DATA

The analysis and interpretation of qualitative data begin with bringing the raw data into some level of order. First, the researcher identifies and selects a set of relevant *categories* or *classes* in which to sort the data. Comparing the data across categories—a step that is typically used in the testing of hypotheses—often follows the initial comparison phase of the analysis. Strauss and Corbin (1998) call this a process of *conceptualizing*. Conceptualizing means reducing the often bulky amount of raw data into workable, ordered bits of information that the researcher can manage with confidence. Kvale (1996) described this act of data categorization as a key qualitative research activity that most distinguishes qualitative strategies from quantitative research.

Researchers can best analyze and interpret raw data if they employ some orderly process. Figure 28.1 displays a model of the first of two such processes. This nine-step process for analyzing and interpreting qualitative data has its roots in the threefold grounded theory interpretation models of Strauss and Corbin (1990) and Neuman (2000), and in information provided in Miles and Huberman (1994, 1998). Each of the nine steps is discussed in more detail below.

Step 1: Preliminary Analysis for Patterns and Structure

Order and structure must be brought to all data if they are ultimately to become *information.* Miles and Huberman (1994) refer to order—the patterns or themes in textual qualitative data—as "gestalts" because they pull together a variety of smaller portions of data into larger "wholes."

A key task of the qualitative researcher is sorting and resorting data to identify *patterns,* from which meaning and definition can be constructed. Finding patterns in the data is a subjective process that often comes naturally to the researcher. Miles and Huberman see this as a potential problem, however, and offer the following caveat:

> The human mind finds patterns so quickly and easily that it needs no how-to advice. Patterns just "happen," almost too quickly. The important thing, rather, is to be able to (a) see *real* added evidence in the same pattern; (b) remain open to disconfirming evidence when it appears. (p. 216)

Figure 28.1   **A Nine-Step Process for Analyzing Qualitative Data**

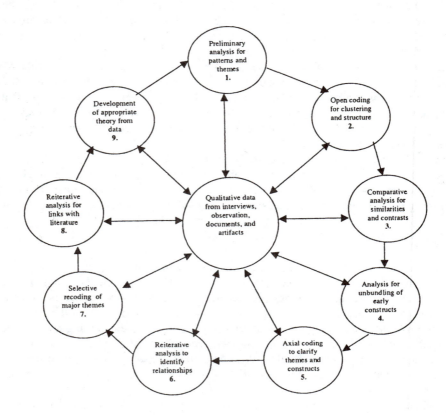

Step 2: Open Coding to Form Clusters and Identify Themes

A key activity in all qualitative data analysis is *clustering*. This entails putting things that are like each other together into groupings or classes. These may be preexisting classes, although this is not the recommended way to begin. More often, the categories are groupings that the researcher creates from smaller collections of ideas that emerge from the data. Coding and categorization go hand in hand during this phase of the analysis.

Straus and Corbin (1998) and Glaser (1992) identified the coding process that occurs in the first phase of the analysis as *open* or *substantive* coding. The goal of this first, open coding process is to begin to form the raw data into meaningful categories with a structure that will guide the researcher in all subsequent analyses and any future data gathering.

There are no limits to how many codes are assigned during the open coding phase or to the inclusiveness (breadth) of each. Miles and Huberman (1994, 219) described the process as a necessary task that can be "applied at many levels of qualitative data; at the level of events or acts, of individual actors, of processes, of settings or locales, of sites as wholes."

In qualitative research, usually little or no categorization is done prior to the data being collected. The categorical codes that emerge at this time are taken from the data they embrace. However, the researcher should keep in mind that one of the goals of coding and categorization is the *reduction of data* into more manageable sets.

Step 3: Comparative Analysis for Similarities and Contrasts

Qualitative research studies require a comparative analysis of the collected data. In grounded theory research, comparisons are an integral part of the entire analysis process. Both Strauss and Corbin (1990) and Glaser (1992) recommended that comparative analysis be an integral step in all studies involving qualitative data. Furthermore, they urged that previously gathered data be continuously compared with every bit of new data. Ragin and Zaret (1983) also considered comparative research to be one of the research tactics that distinguish research on social groups.

Neuman (2000) identified comparison as a "central process" in the analysis of all data. In this central role, comparative analysis has two broad objectives. The first is to find cases or evidence that belong together, based on one or more relevant characteristics; the second is to isolate anomalies in the data—events or cases that do not fit a pattern. Similarities enable the researcher to place the data within their proper categories and to develop new categorical codes that embrace the unclassified phenomenon. Anomalies are the distinct characteristics that are central to the research problem; finding distinctive differences in data is like a prospector finding the mother lode.

Miles and Huberman (1994, 254) considered the process of comparative analysis to be a part of their *drawing and verifying conclusions* step in the analysis of qualitative data. Refuting critics whom they accused of considering the act of making comparisons "odious," they responded:

> Comparison is a time-honored, classic way to test a conclusion. We draw a contrast or make a comparison between two sets of things—persons, roles, activities, cases as a whole—that are known to differ in some other important respect. This is the "method of differences," which goes back to Aristotle if not further.

Miles and Huberman also offered the following caveats to the use of comparisons:

1. "Mindless comparisons are useless." Researchers must be sure that their comparisons are the right ones, and that it makes sense to use them in the analysis.
2. Comparisons should extend beyond the data alone. They should also be compared with what the researcher knows about the things being studied.
3. Researchers should pause before including a comparison in a research report to ask, "How big must a difference be before it makes a difference?" and "How do I know that?"
4. With qualitative comparisons, researchers are concerned with the *practical significance* of the data; they cannot apply the statistical significance tests that are available in quantitative studies.

Strauss and Corbin (1998, 73) placed great importance on the activity of comparative analysis. In their opinion, making comparisons is an integral activity that should be used at all steps in the data analysis process. They define the comparative analysis process as "an analytical tool used to stimulate thinking about properties and dimensions of categories." Strauss and Corbin considered the act of making comparisons to be one of the two essential tasks for development of theory in qualitative research; the other essential task is asking questions and recording subjects' answers in field notes with rich description.

Step 4: Analysis for Unbundling of Early Constructs

In this step, the researcher reviews the coded data to determine whether any categorical constructs make better intuitive sense as two or more factors rather than the one originally assigned. *Unbundling* means that each major category should be reexamined to see if it is really two or more categorical constructs. If an unbundling is warranted, care must also be taken to apply the characteristics originally assigned to the category to each of the newly established subcategories.

Step 5: Axial Coding to Clarify Constructs and Themes

Axial coding affords the researcher a second opportunity to introduce order and structure into the initially coded data. Axial coding can use preestablished codes such as the six categories suggested by Strauss and Corbin (1998), or it can be freely employed without any imposed structure, as Glaser (1992) proposed. Strauss and Corbin added their six categories when they found that the lack of structure at this point made it difficult for beginning researchers to produce clear and cogent theory from the data. Retaining the open and substantive coding levels, they proposed adding a third, intermediate step in the coding/analysis process. They called this intermediate step "axial coding" (Glaser 1992; Kendall 1999). This step was proposed as a way to demystify the grounded theory process. It requires the researcher to place all the initially open-coded data into these six specified categories: (1) conditions, (2) phenomena, (3) context, (4) intervening conditions, (5) actions/strategies, and (6) consequences.

These categories require the researcher to look for antecedents that lead to the particular event or circumstance, in addition to any resulting consequences. It also forces the researcher to reexamine the strategies and processes involved in both the target organization and the research design.

Step 6: Reiterative Analysis to Identify Relationships

Researchers must establish categories and codes for the major and minor constructs within the data, develop meaningful ideas about the data in context, edit and make critical interpretations, and—perhaps most importantly—generate ideas and theories from them. A key activity in this process is identifying *relationships* between constructs and groupings. One way to do this is to diagram the data as a set of boxes, circles, arrows, and lines. Kurt Lewin's "bathtubs and beer barrels" method can be used for this task. Bathtubs (large ovals) are used to represent key ideas, while beer barrels (smaller circles) are used to display antecedents and contributing components or factors. Lines are used to illustrate relationships, with arrows showing the direction of the influence or relationship. Such diagrams make it clear what sorts of relationships, if any, exist between two or more ideas, patterns, constructs, and groupings. Developing diagrams and relationship charts is an important part of the qualitative analysis procedure.

Another procedure sometimes used for this purpose is *power* or *influence analysis*. In this process, the researcher first collects data by observing the way people interact or by questioning them on their perceptions of such factors as power or influence in the organization. The researcher then draws a diagram or chart to illustrate the interactions, relationships, and responses to others within a group or other social setting. Examples of graphic displays of this type include context charts, linkage patterns and knowledge flow charts, and role and power charts.

THE QUALITATIVE DATA ANALYSIS PROCESS

Qualitative data gathering and analysis is carried out in a logical sequence of steps. Jones (1996) has organized this sequence into the twelve-step process shown in Figure 28.2. The twelve steps fall into two equal halves, each with six steps: The first half of the process, involving steps 1 through 6, is the *preparatory* half; while steps 7 through 12 constitute the *analysis and report* portion of the analysis procedure.

Part I: Preparing for Qualitative Research

Steps 1 and 2, *define the research problem* and *establish research objectives* are the initial activities in all research designs. Step 3, *do your homework,* means becoming conversant with the full nature of the subject or topic of interest. Interviews with a few key informants and extensive analysis of the relevant literature are the activities often used in this step.

Step 4, *plan the data-gathering process,* should occur only after the researcher has developed a working familiarity with the subject and study group. The plan should include a preliminary list of the behaviors to be observed, the subjects to be interviewed, the topics to be covered in the interviews, a preliminary coding scheme, and a schedule for each following step in the research process.

Steps 5 and 6, *gain entry into the group* and *become immersed in the setting,* are closely related activities; in fact, they often occur simultaneously. While these are more appropriately tasks in ethnographic research, they are also important in other qualitative research designs. For example, researchers conducting a study of the operating climate within a government agency must first gain permission of the agency director and the compliance of both the managers and agency staff.

Part II: Analyzing and Reporting

The first activity in the second half of the research process is step 7, *take extensive field notes. Field notes* are the notes, recordings, reminders, and other subjective reporting that the researcher records while observing behaviors or interviewing respondents. Not surprisingly, they are the records produced during the process of conducting *field research.* Field research is what is done when researchers want to know something about people, understand behaviors, or describe a group of people who interact in some way (Neuman 2000). Field notes are the detailed written reports and/or diagrams or pictures of what the researcher sees and hears. The term used to describe the required detail needed in field notes is "thick description." Finally, field notes should be written down or transcribed on a regular basis, as soon as possible after the phenomenon occurs.

Taking good field notes is not an easy process; the researcher must make a conscious effort to devote the time and effort necessary to produce good notes because, without them, the final report of the research can only be second-rate. Preparing field notes can be a boring, laborious task that requires self-discipline to be done correctly. The notes contain extensive descriptive detail drawn from memory. Researchers must make it a daily habit—better yet, a *compulsion*—to write their notes and begin to transcribe them immediately after leaving the field. Field notes must be neat and organized because the researcher will be return to them over and over again. Once written, the notes are private and valuable. The researcher must treat them with care, while also ensuring the confidentiality of respondents (Neuman 2000).

An example of how difficult it can be to listen to informants in the field (that is, to gather data) and then transcribe those narratives into meaningful field notes can be found in Jurich's (2001,

Figure 28.2 **The Twelve Steps of Qualitative Fieldwork, Analysis, and Report Preparation**

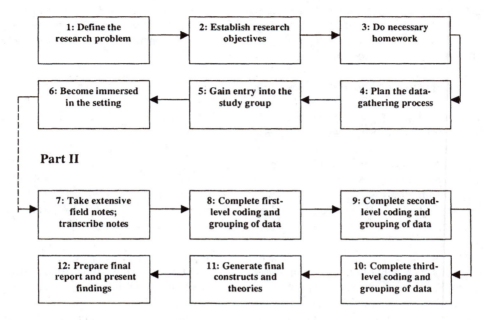

Source: Adapted from Neuman 2000.

S152) story of her lengthy field research project with Native Americans on a South Dakota reservation. She explained her methodological difficulties this way:

> I listened to stories during the day and late into the night, often falling asleep long before conversations were ended. I learned early on that questions were likely to be considered interrogation, intrusive, and were not a frequent form of interaction. So I asked few questions. . . . The stories would get summarized in [my] notebooks. Tape recordings were never part of the fieldwork project. . . . I worked hard to listen and remember, to record as completely as I could the substance of what was said. More often, though, the field notes were thick descriptions of my own experiences of going places and engaging in the practices of reservation life, describing social interaction and processes that were part of my daily life.

Once field notes are transcribed into organized records of the researcher's observations or interviews, they must then be put to a preliminary interpretive analysis. This occurs during steps 8 through 11; it is an ongoing process that begins during the first venture into the field; continues until a final set of codes, categories, and constructs is established; and ends with production of the final report of the research. Miles and Huberman (1994) recommended employing a series of reporting guides or worksheets to ensure that this portion of the process is complete. These include the following guides: (1) a contact summary, (2) a summary of each document analyzed in the study, (3) first-, second-, and third-level coding and grouping of constructs, patterns, and factors discovered in the data, and (4) a final detailed summary of the site in which the activities, behaviors, and events were studied.

First-Level Coding

Step 8, *first-level coding and grouping of data,* begins with preparation of contact summaries and a summary of each document, if any, analyzed for the study. The contact summary is usually nothing more than a single sheet that contains answers to a set of focusing or summary questions about each subject contacted in the study. It often includes demographic information, indications of relative position in the group under study, and other material. It is used to ensure continuity in the responses of all subjects in the study. A document summary is applicable only when documents of any type are acquired for analysis at the research site. The purpose of this guide is to establish a record of the document's significance and how it relates to the actual observations, interviews, or final analysis.

First-level coding is done to develop the initial descriptive codes around which all subsequent data will be organized or grouped. These codes are abbreviations that establish descriptive categories or groupings in the data. Miles and Huberman (1994, 56) defined a *code* as "an abbreviation or symbol applied to a segment of words—most often a sentence or paragraph of transcribed field notes—in order to *classify* the words." Codes should be considered as *categories.* They function as *retrieval* and *organizing devices* that allow the analyst to quickly spot, pull out, and then cluster all the segments relating to the particular question, hypothesis, or concept. Clustering sets the stage for the next level of analysis.

Second-Level Coding

Second-level or *pattern coding* takes place in step 9 of the analysis process. Second-level coding involves establishing *interpretive codes.* Here, the researcher goes beyond simple description and begins to form interpretive labels for categories of behaviors. The goal at this point is to be able to read repeating patterns in the data.

Third-Level Coding

Step 10 involves *third-level* or *thematic development coding* (also called *memoing*). Memoing refers to producing preliminary or partial summary reports for the personal use of the researcher or research team. They might, for example, be used to summarize a pattern or a theme in the data and even be incorporated in their entirety into the final analysis. At the third analysis level, the researcher begins to establish *explanatory* codes that link larger groups of patterns into what are called *themes.* These are the major constructs that will make up the central structure under which the final analysis will occur and be recorded.

Step 11 is a brief description of the events, members, circumstances, and other relevant information that can serve both as a summary of the data-gathering experience and as a memory jogger during the preparation of the final report.

The last step in the process is to combine the notes, constructs, patterns, and themes with the researcher's analyses and synthesize these into a *research report.* This important step in the qualitative research process is not simply putting the researcher's field notes together in one cover. Rather, it involves a number of important activities (Neuman 2000, 395):

> Assembling evidence, arguments, and conclusions into a report is always a crucial step; but more than in quantitative approaches, the careful crafting of evidence and explanation makes or breaks [qualitative] research. A researcher distills mountains of evidence into exposition

and prepares extensive footnotes. She or he weaves together evidence and arguments to communicate a coherent, convincing picture to readers.

REPORTING QUALITATIVE RESEARCH RESULTS

Qualitative research reports can include narrative description, models, diagrams, tables, and verbal and graphic communications tools. They can also exist as films, videos, and collections of photographs, recordings, and any other nonverbal presentation of ideas. Table 28.1 was developed from a combined quantitative and qualitative research study designed to identify the attitudes of small business owners. The areas of concern identified in column 2 were developed from sentence completion items included in the interviews. The examples of responses in column 3 are abbreviated examples of larger statements offered by respondents.

Both quantitative and qualitative data-gathering processes were used in the study. Qualitative methodology consisted of construction techniques (stories from supplied cartoon situations), and sentence completion techniques. These projective techniques were employed to draw out the personal perceptions and attitudes of owners of small businesses. These techniques force the respondent to respond in a manner that reflects his or her own need/value system.

COMPUTER ANALYSIS OF QUALITATIVE DATA

There has been a dramatic growth in the use of computers and the availability of analysis software in the past several decades (Flick 2006; Roberts and Wilson 2002; Tak, Nield, and Becker 1999; Este, Sieppert, and Barsky 1998; Weitzman and Miles 1995; Miles and Huberman 1994). Technology has simplified many necessary but time-consuming and often laborious tasks of the data analysis process

Researchers testing and applying these data analysis packages refer to them collectively as computer assisted qualitative data analysis software (CAQDAS). Originally, the software packages were developed to aid in the analysis of documents and similar textual material. The most popular and effective software programs are those designed for analysis of text material (field notes, results of in-depth interviews, and similar records). Software packages developed for qualitative data analysis include *ATLAS.ti, HyperQual2, NUD*IST, NVivo, MAXQDA,* and others (Flick 2006; Roberts and Wilson 2002; Thompson 2002; Welsh 2002). As the reliability, precision, and ease of classification of these and similar packages continue to improve, they hold the promise of improving data analysis—the task which one author described as "one of the historic pitfalls of qualitative research" (Gobo 2005, 7). However, qualitative researchers have not universally accepted them.

In a public administration example of CAQDAS use in the analysis of textual material, MacMillan (2005) tested both ATLAS.ti and *Diction* (a Windows program) in a study of news reports. ATLAS.ti searched for key words, then coded the data according to demographic categories. *Diction* analyzed political speeches. MacMillan found ATLAS.ti to be effective, but found *Diction* unable to achieve what she described as "fine-grained analysis."

Despite some weaknesses, today's computer programs are capable of efficiently processing large volumes of text material and records, sorting and indexing data, and retrieving information from a variety of different directions (Richards and Richards 1998). Despite this, most data coding, sorting, categorizing, and analysis is still done the way it has been done for more than a hundred years—by hand.

In the taxonomy of analysis software suggested by Richards and Richards, software is divided

Table 28.1

Placing Qualitative Responses into Categories

#	Area of Concern	Examples of Responses	Code
1	Worries about exporting to Pacific Rim	• Spending a lot of money and getting no sales in return. • Korean, Japanese, and Taiwanese firms copy our ideas • Money; getting paid; low profit margins	RIM
2	Getting American products to China	• Lots of red tape • Too difficult for small rewards • Lack of transportation or marketing infrastructure	CHI
3	Finding markets in Australia/NZ	• Buyers there go through brokers (making my costs too high) • They are just like any customer here; buyers there fax us directly with purchases • Believe they would buy from us if they knew about us or our products	AUN
4	Difficulties with customers in Korea	• Can't find proper agents/brokers • Can't get paid; very high import tariffs • Product knockoffs; copyright/trade infringements	KOR
5	Why U.S. products don't sell in Asian markets	• We're not good at promoting them against world competition • They are racists and too nationalistic • U.S. products are too expensive and too low in quality	US
6	Why we don't participate in trade shows in Japan	• Have never tried it • Incredibly frightening thought; it is difficult and expensive • Do it regularly now; very good opportunity	JAP
7	Generic troubles with selling in Taiwan	• Takes lots of time; they won't commit • Tough to meet their price requirements; low labor costs there • Lack of knowledge about the country; don't know the language	TAI
8	Reactions to "Hong Kong is a good market"	• Agree that it's good now, but for how long? • Don't have contacts there • Don't sell as much as we could or should	HON
9	Generic problems with shipping to Asia	• Either profitable or miserable; nothing in between • Extremely complicated • Is easy, straightforward; as smooth as importing from there	ASIA
10	Small companies getting paid for sales in Asia	• No different than any other market • Use Letters of Credit but is a slow process; demand pay before shipping goods	MON

into two broad classifications: (1) general-purpose software packages and (2) special-purpose software developed specifically for data analysis. General-purpose packages include standard word processing programs, database management systems, and text-search software. Richards and Richards identified five categories of special-purpose software:

- Code-and-retrieve software
- Rule-based, theory-building systems
- Logic-based systems
- Index-based systems
- Conceptual, or semantic, network systems

Of these, the two approaches that seem to offer the most promise at this time are logic-based systems and conceptual network systems. Richards and Richards provided an extensive review of a logic-based system they authored, NUD*IST (*Nonnumerical Unstructured Data Indexing, Searching, and Theorizing*). NUD*IST allows the user to code themes and categories by simply attaching labels to segments of the text (Tak, Nield, and Becker 1999). Like a majority of the systems discussed by Richards and Richards, NUD*IST is built around a code-and-retrieve facility. It has been expanded to include a number of different optional processes—something that may turn out to be one of the program's greatest faults. Richards and Richards (1998, 237) offered this caveat about the program:

> NUD*IST appears, compared with the other systems described here, as a rather awkward hybrid, containing features of code-and-retrieve, ways of handling production-rule and other types of conceptual-level reasoning, conceptual representations alternative to conceptual network systems, and database storage facilities, all interacting through interlocking tools. . . . And, perhaps most important, the software offers many ways for a researcher never to finish a study.

Despite the potentially confusing complexity of NUD*IST, it has become one of, if not the most, popular computer software program for analysis of qualitative data. It is particularly popular in education, nursing and other medical studies, and some sociological applications. It is used less often in ethnographic studies and is hardly ever seen in public administration research. In addition, a few innovators in public administration and nongovernment organization research have started to test its capabilities.

The second software program to receive special mention by Richards and Richards was the conceptual network system *ATLAS.ti*. Thomas Mühr developed ATLAS in Germany during the 1980s ATLAS is built on a code-and-retrieve foundation, to which has been added an excellent memoing capability; codes can be assigned to memos as well as the original text. It distinguishing feature, however, is its ability to create conceptual graphic displays that show relationships and linkages. According to Richard and Richards (1998, 240): "Allied with ATLAS's sophisticated text-retrieval system, the graphs support subtle exploration of text via a visually immediate interface that relates the text to the systems or theories in the [setting] being studied."

In conclusion, the application of special-purpose software packages for qualitative data analysis is probably here to stay. As more and more professional researchers discover the capabilities of the packages and more students are exposed to them in their research methods classes, this growth in use should accelerate. As of today, however, because of their complexity—due in large part to their extensive capabilities—most researchers still analyze their data using traditional, minimal techniques and processes.

SUMMARY

Conducting any qualitative research is a time-consuming, complicated, and often confusing task. One of the most problematic components of the process is analyzing qualitative data. The analysis processes for quantitative and qualitative research data are similar in some ways, but different in others. Similarities include the following: (1) data are not just *there;* they must be collected in some way by a researcher; (2) when processed, both quantitative and qualitative data can be used for inference; (3) comparative analyses are used with both data types; and (4) researchers are concerned with both the reliability and validity of all data.

Qualitative data exhibit variety in both form and context. They can also be evaluated and interpreted in a variety of ways. Qualitative data can be words, pictures, artifacts, musical scores, and so on. Each of several different analysis approaches can produce a different outcome with these data.

Qualitative data are gathered during interpretive or postpositivist research studies. They can be written text, transcripts of conversations or interviews, focus-group discussions, records of legal trials, historical or literary documents, ethnographic field notes, diaries, newspaper clippings, or magazine and journal articles. They can also be in the form of photographs, maps, illustrations, paintings, musical scores, tape recordings, films, or any other nonquantitative source. All these data must be analyzed and interpreted before they are meaningful.

There are two parts to the interpretation and analysis of qualitative data. The first is *data management;* the second is *data analysis.* Many different techniques and strategies have been developed for analyzing qualitative data; three are discussed in this chapter. The first is a nine-step process; the second follows twelve steps divided into two halves. Anthropologists developed a third approach for analyzing ethnographic data.

Advances in computer software have resulted in a number of special-purpose software packages for analyzing qualitative data. Two popular programs are NUD*IST and ATLAS.ti. Researchers studying political science and NGO management topics have been slow to adopt these new approaches for analysis, but are now doing so in greater numbers.

ADDITIONAL READING

Jones, Russell A. 1996. *Research Methods in the Social and Behavioral Sciences.* Sunderland, MA: Sinaur Associates.
Miles, Matthew B., and A. Michael Huberman. 1994. *Qualitative Data Analysis.* 2nd ed. Thousand Oaks, CA: Sage.
Neuman, W. Lawrence. 2000. *Social Research Methods.* 4th ed. Boston: Allyn and Bacon.

29

ANALYZING TEXTS, DOCUMENTS, AND ARTIFACTS

Sources of research data include people, their words and actions, publications, material culture, and any item or symbol that communicates a message of any kind. Data-gathering methods include watching how people act; asking them questions about their opinions, attitudes, or perceptions; reading what they have written; watching their movements; listening to their songs and other sounds; rummaging through their garbage; examining their tools and toys; and deciphering their signs, symbols, or facial expressions—the list goes on and on. This chapter discusses some of the ways that researchers go about examining textual material, cultural artifacts, body language, and similar types of written and unwritten communications, records, documents, signs, and symbols.

For convenience, these different sources of research data are grouped into four broad categories. The first is *written texts*—books, periodicals, narratives, reports, pamphlets, and other published materials. Collectively, this group of sources includes most if not all of the mass media. Research using these sources is often called *library research,* or *desk research.*

The second category is *formal and informal documents;* it includes personal messages and assorted types of archival information, such as personal notes and memos, government records and vital statistics, and other informal written materials, including e-mail. Table 29.1 displays the relationship between various sources of data and methods used in their analysis.

The third category of sources is made up of the wide variety of *nonwritten communications.* This group includes such things as graphic displays (graphs, tables, charts), photographs and illustrations, tools and other artifacts, and films and videotapes. The final category includes all *nonverbal signs and symbols.* Among these are the silent messages in body language, facial expressions, gestures, nonverbal symbols and signs, music and dance, animal sounds and behavior, and even noise.

Researchers employ a variety of analysis tools and methods in their study of texts, symbols, and artifacts. Among these are *hermeneutics, content analysis, meta-analysis, semiotic analysis, proxemics, kinesics, discourse analysis, site surveys,* and others.

The analytical approaches used most often in public and nonprofit organization research are the formal literature review; hermeneutic analysis of textual material; content, discourse, and narrative analysis; meta-analysis; archival analysis; and semiotic analysis. Each of these will be discussed in greater detail in the following pages.

Another way to categorize these research approaches might be to look at the formal literature review, meta-analysis, hermeneutics, content analysis, and semiotics as *methods,* and archives, texts, artifacts, and signs and symbols as *sources* of research data. This chapter is structured along

Table 29.1

The Relationship Between Sources, Examples, and Study Methods

Source	Examples	Analysis methods
Written texts	• Professional literature • Mass media • Narratives • Books and stories	Hermeneutics Content analysis Narrative analysis Meta-analysis Literature review
Informal documents and records	• Archival information • Government reports • Vital statistics • Records, documents • Notes and memos	Hermeneutics Content analysis Archival analysis Semiotics
Nonwritten communications and material culture	• Graphs and tables • Photos and drawings • Films and videos • Tools and artifacts	Semiotics Discourse analysis Hermeneutics Site surveys
Nonverbal signs, symbols and other communications	• Body language • Gestures • Music and dance • Nonverbal sounds • Signs • Noise	Semiotics Proxemics Kinesics

these lines, with the discussion of textual sources first discussed in a section on the literature search process. Narrative and discourse analyses are discussed in the content analysis section.

ANALYSIS OF TEXTS AS DATA

In public administration and nonprofit organization research, if not for research in all of the social and administrative sciences, library-based research draws on documents of all types as the sources of data. This is the opposite of the field research methods that have been discussed to this point. In addition to public administration, these types of desk-research projects are common in such fields of inquiry as philosophy, social theory, law, and history, which rely almost exclusively upon documents as the key source (Denscombe 1998). These are also important in studies that draw upon legislative archives for data.

From the researcher's point of view, literature (or documentary) research can be grouped into three key classes. The first is the traditional *literature review* that is or should be a part of all scientific research. A key purpose of the literature review is to provide background information that can then be used to design a complete research project. The second strategy is called *archival studies*. In substance similar to a standard literature review, archival studies draw upon public and private formal documents, records, and other material of a historical nature for data that may or may not be stored in a library. Even when they are, they are generally not open for general access or circulation.

The third approach is what is known as a *meta-analysis* design. In this approach, researchers use other studies as subjects for analysis. Meta-analysis is a quantitative technique for summarizing other investigators' research on a topic; as such, it uses the literature as a source of data in its own right.

THE LITERATURE REVIEW

A crucial early step in the design and conduct of all research is a thorough investigation of the relevant literature on the study topic, the research question, and the methodology followed by others who have studied the same or similar problems. Called a *review of the relevant literature* or, simply, a *literature review,* the process has been defined as "a systematic, explicit, and reproducible method for identifying, evaluating, and interpreting the existing body of recorded work produced by researchers, scholars, and practitioners" (Fink 1998, 3).

Purposes for the Literature Review

The literature review serves three fundamental purposes: First, it shows those who read the research findings that the researcher is aware of the existing work already done on the topic. Second, it identifies what the researcher believes are the key issues, crucial questions, and obvious gaps in the field. Third, it establishes a set of guiding signs that allow readers to see which theories and principles the researcher used to shape the research design and analysis (Denscombe 2002).

Despite the critical importance of the literature review, some researchers either skip this step entirely in the mistaken belief that theirs is a "unique" study problem, or if they do look into the literature of the study topic, field, or discipline, they often take a wrong approach. The literature review is not intended to be just a summary of the articles and books that were read. Nor should a literature review be a list of the authors with whom the researcher agrees or disagrees. The good literature review has a greater purpose than this; it is a source of data in its own right. Among the most meaningful strategic purposes to which the literature review can be put are the following:

1. The review can *trace the historical evolution* of the study problem or key issues, themes, or constructs pertaining to the problem.
2. The review can provide a schematic of the *different schools of thought* that have developed or are developing with regard to the study problem.
3. The review can examine the study problem from several *different disciplines* (for example, looking at welfare reform from the points of view of social work and of economics).
4. The review can examine the positions of *different stakeholder groups,* such as public administrators, citizen groups, and nonprofit organizations.
5. The review can trace *different conceptual schools of thought* that have emerged over time and may currently be taking opposing or conflicting views in the literature (Piantanida and Garman 1999).

The important thing to remember about this list is that these *approaches and strategies are not mutually exclusive.* A good literature review can achieve many goals at the same time. Lang and Heiss (1990) identified two key purposes for reviewing the related literature. First, it hones the researcher's attack on a specific study problem, and second, it provides a point of reference to use when discussing and interpreting the findings of the research. Specifically, a well-conducted literature review can do all of the following:

- Set specific limits for subsequent research
- Introduce the researcher to new and different ways of looking at the problem
- Help the researcher avoid errors and omissions in planning the study
- Suggest new ideas
- Acquaint the researcher with new sources of data and, often, totally different ways of looking at an issue

Figure 29.1   **A Model of the Steps in a Literature Review Process**

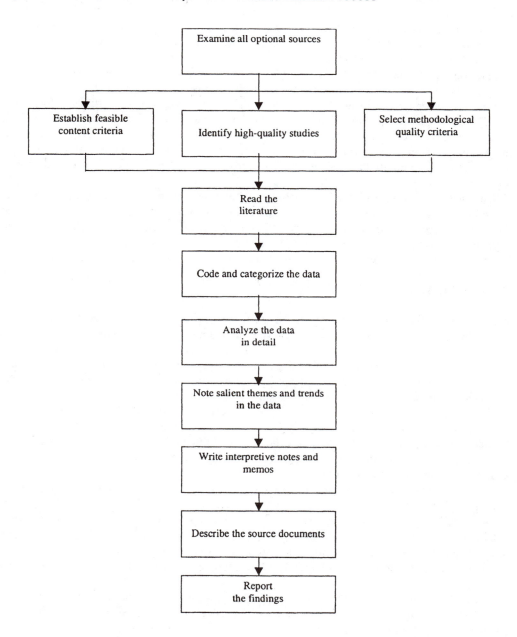

A formal literature review should follow an organized series of steps. The model in Figure 29.1 encourages researchers to study all their options before embarking on their journey through the literature. This means that all potential sources should be considered. Limiting a literature search to a quick perusal of the Internet or a run through a single CD-ROM database is not the way to conduct a thorough, scientific review of the literature.

The second step in the literature review process is made up of three equally important activities. The researcher must establish some basis for selecting articles (content criteria), as well as some methodological criteria. For example, should the studies all be quantitative or qualitative, or can a combination of both be used? Should they all be about the same size? Should the samples discussed all have been selected? These decisions will be based on the study question and may change somewhat when the search itself—the third activity in this step—is underway.

The collected research must then be read in detail. As this occurs, relevant categories of information should begin to stand out. These categories are then coded, with the pertinent information copied onto index cards or worksheets. Repeated salient themes in the literature should be recorded; these often serve as discussion points during the writing of the final research report. As this point, the researcher often begins writing *interpretive memos* that summarize the material and allow the researcher to comment on the content. These memos are sometimes carried into the final report with little or no revision.

During the next-to-last stage in the process, the researcher is encouraged to record all the important bibliographic information on the source documents. This usually includes information about the author(s), the discipline in which they did their research, all information about the source, and any connections to other sources that have been or might also be investigated.

The last step in the process is preparing and presenting a report of the research findings.

RESEARCH WITH ARCHIVAL DATA

Archives, long thought to be of interest only to librarians, have come to be recognized as rich sources of research material in the social sciences, including public administration. They are particularly valuable as a source for cross-checking interview and narrative study data. In this way they contribute to improved validity through triangulation—using several different approaches in a research study. While it is certainly possible for bias and dishonesty to exist in archival data, they are less susceptible to some types of error, including researcher error.

The research element in an archival study is the *record* (Dearstyne 1993). Records are concrete extensions of human memory. They are created and stored to record information, document transactions, justify actions, and provide official and unofficial evidence of events. A record can be any type of saved information. A record can be created, received, or maintained by a person, an institution, or an organization.

Records can be official government reports, recorded e-mail communications, letters, diaries, journals, ledgers, meeting minutes, deeds, case files, election results, drawings and other illustrations, blueprints, agreements, memoranda, and any other type of material that has some historical value. They can exist in many different forms and characteristics. They can be stored in the form of computer tapes or disks; in electronic data storage; as words, figures, and illustrations on paper or parchment; on microfilm and microfiche; or on cassette tape, film, or videotape, among other storage methods.

Records that are established and maintained by organizations or institutions are called *official records*. The *National Historical Publications and Records Commission* recently estimated that there are more than 4,500 historical record repositories in the United States alone. In addition, almost every state has its own historical society and can often direct the researcher to sources not kept in official government archives. A few examples of specific archival records include the following:

1. Private letters and collections
2. Political and judicial documents

3. Voter registration lists
4. The Congressional Record
5. Actuarial records (i.e., vital statistics)
6. Records of quasi-governmental agencies (weather reports, etc.)
7. The mass media
8. Professional and academic journals
9. Company and organization records
10. Personal histories
11. Published and unpublished documents, etc.

Activities of Archivists

Archivists collect, organize, and store documentary evidence of events, operations, correspondence, and organizational functioning. In this way, they perform a valuable service for historians and social science researchers. However, gaining access to archives can sometimes be problematic. If the reaction of one of America's leading archivists, T. R. Schellenberg, is any indication, a guiding principle of archival science might be *a place for everything and everything in its place.* One implication that can be taken away from Schellenberg is: *And that is where there they should stay.*

Researchers, by the very act of researching archival data, must often synthesize, reorganize, re-structure, and condense archival data in order to interpret its meaning. Schellenberg grudgingly admitted this fact, but did so believing that researchers could not really be trusted to leave things the way they found them. He blamed this on their lack of knowledge of the archival profession, but forgave them for their ignorance, as can be seen in the following comments:

> If historians (and other social scientists) fail to preserve the evidential values of records by insisting on a violation of the principle of provenance, their action may be attributed to their ignorance of the archival profession, about which they are expected to know very little, and may for this reason be excused. (Schellenberg 1978, 152)

Regardless of whether you agree that the statement by Schellenberg displays a condescending and biased attitude about the purpose of collections, he was indeed making a valid point; it is one that everyone would be well to remember: As researchers, we all owe future investigators the same right to access to the original archival data that we expect; therefore, researchers must always treat archives with care; they must be left in the state we would like them to be when we find them.

Types of Archives

Webb et al. (2000) group the many sources of stored material into just two broad classes or types of archives: *the running record* (essentially all types of public documents, artifacts, and mass media) and the *episodic and private record* (these are discontinuous and usually not a part of the public record).

Running record archives are the continuous, ongoing records of society. The first thing that comes to mind when we think about this source is the extensive body of vital statistics and other records kept by all levels of governments and the mass media. However, it also includes actuarial records of insurance companies, recorded votes of political officeholders, government budgets, and the like. Like the second type of archive records, these data can exist as words, numbers, pictures, graphic displays, the residue of human activity, and society's refuse.

Webb et al. also alerted the researcher to two classes of potential bias that can creep into public records—*selective deposit* and *selective survival.* Artifacts survive in nature because they are not consumed, not eroded away, and not combined into other artifacts and thus lost to view or memory. For example, ceremonial stones, decorative stone facings, and similar components of Greek and Roman structures have been removed over the centuries to be incorporated into the walls and buildings of later generations. What were once sacred temples of an earlier civilization have become the stables and storehouses of later cultures.

Disappearing Public Records

Changes in political administrations usually result in the filing away and delivery to archival storage of volume after volume of written records. Potentially damaging or embarrassing records somehow get misplaced or "accidentally" removed from the archival record. In other instances, well-meaning historians or social science researchers may be charged with bringing order to a body of unorganized archival records. In the process, they often edit the mass of raw data, unwilling to leave it as they found it. What survives may be what that researcher believed was important. Also, records of diverse events are often grouped together, thereby blurring the real contextual time structure of events. The phenomenon is visible today in the decay and renewal evident in many inner cities. Buildings are abandoned, their materials removed and used for other purposes. What remains for later generations to see is far different from the record as it was originally laid down.

Researchers are encouraged in such instances to fall back on the tried and true practice of *triangulation,* validating the remaining archival record using other sources. These include written records prepared by visitors from other cultures, biographies and histories, others' interpretations of the time, and for phenomena in the not too distant past, the remembrances of participants in the events.

Episodic and Private Archives

It is important to remember that episodic and private record archives are, first, private data. Furthermore, they are usually not as accessible as public records. They tend to be stored for shorter periods and are often destroyed after a set period of time. This accounts for one of the major differences between these two broad classes of archives: it is often not possible to perform longitudinal analyses on private archival data.

Episodic archives can be grouped into three broad classes: company records, institutional records, and personal documents. Company information, such as sales records, has long been used to measure the popularity of, preference for, and loyalty toward a product, event, idea, or service. It is also used to measure the effectiveness of advertising and government informational communications programs. Institutional records are the files of companies, organizations, agencies, and institutions. They can be used to measure job stress by records of absenteeism, tardiness, turnover, and labor union grievances, for example. They can also be used to evaluate agency effectiveness by measuring customer complaints and the content of suggestion programs. Personal records such as letters, memos, collections, artwork, and other possessions are usually the concern of historians and as such have little application for research in public administration.

A Word of Caution Concerning Archives

Caution is advised in the use of archival materials because of the potential distortion that can exist in personal archives (Webb et al. 2000). Low-paid clerical workers often indifferently keep archives with no stake in the accuracy of their product. Because record keepers may feel that the saved material has little value, it may be stored haphazardly. It may be years if not decades before the material is again examined; therefore, their diligence or lack thereof seldom comes to light. When a researcher appears on the scene, however, there is a tendency for their interest to be revitalized, with the unfortunate result of some altering or even destruction of recorded data.

Archive research involves a way of looking at published or previously prepared material and also defines the type of materials that are examined. While this approach to the investigation of archival records of all types can serve as an excellent source of pertinent data for many studies in public administration and nonprofit organization management, it is not without its disadvantages. This final warning was provided by Webb et al. (2000, 84):

> For all their gains [i.e., advantages], however, the gnawing reality remains that archives have been produced for someone else by someone else. There must be a careful evaluation of the way in which the records were produced, for the risk is high that one is getting a cut-rate version of another's errors.

Nontextual Archives: Physical Traces

Physical evidence is another information source that might be considered archival evidence, in that it was recorded for future researchers to interpret. According to Webb et al. (2000), physical evidence is probably the least-used source of data in the social and administrative sciences. However, it does hold what they called "flexible and broad-gauge potential." They identify two broad classes of physical evidence:

- *Erosion measures*—the degree of selective wear or erosion that occurs over time, such as using the rate of wear in museum floor tiles as a measure of exhibit popularity.
- *Accretion measures*—the degree to which materials collect over time. There are two subclasses of accretion measures: (1) *remnants*—only one or a few traces are available for study, and (2) *series*—an accumulative body of evidence remains.

The major advantage of physical evidence is its inconspicuousness. It is, indeed, a *silent* measure of change. What is measured is generated without the subject's knowledge of its use by investigators. This circumvents the problems that arise from the subject's awareness of being measured and removes the bias that comes from the measurement process itself becoming a part of the phenomenon. With all types of physical traces, and particularly when the phenomenon still occurs, index numbers are generated for comparisons, rather than the specific measurements themselves.

PERFORMING A META-ANALYSIS OF TEXT MATERIALS

Lipsey and Wilson (2001) defined *meta-analysis* as a type of survey research in which previously prepared research reports and not people are the subjects of analysis. Meta-analyses are used in order to summarize and compare the results of many different studies; other researchers have produced most if not all of these other studies. Meta-analysis is an excellent way of establishing the state of research findings on a subject—it provides the researcher with the "big picture," rather than simply another discussion of one or a few parts of the question, problem, or issue.

Meta-analyses can only be applied to empirical research reports—that is, studies that employ primary research and data gathering. The technique is not appropriate for qualitative studies or studies that summarize a set of other studies. Although experiments are not required, many meta-analyses have summarized the published findings of experimental research designs.

Advantages and Disadvantages of Meta-Analysis

Lipsey and Wilson (2001) identified four important advantages of the meta-analysis research design. First, the complete process of establishing a coding scheme and criteria for selecting studies (a survey protocol), reading the study reports, coding the material, and subjecting it to a rigid statistical analysis imposes a discipline on the researcher that is sometimes missing in qualitative summarizations and comparative analyses.

Second, the process results in greater sophistication in summarizing research, particularly when compared with qualitative summary attempts. The application of common statistical tests across all the studies can correct for wide differences in sample size, for example. Third, meta-analysis may enable the researcher to find effects or associations that other comparative processes miss. Finally, it provides a way to organize and structure diverse information from a wide variety of study findings.

Meta-analysis is not without its critics, however. Lipsey and Wilson admitted the validity of these criticisms, but were convinced that the strengths of the method far outweigh any such disadvantages. A few of the criticisms that have been cited for the method include the following:

1. The large amount of effort and expertise it requires is an often-cited disadvantage of the method. Properly done, a meta-analysis takes considerably more time than a conventional qualitative research review; many aspects of the method require specialized knowledge, particularly in the selection and computation of appropriate "effect sizes" (i.e., the statistic chosen for comparison across all the studies).
2. Meta-analysis may not be sensitive to some important issues, including but not limited to the social context of the study, theoretical influences and implications, methodological quality, design issues, and procedures.
3. The mix of studies (an *apples and oranges* issue) combined into larger groups may hide subtle differences seen in individual studies.
4. Finally, inclusion of studies that are methodologically weak can detract from the findings in strong studies.

How to Do a Meta-Analysis

Fink (1998, 216) has recommended the following series of seven steps for conducting a meta-analysis:

1. Clarify the objectives of the analysis.
2. Set explicit criteria for including and excluding studies.
3. Justify the methods used for searching the literature.
4. Search the literature using a standardized protocol for including and excluding studies.
5. Devise a standardized protocol to collect data from each study, including study purposes, methods, and outcomes (i.e., effects measured).
6. Describe in detail the statistical method for pooling results.
7. Report the results of the comparative analysis, included conclusions and perceived limitations.

A slightly longer, but possibly more informative, list of steps can be discerned by combining ideas from Lipsey and Wilson's manual on the method with Fink's later review. This summary procedure model is displayed in Figure 29.2.

Statement of the Topic or Question

This step provides the framework upon which all subsequent steps in the process follow. An example of a question statement for a meta-analysis might be: How have mandatory sentencing guidelines affected the number of repeat arrests for crimes in which a weapon was involved?

Identify the Form(s) of Research Relevant to a Meta-Analysis

The "forms" are the types of analysis conducted in the individual research studies. For example, a study that reports an experiment with treatment and control groups, or a study that focuses on correlation between two or more variables. Another example is a standard two-group comparison study, such as a study that compares mean rates of arrests or length of sentences before mandatory sentencing, then repeats the study after imposition of sentencing minimums. This is a typical pre- and posttreatment comparison or hypothesis testing research design.

Select Types of Studies to Be Included in the Analysis

This decision step is similar to the step above, but refers more to the statistical tests used. Four types of tests are regularly used in meta-analyses: (1) central tendency descriptions (such as mean scores), (2) pregroup/postgroup hypothesis test studies, (3) other group contrasts, either pure experiments or nonexperimental grouping comparisons (for example, comparing gender or age groups), and (4) studies employing regression analysis.

Determine Eligibility Criteria

In this step, the researcher determines what criteria to use when deciding which studies to include in the meta-analysis. Examples of types of criteria often used include (1) the distinguishing feature of a study (what made writing about it worthwhile), (2) research subjects (i.e., types or characteristics of respondents used in the study), (3) key variable(s), (4) research designs, (5) cultural and/or linguistic range, (6) time frame involved, and (7) type of publication.

Identify and Locate Sources of Research Reports

At this stage the researcher applies the decision criteria established in the previous step. Lipsey and Wilson urged that the researcher develop a meticulous accounting system so that each study is assigned its own detailed bibliographic entry and its own identification number in order to facilitate future cross-referencing and to ensure that reports are assigned to their appropriate comparison group. A brief description of the subject report should also be prepared at this time.

Some sources and listings for research reports include review articles, references in other studies, computer databases, bibliographies, professional and academic journals, conference programs and proceedings, correspondence with researchers active in the field, government agencies, the Internet, colleges and universities, professional associations, and others.

Figure 29.2   **Steps in a Meta-Analysis Research Design**

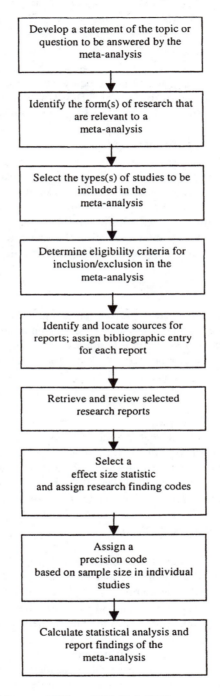

Source: Information from Lipsey and Wilson 2001; Fink 1998.

Retrieve and Review Eligible Research Studies

This step involves several activities. First, the researcher must find bibliographic references to potentially eligible studies, and then obtain a copy of the study for screening. If it is considered to be eligible, it must be coded for inclusion in the meta-analysis.

Select an Effect Size Statistic for Use with the Entire Sample of Reports

In a meta-analysis, a single research finding is a statistical representation of the relationships among the variable(s) of interest. This statistical representation is the effect size statistic that will be used in comparative analysis during the meta-analysis. Research findings in the subject reports are test statistics; each must be coded as a value on the same effect size statistic. This must be the same statistic across the entire sample of reports. For example, if the effect size statistic is the correlation between two or more variables, the variables in all the reports must have been measured at the same level (nominal, ordinal, or interval), with the same correlation statistic employed (Pearson's *r*, Spearman's rho, the chi-square-based phi or Cramer's *V*). Similar restrictions apply for other statistical measures that might be selected (Lipsey and Wilson 2001).

Assign a Precision Code for Each Research Report

A precision code is similar to a weighting system. It is based upon the sample size employed in each subject report. For example, a study in which a sample size of 500 was tested can be expected to be considerably more precise than one in which the sample size was, say, only 5—or even 50. The statistical calculations used in meta-analysis take these precision weights into effect, thus correcting for possible error associated with small samples. The greater the perceived reliability, the greater should be the precision code value assigned to the study.

Calculate Statistical Analysis and Report Findings

Finally, researchers must keep in mind that there are two parts to a meta-analysis coding process. The first part is the information that describes characteristics of the subject report; this is the *study descriptor* portion of coding. Study characteristics include such information as the methods, the measures, sample characteristics and size, constructs developed, and treatments given. The second part of the coding protocol is the part that covers information about the empirical findings contained in the report; this is the "effect sizes" portion of the coding, together with the precision code for each study. Effect sizes are the statistical values that indicate the association between variables.

The first section of this chapter discussed documentary data as a source of data that researchers turn into information. The following section begins a discussion on some of the ways that researchers actually conduct analyses of texts. Texts include signs and symbols, as well as artifacts and other facets of material culture. Methods such as *hermeneutics, semiotics,* and *content analysis* will be discussed.

HERMENEUTIC ANALYSIS OF TEXT MATERIAL

Hermeneutics is a method of analyzing all types of data (particularly written texts) according to a set of principles that requires the analyst to decipher the meaning of the text (1) through the eyes and intent of the writer or creator of the text or artifact, (2) according to the time frame existing at the time of the writing, and (3) considering the political and cultural environmental influences existing at the time of the creation of the text or artifact.

Hermeneutics owes its long history of interpretive applications to the analysis of, first, religious texts, and second, legal documents and written administrative rulings (Gadamer 1975, 1986; Bauman 1992; Alejandro 1993). The term originates from the Greek word *hermeneutikós,* which refers to the act of explaining—making clear or clarifying the obscure (Bauman 1992).

Hermeneutic analysis requires that the researcher take a holistic, or "contextualist," approach to analysis of a problem. The meaning of a text or social phenomenon that is analyzed hermeneutically depends on the whole—that is, the text, the author(s), *and* the context. Meaning cannot be deciphered without understanding the context as well as the text or phenomenon (Wachterhauser 1986).

Hermeneutics is a way of clarifying the meaning of a text by interpreting it *historically.* It looks upon a text as the "medium which links human subjects (i.e., writers of textual material) to their world and to their past . . . it involves identification with the intentions and situation of the (writer)" (Moore 1990, 94). Maas (1999), writing about the hermeneutic analysis of religious texts, explained this two-part focus by describing both a *material* and a *formal* object for the process. The material object is the text or other document that is being explained; the formal object is deciphering the sense of the author at the time the text was written.

Hermeneutic analysis is particularly relevant when studying historical documents, such as past legislation, the records of discourse that occurred over legislative or administrative hearings, and similar applications. In this way, public administration hermeneutics deals with government texts or documents as its material object, with the deciphering of the intent of the framers at the time of the text's creation (i.e., passage or implementation) as its formal object. Thus, legislation that might seem irrelevant today may be interpreted as logical and meaningful when considered in the light of events and circumstances at the time of its enactment.

Principles of Hermeneutics

Several key principles underlie the hermeneutical analysis process. First, *all thought is derived from language and follows the same laws that regulate language.* A writer uses the traditions and conventions of his or her time and particular circumstances, including the same rhetorical logic, sequence of ideas, and rules of grammar in use at the time of the text's creation. Therefore, the analyst who wishes to fully understand the writer and correctly interpret the writer's words must first understand the author's meaning *at the time and place of the writing.* The interpreter must know the context of the text: the writer's language, train of thought, and psychological and historical condition at the time of the writing. Hence, the first principle of hermeneutics is this (Maas 1999, 3): "Find the sense of a book by way of its language (grammatically and philogically) by way of the rules of logic . . . and by way of the writer's mental and external condition (at the time of writing)."

Several other principles follow from this first principle of hermeneutics. Hermeneutic analysis presupposes that the analyst (1) has knowledge of both the grammar and historical evolution of the language in which the work is written, (2) is familiar with the laws of logic and rhetoric, and (3) has knowledge of psychological principles and the facts of history (of the time the work was written).

Hermeneutic Analysis of Nontext Material

While it is used most often as a method for analyzing texts, hermeneutics is applicable to more than this; it is a broadly based theory of interpreting all creations of humankind. Henrietta Moore (1990, 99), describing philosophy's contributions to hermeneutic theory and application, wrote:

> [The] theory of [hermeneutic] interpretation may be extended beyond the written text to encompass other human phenomena which can be said to have textual characteristics. One such phenomenon is meaningful action . . . and action is understood when it can be explained why the individual acted as [he or she] did, and thus can only be explained when a reason or motive for the action can be adduced.

Richardson (1995, 1) also commented on the application of hermeneutic analysis to phenomena other than textual materials, although admitting a sense of puzzlement over the fact:

> Hermeneutics has come forward as that comprehensive standpoint from which to view all the projects of human learning. For those of us who have been puzzled by the new intellectual dominance of hermeneutics, the key is that the term no longer refers to the interpretation of texts only but encompasses all the ways in which subjects and objects are involved in human communication . . . hermeneutics or interpretation has come to be regarded as shorthand for all the practices of human learning.

Moore saw that the problem of analyzing *meaningful action* is at the very heart of much of the research and philosophical speculation in the social sciences, including public administration. She proposed that it be approached with the understanding that the social world is made up of individuals who speak and act in meaningful ways, and added that "these individuals create the social world which gives them their identity and being, and their creations can only be understood through a process of interpretation" (Moore 1999, 111).

Roberto Alejandro applied hermeneutic analysis to public administration issues in his book *Hermeneutics, Citizenship, and the Public Sphere.* He described the key contributions to hermeneutics of German philosopher Hans-Georg Gadamer (*Truth and Method,* 1990). Alejandro discussed two key principles: First, all humans are born into their own tradition, but, because we are all "interpretive beings," we are always working to achieve understanding and interpretation. Second, hermeneutics assumes that mankind's relation to the world is fundamentally and essentially made through language (Alejandro 1993, 34–35).

Meaning and Emphasis in Hermeneutics

Hermeneutics holds that there is always a plurality of meanings available for every human phenomenon. Meaning is not something that just exists; every reader must interpret it. Interpretations will vary from reader to reader, and can only be understood in the light of historical, social, and linguistic traditions. According to Alejandro (1993, 36):

> Interpretation is always a construction of meaning, which is what distinguishes the scientists' endeavor from hermeneutics' purpose. The scientist seeks certainty; hermeneutics seeks clarity. This clarity is anchored in the principle that the construction of meaning that interpretation makes possible is not arbitrary; it is not the outcome of the pure will of the interpreter. The construction of meaning has to consider the boundaries provided by the text [or phenomenon] itself as well as the background provided by the traditions that made it possible.

Bauman (1992, 12) also commented on this difference in emphasis. Because social phenomena —the subject matter of public administration research—are ultimately acts of human beings, they must be understood in a different way than by simply explaining. Men and women do what they do on purpose. True understanding can occur only when we know the purpose, the intent of the actor, his or her distinctive thoughts and feelings that lead up to an action. "To understand a human act . . . [is] to grasp the meaning with which the actor's intention invested it . . . [this is] essentially different from [the goal] of natural science."

In terms of its importance for research on questions in public administration and nonprofit organizations, hermeneutics provides a new way of looking at public issues. The hermeneutic approach assumes that the "constant of history" exists in the mind of every individual and that citizens' actions are inescapably influenced by their beliefs, traditions, and historical events. According to Descombes (1991, 254), *there can be no understanding without interpretation* [author's emphasis].

The Hermeneutic Circle

The process of hermeneutic analysis is less a method than it is a philosophical approach to scientific inquiry. By this is meant that, counter to traditional scientific epistemology that focuses first on explaining and then predicting, the hermeneutic approach is concerned with *interpretation in order to understand*. Achieving understanding, according to Bauman (1992, 17), means following a circular approach "toward better and less vulnerable knowledge."

This path to understanding is called the *hermeneutic circle*. It means beginning by interpreting a single part of the whole, then reevaluating and restating the interpretation in light of information about the time and intent of the event or text. Only then does one move to the next part—again searching the context for greater enlightenment. Merrell (1982, 113) added to understanding of this process by describing the way the analysis moves from the whole to its parts and back to the whole: "When written tests are broken down into isolated segments, those segments can then be relatively easily juxtaposed, compared, and contrasted. That is, they can be subjected to analysis by means of which consciousness of condensed and embedded wholes can be increased." Understanding of parts thus builds on the greater understanding. With each of the parts assessed and reassessed in this way—in a circular analytic process that Bauman described as being "ever more voluminous, but always selective"—full understanding emerges at last.

An Application of Hermeneutic Analysis

Mercier (1994, 42) described how he used the hermeneutic method to examine organizational culture. In his opinion, a hermeneutical analysis of an organization is particularly valuable when management is considering a major shift in strategy. He concluded that a good hermeneutic analysis helps members of the organization recognize that their choices are not as limited as they once believed. Mercier proposed that hermeneutic analysis take place in the following brief sequence of steps:

1. Identification of a "spirit" or central point in an organization's culture ("spirit" refers to what might also be called the *defining characteristic* of the organization)
2. Explanation and interpretation of some of the other puzzling or contradictory elements of the organization through this central point
3. Identification of hard and/or historical elements—related to factors in the environment—that have caused or dramatically influenced the defining characteristic.

In a final word on the hermeneutic method, Wachterhausen (1986, 12) left researchers the following warning, referring to the principle of hermeneutic analysis that establishes and validates many different possible interpretations of a text: "There are no fundamental, underlying 'Truths.' Rather, the rationalistic ideal of discovering a set of self-evident 'foundational' truths from which all legitimate knowledge-claims would follow by strict logical inference is impossible to achieve."

SEMIOTICS: THE ANALYSIS OF SIGNS AND SYMBOLS

Semiotics is a relatively modern interpretive science; it emerged during the middle and last half of the twentieth century as a way of describing how meaning is derived from text, language, and social actions as symbols. The primary social action of interest was initially limited to *language*—in both its written and spoken word forms. However, it was soon applied to analysis of things other than texts, but which could be "read" as text.

Social structure, ritual and myth, material culture, including art and tools: these all became the subject of research into the meaning of their signs and symbols. Today, semiotics is used as a way of interpreting all types of verbal and nonverbal signs and symbols, regardless of the discipline.

The Meaning of Semiotics

Nöth (1990) identified four underlying disciplines that have contributed to the development of the Western semiotic tradition—*semantics* (including the philosophy of language), *logic, rhetoric,* and *hermeneutics.* Other disciplines that helped forge modern semiotics include linguistics, aesthetics, poetics, nonverbal communication, epistemology, and the human sciences in general.

Many definitions of semiotics have been proposed; most relate it in some way to the interpretation of signs and symbols (Peirce 1962; Barthes 1968; Eco 1976; Sebeok 1976; Hodder 1982; Silverman 1983; Nöth 1990; Manning and Cullum-Swan 1998). For example, Nöth (1990) drew upon previous definitive work to give semiotics the following broadest possible definition:

> [The science of signs] has for its goal a general theory of signs in all their forms and manifestations, whether in animals or men, whether normal or pathological, whether linguistic or nonlinguistic, whether personal or social. Semiotics is thus an interdisciplinary approach. (p. 49)

Manning and Cullum-Swan (1998, 251–52), were brief in their suggested definition, referring to semiotics as "the science of signs." They defined a *sign* as "anything that represents or stands for something else in the mind of someone." This definition has two parts: first, an *expression* (such as a word, a sound, a symbol, or the like), and second, a *content,* which is what completes the sign by giving it meaning. Offering another interpretation, Silverman (1983, 14) defined a sign as:

> [S]omething which stands to somebody for something in some respect or capacity. It addresses somebody, that is, it creates in the mind of that person an equivalent sign, or perhaps a more developed sign . . . the sign stands for something, its object. It stands for that object, not in all respects, but in reference to a sort of idea, which I sometimes call the *ground.*

Perhaps the most complete definition of what constitutes a sign was provided by Eco (1976, 16), who defined a sign as "*everything* [his emphasis] that, on the grounds of a previously established social convention, can be taken *something standing for something else.*"

Forms of Signs

Signs come in many different forms. Sebeok (1976) grouped the many different types of signs into six broad classifications: signals, symptoms, icons, indices, symbols, and names. Semiotics pioneer John Peirce, however, developed the most widely used classification system, in 1962. He grouped signs into just three classes: icons, indices, and symbols. An icon is a sign that signifies its meaning by qualities of its own. An index communicates its meaning by being an example of its intended sign, such as a weathercock or a yardstick. Peirce considered the symbol to be a synonym for sign.

Semiotic methodology can be used for either theoretical or applied research studies. The key thing to remember is that the focus of semiotics research should always be on determining the *meaning of signs and symbols,* regardless of the form in which they are encountered.

Researchers do not simply study signs; they focus instead on the *links* between the things that signs represent and the people for whom they have meaning. Symbols are not a reflection of society; rather, they play an active role in forming and giving meaning to social behavior (Hodder 1982). Thus, in order to really understand social behavior, the researcher must begin by interpreting the *contextual meaning* of the signs and symbols of the society.

Political science researchers may use semiotics in any research involving verbal or nonverbal communication. Table 29.2 contains an extensive list of fields and study types that Eco (1976, 9–14) believed belong to the field of semiotics. By extension, they may be of interest to political scientists, public administrators, and managers of nonprofit organizations as well.

A Final Word of Caution about Signs

Anthropologist Christopher Tilley (1989, 16) offered this final caveat regarding the interpretation of signs:

> Meaning . . . resides in a system of relationships between signs and not in the signs themselves. A sign considered in isolation would be meaningless. Furthermore, the meaning of a sign is not predetermined, but is rather of cultural and historical convention. Consequently, it does not matter how a signifier appears, so long as it preserves its difference from other signifiers.

CONTENT ANALYSIS

Content analysis is a quantitative and qualitative method of analyzing the content of written documents, transcripts of films, videos and speeches, and other types of written communication (Denscombe 1998). It has been defined as "any technique for making inferences by objectively and systematically identifying specified characteristics of messages" (Holsti 1969, 14).

The main advantage of content analysis is that it provides the researcher with a structured method for quantifying the contents of a qualitative or interpretive text, and does so in a simple, clear, and easily repeatable format. Its main disadvantage is that it contains a built-in bias of isolating bits of information from their context. Thus, the contextual meaning is often lost or, at the least, made problematic. Furthermore, content analysis has great difficulty in dealing with *implied* meanings in a text. In these situations, interpretive (hermeneutic) analysis may be more appropriate, with content analysis supplementing the primary analysis method.

Content analysis is best used when dealing with communications in which the messages tend

Table 29.2

Examples of Semiotic Research Applications

	Research focus	Description of content
1	Aesthetic texts	Analysis of the aesthetic import of textual material
2	Codes of taste	Present in the culinary and enology fields; how tastes communicate certain images
3	Cultural codes	Behavior and values systems, including etiquette, cultural systems, and social organization of groups and societies
4	Formalized languages	"Languages" of statistics, chemistry, engineering, psychology, etc.
5	Kinesics and proxemics	Movement, gestures, special relationships
6	Mass communications	Coding, sending, receiving, interpreting messages
7	Medical semiotics	Signs and symptoms of the illness they indicate and other symbols forwarded by a patient
8	Musical codes	Musical signs with explicit denotative meanings, such as trumpet calls in the military; music that conveys selected emotional or conceptual meanings, such as tone poems
9	Natural languages	Studies in logic, philosophy of language, etc.
10	Olfactory signs	The "code of scents"; important in atmospherics.
11	Paralinguistic sounds	Sounds without linguistic features, such as grunts, growls, etc.
12	Plot substructure	Mythology, mass communication drama and novels, etc.
13	Rhetoric	An early contributor to the field of semiotics; includes models of oral persuasion, argument, etc.
14	Systems of objects	From architecture to objects in everyday use
15	Tactile communication	Communication systems of the blind, as well as such behaviors as the kiss, embrace, slap on the shoulder, caress.
16	Text theory	The study of text as a "macro unit"; text as a whole unit
17	Visual communication	Graphic displays, advertisements, brands and trademarks
18	Written languages	Includes unknown languages, secret codes, ancient alphabets, cryptography, etc.
19	Zoosemeotics	Communications behavior of nonhumans

Source: Eco 1976.

to be clear, straightforward, obvious, and simple. The more that a text relies on subtle, intricate meanings, the less able is content analysis to reveal the full meaning of the communication. Thus, content analysis is used most often to *describe attributes of messages,* without reference to the intentions of the message sender or the effect of the message on the receiver (Denscombe 1998; Holsti 1969). Counting how many times in a speech a candidate denigrates the character of a political opponent is an example application of content analysis.

The major purpose of all content analysis is to be able to make inferences about one or more variables uncovered in a text. It accomplishes this by systematically and objectively analyzing either the content of the text, the process of communication itself, or both (Sproull 1988). Content analysis takes place in the nine-step process displayed in Figure 29.3.

Figure 29.3   **Steps in Content Analysis Research Design**

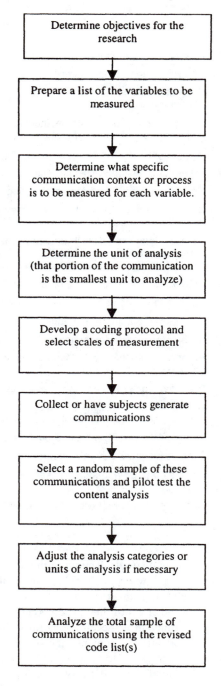

Source: Adapted from Holsti 1969; Sproull 1988; and Denscombe 1998.

The first step in the content analysis process should be a familiar one by now: Establish objectives for the research process. This means determining *in advance* of the research what you want to accomplish by its conduct. Next, assuming that the researcher has some familiarity with the larger issues and/or themes at stake in the phenomenon, a list should be made of what *variables* to be counted in the text. Variables are not the same as words; rather, they tend to be constructs that describe or refer to broader complex issues of behavior or attitude. This list is clearly embedded in the study objectives.

Once the researcher has decided what to look for and where to look for it, he or she must then establish a system for coding the content items and determining how they are going to be counted and recorded. The texts themselves are then collected. Holsti (1969) recommended that at this time researchers should draw a random sample of the materials for a pilot test of the study. The pilot test will provide important clues as to the relative effectiveness of the research design. For example, since the variables of interest are established before measurement takes place, there is a possibility that the variables are not treated significantly in the sample of sources chosen. In that case, the researcher would have to go back and identify new variables for the study.

The final steps in the study involve conducting statistical analysis on the measurements. When possible, these should include correlation analysis and simple hypothesis testing.

Complementary Tools: Narrative and Discourse Analysis

Content analysis is related to several similar research designs, among which are *narrative analysis* and *discourse analysis*. A *narrative* is an oral or written exposition that typically describes the events in the life of a person. A *discourse* is either an oral or written communication designed to inform, rather than entertain. The term "discourse" is often used to identify an *exchange* of communication between two or more speakers or writers.

Narratives have been formally defined as "a means of representing or recapitulating past experience by a sequence of ordered sentences that match the temporal (time) sequence of the events which, it is inferred, actually occurred" (Labov as cited by Cortazzi 1993, 43). A *narrative analysis* is a qualitative approach to the interpretation of texts and, as such, is often used to augment a quantitative analysis of content. Noting the mutually supportive roles of the various methods, Holsti (1969, 11) reminded researchers that:

> [T]he content analyst should use qualitative and quantitative methods to supplement each other. It is by moving back and forth between these approaches that the investigator is most likely to gain insight into the meaning of his [sic] data. . . . It should not be assumed that qualitative methods are insightful, and quantitative ones merely mechanical methods for checking hypotheses. The relationship is a circular one; each provides new insights on which the other can feed.

Narratives are a record of events that have significance for both the narrator and his or her audience (a researcher, for example). Narratives are formally structured; they have a beginning, middle, and an ending. Furthermore, they are organized according to a set of distinct structures with formal and identifiable characteristics (Cortazzi 1993; Coffey and Alkinson 1996).

Cortazzi adapted the narrative evaluation or analysis model developed by W. Labov and J. Waletsky. Table 29.3 summarizes the model. Labov's purpose for developing the model was to illustrate how informal styles of narrative (speech) correlate with a number of extant social characteristics. The specific document selected for analysis might be newspaper stories, speeches at local service clubs, or official records such the *Congressional Record*.

Table 29.3

The Labov/Cortazzi Six-Part Narrative Evaluation Model

Structural element	Comment	Questions
Abstract	A 100-word summary	What was this about?
Orientation	Establishes the situation	Who? What? When? Where?
Complication	Major account of the events that are central to the story	Then what happened?
Evaluation	High point of the analysis	So what?
Result	Outcome of the events or resolution of the problem.	What finally happened?
Conclusion	Returns to the present.	Finish of the narrative

Manning and Cullum-Swan (1998) described several different approaches to the analysis of narratives, among which are *Russian formalism* and *structural methods* such as *top-down* or *bottom-up* approaches. Russian formalism emphasizes the role that form plays in conveying meaning in a narrative. It has been used to analyze the form that Russian fairy tales follow. The same approach has been used to examine myths, poetry, and fiction.

Top-down approaches analyze the narrative text according to a set of culturally established rules of grammar and exposition. These methods are used extensively in education. Bottom-up methods, on the other hand, use elements in the text to build a structure for analyzing the whole. This is the approach followed most often in ethnographic research.

In 1934, Karl Bühler (cited in Merrell 1982) provided an early framework of narrative and discourse analysis that is still relevant today. Bühler saw three main functions for a language. First, it must be *expressive;* the message must serve to convey the emotions or thoughts of the user of the language. Second, it must serve a *signaling* or *stimulative* function; the message must stimulate an expected response by the receiver. And third, it must have a *descriptive* function; the user of the language must be able to use it to describe a particular state of affairs in ways that convey the full picture. Others have added additional functions; the most important of these is an *argumentative* or *explanatory* function, by which language users present alternative thoughts, views, or propositions to the descriptive messages (Merrell 1982).

Discourse Analysis of Communications

Discourse analysis is a method of analyzing oral or written communications in order to identify the formal structure of the message while at the same time keeping a *use-of-the-language* purpose in mind. It can be applied to the same types of messages, texts, and documents that are appropriate for content analysis, albeit for a different purpose. Discourse analysis is strongly associated with the analysis of linguistic structures in the message or text. Potter and Wetherell (1994, 48) referred to this point in their discussion of three particularly pertinent features of discourse analysis:

1. Discourse analysis is concerned with talk and texts as "social practices." It examines the linguistic content—the meaning and the topics discussed—in a message as well as the features of language form, such as grammar and cohesion.

2. Discourse analysis has a "triple concern" with the themes of *action, construction,* and *variability* in the message.
3. Discourse analysis is concerned with the rhetorical or augmentative organization of texts and talks.

Finally, the objective of discourse analysis is to take the focus of analysis away from questions of *how* a text version relates to reality to ask instead how the version is designed to compete success-fully with one or more alternative versions. The following five points direct discourse analysis:

- Variation in theme and message is to be used as a lever in analysis.
- The discourse must be read and analyzed in minute detail.
- A key point in the analysis is the search for rhetorical organization.
- Accountability: Are the points that are made supported?
- Discourse analysis requires cross-referencing with other studies.

EXAMINING MATERIAL CULTURE AND ARTIFACT ANALYSIS

The study of material culture—the tools and other artifacts that are created, used, and left behind by society—is closely related to the science of semiotics. While it owes a great debt to the science of archeology, it is not restricted to the search for meaning among the shards and bones of ancient civilizations. Artifact analysis is a modern science as well; archeologists also study the garbage dumps of today's society.

According to archeologist Ian Hodder, artifact analysis involves a process that begins with the interpretation of signs and symbols, making it a legitimate target for both hermeneutic and semiotic analysis approaches. He defined the term *symbol* as referring to an object or social situation in which a direct, primary or literal meaning also generates an indirect, secondary and figurative meaning.

Hodder (1998) identified the key problem affecting the interpretation of artifacts as the need to locate them within the contexts of their creation, while at the same time interpreting them within the context of the modern researcher. By the very act of being interpreted, the artifact is removed to a new and different context, thus bringing decisive interpretation into question. Potentially, many meanings are possible; the researcher must decide not which is best, but which is most probable. Also related to this problem is the fact that material culture, because it often lasts a long time, either takes on or is given new meanings the longer it is separated from its primary producer. While the artifacts typically retain their original form, their meaning changes: "Material items are continually being reinterpreted in new contexts" (Hodder 1998, 120).

Tilley (1989, 188) also commented on the need to look beyond the individual "piece" of material culture itself when deciphering its meaning: "To understand material culture we have to think in terms that go beneath the surface appearances to an underlying reality. This means that we are thinking in terms of relationships between things, rather than simply in terms of the things themselves." Tilley urged public administration researchers to remember that the interpretation of the meaning and significance of material culture is a contemporary activity; the meaning of the past does not remain in the past, but belongs in the present.

The Interpretation of Material Culture

The interpretation of artifacts requires that the researcher function in a scientific environment that is halfway between the past and present. Interpretation also involves comparing different examples of material culture. This makes the interpretation process problematic, at best. The physical evidence under study is often not what was expected—it has, as Hodder (1998, 121) has noted, "the potential to take on any number of unexpected patterns." Furthermore, because physical evidence cannot talk directly to the researcher, it forces the analyst to evaluate and enlarge his or her own experience and worldview.

At all stages of the evaluation of material culture—from identifying categories and attributes to what Hodder called the "understanding of high-level social processes"—the researcher must work at three levels of interpretation simultaneously:

1. The *context* within which artifacts are deemed to have similar meanings.
2. Inseparable from understanding the context is the *identification of similarities and differences* in the artifacts. By showing that people responded the same way to similar stimuli, patterns are identified.
3. While working with the first two levels of interpretation, the researcher must also establish their relevance in terms of historical theories regarding the data.

Hodder cautioned interpreters of material culture to not get locked into a theory simply because it is fashionable at the time of the research. Observation of material culture and its interpretation are both distinctly theory-laden. As a result, theories can be changed when the researcher is confronted with material evidence to the contrary. In a final word of warning, he discussed controversies over what is seen as a major weakness of artifact analysis: the lack of a method for confirming interpretive conclusions. For all researchers working with material culture, Hodder (1998, 122) proposed these two processes to satisfy the critics of interpretation:

> Perhaps the major difficulty is that material culture, by its very nature, straddles the divide between a universal and natural science approach to materials and a historical, interpretive approach to culture. There is thus a particularly marked lack of agreement in the scientific community about the appropriate bases for confirmation procedures . . . the twin struts of conformation are coherence and correspondence.

As has been shown, material culture interpretation methods involve the simultaneous processes of these three activities: (1) definition of the context of the artifact at its time of creation, (2) identification of patterns of similarities and difference, and (3) the use of relevant theories of social and material culture. The researcher's conclusions must present a coherent picture of the interpretation of the artifacts and at the same time establish a corresponding relationship between the artifacts, their context, and the interpretive conclusion.

SUMMARY

This chapter discussed some of the ways that researchers go about examining texts, cultural artifacts, body language, and similar types of written and unwritten communications, records, documents, signs, and symbols. The different sources of research data were grouped into four broad categories. The first category is *written texts,* which include books, periodicals, narratives, reports, pamphlets, the mass media, and other published materials. Research using these sources is often called *library research,* or *desk research.* The second category is *formal and informal documents;* it includes personal messages and assorted types of archival information, such as personal notes and memos, government records and vital statistics, and other informal written materials, including e-mail.

The third category is the wide variety of *nonwritten communications,* including graphic displays (graphs, tables, and charts), photographs and illustrations, tools and other artifacts, and films and videotapes. The fourth category includes all *nonverbal signs and symbols:* body language, facial expressions, gestures, music and dance, animal sounds and behavior, and even noise.

Researchers employ a variety of analysis tools and methods in their study of texts, symbols and artifacts. Among these are *hermeneutics, content analysis, meta-analysis, semiotic analysis, proxemics, kinesics, discourse analysis,* and *site surveys.* The analysis approaches used most often in public and nonprofit organization research are the formal literature review; hermeneutic analysis of textual material; content, discourse, and narrative analysis; meta-analysis; archival analysis; and semiotic analysis.

ADDITIONAL READING

Banks, Marcus. 2001. *Visual Methods in Social Research.* London: Sage.
Cook, Michael. 1986. *The Management of Information from Archives.* Aldershot, UK: Gower.
Lipsey, Mark W., and David B. Wilson. 2001. *Practical Meta-Analysis.* Thousand Oaks, CA: Sage.
Tilley, Christopher, ed. 1990. *Reading Material Culture.* Oxford: Basil Blackwell.
Webb, Eugene J., Donald T. Campbell, Richard D. Schwartz, and Lee Sechrest. 2000. *Unobtrusive Measures.* 2nd ed. Thousand Oaks: Sage.

PART 7

PREPARING THE RESEARCH REPORT

30

WRITING THE RESEARCH REPORT

Once research data has been collected, tabulated, and analyzed, the researcher must then organize the information and choose a structure for presenting the findings of the study and the researchers' conclusions. There are many different ways to do this. One way is to use *chronological* organization. A second approach is to move from the *general to the specific* or *from the specific to the general*. The researcher could use the points in the *definition of the study question or the research hypotheses* as a discussion structure. This could mean starting a paragraph with a point or a hypothesis, then using material from the literature to show how the point is applied in practice. Many other approaches are also possible.

There are no ironclad rules to follow when deciding how to organize research findings and present ideas. However, it is recommended that the report writer avoid jumping around from one point to another with no underlying plan. Remember: A fundamental goal is for your writing to be *read*. For that to happen, it must be *interesting and readable*. This requires adopting a structure and sticking to it.

STRUCTURING THE RESEARCH REPORT

The key step in organizing and presenting ideas is to select a *point of view*. This involves deciding how to structure the paper so that the ideas flow smoothly from section to section. The chances of the paper being read can often be improved by following a simple, standard structure and using a writing style consistent with the writing in that field of study. Later, if the researcher tries to publish a research paper, the format *must* meet the specific structure and style requirements of the selected journal. For now, concentrate on meeting as many of the following requirements as possible.

Points of View for Research Reports

Different disciplines in the social and administrative sciences and the humanities recommend a variety of ways to structure or organize written reports. A valuable overview of some of the different directions or points of view that researchers can take when planning and writing reports of their findings has been suggested by Sorrels (1984, chapter 6), who lists these seven different points of view (or "patterns") that are often chosen:

1. The *indirect pattern,* which moves from factual parts to a general conclusion
2. The *direct form,* which reverses the indirect order, moving from a general conclusion to the facts that support it
3. A *chronological pattern,* which moves the reader through an order of events, such as a sequence of dates
4. A *spatial pattern,* which moves the reader from one department or location to others in a logical sequence
5. An *analytical organization,* in which the whole is separated into its parts, with each part addressed completely before moving onto the next part
6. A *comparative pattern,* in which parts of a whole are compared point by point
7. A *ranked method,* where portions of the paper are presented in the order of their importance or impact; this may be in ascending or descending order

SECTIONS OF THE FINAL REPORT

This section provides a brief discussion of each of the major report components found in public administration and nonprofit organization research reports. This represents a summary or compendium of many different report style recommendations. As they scan published papers and books, researchers are likely to encounter a host of variations from this list of components. Keep in mind that most researchers and business writers in general do not regularly follow any one style or format for their reports, but allow themselves some flexibility. With this in mind, the format and style presented here have been designed to meet most writing requirements and can be safely followed in most instances.

Written research reports contain, at most, nine or ten parts or sections. These are usually organized in the manner presented in Box 30.1. However, it is also important to remember that not all papers and reports follow this format, and not all include every one of these major components.

Notice that this list does not include any mention of charts, tables, graphs, illustrations, drawings, models, or other graphic communication tools. That is because these tools are not limited to any one section. Naturally, graphic items are seldom if ever found on the title page or in the abstract or references. However, this is not to say that they cannot be used in any or all of the other sections. When used correctly, graphic tools greatly improve the ability of a report to communicate. They allow the researcher to present detailed information *clearly, succinctly,* and at a glance, regardless of where they are used in the report.

The Title and Title Page

The title is one of the most important components of a paper. It should leap off the page and grab the reader's attention. This does not mean that it should be "cute." In fact, always avoid using anything that smacks of being cute. Never use slang in writing. If for some reason slang must be used for effect, it should always be set off in quotation marks or in italics.

Most students and beginning researchers tend to use titles that are too general or that do not say anything about what the research or assignment involves. For example, "A Report in Compliance with the Research Assignment of February 2." is not an appropriate title, even if it is true.

Do not make the title too long; eight to twelve words should be the maximum. On the other hand, do not be terse (abruptly brief). Research papers are not newspaper stories; short, tricky headlines as titles are not appropriate—even if they are explained in the first section of the paper.

> ## Box 30.1
> ### Major Components of a Research Report
>
> 1. Title Page
> 2. Abstract
> 3. Introduction or rationale for the study
> 4. Review of the literature examined for the study
> 5. Discussion of the methodology used for the study
> 6. Complete discussion of the results or findings
> 7. Conclusions and/or recommendations
> 8. Detailed list of the references and/or sources cited
> 9. Appendices

Elements of a Good Title

Box 30.2 lists the components of a good title. The purpose of the title is to tell the reader what the paper is about—and to capture the reader's interest so that the full finished product is examined.

A *review* is a secondary literature research strategy. The researcher studies the issue by reading all available information about the topic. Then, a synthesis of that information is presented in the research report. This *qualitative research* method is known as a literature review.

It is a good idea to include the research *method* followed in the title of the final report as often as possible. Some examples of titles for reports in these types of studies include the following:

Examples of Titles for Qualitative Studies

- "An Ethnographic Analysis of Community Meetings for Overcoming Negative Public Attitudes toward Public Safety Planning"
- "Using Personal Interviews to Measure Citizen Confidence in State Educational Achievement Requirements"

Examples of Titles for Quantitative Studies

- "A Factor Analysis of Consumer Attitudes about Smoking"
- "A Time Series Analysis of Minority Hiring Data"

The title page should include the title of the paper, the name of the author or authors (usually in alphabetical order based on the first letter of the last name), and any other relevant information. A format example for title pages is shown in Figure 30.1. An example of a title page for a master's thesis follows in Figure 30.2.

The Abstract

The *abstract* is a concise summary of the research study and report. It is placed at the top of the first page of the paper, immediately below the title and before the introduction section. While

---

Box 30.2
Elements of a Good Title

Good titles include:

- The topic of the study
- The specific application or dimension of the topic studied (Innovations, Revisions, Results, Effects, Use of, New Ways of, etc.)
- The agency, location, people, industry, or other such relevant focus
- Key methodology used (qualitative, quantitative, etc.).

Figure 30.1   **Components of a Title Page for a Research Report**

THE TITLE OF THE REPORT

by
Author's Name

Name of the group, team, or organization
Name of the parent agency
Submission date of the report

---

most reports are typed double-spaced, the abstract is usually typed single-spaced and indented five spaces on both sides of the paper.

Typically, the abstract ranges from 100 to 200 words. In some journals, instructions for authors call for the abstract to be less than 100 words. Whatever length, in this short space the abstract must inform readers what was done, how it was done, the most significant results or findings, and what readers will find when they read the entire paper.

Abstracts are found in all professional journal articles and in the long-form listing of papers included in such CD-ROM databases as *ABI-Inform* and others. Abstracts contain enough information to accurately inform the reader of the key ideas in a paper, while also encouraging the reader to read the full paper.

Figure 30.2 **Title Page for a Master's Degree Thesis**

THE PRIVATE vs. PUBLIC POWER FIGHT IN SEATTLE,
1930–1934

A Study of the Efforts of Three Daily Newspapers
to Influence Public Opinion

by

David E. McNabb

A thesis submitted in partial fulfillment of the requirements for the degree of
Master's of Arts in Communications

University of Washington
Seattle, Washington

Source: McNabb 1968.

In a report prepared for internal distribution, such as a study done for management of a nonprofit organization, the abstract is replaced by a slightly longer summary called an executive summary. While abstracts follow normal sentence construction, the executive summary may be presented in outline or "bulleted" form. The executive summary is often used to guide an audience through an oral presentation of the paper.

A Sample Abstract

In the 123-word abstract displayed in Box 30.3, the authors explain that the paper is about a survey of the perceptions and attitudes on environmental and social issues held by students in Canada, Taiwan, and the United States. It explains who members of the sample are and provides a rationale for conducting the research. A brief suggestion of the results is also included.

The Introduction

In some professional journal formats, this section may be called the *background* section. In others it is referred to as the *rationale for the study*. In some journals, the section may have no label or headline. Most public administration and administrative science journals continue to use the *introduction* label.

The purpose of the *introduction* section is to explain in some detail what the study and paper are all about. Beyond this, there are few specific rules about what goes in the introduction, only

Box 30.3
An Example of a Journal Paper Abstract

Abstract

This paper presents findings of a cross-cultural survey of university students' perceptions of the importance of environmental and social issues, and of programs to deal with these issues. Students in undergraduate and graduate courses in Canada, Taiwan, and the United States were surveyed. The study grew out of discrepancies seen in various cultures' priorities for resolving environmental problems. The researchers developed a list of 45 environmental and/or social problems and 20 statements about how organizations deal with environmental problems. The findings supported the propositions that different countries have different ideas about global environmental problems, that more international cooperation is needed, and management education must include more comprehensive discussions of environmental problems to prepare researchers to function in the sustainable-growth economies of the future.

suggestions. Here are some suggestions the researcher should consider the before writing an introduction for a report or paper.

The introduction section is where readers are introduced to the full scope of the study topic. It includes background information on the topic or situation, the researcher, any funding agencies involved in the study, and any other relevant preliminary information. It is the place to state why the topic was selected and to list the steps taken in developing the study. The introduction explains how or why the study was first considered and what the researcher hoped to learn by studying this particular topic.

The introduction sometimes includes a brief discussion of key items of the literature so that readers can see how the research relates to other work done on this topic. Special care must be taken to avoid simply repeating what others have written, however. It is important that the researcher interprets others' reports and indicates how they relate to the new study.

The introduction is the first place where writing should begin to sparkle. This section must be carefully written and rewritten. It is the first chance to hook the people who are in a position to judge your research and writing.

The following statement from the "Information for Contributors," which appears in every issue of the *Academy of Management Review*, emphasizes the importance of careful presentation of your ideas:

> Manuscripts submitted will be judged primarily on their substantive content, but writing style, structure, and length also will be considered. Poor presentation is sufficient reason for reviewers to reject a manuscript. Clarity and logical presentation are necessary; also, a provocative, challenging orientation that stimulates debate is appreciated, assuming professionalism is maintained.

To summarize, the introduction section should include the following:

- A brief (no more than one or two paragraphs) review of the background of the study
- A statement explaining why the topic was selected
- If appropriate, a brief introduction to other research on the subject
- An indication of what will be presented in the pages to follow
- Any additional information that logically could be considered as an introduction to the research project, study, topic, or paper

Review of the Literature

The section that follows the introduction is the *review of the literature*. It should contain the majority of the analysis of what other researchers and authors have said about the topic. This is where results of the library and/or Internet investigation are presented. Since everything included in this section comes from the work of others, the researcher must be careful to always cite sources; the person who did the work first *must* be given appropriate credit.

For research papers that follow a document analysis strategy, this section might more appropriately be called the *discussion section*. For example, for a paper about how managers in public organizations exercise one or more aspects of good leadership, all data might come from already published sources, such as one or more broadly focused management journals like *Business Week, Harvard Business Review,* or similar sources on CD-ROM or the Internet. Once this is complete, the researcher might then carry out a more extensive search of the public administration literature for specific articles on managers in the public sector. This is not as difficult as it sounds because good examples tend to get lots of attention in the media.

The researcher may include introductory paragraphs defining the topic and variables in question; in this example it means describing specific leadership traits. Then, the literature that addressed each of the traits might be examined. Or, the researcher might be asked to prepare a more structured study that involves observing leadership traits as exhibited by managers in the researcher's own organization. The method of gathering this data may be either qualitative, quantitative, or a combination of the two research methods. In this situation, the literature search can provide suggestions about what traits might be more important than others, how leadership traits are or might be measured, and other relevant foundation material.

Research and Theory

Developing new ideas and concepts requires that a researcher first have a thorough grounding in *existing* theory. This comes from a comprehensive review of the literature on the topic. Sources may be personal interviews the researcher conducts with experts. They may be from the extensive body of domestic and international professional and/or occupational literature or from current and past textbooks. Or they may be from other published materials such as newspapers, encyclopedias, yearbooks, unpublished papers, opinion pieces by other scholars, or from material prepared expressly for and carried only on the Internet.

To summarize this discussion, a review of the literature (or discussion section in a shorter paper) should do the following:

- Review earlier work done in the field
- Explain how earlier work relates to this investigation
- Give examples of directions being taken by other investigators
- Give a sense of continuity or closure to your work
- For a shorter paper, it may provide the body of your ideas and results of the study

Methodology

Sometimes called *research methods,* or *methods and materials,* or simply the *methods* section, this is the part of the report that explains how the work was done. In research studies, this section describes in some detail how data were collected and processed.

Was the study completely a library study? Was the research limited to a study of Internet sources? If so, why? Was a custom-designed questionnaire developed, or was an existing questionnaire used for the survey? Why? Was the data gathered by observation? If so, was the researcher functioning as a full participant or as unobtrusive bystander? Did the research involve conducting a series of personal interviews? Was an experiment designed and carried out? These are only a few of the many different ways to gather information. The method chosen will depend upon the nature of the study problem, the relevant study variables, and the resources available to the researcher.

Methods and Data Differences

It might be worthwhile here to briefly review one of the key differences in data as it relates to study methodology. This is the *primary-secondary data* dichotomy. *Primary* data are data that the researcher generates; they can be considered to be specific to the research project at hand. An example is the collective responses to the questions in a questionnaire (also called a *survey instrument*) that are acquired from a sample of subjects. *Secondary* data, on the other hand, are data that were collected by someone else for a different purpose. Examples include published economic or demographic statistics. Typically, secondary data are cheaper and quicker to gather. Primary data tend to be the more reliable of the two data types. There is a place and purpose for both. If the study is library or Internet research for a short paper, it will involve gathering secondary data exclusively. If the research study means conducting an experiment to evaluate citizens' responses to various public service announcements, it means gathering primary data.

When gathering secondary data, remember that every source of information used must be identified in the paper. This means including a complete bibliographic citation, including page numbers for actual quotes included in the paper (page numbers should *not* be used with source citations when they are paraphrased).

Research means studying published books and articles in the library or checking sources over the Internet. It can require examining artifacts or observing behavior in the field. It can involve developing a set of questions and asking people to respond to a questionnaire. Or, it can require carefully designing and conducting an experiment with human subjects. In every case, the researcher must describe exactly what and how it was done. That information goes here, in the *methods* section of the research paper.

The Results or Findings Section

Once readers have been told what was researched and how it was done, it is time to tell them what the research revealed—what it accomplished. Sometimes this section is called the *discussion section,* or simply *results* or *findings.* This is where readers are presented the final results of the research effort; in the process, it explains the reasons for conducting the research in the first place.

This information must be presented clearly, factually, simply, and without editorial comment. This section is not the place for the researcher to introduce opinions or reactions; conclusions, judgments, or evaluations of the information should not be interjected. The job of the author is simply to *explain what the data reveal*—nothing more.

Do not "editorialize" about the data in this section. Remain cool and objective; simply "tell it like it is." Avoid negative opinions; don't say a manager was "really stupid." However, it is possible to describe the behavior that makes you or others think that he or she was. Let the readers make their own evaluations and conclusions; never tell them how to think.

Writing in First Person or Third Person

Typically, quantitative research reports are written in the third person, while qualitative study reports may be written in either the first person or third person. It is a good thing to get in the habit of using the form used most often in the field of interest or study. For example, authors are strongly encouraged to avoid using the first person approach ("I") in reports on business or economics research, whereas many public administration journals include papers written in both forms. The topic and research methodology followed should dictate the form to use.

As a rule of thumb, however, it is difficult to get into trouble when writing clearly and objectively in the third-person format. However, it is also important to know that many instructors require that personal opinions are included in class writing to encourage students to develop critical thinking skills. Whenever the issue comes up, it is best to comply with one of the first requirements of all writing in organizations: Write for your audience. To summarize, here are some key points for the *results* section:

- Third person is the preferred style for business and economics papers; public administration papers are written in either first- or third-person format.
- Unless specifically asked for your opinion, do not give it in the results section; it goes in the conclusions section.
- Do not "editorialize" about the study results in the findings section. Remain cool and objective.
- Avoid negative opinions; let the readers come to their own conclusions.
- Use clear, objective writing.

Conclusions and/or Recommendations Section

Writing a research report is much like writing a speech. In both cases, the writer selects a topic, finds something out about the topic, and then writes about it. The writer closes with a summary and shares conclusions about the process with an audience. People who teach speechmaking have reduced this to a three-part structure: (1) tell your audience what you are going to tell them, (2) tell them, then (3) tell them what you told them.

In a sense, we have been following these directions as we moved from section to section in this chapter. In the introduction, readers were told what the research and report were going to be about. The methodology section described the way the data were gathered and processed. The results section presented the main body of your research findings. Now is the time to wrap things up by telling the audience what was learned from the research.

A good conclusions section can be one of the most valuable components of a paper (Markman, Markman, and Waddell 1989)—part conclusion, part summary, and part recommendations. This section can be used for several different purposes. First, it provides an opportunity to summarize the main ideas gleaned from the literature and also permits repeating any critical findings from experimental research. Second, it allows the researcher to *interpret* the findings and to present a subjective interpretation in his or her own words. In a good public administration paper, this may be the only place where the researcher can be "original." To this point, the writing remained completely objective, with only the *facts* reported.

Finally, the conclusions section gives the researcher a chance to prove that the research idea, design, and project were valid and "worth the doing." Now, however, the researcher must explain what it all means. To do this well requires the researcher to finally be creative, analytical, and persuasive. At the same time, the author tries to influence the audience or to convince them that the presented interpretation is the "right" one.

This section should begin with a brief summary of the research, then present your interpretation, and close with what you see as implications of the findings, or with your recommendations.

To summarize, the conclusions section should:

- Summarize the main ideas
- Say what these ideas mean
- Include a personal interpretation of the findings (your *opinions*)
- Convince readers that the research was worth the effort
- Make recommendations, if any, to the reader

References (Bibliography)

In the references, the writer identifies all sources of information. Typically, there are two parts to this section: (1) the location of the information used in your study; and (2) an alphabetically listed compilation of all sources cited, studied, or examined during the study. The first part of this section is known as the *notes* or *sources cited* section and can be presented in the report as *endnotes, footnotes,* or *in-text citations.* Notes are presented in chronological order as they appear in the paper, from the first to the last. In-text citations are included in the body of the paper; they appear as the source information is used.

Writers may use footnotes, endnotes, or in-text citations to inform readers of the location of their information sources. "Location" information is needed for others to either replicate the study or test for flaws. For papers of ten or twelve pages, authors are no longer required to use endnotes or footnotes. This does not mean that authors can use the work of others as their own. Doing so is *plagiarism,* and plagiarism is theft. The practice is unethical, immoral, and in most cases, illegal. At some universities and colleges, students can be expelled for plagiarism.

What it does mean is that the citations issue can be dealt with by placing the author's name and date of publication in parentheses at the beginning or end of the section dealing with that work. This is called an *in-text citation.* The in-text citation method is growing in popularity; most publications and organizations prefer that this method be used exclusively. It is the method used throughout this book.

The *references* or *bibliography* contains complete bibliographic information about all sources used in the study. Many different styles for presenting bibliographic information are used in research writing. It is usually best to follow the style used by the most influential writers in the field or the "best" journal in the discipline. The *references* section of the research paper must include a complete bibliographic entry for every source used in the research. If a source has been examined for the study but not used, it is not necessary to include it in the bibliography.

The information used as background for a research project can come from published books; periodicals (magazines, newspapers, journals); interviews or surveys; films; electronic sources such as the Internet; government or company brochures, reports or pamphlets; television programs; or other sources. There are a variety of rules governing how to list these sources, both as notes and references.

In the past, some stylebooks called for both notes and references to be included. Today, however, in-text citations are usually substituted for endnotes or footnotes. Most periodicals require in-text citations be used instead of endnotes or footnotes, together with a formal bibliography at the end of the paper.

The Appendix

The *appendix* is the last component of a research paper. This word has two plural forms: *appendixes* or *appendices;* either can be used. The *appendix* is where to place any attachments that might relate to the paper but that cannot or should not be placed in the body of the paper itself. Examples include a brochure or advertisement, a copy of the questionnaire used in a research study, a complicated mathematical table, or a copy of an article from a magazine, journal, or a newspaper.

There are no limits to what can or should be included in the appendices. The wide variety of materials that could qualify suggests that there is no one rule or special format to follow for appendices. Style manuals with recommendations pertaining to the appendix tend to agree with the following conclusions, however:

- Research papers for public administration, business, or economics seldom require an appendix or appendices.
- When they are used, they should be attached after the bibliography.
- While it is not completely necessary, a single title page (with the label *Appendix*) placed before all the attached material is commonly used.
- Only the number of the appendix title page is noted in the table of contents.
- When more than one appendix is used, the word *Appendices* is placed in the table of contents and on the section title page.
- More than one appendix may be labeled: Appendix A, Appendix B, Appendix C, etc.

STYLE AND FORMAT IN RESEARCH WRITING

The words *style* and *format* are often used interchangeably to refer to the way a paper is put together, but they mean different things. *Format* refers to the way the research paper is structured or organized. It includes headlines, subheads, and the order of the components of the paper. *Style,* on the other hand, refers to the choice of words and sentences used in the report. It includes punctuation and grammar.

Format often varies from discipline to discipline, journal to journal, and depending on the purpose of the paper. Sometimes, *style* refers to the *writing rules* of organizations such as the American Management Association or the University of Chicago Press. At other times, style means the subjective, creative, artistic part of writing: selecting words that sparkle, using the active rather than the passive voice, and using a variety of sentence lengths.

Textbooks with rambling sentences, no paragraph breaks, no headings or subheads, few interesting graphic displays, the researcher and offensive or patronizing language are not easy to read or understand. Most people prefer textbooks and articles that can be easily read and understood. These are the examples to use as models for your own writing. Good writing *can* be learned, just as poor writing can be avoided.

When editors talk about style, they mean either one or all of these writing features: (1) an author's choice of words and sentences, (2) the author's use of the basic rules of grammar and punctuation, or (3) the mechanics of footnotes, endnotes, in-text citations, and various ways of recording bibliographic (reference) notation. This section is about the third component of style: *notes, citations,* and *reference notation.* It is also a brief introduction to several of the most commonly used notation styles: the Modern Language Association (MLA)style, the American Psychological Association (APA) style, and the University of Chicago Press (Chicago style). Style references in several disciplines are also explained.

ENDNOTES, FOOTNOTES, AND IN-TEXT CITATIONS

Endnotes, footnotes and in-text citations are tools used to show the reader where you found your information. Endnotes are footnotes placed at the end of the paper, just before the bibliography. Footnotes are placed on the bottom of the page on which the material they refer to is introduced. An identifying number or symbol is placed at the end of the material to which the footnote applies and repeated at the beginning of the reference information. Superscript is the preferred font for the notations; [1] is an example of superscript.

Both endnotes and footnotes allow the researcher to include additional or parenthetical information that is not otherwise considered part of the regular flow of the paper. They may be personal observations, comments, or questions about the sources. They may also be *asides*—information that adds to the understanding or fuller appreciation of a point in the paper itself. However, their primary purpose is to tell the reader the source of the ideas. Unless the ideas are exclusively the researcher's, their source must always be cited.

Endnote and footnote entries are made in numerical order, from the first to the last. The first time a source is mentioned, a complete bibliographic entry is included with the same format required for a complete bibliography. If the endnote or footnote is additional or parenthetical information and not a citation, it should be written using complete sentences with proper punctuation. With endnotes or footnotes, the complete citation is included in only the first note. After the first entry, all subsequent entries use only the author's last name. The Latin phrases *Ibid.* and *Op. cit.* are rarely used in research reports or other scientific writing and should be avoided.

Formats for In-Text Citations

Today, the preferred way of noting sources in the body of a paper is the in-text citation method. It is easy and quick to use. In-text citations appear in parentheses as they occur in the paper, in chronological order. They consist of the author's last name and the year of publication, without commas or periods, unless followed by a page number. Page numbers are added if a direct quote is used; place a comma between the date and page number.

Say, for example, that you are writing a paper about religion and government. One of your sources discusses parables in modern government literature. If you use an idea found in the source but express it in your own words (i.e., paraphrase), you need not place it in quotation marks. At the end of the reference to that work, add the following notation: "(Last Name 2000)." Beyond this, no end- or footnote notation is required. However, if there is a quote from the work, you must add the page number after the date, thus: (Last Name 2000, 223).

Use of Notes in Large Reports

For large papers and research reports (forty pages or longer), some editors suggest that it is better to use footnotes or endnotes instead of in-text citations. However, if the paper is to be published in a professional journal, the system required by the journal must be used. If it is a paper for a class, follow the instructor's requirements. Here is a good "rule of thumb" to follow: If the paper is shorter than twenty pages or so, do not use endnotes or footnotes; if the paper is longer than twenty pages, use endnotes or footnotes. Other than this, use them if doing so makes the paper easier to read or understand

Bibliographic Style

Most style manuals have grouped source materials into three broad categories: (1) books, (2) periodicals (magazines, journals, and newspapers), and (3) miscellaneous, including pamphlets, brochures, annual reports, letters, speeches, interviews, films, and other sources. Today, a fourth category has been added: *electronic sources*. These include the Internet, CD-ROMs, and miscellaneously electronically accessed databases.

A word of caution: There is a lack of agreement on which is the best or most appropriate way to list citations. Almost every discipline has its own format. It is up to you to determine which format is accepted or preferred in the organization for which the paper is written; follow that style. Considerable disagreement also exists on citation formats for electronic sources. Several different citation guides are listed in this guide; one is the *Columbia Guide to Online Style* (1998), published by Columbia University Press.

Although most public administration programs require students to follow APA style, many public administration, management, and economics publications follow format requirements that are established or promoted by their respective professional associations. Those formats may differ somewhat from the three main style formats: APA, MLA, and the University of Chicago Press style. Communications courses also have format requirements of their own; they often follow a newspaper style established by either the Associated Press (AP) or United Press International (UPI). Citation formats for papers written for natural sciences also vary somewhat from the three major styles.

This section also includes some style requirements for government, law, business, and economic disciplines. The following is a summary of style information:

- Most style manuals group sources into three categories: books, periodicals and miscellaneous. Today, a fourth category is also used: electronic sources.
- There are many different ways to cite sources: Use *one* and stick to it.
- These three major styles are the standard forms in use (often with some variation): APA, MLA, and Chicago.
- Some disciplines recommend using either Associated Press (AP) style or United Press International (UPI) style.
- Never create your own style; never mix styles within the same paper.
- Style manuals have been written for many occupations. Find the one used in your industry or discipline and use it for all writing.

MAJOR BIBLIOGRAPHY STYLES

Bibliography style refers to the way researchers indicate the names and locations of their sources. Most, but not all, public administration writing follows the style of the American Psychology Association (APA). This information is included at the end of a paper, a report, or a book. It includes all sources used in the project. Typically, bibliography styles require most if not all of the following information:

1. Author(s) name(s)
2. Title of the section, if a part of a book
3. Title of the book, article, pamphlet, or other source
4. Name of the editor, translator or compiler, if appropriate
5. Edition of the work if other than the first
6. Name(s) or number(s) of the volume(s) used, if a multivolume work
7. Name of the series, if part of a series of books
8. Place of publication (city)
9. Name of the publisher
10. Date of publication
11. Journal volume, edition number
12. Page numbers, if quoted from a work or if the work is part of a compendium
13. Any other relevant bibliographic information and/or annotation

APA Style

The American Psychological Association (APA) prefers that authors use in-text citations without footnotes or endnotes, with references placed in an end-of-paper "Works Cited" section. This applies for all papers, regardless of length. All source listings should include the author(s) name, title of the work, and publication information. Page numbers are required for all direct quotes. Publication dates are placed in parentheses immediately after the author's name.

APA style requires you to underline a title if you do not have access to an italic typeface. Do not indent the first line of a listing; instead, indent the second and each subsequent line three spaces (MLA requires a five-space indentation). *All* authors' names must be listed—do not use *et al.* (*et alia,* which in Latin means "and others"). All names must be inverted (listed last name first).

If you do not have an author's name, alphabetize the listing by the first word of the title (except for short words such as *the, a,* or *an*). Capitalize the first letter of only the first word in book, journal, and newspaper titles (except for proper nouns). Capitalize short titles like *Business Week.* Do not put quotation marks around the titles of journal articles.

Use double space or space-and-a-half for listings. APA also recommends dropping short labels as "Press," "Co.," "Corp.," or "Inc." after the name of the publisher. Books printed by university presses are usually typed out in full, thus "Oxford University Press."

Periodical citations include the name(s) of the author(s), date of publication, title or headline of the article, and name of the periodical; use initial capital letters for periodical title names (Examples: *Business Week, Journal of Macroeconomics, Journal of State and Local Government).* Volume and issue numbers, when available, are also included, appearing just before page numbers.

Other sources include pamphlets, government or company brochures, dissertations, conference proceedings, personal letters and interviews, and annual reports. These are all legitimate published sources and should be listed in the bibliography in the same way as books and periodicals.

Formats for Reference Lists

Information for these format recommendations can be found in the 5th edition of the APA's *Publication Manual of the American Psychological Association* (2006). Keep in mind that only the works cited in your paper should be included in the references list. List entries by the last name of the authors; where there is no author identified, list by the first major word in the title. All entries should be double spaced. Two or more works by the same author should be listed in chronological order, with the earliest work listed first. Use two spaces after each element in the entry, with periods separating sections, when punctuating reference entries.

When preparing a paper for a social science journal that uses APA style, the style manual calls for entries to be listed differently than they will appear in the final published order. Instead of typing entries flush left with hanging indents for each following line, APA style requires the first line of the entry to be indented five spaces, with no hanging indents for subsequent lines (this is a mechanical requirement for typesetting purposes). If the entries are typed the way they will be read, use the traditional flush left for the first line and hanging indents (five spaces) for each subsequent line.

APA is one of the few styles that call for the first names of entry authors to be omitted, with only the first letter of the name used instead. For example, instead of *Jones, James B.,* use *Jones, J.B.* The names of *all* authors are presented with last name first, followed by initials of first and middle names. Styles for the major categories of references assume that users will have access to italic type for publication titles. If not, substitute underlining the title in place of italics. The following examples are presented as they are required in APA style, not as they will appear in a published document.

Journals

Author's last name, initials. (year). Article title with only the first word capitalized, without quotation marks. *Journal Title,* volume number as an Arabic numeral (issue number), page numbers, omitting pp.

1. Papers with One Author:

Jones, J. B. (2005). Legislative deadlock: The history of the 2004 legislative session. *Journal of Legislative Affairs,* 12 (3), 37–55.

2. Papers with Two or More Authors:

Shirley, J. E., Johnston, A. B., & Sarakofski, T. O. (2006). Online training for public sector first-level supervisors. *Journal of Education and Training,* 37 (6), 432–437.

Magazine and Newspaper Articles

Crookshank, N. B. (2006, March 21). Minority participation in border state municipal elections. *Newsweek,* 49–51.

Books

Marshall, B. C. (2004). *Understanding social science research* (3rd ed.). New York: Brownstone.

Section in an Edited Book or Anthology

Batten, D. B. (2005). Communities of practice in Oregon. In D. E. Wilson (Ed.), *Knowledge management in state government* (pp. 87–108). London: Updegraff.

Electronic References

A reference of an Internet source should provide a document title or description, a date (either of publication or accessed), and an Internet address. The Internet address is the uniform resource locator (URL). If the authors of the document are known they should also be included. An example is the following citation for the American Psychological Association's 2003 URL for Electronic Resources:

APA. (2003). *Electronic references.* Washington, DC: The American Psychological Association. *APA style.org.* Accessed August 3, 2006 from http://www.apastyle.org/elecmedia.html

Government Publications

1. No Author Identified:

U.S. Government Printing Office. (2003). *The president's management agenda.* Washington, DC: Author.

2. Author Identified:

Henley, M. T. (2004). *Reducing duplication in government ICT spending.* Washington, DC: Office of Management and Budget.

Using MLA Style

According to the Modern Language Association of America (MLA), all sources included in a bibliography include three main components: author(s), title, and publication information. All other style formats are in agreement with these requirements; they differ, however, in the way and the order in which they are presented.

MLA requires that the bibliography be in two sections. First, place citations for all sources cited in the body of the paper in a section titled "Works Cited." All other sources referenced but not cited can go into a "References" or "Bibliography" section.

Twelve or more types of book listings are described in the MLA style manual. These range from books with a single author to multiple or unknown authors. Also included are compilations by editors, various editions or volumes in a series, parts of books, the forward or preface, encyclopedias, and dictionaries. Only a few of the most commonly encountered versions are listed here. When the name of a book's author is not known, the title of the book or journal is substituted.

MLA style calls for two spaces between citation components (for example, between the author's name and title of the work). If you do not have access to an italic typeface for the title, underline it instead. Do not indent the first line of each bibliography or note listing; instead, indent the second and each subsequent line five spaces.

Use double space or space-and-a-half for all listings. MLA also recommends omitting short labels, such as "Press," "Co.," "Corp.," or Inc. after the name of the publisher. An exception to this rule is for books printed by university presses: Instead of typing "Oxford University Press," use "Oxford UP." Some specific examples are shown below.

Books

1. Books with one author:

Aldershot, Benjamin B. *Writing for Fun and Profit*. Chicago: Winslow, 1997.

2. Books with two or more authors:

West, Barbara A., and Janet C. Lagerquist. *Principles of Qualitative Research*. London: Oxford UP, 1998.

(Only the first author is listed last name first; separate the names of two or more authors by commas.)

3. Books with editors:

Andreeson, Elizabeth, ed. *Strategies for Competing after 2000*. Homewood, IL: Business Books, 1999.

4. Author with an editor (article in an anthology):

Marshall, Jay B. "From Cottage to Factory." *Wool and the Industrial Revolution in Britain*. Ed. James B. Galloway. Liverpool: Liverpool UP, 1990: 87–102.

Note that the title of the article or chapter in this book is in quotation marks; the book's editor comes after the book title, with "Ed." (for "Edited by") before the editor's name; the pages of the article or chapter are noted after the date, separated by a colon.

5. Books, second or later edition:

Smith, Alfred E. *Principles of Nonprofit Organization Management*. 6th ed. San Jose: Lighthouse, 1998.

6. Article in an encyclopedia:

"Ethics." *Encyclopedia Britannica*. 15th ed. 1995.

Periodicals (Magazines, Journals, and Newspapers)

Several different terms are used here to refer to what are commonly known as magazines, or what libraries call *periodicals*. Periodicals appear as often as daily or as seldom as once or twice a year. They may be of general or special interest. They may carry news of an industry sector, a career field, or may be about research or new developments in a discipline. Because the articles usually go into some depth on a specific idea, problem, or question, they are excellent sources of information for papers. Most but not all periodicals include the name of the author(s) and titles or headlines for each of the articles.

Newspapers are published daily, weekly, every one or two weeks, or monthly. Not all newspaper articles include the author's name (the author's name is sometimes called a *byline*). Newspaper articles are usually current; they include what is news *today*. However, most of the time they do not go into much depth, but there are exceptions such as the *Wall Street Journal* and Sunday edition of *The New York Times*.

A reference listing of a periodical article must include the name of the author, title of the article, name of the periodical, month and year of publication, and page numbers. Newspaper article citations also include the day of publication and section, if available. If the article is broken into two or more sections—for example, starting on pages 33–40 and continued on pages 101–105, use 33+, not 33–105. Following are some of the most commonly used ways to present source citations.

1. Article in a weekly publication:

Serenski, Sergi V. "Cost Accounting Is Sexy." *Business Week* 22 February 1998: 35–36.

2. Article in a monthly or quarterly journal:

Rice, Jerry B. "Tracking the Cost of Professional Football Admissions." *Journal of Accounting* (January 1991): 64–72.

3. Unknown author:

"Boeing Employment Cuts Go Deep." *Time* 3 December 1998: 20–21.

4. Article in a newspaper:

Sorenson, Theodore X. "Microsoft Foes Throw Rocks at Windows." *Tacoma News-Tribune* 5 October 1999: B1.

Other Sources

1. A government pamphlet or brochure, no author listed:

U.S. Dept. of Agriculture. *Regulations for Applying Pesticides.* Washington: GPO. 1990.

("GPO" is the U.S. Government Printing Office, where most federal publications are published and distributed.)

2. Company pamphlet, brochure, or annual report:

The Boeing Co. *1997 Annual Report.* Seattle: The Boeing Co., 1998.

3. Unpublished (Ph.D.) dissertation or (M.A.) thesis:

McNabb, David E. *Segmenting the Market for Post-Secondary Education.* Diss. Oregon State U., 1980.

4. A personal letter:

LeBlank, Peter A. Letter to the author. 25 June 1997.

5. A personal interview:

Jones, Edward S. Personal interview. 30 January 1996.

6. Published proceedings of a conference:

Sepic, F. Thomas, and David E. McNabb. *Organization Climate and an Organization's Readiness for Change.* Proc. of Western Decision Sciences Institute, 1994. Reno, Fullerton: Cal-State Fullerton U, 1994.

Electronic Sources

Researchers and authors are turning to electronic sources for much if not most of their secondary information. Changes in these sources are occurring rapidly as the World Wide Web and online databases become preferred sources for research information. The following recommendations are from James-Catalao's *Researching on the World Wide Web* (1996), Harnack and Kleppinger's (1997) manual: *ONLINE! A Reference Guide to Using Internet Sources,* and Li and Crane's (1996) publication, *Electronic Styles: A Handbook for Citing Electronic Information.* A citation for a Web source must include as much of the following information as is available: author(s), title of the piece, date it was placed on the Web, address and other retrieval information, and date the user accessed the article. The following recommendations have been adapted to comply with MLA style requirements.

1. World Wide Web sources:

U.S. Dept. of Labor. "The Occupational Safety and Health Act of 1970 (OSH Act)." *Small Business Handbook: Safety and Health Standards.* November 1997. http://www.dol.gov/dol/asp/public/programs/handbook/osha.htm. 2 December 1998.

Gillmor, Dan "Nader May Be the True Microsoft Threat." 27 October 1997. http://www.computerworld.com. 23 November 1998.

2. An e-mail source:

McNabb, David E. *Students' Attitudes on Environmental Issues.* 4 November 1998. E-mail available from Prof. Samuel Goldberg: sgoldberg@oregonstateu.edu.

Chicago Style

The editorial staff of the University of Chicago Press, a major publisher of works by academic authors, printed its first *Manual of Style* for writers in 1906. Since that time, the manual has gone through at least fourteen revisions, with more on the way. The *Chicago Manual of Style* describes the use of both footnotes and in-text citations. A full biographic listing is required in the end-of-work references section.

When available, all listings should include the author(s), title of the work, and publication information. Page numbers are required for all direct quotes. Publication dates are placed at or near the end of the listing, immediately before the page numbers. Chicago style requires titles of journals and books to be in italics. Bibliographic listings are presented in alphabetical order, single-spaced, with two spaces between each listing.

Only the first author's name should be inverted (listed last name first); others are listed first name, middle initial, last name. If there is no author's name, alphabetize the listing by the first word of the title. *All* authors' names must be listed. Capitalize the first letter of *all* words in book, journal, and newspaper titles. Put quotation marks around the titles of journal articles.

Chicago style requires these items to be listed in the following order in book citations:

- Name of the author or authors, editors, or institution responsible for the writing of the book
- Full title of the book, including subtitle
- Series, if any
- Edition if not the first
- Publication city
- Name of the publisher
- Date of publication

Periodical citations should include as many of the following as possible:

- Name(s) of the author(s)
- Title of the article
- Name of the publication
- Volume (and number) of the periodical
- Date of the volume or of the issue
- Page numbers of the article

The following information for electronic sources has been adapted to come as close as possible to Chicago style guidelines. Electronic sources must include as much of the following information as is available:

1. Known author:

- Name(s) of author(s)
- Date that the piece was placed on the Web
- Title of the piece (including edition number, if not the original)
- Type of medium
- Producer (optional)
- Available: supplier or database identifier or number
- Date that the user accessed the article.

2. Unknown author:

- Title (edition)
- Type of medium
- Year
- Producer
- Available: supplier or database identifier or number
- Access date

Other Style Manuals

Many different style manuals offer help in writing. While they vary in their recommendations, they serve a common purpose—as a guide to the "proper" way to present a written report. Some of the manuals are slim pamphlets; others are full-size books. Some manuals give suggestions and rules for all aspects of researching; others are only guides to citing sources. The following is a partial list of available style manuals; most can be found in any college or university library.

General

*The Complete Guide to Citing Government Information Sources: A Manual for Writers and
    Librarians*
Electronic Styles: A Handbook for Citing Electronic Information
The Little, Brown Guide to Writing Research Papers
The McGraw-Hill Style Manual
Manual for Writers of Term Papers, Theses and Dissertations (Kate Turabian)
A Manual of Style: U.S. Government Printing Office
Prentice-Hall Handbook for Writers

For Specific Disciplines

Environment and Earth Sciences: *Suggestions to Authors of the Reports of the United States Geological Survey.* (Originally an internal USGS document, this manual has been made available to the public and serves as a guidebook for all writing in the earth sciences.)

Education: *Journal Instructions to Authors: A Compilation of Manuscript Guidelines from Education.*

Computer Topics: *Electronic Styles: A Handbook for Citing Electronic Information.*

Journalism: *A Broadcast News Manual of Style; UPI Stylebook* (United Press International); *AP Stylebook* (Associated Press).

Law: *The Bluebook: A Uniform System of Citation.*

Social Science: *Writing for Social Scientists: How to Start and Finish Your Thesis, Book or Article.*

STYLE REQUIREMENTS FOR PUBLIC ADMINISTRATION
RESEARCH REPORTS

Style recommendations of the American Society for Public Administration can be found in such journals as the *State and Local Government Review*. This journal uses *The Chicago Manual of Style* system for in-text citations.

1. *Cover page*: The cover page includes the title of the paper and the author's name, position, and organizational affiliation (for a class paper, the course number and name). At the top of the first paper only the title is repeated.

2. *Abstract*: An abstract of no more than 100 words should be placed on the first page between the title and start of the paper's text.

3. *Headings*: The introduction section does not have a heading. Do not number any headings or subheadings. Headings are typically used for the findings and conclusions sections. Other headings may be used at the discretion of the author.

4. *Summary*: Papers should *not* end with a summary section. If relevant, a summary may be included in the author's conclusion section.

5. *Tables, graphs, figures*: When the paper is distributed within an organization, the tables, graphs, and figures should be inserted at the appropriate spots in the paper itself. When sending the paper to a journal for publication, tables, graphs, and figures should be attached as separate sheets at the end. Authors must explain all tables, graphs, and figures in the body of the paper itself. All tables, graphs, and figures *must* be numbered and titled, with a descriptive legend. A reference to the table *must* be included in the body of the text. Titles, column headings, captions, and so on must be clear and to the point. When submitting the paper to a journal, tables must be numbered with Roman numerals (e.g., Table IX). For papers distributed within an organization, either Roman numerals or Arabic numbers may be used.

   Figures must be numbered with Arabic numerals (e.g., Figure 9.1 for the first figure in Chapter 9). Each figure number must have a title followed by a written descriptive legend.

6. *Footnotes*: Authors should avoid the use of notes as much as possible. If notes must be used, they should be numbered sequentially. A listing of endnotes typed on a separate page must be placed before the references section.

7. *Citations*: The first line of the citation should be flush left; all other lines are to be indented three spaces. Do not number the citations. In the body of the paper, use in-text citations format for documentation: Jones and Smith (1997) found that . . .

   If the in-text citation deals with a quotation, the page number must be added after the date of publication, separated by a comma: (Jones and Smith 1997, 25).

8. *References*: The references section should include only works cited in the text, typed on a separate page(s) under the heading "References." References are listed alphabetically according to the last name of the first author.

Finance and Economics Research Reports

The *Journal of Macroeconomics* and the *Journal of Economic Perspectives* are examples of finance periodicals that follow *Chicago Manual of Style* requirements as established by the American Finance Association. Examples of style requirements can be found in the *Journal of Macroeconomics*, among others.

Administrative and Management Reports

Papers written for public and nonprofit management topics typically follow style requirements established by the American Academy of Management. Examples and guidelines for authors can be found in the *Academy of Management Review* and other periodicals published by the Academy (PO Box 3020, Briarcliff Manor, New York, 10510–8020).

Professional organizations often ask that all papers be double-spaced and typed in a plain twelve-point typeface (font). If it is impossible to italicize in the paper, underlining is allowed. Boldface type should be used for the title and headings. Tables should be typed in the same font used for the body of the paper. A title page is required. An abstract of seventy-five or fewer words should be included under the title near the top of the second page. The abstract should state the purposes for the research; include any theoretical basis for the hypotheses, analyses, major results, and implications of the findings.

SUMMARY

Both format and style were discussed in this chapter. *Format* refers to the logical way papers and reports are structured or organized. *Style* refers to the choice of words, the way words are used in sentences, and how sentences are formed into paragraphs. It includes punctuation and grammar. A related aspect of style is the form used to present references and works cited in a research paper.

Research reports often have nine major components. These are (1) the title and title page, (2) an abstract, (3) an introduction or rationale for the study, (4) a review of the literature, (5) a discussion of the methodology used for the study, (6) a complete discussion of the results produced by the study, (7) the conclusions and/or recommendations, (8) references, and (9) appendices, if any.

Most professional public administration and nonprofit organization publications follow the in-text citation model. All references used in the paper should appear in a separate section at the end of the report but before any appendices, tables, or figures. This section starts on a new sheet, continuing the pagination used in the body of the paper. The word "References" should be flush left or centered in capital letters, at the top of the section. All references should be double-spaced and use hanging indents equal to five spaces.

Citations should be in alphabetical order by the last name of the author or first author in multiple-author works or by the organization for a corporate author (e.g., *Seattle Times*). When more than one work by the same author or authors is used, the most current one is listed first. If there are two or more works with the same publication date, use lowercase letters to distinguish them (1987a, 1987b, 1987c).

Reference listings use authors' last names and initials. Additional authors of a work are also presented with the last name first followed by their initials. Italicize titles of publications (underline if unable to use italics).

Some tips for producing a research report that reflects favorably on you and your work are: (1) write in the active voice; (2) use past tense when describing the research project; (3) arrange citations in alphabetical order according to the last name of the first author or name of the publishing organization if no author is listed; (4) in the bibliography, list only the sources you have cited; (5) format authors' initials in the style used in your discipline; (6) put the date of publication immediately after the author(s)' name(s); (7) capitalize only the first word of an article or book chapter title and do not put the title in quotation marks; (8) italicize (or underline, if necessary; not both) the title of the journal and/or book; (9) in citations for direct quotes, include the page number after the year; separate the year and page number with a comma and a space; (10) multiple works by the same author in the same year should be distinguished by letters (1999a, 1999b, 1999c, etc.); (11) include charts, graphs, illustrations, and tables in the body of the paper and discuss the contents of each item in the paper as near to the item as possible; (12) place TABLE and its number above each table, and FIGURE and a number beneath graphs and other illustrations.

ADDITIONAL READING

APA. 2001. *Publication Manual of the American Psychological Association.* 5th ed. Washington, DC: American Psychological Association.
Baugh, L. Sue. 1995. *How to Write Term Papers and Reports.* Lincolnwood, IL: VGM Career Horizons.
Becker, Howard S. 1986. *Writing for Social Scientists.* Chicago: University of Chicago Press.
Williams, Joseph M. 1990. *Style: Toward Clarity and Grace.* Chicago: University of Chicago Press.

REFERENCES

Abdellah, Faye G., and Eugene Levine. 1994. *Preparing Nursing Research for the 21st Century.* New York: Springer.

Achinstein, Peter. 1970. "Concepts of Science: A Philosophical Analysis." In *The Way of Science,* ed. Frank E. Egler, 40–47. New York: Hafner Publishing.

Adams, Gerald R., and Jay D. Schvaneveldt. 1985. *Understanding Research Methods.* New York: Longman.

Adler, Patricia A., and Peter Adler. 1998. "Observational Techniques." In *Collecting and Interpreting Qualitative Methods*, ed. Norman K. Denzin and Yvonna S. Lincoln. Beverly Hills: Sage.

Agger, Ben, and Tim Luke. 2002. "Politics in Postmodernity: The Diaspora of Politics and the Homelessness of Political and Social Theory." In *Theoretical Directions in Political Sociology for the 21st Century,* volume 11, ed. Betty A. Dobratz, Timothy Buzzell, and Lisa K. Waldner, 159–195. Boston: JAI.

Alasuutari, Pertti. 1995. *Researching Culture: Qualitative Method and Cultural Studies.* London: Sage.

Aldenderfer, Mark S., and Roger K. Blashfield 1984. *Cluster Analysis.* Beverly Hills: Sage.

Alejandro, Roberto 1993. *Hermeneutics, Citizenship, and the Public Sphere.* Albany: State University of New York Press.

Alexander, Jeffrey C. 1985. *Positivism, Presuppositions, and Current Controversies.* Vol. 1 of *Theoretical Logic in Sociology.* Berkeley: University of California Press.

Allen, K. R., and K. M. Barbar. 1992. "Ethical and Epistemological Tension in Applying a Postmodern Perspective to feminist Research." *Psychology of Women Quarterly* 16(1): 1–15.

Allman, Dwight D. 1995. "Nietzscheanism Contra Nietzsche." *Perspectives on Political Science* 24(Spring): 69–76.

American Association of Fundraising Counsel (AAFRC). 2004. "Americans Give $241 Billion to Charity in 2003." Press release, American Association of Fundraising Counsel. Accessed June 6, 2006 from www. aafrc.org/press_releases/trustreleases/americansgive.html.

American Psychological Association (APA). 2003. *Electronic References.* Washington, DC: The American Psychological Association. Accessed August 3, 2006 from www.apastyle.org/elecmedia.html.

Ammons, David N., Charles Coe, and Michael Lombardo. 2001. "Performance-Comparison Projects in Local Government: Participants' Perspectives." *Public Administration Review* 61(1): 100–110.

Anastas, Jeane W., and Marian L. MacDonald. 1994. *Research Design for Social Work and the Human Services.* New York: Lexington Books.

Annells, Merilyn. 1996. "Grounded Theory Method: Philosophical Perspectives, Paradigm of Inquiry, and Postmodernism." *Qualitative Health Research* 6(3): 379–394.

Argyris, Chris, Robert Putnam, and Diana M. Smith 1985. *Action Science.* San Francisco: Jossey-Bass.

Arneson, Pat. 1993. "Situating Three Contemporary Qualitative Methods in Applied Organizational Communication Research: Historical Documentation Techniques, the Case Study Method, and the Critical Approach to Organizational Analysis." In *Qualitative Research: Applications in Organizational Communications,* ed. Sandra L. Herndon and Gary L. Kreps, 159–173. Cresskill, NJ: Hampton Press.

Association for Research on Nonprofit Organizations and Voluntary Action (ARNOVA). 2006. *Nonprofit and Voluntary Sector Quarterly.* Association for Research on Nonprofit organizations and Voluntary Action Webpage. Accessed May 18, 2006 from www.arnova.org/nvsq.php.

Babbie, Earl. 2001. *The Practice of Social Research.* Belmont, CA: Wadsworth/Thompson Learning.

Bailey, Mary T. 1994. "Do Physicists Use Case Studies? Thoughts of Public Administration Research." In *Research in Public Administration: Reflections on Theory and Practice,* ed. Jay D. White and Guy B. Adams, 183–196. Thousand Oaks, CA: Sage.

Barnet, Sylvan. 1993. *Critical Thinking, Reading, and Writing.* Boston: St. Martin's Press.

Barnett, Marva T. 1987. *Writing for Technicians.* 3rd ed. New York: Delmar.

Bartels, Larry M., and Henry E. Brady. 1993. "The State of Quantitative Political Methodology." In *Political Science: The State of the Discipline*, ed. Ada W. Finifter. Washington, DC: American political Science Association.

Barthes, Roland. 1968. *Elements of Semiology.* Annette Lavers and Colin Smith, trans. New York: Hill and Wang.

Baruch, Yolanda, and Nelson Ramalho. 2006. "Communalities and Distinctions in the Measurement of Organizational Performance and Effectiveness Across For-profit and Nonprofit Sectors." *Nonprofit and Voluntary Sector Quarterly* 35(1): 39–65.

Baugh, L. Sue. 1995. *How to Write Term Papers and Reports.* Lincolnwood, IL: VGM Career Horizons.

Bauman, Zygmunt. 1992. *Hermeneutics and the Social Sciences.* Aldershot, UK: Gregg Revivals.

Barzun, Jacques, and Henry F. Graff. 1970. *The Modern Researcher.* 2nd ed. New York: Harcourt, Brace, and World.

Becker, Fred, and Valerie Patterson. 2005. "Public-private Partnerships: Balancing Financial Returns, Risks and Roles of the Partners." *Public Performance & Management Review* 29 (2): 125–144.

Becker, Howard S. 1986. *Writing for Social Scientists.* Chicago: University of Chicago Press.

Bennet, Andrew. 2004. "Letter from the Section President." *Qualitative Methods* 2(2): 1.

Bennett, Spencer, and David Bowers. 1976. *An Introduction to Multivariate Techniques for Social and Behavioral Sciences.* London: Macmillan.

Berenson, Mark L., and David M. Levine. 1996. *Basic Business Statistics: Concepts and Applications.* 6th ed. Upper Saddle River, NJ: Prentice Hall.

Berg, Bruce L. 1995. *Qualitative Research Methods for the Social Sciences.* Needham. MA: Allyn and Bacon.

Bernard, H. Russell. 1988. *Research Methods in Cultural Anthropology.* Beverly Hills, CA: Sage.

———. 1994. *Research Methods in Anthropology.* 2nd ed. Thousand Oaks, CA: Sage.

———2000. *Social Research Methods.* Thousand Oaks, CA: Sage.

Bevir, Mark, and R. A. W. Rhodes. 2002. "Interpretive Theory." In *Theory and Methods in Political Science.* 2nd ed., ed. David Marsh and Gerry Stoker, 132–152. Houndmills, UK: Palgrave MacMillan.

Beyerstein, Barry L. 1995. *Distinguishing Science from Pseudoscience.* Monograph prepared for The Center for Curriculum and Professional Development. Victoria, BC: Simon Fraser University.

Binmore, Ken, Aland Kirman, and Pietro Tani, eds. 1993. *Frontiers of Game Theory.* Cambridge, MA: MIT Press.

Blyler, Nancy. 1998. "Taking a Political Turn: The Critical Perspective and Research in Professional Communications." *Technical Communication Quarterly* 7(1): 33–53.

Borzaga, Carlo, and Ermanno Tortia. 2006. "Worker Motivations, Job Satisfaction, and Loyalty in Public and Nonprofit Social Services." *Nonprofit and Voluntary Sector Quarterly* 35(2): 225–248.

Boskoff, Alvin. 1972. *The Mosaic of Sociological Theory.* New York: Crowell.

Box, Richard C. 1992. "An Examination of the Debate Over Research in Public Administration." *Public Administration Review* 52(1): 62–69.

Box, Richard C., and Cheryl S. King 2000. "The Truth is Elsewhere: Critical History." *Administrative theory and Praxis* 22(4): 751–771.

Boyte, Harry C. 2000. "The Struggle against Positivism." *Academe* 86 (July/August): 46–51.

Bredemeier, Harry C., and Richard M. Stephenson. 1967. "The Analysis of Culture." In *The Study of Society,* ed. P.I. Rose, 119–133. New York: Random House.

Brewer, Gene A., James W. Douglas, Rex L. Facer II, and Laurence J. O'Toole Jr. 1999. "Determinants of Graduate Research Productivity in Doctoral Programs of Public Administration." *Public Administration Review* 59(5): 373–382.

Bryant, Christopher G.A. 1985. *Positivism in Social Theory and Research.* New York: St. Martin's Press.

Bryson, John M. 2004. *Strategic Planning for Public and Nonprofit Organizations.* 3rd ed. San Francisco: Jossey-Bass/Wiley.

Bureau of Labor Statistics (BLS). 2005. "Volunteering in the United States, 2005." U.S. Department of Labor: Bureau of Labor Statistics. Accessed June 3, 2006 from www.bls.gov/news.release/pdf/volun.pdf.

Button, Graham, ed. 1991. *Ethnomethodology and the Human Sciences.* New York: Cambridge University Press.

California State University-Sacramento. 2005. "Research and Sponsored Projects: Proposal Development Handbook." Accessed December 29, 2005 from www.csus.edu.rsp/Chapter6.htm.

Capital Research Center (CRC). 2006. "Philanthropy Notes: May 2006" (Press release). Washington, DC: Capital Research Center. Accessed June 6, 2006 from www.capitalresearch.org/news/news.asp?ID=404.

Cartwright, Dorwin, ed. 1951. *Field Theory in Social Science: Selected Theoretical Papers by Kurt Lewin.* New York: Harper and Row.

Case Western Reserve University. 2006. "Mandel Center for Nonprofit Organizations." Cleveland, OH: Case Western Reserve University. Accessed June 6, 2006 from www.cwru.edu/mandelcenter/research/.

Cassell, Catherine, and Gillian Symon, eds. 1997. *Qualitative Methods in Organizational Research.* Thousand Oaks, CA: Sage.

Cattell, Raymond B. 1978. *The Scientific Use of Factor Analysis in the Behavioral and Life Sciences.* New York: Plenum Press.

Child, Dennis. 1990. *The Essentials of Factor Analysis.* 2nd ed. London: Cassell.

Cleary, Robert E. 1992. "Revisiting the Doctoral Dissertation in Public Administration: An Examination of the Dissertations of 1990." *Public Administration Review* 52(1): 55–61.

Coffey, Amanda, and Paul Alkinson. 1996. *Making Sense of Qualitative Data.* Thousand Oaks, CA: Sage.

Cohen, Ronald. 1973. "Generalizations in Ethnography." In *Handbook of Method in Cultural Anthropology,* ed. Raoul Naroll and Ronald Cohen, 31–50. New York: Columbia University Press.

Coleman, Sally S., Gene Brewer, and Jeffrey Brudney. 1999. "Reconciling Competing Values in Public Administration: Understanding the Administrative Role Concept." *Administration and Society* 31 (2): 171–204.

Collins, Harry, and Trevor Pinch. 1993. *The Golem: What Everyone Should Know about Science.* Cambridge: Cambridge University Press.

Columbia University. 1998. *Columbia Guide to Online Style.* New York: Columbia University Press.

Comstock, Donald E., and Russell Fox. 1993. "Participatory Research as Critical Theory: The North Bonneville, USA, Experience." In *Voices of Change: Participatory Research in the United States and Canada,* ed. Peter Park, Mary Brydon-Miller, Budd Hall, and Ted Jackson, 103–24. Westport, CT: Bergin and Garvey.

Cook, Ronald G., and David Barry. 1995. "Shaping the External Environment: A Study of Small Firms' Attempts to Influence Public Policy." *Business and Society* (December): 1–18.

Cooper, Charles W., and Edmund J. Robins. 1962. *The Term Paper: A Manual and Model.* 3rd ed. Stanford, CA: Stanford University Press.

Cooper, Terry L. 1998. *The Responsible Administrator: An Approach to Ethics for the Administrative Role.* 4th ed. San Francisco: Jossey-Bass.

Cooper, John C. B. 1987. *Country Crediworthiness: The Use of Cluster Analysis and Discriminant Analysis.* Glasgow: Glasgow College of Technology.

Cortazzi, Martin. 1993. *Narrative Analysis.* London: Falmer Press.

Cozzetto, Don A. 1994. "Quantitative Research in Public Administration: A Need to Address Some Serious Methodological Problems." *Administration and Society* 26(3): 337–343.

Creswell, John W. 1994. *Research Design: Qualitative and Quantitative Approaches.* Thousand Oaks, CA: Sage.

Crotty, Michael. 1998. *The Foundations of Social Research.* London: Sage.

Cunningham, J. Barton. 1995. "Strategic Considerations in Using Action Research for Improving Personnel Practices." *Public Personnel Management* 24(4): 515–540.

Dalgleish, Leonard I., and David Chant. 1995. "A SAS Macro for Bootstrapping the Results of Discriminant Analysis." *Educational and Psychological Measurement* 55(August): 613–624.

Dastmalchian, A., P. Blyton, and R. Adamson. 1991. *The Climate of Workplace Relations.* London: Routledge.

De Laine, Marlene. 2000. *Fieldwork, Participation and Practice: Ethics and Dilemmas in Qualitative Research.* London: Sage.

Dearstyne, Bruce. 1993. *The Archival Enterprise.* Chicago: American Library Association.

Denhardt, Katherine G. 1989. "The Management of Ideals: A Political Perspective on Ethics." *Public Administration Review* 49(1): 187–193.

Denison, Dwight V., and Robert Eger III. 2000. "Tax Evasion from a Policy Perspective." *Public Administration Review* 60(2): 163–172.

Denscombe, Martyn. 2002. *Ground Rules for Good Research.* Buckingham, UK: Open University Press.

Denzin, Norman K and Yvonna S. Lincoln, eds. 1994a. "Introduction: Entering the Field of Qualitative Research." In *Handbook of Qualitative Research,* ed. Norman K. Denzin and Yvonna S. Lincoln, 1–34. Thousand Oaks, CA: Sage.

———. 1994b. *Handbook of Qualitative Research.* Thousand Oaks, CA: Sage.

———. 1998. *Strategies of Qualitative Inquiry.* Thousand Oaks, CA: Sage.

DePoy, Elizabeth, and Ann Hartman. 1999. "Critical Action Research: A Model for Social Work Knowing." *Social Work* 44(6): 560–570.

Descombes, Vincent. 1991. "The Interpretation of Texts." In *Gadamer and Hermeneutics*, ed. Hugh J. Silverman, 247–268. London: Routledge.

Dirkx, John M. and Benita J. Barnes. 2004. "What do We Really Mean by a 'Qualitative' Study? An Analysis of Qualitative Research in Adult and Continuing Education." Paper presented at the Midwest Research-to-Practice Conference in Adult, Continuing and Community Education, October 6–8, Indianapolis, IN: Indiana University.

Dood, Janet S., ed. 1986. *The ACS Style Guide: A Manual for Authors and Editors.* Washington, DC: American Chemical Society.

Dunteman, George T. 1994. "Principle Components Analysis." In *Factor Analysis and Related Techniques*, ed. Michael S. Lewis-Beck, 157–245. London: Sage.

Dusche, Richard A. 1994. "Research on the History and Philosophy of Science." In *Handbook on Science Teaching and Learning,* ed. Dorothy L. Gabel, 443–465. New York: Macmillan.

Duveen, Gerard. 2000. "Piaget, Ethnographer." *Social Science Information.* 39(1): 79–97.

Easton, David. 1962. "The Current Meanings of 'Behavioralism' in Political Science." In *The Limits of Behavioralism in Political Science,* ed. James C. Chatsworth, 1–25 Philadelphia: American Academy of Political and Social Science.

Eco, Umberto. 1976. *A Theory of Semiotics.* Bloomington: Indiana University.

Eisenberg, Pablo. 2004a. "Solving the Nonprofit Leadership Crisis Will Take Much Work." *Chronicle of Philanthropy* 17(5) (December 9): 44.

———. 2004b. "Have Nonprofits Lost Their Integrity?" *Chronicle of Philanthropy,* 17(3) (December 11): 48.

Eisner, Elliot W. 1997. "The New Frontier in Qualitative Research Methodology." *Qualitative Inquiry* 3(2): 259–274.

Ellsberg, Mary, and Lori Heise. 2005. *Researching Violence Against Women.* Geneva: World Health Organization.

Emerson, Robert M., Rachel I. Fretz, and Linda L. Shaw. 1995. *Writing Ethnographic Fieldnotes.* Chicago: University of Chicago Press.

Este, David, Jackie Sieppert, and Allan Barsky. 1998. "Teaching and Learning Qualitative Research with and without Qualitative Data Analysis Software." *Journal of Research on Computing in Education* 31(2): 138–155.

Farr, James, John S. Dryzek, and Stephen T. Leonard, eds. 1995. *Political Science in History.* Cambridge, UK: Cambridge University Press.

Fay, Brian. 1975. *Social Theory and Political Practice.* London: Allen and Unwin.

Fernandez, Sergio, and Ross Fabricant. 2000. "Methodological Pitfalls in Privatization Research: Two Cases from Florida's Child Support Enforcement Program." *Public Productivity and Management Review* 24(2): 133–144.

Fetterman, David M. 1989. *Ethnography: Step by Step.* Newbury Park, CA: Sage.

Fink, Arlene. 1998. *Conducting Research Literature Reviews.* Thousand Oaks, CA: Sage.

Fischer, Frank. 1998. "Beyond empiricism: Policy Inquiry in Postpositive Perspective." *Policy Studies Journal* 26(2): 129–46.

Fischler, Raphael. 2000. "Case Studies of Planners at Work." *Journal of Planning Literature* 15(2): 184–195.

Fitz-Gibbon, Carol Taylor, and Lynn Lyons Morris. 1987. *How to Analyze Data.* Newbury Park, CA: Sage.

Flick, Uwe. 1999a. "Qualitative Methods in the Study of Culture and Development: An Introduction." *Social Science Information* 38(4): 631–658.

———. 1999b. "Social Constructions of Change: Qualitative Methods for Analyzing Developmental Processes." *Social Science Information* 38(4): 625–629.

————. 2006. "Qualitative Research in Sociology in Germany and the US—State of the Art, Differences and Developments." *Forum: Qualitative Social Research* 6(3): 1–19. Accessed August 1, 2006 from http://www.qualitative-research.net/fqs-texte/3-05/05-3-23-e.htm.

Folz, David H. 1996. *Survey Research for Public Administration.* Thousand Oaks, CA: Sage.

Fong, Margaret L. 1992. "When a Survey Isn't Research." *Counselor Education and Supervision* 31(4): 194–196.

Fowler, H. Ramsey, and Jane E. Aaron. 1995. *The Little, Brown Handbook.* 6th ed. New York: HarperCollins.

Fox, Richard G. 1977. *Urban Anthropology: Cities in Their Cultural Settings.* Englewood Cliffs, NJ: Prentice Hall.

Fredericksen, Patricia, and Rosanne London. 2000. "Disconnect in the Hollow State: The Pivotal Role of Organizational Capacity in Community-Based Development Organizations." *Public Administration Review* 60(3): 230–239.

Freedman, Paul. 1960. *The Principles of Scientific Research.* 2nd ed. London: Pergamon Press.

Gabel, Dorothy L. 1995. "An Introduction to Action Research." Presidential address at the National Association for Research in Science Teaching annual meeting. San Francisco, CA. April 24. Accessed November 14, 2000 from www.phy.nau.edu.

Gadamer, Hans-Georg. 1975. "Hermeneutics and Social Science." *Cultural Hermeneutics* 2: 307–316.

————. 1986. "Text and Interpretation." In *Hermaneutics and Modern Philosophy*, ed. Bruce R. Wachterhauser, 377–396. Albany: State University of New York.

Galston, Wiliam A. 1993. "Political Theory in the 1980s: Perplexity Amidst Diversity." In *Political Science: The State of the Discipline II*, ed. Ada W. Finister, 27–54. Washington, DC: American Political Science Association.

Garafalo, Charles, and Dean Geuras. 1999. *Ethics in the Public Service: The Moral Mind at Work.* Washington, DC: Georgetown University Press.

Garrick, John. 1999. "Doubting the Philosophical Assumptions of Interpretive Research." *International Journal of Qualitative Studies in Education* 12(2): 147–157.

Garson, G. David, and Samuel Overman. 1983. *Public Management Research in the United States.* New York: Praeger.

Geertz, Clifford. 1973. *The Interpretation of Cultures: Selected Essays.* New York: Basic Books.

Geuss, Raymond. 1981. *The Idea of a Critical Theory: Habermas and the Frankfurt School.* Cambridge: Cambridge University Press.

Gibaldi, Joseph, and Walter S. Achtert. 1988. *MLA Handbook for Writers of Researcher Papers.* New York: Modern Language Association of America.

Gill, Jeff, and Kenneth J. Meier. 2000. "Public Administration Research and Practice: A Methodological Manifesto." *Journal of Public Administration Research and Theory* 10(1): 157–199.

Gill, John, and Phil Johnson. 1991. *Research Methods for Managers.* London: Chapman.

Glanz, Jeffrey. 1999. "A Primer on Action Research for the School Administrator." *Clearing House* 72(5): 301–305.

Glaser, Barney G. 1972. *The Research Adventure: Promise and Problems of Field Work.* New York: Random House.

————. 1992. *Emergence vs. Forcing: Basics of Grounded Theory Analysis.* Mill Valley, CA: Sociology Press.

Glaser, Barney G., and Anselm L. Strauss. 1967. *The Discovery of Grounded Theory: Strategies for Qualitative Research.* Chicago: Aldine.

Glorfeld, Louis W. 1995. "An Improvement on Horn's Parallel Analysis Methodology for Selecting the Correct Number of Factors to Retain." *Educational and Psychological Measurement* 55(June): 377–393.

Gobo, Giampietro. 2005. "The Renaissance of Qualitative Methods." *Forum: Qualitative Social Research* 6(3). Accessed August 1, 2006 from http://www.qualitative-research.net/fqs-texte/3-05/05-3-42-e.pdf.

Goddard, John, and Andrew Kirby. 1976. *An Introduction to Factor Analysis.* Norwich, UK: University of East Anglia.

Golden, M. Patricia, ed. 1976. *The Research Experience.* Itasca, IL: Peacock.

Goldman, Aron P. 2005. "Encouraging Innovation: a Task for Congress." *Chronicle of Philanthropy* 17(11) (March): 39–41.

Goss, Robert P. 1996. "A Distinct Public Administration Ethics?" *Journal of Public Administration Research and Theory* 6(October): 573–598.

Gottfredson, Gary D. 1996. "The Hawthorne Misunderstanding (and How to Get the Hawthorne Effect in Action Research)." *Journal of Crime and Delinquency* 33(1): 28–49.

Gubanich, Alan A. 1991. *Writing a Scientific Paper.* Dubuque: Kendall/Hunt.

Gubba, E.G. and Yvonna A. Lincoln. 1998. "Competing Paradigms in Qualitative Research." In *The Landscape of Qualitative Research*, ed. N.K. Denzin and Y.S. Lincoln, 195–220. Thousand Oaks, CA: Sage.

Gummesson, Evert. 1991. *Qualitative Methods in Management Research.* Newbury Park, CA: Sage.

Gunnell, John G. 1983. "Political Theory: The Evolution of a Subfield." In *Political Science: The State of the Discipline*, ed. Ada W. Finifter, 3–45. Washington, DC: American Political Science Association.

Gurman, Pamela J., ed. 1997. *Written Communications Resources Digest.* Needham Heights, MA: Simon and Schuster.

Gustavsen, Bjorn. 1996. "Action Research, Democratic Dialogue, and the Issue of 'Critical Mass' in Change." *Qualitative Inquiry* 2(1): 90–104.

Habermas, Jürgen, 1979. *Communication and Evolution of Society.* London: Heinemann.

Hacker, Diana. 1992. *A Writer's Reference.* 2nd ed. Boston: Bedford Books.

Haig, Brian. 1995. "Grounded Theory as Scientific Method." *Philosophy of Education Society Yearbook.* Accessed November 2, 2000 from www.ed.uiuc.edu/EPS.

Hall, Michael H., Cathy W. Barr, M. Easwaramoorthy, S. Wojciech Sokolowski, and Lester M. Salamon. 2005. *The Canadian Nonprofit and Voluntary Sector in Comparative Perspective.* Toronto: Imagine Canada. Accessed June 3, 2006 from www.nonprofitscan.ca/Files/misc/jhu_report_en.pdf.

Hall, Michael H., David Lasby, Glenn Gumulka, and Catherine Tyron. 2006. *Caring Canadians, Involved Canadians: Highlights from the 2004 Canada Survey of Giving, Volunteering, and Participating.* Ottawa: Statistics Canada.

Hall, Michael, Larry McKeown, and Karen Roberts. 2001. *Caring Canadians, Involved Canadians: Highlights from the 2000 National Survey of Giving, Volunteering and Participating.* Catalogue No. 71-542-XIE. Ottawa: Statistics Canada.

Hall, Peter D. 2005. "Historical Perspectives on Nonprofit Organizations in the United States." In *The Jossey-Bass Handbook of Nonprofit Leadership and Management.* 2nd ed., ed. Robert D. Herman and associates, 3–38. San Francisco: Jossey-Bass/Wiley.

Hall, Wendy A., and Peter Callery. 2001. "Enhancing the Rigor of Grounded Theory: Incorporating Reflexivity and Relationality." *Qualitative Health Research* (March): 257–272.

Hansen, Philip and Alicja Muszynski. 1990. "Crisis in Rural Life and Crisis in Thinking: Directions for Critical Research." *Canadian Review of Sociology and Anthropology* 27(February): 1–23.

Hanson, N.R. 1958. *Patterns of Discovery: An Inquiry into the Conceptual Foundations of Science.* Cambridge: Cambridge University Press.

Harding, Sandra. 1987. "Is There a Feminist Method?" In *Feminism and Methodology: Social Science Issues*, ed. Sandra Harding, 1–14. Bloomington: University of Indiana Press.

———. 2006. *Science and Social Inequality: Feminist and Postcolonial Issues.* Urbana: University of Illinois Press.

Harnack, Andrew, and Eugene Kleppinger. 1997. *ONLINE! A Reference Guide to Using Internet Sources.* New York: St. Martin's Press.

Harrison, Jon. 2006. "Grants and Related Sources." East Lansing: Michigan State University Libraries (January 26). Accessed June 6, 2006 from www.lib.msu.edu/harris23/grants/zphilrees.htm.

Harvey, Don, and Donald R. Brown. 1996. *An Experiential Approach to Organizational Development,* 5th ed. Upper Saddle River, NJ: Prentice Hall.

Hempel, Carl. 1966. *Philosophy of the Natural Sciences.* Englewood Cliffs, NJ: Prentice-Hall.

Herman, Robert D and Associates, eds. 2005. *The Jossey-Bass Handbook of Nonprofit Leadership and Management.* San Francisco: Jossey-Bass.

Hernández-Murillo, Rubén, and Deborah Roisman. 2005. "The Economics of Charitable Giving." Federal Reserve Bank of St. Louis. Accessed June 6, 2006 from http://stlouisfed.org/publications/re/2005/d/pages/charity.html.

Heron, John. 1996. "Co-operative Inquiry and Related Forms of Research." *Co-operative Inquiry* (Extract from Chapter 1). London: Sage.

Hobson, Mellody. 2005. "Make Your Contribution Count." *ABC News.* September 25. Accessed June 7, 2006 from http://abcnews.go.com/WNT/MellodyHobson/story?id=115047

Hodder, Ian. 1982. *Symbols in Action.* Cambridge, UK: Cambridge University Press.

Holsti, Ole R. 1969. *Content Analysis for the Social Sciences and Humanities.* Reading, MA: Addison-Wesley.

Hughes, John, and Wes Sharrock. 1997. *The Philosophy of Social Research.* 3rd ed. London: Longman.

Houston, David J., and Sybil M. Delevan. 1990. "Public Administration Research: An Assessment of Journal Publications." *Public Administration Review* 50(1): 674–681.

Huberty, Carl, and Laureen L. Lowman. 1997. "Discriminant Analysis via Statistical Packages." *Educational and Psychological Measurement* 57(October): 769–784.

Hutcheson, Graeme, and Nick Sofroniou. 1999. *The Multivariate Social Scientist.* London: Sage.

Indiana University Center on Philanthropy (IUCOP). 2002. "America Gives: Survey of Americans' Generosity after September 11." Indiana University Center on Philanthropy, January. Accessed June 6, 2006 from www.philanthropy.iupui.edu/AmericaGivesReport.pdf.

Institute of Development Studies (IDS). 2000. "Civil Society and Governance Programme: Overview." Institute of Development Studies: Civics and Governance. Accessed June 1, 2006 from www.ids.ac.uk/ids/civsoc/about.html.

Ironstone-Catterall, Penelope. 2006. "Feminist Research Methodology and Women's Health: A Review of the Literature." National Network on Environments and Women's Health (Canada) and York University White Paper. Accessed July 28, 2006 from www.yorku.ca/nnewh/english/pubs/workpap2.pdf.

Jacques, Elliott. 1951. *The Changing Culture of a Factory: A Study of Authority and Participation in an Industrial Setting.* London: Tavistock Institute.

James-Catalao. Cynthia N. 1996. *Researching on the World Wide Web.* Rocklin, CA: Prima.

Janesick, Valerie J. 1994. "The Dance of Qualitative Research Design." In *Handbook of Qualitative Research,* ed. Norman K. Denzin and Yvonne S. Lincoln, 209–219. Thousand Oaks, CA: Sage.

Jones, Russell A. 1996. *Research Methods in the Social and Behavioral Sciences.* 2nd ed. Sunderland, MA: Sinauer.

Jurich, Katarin. 2001. "Getting the Story Straight: Grounded Theory, Hermeneutics and the Practice of Fieldwork on the Plains of South Dakota." *Sociological Perspectives* 43(4): S149–162.

Kalinosky, Kathy. 1997. "Action Research and Learner Participation in a Homeless Shelter." *New Directions for Adult and Continuing Education* 73(1): 52–55.

Kaplan, Robert S. 1998. "Innovation Action Research: Creating New Management Theory and Practice." *Journal of Management Accounting Research* 10(1): 89–119.

Kaplan, Robert S. and David P. Norton. 1996. *The Balanced Scorecard.* Boston: Harvard Business School Press.

Kaufman, Herbert. 1960. *The Forest Ranger: A Study in Administrative Behavior.* Baltimore: Johns Hopkins University Press.

Keller, Julia. 1998. "Cyber-goofs Point Out Need for Fact Checking." *Seattle Times*, December 27, C-2.

Kelly, Michael F., Linda Bennett, and Lin Moore. 2002. "Preparing High Quality Research Proposals for ACEI." Presentation at 2002 ACEI Annual Conference. San Diego, CA: Association for Childhood Education International. Accessed December 29, 2005 from www.acei.org/PrepHighQualityResearch-Proposals.ppd

Kendall, Judy. 1999. "Axial Coding and the Grounded Theory Controversy." *Western Journal of Nursing Research* 21(6): 743–758.

Kennedy, X.J., and Dorothy M. Kennedy. 1987. *The Bedford Guide for College Papers.* New York: St. Martin Press.

Keping, Yu. 2000. "The Emergence of Chinese Civil Society and Its Significance for Governance." Paper prepared for the UK Ford Foundation Civil Society and Governance Programme, Institute of Development Studies. Accessed June 1, 2006 from www.ids.ac.uk/ids/civsoc/final/china/chn8.doc.

Kerlinger, Fred N., and Elazar J. Pedhazur. 1973. *Multiple Regression in Behavioral Research.* New York: Holt, Rinehart, and Winston.

Kerr, Brinck, William Miller, and Margaret Reid. 2002. "Sex-Based Occupational Segregation in U. S. State Bureaucracies, 1987–97." *Public Administration Review* 62 (4): 412–423.

Kidder, Louise H. 1986. *Research Methods in Social Relations.* New York: Holt, Rinehart and Winston.

Kim, Taeyong. 1995. "Discriminant Analysis as a Prediction Tool for Uncommitted Voters in Preelection Polls." *International Journal of Public Opinion Research* 7(Summer): 110–127.

Kim, Jae-on and Charles W. Mueller. 1994. "Introduction to Factor Analysis." In *Factor Analysis and Related Techniques,* ed. Michael S. Lewis-Beck, 1–74. London: Sage.

Kincheloe, Joe L., and Peter L. McLaren. 1984. "Rethinking Critical Theory and Qualitative Research." In *Handbook of Qualitative Research,* ed. Norman K. Denzin and Yvonne S. Lincoln, 138–157. Thousand Oaks, CA: Sage.

King, Cheryl S., Kathryn M. Felty, and Bridget O. Susel. 1998. "The Question of Participation: Toward

Authentic Public Participation in Public Administration." *Public Administration Review* 58(July/August): 317–326.

King, James R. 1999. "Am Not! Are Too! Using Queer Standpoint in Postmodern Critical Ethnography." *International Journal of Qualitative Studies in Education* 12(5): 473–491.

Kiniry, Malcolm, and Mike Rose, eds. 1990. *Critical Strategies for Academic Writing*. Boston: Bedford Books.

Klecka, Willaim R. 1980. *Discriminant Analysis*. Beverly Hills, CA: Sage.

Klein, Heinz K., and Michael D. Myers. 1999. "A Set of Principles for Conducting and Evaluating Interpretive Field Studies in Information Systems." *MIS Quarterly* 23(1): 67–98.

Kluckholm, Clyde. 1967. "The Study of Culture." In *The Study of Society,* ed. P.I. Rose, 74–93. New York: Random House.

Koliba, Christopher J. 2000. "Good Governance Functions of Civil Society Organizations in the United States." Paper prepared for the UK Ford Foundation Civil Society and Governance Programme, Institute of Development Studies. Accessed June 1, 2006 from www.ids.ac.uk/ids/civsoc/final/usa/USA19.doc.

Konecki, Krysztof. 1997. "Time in the Recruiting Search Process by Headhunting Companies." In *Grounded Theory in Practice,* ed. Anselm Strauss and Juliet Corbin, 131–145. Thousand Oaks: CA: Sage.

Kornblum, William. 1996. "Introduction." In *In the Field: Readings on the Field Research Experience*. 2nd ed., ed. Carolyn D. Smith and William Kornblum, 1–7. Westport, CT: Praeger.

Kuechler, Manfred. 1998. "The Survey Method." *American Behavioral Scientist* 42(2): 178–200.

Kuhne, Gary W., and Allen Quigley. 1997. "Understanding and Using Action Research in Practice Settings." *New Directions for Adult and Continuing Education* 73(1): 23–40.

Kuhns, Eileen, and S.V. Martorana, eds. 1982. *Qualitative Methods for Institutional Research*. San Francisco: Jossey-Bass.

Kumar, Ranjit. 1996. *Research Methodology*. London: Sage.

Kvale, Steiner. 1996. *Interviewing: An Introduction to Qualitative Research*. Thousand Oaks, CA: Sage.

Lan, Zhiyong, and Kathleen K. Anders. 2000. "A Paradigmatic View of Contemporary Public Administration Research." *Administration and Society* 32(2): 138–166.

Lance, Charles E., and Robert J. Vandenberg. 2002. "Confirmatory Factor Analysis." In *Measuring and Analyzing Behavior in Organizations*. Fritz Drasgow and Neal Schmitt, eds. San Francisco: Jossey-Bass: 221–254.

Lang, Gerhard, and George D. Heiss. 1990. *A Practical Guide to Research Methods*. 6th ed. Lanham, MD: University Press of America.

Lapin, Lawrence L. 1993. *Statistics for Modern Business Decisions*. 3rd ed. Fort Worth, TX: Dryden.

Lastrucci, Carlo L. 1967. *The Scientific Approach: Basic Principles of the Scientific Method*. Cambridge: Schenkman.

Lasswell, Harold D. 1953. "Why Be Quantitative?" In *Reader in Public Opinion and Communication,* ed. Bernard Berelson and Morris Janowitz, 265–272. Glendoe, IL: Free Press.

Lathrop, Richard G. 1969. *Introduction to Psychological Research*. New York: Harper & Row.

LeCompte, Margaret D., and Jean J. Schensul. 1999. *Designing and Conducting Ethnographic Research*. Walnut Creek, CA: AltaMira Press.

Lee, Thomas W. 1999. *Using Qualitative Methods in Organizational Research*. Thousand Oaks, CA: Sage.

Lee, Chung-Shing, J. Thad Barnowe, and David E. McNabb. 1999. "Environmental Issues in Taiwan and the USA: Public Perceptions, Attitudes and Priorities." Paper presented at the 2002 Pan-Pacific Conference, Santiago, Chile.

Leedy, Paul D. 1974. *Practical Research: Planning and Design*. New York: Macmillan.

Lehmann, Donald R. 1985. *Market Research and Analysis*. 2nd ed. Homewood, IL: Irwin.

Lehmkuhl, L. Don. 1996. "Nonparametric Statistics: Methods for Analyzing Data Not Meeting Assumptions Required for the Application of Parametric Tests." *Journal of Prosthetics and Orthodontics* 8(3): 105–113.

Leiter, Kenneth. 1980. *A Primer on Ethnomethodology*. New York: Oxford University Press.

Lenkowsky, Leslie, and James L. Perry. 2000. "Reinventing Government: The Case of National Service." *Public Administration Review* 60(4): 298–307.

Lessor, Roberta. 2000. "Using the Team Approach of Anselm Strauss in Action Research: Consulting on a Project in Global Education." *Sociological Perspectives* 43(4): S133–48.

Lester, James D., Sr. and James D. Lester Jr. 1992. *The Research Paper Handbook*. Glenview, IL: Scott Foreman.

Letts, Christine W., William P. Ryan, and Allen Grossman. 1999. *High Performance Nonprofit Organizations: Managing Upstream for Greater Impact.* New York: Wiley.

Lewicki, R.J., R.D. Bowen, D.R. Hall, and F.S. Hall. 1988. *Experiences in Management and Organizational Behavior.* 3rd ed. New York: Wiley.

Li, Xia, and Nancy B. Crane. 1996. *Electronic Styles: A Handbook for Citing Electronic Information.* Medford, NJ: Information Technology Today.

Light, Paul C. 2000. *Making Nonprofits Work: A Report on the Tides of Nonprofit Management Reform.* Washington, DC: The Brookings Institution.

Lincoln, Yvonna S. 1997. "From Understanding to Action: New Imperatives, New Criteria, and New Methods for Interpretive Researchers." *Theory and Research in Social Education* 26(1): 12–29.

Lindzey, Gardner. 1961. *Projective Techniques and Cross-Cultural Research.* New York: Appleton-Century-Crofts.

Linz, Juan J. 1969. "Ecological Analysis and Survey Research." In *Quantitative Ecological Analysis in the Social Sciences*, ed. Mattei Dogan and Stein Rokkan, 91–131. Cambridge, MA: Massachusetts Institute of Technology.

Lippitt, Ronald, Jeanne Watson, and Bruce Westley. 1958. *The Dynamics of Planned Change.* New York: Harcourt, Brace.

Lipsey, Mark W., and David B. Wilson. 2001. *Practical Meta-Analysis.* Thousand Oaks, CA: Sage.

Lipsky, Michael. 1980. *Street-Level Bureaucracy.* New York: Russell Sage.

Locher, Brigit, and Elisabeth Prügl. 2001. "Feminism and Constructivism: Worlds Apart or Sharing the Middle Ground?" *International Studies Quarterly* 45 (March): 111–129.

Locke, Karen. 1996. "Rewriting the Discovery of Grounded Theory After 25 Years?" *Journal of Management Inquiry* 5(3): 239–46.

Locke, Lawrence F., Waneen W. Spirduso, and Stephen J. Silverman. 1999. *Proposals That Work.* 4th ed. Thousand Oaks, CA: Sage.

Long, Scott. 1983. *Confirmatory Factor Analysis.* Beverly Hills, CA: Sage.

Loor, Maurice. 1983. *Cluster Analysis for Social Scientists.* San Francisco: Jossey-Bass.

Lowndes, Vivian. 2002. "Institutionalism." In *Theory and Methods in Political Science,* 2nd ed., ed. David Marsh and Gerry Stoker, 90–108. Houndmills, UK: Palgrave Macmillan.

Luckert, Kate. 2005. "Nonprofit Organizations (Definition and Examples)." Case Western Reserve University: Learning to Give. Accessed June 14, 2006 from www.learningtogive.org/papers/index.asp?bpid=41&print=yes.

Maas, A.J. 1999. "Hermeneutics." *The Catholic Encyclopaedia,* Vol. 7. Online edition. Accessed August 8, 2000 www.newadvent.org/cathen/0/2/1anum.

MacMillan, Katie. 2005. "More Than Just Coding? Evaluating CAQDAS in a Discourse Analysis of News Texts." *Forum: Qualitative Social Research,* 6(3). Accessed August 1, 2006 from www.qualitative-research.net/fqs-texte/3-05/05-3-25-e.pdf.

Malhotra, Naresh K. 1999. *Marketing Research: An Applied Orientation.* 3rd ed. Upper Saddle River, NJ: Prentice Hall.

Maner, Martin. 2001. *The Research Process,* 2nd ed. New York: McGraw-Hill.

Manning, Peter K., and Betsy Cullum-Swan. 1998. "Narrative, Content, and Semiotic Analysis." In *Collecting and Interpreting Qualitative Materials,* ed. Norman K. Denzin and Yvonna S. Lincoln, 246–273. Thousand Oaks, CA: Sage.

March, James. 1977. "Administrative Practice, Organizational Theory, and Political Philosophy: Ruminations on the Reflections of John M. Gauss." *Political Science and Politics* 30(4): 689–698.

Margulies, N., and J. Wallace. 1973. *Organizational Change: Techniques and Applications.* Glenview, IL: Scott Foresman.

Markman, Roberta H., Peter T. Markman, and Marie L. Waddell. 1989. *10 Steps in Writing the Research Paper.* 4th ed. New York: Barron's Educational Series.

Marrow, Alfred J. 1977. *The Practical Theorist: The Life and Work of Kurt Lewin.* New York: Teachers College Press.

Marsh, David, Gerry Stoker, and Paul Furlong 2002. " A Skin, Not a Sweater: Ontology and Epistemology in Political Science." In *Theory and Methods in Political Science.* 2nd ed., ed. David Marsh and Gerry Stoker, 17–41. Houndmills, UK: Palgrave Macmillan.

Marshall, Catherine, and Gretchen B. Rossman. 1999. *Designing Qualitative Research.* 3rd ed. Thousand Oaks, CA: Sage.

Martin, Lana A. 2000. "Effective Data Collection." *Total Quality Management* 11(3): 341–345.

Mattson, Dale. 1986. *Statistics: Difficult Concepts, Understandable Explanations.* Oak Park, IL: Bolchazy-Carducci.

Maxwell, Albert E. 1977. *Multivariate Analysis in Behavioral Research.* London: Chapman and Hall.

Maykut, Pamela, and Richard Morehouse. 1994. *Beginning Qualitative Research: A Philosophic and Practical Guide.* London: Falmer Press.

McClintock, Norah. 2004. *Understanding Canadian Volunteers.* Toronto: Canadian Centre for Philanthropy.

McCurdy, Howard E., and Robert E. Cleary. 1984. "Why Can't We Resolve the Research Issue in Public Administration?" *Public Administration Review* 44(1): 49–55.

McDaniel, Carl Jr., and Roger H. Gates. 1993. *Contemporary Marketing Research.* Fort Worth, TX: West.

McDonald, Gael. 2000. "Business Ethics: Practical Proposals for Organizations." *Journal of Business Ethics* 25(1/2): 169–84.

McKelvey, Bill. 2002. "Emergent Order in Firms: Complexity Science vs. The Entanglement Trap." In *Complex Systems and Evolutionary Perspectives of Organizations: Applications of Complexity Theory to Organizations,* ed. Eve Mitleton-Kelly. New York: Elsevier.

McKeown, Larry, David McIver, Jason Moreton, and Anita Rotondo. 2004. *Giving and Volunteering: The Role of Religion.* Toronto: Canadian Centre for Philanthropy. Accessed June 9, 2006 from www.givingandvolunteering.ca/pdf.reports/Religion.pdf.

McMillian, James H., and Sally Schumacher. 1997. *Research in Education.* 4th ed. New York: Addison Wesley Longman.

McNabb, David E. 1968. The Private vs. Public Power Fight in Seattle, 1930–1934. Unpublished master's thesis. Seattle: University of Washington.

———. 1980. Experimental Methodology for Segmenting the Postsecondary Educational Market. Unpublished Ph.D. dissertation. Corvallis, OR: Oregon State University.

———. 1991. "Shaping the 18th-Century Consumer Society: The *London Post* and *General Advertiser,* 1734–1809." Proceedings of the 16th Annual European Studies Conference (October), Omaha, Nebraska.

McNabb, David E., and F. Thomas Sepic. 1995. "Culture, Climate and Total Quality Management: Measuring Readiness for Change." *Public Productivity and Management Review* 18(4): 369–385.

McWilliam, Carol L. 1996. "Creating Understanding that Cultivates Change." *Qualitative Inquiry* 2(2): 151–176.

Meacham, Shuaib J. 1998. "Threads of a New Language: A Response to Eisenhart's 'On the Subject of Interpretive Review.'" *Review of Educational Research* 68(4): 401–407.

Meier, Kenneth J. and Vicky M. Wilkins. 2002. "Gender Differences in Agency Head Salaries." *Public Education Review* (July/August): 405–411.

Melia, Kathy M. 1996. "Rediscovering Glaser." *Qualitative Health Research* 6(3): 368–379.

Mercier, Jean. 1994. "Looking at Organizational Culture Hermeneutically." *Administration and Society* 261(May): 28–47.

Merrell, Floyd. 1982. *Semiotic Foundations: Steps Toward an Epistemology and Written Texts.* Bloomington: Indiana University Press.

Merriam, Sharan B., and Edwin L. Simpson. 1989. *A Guide to Research for Educators and Trainers of Adults.* Melbourne, FL: Krieger.

Merton, Robert K. 1967. "Research and Sociological Theory." In *The Study of Society,* ed. P.I. Rose, 35–48. New York: Random House.

Miles, Matthew B., and A. Michael Huberman. 1984. *Qualitative Data Analysis: A Sourcebook of New Methods.* Beverly Hills, CA: Sage.

———. 1994. *Qualitative Data Analysis: A Sourcebook of New Methods.* 2nd ed. Beverly Hills, CA: Sage

———. 1998. "Data Management and Analysis Methods." In *Collecting and Interpreting Qualitative Materials,* ed. Norman K. Denzin and Yvonna S. Lincoln, 179–210. Thousand Oaks, CA: Sage.

Miller, Delbert C. 1991. *Handbook of Research Design and Social Measurement.* 5th ed. Newbury Park: Sage.

Miller, Steven I. and Marcel Fredericks. 1999. *Handbook of Research Methods in Public Administration.* New York: Marcel Dekker.

Minkel, J.R. 2006. "T Cells for Brain Cells." *Scientific American* 294(1): 21–22.

Mitchell, Jerry. 1998. "Ethical Principles for Public Administration Research." In *Teaching Ethics and Values in Public Administration Programs,* ed. James Bowman and Donald. Menzel, 305–320. Albany: State University of New York Press.

Mitchell, Marilyn L. 1998. *Employing Qualitative Methods in the Private Sector.* Thousand Oaks, CA: Sage.

Moore, Henrietta. 1990. "Paul Ricoeur: Action, Meaning, Text." In *Reading Material Culture: Structuralism, Hermeneutics, and Post-structuralism*, ed. Christopher Tilley, 85–120. Oxford: Blackwell.

Morse, Janice M. 1994. "Designing Funded Qualitative Research." In *Handbook of Qualitative Research*, ed. Norman K. Denzin and Yvonna S. Lincoln, 220–235. Thousand Oaks, CA: Sage.

Munhall, Patricia L., and Carolyn J. Oiler. 1993. *Nursing Research: A Qualitative Perspective.* Norwalk, CT: Appleton-Century-Crofts.

Myers, M.D. 1997. "Qualitative Research in Information Systems." *MIS Quarterly* 21(2): 241–242. *MISQ Discovery,* updated version. Accessed April 28, 1999 from www.misq.org/misqd961/world/.

Nakano, Lynne Y. 2000. "Volunteering as a Lifestyle Choice: Negotiating Self-Identity in Japan." *Ethnology* 39(2): 93–107.

Narotzky, Susana. 2000. "The Cultural Basis of a Regional Economy: The Vega Baja del Segura in Spain." *Ethnology* 39(1): 1–14.

National Center for Charitable Statistics (NCCS). 2006. "Conclusion and Manual: Introduction." The Urban Institute: National Center for Charitable Statistics. Accessed June 2, 2006 from http://nccs2.urban.org/ntee—cc/index.htm

National Endowment for the Humanities (NEH). 2001. *Research Misconduct Policy.* Washington, DC: National Endowment for the Humanities. Accessed April 12, 2005 from www.neh.gov/grants/guidelines/researchmisconduct.html.

Neef, Nancy A., Brian A. Iwata, and Terry J. Page. 1986. "Ethical Standards in Behavioral Research." In *Research Methods in Applied Behavior Analysis: Issues and Advances,* ed. Alan Poling and R. Wayne Fuqua, 233–263. New York: Plenum Press.

Nel, Juan, and Johan Kruger. 1999. *From Policy to Practice: Exploring Victim Empowerment Initiatives in South Africa.* Pretoria: CSIR.

Neuman, W. Lawrence. 2000. *Social Research Methods: Qualitative and Quantitative Approaches.* 4th ed. Boston: Allyn and Bacon.

Nonprofit Resource Center. 2006. "What is a Nonprofit Organization?" Sacramento, CA: Nonprofit Resource Center. Accessed June 14, 2006 from http://www.nonprofitresourcectr.org/intro.html

Northrop, Alana, and Kenneth L. Kraemer. 1982. "Contributions of Political Science and Public Administration to Qualitative Research Methods." In *Qualitative Methods for Institutional Research,* ed. Eileen Kuhns and S.V. Martorana, 43–54. San Francisco: Jossey-Bass.

Norusis, Marija J. 2000. *SPSS For Windows Base System User's Guide* (Version 10.0). Chicago: SPSS.

———. 2005. *SPSS 14.0 Guide to Data Analysis.* Upper Saddle River, NJ: Prentice Hall.

Nöth, Winfried. 1990. *Handbook of Semiotics.* Bloomington: Indiana University.

Oakley, Ann. 2002. *Experiments in Knowing.* Cambridge, UK: Polity Press.

Office of Management and Budget (OMB). 2002. *The President's Management Agenda.* Washington, DC: Office of Management and Budget. Accessed June 3, 2006 from www.whitehouse.gov/omb/budget/fy2002/mgmt.pdf.

Olin and Uris Libraries. 2006. "The Seven Steps of the Research Process." Ithaca, NY: Cornell University. Accessed June 25, 2006 from www.library.cornell.edu/olinuris/ref/research/skill1.htm.

Oliver, Paul. 1997. *Teach Yourself: Research for Business, Marketing and Education.* Chicago: NTC Publishing Group.

Oppenheim, A.N. 1992. *Questionnaire Design, Interviewing, and Attitude Measurement.* 2nd ed. New York: St. Martin's Press.

Organ, Dennis W., and Thomas S. Bateman. 1991. *Organizational Behavior.* 4th ed. Homewood, IL: Irwin.

Orlans, Harold. 1967. "Ethical Problems in the Relations of Research Sponsors and Investigators." In *Ethics, Politics, and Social Research*, ed. Gideon Sjoberg. Cambridge, MA: Schenkman.

Oskamp, Stuart. 1977. *Attitudes and Opinions.* Englewood Cliffs, NJ: Prentice-Hall.

O'Sullivan, Elizabethann, and Gary R. Rassel. 1995. *Research Methods for Public Administrators.* 2nd ed. White Plains, NY: Longman.

Page, Nanette, and Cheryl E. Czuba. 1999. "Empowerment: What Is It?" *Journal of Extension* 37(5).

Patton, Michael Q. 1980. *Qualitative Evaluation Methods.* Beverly Hills, CA: Sage.

———. 1990. *Qualitative Evaluation and Research Methods.* 2nd ed. Newbury Park, CA: Sage.

Paxton, Patsy, and Stephen J. Cox. 2000. "Preparing Research Proposals." New Zealand: Wintec. Accessed December 29, 2005 from www.wintec.ac.nz/files/research%20connections/PreparingResearchProposals.doc.

Payne, R.L. 1971. "Organizational Climate: The Concept and Some Research Findings." *Prakseologia* 39(1): 40.

Pechenik, Jan A. 1987. *A Short Guide to Writing About Biology*. New York: HarperCollins.

Peirce, John R. 1962. *Symbols, Signals, and Noise*. London: Hutchinson.

Pelto, Pertti J. 1970. *Anthropological Research: The Structure of Inquiry*. Cambridge: Cambridge University Press.

Pennings, Paul, Hans Keman, and Jan Kleinnijenhuis. 1999. *Doing Research in Political Science*. Thousand Oaks, CA: Sage.

Pennock, J. Roland. 1966. "Political Philosophy and Political Science." In *Political Research and Political Theory*, ed. Oliver Garceau. Cambridge: Harvard University.

Pernanen, Kai. 1993. "Research Approaches in the Study of Alcohol-Related Violence." *Alcohol Health and Research World*. 17(2): 101–108.

Perry, James L., and Kenneth L. Kraemer. 1986. "Research Methodology in the *Public Administration Review, 1975–1984*." *Public Administration Review* 46(2): 215–226.

Peterson, Karen S. 2001. "Would I Lie to You?" *USA Today*, July 5, 8D.

Peters, Thomas J., and Robert W. Wateman. 1982. *In Search of Excellence: Lessons from America's Best Run Companies*. New York: Harper and Row.

Petrick, Joseph A., and John F. Quinn. 1997. *Management Ethics: Integrity at Work*. Newbury Park, CA: Sage.

Pfiffner, John M. 1940. *Research Methods in Public Administration*. New York: Ronald Press.

Phillips, Bernard S. 1976. *Social Research: Strategy and Tactics*. 3rd ed. New York: Macmillan.

Phillips, Denis C. 1987. *Philosophy, Science, and Social Inquiry*. Oxford: Pergamon.

Piantanida, Maria, and Noreen B. Garman. 1999. *The Qualitative Dissertation*. Thousand Oaks, CA: Sage.

Plotkin, Henry. 1994. *The Nature of Knowledge*. London: Allen Lane/Penguin Press.

Poister, Theodore H. 1978. *Public Program Analysis: Applied Research Methods*. Baltimore: University Park Press.

Poister, Theodore H., and Richard H. Harris, Jr. 2000. "Building Quality Improvement Over the Long Run: Approaches, Results, and Lessons Learned from the PennDOT Experience." *Public Productivity and Management Review* 24(2): 161–176.

Potter, Jonathan, and Margaret Wetherell. 1994. "Analyzing Discourse." In *Analyzing Qualitative Data*, ed. Alan Bryman and Robert B. Burgess, 47–66. London: Routledge.

Public Health Agency of Canada (PHAC). 2005. "Voluntary Sector Surveys." Ottawa: Public Health Agency of Canada, Office of the Voluntary Sector. Accessed June 1, 2006 from www.phac-aspc.gc.ca/vs-sb/surveys/index.html.

Punnett, Betty J., and Oded Shenkat. 1996. *Handbook for International Management Research*. Cambridge: Blackwell.

Quigley, B. Allan. 1997. "The Role of Research in the Practice of Adult Education." *New Directions for Adult and Continuing Education* 73(Spring): 3–22.

Quigley, B. Allan, and Gary W. Kuhne, eds. 1997. *Creating Practical Knowledge Through Action Research: Posing Problems, Solving Problems, and Improving Daily Practice*. San Francisco: Jossey-Bass.

Rabin, Jack, W. Barkley Hildreth, and Gerald J. Miller, eds. 1989. *Handbook of Public Administration Research*. New York: Dekker.

Racker, Efraim. 1997. "A View of Misconduct in Science." In *Research Ethics*, ed. Deni Elliott and Judy E. Stern, 34–51. Hanover, NH: University Press of New England.

Raelin, Joseph A. 1997. "Action Learning and Action Science: Are They Different?" *Organizational Dynamics* 26(1): 21–35.

Ragin, Charles, and David Zaret. 1983. Theory and Method in Comparative Research: Two Strategies." *Social Forces* 61(3): 731–754.

Ray, Larry J. 1993. *Rethinking Critical Theory*. London: Sage.

Reason, Peter. 1998. "Three Approaches to Participative Inquiry." In *Strategies of Qualitative Inquiry*, ed. Norman K. Denzin and Yvonna S. Lincoln, 261–291. Thousand Oaks, CA: Sage.

Reisman, David. 1979. "Ethical and Practical Dilemmas of Fieldwork in Academic Settings: A Personal Memoir." In *Qualitative and Quantitative Social Research*, ed. R.K. Merton, J.S. Coleman, and P.H. Rossi, 210–231. New York: Free Press.

Reynolds, Paul D. 1979. *Ethical Dilemmas and Social Science Research*. San Francisco: Jossey-Bass.

Richards, Thomas L., and Lyn Richards. 1998. "Using Computers in Qualitative Research." In *Collecting and Interpreting Qualitative Materials,* ed. Norman K. Denzin and Yvonna S. Lincoln, 211–245. Thousand Oaks, CA: Sage.

Richardson, Frank C., and Blaine J. Fowers. 1998. "Interpretive Social Science." *American Behavioral Scientist* 41(4): 465–495.

Richardson, Kurt A. 1995. "Postmetaphysical Hermeneutics: When Practice Triumphs Over Theory." *Premise* 2(8): 8–19.

Roberts, Marylyn. 1992. "Predicting Voter Behavior via the Agenda-Setting Tradition." *Journalism Quarterly* 69(Winter): 878–892.

Roberts, Carol A. 1999. "Drug Use Among Inner-City African American Women: The Process of Managing Loss." *Qualitative Health Research* 9(5): 620–639.

Roberts, Kathryn A., and Richard W. Wilson. 2002. "ICT and the Research Process: Issues Around the Compatibility of Technology with Qualitative Data Analysis." *Forum: Qualitative Social Research* 3(2). Accessed August 1, 2006 from www.qualitative-research.net/fqs-texte/2–02/2–02robertswilson-e.htm.

Robinson, Viviane M.J. 1994. "The Practical Promise of Critical Research in Education." *Educational Administration Quarterly* 30(1): 56–77.

Robrecht, Linda C. 1995. "Grounded Theory: Evolving Methods." *Qualitative Health Research.* 5(2): 169–178.

Robson, Colin. 2002. *Real World Research.* Oxford: Blackwell.

Rodgers, Robert, and Nanette Rodgers. 1999. "The Sacred Spark of Academic Research." *Journal of Public Administration Research and Theory* 9(3): 473–492.

Rohr, John A. 1998. *Public Service, Ethics, and Constitutional Practice.* Lawrence: University Press of Kansas.

Rosenthal, Robert, and Ralph L. Rosnow. 1991. *Essentials of Behavioral Research.* 2nd ed. New York: McGraw-Hill.

Rothman, Jack. 1974. *Planning and Organizing for Social Change: Action Principles from Social Science Research.* New York: Columbia University.

Rowlands, Bruce. 2005. "Grounded Theory in Practice: Using Interpretive Research to Build Theory." *Electronic Journal of Business Research Methods* 3 (1): 213–222.

Runyon, Melissa K., Jan Faust, and Hellen Orvaschel. 2002. "Differential Symptom Patterns of Posttraumatic Stress Disorder (PTSD) in Maltreated Children With and Without Concurrent Depression." *Child Abuse and Neglect* 26(January): 39–53.

Rutgers, Mark R. 1997. "Beyond Woodrow Wilson: The Identity of the Study of Public Administration in Historical Perspective." *Administration and Society* 29(3): 276–300.

Salkind, Neil J. 2000. *Exploring Research.* 4th ed. Upper Saddle River, NJ: Prentice Hall.

Sanders, David. 2002. "Behavioralism." In *Theory and Methods in Political Science.* 2nd ed., ed. David Marsh and Gerry Stoker, 45–64. Houndmills, UK: Palgrave Macmillan.,

Sarantakos, Satirios. 2004. *Social Research.* Houndmills, UK: Palgrave.

Saxonhouse, Arlene. 1993. "Texts and Canons: The States of the 'Great Books' in Political Science." In *Political Science: The State of the Discipline II,* ed. Ada W. Finifter, 3–27. Washington, DC: American Political Science Association.

Schein, Edgar H. 1992. *Organizational Culture and Leadership.* 2nd ed. San Francisco: Jossey-Bass.

———. 1996. "Culture: The Missing Concept in Organization Studies." *Administrative Science Quarterly* 41(2): 229–240.

Schellenberg, James A. 1978. *Masters of Social Psychology.* Oxford: Oxford University Press.

Schmuck, Richard A. 1997. *Practical Action Research for Change.* Arlington Heights, IL: SkyLight.

Schulz, Amy J., and Leith Mullings, eds. 2006. *Gender, Race, Class, and Health.* San Francisco: Jossey-Bass.

Schulze, Salomé. 2003. "Views on the Combination of Quantitative and Qualitative Research Approaches." *Progressio* 25(2): 8–20.

Schwandt, Thomas A. 1997. *Qualitative Inquiry: A Dictionary of Terms.* Thousand Oaks, CA: Sage.

Scott, Judy E. 2000. "Facilitating Interorganizational Learning with Information Technology." *Journal of Management Information Systems* 17(2): 81–114.

Seaman, Catherine C., and Phyllis J. Verbonick. 1982. *Research Methods.* 2nd ed. New York: Appleton-Century-Crofts.

Sebeok, Thomas A. 1976. *Contributions to the Doctrine of Signs.* Lanham, MD: University Press of America.

Seech, Zachary. 1993. *Writing Philosophy Papers.* Belmont, CA: Wadsworth.

Selltiz, Claire, Lawrence S. Wrightman, and Stuart W. Cook. 1976. *Research Methods in Social Relations.* New York: Holt, Rinehart and Winston.

Selznick, Philip. 1949. *TVA and the Grass Roots: A Study in the Sociology of Formal Organization.* Berkeley: University of California Press.

Shahariw-Kuehne, Valerie. 1998/1999. "Building Intergenerational Communities Through Research and Evaluation." *Generations* 22(4): 82–88.

Shaughnessy, John J., and Eugene B. Zechmeister. 1994. *Research Methods in Psychology.* 3rd ed. New York: McGraw-Hill.

Shelly, Gary B, Thomas J. Cashman, and Misty E. Vermatt. 1995. *Microsoft Office: Introductory Concepts and Techniques.* Danvers, MA: Boyd and Fraser.

Shepsle, Kenneth A. 1995. "Studying Institutions: Some Lessons from the Rational Choice Approach." In *Political Science in History*, ed. James Farr, John S. Dryzek, and Stephen T. Leonard, 276–295. Cambridge, UK: Cambridge University Press.

Siegel, Andrew. 2002. *Practical Business Statistics.* 5th ed. New York: McGraw-Hill/Irwin.

Siegel, Sidney. 1956. *Nonparametric Statistics for the Behavioral Sciences.* New York: McGraw-Hill.

Silverman, Kaja. 1983. *The Subject of Semiotics.* Oxford: Oxford University Press.

Small, Stephen A. 1995. "Action-Oriented Research: Models and Methods." *Journal of Marriage and Family* 57 (November): 941–956.

Smith, Charles B. 1981. *A Guide to Business Research.* Chicago: Nelson-Hall.

Smith, Kevin B., and Michael J. Licari. 2006. *Public Administration: Power and Politics in the Fourth Branch of Government.* Los Angeles: Roxbury.

Somit, Albert, and Joseph Tanenhaus 1967. *The Development of American Political Science: From Burges to Behavioralism.* Boston: Allyn and Bacon.

Soni, Vidu. 2000. "A Twenty-First Century Reception for Diversity in the Public Sector: A Case Study." *Public Administration Review* 60(5): 395–408.

Sorrels, Bobbye D. 1984. *Business Communications Fundamentals.* New York: Macmillan.

Sproull, Natalie L. 1988. *Handbook of Research Methods.* Metuchen, NJ: Scarecrow Press.

Stack, Carol. 1996. "Doing Research in the Flats." In *In the Field: Readings on the Field Research Experience,* 2nd ed., ed. Carolyn D. Smith and William Kornblum, 21–25. Westport, CT: Praeger.

Stake, Robert E. 1994. "Case Studies." In *Handbook of Qualitative Research,* ed. Norman K. Denzin and Yvonna S. Lincoln, 236–247. Thousand Oaks, CA: Sage.

Stallings, Robert A., and James M. Ferris. 1988. "Public Administration Research: Work in PAR, 1940–1984." *Public Administration Review* 48(1): 580–587.

StatSoft, Inc. 2002. *Nonparametric Statistics.* Accessed May 19, 2002 from http://www.statsoft.com/textbook/stnonpar.html.

Stein, Harold, ed. 1952. *Public Administration and Policy Development: A Case Book.* New York: Harcourt, Brace and World.

Stillman, Richard J., and Jos C. N. Raadschelders. 2006. "Why PAR?" *Public Administration Review* 66(1): 1–5.

Stivers, Camilla. 2000. "Public Administration Theory as a Discourse." *Administrative Theory and Praxis* 221(2): 132–139.

Stoker, Gerry, and David Marsh. 2002. "Introduction." In *New Perspectives on Historical Writing.* 2nd ed. Cambridge, UK: Polity Press.

Stone, Eugene F. 1978. *Research Methods in Organizational Behavior.* Santa Monica, CA: Goodyear.

Strauss, Anselm, and Juliet Corbin, eds. 1997. *Grounded Theory in Practice.* Thousand Oaks, CA: Sage.

———. 1998. *Basics of Qualitative Research.* 2nd ed. Thousand Oaks, CA: Sage.

———. 1990. *Basics of Qualitative Research: Grounded Theory Procedures and Techniques.* Newbury Park, CA: Sage

Stringer, Ernie, ed. 1997. *Community-Based Ethnography: Breaking Traditional Boundaries of Research, Teaching, and Learning.* Mahwah, NJ: Lawrence Erlbaum.

Strunk, William Jr., and E.B. White. 1979. *The Elements of Style.* 3rd ed. Boston: Allyn and Bacon.

Suchman, Edward A. 1967. *Evaluative Research: Principles and Practice in Public Service and Social Action Programs.* New York: Russell Sage Foundation.

Suppe, Frederick. 1988. "The Structure of a Scientific Paper." *Philosophy of Science* 65(4): 381–405.

Tak, Sunghee H., Margaret Nield, and Heather Becker. 1999. "Use of a Computer Software Program for

Qualitative Analyses—Part 1: Introduction to NUD*IST (N1)." *Western Journal of Nursing Research* 31(1): 111–118.

Taxpayers for Common Sense (TFCS). 2001. "Senator William Proxmire and the History of the Golden Fleece Award." Accessed July 7, 2001 from www.taxpayer.net/proxmire.html.

Tibbetts, Arn. 1987. *Practical Business Writing.* Boston: Little, Brown.

Thompson, James R. 2000. "Reinvention as Reform: Assessing the National Performance Review." *Public Administration Review* 60(6): 508–521.

Thompson, Robert. 2002. "Reporting the Results of Computer-assisted Analysis of Qualitative Research Data." *Forum: Qualitative Social Research* 3(2). Accessed August 1, 2006 from http://www.qualitative-research.net/fqs-texte/2-02/2-02thompson-e.pdf.

Tilley, Christopher. 1989. "Interpreting Material Culture." In *The Meaning of Things: Material Culture and Symbolic Expression,* ed. Ian Hodder, 185–194. London: HarperCollins Academic.

Trochim, William K. 2002. *Positivism and Post-Positivism.* http://trochim.human.cornell.edu/kb/positivism. Accessed June 10, 2002.

Tucker, David J., and David H. Sommerfeld. 2006. "The Larger they Get: The Changing Size Distribution of Private Human Service Organizations." *Nonprofit and Voluntary Sector Quarterly* 35(2): 183–203.

Tufte, Edward R. 1983. *The Visual Display of Quantitative Information.* Cheshire, CT: Graphics Press.

Turner, Roy, ed. 1974. *Ethnomethodology: Selected Readings.* Harmondswork, UK: Penguin.

University of Chicago. 1993. *A Manual of Style.* 14th ed. Chicago: University of Chicago Press.

University of San Francisco. 2006. "Pioneering Nonprofit Research and Education." University of San Francisco Institute for Nonprofit Organization Management. Accessed June 6, 2006 from www.inom.org.

Van Evera, Stephen. 1997. *Guide to Methods for Students of Political Science.* Ithaca, NY: Cornell University Press.

Velasquez, Manuel. 1998. *Business Ethics: Concepts and Cases.* 4th ed. Upper Saddle River, NJ: Prentice Hall.

Verplanck, William S. 2002. "Fifty-Seven Years of Searching Among Behaviorisms: A Memoir." Speech given at the Second International Congress on Behaviorism and the Sciences of Behavior. Palermo, Italy. Accessed May 7, 2001 from http://webutk.edu/~wverplan/bibn049.

Wachterhauser, Brice. 1986. "History and Language in Understanding." In *Hermeneutics and Modern Philosophy,* ed. Brice Wachterhauser, 5–61. Albany: State University of New York.

Waddington, David. 1997. "Participant Observation." In *Qualitative Methods in Organizational Research,* ed. Catherine Cassell and Gillian Symon, 107–122. Thousand Oaks, CA: Sage.

Walizer, Michael H., and Paul L. Wienir. 1978. *Research Methods and Analysis: Searching for Relationships.* New York: Harper and Row.

Walker, Robert, ed. 1985. *Applied Qualitative Research.* Aldershot, UK: Gower.

Waller, Alisha A. 2005. "Work in Progress—Feminist Research Methodologies: Why, What and How." Paper presented at the 35th ASEE/IEE Frontiers in Education Conference, October 19–22, Indianapolis, IN. Accessed July 27, 2006 from http://fie.engrng.pitt.edu/fie2005/papers/1588.pdf.

Wapner, Paul. 2002. "The Sovereignty of Nature? Environmental Protection in a Postmodern Age" *International Studies Quarterly* 40 (June): 167–187.

Wasby, Stephen L. 2001. "Proposal Writing—A Remedy for a Missing Part of Graduate Training." *PS: Political Science and Politics* 34(2): 309–312.

Wasson, Chester R. 1965. *Research Analysis for Marketing Decision* [sic]. New York: Appleton-Century-Crofts.

Waterston, Alice 1999. *Love, Sorrow, and Rage: Destitute Women in a Manhattan Residence.* Philadelphia: Temple University Press.

Webb, Eugene J., Donald T. Campbell, Richard D. Schwartz, and Lee Sechrest. 2000. *Unobtrusive Measures,* rev. ed. Thousand Oaks, CA: Sage.

Webb, Thomas W. 1999. "A Journey Toward the Ontological (an Epistemological) Position of the Approach to Experimental Pedagogy to Project Work." In *Project Studies—A Late Modern University Reform?* ed. S. Olesen and Jens J. Jensen, 257–275. Denmark: Roskilde University Press.

Weitzman, Eben A., and Matthew B. Miles. 1995. *Computer Programs for Qualitative Data Analysis: A Software Sourcebook.* Thousand Oaks, CA: Sage.

Welsh, Elaine. 2002. "Dealing with Data: Using NVivo in the Qualitative Data Analysis Process." *Forum: Qualitative Social Research* 3(2). Accessed August 1, 2006 from http://www.qualitative-research.net/fqs-texte/2-02/2-02welsh-e.pdf.

Werther, William B. Jr., and Evan M. Berman. 2001. *Third Sector Management: The Art of Managing Nonprofit Organizations*. Washington, DC: Georgetown University Press.

Westmarland, Nicole. 2001. "The Quantitative/Qualitative Debate and Feminist Research: A Subjective View of Objectivity." *Forum: Qualitative Social Research* 2(1). Accessed July 27, 2006 from www.qualitative-research.net/fqs-texte/1-01/1-01westmarland-e.pdf.

Whelan, Robert K. 1989. "Data Administration and Research Methods in Public Administration." In *Handbook of Public Administration*, ed. Jack Rabin, W.B. Hildreth, and G.J. Miller, 657–682. New York: Dekker.

White, Jay D. 1999. *The Narrative Foundations of Public Administration Research*. Washington, DC: Georgetown University Press.

———. 1986. "Dissertations and Publications in Public Administration." *Public Administration Review* 46(5): 227–239.

White, Jay D., and Guy B. Adams, eds. 1994. *Research in Public Administration*. Thousand Oaks, CA: Sage.

Whiting, Beatrice, and John Whiting. 1973. "Methods for Observing and Recording Behavior." In *A Handbook of Method in Cultural Anthropology*, ed. Raoul Naroll and Ronald Cohen, 282–315. New York: Columbia University Press.

Wildavsky, Aaron. 1993. *Craftways: On the Organization of Scholarly Work*. 2nd ed. New Brunswick, NJ: Transaction.

Wilhelm, Mark. 2002. "The Distribution of Giving in Six Surveys." Indianapolis: Indiana University/Purdue University, November. Accessed June 6, 2006 from www.philanthropy.inpui.edu/SurveyComparisons-Wilhelm.pdf.

Williams, Terry. 1996. "Exploring the Cocaine Culture." In *In the Field: Readings on the Field Research Experience*, 2nd ed., ed. Carolyn D. Smith and William Kornblum, 27–32. Westport, CT: Praeger.

Wilson, James Q. 1989. *Bureaucracy: What Government Agencies Do and How They Do It*. New York: Basic Books.

Woller, Gary M., and Kelly D. Patterson. 1997. "Public Administration Ethics: A Postmodern Perspective." *American Behavioral Scientist* 41(1): 103–108.

Wong, Paul T.P. 2002. "How to Write a Research Proposal." Langley, BC: Trinity Western University. Accessed December 29, 2005 from www.meaning.ca/archives/archive/art_how_to_write_P_Wong.htm.

Worlcott, Harry F. 1995. *The Art of Fieldwork*. Walnut Creek, CA: AltaMira Press.

Wright, Alex. 2004. "A Social Constructionist's Deconstruction of Royal Dutch Shell's Scenario Planning Process." University Working Paper Series 2004, No. WP004/04. Wolverhampton, UK: University of Wolverhampton.

Yeager, Samuel J. 1989. "Classic Methods in Public Administration Research." In *Handbook of Public Administration*, ed. Jack Rabin, W.B. Hildreth, and G.J. Miller, 683–793. New York: Dekker.

Yin, Robert K. 1994 *Case Study Research: Design and Methods*. 2nd ed. Thousand Oaks, CA: Sage.

Zikmund, William G. 1994. *Business Research Methods*. Fort Worth, TX: Dryden.

AUTHOR INDEX

SUBJECT INDEX

ABOUT THE AUTHOR

Dr. David E. McNabb is professor emeritus at Pacific Lutheran University. He has recently held visiting professorships at the Stockholm School of Economics–Riga, Evergreen State College, the University of Maryland-UC (Europe), and the University of Washington–Tacoma. He earned his Ph.D. at Oregon State University, an MA at the University of Washington, and a BA at California State University, Fullerton. He served as director of communications for a caucus of the Washington House of Representatives and as director of economic development for the city of Fullerton, California. He has authored four books and more than sixty articles and conference papers. The first edition of *Research Methods in Public Administration and Nonprofit Management: Quantitative and Qualitative Approaches* received the 2004 Grenzebach Research Award for Outstanding Published Scholarship. He is a member of the Academy of Management, the American Society for Public Administration, and the American Political Science Association.